Marginalized Religion and the Law in the Roman Empire

Marginalized Religion and the Law in the Roman Empire

K. P. S. JANSSEN

OXFORD
UNIVERSITY PRESS

OXFORD
UNIVERSITY PRESS

Great Clarendon Street, Oxford, OX2 6DP,
United Kingdom

Oxford University Press is a department of the University of Oxford.
It furthers the University's objective of excellence in research, scholarship,
and education by publishing worldwide. Oxford is a registered trade mark of
Oxford University Press in the UK and in certain other countries

Published in the United States of America by Oxford University Press
198 Madison Avenue, New York, NY 10016, United States of America

British Library Cataloguing in Publication Data
Data available

Library of Congress Control Number: 2024940806

ISBN 9780192856104

DOI: 10.1093/9780191946400.001.0001

Printed and bound by
CPI Group (UK) Ltd, Croydon, CR0 4YY

Contents

Acknowledgements

Just as Rome was not built in a day, no book is ever truly written alone—and this is doubly true for projects that, like this one, find their origins in doctoral research. I am particularly grateful to Jürgen Zangenberg and Luuk de Ligt, who acted as my supervisors during my time as a PhD candidate at Leiden University, and whose generous support, constructive feedback, and great erudition has been absolutely invaluable both before and after my defence. I feel incredibly fortunate to have experienced their mentorship, and am equally grateful for their continued guidance.

A great number of friends and colleagues were kind enough to comment on various stages of this project, and directly or indirectly helped me to develop my ideas. Although lists of this kind can ultimately rarely deliver the degree of comprehensiveness they seem to promise, I am especially grateful to Kim Beerden, Maurits Berger, Jan Bremmer, Diederik Burgersdijk, Liesbeth Claes, Kimberley Czajkowski, Elsemieke Daalder, Roald Dijkstra, Rebecca Flemming, Jaap Jan Flinterman, Miko Flohr, Bas ter Haar Romeny, Ab de Jong, Egbert Koops, Patricia Kret, Glyn Muitjens, Paul du Plessis, Ineke Sluiter, Rens Tacoma, and Rick Verhagen, as well as the anonymous reviewers for OUP, whose comments, insights, and suggestions were extremely valuable. This overview, again, should not be taken as exhaustive, and any remaining errors are of course my own. I would also like to extend my thanks to the colleagues at the Leiden University Centre for the Arts in Society (LUCAS) and the Leiden University Institute for History (LUIH), and especially to the members of the departments of Classics and Ancient History, for creating a true academic home filled with sharp and supportive minds. The support and numerous opportunities for academic exchange provided by the Dutch National Research School in Classical Studies OIKOS have likewise been greatly appreciated.

I am deeply grateful to my editors at Oxford University Press, Charlotte Loveridge and Henry Clarke, who were unfailingly helpful and patient in their assistance, and in responding to my (many) queries. Thanks likewise goes out to the American Numismatic Society, the Dutch National Museum of Antiquities (Rijksmuseum van Oudheden, Leiden), and the Münzkabinett, Staatliche Museen zu Berlin, for allowing me to reproduce the various images in this volume. The book grants awarded to me by the Fonds Marinus de Jonge during my PhD have long since proved highly useful, but were especially appreciated when working on my manuscript during plague-times.

Finally, there are those who are ultimately this book's bedrock. The generous kindness of Simon and Jenny Peters has been with me from the beginning, and my friends and family continue to be an inspiration. I am more grateful than I can say to Bas Clercx, Redmer Kronemeijer, Maaike van der Plas, Anne van Schaik, Caspar Sundholm, and especially to my mother and father, whose firm encouragement, support, and enthusiasm never cease to make writing—and everything else—worthwhile.

List of Figures

Introduction

0.1 Marginalized Religion and the Law: A Comparative Approach

In 204 BCE, a new deity entered the city of Rome. Her arrival had been much anticipated: while the Second Punic War was by now nearing its end,[1] the conflict had nevertheless proved highly taxing, and a variety of strange omens only seemed to confirm the need for increased divine support.[2] However, the integration of this new goddess, known both as Cybele and as Magna Mater, within the Roman cultic landscape was hardly uncomplicated. On the one hand, our sources report that she was received with all due honours, to the extent that the senate took a vote to determine who was the best man in Rome, and therefore worthy of welcoming her.[3] The cult of the goddess also became a prominent part of Roman religious life, and her image was even housed in a temple on the Palatine hill.[4] On the other hand, Roman authors frequently emphasize the cult's distinctly 'foreign' character, and some of its practices were considered so alien that native Romans were allegedly banned from participating in them.[5] Despite becoming an established part of the religious calendar, then, the rites of Magna Mater—with their loud music and castrated priests with long hair, prominent jewellery, and colourful

[1] For the idea that the war was at this stage largely won, and that the introduction of the Magna Mater cult in Rome was therefore unrelated to the conflict, see e.g. Beard (2012), 328–9; Gruen (1990), 6–7; Orlin (2010), 78–82.

[2] Despite the discrepancies between the two accounts, these omens are mentioned in both Livy, *Ab Urbe Condita* 29.10 and Ovid, *Fasti* 4.255–65. Livy's account may be found in, among others, the Oxford Classical Text edition by Conway and Johnson (1963) and the Teubner edition by Walsh (1986). For Ovid's *Fasti*, see Fantham (1998).

[3] Livy, *Ab Urbe Condita* 29.11 and 29.14.

[4] The fact that the goddess's temple was housed within the *pomerium* is notable, as Augustus appears to have banned the cult of Isis from being housed within its sacred boundaries. See Cassius Dio, *Historiae Romanae* 53.2.4. For the idea that the Roman elite in particular was heavily involved in the cult, and often continued to use very 'traditional' Roman forms of worship in this context, see Beard (2012), 348–9; Beard, North, and Price (1998), 160.

[5] The description in Ovid, *Fasti* 4.179–372 in particular seems to waver between emphasizing the cult's long-standing connection to Rome by linking it to Troy and Aeneas, and dwelling on its more 'alien', ecstatic elements—particularly its use of music and the self-castration of its priests. For a similar angle, see Juvenal, *Saturae* 6.511–16. The idea that native Romans were banned from becoming priests of the goddess is mentioned in Dionysius of Halicarnassus, *Antiquitates Romanae* 2.19, although the validity of this claim is in doubt—see Beard (2012), 341. Dionysius' account may be found in the Loeb edition by Cary (1937). For editions of Juvenal's *Saturae*, see Braund (2004) and Nadeau (2011).

flowing robes—also appear to have been, on some level, fundamentally shocking to Roman religious sentiments.

These ambivalent attitudes towards the cult of Magna Mater are highly illustrative of the complex relationship between Roman society and the wide variety of religious groups and practices within its territories. On the one hand, traditional Roman polytheism has often been seen as almost proverbially religiously tolerant. Whether this reputation is entirely deserved or not,[6] the frequency with which new, non-Roman elements were incorporated within the existing religious landscape, and the wide variety of ways in which this occurred, nonetheless remain notable, and rightly continue to be the subject of extensive discussion.[7] On the other hand, this episode also illustrates that this remarkable religious heterogeneity was not always entirely comfortable, and that the presence of groups and practices that were perceived as stretching or crossing the limits of acceptable religious behaviour led to repeated attempts to define what exactly those limits were.[8] At least part of this debate took place in the legal sphere, and throughout the ancient sources references to legal interactions between the Roman authorities and (members of) religious groups that were in some way excluded from the perceived centre of Roman society, and may thus be described as marginalized, appear with some regularity.[9] Such attempts to formally regulate religious life have received particular scholarly attention—and given how illuminating a legal approach is to our understanding of Roman religious life, this is hardly suprising. Most obviously, the legal measures taken by the Roman authorities had a practical impact on the day-to-day lives of the inhabitants of the empire, and to understand them is therefore likewise to understand a fundamental part of the wider societal context in which marginalized religious groups developed and functioned. In addition, legal interactions often provide a fascinating insight into the moral values and concerns of the society from which they originated. Pronouncements regarding the legality or illegality of certain practices are unavoidably man-made, and their very existence requires the involvement of societal groups (or individual members thereof), who carry with them specific notions of what is both

6 For the idea that polytheism is 'by definition tolerant and accommodating', see e.g. Bowersock (1990), 6. This idea, however, has increasingly come under scrutiny. For these critical perspectives, see Ando (2016[b]), 254–5; Beard, North, and Price (1998), 212; Dijkstra and Raschle (2020), 4–7; and Garnsey (1984). The latter author offers a fascinating discussion of the pitfalls of applying the term 'tolerance' to the ancient world. See Raschle (2020) for a discussion of mechanisms of both inclusion and exclusion.

7 See, non-comprehensively, Beard, North, and Price (1998); Orlin (2010); Rives (2007); Rüpke (2016[a]); and Wendt (2016).

8 Beard, North, and Price (1998), 211–44; Rüpke (2016[b]).

9 The term 'marginalization' is here intended to refer to the practice of excluding certain groups or individuals from the perceived societal centre, or designating them as deviating from the accepted societal norms. This exclusion could, and can, take legal, political, and social forms, and may not appear uniformly across all areas of life. A particular group may for example be strongly integrated in an economic sense, while being excluded from the centre of social or political power. See Knapp (2016).

morally right and legally expedient. Legal disagreements can be especially telling in this regard, as they allow us to study in some detail which arguments were used in such debates, and which were ultimately considered persuasive. The ability of societies to shape their laws 'in their own image', it may therefore be argued, allows legal measures to reflect how societies see themselves, and what they aspire to be.[10] By investigating the legal treatment of marginalized religious groups, we can thus go beyond the personal opinions of individual authors,[11] and instead gain more comprehensive insights into these communities' position in the Roman world.

While the legal positions of the various marginalized religious groups that existed in the Roman Empire have each been the subject of extensive research, it is notable that their respective legal positions have widely been discussed in isolation. This holds especially true for early Christianity, where the lack of comparison with other contemporary religious groups has moreover been particularly problematic. Previous studies have overwhelmingly focused on the legal position of Christianity per se, which has served to (explicitly or implicitly) reinforce the common perception that this group received unusually harsh treatment at the hands of the Roman authorities without testing the applicability and limits of this assumption.[12] However, the same holds true for other groups that were in

[10] See e.g. Cotterrell (1984), 11 and Harries (2007), 131. While it is not possible to go into detail here, the idea that legal measures are reflective of the society from which they emerged has been explored by sociologists from a number of angles. Perhaps most concisely, it has been argued that 'law is the visible "index" of [the] invisible moral milieu'. For this turn of phrase, see Cotterrell (1984), 79, where the author summarizes Durkheim (1900). For a recent German translation of the latter work, see Miethling and Hartmann (2009). The opening paragraphs of many modern constitutions provide fascinating examples of legal measures acting as a form of self-representation. It may be noted, for instance, that the constitution of the Federal Republic of Germany that was implemented after the Second World War focuses strongly on human dignity (*die Würde des Menschen*; Article 1, 1949), while the constitution of the United States of America emphasizes its departure from the British monarchical system by ascribing legislative power to 'we the people' in its preamble. For the importance of law to self-definition and identity in the ancient world, see Ando (2011), 3 and (2015[b]), 47 and Schröder (1996).

[11] For an exploration of the way in which various individual Roman authors discuss religious matters, see Davies (2004).

[12] A more thorough analysis of existing scholarship regarding the legal treatment of early Christians will be presented in section 4.1. For explicit references to the (perceived) unique position of Christianity in the Roman world, see especially Ste Croix (1974[a]), 242. This foundational study maintains that both Christianity itself and its harsh legal treatment were without precedent in the Roman world. For a similar argument in a more recent work, see Rives (2011[b]), 199 and Lane Fox (1986), 271, the latter of whom focuses on the swift spread of Christianity. Ando (2008), 96–100 holds that traditional Graeco-Roman religion was ill-equipped for the systematic implementation of a so-called *Reichsreligion*, due to the fact that so much of its practices were tied to specific locations or objects, and argues in Ando (2008), 119 that, aside from the imperial ruler cult, Christianity is the only religious movement of the period to claim that its object of worship was ubiquitously present throughout the empire. Throughout the rest of his work, Ando emphasizes the differences between Christianity and traditional Roman religious beliefs and practices on a notable number of occasions. While Moss (2013) and Nixey (2017) both make significant efforts to nuance the common perception of early Christians as a perpetually harassed and oppressed minority, they, too, overwhelmingly discuss the legal treatment of Christianity as an isolated case.

some way perceived to fall outside of the religious norm, which have likewise overwhelmingly been studied in their own right.[13] Broader studies on religion in the Roman world, by contrast, often pay comparatively little attention to the specific, individual legal treatment of each of the empire's many religious groups, or indeed the legal perspective in general, and instead tend to limit themselves to more wide-ranging statements about societal attitudes towards 'un-Roman' beliefs and practices in general, and the possible existence of an imperial religious policy.[14] In these studies, too, a methodical comparison between various marginalized religious groups has widely been omitted, in spite of recent calls to provide a more holistic perspective on the legal position of religious groups in the ancient world.[15] The present study therefore aims to thoroughly contextualize the legal treatment of a well-attested selection of these marginalized religious groups within the wider Roman legal framework, not only by adopting a comparative approach that, as has been remarked, has so far proved to be remarkably rare but also by incorporating recent findings in the field of Roman law and administration, which provide valuable information about the backdrop against which the relevant interactions took place. In doing so, it hopes to shed a new light on the religious landscape of the Roman world by systematically analysing the way in which these marginalized religious groups were embedded in, and interacted with, the Roman legal system of the imperial period.

0.2 Sources and Scope

Since legal interactions between the Roman authorities and marginalized religious groups did not occur in a vacuum, this study will open by analysing the legal and administrative framework in which these events took place (Chapter 1). This chapter, which is intended to provide a concise and accessible introduction to a broad and complex field, will include a discussion of the various sources from which Roman legal measures could be derived, as well as the procedures that were used to resolve legal disputes, before delving into an analysis of the

[13] See for instance Cramer (1954); Fögen (1993); and Ripat (2011) for studies focused on the legal position of divination; Rajak (2002[b]) and Schuol (2007) for that of Judaism. For a rare example of a comparative study, albeit on a limited scale, see Raschle (2020).

[14] See, among others, Ando (2008); Baudy (2006); Beard, North, and Price (1998), 211–44; Orlin (2010); MacMullen (1966); Rüpke (2014) and (2016[b]); Watson (1992), 58–62.

[15] See Corke-Webster (2017[b]), 406, who focuses on Christianity in particular, but especially Wendt (2015[a]) and (2016), who argues that both Jewish and Christian groups in particular should be viewed within the context of the rising popularity of freelance religious experts in the first and second century CE. While this analysis has much to recommend it, the legal angle receives little systematic attention. In addition, Wendt largely limits her discussion to individuals that drew the attention of the Roman authorities, while the question of the extent to which larger groups or communities could collectively be seen as 'freelance experts' remains underexplored.

workings of Roman governance in the provinces, which was an essential component of many of the relevant interactions.

This first chapter will be followed by three case studies, which will serve to illustrate how this wider framework was applied to the treatment of marginalized religious groups. The intent, it should be noted, is not to present a fully comprehensive overview of 'Roman religious policy' by analysing every single legal measure dealing with religious groups that has been transmitted to us, but rather to allow for a detailed discussion of a more limited number of cases. The religious groups that will be discussed in the following chapters each had their own distinct character and held different positions in the Roman world, but they were nevertheless all frequently perceived as 'alien' or 'other', and often had a strained relationship with both their immediate neighbours and the Roman authorities. The similarities and differences between their respective interactions with the Roman authorities, then, collectively allow for deeper insight into the underlying principles that shaped Roman attitudes towards marginalized religion in general. The relevant groups have been selected as *comparanda* for a number of different reasons, of which the number and scope of the available sources is perhaps most conspicuous. While groups such as the Celtic druids, participants in the Bacchanalia, and the followers of the goddess Isis each had their notable confrontations with the Roman authorities, and have received their share well-deserved scholarly attention, the number of references to legal interactions involving these groups is relatively small,[16] which makes it more difficult to determine whether any particular case was indeed representative of a larger pattern. Furthermore, the selection has been limited to religious movements and communities whose encounters with the Roman authorities took place during approximately the same period, which allows for a more clear-cut comparison.[17]

The first group on which we will focus our attention is a group that may best be indicated by the collective moniker of 'private diviners' (Chapter 2).[18] The surviving

[16] The circumstances surrounding the implementation of the famous *Senatus Consultum de Bacchanalibus* were transmitted in Livy, *Ab Urbe Condita* 39.8–18. The text of the senatorial decree has survived in the form of an inscription from Tiriolo, Italy, and may be found in *Corpus Inscriptionum Latinarum* I^2.2.581 (now in the Kunsthistorisches Museum, Vienna). Measures against druids are referenced by Pliny the Elder, *Naturalis Historia* 30.4 (13) and Suetonius, *De vita Caesarum: Claudius* 25.5. Tacitus, *Annales* 14.30 mentions the burning of the druids' sacred groves in the context of military conflict. Legal interactions surrounding the cult of Isis are mentioned in Cassius Dio, *Historiae Romanae* 40.47.3–4, 42.26.2, 53.2.4, and 54.6.6; Flavius Josephus, *Antiquitates Iudaicae* 18.3.4 (65–80); Suetonius, *De vita Caesarum: Tiberius* 36; Tacitus, *Annales* 2.85; Tertullian, *Ad Nationes* 1.10.17–18 (citing Varro); Valerius Maximus, *Facta et Dicta Memorabilia* 1.3 (*De Superstitionibus*).4.

[17] Since this study is focused on groups that were, at least to some extent, perceived as religious 'outsiders', a thorough discussion of legal interactions involving the so-called imperial cult has been omitted. For a select number of valuable studies in this vast field, see Gordon (2011); Gradel (2002); Herz (2007); and Price (1984).

[18] While the terminology used in ancient sources to refer to this group is notably diverse, there are nevertheless good reasons to assume that private practitioners of divination were, for legal purposes, regarded as a joint legal category. For more details on the subject, see section 2.2.

collection of accounts referencing legal measures dealing with this group is notably large, and may overwhelmingly be dated to the first and second centuries CE, making them a fascinating example of the legal treatment of marginalized religious groups during the early imperial period. Furthermore, these diviners regularly appear to have been seen as suspicious 'outsiders', whose religious beliefs and practices were closely associated with transgression and disruption but nevertheless held significant appeal. As a result, private diviners have on occasion been indicated as a useful foil for other marginalized religious groups,[19] and it pays to investigate their legal positions in more detail.

A second group whose treatment allows us to gain valuable insights into the legal treatment of marginalized religion in the Roman world consists of the various Jewish communities in the empire (Chapter 3). Once again, we have access to a significant number of sources that date from the imperial period, which provides ample opportunity for comparing and contrasting the treatment of this group to that of others. The value of this comparison is further increased by the fact that the religious life of Jewish groups, rather than involving a plurality of gods and goddesses, was focused on a single supernatural power to the exclusion of all others, which differentiated them from the overwhelming majority of the inhabitants of the Roman world. At the same time, however, it has been argued that Jewish communities were met with rather more lenient attitudes than their proverbially persecuted Christian counterparts and could even count on the support of Roman authorities on a notable number of occasions. The balance between inclusion and exclusion has proved to be a central theme in the study of ancient Judaism,[20] and an analysis of the extent to which Jewish groups were treated differently than others, and the reasons behind such disparities, is thus essential for our understanding not only of the position of Jewish communities themselves but also of the wider religious, socio-political, and legal framework in which their interactions with the Roman authorities took place.

Finally, no study of marginalized religion would be complete without an analysis of the legal position of early Christianity, which has received almost incomparable amounts of scholarly attention. Historically, the aforementioned idea that the Christian community was fundamentally threatened by suppression, persecution, and martyrdom during the early centuries of its existence has been deeply influential: images of Christians from ages past suffering, and often dying, for their beliefs can be found in museums all over the world, and these same figures are likewise frequently alluded to in the names of churches, schools, and even

[19] See, for instance, Wendt (2015[a]), who includes both diviners and Jewish and Christian practitioners in her category of freelance religious experts. The connection between Christians and diviners is also made by Beard, North, and Price (1998), 237–8, although on a much more limited scale. For a similar link between Christians and magicians, rather than diviners, see Benko (1984), 103–32.

[20] See, non-comprehensively, Avidov (2009); Barclay (1996) and (2004); Feldman (1993); Goodman (2007[a]); Gruen (2002); Schäfer (1997); Schwartz (2014).

cities. This focus on persecution has not only proved to be foundational for the church itself, with martyrs taking on the role of the movement's heroes from early on,[21] but has also retained a strong presence in the popular consciousness to this day. Martyr narratives were instrumental in ensuring that the relationship between Christians and the Roman authorities is still overwhelmingly perceived as remarkably, or even uniquely, hostile, and the often spectacularly gruesome nature of such stories may be argued to have only enhanced the enduring general fascination with the treatment of Christian communities in the Roman world. Given the centrality of legal interactions to such accounts, it is little wonder that even early Christians themselves discussed (and to an extent analysed) the way in which the Roman authorities responded to the Christian phenomenon,[22] and that later researchers have continued this tradition by extensively debating the formal legal basis of such interactions. The study of early Christianity, then, particularly stands to gain from a broader perspective on the legal treatment of marginalized religious groups in the Roman world, in which Christians are not treated as the proverbial outsiders by default, but rather placed back within the wider administrative context of the Roman world and treated as part of the existing contemporary legal system.

Throughout the following chapters, a wide variety of sources will be used to chart and analyse the many interactions between the Roman authorities and members of the aforementioned religious groups.[23] Despite this study's focus on legal and administrative matters, legal texts in the strict sense of the word make up only a relatively small part of the relevant corpus, as religious matters are only rarely referenced in the surviving legal collections, the value of which is furthermore complicated by their late date of compilation. The majority of sources that refer to legal interactions with religious groups are instead contained in the work of various historians from the Graeco-Roman world, and the context they provide will inevitably be central to the following analysis—even if they are not without

[21] The idea that stories of martyrdom contributed to the growth of the church was brought forward as early as the second century CE—see Tertullian, *Apologeticus pro Christianis* 50.13, where the author proclaims that *semen est sanguis Christianorum*: 'the blood of Christians is seed [for the church]'. The numbering system used in references to this text is that of the Loeb edition of Glover and Rendall (1931). See also the older edition of Oehler, Mayor, and Souter (1917), which has recently been made digitally available. For the persisting cultural power of Christian martyrdom, see also Lane Fox (1986), 419–20 and Nixey (2017), 56–9. For the connection between Christian martyrdom and the wider paradigm of 'heroic death' in antiquity, see Lane Fox (1986), 436–7; van Henten and Avemarie (2002); and Moss (2012[a]), 23–48.

[22] While a number of Christian authors reference the issue, as will be discussed in more detail in Chapter 4, the most prominent and extensive examples may be found in the works of Tertullian. Particularly relevant is Tertullian, *Apologeticus pro Christianis* 2, where the author discusses perceived inconsistencies in the Roman treatment of Christians, as well as *Apologeticus pro Christianis* 21.1, where he contrasts Christianity with Judaism. The latter, Tertullian argues, had been pronounced *licita* (approved or permitted by law), thereby implying that Christianity had not received the same treatment. It should be noted, however, the term *religio licita* does not appear to have been used in a technical sense, as is remarked e.g. by Rüpke (2001), 42.

[23] Unless otherwise indicated, all translations of Greek and Latin sources in this study are my own.

their biases and must therefore be treated with due caution. A similarly critical approach must be adopted in the case of sources written by members of the various marginalized groups under discussion themselves, particularly the so-called Martyr Acts. While these accounts of the trials and executions of early Christians often contain references to miracles and other supernatural events, and were frequently composed significantly after the events they describe, some of these texts may nevertheless provide us with valuable information. On a select number of occasions we are furthermore able to access legal and administrative practice more directly, either through papyrological evidence or via correspondence that has been transmitted to us in other ways.

For the sake of coherence, this study will focus primarily on the imperial period up to the middle of the third century CE, which may be seen as an important transitional period in the history of the Roman Empire. These decades witnessed not only the increased focus on the collection of precedents and attempts to create legal coherence that characterized the Severan period, but also Caracalla's grant of universal Roman citizenship to all free inhabitants of the empire. Due to these significant changes, the period also marked a shift in the legal position of various marginalized religious groups within the Roman territories, and the latter half of the third century CE will therefore be beyond the scope of this study.[24] Due to the importance of precedents for our analysis, however, republican examples of the Roman authorities' legal interactions with diviners and Jewish communities will be included. Given the significant size of the relevant corpora, a succinct overview of all cases discussed in chapters 2, 3, and 4 may be found in the appendices, alongside the available sources for each particular interaction and other relevant information.

0.3 Methodology and Terminology

In its investigation of the similarities and differences between the interactions of the aforementioned marginalized religious groups and the Roman authorities, this study will focus not just on the legal basis for their respective treatments in itself but especially on the considerations, mechanisms, and formal procedures from which these treatments emerged. If we are to analyse these underlying principles systematically, however, it is essential to take into account not only

[24] Traditionally, the year 249/250 has been seen as a one of the great turning points in the legal treatment of Christians in the Roman world due to the implementation of Decius' edict of universal sacrifice, as suggested by (among many others) Leppin (2007), 100; Rives (2007), 199; and Ste Croix (1974[a]), 211. For the argument that the Severan period marked a shift in the legal position of Jewish communities, see Harker (2012), 286; Linder (2006), 135–6 and 139. The effect that the increased collection of precedents had on the way in which the legal position of diviners was perceived will be discussed in more detail in section 2.10.

legal measures in the strict sense of the word, but instead on the entirety of the legal process. Investigating the creation and enforcement of particular measures alongside their contents will help us to gain a more nuanced understanding of both the origins and the long-term significance of these regulations and to more closely analyse the principles, institutions, and procedures that underpinned them. Furthermore, this approach allows us to embed legal dealings between members of marginalized religious groups and the Roman authorities in their historical context, which would have been all too easily lost if we were to focus on the contents of these measures alone, and to trace the differences between historical periods and individual events in some detail. Even studies that emphasize the often sporadic nature of Roman dealings with marginalized religious communities have a tendency to present a rather homogenized picture of the relevant interactions, and while detailed studies of specific events of course exist, more general analyses often present their conclusions without differentiating between various individual cases—although in the case of Christianity the famous correspondence between Pliny the Younger and the emperor Trajan, which is almost always central to discussions of the subject, could be considered an exception. While such an approach can, and has, certainly yielded valuable results, it does almost inevitably emphasize similarities over differences, thereby obscuring the possibility for non-linear developments and ad hoc decision-making. Likewise, a focus on the entirety of the legal process allows for the careful consideration of the role of legal actors beyond the limited sphere of Roman authorities—including not only local elites and the general population of the empire but also marginalized communities and individuals themselves, as well as the nature of interaction between these different parties.

Throughout this study we will therefore distinguish between the origins, contents, and implementation of legal measures dealing with marginalized religious groups, each of which will be analysed with the help of a number of central questions. When analysing the various factors that contributed to the first of these stages in the legal process, we should in particular take into account the temporal and local circumstances from which a particular interaction emerged, including not only when and where the relevant events took place but also who took the initiative. In this regard, it is especially important to consider whether the Roman authorities became involved in response to particular events, or rather acted without being prompted to do so. If the former, the scale of these events should likewise be taken into account: a measure taken in response to an empire-wide crisis or other notable events of a similar scale may well have had very different implications, and should therefore be evaluated differently, than a regulation that emerged in the wake of more localized difficulties. A final question belonging to this category concerns the use of precedent. While this term should not necessarily be taken to imply that Roman officials were legally obligated to follow rulings made by their predecessors, as is often the case when the word is used in a modern context,[25] it nevertheless remains important to consider whether measures from the past were invoked as examples for the correct course of action in the present—and if so: when and by whom. For this reason, the various occasions on which the Roman authorities encountered the specific religious groups under discussion in the following chapters will be discussed in chronological order as much as possible.

The second set of questions includes issues that are more particularly related to the contents of the relevant legal measures and is most especially concerned with what exactly was being regulated. This may include specific behaviours or actions, although we must also consider the possibility that such regulations were instead concerned with more fundamental matters like the possession of certain knowledge—or indeed simply belonging to a particular group. We may then ask whether the behaviour, knowledge, or community targeted by the legal measure is being permitted, modified, or repressed, and whose wishes and perspectives are being favoured in doing so. Similarly relevant is the number of people to whom the measure applied: did a measure impact a specific individual, or was it aimed at a larger group of people—and if so: how many? Finally, we must consider the character and purpose of additional legal actions attached to the measure in question. In case of repressive measures, this requires us to consider whether a measure involved punishment, and, if it did, the nature of this punishment. However, procedures that were not intended as retribution as such, but rather contributed to the legal proceedings in some other way (for instance as a method of truth-finding), must likewise be considered.

The last category consists of questions that deal with the implementation or enforcement of legal measures. We must first ask ourselves who was involved in the implementation of the relevant decisions, including different levels of Roman government, local institutions, and potentially private individuals. The temporal and geographical scope of the implementation is likewise relevant: to what extent were measures, once taken, uniformly enforced in the empire's different territories? Did they remain in place for longer periods of time, or instead gradually or suddenly fall into disuse? In this regard, it is especially important to consider the possible repetition of the same or similar legal measures, since this may serve as an indication that previous rulings were in need of recurring confirmation or reinforcement.[26] Finally, we must take into account the possibility that some measures may have been altered or modified after the fact, whether by appealing

[25] For a more detailed exploration of the concept of precedent as it relates to Roman administration, see Chapter 1.

[26] This idea is expanded upon by Harries (1999), 77–98, who argues that repetition of similar measures is a sign of increasing strength, rather than the initial weakness of the regulation in question. While she may very well be right in arguing that repetitions led to the reinforcement of existing measures, it should nevertheless be noted that investigating the circumstances under which such repetitions took place remains especially important.

previous verdicts or by attempts to implement an altered, and possibly contradictory, measure in response.

In addition to focusing on the entirety of the legal process, rather than legal measures in themselves, this study will furthermore extend beyond the fairly narrow scope of laws in the strict sense of the word, which are generally referred to as *leges* in the works of the Roman jurists. Such a narrow focus would severely limit the available corpus, and exclude a great number of relevant sources and events from consideration. The case studies that are discussed in the following chapters will therefore also include trials and other administrative actions, so as to better represent the diverse range of legal procedures that existed in the Roman world.[27] For this reason, the terms 'legal measure' and 'legal interaction' will generally be preferred over 'legislation' when discussing the legal actions of the Roman government in general, although the latter phrase may be used in specific cases.

The term 'religious groups' likewise demands clarification. The debate about the nature, and indeed the very existence, of 'religion' in the ancient world is a long one, and disagreement surrounding certain fundamental points persists. In particular, the applicability of modern terminology surrounding the phenomenon to the Graeco-Roman period remains a point of significant contention. It has, for example, repeatedly been argued that neither ancient Greek nor Latin had a word for 'religion', and that terms that may at first seem similar (like the Latin *religio*) in fact have different connotations. This observation has been used to claim that religion, as a concept and area of life distinct from the secular, is a more recent phenomenon than is often assumed.[28] However, while it would indeed be difficult to straightforwardly project modern notions of 'religion' onto the ancient world and to assert that the inhabitants of the Roman Empire were familiar with organized, institutionalized religion akin to what we know today, this should not be taken to mean that the existence and societal relevance of beliefs and practices that are most succinctly described as 'religious' can be easily dismissed.[29] People throughout the ancient world sincerely believed in their gods and other supernatural beings and made significant efforts to interact with them and win their

[27] For more on this subject, see Chapter 1.

[28] Barton and Boyarin (2016); Nongbri (2013). This lack of a distinct terminology for 'religion' has also been pointed out by, among others, Mason (2007), 480–2 and Rives (2007), 4–6 and 13–53, both of whom are similarly critical of the idea of 'religions' in the ancient world, and likewise point out that the Latin term *religio* originally did not correspond with 'religion' as it is most often defined today. For the difficulties inherent in investigating ancient religion, see also Rüpke (2016[a]), 17–22. Defining related terms like *superstitio*, or its Greek cognate *ἀσέβεια*, has likewise proved problematic, as has the interpretation of the term 'atheism' as it was applied by ancient authors. For a number of notable studies on these issues, see Bowden (2008); Bremmer (2006); Edwards (2013); Gordon (2008); Martin (2006); Rüpke (2016[b]), especially 1–11; and Sedley (2013).

[29] For the argument that the complete rejection of the term 'religion' in discussions about the ancient world makes it difficult to know 'what we are talking about', see Petersen (2017).

favour.[30] Nevertheless, the question remains whether we can rightly speak about 'religious groups', or even the plural 'religions', in an ancient context. Such terms could suggest the existence of 'a plurality of self-contained and neatly separated religious traditions or systems',[31] each with an implied internal coherence and shared sense of identity that did not necessarily exist. To refer to 'religious groups' without further comment, then, risks simplifying a highly complex and diverse religious landscape, in which borders were frequently porous.[32] For our present purposes, however, the internal perspective of specific religious practitioners is less relevant than that of Roman officials and jurists, who were quite willing and able to group together those they believed were engaged in similar religious practices, and/or shared similar beliefs. In what follows, the term 'religious group' will therefore be taken to refer to a group of people who were, from a legal perspective, perceived to share similar, although not necessarily identical, ways of thinking about, and interacting with, the supernatural.[33] Such groups need not have been governed by a single organizing structure, or indeed demanded the exclusive allegiance of those thought to belong to them. As will be discussed in more detail in the following chapters, however, each of the religious groups discussed in this study was, in its own way, recognized as a legal category.

A final terminological note concerns the word 'persecution', which is particularly prevalent in discussions of the legal treatment of Christians in the Roman Empire. While the use of such terms makes it easier to briefly and succinctly refer to the totality of legal interactions involving this group, or indeed other repressive measures taken by the Roman authorities (and is at least partially understandable for that reason), the phrase must in this author's opinion nevertheless be avoided. The word 'persecution' carries with it significant connotations of systematic violence and oppression, and can likewise be taken to refer to deliberate and active inquisitorial actions in order to achieve this goal.[34] The term therefore implies much about the intentions and procedures behind the Roman treatment of marginalized religious groups that may substantially colour our analysis from the outset, while not necessarily being rooted in the available sources. For this reason, each individual case discussed in this study will be judged on its own merits, and various alternative terms will be used in an attempt to convey the nature of events

[30] This much has been acknowledged even by authors who are otherwise fundamentally critical of applying the concept of 'religion' to the ancient world—see Barton and Boyarin (2016), 4–5; Nongbri (2013), 4. While it is almost impossible to exhaustively discuss the existing scholarship on the subject here, it bears mentioning that the term 'embedded religion' has been used to describe the ubiquitous presence of religion in the ancient world with some frequency, although it has since become less popular. See Beard, North, and Price (1998), 43; Beerden (2013), 32; Oakman (2005); Rüpke (2001), 13. Nongbri (2008) is particularly critical of this concept.

[31] Rüpke (2004), 179.

[32] Rives (2007), 52; Rüpke (2004), 179.

[33] This definition of 'religion' incorporates and adapts elements from the definitions offered by Beerden (2013), 30; Rives (2007), 52; and Rüpke (2014), 5.

[34] Oxford English Dictionary, *ad loc.* 1b and 1d. For a similar argument, see Bryen (2014[a]), 253–4 and Moss (2013), 159–62.

described in the sources as carefully and accurately as possible to allow for a more specific comparison between different cases. Preference will therefore be given to terminology that describes the formal character of the measure in question (like trial, expulsion, confiscation of property, protective measure, etc.), rather than the intentions behind it.

Marginalized Religion and the Law in the Roman Empire. K. P. S. Janssen, Oxford University Press.
 DOI: 10.1093/9780191946400.003.0001

1

Roman Law and Administration

1.1 Introduction

In order to understand the ways in which Roman officials engaged with marginalized religious groups within their territories, it is necessary to first discuss the wider context in which such interactions took place. Each of the individual encounters discussed in this study occurred within the legal and administrative framework of the Roman world and was therefore fundamentally shaped by its underlying principles. To ignore this fact is to risk artificially disconnecting legal responses to these groups from their societal background,[1] and to treat them as isolated, atypical incidents unrelated to the 'ordinary' legal system. This chapter's discussion of the legal actors, institutions, and procedures that collectively shaped Roman law and administration therefore provides an important basis for later analyses. The field has undergone significant developments in recent years: scholarship has increasingly moved away from the traditional perception of Roman government, and its legal system in particular, as both uniform and highly standardized,[2] and has instead shifted its focus to the significant diversity of Roman administrative practices, as well as the important role played by interactions between different actors within this process.[3] While this diversity makes it

[1] The extent of the connections between Roman law and its societal context is a matter of some debate. In scholarship the two were (and to an extent are) often treated as separate entities, due to the fact that Roman law was long considered its own field, quite distinct from Roman history—see Meyer (2004), 3–4; Pölönen (2006), 399–402 and (2016). It has been suggested by some, especially Watson (1995), 64–73 and (2007), that private law in particular was a similarly isolated field in the Roman world itself. From this perspective, the specialist work of Roman elite jurists had little to do with legal practice and the social realities from which legal situations emerged—or indeed with the needs and values of wider society and changes therein. However, it has increasingly, and convincingly, been argued that law should be seen as a social phenomenon, and important insights have been gained from this perspective. See, non-exhaustively, Bryen (2014[b]), 349; Cairns and Du Plessis (2007); Crook (1967) and (1996); De Angelis (2010); Du Plessis, Andro, and Tuori (2016); Harries (2006), 12; Schiavone (2012). For the acknowledged challenges of such interdisciplinary work, see Du Plessis (2013), 2.

[2] This development has likewise been observed by e.g. Czajkowski and Eckhardt (2020), 3–4; Meyer (2004), 3; and Tuori (2007). It should be noted the period after the *Constitutio Antoniniana* of 212 CE is particularly central to this debate.

[3] See, among others, Ando (2000), (2010), and (2024); Bang (2013), 438–42; Capogrossi Colognesi (2014); Dolganov (2019); Humfress (2007) and (2013); Kokkinia (2004); Richardson (2016); and Roselaar (2016). For a more historiographical approach, see Bryen (2014[b]), who also provides an extensive bibliography on the subject. For a note on the limitations of the available evidence, see Burton (2002). It should be noted that Burton chooses not to distinguish between various types of imperial pronouncements, instead choosing to regard all of these as 'imperial constitutions' and

difficult to exhaustively discuss the many intricacies and nuances of Roman administration within the scope of a single chapter, the room this approach provides for the perspectives of a broad range of societal groups, including those who did not belong to the traditional Roman elite, is absolutely invaluable for our understanding of the treatment of marginalized religious groups. It thus remains important to present an overview of the most important principles and tendencies involved in the governance of the Roman Empire, including aspects of both public administration and the legal system in a narrower sense.

As a starting point, we will first consider the different types of legal measures that existed within the Roman administrative framework, and the authoritative sources from which they could be derived (section 1.2). The Roman legal system allowed for a number of procedures through which regulations could be created, and an exploration of the different possibilities provides insight into both the relevant legal terminology and the different Roman institutions that could be involved. On this basis we can then discuss the procedures through which these measures could be enforced and the ways in which legal conflicts could be resolved once they emerged (section 1.3). Since many of the interactions between Roman officials and members of marginalized religious groups took place in the context of trials, these proceedings, and the involvement of the Roman authorities therein, warrant special consideration, but alternative ways of upholding the legal order will also be discussed. The final part of this chapter (section 1.4) will then take a more detailed look at the workings of the Roman government in the provinces, where many of the known confrontations between Roman officials and members of marginalized religious groups took place. While many of the governmental tools and structures that would over time come to play a significant role in ruling the empire as a whole found their origins in Rome itself, and thus reflected the needs and conditions of the original *urbs*,[4] it can hardly be

'authoritative rule-making and decision-making by the imperial state', which complicates his attempts at nuancing the idea that the Roman authorities were primarily reactive in their approach to provincial administration. See Burton (2002), 252. Within scholarship on Roman law in the stricter sense of the word, recent years have witnessed an increased focus on legal actors beyond the specialist jurists, including the magistrates, advocates, and judges, who, while not having the jurists' level of expertise, nevertheless played an important role in the legal process. See Du Plessis (2016), 4; Pölönen (2016), 16; Tellegen-Couperus and Tellegen (2013).

[4] An example of the continued relevance of the administrative and legal structures of the city of Rome itself, even after the expansion of the empire, can be found in the works of the Roman jurist Gaius, whose *Institutiones* are one of the most important available contemporary sources for Roman legal procedures. Although Gaius wrote around the middle of the second century CE, he prominently includes references to Roman institutions that were strongly tied to the physical space of the capital, like the senate and the Roman people's assemblies—as will be discussed in more detail in section 1.2. See, for example, *Institutiones* 1.98–100. The jurist's continued interest in the capital's traditional institutions, however, is hardly surprising, not only due to Rome's symbolic status but also for practical reasons. Even for many magistrates who were posted elsewhere in the Roman territories, the legal practices of the city were at least passingly familiar due to their previous careers and could thus serve as a useful basis for their work in the provinces. It is little wonder, then, that Gaius repeatedly equates the role of the governor in the provincial legal system to that of the praetor in Rome—see

overemphasized that they did not function in a socio-political vacuum. The expansion of Roman rule over large parts of the Mediterranean world meant that Roman magistrates and institutions had to interact with the existing power structures of the various provinces, and it required the latter's incorporation within the wider administrative framework of the empire. This discussion of the complex ways in which the layers of government related to each other in these parts of the Roman world will include both the role of local, pre-existing norms and institutions, and the interplay between the centralized Roman authorities and their representatives in the provinces. In keeping with the scope of this study, this chapter will be primarily concerned with the workings of Roman administration during the imperial period up to the middle of the third century CE. Whenever necessary, however, institutions and practices from the republican period will likewise be discussed, particularly when they provide insight into the development of Roman law and administration, or when their existence continued to be relevant during the principate.

1.2 Sources of Law

The different ways in which new legal measures could be created, and the technical distinctions between them, were a point of scholarly interest even within the Roman world itself. For large parts of Roman history, but particularly in the late second and early third centuries CE, professional jurists attempted to analyse and systematize various aspects of the legal system of which they were a part, composing a range of writings that continue to be central to our understanding of Roman law.[5] These works included not only commentaries and collections of legal opinions, which often provide access to earlier legal measures by quoting, discussing, and often synthesizing relevant passages,[6] but also handbooks meant for those who practised and studied law, which provide the reader with a broader sense of law's institutional framework. While the works of the jurists are primarily concerned with private law,[7] and furthermore overwhelmingly survive only in

e.g. *Institutiones* 1.6, 1.29, 1.102, 1.183, 2.24–5, and 2.278. The continued importance of Rome even after the expansion of the empire is also underscored by Williamson (2005), 423. For a discussion of the effect the expansion of the Roman territories may have had on Roman attitudes to law, see Schiavone (2012), 240ff.

[5] For the centrality of the works of the jurists for our knowledge of Roman law, and the limitations this brings with it, see Ibbetson (2015), 35–9; Schiavone (2012), 31–41.

[6] For the different types of works composed by these jurists, see Ibbetson (2015), 37 and Jolowicz and Nicholas (1972), 376–7.

[7] Private law was undoubtedly the area that was most systematically and thoroughly developed in the Roman world, while works dealing with the fields of public law, administrative law, and criminal law are much more limited in both scope and number. See Jolowicz and Nicholas (1972), 404 and Ste Croix (1974[a]), 220 for the argument that the level of development of criminal law in the Roman world would never match that of private law. The idea that the Roman legal system was primarily used to

the form of selected fragments incorporated in Justinian I's *Corpus Iuris Civilis*,[8] they thus nevertheless shed an important light both on the spectrum of existing procedures and on the different parties that were commonly involved in the legal process.

This holds especially true for the *Institutiones*, which contains an overview of the most important Roman legal institutions and was included in the *Corpus Iuris Civilis* to serve as a basic handbook for students of the law in the Byzantine period. Much of its contents, however, derive from a substantially earlier work of the same name that was written by the jurist Gaius around 161 CE.[9] Gaius' *Institutiones* appears to have been considered highly authoritative, as is evidenced not only by its prominent presence in the *Corpus* but also by the fact that it is the only work by a Roman jurist to survive separately from the *Digesta* in an almost complete form.[10] As a result, the text provides a useful point of entry to the basic workings of the Roman legal system in the imperial period, and a passage from the opening of the first book in particular serves as a convenient starting point for any discussion of the sources from which legal measures could be derived:

> *Constant autem iura populi Romani ex legibus, plebiscitis, senatusconsultis, constitutionibus principium, edictis eorum qui ius edicendi habent, responsis prudentium.*[11]
>
> The laws of the Roman people consist of *leges*, *plebiscita*, decrees of the senate, orders of the emperors, the edicts of those who have the right to issue them, and the responses of experts.

settle conflicts between private individuals is also supported by Kelly (2011), 163–5 and Schiavone (2012), 107, the former of whom argues that economic disputes made up more than half of the known cases from Roman Egypt in the first three centuries CE. Mommsen (1871–88) and (1899) are widely considered foundational studies on Roman administrative and criminal law, respectively, although they are now considered outdated in important ways. For a more recent analysis of the latter, see Robinson (1995).

[8] The writings of the Roman jurists are overwhelmingly contained in the *Digesta*, which despite being one of the most important sources for this type of legal writing likely only contains approximately 5 per cent of the corpus that was originally available to its compilers—see Honoré (2010), 9. The other parts of the *Corpus* are the *Codex*, which collects imperial pronouncements from the time Hadrian onwards, and the *Novellae*, which cover Justinian's own new laws. The *Corpus Iuris Civilis* is so fundamental to the study of Roman law that it would be almost impossible to enumerate every available edition of its text. For an overview of the most important scholarship on each individual part of the *Corpus*, see Kaiser (2015). For the Latin text, see Mommsen, Krueger, Schoell, and Kroll (2014). The German edition of Behrends, Knütel, Kupisch, and Seiler (1995–2012) is still a work in progress, and at the time of writing contains the *Institutiones* and part of the *Digesta*. For a Dutch edition, see Spruit et al. (1993–2011).

[9] Ibbetson (2015), 29; Schiemann (2006).

[10] Ibbetson (2015), 37; Kaiser (2015), 133. The independent textual tradition of Gaius' *Institutiones* is based on a palimpsest codex from Verona, which contains a copy of the work that may be dated to the fifth or sixth century CE. For a critical edition of this text, along with a commentary, see Zulueta (1946–53). For its transmission, see Nelson (1981), especially pp. 44–6.

[11] Gaius, *Institutiones* 1.2. The distinction between *lex* and *plebiscitum* will be discussed in more detail later in this section. Since both terms carry connotations that are difficult to convey in English, they have been left untranslated.

In this passage, Gaius gives a clear and concise overview of the various sources of law he considers to be of importance to his readers, focusing specifically on those that had been put in writing. The extent to which Roman jurists understood unwritten rules or customs to constitute a direct source of law is a matter of some debate within scholarship. While some jurists, like Gaius, exclude it from their lists,[12] others in a similar context distinguish between *ius scriptum* and *ius non scriptum* (written and unwritten law), and thereby seem to leave open the possibility that uncodified rules could be equivalent to written law.[13] However, this conceptualization of custom as a distinct, independent source of law has been argued by some not to have been developed until the later imperial period, and it has therefore been suggested that the idea of an unwritten 'customary law' must be regarded as 'post-classical'.[14] Indeed, the position of custom within Roman law and administration during the principate, and likely the republic as well, appears to have been a complicated one. The phraseology used to discuss the concept is notably varied, as evidenced by the simultaneous occurrence of terms like *mos* (*maiorum*), *usus*, and *consuetudo*, and does not appear to have been consistently applied.[15] In addition, written sources of law appear to have been favoured over customs: while a number of jurists note that long established custom could be used in particular legal situations to determine the appropriate outcome, they qualify this by stating that it should do so in cases where no clear written law is available (*de quibus causis scriptis legibus non utimur*),[16] and that custom certainly should not be preferred over written law where the two contradicted each other, or where custom upheld a practice that was opposed to *ratio*.[17] Nevertheless, custom can

[12] Particularly Papinian, see *Digesta* 1.1.7.

[13] The distinction between *ius scriptum* and *ius non scriptum* is made explicitly by Ulpian in *Digesta* 1.1.6.1, and is alluded to by Gaius' contemporary Julianus and others in *Digesta* 1.3.32ff. It appears again in Justinian's *Institutiones* 1.2.3. and 1.2.9–11. Gaius himself may be referring to custom as a source of law in *Institutiones* 3.82. For the idea that disagreements between jurists were not uncommon, see Ibbetson (2015), 37.

[14] See especially Schiller (1938), 271 and 281, as well as the discussions of this idea by Humfress (2011); Ibbetson (2015), 39–42; and Jolowicz and Nicholas (1972), 353–5. Naturally, the moniker 'post-classical' is mostly ascribed to Justinian's *Institutiones*, although Ulpian and his contemporaries are also linked to this later increased juristic interest in custom by Ibbetson (2015), 41–2. While it has been suggested that references to custom as a source of law by Julianus and other classical jurists are later interpolations, this idea has been rejected by Jolowicz and Nicholas (1972), 354 and Schiller (1938), 271 n. 11. See Ibbetson (2015) 39–40 for the idea that Julianus' discussion of the subject ultimately differed little from Gaius' insistence that consensus among jurists had force of law. Zulueta (1946–53), vol. 2, 13–14 similarly suggests that Gaius (and Papinian) likely 'did not regard [custom] as a source of law distinct from jurisprudence'. For an alternative reading of Julianus' comments, which sees them as a 'dynamic, problem-solving text' directed at handling specific legal difficulties in the Roman provinces, see Humfress (2011).

[15] Jolowicz and Nicholas (1972), 354.

[16] *Digesta* 1.3.32.pr; see also *Digesta* 1.3.33, 1.3.37, 1.3.38.

[17] *Digesta* 1.3.39, 22.1.1.pr. A later example may be found in *Codex Iustiniani* 8.53.2. While *Digesta* 25.4.1.15 does contain an example of custom prevailing over the stipulations of the praetor, it is notable that the provisions in this particular case are characterized as having been made *leviter*, which would make insisting on strict adherence unequitable.

hardly be said to have been without standing altogether: the concept of ancestral customs had great symbolic resonance throughout the Mediterranean world, both in the legal sphere and outside of it, and furthermore came with important social and moral connotations.[18] It is telling that jurists used customs as an argument in a variety of contexts throughout the imperial period, and it is very likely that other participants in the legal process did the same—whether the traditions and ancestral practices referred to were truly as well established as they were claimed to be or not.[19] Whether or not custom was truly seen as an independent source of law or not, it may thus be argued that tradition and ancestral practices played a substantial part in Roman provincial administration, as will be discussed in more detail in section 1.4, as well as Chapter 3 in particular.

Despite his omission of unwritten sources of law, however, Gaius' subsequent analysis of their written counterparts is noticeably thorough. He makes no attempt to rank the written sources of law in order of importance, thus highlighting their diversity and the wide range of legal options that were available to Roman decision-makers. Gaius starts out by discussing *leges* and *plebiscita*. These terms refer to two different types of legal measures that are united by the fact that their validity depended on the authority of one of the Roman assemblies, and thus formally on the will of the people—although the proposals up for vote were often prepared and formulated by one or multiple magistrates.[20] While both types of regulations were historically of great importance, and were likely included in Gaius' summary for that reason, the procedures that created them had become mostly obsolete in the jurist's own time. After the transition from republic to principate the practice of passing laws through Rome's assemblies nominally remained in place for at least a number of decades, but by the end of the first century CE it had largely disappeared.[21]

By contrast, the importance of the *senatus consultum* appears to have grown over the course of the imperial period, although Gaius records that its status had

[18] See Schröder (1996), 158–206 for an exploration of the way in which the concept of ancestral law was used in the works of Greek and Roman authors, as well as in inscriptions. For the importance of ancestral customs in the religious sphere, see Guettel Cole (2008), 57.

[19] Humfress (2011), 29–33 and 47. For a similar argument, see Ando (2011), 2, who argues that later laws were generally presented as honouring tradition, even when their contents differed, or even contradicted each other. This suggests that the idea of traditional practices was rhetorically highly significant, even if these customs were not always honoured in practice.

[20] Ibbetson (2015), 30; Johnston (1999), 3. *Leges* were created by the *comitia tributa* and the *comitia centuriata*, which admitted all Roman citizens, while *plebiscita* were made by the *concilium plebis*, which admitted only plebeians. Gaius discusses these matters in *Institutiones* 1.3. For more information on the differences between these institutions, see Gizewski (2006) and Lintott (1999), 40–64. The *comitia curiata* had ceased to have legislative powers in republican times. See Jolowicz and Nicholas (1972), 86 n. 4. While Williamson (2005) likely goes too far in suggesting that statutes created by these assemblies, during the republican period at least, were meant to reflect broad societal consensus, the symbolic value of legal measures being created by the people's assemblies in nevertheless not to be underestimated.

[21] Ibbetson (2015), 30; Jolowicz and Nicholas (1972), 355–6; Robinson (1997), 12.

been a matter of debate.[22] While the senate was historically of great importance when it came to international relations, and its approval was indispensable for the formal ratification of treaties and alliances, it traditionally did not have the power to create laws on its own authority.[23] The senators were initially limited to ratifying laws made by the *comitia* and to advising magistrates who were planning to propose the law, as was decreed by custom.[24] The term *senatus consultum* originally referred to this advisory function, but over time came to denote decisions made by the senate that had force of law. However, it is unlikely that the senate often took legislative initiative, and in practice the body seems to have functioned primarily as an extension of imperial power.[25] Nominally, a measure would be proposed by the senate, which could lend early emperors in particular a sense of republican legitimacy. In practice, however, it would have been very clear that no motion could be passed without the emperor's approval.

This is not to say that the emperor was limited to acting via traditional republican institutions. While these initially remained in place during the early principate,[26] the emperor's power to create laws gradually grew, and became more distinct.[27] It is little wonder, then, that the will of the emperor was widely recognized as a primary source of law by Roman jurists. The adage *quod principi placuit legis habet vigorem*, 'what pleases the emperor has the force of law', is repeated both in Ulpian and Justinian's *Institutiones*,[28] and Gaius likewise explicitly states that the legal standing of imperial measures has never been doubted.[29] However, it remains important to distinguish between the various ways in which the emperor could issue such decisions. Of the three categories distinguished by Gaius, the *edicta* are most straightforward: this type of measure was intended to directly create a new regulation or to amend one that already existed.[30] This category may also be said to include the *mandata*, a set of administrative instructions given to Roman officials by the emperor at the beginning of their term in office, the relevance of which for provincial administration will be discussed in more detail

[22] Gaius, *Institutiones* 1.4: *Senatusconsultum est quod senatus iubet atque constituit; idque legis vicem optinet, quamvis fuerit quaesitum*: 'a *senatusconsultum* is what the senate orders and determines. It has the force of law, although this has been questioned.'

[23] Capogrossi Colognesi (2014), 247–8; Jolowicz and Nicholas (1972), 40–2; Lintott (1999), 86–8.

[24] For the legislative position of the senate in republican times, see Ibbetson (2015), 30–1 and Jolowicz and Nicholas (1972), 33–4. It is notable, however, that the *Tabula Heracleensis*, which likely dates to around the middle of the first century BCE, mentions *senatus consulta* as a source of law alongside *leges* and *plebiscita* in lines 52 and 72, suggesting that they were at this point seen as source of law of equivalent standing. See Crawford (1996), 382.

[25] Capogrossi Colognesi (2014), 248; Jolowicz and Nicholas (1972), 363–5; Robinson (1997), 6–7 and 12.

[26] This symbolic republicanism to an extent appears to be reflected even in Gaius' *Institutiones*. See Ibbetson (2015), 31–2.

[27] Jolowicz and Nicholas (1972), 366.

[28] See *Digesta* 1.4.1 and Justinian, *Institutiones* 1.2.6, respectively.

[29] Gaius, *Institutiones* 1.5.

[30] Ibbetson (2015), 32.

in section 1.4.2.[31] Until the late third century CE, notably few *edicta* appear to have had a general, empire-wide application. Instead, it may be argued that most were created for specific groups or geographical areas—as we shall once again see when discussing the role of the emperor in the governance of the provinces.[32] The primary distinguishing feature of the *edicta*, then, is that they were essentially the result of the emperor's own initiative, which stands in contrast to the other, more ad hoc types of imperial measures mentioned by Gaius, like the *decreta*. This type of measure was the result of the emperor responding to specific legal cases in the role of the judge, after which his verdicts could gain relevance as potential precedents in other lawsuits and could thereby begin to function as more far-reaching regulations.[33] The last category, the *epistulae*, consisted of all imperial communications. These included letters responding to questions asked by Roman officials, especially those in the provinces, but also replies to the petitions of various communities or private individuals. The legal measures that were created in response to such questions are also known as *rescripta*,[34] and although the actual text of such rulings was often written by specially designated and trained imperial secretaries,[35] it is difficult to overstate their importance. The legal pronouncements in these messages were imbued with the emperor's authority, and *rescripta* therefore allowed the imperial administration to directly respond to very particular situations, while also contributing to the ever growing corpus of imperial rulings on a variety of subjects—the collection of which for future reference could allow them to significantly increase in influence.[36]

[31] The *mandata* are treated as a separate category by Jolowicz and Nicholas (1972), 370–1, while Ibbetson (2015), 32 includes them among the *edicta*.

[32] Ibbetson (2015), 32. For a more elaborate discussion of recent debate on this subject, see section 1.4.2.

[33] Ibbetson (2015), 32. It should be noted that such cases always took the form of a *cognitio* procedure. See Jolowicz and Nicholas (1972), 368. For the role of the emperor as supreme judge and the development therein, see Tuori (2016), in which it is argued that the way for the emperor's role as judge was prepared by, among other factors, the existing system of *clientela* and the jurisdictional role of pre-existing magistrates like the praetor and the provincial governor. For the importance attached to previous judgements as a precedent for later cases, see Ando (2015[a]).

[34] For the different forms rescripts could take, see Jolowicz and Nicholas (1972), 368–9. Sirks (2001), 129 argues that the rescript system found its origins in the republican practice of making requests to patrons by way of a *libellus*.

[35] For the involvement of jurists in the office *a libellis*, which was intended to respond to questions that were addressed to the emperor in person, see Liebs (2010), 165–8. For the argument that this did not mean a lack of involvement on the emperor's part, see Ibbetson (2015), 33.

[36] Millar (2004), 38. The significant potential influence of imperial rescripts, particularly in the work of Roman jurists, can be observed in Justinian's *Codex*, in which a notable number has been included, as well as in Ulpian's assertion that imperial rescripts had general validity throughout in the empire in *Digesta* 47.12.3.5. For the importance that widely appears to have been attached to archiving imperial proclamations of various kinds, see Ando (2000), 91–6 and Ibbetson (2015), 33. It should be noted, however, that despite the fact that such pronouncements would by definition have had legal authority due to the fact that they were issued by the emperor, only a very select number of members of the general public, aside from the original petitioner, would have had access to imperial rescripts, which would have significantly limited their influence in actual practice. For measures intended to be generally applicable, the edict thus would have been the appointed method. For this, see Sirks (2001), 127–8, 131–2, and 135.

The emperor, however, was not the only magistrate who could issue legal measures. Gaius names 'the edicts of those who have the right to issue them' as an important source of law, and includes aediles, provincial magistrates, and especially the peregrine and urban praetors, in this category.[37] While the position of the provincial governor is more centrally important to the present study, and will therefore be discussed more thoroughly later in this chapter, Gaius' prominent inclusion of the *praetor urbanus* in particular is, in itself, hardly surprising.[38] This was the magistrate who was traditionally responsible for the bulk of judicial matters within the city of Rome, and the edict he issued at the beginning of his term in office originally formed the formal basis for that year's legal proceedings in the capital.[39] Since the praetorian edict dealt exclusively with private law, however, we need not delve into the details of its functioning here. For now, it is sufficient to remark that the importance of the praetorian edict for civil procedures in the capital gradually diminished, giving way to the so-called *cognitio* proceeding that also became prevalent in criminal cases, as will be discussed in more detail in section 1.3.

The final source of law mentioned by Gaius underlines the important position jurists like himself held in Roman administration. Since many Roman magistrates received limited formal legal training,[40] the advice of legal experts who had access to relevant knowledge and examples was of great importance even in republican times, and it is therefore little wonder that the so-called *responsa prudentium* are

[37] Gaius, *Institutiones* 1.6. The rulings of these magistrates are also collectively described as the *ius honorarium*.

[38] The *praetor urbanus* was only responsible for civil cases between Roman citizens. Disputes between citizens and non-citizens were treated by the *praetor peregrinus*, a position that existed from 242 BCE onwards. In such cases, the *praetor peregrinus* made use of the so-called *ius gentium*, a form of law that was considered to apply to all peoples, rather than being limited to Roman citizens. See Jolowicz and Nicholas (1972), 102–7. The term *praetor* is also used to refer to the magistrates who concerned themselves with criminal cases in the so-called *quaestiones perpetuae*, about which more will be said in section 1.3.

[39] Johnston (1999), 3. Rather than being a law in itself, the praetorian edict contained a list of legal remedies that could be used by an injured party to seek reparations arising from the other party's obligations. In essence, then, this edict determined only which types of cases could be brought to trial in the next year, and which could not. Originally, the urban praetor had the right to alter the edict by adding new remedies, amending existing ones, and removing those that were no longer of use—see Galsterer (1996), 398; Johnston (1999), 4. As remarked by Jolowicz and Nicholas (1972), 99–100, this flexibility has at times been seen as the basis for the edict's important status, since it allowed the praetor to respond to relevant developments when they occurred. Gradually, however, the edict became fixed, and (as in the case of the senate) we may ask ourselves to what extent the praetor and other magistrates retained their independence after the end of the republic. See Ibbetson (2015), 28; Johnston (1999), 4; Jolowicz and Nicholas (1972), 356–7. In the early second century CE, Hadrian officially standardized the praetorian edict, thus creating what is commonly known as the *edictum perpetuum*. For the argument that important steps in this direction were already made during the late republican and early imperial periods, see Schiavone (2012), 325 and 353–61. See Peachin (2001), 110–11 for the idea that this codification did not put an end to legal debate surrounding the edict.

[40] Johnston (1999), 5. The extent to which so-called lay judges in particular were trained in the law has become a matter of some debate. For a discussion of this issue, see Metzger (2004).

included among Gaius' sources of law.[41] It is generally acknowledged that jurists contributed significantly to the Roman legal process, and Roman legal culture in general,[42] by collecting earlier pronouncements on specific issues, and by using them to establish what they believed to be the 'correct' legal rule—which they could do by expanding the application of a particular existing rule to cover new situations, or (as will also be discussed in Chapter 2) by attempting to create coherence between previous measures that did not originally exist.[43] Thus, while the opinions of the jurists were likely not universally binding, they could certainly be considered important guidelines, and this authority would only have increased if they obtained an imperial endorsement.[44]

1.3 Upholding Public Order: Trials and Police Actions

Rather than being limited to laws in the strict sense of the word, then, the Roman legal system included a number of different ways of creating legal measures, many of which involved a degree of flexibility, or indeed a range of different parties—including those beyond the formal sphere of the Roman government. A similar pattern emerges when we investigate the procedures through which such measures could be enforced and that contributed to upholding public order. While it has widely been observed that the latter in particular was one of the Roman authorities' primary concerns,[45] they were not the only ones to contribute to achieving this goal. One key way of targeting those whose actions were perceived to transgress societal norms was the trial, and significantly the responsibility for bringing cases to court rested not with public officials but rather with private individuals. While government involvement would eventually increase, private

[41] Gaius, *Institutiones* 1.7.

[42] For the importance of the jurists throughout Roman legal history, see Frier (1985), 272; Humfress (2007), 62–92; Schiavone (2012), 32–3 and 137.

[43] Ibbetson (2015), 35–9; Jolowicz and Nicholas (1972), 362–3.

[44] It has widely been assumed that, from Augustus onwards, jurists who were considered to be particularly skilled and learned could be granted the right to speak with imperial approval and authority—see e.g. Capogrossi Colognesi (2014), 320; Ibbetson (2015), 38; Jolowicz and Nicholas (1972), 359–63, who base their arguments primarily on the account of the jurist Pomponius in *Digesta* 1.2.2.48–50. Augustus' involvement, however, has been doubted by e.g. Robinson (1997), 7–9. The increased power of the jurists this measure implies may seem a better fit for the time of Hadrian, who is said to have made certain innovations concerning this practice (although their nature, too, remains uncertain), and the available sources on the *ius respondendi* in general are exceedingly difficult to interpret—especially the account of Pomponius in *Digesta* 1.2.2.49, which contains some puzzling difficulties. The same holds true of Gaius' suggestion that consensus among these authorized jurists created a *de facto* law, which subsequently had to be followed by judges in relevant cases—see Gaius, *Institutiones* 1.7. This statement has given rise to substantial debate about its interpretation, and much regarding its implications and the *ius respondendi* in general remains unclear. For an elaborate overview of the debate on both issues, see Tuori (2004). The balance of power between emperor and jurists is discussed in Peachin (2001).

[45] See e.g. Garnsey and Saller (1987), 20.

initiative would remain of central importance in both civil and criminal proceedings for the rest of the principate,[46] and the inhabitants of the empire overwhelmingly remained the ones who decided whether litigation was indeed necessary to resolve any conflicts in which they might be involved, or whether they would instead opt for one of the possible alternative methods of dispute resolution—some of which avoided the legal system entirely.[47]

When trial proceedings did occur, they could take a number of different shapes. Of these, the so-called *formula* trial has traditionally been considered most significant due to its prevalence and distinct structure: this type of procedure consisted of two stages,[48] and was reserved for civil cases, which likely made up the more prominent part of legal proceedings that took place in the city of Rome.[49] This type of trial was therefore firmly linked to the aforementioned edict of the urban praetor, which restricted the types of cases that could be brought forward.[50] In the case of criminal trials, which are of greater importance to the

[46] For the role of private accusers in civil cases, see Johnston (1999), 112; Metzger (2015), 282 and 285; and Rüfner (2016), 263–4. The praetor could in theory grant the accuser possession of the accused's property in order to satisfy the former's demands, should the latter fail to appear during the trial. See Johnston (1999), 123–4. For the idea that trials may well have been used to escalate disputes, rather than resolve them, see Kelly (2011), 287–326. For the importance of private initiative in criminal cases, see Harries (2007), 8 and 31; Lintott (2015), 301; and Robinson (1995), 4–5. The fear of private accusers who made their claims in exchange for a reward, also known as *delatores*, features prominently in Roman literature. See Robinson (2007).

[47] For the spectrum of methods of conflict resolution available in the Roman world, including mediation and arbitration, see Bablitz (2016). See Humfress (2007), 31–6 for the persistence of these practices in late antiquity, as well as the argument that most inhabitants of the Roman Empire would avoid litigation if possible.

[48] During the first stage of the proceedings, the respective parties had to appear before the praetor and agree on the exact legal basis for the trial with the help of their lawyers. The judge (*iudex*) who would preside over the subsequent trial also had to be appointed by the praetor with the consent of both parties—see Jolowicz and Nicholas (1972), 200–1 and Schulz (1951), 19. If they were unable to agree, a judge could be chosen from lists of eligible candidates compiled for this purpose, which likely consisted of senators and *equites*, for which see Jolowicz and Nicholas (1972), 176–8 and Johnston (1999), 127. There may have been some additional criteria, although none of these related to legal expertise. The second stage of the proceedings then fell under the jurisdiction of this judge, who was in turn responsible for determining liability. See Schulz (1951), 13. The right to pronounce such verdicts is referred to as *iudicatio*. It is important to note that these judges were private persons (see the term *iudex privatus*, Metzger (2015), 277), and are themselves unlikely to have received consistent legal training—see Johnston (1999), 126 and Metzger (2004), 259. For the difficulties this lack of legal background could cause, see the personal experiences related in Aulus Gellius, *Noctes Atticae* 14.2. Since the praetor and the respective parties generally lacked legal training as well, the presence of lawyers, who were often the only ones with any real legal expertise, was often indispensable. See Schulz (1951), 22–3.

[49] The earlier type of proceeding known as *legis actio* had largely disappeared by the second century BCE, and therefore need not be discussed here. For more details, see Metzger (2015), 278 and 281–3. For the argument that a lot of cases that would today fall under criminal law were seen as civil matters in the Roman world, see Lintott (2015), 301–2. For a more elaborate discussion on what exactly criminal law entailed, see Riggsby (2016).

[50] As noted in n. 39 of this chapter, this edict was not a set of regulations, but rather an overview of the different legal remedies available to those who felt that they had been wronged. The praetor, then, was not himself responsible for passing legal judgement on the case at hand and only had the authority to determine whether a specific claim could be legally pursued, thus Schulz (1951), 13 and 19. The praetor's authority in such matters is referred to as *iurisdictio*. His official permission for the case to

present study, the official procedure looked differently even in the city of Rome itself, and was originally more flexible than its civil counterpart.[51] By the middle of the second century BCE, however, permanent tribunals for a number of specific criminal accusations (the so-called *quaestiones perpetuae*) began to emerge, in which charges were first judged on their validity by the relevant praetor, before being tried by a jury in a *iudicium publicum*.[52]

While two-step procedures continued to be used for certain cases until well into the imperial period, and was formally streamlined under Augustus,[53] they would gradually be replaced by another type of trial in which the entire procedure fell under the jurisdiction of a single magistrate or institution. This type of trial is commonly known as the *cognitio* procedure, but is (particularly in scholarship on early Christianity) also frequently referred to as the *cognitio extra ordinem* or *cognitio extraordinaria*—although it should be noted that the technical meaning and usefulness of the designation 'extra-ordinary' is in dispute.[54] The origins and development of this type of procedure in the empire's capital are difficult to trace,[55] and there likely were significant differences between individual lawsuits beyond the fact that they fell under the responsible magistrate's authority in their entirety.[56]

Nevertheless, the gradual transition to the *cognitio* trial marks an important shift in Roman legal culture: while the magistrate in question still had the right to appoint a different judge to act as his replacement if he so chose, this was now his prerogative, and no longer dependent on the mutual agreement of the parties involved.[57] The procedure therefore represents a departure from Roman republican values by attributing more power to the imperial bureaucracy,[58] while also allowing for a greater degree of flexibility by allowing for lawsuits and verdicts

proceed was given in the form of a *formula*, after which this type of trial is named. This type of document instructed the chosen judge to pronounce a specific verdict, usually by stating 'if x is guilty of y, condemn him to z', although clauses could be added or removed if this was agreed upon by the respective parties. See Johnston (1999), 114. Due to the highly specific phrasing of the praetorian edict, the formal charge had to be carefully chosen. The respective parties might thus favour different complaints in order to increase their personal chances of success, which explains the involvement of the praetor as a third party.

51 The earliest known criminal trials were conducted by a magistrate—possibly with the involvement of an assembly of the Roman people. For this reason, this type of proceeding has also become known as a *iudicium populi*. See Bauman (1996), 5; Harries (2007), 14–16; and Robinson (1995), 1. For a brief discussion of the debate surrounding the involvement of a people's assembly, see Lintott (2015), 304.

52 Bauman (1996), 5; Harries (2007), 18–20; Lintott (2015), 308–14; and Robinson (1995), 2–6.

53 Bauman (1996), 5; Harries (2007), 20; Lintott (2015), 314–17; and Robinson (1995), 2 and 6–7.

54 See e.g. Ando (2015[a]), 112; Harries (2007), 9 and 29–33; Metzger (2015), 295 n. 25; Robinson (1997), 67–8; Rüfner (2016), 257; Streeter (2006), 14; Willems (2023), 493.

55 Metzger (2015), 287; Rüfner (2016), 258.

56 Rüfner (2016), 257–8; Santalucia (1994), 210–11; Schulz (1951), 14–15; Willems (2023), 493–4.

57 Harries (2007), 30; Schulz (1951), 14–15.

58 Jolowicz and Nicholas (1972), 396–7; Riggsby (2016), 319; Rüfner (2016), 258 and 266; Santalucia (1994), 210–11; Tuori (2016), 4–5; Willems (2023), 495–6. This development was also visible in the physical locations in which legal procedures took place. For a thorough analysis, see Färber (2014).

outside the confines of the *quaestiones perpetuae*, which came to be perceived as overly rigid.[59] Innovations outside the boundaries of the established procedures were implemented for both civil and criminal cases on a number of different occasions from Augustus onwards (for which see also Chapter 2),[60] and it is all but certain that even at an early date emperors themselves were not bound by traditional regulations of the *quaestiones perpetuae* when exercising their judicial authority.[61] The same was likely true for other institutions: the senate was allowed to conduct criminal trials on a number of occasions,[62] and by the Severan period, the urban prefect held jurisdiction over all criminal cases in the city of Rome and the surrounding area.[63] Most significant, however, was the prevalence of *cognitio* proceedings in the provinces, where they appear to have been widely, although likely not exclusively, used—for instance in trials against Christians, as will be discussed in more detail in Chapter 4.[64] Given the fact that law and administration in the provinces were united under the jurisdiction of the governor,[65] it is hardly surprising that the *cognitio* procedure is in evidence in these regions from a relatively early date. In Rome itself, the *quaestiones perpetuae* likely retained some of their importance well into imperial period, but even in the capital the *cognitio* procedure appears to have become increasingly commonplace by the third century CE, although it is unknown when it fully supplanted the *iudicium publicum* in practice.[66]

The gradual transition towards the *cognitio* procedure brought with it a number of notable consequences,[67] the most important of which for our current purposes was the fact that magistrates were less restricted in the way they chose to conduct

[59] Civil trials underwent a similar shift, although likely at a later date. See Bauman (1996), 5–6; Harries (2007), 20–7; Lintott (2015), 322; Metzger (2015), 288; Robinson (1995), 10; Santalucia (1994), 211; Tuori (2016), 295; Willems (2023), 494–5.

[60] Bauman (1996), 5–6; Johnston (1999), 47–9 and 121; Lintott (2015), 318–19; Metzger (2015), 287; Rüfner (2016), 258–60; Schulz (1951), 15.

[61] Rüfner (2016), 260; Santalucia (1994); 212–13; Willems (2023), 495–6. The former is unsure whether the special position of the emperor contributed to the development of the *cognitio* procedure. See Robinson (1995), 9 for the argument that imperial verdicts were likely shaped by the procedures of the *iudicium publicum*.

[62] Lintott (2015), 320–1; Robinson (1995), 8; Santalucia (1994), 218–23.

[63] Fuhrmann (2012), 131; Lintott (2015), 322–3; Robinson (1995), 10–11; Santalucia (1994), 213–14, the latter of whom argues that this authority was derived from the emperor himself and was delegated to the relevant officials.

[64] See Knapp (2016), 371 for the argument that all criminal trials in the provinces were *extra ordinem*, meaning that they took place at the discretion of the magistrate. There is, however, some evidence that *formula* trials were also used in civil cases outside of Rome, although this practice seems to have disappeared by the second half of the second century CE. See also Harries (2007), 7 and 30; Lintott (2015), 322; Metzger (2015), 287; Robinson (1995), 11; Rüfner (2016), 261–2; Santalucia (1994), 215; Tuori (2016), 40 and 294; Willems (2023), 296–8.

[65] For the increased criminal jurisdiction of the governor over the course of the imperial period, see Santalucia (1994), 215–17.

[66] Jolowicz (1954), 407–8; Jolowicz and Nicholas (1972), 398; Lesaffer (2004), 90–1; Lintott (2015), 323; Santalucia (1994), 210. For civil cases, the *formula* procedure was only formally abolished in 342 CE.

[67] For a number of other innovations, most intended to limit the ways in which accusations could be brought forward, see Santalucia (1994), 224. Rüfner (2016), 257–8 argues that not all changes in

trials and in deciding with cases were accepted and which were not.[68] In these trials, a magistrate's decision could therefore be influenced not only by the facts of the case and the established procedures and regulations but also by the particular circumstances under which the relevant events took place and the perspectives of the parties involved.[69] It has for instance been argued that this type of procedure allowed magistrates to conduct their own investigations on the basis of a broader range of reports they received from private individuals without the need for a formal accusation according to highly specific procedures, which would have served to make Roman courts more accessible.[70] Similarly, under the *cognitio* procedure magistrates appear to have been at greater liberty to inflict the type of punishment they themselves believed to be most appropriate, rather than being confined by the measures prescribed by the *quaestiones perpetuae*.[71] This means that the socio-political status of the accused could become particularly relevant: those who held Roman citizenship could often expect a more circumspect treatment than those who did not, and social status in general could play an important part in determining the type of punishment that was ultimately administered. Likewise, witnesses of higher social standing were often given greater credulity and could have a better chance of making their voices heard.[72]

Aside from trials, which generally continued to be instigated by complaints made by private individuals in response to unwanted behaviour, whether formally or informally,[73] law and order could also be upheld in other ways. Although the idea that the city of Rome, and the Roman territories in general, did not have a police force as we know it today is by now well established,[74] there nevertheless appears to have been at least some expectation that the authorities should address

trial proceedings that emerged alongside the *cognitio* trial can indeed be said to have been the result of the disappearance of the *formula* trial.

[68] See e.g. Bauman (1996), 5; Harries (2007), 7; Lintott (2015), 322; Rüfner (2016), 258–60; Willems (2023), 294–5.

[69] Harries (2007), 32–3. For the argument that at least some of this flexibility was retained even in late antiquity, and that Roman judges of the period were therefore part of 'an ongoing process of legal interpretation and law-making', see Humfress (2007), 55–61.

[70] Lintott (2015), 322; Robinson (2007), 218–19; Rüfner (2016), 266.

[71] Harries (2007), 22, 27, and 37; Robinson (1995), 10; Santalucia (1994), 225.

[72] Garnsey (1968), 53 and (1974); Meyer (2016); Rüfner (2016), 265; Santalucia (1994), 215–16 and 225; Taylor (2016). For a discussion of the argument that the nature of the punishment was up to the personal discretion of the judge during the early principate, while more fixed rules gradually (although not straightforwardly) started to develop in later periods, see Bauman (1996), 124–40. Nevertheless, status may well have been an influential factor even at an earlier stage, albeit in less formally regulated ways. See also Lintott (2015), 325.

[73] Accusations brought forward by private individuals were likely still essential for opening a procedure on many occasions even in *cognitio* trials. See Fuhrmann (2016), 297 and Rüfner (2016), 263, but also Santalucia (1994), 223. While Santalucia (1994), 224 notes that limitations on the way in which accusations could be brought forward were gradually imposed, it is unclear when these measures were introduced. For the fact that accusers could receive punishment for making false accusations, see Santalucia (1994), 223–4.

[74] See e.g. Fuhrmann (2012), 5–6; Kelly (2013), 213–16; Lintott (1968), 4; Nippel (1995), 2.

major disruptions like riots, as well as other forms of criminality.[75] Both in the capital and in the provinces, then, there existed a diverse range of institutions that could help to combat disruptions of the peace. With regard to Rome itself, military forces were traditionally not allowed to enter the sacred boundary of the *pomerium*,[76] and there likewise originally does not appear to have been a specific magistrature that was responsible for upholding public order,[77] but this does not mean that the authorities had no way of taking action when required. During the republican period, such actions primarily involved magistrates with *imperium*, who could use a variety of measures to impose their will with the help of their personal guard of *lictores* (a principle known as *coercitio*),[78] as well as lower magistrates like the aediles and the *tresviri capitales*, whose duties also included upholding public order.[79] From the early principate onwards, the use of military force in the capital appears to have become increasingly acceptable, especially in the case of riots and other major disturbances,[80] and a growing number of organizations intended to maintain the peace emerged, of which the urban and praetorian cohorts and the *vigiles* were most important.[81] A similarly diverse approach emerges in the provinces. Roman military forces were repeatedly used in cities throughout the empire to combat riots or other substantial disturbances, especially during the imperial period, but they were not the only form of law enforcement available. Local civilian police forces and other regionalized custodial institutions are attested in many parts of the empire, and their role in upholding public order was very likely essential, particularly with regard to day-to-day affairs.[82]

Despite the availability of these various institutions, however, it should be noted that there does not appear to have been a standard procedure for dealing with public unrest: much depended on the nature of the disturbances, the status and position of those involved, the level of popular support for active intervention, and on the attitude of the responsible magistrate.[83] Roman officials could indeed take significant action, and even suspend protections normally granted to those accused of criminal behaviour, when they believed the situation called for it.[84] In particular, cases in which the safety of the Roman state or the person of the emperor was considered to be at risk were given top priority, and under such circumstances the various options available within the Roman legal system would

[75] Kelly (2007); Kelly (2013), 411–12.

[76] Kelly (2013), 414; Nippel (1995), 4.

[77] Nippel (1995), 5.

[78] Nippel (1995), 5. For the argument that these powers ultimately had limited effect, see Lintott (1968), 89.

[79] Kelly (2013), 412; Lintott (1999), 131–3; Nippel (1995), 21–6. See Galsterer (1996), 402–3 for the specific function and jurisdiction of the *tresviri*.

[80] Fuhrmann (2012), 113–18 and 123–45; Fuhrmann (2016), 301–3; Kelly (2016), 379.

[81] Fuhrmann (2012), 113–18; Kelly (2013), 412–13; Nippel (1995), 90–8.

[82] See Fuhrmann (2012), 55–82; Fuhrmann (2016), 299–308; Kelly (2016), 379–80; Nippel (1995), 103–6.

[83] Fuhrmann (2012), 241; Kelly (2007); Kelly (2016), 383–4; Nippel (1995), 112.

[84] Kelly (2016), 380–1.

have been used to full effect. Depending on the context and scope of the events, such disturbances could lead to a *cognitio* procedure before special courts, or even the emperor himself, or be met with large-scale military intervention.[85] In many smaller cases, however, the Roman authorities were likely less actively involved, and it has been argued that the official institutions were not, ultimately, sufficient to address the significant amount of larger and smaller disruptions of public order that occurred on a daily basis. It is therefore likely that the inhabitants of the empire had to be actively involved in ensuring their own safety,[86] and our sources frequently refer to the use of private security by wealthier households,[87] as well as people calling out for help from their neighbours, their patrons—or even the gods.[88]

1.4 Roman Administration in the Provinces

The governance of the Roman Empire, with its notable size and diversity, came with its own particular set of challenges. As Roman rule expanded across the Mediterranean world, it encountered a wide variety of established socio-political structures, institutions, and regulations that could diverge significantly from what Roman administrators were used to. If we are to understand the workings of the empire, it is therefore essential to consider in more detail what role these differing circumstances played in governing the provinces, how the institutions and practices discussed in previous paragraphs functioned within this provincial context, and how the various layers of government interacted with each other. Before delving further into these issues, however, a word of caution is in order. It should be noted that the available source material on Roman provincial administration is fragmentary in nature, which imposes certain limitations: while the subject was certainly reflected on by contemporary Roman authors, no systematic analysis survives in complete form. Even Ulpian's *De Officio Proconsulis*, which as the title suggests was intended to provide an elaborate discussion of the duties and responsibilities of the provincial governor, has been transmitted only in the form of specific passages cited in the *Digesta*, and thus cannot answer all questions that modern scholars might have.[89] Epigraphical and papyrological material can fill in

85 Kelly (2016), 378–83. For the developing connotations of the term *maiestas* over the course of the republican and imperial periods, see Williamson (2016).

86 The extent to which the inhabitants of Rome in particular actually self-policed on a community level is a matter of some debate. Nippel (1995), 35–46 suggests that a degree of self-policing was likely inevitable, while also noting that the line between self-policing and causing further disruption could be a fine one. For a critical perspective on the issue, see Kelly (2013), 416–21.

87 Fuhrmann (2012), 49–52; Kelly (2013), 421–3; Nippel (1995), 36–9.

88 Fuhrmann (2012), 46–52; Nippel (1995), 24.

89 The work's third-century date is similarly problematic. See Harries (2014) for the influence of Ulpian's personal background on his views on the office of the proconsul.

at least part of the gaps and is essential for shedding a much-needed light on the way in which the inhabitants of the provinces perceived and dealt with the Roman authorities. Here too, however, we should be aware of the limitations inherent in these types of sources: not only is the surviving corpus a selection of the documents that originally circulated, created both deliberately and by historical chance, but the available material is also unevenly spread across the different regions of the empire, and suffers from important lacunas.[90] We should therefore be aware that an overview of Roman governance in the provinces of this scope almost inevitably includes certain generalizations, whether intentional or not.[91]

Nevertheless, it remains possible to reach a number of important general conclusions with regard to the general principles and underlying mechanisms that shaped the governance of the empire. In order to do so we will first investigate the power structures present within the provinces themselves, focusing in particular on the role of the Roman governor (section 1.4.1). As the highest official in the territories assigned to him, the governor wielded significant authority, and an understanding of his jurisdiction and duties, as well as the powers and limitations of his office, must therefore be central to any discussion of Roman administration in the provinces. In this context, the role of the local population, including its elites, laws, and institutions, must also be considered. We will then turn to the relationship between provinces and the central government (section 1.4.2) and investigate the nature of the latter's interactions with both lower Roman officials and the population of different parts of the empire. Pivotal to this discussion will be the extent to which the emperor and his officials were directly involved in legal life in the provinces and the methods they used to do so.

1.4.1 Governors and locals

As the primary representative of Rome in the province appointed to him, it was the governor who held supreme legal and administrative authority in the territories under his jurisdiction.[92] Originally, the position was primarily a military one. During the republican era, the term *provincia* was used to refer to a task assigned to an individual official, governor or otherwise, and this concept was so central to

[90] Czajkowski and Eckhardt (2020), 4 and 11; Eck (2009), 195–202. See Bruun (2015) and Rowe (2015) for the limitations of epigraphy when discussing matters of Roman law and administration. Bruun in particular remarks, among his other points, that communities and individuals were more likely to record rulings that were in their favour, thus skewing our perception of the types of regulations that were issued in historical practice. For the argument that epigraphy is nevertheless a highly useful source for the study of Roman law, see Beggio (2016). A similar argument regarding papyrology is made by Alonso (2016). See Meyer (2004) for the importance of *tabulae* in Roman legal practice.

[91] For a recent study devoted to tracing the similarities and differences between the ways in which different regions of the empire engaged with the Roman legal order in much more detail, see Czajkowski, Eckhardt, and Strothmann (2020).

[92] See *Digesta* 1.16.7.2, which provides a citation of Ulpian, *De Officio Proconsulis* 2 to this effect.

the organization of Rome's armies that, in the context of provincial administration, it gradually came to denote the geographical area over which the official in question's authority extended.[93] Especially during the second century BCE, this authority assigned to governors gradually came to include taxation and legal activity, which became increasingly central to their work.[94] While those who held the office could hold a number of different titles, the primary responsibility of all governors was ultimately to maintain peace, quiet, and good order in their respective provinces, and thereby to ensure the stability of the empire.[95] The importance of this part of the governor's duties was already recognized in the Roman world itself, as for instance in one of the letters from Trajan to his governor Pliny the Younger:

> *Sed ego ideo prudentiam tuam elegi, ut formandis istius provinciae moribus ipse moderareris et ea constitueres, quae ad perpetuam eius provinciae quietem essent profutura.*[96]
>
> But I have selected you, with your good judgement, for this very reason: so that you may yourself regulate the shaping of the practices of that province of yours and implement what is beneficial for the perpetual peace of that province.

The success of a governor's term in office, then, depended in large part on his ability to ensure the internal stability of his territories and their continued compliance with Roman rule. In order to achieve this goal, governors could to a certain extent take the measures they believed to be appropriate: they were the primary holder of legal power within their provinces, and therefore had the right, though not the obligation, to judge any case in which they took an interest, or that

[93] Díaz Fernández (2021); Drogula (2021); Lintott (1993), 22–7; Richardson (2015), 45–8 and (2016), 112–13.

[94] Lintott (1993), 55 and 70–91; Richardson (2015), 46 and (2016), 113–14.

[95] In the republican period, governors could hold the title of either *proconsul* or *propraetor*. For the argument that the former remained primarily military-oriented for longer, while the latter's military authority was more significantly restrained, causing attention to shift to administrative affairs, see Drogula (2005), 165–6. In the imperial period, the terms *praefectus*, *procurator*, *legatus Augusti*, and *proconsul* were all used, and a formal distinction between imperial and senatorial provinces may be made. Governors of the latter type officially derived their authority from the consent of the senate and people of Rome, and therefore formally reported to them rather than to the person of the emperor. Nevertheless, this distinction is unlikely to have had a truly significant impact on the relationship between governor and emperor in practice: senatorial governors, too, received a set of instructions from the emperor at the beginning of their term in office, as argued by Jolowicz and Nicholas (1972), 370. See Bowman (1996), 346–7 for the differences in the mode and duration of appointment of the various types of governors, and Bowman (1996), 369–70 for the ranks they held. For the argument that the day-to-day administrative practice of the different types of governors diverged little in practice, see Ando (2006), 179 and Galsterer (1996), 411 and (2000), 346. See Drogula (2005) for the argument that the development of the governor's position over the course of the imperial period found its roots in traditional republican values.

[96] Pliny the Younger, *Epistulae* 10.117. The Latin text used is the version presented by Mynors (1963). For the repetition of *provincia* in this phrase as a sign of 'the bureaucrat's struggle to be explicit', see Coleman (2012), 224–5. The governor's responsibility of maintaining peace and quiet in his province is also emphasized by the jurists Paul and Ulpian in *Digesta* 1.18.3 and 1.18.13.

was brought before them.[97] Criminal jurisdiction and the application of capital punishment in particular appear to have become the particular prerogative of the governor by the Severan period at the latest, to the exclusion of local officials.[98] Governors likewise had significant discretion in deciding the level of punishment they believed to be most appropriate for the majority of the principate and were free to take police measures to ensure public order.[99]

In exercising this significant authority, however, the governor had to take certain logistical considerations into account. In order to effectively maintain public order, governors routinely travelled around their provinces, and the legal and administrative centre of the region travelled with him to the various cities and towns on his itinerary.[100] The governor's entourage consisted not only of his own staff, including soldiers, secretaries, and advisors of various kinds, but also of provincial notables—to name only those officially involved in the business of government.[101] Wherever the governor went, great numbers of people followed to make use of this important opportunity to gain access to the highest authority present in the region and to ask him for advice, legal judgements, and other kinds of assistance. Such visits to different parts of the province were also an important administrative tool for governors themselves, since these travels allowed them to personally survey the areas for which they were responsible, to make the acquaintance of the local notables, and to present themselves as capable (and potentially generous) administrators—thereby solidifying the power of Rome, as well as their personal authority.[102]

In addition to these practical considerations, the governor's power was also not without its legal limitations. Of course, the emperor's power superseded that of the governor from the late first century BCE onwards, but even setting aside imperial legal measures directed at the territories under the governor's jurisdiction (which will be discussed in more detail in section 1.4.2), there were a number

[97] This notable independence in legal affairs is attested for both the republican and the imperial periods. See Fuhrmann (2012), 171; Galsterer (1996), 404–5; Lintott (1993), 65–9; Richardson (2016), 116–17. Ando (2006), 190–1 notes that governors could choose to conduct cases either by *formula* trial or through a *cognitio* procedure. For the governor's authority in his province, which was only exceeded by that of the emperor, see also Ulpian's comment to this effect in *Digesta* 1.18.4. Governors' ability to delegate even cases redirected to them by the emperor is discussed by the second-century Julian in *Digesta* 1.18.8.

[98] Galsterer (2000), 351.

[99] Bauman (1996), 136–9; Harries (2007), 37; Robinson (1995), 10.

[100] Burton (1975); Fuhrmann (2012), 173; Richardson (2015), 51. See Färber (2014), 173–4 for the continued flexibility of provincial legal spaces in the early imperial period. The presence of the emperor, when he chose to travel beyond the capital, likely had a very similar effect, as for instance in the case of Hadrian. See Millar (1977), 28–40.

[101] Lintott (1993), 50–2. See also Fuhrmann (2012), 172–4 and 186–7, who remarks on the 'unsavoury' hangers-on, like pimps, hustlers, and sex workers, who would have accompanied the governor in a less official capacity.

[102] See Slootjes (2004) for the various ways in which late antique governors could act as a benefactor, and the complexities of doing so. Kokkinia (2004) presents an analysis of the various alternative ways in which governors could interact with the inhabitants of their province.

of additional regulations to which he had to adhere. First among these was the so-called *lex provinciae*, which in certain (although notably not all) provinces provided a general framework for the administration of that region.[103] Where they existed, these *leges* established the administrative geography of the province, made arrangements for the collection of its taxes, and determined the status of various cities, as well as their inhabitants and magistrates.[104] However, references to the specific legal measures that would apply in the region were very likely omitted.[105] This gap appears to have been at least partially filled by the edict that was traditionally issued by the governor before he departed for his province.[106] This edict likely mirrored that of the *praetor urbanus* in Rome by detailing the matters on which the governor would pronounce judgement and the way in which he would do so during his time in office, although there is some evidence to suggest that governors originally were at greater liberty to alter the edicts of their predecessors as they saw fit, and that the edicts of different provinces could diverge to a certain extent.[107]

Gradually, however, the governor's edict appears to have become more standardized, as had been the case with the praetorian edict. By the time of Hadrian, the various provincial edicts seem to have converged so much as to have become virtually indistinguishable,[108] and indeed the title of Gaius' commentary *Ad Edictum Provinciale*, with its notable use of the singular, suggests that only one provincial edict existed at his time of writing. In any case, the edicts of the various governors likely served as an important source of law throughout much of the Roman world. While governors do not appear to have been strictly bound by them, and retained the right to instead reach for the greater flexibility provided by the *cognitio* procedure, these edicts could establish an important legal

[103] The *leges provinciarum* likely originated as decrees by individual commanders after Roman conquest and were later confirmed by the senate. For the argument that the existence of such a law can only be attested in a select number of provinces with any degree of certainty, see Czajkowski and Eckhardt (2020), 7–8; Galsterer (1986), 16; Lintott (1993), 28–32; and Richardson (1994), 589. Four measures are commonly cited as examples of such *leges*. The *lex Pompeia* applying to Bithynia-Pontus is referenced in Pliny the Younger, *Epistulae* 10.79, 10.80, 10.114, and 10.115. For the Sicilian *lex Rupilia*, see Cicero, *In Verrem* 2.2.32–42 and 2.2.90, as well as Valerius Maximus, *Facta et Dicta Memorabilia* 6.9.8. Cicero, *Epistulae ad Familiares* 13.48 seems to reference a *lex* for Cyprus created by P. Lentulus Spinther. Finally, a possible *lex Cornelia* applying to Asia may be found in Sherk (1969), no. 65 D, 82–4. For the suggestion that the *leges provinciarum* were not ratified by the Roman assemblies, despite what the term *lex* may suggest, see Richardson (2015), 48.

[104] Galsterer (1986), 16; Jolowicz and Nicholas (1972), 69–70; Richardson (1994), 589.

[105] Galsterer (1986), 16.

[106] This practice was already well established in the late republican period. See Jolowicz and Nicholas (1972), 70; Richardson (2015), 50 and (2016), 116. For the argument that governors in imperial provinces are unlikely to have issued such an edict, see Amelotti (1999).

[107] Ando (2006), 190; Galsterer (1986), 17; Johnston (1999), 9; Jolowicz and Nicholas (1972), 358; Richardson (1994), 589–90, (2015), 50, and (2016), 116. See also Cicero, *Epistulae ad Atticum* 6.1.15.

[108] Johnston (1999), 9; Jolowicz and Nicholas (1972), 358; Richardson (2015), 51. The latter remarks that specifications for individual provinces were likely added as an appendix after the standardization of the edict. For a possible reference to Hadrian's unifying legal policy in the work of Aelius Aristides, see Cortés-Copete (2019).

framework, as well as certain general guidelines that could be invoked by both officials and inhabitants of the province. This appears to have been true even for those who did not hold Roman citizenship themselves but nevertheless believed references to Roman practices to be beneficial for their cause, and therefore included them in their legal arguments. Roman law, then, could play a significant part in provincial administration, and likely did so even before the implementation of universal Roman citizenship in the *Constitutio Antoniniana* in 212 CE.[109]

In addition to these Roman legal frameworks, the governor had to take care to consider the local circumstances he encountered during his time in office. Since the number of Roman officials present in a particular province would generally have been comparatively small, both the governor and the central authorities were strongly dependent on local structures and institutions built on pre-existing circumstances (albeit with certain Rome-imposed regulations),[110] whose collaboration allowed them to govern the region effectively.[111] Governors were highly reliant on self-reporting in their efforts to govern their province and uphold public order, and were often confronted with substantial amounts of petitions and legal cases brought forward by their subjects.[112] A good relationship with the

[109] It has been suggested that the governor's edict, like the praetorian edict, would only have applied to Roman citizens, and would thus only have been of limited relevance in the provinces before 212 CE, for which see Jolowicz and Nicholas (1972), 358. Richardson (1994), 589 counters that there is substantial evidence to suggest that governors did not limit themselves to cases involving Roman citizens. Indeed, Roman legal practices likely had a significant influence in the provinces. It has been argued that they were part of the 'way of thinking' of Roman officials in the provinces, even those who had not received legal training themselves, among others by Ando (2006), 189, as well as Dolganov (2019), 59, and this may indeed help to explain the frequency with which the role of the provincial governor is compared to that of the Roman praetor in e.g. Gaius, *Institutiones* 1.6, 1.29, 1.102, 1.183, 2.24–25, and 2.278. Furthermore, Roman law enjoyed a degree of standing in the provinces, and there are good reasons to assume that even non-citizens attempted to use it on occasion. It has convincingly been argued by Anna Dolganov that litigants in Roman Egypt, at least, could enlist the help of a lawyer to 'speak the language of Roman courts' even before the advent of universal Roman citizenship, and could use arguments from different legal systems if this suited their case. See Dolganov (2019), as well as Ando (2015[a]), 112; Czajkowski and Eckhardt (2018); Humfress (2013), 81 and 86; Hurlet (2019), 136; Merola (2020), 488. While Dolganov limits herself to material from Roman Egypt, similar arguments have been made on the basis of the famous Babatha archive, which dates from the early second century CE. See Oudshoorn (2007) and Czajkowski (2017). Wolf (2015), 67 notes that the use of Roman law is also attested in Dacia. For the prevalence of specialists in Roman law in the eastern parts of the Empire, see Jones (2007). For the idea that the early usage of Roman law by non-citizens contributed significantly to preparing the way for the 'dramatic shift' of the *Constitutio Antoniniana*, rather than becoming more prominent only after the advent of universal citizenship, see Dolganov (2019), 60. Caracalla's motivation for including all free inhabitants of the empire in Roman citizenship are in dispute. See Garnsey (2004), 134 and Hekster (2008), 47–50.

[110] While it is widely acknowledged that Roman provincial administration was inclined to make use of pre-existing power structures, it should be noted that the Roman authorities did impose restrictions on their functioning. For this, see Ando (2006), 181–2; Burton (2001), 205–7 and 210–14; Lintott (1993), 54–5.

[111] Ando (2006), 180–1; Burton (2001), 202–3; Capogrossi Colognesi (2014), 303–8; Czajkowski and Eckhardt (2020), 8–9; Galsterer (2000), 345; Garnsey and Saller (1987), 26; Lintott (1993), 54; Roselaar (2016), 124.

[112] Burton (1975); Drogula (2005), 377–9; Eck (2009), 203–7; Fuhrmann (2012), 174 and (2016), 297. It should be noted that governors often lacked expertise both in the character of their province and the law, and therefore needed assistance, as argued in Czajkowski and Eckhardt (2020), 8 and Fuhrmann (2012), 172. While some governors likely did have such expertise, this was by no means a formal requirement.

local elite was likewise of central importance, and its members were in a position to both aid and hinder a governor in enforcing his authority.[113] Certain cities retained a degree of autonomy alongside their own magistracies and laws,[114] the latter of which likely continued to be employed alongside Roman legal practices by those who saw benefit in using them both before and after the *Constitutio Antoniniana*'s grant of universal Roman citizenship.[115] Local institutions, whatever their particular status, remained essential for the governance of the empire, and could be especially helpful in the day-to-day business of provincial administration, while also granting status to those who held the relevant offices.[116] City governments widely assisted in the collection of taxes, as well as in upholding public order,[117] while local courts or officials could handle certain types of legal

[113] Humfress (2013), 77; Kokkinia (2004), 57. See Rizakis (2007) for the way in which local elites functioned within the Roman Empire. Harries (2014), 197–200 points out Ulpian's belief that it was essential for governors to take the wishes of the inhabitants of their province into account.

[114] See Galsterer (2000), 348–9 for the different types of judicial status that could be granted to the cities of the empire. For the right of certain favoured cities to maintain their own laws, see Ando (2006), 184 and Galsterer (1986), 18–19, as well as Cicero, *In Verrem* 2.2.90 for a practical example. It should be noted, however, that governors could still intervene in these cities if they so wished or were asked to do so—thus Galsterer (2000), 349; Lintott (1993), 39.

[115] There are good reasons to assume that local, pre-existing sources of law continued to be used within the empire both before and after the implementation of the *Constitutio Antoniniana*. Although interpretations of the specific degree of influence of these local traditions vary, their continued existence has been acknowledged, among others, by Alonso (2020); Amelotti (1999); Ando (2016[a]), 290–1; Capogrossi Colognesi (2014), 308–12 and 314–16; Czajkowski (2019[b]), 110–11; Czajkowski and Eckhardt (2020), 4; Dolganov (2019), 59; Galsterer (1986), 24; Hekster (2008), 52; Humfress (2013), 88–93; Merola (2020), 488–9; Tuori (2007), 51. For the idea that Roman jurists were well aware of this legal diversity, see Vonken (2013), §263, as well as Gaius, *Institutiones* 1.55. The idea that the *Constitutio Antoniniana* constituted a swift and full replacement of local law by Roman law, then, is now widely regarded critically, as is the view that substantial differences with regard to the adoption of Roman law existed between the eastern and western parts of the empire. While the influence of local legal traditions in the East, and in Egypt in particular, has been widely recognized, among others by Amelotti (1999); Garnsey (2004); Humfress (2011), 35; and Mitteis (1891), sources from the West are comparatively scarce. It has therefore on occasion been argued that the East, with its long-standing strongly urbanized environment, held on to its own old and complex legal systems more fervently, whereas the West did not have such a well-established tradition, and adopted Roman law with relative ease. For important discussions of this subject, see Czajkowski and Eckhardt (2018) and (2020), 4 and 11; Humfress (2011), 44; Jolowicz and Nicholas (1972), 69; Meyer (2004), 183–4; and Mitteis (1891), 8. In a contrasting view, Bowman (1996), 344 has argued that the East took to Roman rule more quickly, due to the fact that the concept of centralized legal institutions would have been more familiar to its inhabitants. Any attempts to compare the ease with which Roman law and administration was adopted in both parts of the empire, however, must reckon with the lack of evidence from the western provinces. Whatever the case, it seems clear that the Roman Empire knew a significant legal diversity, and that the exact relationship between Roman and local law was repeatedly up for negotiation. See Galsterer (2000), 345; Humfress (2011), 44 and (2013), 92; Merola (2020), 488–92. A similar point regarding the construction of local identities in a wider sense, see Ando (2010), as well as (2016[b]), which argues that Roman authorities actively encouraged the continuation of local religious traditions. Wolff (1979) makes the case that local law and Roman law cannot be said to have competed with each other, since the two were—in his view—not on equal footing.

[116] See Ando (2006), 181, as well as Roselaar (2016), for an overview of the relevant local institutions and their responsibilities, as well as their usefulness to Roman rule.

[117] For the collection of taxes, see Bowman (1996), 362 and Galsterer (2000), 356–7. For local means of upholding public order, see Fuhrmann (2012), 45–87. Fuhrmann argues that a Roman police force was present in most provinces, and that it appears to have grown in size in the second century CE. However, these soldiers were likely not meant to be involved in disputes between civilians, although individual inhabitants of the provinces may nonetheless have encouraged them to do

cases, or assist the governor in administering justice in other ways.[118] It would be unwise, then, to characterize the role of the local population as wholly deferential. Indeed, members of the local elite, and inhabitants of the province in general, often played a significant part in the administration of their region by encouraging the governor to follow a specific course of action,[119] and they could likewise create significant difficulties when dissatisfied with his performance. Governors could formally be tried for misconduct only after their term in office was over, but a failure to balance the intricacies of local politics and the interests of various factions (for which see Chapters 3 and 4 in particular) could still result in complaints being made even during his time in office, which he would have been eager to avoid, and which could cause significant damage to his career—as is perhaps most clearly demonstrated by the fate of the Alexandrian governor Aulus Avilius Flaccus (which is discussed in more detail in section 3.10), and a number of Pliny the Younger's predecessors in Bithynia-Pontus and some of his other contemporaries.[120]

It thus becomes clear that cooperation between the governor and local institutions was essential for the successful administration of the provinces, and that these actors were strongly interdependent. While it is true that the governor's

so. See Fuhrmann (2012), 214–15. For the limited scope of Roman bureaucracy, see Garnsey and Saller (1987), 20–40; Lintott (1993), 54.

[118] Bowman (1996), 366; Czajkowski (2019^{b}), 121–2; Fuhrmann (2012), 174; Roselaar (2016), 130–1. In certain cities, local magistrates seem to have had limited jurisdiction and were allowed to hear civil disputes, while criminal cases had to be left to a higher (Roman) authority. See Galsterer (2000), 351. While this does not appear to have been the case throughout the empire, Severan jurists ultimately ascribed only inferior jurisdictions to municipal magistrates, as may be seen in *Digesta* 50.1.26. See also the earlier *Lex Irnitana* 84, which dates from the Flavian period and excludes the local *duoviri* from criminal jurisdiction.

[119] Galsterer (2000), 358; Harries (2007), 31–3; Lendon (1997), 6–7 and 194–201. See Slootjes (2004), 61–2, particularly n. 7, for the argument that the governor would often consult locals upon his arrival in the province in order to establish what *beneficia* they expected from him. An interesting example of the local elite spurring a governor into action may be found in an edict from Antioch in Pisidia (93 CE), in which the governor makes provisions for the grain supply of the city after prices had risen significantly due to bad harvests—but only at the instigation of the *duoviri* and *decuriones* of the city. For more details, see Erdkamp (2005), 286–8 and Robinson (1924). On p. 12, Robinson suggests that the local authorities were unable to resolve the situation themselves, whereas Erdkamp (2005), 287 argues that the enforcement of the edict remained the responsibility of the local magistrates and that the governor simply lent his authority to the decision. In either case, it should be noted that both the governor's involvement and the initiative of the locals was necessary for the enactment of this measure.

[120] See Fuhrmann (2012), 173–7 and Kokkinia (2004), both of whom also note that the inhabitants of a city seldom formed a unified community and that the governor had to be aware of the various factions present in a certain region. See also Richardson (2016), 114, as well as Pliny the Younger, *Epistulae* 10.34, which references Roman concerns surrounding factionalism. Tuori (2016), 295 makes the argument that inhabitants of the provinces may have been inspired to seek out imperial assistance in legal matters because the local courts could be dominated by their opponents. For the suggestion that the performance of the governor was the subject of debate in the *κοινά*, or associations of the different cities in a specific province, see Galsterer (2000), 347. For the development of trials against governors who were perceived to have managed their province badly in some way, see Lintott (1993), 97–107. For Pliny's involvement (in various capacities) in trials against provincial governors, and the complexities of these proceedings, see Pliny the Younger, *Epistulae* 2.11, 3.4, 3.9, 4.9, 5.20, 6.29, 7.6, 7.10, and 10.3a.

power was more overt, he frequently relied on the local population to inform him about issues that warranted his attention and to aid the Roman authorities in governing the region effectively. On the other hand, the locals depended on the goodwill of the governor to provide them with an administrative policy that suited their needs. Neither party, then, could successfully function without the other, and negotiation—whether implicit or explicit—between the various levels of government, as well as different forms of law,[121] was essential to Roman administration in the provinces.

1.4.2 Centre and province

The importance of negotiation and interdependence between different levels of government is further underscored by the role the central authorities, and especially the emperor, played in the administration of the provinces. During the republican period, governors had formally been representatives of the senate and the people of Rome,[122] and the former in particular could be an important factor in the government of the empire. The importance of the central authorities only increased during the principate, when governors became answerable to the imperial administration and were reliant on its approval.[123] However, it should also be noted that both the senate and the emperors were, in turn, likewise dependent on lower officials both for information and for representing and upholding Roman authority: they were the ones who were physically present in the province in question and were thus able to be directly involved in, and aware of, its affairs. On the one hand, this meant that governors could have significant influence on the central authorities' attitude towards a particular subject through the way in which they represented the situation, and the suggestions they offered.[124] On the other hand, travel times between the provinces and the current centre of government, wherever it happened to be, could be significant, and the possibilities for speedy and direct communication about urgent matters were thus limited, while more

[121] For the distinction between 'normative' and 'jurisdictional' legal pluralism, see Czajkowski (2019[b]), where it is argued that different norms might be acknowledged and applied within the Roman world, and that there existed the option for alternative dispute resolution beyond the legal fora provided by the state. For the argument that pluralism, of law as well as other areas of life, was an essential characteristic of ancient empires, see Ando (2015[b]), 53–4.

[122] See Drogula (2021), 20–1 and Lintott (1993), 46–8 for the role of the senate and the people's assemblies in the appointment of governors.

[123] Eck (2016), 108. The idea that the Roman Empire was governed by a strong, centralized authority has historically been highly significant. See for instance Mommsen (1871–88, vol. 2.2), 709, who argues that this central authority consisted of both the *princeps* and the senate—a construction he refers to as the *dyarchia*. This suggestion has come to be regarded with suspicion and is now usually rejected.

[124] See for instance Pliny the Younger, *Epistulae* 10.41 and 10.42, as well as 10.96 and 10.97. A more elaborate discussion may be found in Janssen (2021[b]).

straightforward day-to-day affairs would hardly have been worth the effort.[125] To an extent, then, it was in a very practical sense almost unavoidable that the central authorities depended on lower officials to handle the majority of government matters in their province, and a degree of self-reliance on the governor's part would therefore have been not only beneficial but also simply necessary.

Nevertheless, there were still a number of different ways in which the central authorities could be involved in provincial government. With regard to the republican period, our sources indicate that the senate issued instructions on specific important issues from the early second century BCE onwards—which, while not amounting to an exhaustive set of regulations, nevertheless meant that governors could be held accountable if they went against previously established agreements.[126] This oversight only increased during the imperial period. At the beginning of their term in office, governors were provided with the aforementioned imperial *mandata*—a collection of administrative guidelines that set certain limitations to the governor's actions and raised particular issues to which he should devote especially close attention.[127] These *mandata*, however, are unlikely to have covered every situation the governor would encounter in his administrative practice, which meant that communication between governor and emperor rarely ended there. While governors could certainly rely on their personal discretion, they appear to have asked for imperial guidance and approval with some frequency. The tenth book of Pliny the Younger's letters, which is devoted to his correspondence with Emperor Trajan, serves as a fascinating example of the wide variety of subjects about which emperors could be consulted by their subordinates: in Pliny's letters we find references to building projects, regulations regarding the upkeep of orphans, and the location of a burial site—to name only a few of the issues about which the author requested the emperor's advice.[128] While Pliny's collection is the only extensive example of a correspondence between governor and emperor known to us, it is very likely that other governors sent similar

[125] The communicative limitations the governor faced in the management of his province described by Burton (1975), 106 would have applied *a fortiori* to communication between governor and emperor. See also Ando (2024), 132; Millar (2004), 24 and 34–5; Öhler (2021), 273.

[126] Lintott (1993), 43–5 and 97.

[127] For the idea that *mandata* increased in number over time, and likely contained general guidelines as well as instructions applying to specific provinces, see Eck (2016), 107. Millar (1977), 317 suggests that *mandata* were 'the only positive communication from the emperor to an office-holder in the entire course of his functions'. It should be noted that Millar (1966), 164 is likely mistaken in his claim that *mandata* were only issued from the early second century CE onwards. For this, see Ando (2024), 132–3 and Bowman (1996), 348, who suggest that these instructions were already issued in the early years of the principate. The disbanding of the disruptive *collegia* of Bithynia-Pontus appears to have been one of Pliny the Younger's *mandata*. See Pliny the Younger, *Epistulae* 10.96.7–8.

[128] For the authenticity of these letters, see section 4.6.1. Drogula (2005), 1 suggests that Pliny cannot be seen as a 'normal' governor due to the fact that he was sent on a special mission by Trajan—although it should be noted that many of the cases mentioned here were hardly part of Pliny's assignment.

queries with some regularity, as may also be seen in Chapter 4.[129] Such communications were, in a sense, an insurance policy: they showed the governor's respect and deference towards his superior, while also ensuring that the governor's actions complied with the emperor's wishes, thereby reducing the risk of unprompted imperial intervention, or even retribution, in case disturbances arose and the governor faced accusations of maladministration after his time in office.[130] The inhabitants of the provinces, too, could ask the emperor for his judgement, advice, or approval, and the available evidence (including the sheer number of imperial rescripts cited in the *Digesta*) suggests that they did so with some frequency.[131] This practice found its origins in the republican period, when communities throughout the empire attempted to influence Roman policy in a variety of ways (see also Chapter 3),[132] and it certainly did not disappear during the principate. Pliny's letters reference a number of cases in which the governor served as an intermediary between the emperor and the local population, but the inhabitants of the empire could also approach the emperor in more direct ways.[133] In particular, the emergence of imperial power meant that there was now an authority above the governor to whom legal cases could be appealed, which appears to have been formally possible during republican times but was extremely difficult in practice.[134] In addition to legal appeals, delegations could be sent to Rome to request specific measures, and petitions in writing (*libelli*) were likewise frequently used.[135] It should be noted, however, that emperors could just as well refer matters back to the governor or other (lower) officials, when they felt that the case in question could best be handled 'on location'.[136]

It may be argued, then, that emperors relied heavily on the initiative of their officials and subjects, and therefore took an approach to provincial administration

[129] Eck (2000), 266–8. See also Aelius Aristides, *Orationes* 26.31–2 (also known as the *Roman Oration*) for the assertion that governors consulted the emperor even about the smallest of matters.

[130] For the idea that the emperor could openly intervene in the provinces with relative ease if the governor mishandled his affairs, or matters escalated in a different way, see Bowman (1996), 347–8 and Richardson (2016), 119.

[131] For the argument that this allowed Roman legal officials to 'directly influence the law applied in the provinces', see Tuori (2016), 294.

[132] Morrell (2022).

[133] See Pliny the Younger, *Epistulae* 10.47, 10.59, 10.75, 10.83, and potentially 10.90 and 10.92. For communications between emperor and province in general, see also Eck (2000), 268–71; Fuhrmann (2012), 148–9; and Galsterer (1996), 407–8.

[134] Lintott (1993), 45–6 and 65–9.

[135] For delegations being sent to the emperor, and the regional differences in this regard, see Ziethen (1994). Eck (2000), 269 notes that emperors attempted to limit the number of ambassadors per delegation. Hauken (1998), i argues that petitions became strictly formalized from Hadrian onwards.

[136] Eck (2000), 271 and (2009), 203; Fuhrmann (2012), 148–9. A notable number of cases in which the emperor referred certain cases back to the governor may be found in Pliny the Younger, *Epistulae*. See e.g. 10.40, 10.69, 10.76, 10.84, 10.109, and 10.117. Similar examples from epigraphic sources may be found in Hauken (1998), 2–28, 74–139, and 140–61, while Elliot (2004), 55–60 argues that emperors often delegated boundary disputes to lower officials. See Galsterer (1996), 407–8 for cases being delegated to other Roman officials.

that was to an important extent reactive. This idea has been most famously championed by Fergus Millar, whose seminal discussion of the 'petition and response' model rightly continues to be highly influential,[137] and it may indeed be suggested that the notable flexibility and diversity of Roman administration contributed significantly to its success.[138] This diversity was likely further enhanced by the fact that the central authorities generally appear to have created measures on a province-by-province (or even case-by-case) basis, whether or not they themselves took the initiative for intervention. The number of known centralized legal measures, particularly edicts, that were applicable to the entirety of the empire remains limited until the third century CE, while evidence for imperial regulations directed at particular provinces is noticeably more prevalent.[139] Thus, while the emperors certainly could, and on occasion did, make regulations that applied to the entirety of the empire,[140] a significant portion of Roman administration seems to have been concerned with local situations and circumstances. Indeed, the Roman authorities on occasion appear to have favoured this approach over more unifying tendencies: emperors sometimes explicitly resisted attempts to apply a measure made for one province to another part of the empire, and they could likewise decline to make a pronouncement *in universum*, thus implying a tendency to distinguish not only between provinces but also between cities, and even between individual cases.[141] This focus on specific circumstances also meant that legal measures did not necessarily remain in place indefinitely once they had been issued: while the praetorian and provincial edicts gradually attained a permanent status, it is notable that communities or individuals appear to have asked for the confirmation of previously granted privileges with some frequency, particularly after the ascension of a new emperor, while other measures, like the *mandata*, also appear to have been subject to repeated renewals or

[137] Bowman (1996), 368; Fuhrmann (2012), 150; Galsterer (1996), 407–8; Harries (1999), 88; Millar (1977). For the practical difficulties presented by strong centralized control, see Galsterer (1986), 24–7.

[138] Ando (2015^{b}), 53–4; Bowman (1996), 368; Capogrossi Colognesi (2014), 303; Czajkowski and Eckhardt (2020), 12.

[139] Bowman (1996) 350; Ibbetson (2015), 32. For the idea that the central imperial government was primarily concerned with military matters, upholding public order, taxation, and a number of other areas that were considered to be of importance for performing these tasks, see Sirks (2015), 340–2. Similar points are made by Humfress (2013), 76 and Galsterer (1986), 26–7. For the application of certain measures to specific regions, including Italy itself, see also Gaius, *Institutiones* 1.185, 2.63, and 3.121–2.

[140] For the argument that this aspect of Roman administration has been unfairly relegated to the sidelines, see Ando (2024), 135–6.

[141] See Ibbetson (2015), 32. For the idea that the *mandata*, too, included province-specific instructions, see Eck (2016), 107. Practical examples of regulations specifically dealing with local circumstances may be found in e.g. Pliny the Younger, *Epistulae* 10.34, 10.65, 10.66, 10.97, and 10.113. For the idea that the specific circumstances of individual legal cases continued to be a central part of the Roman legal process even in late antiquity, at least in part due to the acknowledged interpretative role of judges, see Humfress (2007), 61.

supplementations.[142] While it has been argued that this should not be taken to mean that imperial *edicta* necessarily lost their force when the emperor who had issued them died, and that they could in fact be invoked in later periods without the need for formal renewal,[143] it should be noted that the initiative for this often appears to have been taken by the inhabitants of the province, and thus depended both on the accessibility of previous rulings and the extent to which they were considered useful by the general population.[144] This means that Roman administration was not only often localized, but that its regulations could also be subject to renegotiation at a later date.[145]

In spite of the often reactive and localized character of imperial legal measures, however, the amount of influence and authority wielded by the emperor can hardly be overstated, and it must be remembered that he was at the very centre of the Roman government, with both lower officials and the inhabitants of the provinces being strongly dependent on his approval.[146] It has therefore been suggested that our perception of imperial governance has been skewed by the fragmentary nature of the available sources, and that epigraphic and documentary evidence for centralized, empire-wide policies that more clearly reflect the emperor's importance may well continue to grow in the coming years. We should therefore, the argument goes, be careful not to dismiss the possibility for wide-ranging imperial measures by default.[147] Although this line of thinking must necessarily

[142] Eck (2016), 107–8; Galsterer (2000), 360; Harries (1999), 84; Jolowicz and Nicholas (1972), 370. For the importance, and prevalence, of embassies to a new emperor, see Ziethen (1994), 115–31, as well as Eck (2009), 195.

[143] See Jolowicz and Nicholas (1972), 367, who suggest that the continued validity of imperial edicts was in doubt in the early principate but soon became well established. This argument is made on the basis of Wilcken (1921), 133–44.

[144] Ando (2015[a]) and (2024), 136. See Ando (2000), 96–117 for the procedures that played a part in the promulgation of a new legal measure. See Ando (2000), 96–117 and (2024), 134–6 for the idea that new edicts would normally have been publicly displayed for a certain period of time in the regions to which they applied, and were thus available to the public. If these edicts were particularly significant for the community in question, they might be engraved in a visible location (a practice that is, for example, referenced in the case of certain Jewish communities), but the overwhelming majority of imperial proclamations would have been archived by the authorities—and possibly transcribed by private individuals who took an interest. See Ando (2000), 91–6. While such archives would have made previous proclamations at least theoretically accessible to some extent—at least if we assume that they were properly maintained and open to the public—this does not mean that each imperial edict would have been continuously upheld, or even remembered, in practice. For the limitations of Roman archival practices, see Haighton (2010), as well as Pliny the Younger, *Epistulae* 10.65, in which Pliny expresses his suspicions that the text of a legal measure presented to him by the people involved might not be entirely correct, and recommends the consultation of the imperial archives to make sure. For a debate on the role of both provincial and central archives in the compilation of the *Codex Theodosianus*, see Harries (1993); Matthews (1993); and Sirks (1993). Sirks (2001), 127–8, 131–2, and 135 provides a critical perspective on the accessibility of imperial rescripts.

[145] For the idea that late antiquity, too, witnessed 'an ongoing process of legal interpretation and law-making, which was driven by concrete cases rather than abstract principles or values', in which legal interpretation was of great importance, see Humfress (2007), 61. Cf. Harries (1999), 81 and 86.

[146] Ando (2024), 133; Bowman (1996), 350.

[147] Ando (2006), 192 and (2024), 136; Bruun (2015), especially 294; Edmondson (2015), particularly 132–3. Each of these authors is, in their own way, careful to suggest a change in nuance, without dismissing the premise that the imperial authorities often acted reactively altogether.

remain largely speculative, even without further evidence in this direction the sheer prevalence of petitions, questions, and requests directed at the emperor by his subjects (and the care with which such decisions were on occasion documented)[148] is in itself highly indicative of both the symbolic and practical importance of imperial responses, and it is almost undeniable that the emperor acted as a unifying force above and behind the empire's institutional and legal diversity.[149] Previous imperial pronouncements were an important source of potential precedent, and while it is unlikely that they were at all times easily available (or in fact regarded as universally binding), there is substantial evidence that private individuals and communities invoked such rulings when it suited their needs—even if the Roman authorities, as we have seen, were not always enthusiastic about attempts to reference measures that had originally been issued for a different part of the empire.[150]

For most of the principate, then, the nature of Roman provincial administration was characterized by an intricate interplay between the emperor, his governors, and the general population of the empire and their local notables. However, it may be suggested that the centralized imperial authorities' direct influence gradually increased, particularly from the late second and third centuries CE onwards. This period witnessed a growing interest in the collection and systematization of

[148] See Ando (2000), 91–6.

[149] See especially Ando (2000), 79 and (2024), 136; as well as Edmondson (2015). For the increasing number of petitions directed at emperors themselves from the time of Hadrian onwards, which may be seen as proof for increasing centralization, see Eck (2000), 271 and (2016), 108 and Ibbetson (2015), 33. See also Tuori (2016) for the emerging perception of the emperor as the supreme judge, and Meyer (2004), 229–30 and 296 for the suggestion that laws in the Roman world came to derive their authority from the almost super-human position of the emperor, rather than the other way around.

[150] Ando (2024), 136; Harries (1999), 81 and 86. Ando (2006), 185 suggests that the use of precedent was so important and ubiquitous that it contributed to the creation of legal uniformity throughout the empire. However, it remains important to distinguish between the widespread use of precedent and the conscious creation of legal uniformity: the first suggests voluntary participation in the Roman 'system', as well as a bottom-up initiative, whereas the latter suggests the centralized creation and enforcement of policy. While the results might be similar, they suggest notably different ways of thinking. The fact that Pliny the Younger, *Epistulae* 10.65 references an imperial edict being read to him (*recitabantur autem apud me edictum*) suggest that this particular precedent, at least, was brought forward by the inhabitants of the province who came before him with their request, not by the governor himself. For similar examples see e.g. Pliny the Younger, *Epistulae* 10.68 and 10.72. For the idea that collections of precedents were made available to governors from the reign of Diocletian onwards, see Richardson (2016), 121–2. Dolganov (2019), 35 argues that the rulings of provincial governors were actively collected in order to be used as precedent, while Ando (2015[a]) notes that imperial rulings, too, were primarily invoked not by Roman magistrates but by those who brought a case to court. See also Pliny the Younger, *Epistulae* 10.65 for the idea that the legal measures presented as evidence to Roman officials could at times be of dubious authenticity. For the argument that the extent to which imperial rescripts were generally valid was very much in flux and depended on their use in practice, see Nörr (1981). For the related argument that imperial rescripts were formally universally valid but were for a long time simply too inaccessible to function that way in practice, see Sirks (2001), 127–8, 131–2, and 135. It should be emphasized that the term 'precedent' is not meant to imply that magistrates were bound to follow previous rulings in similar cases. While the term is used in this way in later periods, the same does not hold true for Roman law—although, as we have seen, such rulings could carry a certain weight.

imperial legal proclamations on the part of Roman jurists, alongside an apparent increase in the number of laws that were directed at the entirety of the empire.[151] The previously mentioned standardization of the praetorian and provincial edict under Hadrian can be seen as an earlier sign of this tendency towards centralization and bureaucratization, and it may be suggested that the growth in the number of Roman soldiers acting as a military police force for the provinces in the same period reflects a similar pattern.[152] Even from the late second century onwards, however, there are indications that an important degree of administrative diversity continued to exist: as discussed, local laws and customs continued to be invoked on an important number of occasions even after the introduction of universal Roman citizenship by the *Constitutio Antoniniana*,[153] and it has been argued that the growing complexity of the governor's responsibilities led to increased pressure and involvement from local elites.[154] Such factors would have contributed to a continued diversity in the implementation of imperial measures, and despite the fact that centralized governance was formally gaining in importance, many aspects of provincial administration continued to be shaped both by lower-ranking officials, like governors, and by the attitudes and cooperation of the general population.

1.5 Conclusion

When investigating the legal and administrative framework in which interactions between the Roman authorities and members of various religious groups took place, it thus becomes clear that the different layers of government were strongly interdependent. This pattern emerged during the republican period, and while the emperor was without a doubt the highest political authority in the Roman world during the principate, and could exert a great deal of influence in that capacity, he was also reliant on his governors and the inhabitants of the provinces to provide him with information about matters that required his attention and to enforce his decisions once he had made them. This reliance on lower officials meant that governors were central to maintaining public order in the empire and could influence the emperor's decision by the way in which they represented the affairs about which they consulted him. The governor's powers were substantial, and he could often operate with significant independence, especially within the

151 Humfress (2013), 75–6; Ibbetson (2005), 191–2; Richardson (2016), 121–2; and Sirks (2015), 335–7. For the difficulties that the later editorial work of Justinian's jurists in particular poses to the historian, see Galsterer (1996), 397. See Ibbetson (2015), 32 for the increase in centralized legal measures.

152 Fuhrmann (2012), 244.

153 For a more elaborate discussion of this subject, see n. 115 of this chapter. See also Humfress (2007), 18–19, who rightly notes that the interpretative efforts of legal professionals remained highly significant for the practice and development of Roman law even during this period of increased codification.

154 Roueché (1998), 34–5.

context of *cognitio* proceedings. In doing so, however, he had to take both the wishes of the emperor, and those of the local population (and particularly the local elite), into account: the goodwill of the emperor was essential for any Roman official who wished to maintain his position, while local institutions were indispensable for a form of government that had a limited administrative infrastructure of its own. Furthermore, the inhabitants of the various provinces could threaten legal action against a governor when they believed him to have acted in a way they found unjust or undesirable, and the petitions and complaints of private individuals and local communities were responsible for instigating many of the actions of the Roman authorities. Finally, the inhabitants of the provinces in turn also depended on both governor and emperor to provide measures that suited their needs—and possibly even grant political privileges. In practice, then, Roman administration contained both bottom-up and top-down approaches to government, and none of the relevant actors could simply impose his will on the others without consequence. Instead, the administration of the Roman provinces may be seen as a process of almost continuous negotiation and re-negotiation between various levels of government and the inhabitants of the empire, which was necessary for maintaining (and restoring) the balance between the different parties.

In large part due to this frequent need for negotiation between various legal actors, diversity and flexibility were essential features of Roman administrative proceedings. While wide-ranging centralized enactments were issued on occasion, it can hardly be denied that the possibility for private petitions, as well as appeals, was likewise built into the system—or that these options were frequently employed, as is evidenced by the prevalence of imperial *rescripta*. Similarly, the enquiries of lower Roman officials, particularly governors, could play an important part in the creation of new measures, and these same lower magistrates were overwhelmingly responsible for their implementation, as well as for the handling of many of the local enquiries and requests we know confronted them. The Roman authorities, then, often took a reactive approach to the governance of the provinces, and many of its measures were originally both ad hoc and intended to be local in nature. The institutionalized flexibility of Roman administration likewise becomes visible in the fact that measures appear to have been frequently repeated, both within the territories for which they were originally intended and elsewhere. Private individuals and local communities appear to have been an essential moving force in this regard: they could ask for the confirmation of previously granted privileges after a change in imperial or gubernatorial leadership or bring forward relevant cases from the past as a potential precedent. While there was no guarantee that such suggestions would be accepted, the importance that was attached to both precedent and ancestral custom throughout the Mediterranean world, and the Roman Empire in particular, allowed the local population to shape the legal landscape to its advantage. This is further evidenced by the fact that, both before and after the *Constitutio Antoniniana* of 212 CE, local law and Roman law were often applied alongside each other in the same region as best suited the needs of those involved in the relevant legal proceedings, as well as local interests and sentiments. Previous imperial pronouncements would have been especially useful in this type of legal negotiation, since their origins would have lent them an important degree of authority. It may therefore be argued that an interplay between tradition and current reality existed alongside the interactions between various levels of government: legal measures were often created to suit specific circumstances, but tradition and precedent could be considered a significant indicator of the shape such measures should take. The nature of the legal framework that was applied to specific cases, then, appears to have been determined by an interplay between emperor, governor, local elites, and general population that was very similar to the negotiations that were so essential for the creation and implementation of legal and administrative measures in general, and usually appears to have been correspondingly flexible and localized as a result.

Marginalized Religion and the Law in the Roman Empire. K. P. S. Janssen, Oxford University Press.
 DOI: 10.1093/9780191946400.003.0002

2
Divination in Roman Legal Measures

2.1 Introduction

In 63 BCE a heavily pregnant woman and her husband were struck by strange visions: she dreamed that her intestines expanded to the point that they covered the entire world, while he witnessed a ray of sunshine emerging from his wife's womb. Both visions appeared to predict their child's future importance, as did the other signs of great things to come that the prospective mother had received. Before the conception of her child, she had fallen asleep in the temple of Apollo and dreamed that she was having intercourse with a snake. She later considered this dream to be a sign of her child's divine parentage.[1] The woman's name was Atia Balba Caesonia, and she and her husband Gaius Octavius were about to become the parents of the boy who would grow up to become Emperor Augustus.

While it would be easy to dismiss this story as an anomaly due to the unique status of the people involved, it is commonly accepted that divination played an important role in most ancient societies.[2] The exact methods that were applied and the cultural setting of the practice may have varied significantly, but the urge to obtain hidden knowledge, often about a personal or collective future, was undeniably widely represented—and even powerful.[3] The aforementioned dreams surrounding Augustus' birth are just one case in which divinatory signs were significant on a larger political scale, but finding other examples, both from the republican and the imperial periods, is a relatively simple matter. We need

[1] Cassius Dio, *Historiae Romanae* 45.1.2–3; Suetonius, *De vita Caesarum: Augustus* 94.4. A significant number of critical editions of Suetonius' *De vita Caesarum* is available. See, for instance Kaster (2016[a]) in the Oxford Classical Texts series. The most accessible version of Cassius Dio's surviving works, including fragments, may be found in the Loeb edition of Cary and Foster (1914–27), the numbering of which will be followed throughout this study. Editions and commentaries on individual books are easier to come by. The more recent Budé editions have focused on Dio's account of the transition from republic to empire, but otherwise the series at the time of writing remains regretfully incomplete. It should be noted that large parts of Dio's work survive only in the form of epitomes composed by the Byzantine scholars Xiphilinus and Zonaras. While both are generally considered to give a fair representation of Dio's original account, and frequently include verbatim quotations, their writings should still be treated with caution due to their tendency to rephrase, heavily abbreviate, and omit certain parts of the narrative entirely—see Burden-Strevens (2019), 14; Davenport (2014), 98–9; Millar (1964), 1–4; Simons (2009), 28–32; Schulz (2019), 176–7. For this reason, references to the epitomized portions of Dio's work are preceded by 'ep.' throughout this study.

[2] Johnston (2004), 370–91.

[3] For a more thorough discussion of the term 'divination' as it relates to the ancient world, see section 2.2.

only think about traditional Roman institutions like the *haruspices*, the Sibylline books, the consultation of *prodigia* before elections and other major events,[4] the presence of diviners at the courts of various emperors,[5] or even Rome's infamous sacred chickens,[6] to see that the political importance of divination in the Roman world cannot simply be dismissed.[7] Material remnants of the presence of professional diviners, like a marble owl that likely once served as a shop sign for one of Rome's many private practitioners (see Figure 1)[8] and the sanctuary of Fortuna Primigenia at Praeneste,[9] furthermore show that divination was not just available to the happy few, but rather to everyone who sought it out. These finds suggest that all levels of Roman society were concerned with gaining hidden knowledge—whether about their own personal welfare or that of the state.

The clear prevalence and importance of divination did not mean, however, that the practice was universally regarded in a favourable light. Certain members of the Roman elite appear to have taken an alternative view, as becomes clear in Cicero's *De Divinatione*, the highly critical tone of which seems to suggest that divination was not universally trusted, or indeed respected.[10] Most especially, however, the complicated and ambiguous position divination held in Roman society is illustrated by the various attempts made by Roman authorities to

[4] See Santangelo (2012) for the argument that divination and law were closely connected in the late Roman Republic.

[5] Cramer (1954), 81–146.

[6] For the tale of the sacred chickens, which were likely used to give an indication of the presence or absence of divine favour in war, see Cicero, *De Natura Deorum* 2.3.7.

[7] For a thorough exploration of the importance of divination in the time of the Roman Republic, see Rasmussen (2003). See Santangelo (2013), 265–6 for the suggestion that 'debate on prediction and divination had become a thing of the past' after Augustus took control over divination. As will be discussed throughout this chapter, however, imperial control over divination can hardly be assumed to have been stable.

[8] Much about this statue, which is generally known as the Owl of Thoms and can be found in the Dutch National Museum of Antiquities (Rijksmuseum van Oudheden; Leiden), remains unclear. At the very least, we know that the piece was acquired in Italy, possibly Rome, in the early 1700s, although its exact provenance remains unknown—see Bastet and Brunsting (1982), nr. 118; Halbertsma (1995), 83 and (2003), 12. It was originally dated to the early imperial period, or to the first century CE, and is at the time of writing still listed as such on the museum's website, where it can be found under the inventory number ZM-7. See Bastet and Brunsting (1982), nr. 118 and Halbertsma (1995), 83. In recent years, however, the description in the museum itself has been changed to include a second-century CE date—which is also adhered to by the collection's curator in Halbertsma (2003), 13, although without further explanation. Correspondence with Professor Halbertsma, who was kind enough to respond to enquiries on the subject, revealed that the date was adjusted to the second century in analogy to the dating of human portraits: in the first century the pupils of the eyes were omitted in portraiture, while they were more generally carved into the material in the second century. As the owl's piercing gaze can be at least in part explained by the fact that its pupils are chiselled into the marble, a second-century date was considered to be more likely. For the slightly stilted Greek of the inscription and its reading, see Beerden (2013), 96 n. 181 and Halbertsma (2003), 12.

[9] The presence of an oracle connected to this sanctuary is mentioned by Cicero, *De Divinatione* 2.41.85–7. The sanctuary appears to have appealed to women in particular. See Coarelli (1987), 67–8. For a more elaborate description of the site, see Coarelli (1987), 35–84.

[10] The extent to which this work of Cicero's reflects his own views on divination has been the subject of debate. For a summary of the relevant arguments, see Wardle (2006), 8–28.

Figure 1 Marble statue of an upright owl crushing a mouse underneath its left claw, which likely served as a shop sign for a private diviner (Rijksmuseum van Oudheden, Leiden). The statue is generally known as the Owl of Thoms. While its exact provenance is unknown, it was likely found in Italy and dates from the second century CE. The Greek inscription on the statue's base should most likely be read as 'Archates Petrios the diviner (μάντις) predicts the future for four asses'.

Image courtesy of the Dutch National Museum of Antiquities/Rijksmuseum van Oudheden; Leiden, The Netherlands.

regulate the divinatory practices of their subjects. The available corpus of ancient sources mentioning legal measures involving divination is nothing short of remarkable: references to trials and legal proclamations related to the practice appear in the works of historians like Suetonius, Tacitus, and Cassius Dio with noteworthy frequency, and are likewise present in the writings of Roman jurists. The types of legal interaction referred to are similarly diverse: we are told not only about trials involving professional practitioners of divination, as well as those who consulted them, but also about attempts to expel diviners from a specific region, and attempts to regulate access to divination in a number of other ways.[11]

The legal position of divinatory practices in the Roman world has, however, received comparatively little attention in scholarship. More frequently, researchers have chosen to focus on the gradual incorporation of astrology as an (at least initially) 'foreign' form of divination specifically into the Roman cultural and intellectual landscape,[12] or on the political role divination could play during the imperial period.[13] Legal measures, on the other hand, are often only briefly referred to.[14] When they are, the view that the legal position of divination was determined by certain specific restrictions on the practice that were enforced throughout the Roman Empire and remained in force for well over two centuries, most prominently championed by Frederick Cramer, continues to be prevalent—despite the fact that it, as we shall see, rests on shaky ground.[15] A re-evaluation of the available sources, as well as the legal mechanisms described in them, is

[11] The argument made by Fögen (1993), 54 and 84, namely that 'Recht' regarding divination did not emerge until the time of Diocletian, is based on a notably narrow definition of the ways in which the Roman authorities could exercise their power and does not take into account the possibility for legal interactions without the framework of a wide-ranging, general law.

[12] See e.g. Barton (1994[a]) and (1994[b]); Green (2014); Grothoff (2016). While the focus of Cramer (1954) is on the legal and political position of astrology, he, too, opens his book with an analysis of the emergence of the practice in the Roman world.

[13] Barton (1994[b]); Domenicucci (1996); Grothoff (2016); Morgan (2000); Potter (1994); Wildfang (2000).

[14] The primary exceptions to this trend are Cramer (1954); Desanti (1990); and Fögen (1993). For an overview of the legal interactions that will be discussed in this chapter, see Appendix 1.

[15] See Cramer (1954). Cramer's primarily astrology-focused study, alongside an elaborate analysis of the various ways in which astrology became involved in Roman law and politics, contains a detailed inventory of all sources he deems relevant to his argument. Although the systematic nature of his work has contributed greatly to its significant influence, and not without reason, Cramer's conclusions are not without their flaws. On the one hand, his list of relevant cases on a notable number of occasions includes sources whose references to divination are far from straightforward. On the other hand, he is inclined to emphasize the importance of accusations of illicit divination in high-profile trials, while perhaps understating the role played by other accusations in the available accounts, as well as the wider circumstances surrounding the relevant trials. For the idea that specific measures against divination remained in place throughout the empire for long periods of time, see especially Cramer (1954), 249–75. Cramer does, however, see expulsions of diviners as temporary measures—see p. 233. The influential nature of Cramer's work is also commented upon by Ripat (2011), 115. Fögen (1993) likewise assumes the existence of a general, empire-wide law but places its inception at a significantly later date. For an alternative framework, which places divination in the context of Roman discomfort about freelance religious experts, see Wendt (2016).

therefore in order, and would not only shed light on the legal treatment of diviners in particular, but also serve to increase our understanding of the way in which the Roman authorities could interact with various religious groups in their territories—particularly those who could easily be perceived as operating outside acceptable societal norms.

2.2 Terminology and Definitions

Before delving into the specifics of these legal interactions, however, it is essential to first consider the relevant terminology used in both the available ancient sources and modern discussions of the issue. An important number of influential modern studies have chosen to employ the monikers of 'astrology' and 'astrologers' to describe the practice they believe to have been targeted by the Roman authorities and those involved in it, while more general terminology related to 'divination' is, by contrast, avoided.[16] At first sight, this distinction may seem to be an unimportant one. However, the use of astrology-related terminology brings with it its own set of assumptions connected to the position and status of the practice in Roman society, which has often been described as ambiguous to say the least. On the one hand, it has been argued by some that astrology was seen as a distinctly 'foreign' or 'alien', and therefore inherently suspicious, phenomenon.[17] On the other hand, however, after the transition from republic to empire the practice also appears to have become increasingly important, until it was, as Steven Green phrases it, 'at the heart of Roman political life'.[18] This shift in status notwithstanding, astrology does not appear to have been universally appreciated, or even accepted, which made its position notably complex. It is perhaps little wonder, then, that the historian Tacitus described astrologers as 'a class of men [...] that will always be forbidden in our state, yet will always be retained', when expressing his dissatisfaction with the significant influence these diviners could have on imperial decision-making in spite of their dubious reputation.[19] Against this backdrop, it becomes especially important to consider the nomenclature that

[16] In this regard, too, the influence of Cramer (1954) continues to be felt. For examples of authors who use the terminology of astrology to discuss the general corpus of legal measures involving divination, see among others Barton (1994[a]), 49–52; Beard, North, and Price (1998), *passim*; Green (2014).

[17] See e.g. Beard, North, and Price (1998), 160–1; Raschle (2020). See Barton (1994[a]), 32–7 for the argument that astrology was originally associated with the lower social classes of Roman society before gradually being adopted by the elite as part of 'Greek' culture. The position of philosophers in Roman society appears to have been equally ambivalent. See MacMullen (1966), 62. For the wider category of diviners as proverbial 'outsiders' in a more general sense, see also MacMullen (1966), 128–62.

[18] Green (2014), 2.

[19] *Genus hominum* [...], *quod in civitate nostra et vetabitur semper et retinebitur*; Tacitus, *Historiae* 1.22.

was used to discuss the relevant legal measures within the ancient sources themselves. On the one hand, the consistent use of astrological terminology would suggest that there was something considered to be inherently dangerous about that practice in particular that led to the creation of legal measures against it, while practitioners of other types of divination were left well alone. On the other hand, however, if the legal interactions in our corpus did not exclusively involve astrology, but rather dealt with a variety of divinatory practices, we might then infer that what was at stake was not the method of divination used but instead some other factor that determined which practices and people were targeted and which were not. The distinction between 'astrology' and 'divination' is thus relevant both for our understanding of the motives behind these measures and for discerning the practical process of enforcing them.

The Greek and Latin texts included in our corpus use a notably diverse range of terms to indicate the divinatory practices targeted by legal measures. Aside from terminology that references fate-telling (*fatidicus*)[20] or fore-telling (*προλέγειν*, *praedicere*),[21] our sources contain a number of nouns used to indicate those who practised divination. In Latin, the most common terms are *chaldaeus*[22] and *mathematicus*,[23] but words like *vates*,[24] *magus*,[25] *somniorum interpres*,[26] *haruspex*,[27] (*h*)*ariolus*,[28] *vaticinatus* or *vaticinator*,[29] *astrologus*,[30] and various phrases that indicate predictions rather than the ones who made them, are also used in similarly legal contexts. The Greek terminology is more limited with regard to the number of different words that are employed, although not

[20] Suetonius, *De vita Caesarum: Augustus* 31.1. In each of the following footnotes on terminology, references are presented in the chronological order of the events they describe, which is also the order in which they appear in Appendix 1.

[21] Cassius Dio, *Historiae Romanae* 59.29.4; Tacitus, *Annales* 11.4; Cassius Dio, *Historiae Romanae* ep.67.16.2.

[22] Valerius Maximus, *Facta et Dicta Memorabilia* 1.3 (*De Superstitionibus*).3; Tacitus, *Annales* 2.27; Ulpian, *De Officio Proconsulis 7* in *Leg. Mos. et Rom. Coll.* 15.2.1; Tacitus, *Annales* 3.22; Tacitus, *Annales* 12.22; Tacitus, *Annales* 12.52; Tacitus, *Annales* 16.14; Scriptor Historiae Augustae, *Septimius Severus* 4.3; Scriptor Historiae Augustae, *Septimius Severus* 15.5.

[23] Tacitus, *Annales* 2.32; Suetonius, *De vita Caesarum: Tiberius* 36; Ulpian, *De Officio Proconsulis 7* in *Leg. Mos. et Rom. Coll.* 15.2.1; Tacitus, *Annales* 12.52; Tacitus, *Historiae* 1.22; Suetonius, *De vita Caesarum: Otho* 4.1; Tacitus, *Historiae* 2.62; Suetonius, *De vita Caesarum: Vitellius* 14.4; Jerome, *Chronicon* AD 89–90 and 93–4; Suetonius, *De vita Caesarum: Domitianus* 15.3; Scriptor Historiae Augustae, *Septimius Severus* 2.8; pseudo-Paul, *Sententiae* 5.21.3.

[24] Livy, *Ab Urbe Condita* 25.1.8; Scriptor Historiae Augustae, *Septimius Severus* 4.3; Scriptor Historiae Augustae, *Septimius Severus* 15.5.

[25] Tacitus, *Annales* 2.27; Tacitus, *Annales* 2.32; Tacitus *Annales* 12.22; Tacitus *Annales* 16.30.

[26] Tacitus, *Annales* 2.27.

[27] Suetonius, *De vita Caesarum: Tiberius* 63; Suetonius, *De vita Caesarum: Domitianus* 16.1; pseudo-Paul, *Sententiae* 5.21.3.

[28] Ulpian, *De Officio Proconsulis 7* in *Leg. Mos. et Rom. Coll.* 15.2.1; pseudo-Paul, *Sententiae* 5.21.3.

[29] Ulpian, *De Officio Proconsulis* 7 in *Leg. Mos. et Rom. Coll.* 15.2.3 and 15.2.5; pseudo-Paul, *Sententiae* 5.21.1 and 5.21.3

[30] Scriptor Historiae Augustae, *Septimius Severus* 2.8; Ulpian, *Ad Edictum* 77 in *Digesta* 47.10.15.13.

necessarily in their meaning. In the relevant corpus, ἀστρολόγος,[31] γόης,[32] and μάντις[33] are all used with some frequency, while χαλδαῖος appears only once.[34] In total, then, we are dealing with thirteen different terms that denote practitioners of some kind of divination, which can in turn be divided into three distinct categories.

Firstly, there are the words that in their literal translation may be taken to refer to a person we can describe as an astrologer proper—someone who gains access to hidden knowledge by way of observing and interpreting the position of the 'heavenly bodies'. Of these, the Latin *astrologus*, which appears to have been rarely used in texts referring to legal procedures, and its Greek equivalent ἀστρολόγος require little to no explanation. However, this category also includes the less obvious *chaldaeus*, as well as its Greek counterpart χαλδαῖος, which in a literal sense refers to a Mesopotamian people that became strongly associated with astrological knowledge over the course of the Hellenistic period, eventually causing this geographical term to be used as a professional denomination.[35] Likewise, the term *mathematicus* can be considered to refer to astrology, rather than any other form of divination, due to the fact that both astrologers and mathematicians were involved in the making of calculations. From the middle of the first century onwards, the word predominantly referred to the divinatory practice, although its more literal meaning continued to be used.[36]

The second category contains words that refer to those practising forms of divination other than astrology, or to divination in general. *Somnium interpres*, as is implied by its literal translation, specifically refers to a person who practises oneiromancy, or divination based on dreams, while the terms *haruspex* and *(h)ariolus* traditionally indicated someone versed in the art of extispicy, the reading of entrails. However, the latter two words are also used without any specific reference to the reading of entrails, and can thus also be used to mean prophet, diviner, or soothsayer more generally—a meaning that is shared by *vates* and *vaticinatus* or *vaticinator*, as well as μάντις in the Greek sources. It bears mentioning that details about the divinatory process are noticeably scarce in the

[31] Cassius Dio, *Historiae Romanae* 49.43.5; Cassius Dio, *Historiae Romanae* 57.15.8; Cassius Dio, *Historiae Romanae* ep.61.33.1; Cod. Paris. suppl. gr. 607A; Cassius Dio, *Historiae Romanae* ep.64.1.4; Cassius Dio, *Historiae Romanae* ep.65.9.2; Cassius Dio ep.67.12.2. The term ἀστρονόμος occurs once in Zonaras 11.15.D.

[32] Cassius Dio, *Historiae Romanae* 49.43.5; Cassius Dio, *Historiae Romanae* 57.15.8; Cod. Paris. suppl. gr. 607A; Zonaras 11.15.D.

[33] Cassius Dio, *Historiae Romanae* 56.25.5; Plutarch, *Galba* 23.4.

[34] Plutarch, *Galba* 23.4.

[35] Grothoff (2016), 201–3. This process is not specific to astrologers—see for instance the term *Thraex* used to denote a specialization among gladiators, or potentially the word *Galli* to refer to the priests of Magna Mater, whom Ovid claimed originally hailed from the Phrygian territory around the river Gallus. See Ovid, *Fasti* 4.361–4. For the argument that ethnic identities like that of Chaldaean were often 'constructed, fluid, and performative, rather than natural, static, and assumed', see Wendt (2016), 113.

[36] Grothoff (2016), 223.

overwhelming majority of sources, and it is therefore generally best to translate the aforementioned terms as 'diviner', unless more specific information is offered.

Finally, we find that terms that usually refer to those involved in magic, namely *magus* and γόης, are also occasionally used to indicate diviners.[37] For the purpose of this analysis, only the instances in which these two terms are used in a divinatory context, or along with other terms that refer to divination, are included. It should be noted, however, that both words can also be used outside of this context to indicate perceived magical arts in general, without any specific reference to divination.[38] While legal measures against magic in a broader sense were on occasion implemented in the Roman Empire, the extent to which such measures found their basis in regulations intended to punish wrongful death or other concrete harm remains an important point of debate that is best addressed separately.[39] For this reason, passages in which the use of magic is mentioned without any reference to divinatory practices are not included in our corpus.

Given the diversity of the terminology used in our sources, it becomes likely that the legal distinction between astrologers and other types of diviners was not as firm as it is often assumed to have been. While astrology-related terminology is certainly most prevalent, not all of the monikers used to describe the practitioners involved in the relevant legal interactions can simply be translated as 'astrologer', with all the connotations that come with the term. Rather, references to the type of divination used often remain ambiguous or include practices that did not involve astrology at all. A particularly interesting example of the use of diverse terminologies are the writings of the third-century jurists, who cite and collect a number of earlier measures on the issue. Remarkably, both the writings of Ulpian and those traditionally ascribed to the jurist Paul use multiple terms to describe diviners directly alongside each other rather than just one, which suggests the absence of coherent legal jargon at their time of writing. It is clear, however, that the connection between these terms was expected to be evident to the

[37] A similar phenomenon occurs in Cassius Dio, *Historiae Romanae* 52.36.3, where Dio presents Maecenas as using the term μαγευτής to refer to diviners who are not officially sanctioned and who mislead the people by 'speaking truths sometimes, and falsehoods more often'. In this passage, Dio's Maecenas attempts to persuade Augustus that he should take strong actions to prevent traditional Roman religious practices from falling into disuse, but no specific historical measures are mentioned.

[38] For a discussion of the use of the word *magus*, as well as an interesting distinction between the usage of the word and its related terms in poetry and prose, see Rives (2010), 53–77. For the idea that *magi* were often linked to divination, see Rives (2010), 61, 64, and 66.

[39] See Rives (2006) and (2011[a]). See Sánchez-Moreno Ellart (2009) for the argument that legal measures against divination were likely not derived from previous regulations against magic. This analysis rightly rejects the connection between the treatment of divination and the *Lex Cornelia de Sicariis et Veneficiis* made by Desanti (1990), 39–41. A full exploration of the relationship between the concepts of 'magic' and 'religion' is beyond the scope of this study. An overview of the various distinguishing factors that have been suggested may be found in Versnel (1991). See Sandwell (2005) for the use of this set of terms in the Christian Roman Empire.

reader. The passage attributed to Paul (henceforth referred to as pseudo-Paul)[40] makes mention of '*mathematicos, hariolos, haruspices, vaticinatores*',[41] without even distinguishing between the various diviners with a conjunction. Ulpian's text likewise refers to *mathematicis, chaldaeis, ariolis*, and even adds an *et ceteris* for good measure—which is particularly telling because it is used in the context of a reference to an earlier expulsion measure from the time of Tiberius, and is thus more likely to include a paraphrase.[42] While it is true that these sources date from a later period, they thus nonetheless show that their authors did not perceive earlier measures as having been aimed at astrologers exclusively, but rather as broader proclamations against a spectrum of divinatory practices. This approach is consistent with the earlier sources. As will be discussed more thoroughly throughout this chapter, the common thread in trials against individual diviners and those who consulted them was generally the type of question that was asked and not the type of divination that was used. Additionally, in cases that involved the expulsion of diviners, astrological terminology is used alongside phrases referring to other types of divination in a number of crucial examples, particularly the aforementioned expulsion orders dated to the time of Tiberius.

However, even in cases where astrology-related terms are used in isolation, we should be careful not to draw far-reaching conclusions. As Pauline Ripat has convincingly shown, astrology was regularly conflated with other types of divination, and individual practitioners often possessed knowledge of more than one divinatory technique, which made it difficult, if not impossible, to delineate who was an astrologer and who was not.[43] In addition, it has been remarked that astrological terminology often carried negative, derogatory connotations, which suggests that terms like *chaldaeus*, *mathematicus*, or *astrologus* were used as slurs, which practitioners were reluctant to apply to themselves.[44] The application of these terms, then, was subject to negotiation,[45] and the particular type of divination used by a particular practitioner was not necessarily the only factor involved in

[40] It should be noted that the *Sententiae* are very likely pseudepigraphal, and therefore cannot be attributed to the historical Paul with any degree of certainty. Their validity and authority were, however, confirmed by Constantine, which demonstrates that use of the work in government circles was already well established by the early fourth century CE, making it a relevant source in spite of its dubious attribution. See Bauman (1996), 121; Giaro (2006); Honoré (2002), 206; Liebs (2005), 41–4.

[41] Pseudo-Paul, *Sententiae* 5.21.3. The Latin text of both the passage from the *Sententiae* and the passages by Ulpian quoted in the *Legum Mosaicarum et Romanarum Collatio* (*Leg. Mos. et Rom. Coll.*) may be found in Baviera (1940), 406–7 and 579–80. A more recent edition of the *Sententiae* with a Dutch translation may be found in Spruit and Bongenaar (1984). The commas in this passage are my own.

[42] Ulpian, *De Officio Proconsulis* 7, transmitted in *Leg. Mos. et Rom. Coll.* 15.2.1. The text of this part of the *collatio* may be found in Frakes (2011), 190–1, with an English translation on pp. 232–3; Hyamson (1913), 128–9 and Smits (1934), 128–9. For the date and authorship of the *collatio*, see Frakes (2011), 1–151 and Liebs (1987), 162–74. The measure from the time of Tiberius will be discussed in section 2.6.3.

[43] Ripat (2011), 131–2. [44] Grothoff (2016), 374. [45] Grothoff (2016), 383–4.

determining who was described as an astrologer, and who was not. This once again suggests that the group targeted by these legal measures was likely larger than is implied by a strict adherence to astrological terminology, and it is therefore doubtful that those described as astrologers were a distinct, recognizable group separate from other types of divinatory practitioners.

When taking the terminology that is used in ancient sources into consideration, it thus becomes likely that legal measures were not limited to those who used astrological means to obtain hidden knowledge, and that they instead targeted aspects of the divinatory process other than the specific method that was being used. In that sense, it is probable that astrology was no more likely to be targeted than any other form of divination, and that astrologers were simply included as one of the various possible groups of diviners to whom measures could be applied. To speak simply of 'astrology' is therefore not sufficient, and for this reason the term 'divination' will be used throughout this chapter to indicate the spectrum of methods and divinatory specialisms that were included in Roman legal measures. In turn, the term 'astrology' will only be used when our sources make clear reference to the use of the heavenly bodies to gain access to hidden knowledge or as a literal translation in cases where they employ specific nomenclature that refers to this practice.

Thus far, we have primarily used the word 'divination' to indicate a range of different practices that appear in accounts of Roman legal measures, in contrast to the narrower concept of astrology. It remains necessary, however, to briefly discuss how the term itself should be defined. The religious connotations of the practice are often lost in translation when it is discussed in a socio-political or legal context,[46] and for this reason divination may at first glance seem to be 'the odd one out' in an analysis of Roman legal measures dealing with marginalized religious groups. Many modern readers will likely be less inclined to recognize divination as an example of religious behaviour, let alone to see diviners as a religious group akin to Jewish and Christian communities.[47] Astrologers in particular have been described as an 'amorphous, self-selecting social category', the treatment of which is best analysed according to a modern theoretical framework used to discuss subcultures,[48] or as scientific, rather than religious, practitioners.[49] The practice is therefore often presented as a social phenomenon, instead of a religious concept, and the focus of such analyses is often on the inherent 'otherness' that was supposedly ascribed to the practice and those involved in it by

[46] For the argument that Ulpian, *De Officio Proconsulis* 7 describes divination in 'purely non-religious terms', see Rüpke (2016[b]), 65–6. The fact that the latter paragraphs of this passage explicitly reference divine inspiration serves to disprove this argument.

[47] For the idea that the concept of religion is generally defined according to the maxim 'I know it when I see it', see Nongbri (2013), 15.

[48] Ripat (2011), 116.

[49] Barton (1994[b]); Grothoff (2016). While Wendt (2015[a]) and (2016) describe diviners as practitioners, both works do place them in a religious context.

Roman society. This reluctance to see astrology as a religious concept is not helped by the prevalent modern view that anything to do with astrology cannot possibly be serious enough to warrant any real belief on the one hand,[50] and the idea that it became popular among the Roman elite at least in part because it was perceived as a semi-intellectual pastime linked to other traditionally 'Greek' pursuits like to philosophy on the other.[51]

There are, however, good reasons to describe divination, and therefore astrology, as a religious practice. While the exact phrasing differs, most definitions of divination in one way or another describe the practice as a human attempt to gain access to hidden knowledge through perceived contact with the supernatural.[52] This contact occurred by way of perceived signs, which could be invoked or recognized, and thereafter had to be interpreted, often with the help of a divinatory expert.[53] Divinatory signs could take many different forms, but all of them assumed not only that the supernatural existed, but also that communication with such an entity or entities was possible.[54] When regarded as such, it is difficult to deny that divination fits well within the definition of religion established in the Introduction, of which the perceived presence of the supernatural and the possibility of interacting with it in some way are likewise essential features. While divination need not be focused on one or more specific deities, or indeed demand the exclusive allegiance of those involved in it, the practice thus neatly fits within the scope of religious behaviour, especially according to those definitions that see religion as a 'communicative action' with supernatural entities whose presence is considered to be self-evident.[55] If we are to understand the context of Roman legal measures on divination, we must therefore assume that the practice held at

[50] This belief is referenced in Barton (1994[b]), 27; Green (2014), 1; Santangelo (2013), 7. See especially Cumont (1912), xix: 'how could this absurd doctrine arise, develop, spread, and force itself on superior intellects for century after century?'

[51] Barton (1994[a]), 33–7; Green (2014), 65–9. For the idea that philosophy, like divination, held an ambivalent position in Roman society, see MacMullen (1966), 62.

[52] The classification 'perceived' has here been included not necessarily to indicate academic distance from ancient practices, but rather to avoid the presupposition that belief in divination was equally shared throughout the Roman world. While it is very likely that those who consulted divinatory experts, at the very least, believed that their attempts to contact the supernatural were valid, the same need not have been true for the Roman authorities involved in legal interactions with these practitioners.

[53] See Beerden (2013), 19–21 for a discussion of various possible definitions for divination. While Beerden's own definition rightly includes a diagnostic element of divination, this chapter will be primarily concerned with its prognostic elements due to the nature of the events described in our sources. It is important to remember, however, that divinatory methods could also be used to determine the cause of current circumstances, and possibly find a way to improve them. For a rare example of this in the present corpus, see Ulpian, *Ad Edictum* 77 in *Digesta* 47.10.15.13. A more thorough discussion of this source may be found in Sánchez-Moreno Ellart (2009), and in section 2.10 of this chapter.

[54] Beerden (2013), 116–22. See pp. 28–32 and 113 for the central importance of the supernatural in the context of divinatory practices.

[55] Rüpke (2014), 5. A similar line of thinking may be found in Wendt (2016), 32–4 and Raschle (2020), 100. For an indication that divination was likewise included under the moniker of religious behaviour in antiquity itself, see e.g. Cassius Dio, *Historiae Romanae* 52.36.

least some religious importance for a significant portion of the population—as is indeed suggested by the wide variety of evidence for the practice throughout Roman history.

2.3 Outline and Central Questions

This chapter will present an analysis of the known interactions between the Roman authorities and those involved in divination. As stated in the introduction to this study, these different examples will be presented in chronological order as much as possible, beginning with a number of early cases dating to the republican period. While this means that different types of legal interactions (including, among others, expulsions of diviners and trials against individuals involved in the practice) will be discussed concurrently, rather than as distinct practices, this method does allow us to trace the development of, and connections between, existing measures in more detail, and furthermore to pay close attention to the possible reiteration of such measures. Adhering to a chronological order, then, allows us to firmly embed each case in its historical context, which is essential for our understanding of the way in which measures against diviners were created, shaped, and enforced. It bears repeating, however, that an overview of all relevant cases may be found in Appendix 1 for reference.

As is the case throughout this study, care will be taken to incorporate all stages of the legal process, including issues pertaining to the origins, contents, and implementation of the relevant legal measures. In doing so, there are a number of issues that deserve special attention in this particular case. First among these is the question to which region particular measures were meant to be applied. As will be pointed out throughout this chapter, a significant number of the known interactions between diviners and the Roman authorities took place in Rome and Italy, and it is therefore important to consider to what extent regulations that originated in this region were also implemented in other parts of the empire, or resulted in the creation of similar measures in the provinces. This is especially important due to the aforementioned tendency in scholarship to assume that a select number of restrictions on divination remained in force throughout the empire for a significant period of time, and therefore determined the legal treatment of diviners throughout the Roman territories.[56] On a related note, we must also ask ourselves whether legal measures involving diviners were created at the direct initiative of the Roman authorities, or if they were intended as a response to a particular situation or event.[57]

[56] See especially Cramer (1954), 249–75.

[57] For different variants of the latter view, see Potter (1994), 174–6; Ripat (2011), 144–50; and Sánchez-Moreno Ellart (2009), the last of whom refers to the expulsions of astrologers as 'police acts'.

With regard to the contents of these legal measures, it must furthermore be considered what exactly was being targeted: did the Roman authorities simply mean to regulate participation in divinatory practices, or did they instead intend a more far-reaching regulation and suppression of divinatory knowledge in general? This issue was already discussed in the works of Roman jurists,[58] and is particularly relevant due to its possible similarities to the question posed to Emperor Trajan by Pliny the Younger, who wondered whether Christianity was in itself a punishable offence (*nomen ipsum*), or whether Christians should be punished for crimes connected to their beliefs (*flagitia cohaerentia nomini*).[59] In both cases, we are dealing with a possible attempt to make a legal distinction between belief and practice, and the way this issue played out in the case of diviners therefore warrants special consideration.

A final issue that must be kept in mind, is the extent to which legal measures on divination were subject to repetition. Even in antiquity itself, the apparent lack of effectiveness of attempts to regulate divination was commented upon,[60] and it is therefore important to consider whether these measures, as some have argued, were indeed meant to be enforced for longer periods of time,[61] or were instead intended as more short-term actions. Finally, it should be noted that many of the aforementioned questions tie into an underlying debate about the Roman authorities' motivations for acting against divinatory practices. Some authors have firmly rejected accusations of 'imperial hypocrisy', which would have allowed emperors to ban certain types of divination while also participating in the practice themselves, and ultimately assume a deeply held belief in divination on the part of various emperors.[62] From this point of view, emperors attempted to regulate divination because they were afraid of what diviners might reveal about them and their reign, and were thus bound to take the practice seriously. Others, however, have suggested that Roman officials were not so much concerned with diviners' actual knowledge, but rather with their influence on the general population,[63] while others again have claimed that legal interactions involving divination were primarily seen as political in nature.[64] Of course, not all of these possibilities necessarily exclude each other, but it remains important to keep this issue in mind when discussing our sources.

[58] Pseudo-Paul, *Sententiae* 5.21.4 and Ulpian, *De Officio Proconsulis 7* in *Leg. Mos. et Rom. Coll.* 15.2.1–3.

[59] Pliny the Younger, *Epistulae* 10.96.2.

[60] Tacitus, *Annales* 12.52 and *Historiae* 1.22.

[61] See e.g. Cramer (1954); Santangelo (2013), 254.

[62] See especially Cramer (1954), 233. Claims of imperial hypocrisy continued to be brought forward after Cramer's time—see e.g. Green (2014), 102.

[63] Ripat (2011).

[64] Green (2014), 102–4; Sánchez-Moreno Ellart (2009). These last two motivations show some similarities to the so-called 'manipulation hypotheses' discussed in Rasmussen (2003), 25–6.

2.4 Divination in the Republic: Early Interactions

While the overwhelming majority of the known legal interactions between Roman officials and those involved in divinatory practices took place in the imperial period, three additional cases from the republican era appear in the ancient sources. The last of these took place during the rule of the second triumvirate, and can be easily connected to later Augustan measures on the same subject due to the central involvement of Octavian's faction. The two older republican measures lack such an immediate connection and predate their counterparts by more than a century in one case, and almost two in the other. Despite these early dates, however, it remains important to briefly consider the context and contents of these events in order to gain an insight into the extent to which this legal tradition may have influenced later incidents.

2.4.1 Suppression of diviners and foreign priests during the Second Punic War

The earliest known attempt to regulate divination was recorded by Livy in his *Ab Urbe Condita* (Appendix 1.1).[65] Livy dates these events to 213 BCE, in the middle of the Second Punic War, and claims that the recent misfortunes Rome had experienced in the conflict had led the inhabitants of the capital to adopt certain foreign rituals in an attempt to find some sense of security.[66] At first, these rites were only practised in private, but gradually the new-fangled priests and diviners (*sacrificuli ac vates*) increased their hold on their supporters, until they began to exercise their beliefs in public, even on the Forum and the Capitol.[67] This type of behaviour did not go unnoticed, and according to Livy's description those not caught up in the new religious movements were unambiguous in their dislike for what they saw as the abandonment of traditional piety and potentially as an attempt by these religious leaders to trick their followers for profit.[68] Official

[65] While questions have rightfully been raised about the historical accuracy of Livy's account, there are some indications that the essence of this episode, at least, is reliable. Livy famously made use of earlier authors, who in turn used a variety of sources. It has been argued that by the late third century BCE the chronicles of the *pontifex maximus* had been put into writing. Given the religious nature of this part of Livy's narrative, this interaction with diviners may well have been recorded in these chronicles when it first occurred. See Forsythe (1999) and Kierdorf (1990), 202–3. For critical editions of Livy's account see, among others, the Oxford Classical Text of Conway and Walters (1963), or the Teubner edition of Dorey (1976).

[66] For a discussion of the so-called 'stress hypothesis', which holds that the appearance of perceived divinatory signs was caused by mass hysteria, see Rasmussen (2003), 25.

[67] Livy, *Ab Urbe Condita* 25.1.6–8.

[68] Livy, *Ab Urbe Condita* 25.1.8–9 refers to these people as the *boni*. This phrasing may suggest that those objecting to the new religious practices were members of the Roman elite. However, since the account offers no additional details, this idea ultimately cannot be proven.

complaints were brought before the senators, who then proceeded to reprimand the *aediles* and the *tresviri capitales*, who were supposed to safeguard public order, for their failure to act sooner.[69] Devotees were subsequently driven from the Forum, but they appear to have resisted, and riots were only narrowly avoided.[70] The senate finally turned to one of the praetors,[71] who ordered the senate's commands to be officially proclaimed before the public, and furthermore issued an order mandating that any books on prophecy and ritual were to be handed over, and that no foreign rite should be performed in public.[72]

Livy's description of these events contains a number of noteworthy elements. First among these is his claim that the measures against these diviners were instigated by complaints made by members of the public, who were particularly concerned with the civic unrest that was arising within the city in a time of war, which was further exacerbated by a significant influx of people from the countryside.[73] The origins of the ensuing measure, then, may be found in local circumstances, and its character likewise appears to have been local in nature: the senate's order focused on removing those involved in foreign religious practices from Rome's public spaces, and the praetor's measure was likewise focused on circumstances in the city itself. It should also be noted that diviners and other private religious practitioners were seen as a potential threat to public order, but not necessarily as fundamentally or inherently dangerous. The senate originally believed that the matter could have been resolved by the *aediles* and the *tresviri capitales*, both of whose jurisdiction was normally limited to relatively low-level disturbances.[74] Although the matter was thereafter referred to the praetor, he does not appear to have mandated any punishment for previous behaviour, but instead focused on removing the cause of the disturbances by requiring the inhabitants of the city to hand over any writings related to the offending practices and to stop performing their rites in public. Adherence to these new and foreign rituals, then, did not in itself become a banned practice—only their display in public, and especially in consecrated spaces, was restricted, as this would have been especially inflammatory.[75] In this context, the confiscation of handbooks and sacred

[69] See Galsterer (1996), 402–3 for the function and jurisdiction of the *tresviri*. Nippel (1995), 21–6 discusses both institutions.

[70] Livy, *Ab Urbe Condita* 25.1.9–10.

[71] The name of this praetor, as well as his exact designation, is disputed. Livy mentions the *praetor urbanus* Marcus Aemilius, but it has been suggested he was in fact *praetor peregrinus*, and that his urban colleague Marcus Atilius is therefore meant instead. See Broughton and Patterson (1951), 263 and 266 for the suggestion that Marcus Atilius may have performed the duties of both praetors after Aemilius' departure from Rome.

[72] Livy, *Ab Urbe Condita* 25.1.12.

[73] For a similar argument, see Nippel (1995), 22.

[74] Fuhrmann (2016), 299; Nippel (1995), 22.

[75] In this regard, we might observe certain similarities between Livy's description of these events, and that of the *Senatus Consultum de Bacchanalibus* in *Ab Urbe Condita* 39.8–18. There, too, Roman officials are disinclined to ban the new cult completely, instead requiring devotees to request formal permission before they can participate. The procedure, in which the senate urges the city magistrates to take action after complaints by the Roman populace, is likewise similar.

texts was likely intended to limit access to these practices, and to thereby prevent them from spreading further.

2.4.2 The expulsion measure of Cn. Cornelius Hispalus

After this first attempt to regulate divination in the capital, we hear of no further measures targeting the practice until 138 BCE, when a second republican legal measure (Appendix 1.2) is said to have been issued.[76] The event was recorded as part of Valerius Maximus' *Facta et Dicta Memorabilia* (*c.* first century CE),[77] and has been transmitted in two versions, the older of which is likely closer to Valerius' original text.[78] Despite the complex transmission of this passage, the essence of both versions is largely similar: the *praetor peregrinus* Cn. Cornelius Hispalus issued a measure that ordered astrologers (*chaldaei*) to leave Rome and the Italian peninsula within ten days. The precise context of this expulsion is not mentioned, although the older version of the passage suggests that the astrologers were accused of spreading a *quaestuosam* [...] *caliginem*, or profitable darkness, because they used their predictions to ensnare the more gullible members of the public and made a profit by telling lies.[79] The more recent version is briefer in its description of the astrologers' alleged misbehaviour, stating that the goal of the measure was to prevent them from 'selling their foreign science', which seems to imply a similar motivation on the part of the authorities.[80] Both versions also connect the expulsion of the astrologers to a similar measure directed at the Jewish inhabitants of Rome, once again citing attempts to include Romans in their 'foreign' beliefs as the reason for the expulsion (Appendix 2.4).[81]

[76] Although the names in this passage have become corrupted, as discussed by Stern (1974), 357–60 and Wardle (1998), 148, the mention of the consular names does allow for a fairly reliable dating of the measure. It also suggests that Valerius Maximus may have drawn from a source based on the Roman annals, possibly Livy, although the relevant books of *Ab Urbe Condita* are now lost, and only fragments of the relevant epitome survive. The correct name of the *praetor peregrinus* was likely Cn. Cornelius Scipio Hispanus—thus Stern (1974), 358.

[77] Valerius Maximus, *Facta et Dicta Memorabilia* 1.3 (*De Superstitionibus*).3.

[78] The relevant passage has only been transmitted in epitomes of Valerius Maximus' writings. The oldest known edition of the first summary dates from the ninth century and has been attributed to Iulius Paris (Cod. Par. Vat.), while the second survives in a version dated to the fourteenth century and is attributed to Ianuarius Nepotianus (Cod. Nep.). Both authors seem to have created their original compilations in the fourth to fifth century CE. See Briscoe (1998), xiii and xxi; as well as Stern (1974), 357. It has been suggested that Paris mostly remains faithful to Valerius' language, whereas Nepotianus abbreviated in more significant ways. See Wardle (1998), 18–19.

[79] Valerius Maximus, *Facta et Dicta Memorabilia* 1.3 (*De Superstitionibus*).3, Cod. Par. Vat. A similar accusation is levied against the diviners in the previously discussed passage from Livy, *Ab Urbe Condita* 25.1.8.

[80] Valerius Maximus, *Facta et Dicta Memorabilia* 1.3 (*De Superstitionibus*).3, Cod. Nep.

[81] Valerius Maximus, *Facta et Dicta Memorabilia* 1.3 (*De Superstitionibus*).3, Cod. Nep. and Cod. Par. Vat. For the various expulsions of Jews from Rome, see Chapter 3. This incident is discussed from the perspective of Judeo-Roman relations in section 3.4.

The events of 213 BCE described by Livy and those surrounding the expulsion of 139 BCE share a number of crucial characteristics, despite the fact that the measures taken by the Roman authorities were ultimately different in character. In both instances, action appears to have been taken in response to a general sense of unease, and possibly even anger, about the diviners' practices. Livy's account explicitly points out the outrage felt by parts of the populace when they saw that diviners and other religious practitioners had taken over parts of the city. Likewise, the terminology used to describe the events of 139 BCE (in the oldest known version of Valerius' account at least) is strongly focused on the disruptive nature of the astrologers' divinatory practices, and directly references their allegedly deceptive character. Although the passage itself does not offer concrete evidence that Hispalus' expulsion order was a direct response to specific cases of socio-political unrest, some connection to the upheavals of the period, which have been ascribed to growing discontent among the Roman proletariat, cannot be completely ruled out.[82] The danger attributed to these divinatory practitioners, then, appears to have been twofold: on the one hand, the available accounts suggest that they swindled their customers by asking payment for possibly fallacious information, which in itself may well have caused tensions with unsatisfied customers. It is therefore possible that *praetor peregrinus* Hispalus acted in response to complaints made by inhabitants of the city, as had been the case in 213 BCE. On the other hand, and perhaps more importantly, certain people appear to have lent credence to the information provided by the astrologers and followed their guidance, leading these practitioners to be seen as a threat to public order.[83]

The less than favourable sentiments towards diviners on the part of the Roman authorities in both 213 and 139 BCE furthermore appear to have been exacerbated by the fact that they were, at this stage, apparently regarded as an essentially foreign phenomenon, as becomes clear not just from the phrasing that is used in both accounts, but also from the fact that the 139 BCE expulsion was ordered by the *praetor peregrinus*, who dealt with cases involving foreigners, rather than by his urban counterpart. The forms of unsanctioned, private divination practised in these cases therefore appear to have been relatively new phenomena, and it is very likely that astrology in particular was still seen as essentially un-Roman at this point in time. This is not to say, however, that these measures should be understood as putting in place measures intended to ban these 'foreign' cults long term. Instead, both appear to have been implemented in order to provide a solution to specific disruption in public order, and while the question of who 'belonged' in Roman society very likely played a part in determining who was targeted, neither measure appears to have had long-term consequences. We hear

[82] Cramer (1954), 234–5.

[83] Kneppe (1988), 173 and Rives (2007), 190. See also Sánchez-Moreno Ellart (2009), 213, who refers to this action as a 'police measure'.

of no further interactions between the Roman authorities and diviners in the following decades, and this century-long silence on measures against diviners that followed this measure makes it unlikely that any direct legal connection between this expulsion and the next existed.

2.4.3 The expulsion measure of Marcus Agrippa

The third known measure against diviners dates from 33 BCE (Appendix 1.3) and was issued by Octavian's right hand man Marcus Agrippa, who then held the office of aedile.[84] Since this case is only mentioned by Cassius Dio, who wrote centuries after the event and devoted only a single sentence to the proclamation, context is once again lacking. Without any further elaboration, we are simply told that Agrippa expelled astrologers and other charlatans (ἀστρολόγοι and γόητες, respectively) from Rome. Fortunately, however, Dio included this event in a list of other measures taken by the aedile, which may offer some indication of the reasons behind the expulsion. According to Dio's catalogue, Agrippa's measures fit well within the traditional responsibilities of the aedile and were primarily concerned with upholding public order within the city of Rome. This included not only the restoration of public buildings and the maintenance of the city's sewers at his own expense, but also distribution of bread and salt, the organization of public games, free access to both bathhouses and barbers, and the distribution of certain much-needed goods.[85] Such measures undoubtedly served to make Agrippa, and by extension Octavian, popular with the Roman masses, which would have been symbolically important at the very least in a period during which relations between Octavian in the West and Mark Antony in the East continued to worsen.[86] Since unfavourable predictions could have a negative effect on the public's attitude towards Octavian's faction, and could therefore be the cause of unrest in the empire's capital, it is likewise very well possible that there were some political motivations behind the expulsion. The suggestion, however, that astrologers directly attempted to support Mark Antony because of their Eastern heritage lacks any strong foundation.[87] In fact, it is far from clear that astrology was still considered distinctly 'foreign', since by the end of the republic the practice appears to have become more and more accepted among members of the Roman elite.[88] Furthermore, the inclusion of charlatans (γόητες) in the expulsion suggests that Agrippa meant to target a wider group and not just

[84] Cassius Dio, *Historiae Romanae* 49.43.5.
[85] Cassius Dio, *Historiae Romanae* 49.43.1–4.
[86] For a similar argument, see Raschle (2020), 102 and Ripat (2011), 118.
[87] For this suggestion, see Cramer (1954), 83 and 237; Freyburger and Roddaz (1994), 189; and Roddaz (1984), 154–5.
[88] Green (2014), 67 references Cicero, *De Divinatione* 2.47.99 to argue that astrology had come to be adopted by Rome's elite at this point.

those who could be suspected of political disloyalty on the basis of ethnic profiling. It therefore seems more likely that the expulsion of astrologers and magicians was seen as a way to enhance the standard of living in the city in a more general sense and limit the chance of disturbances at the same time.

When comparing the three republican measures against diviners, then, it becomes clear that they have a number of important features in common. The most obvious, and simultaneously most important, point of similarity is the fact that all three measures applied primarily to the city of Rome. The inclusion of the Italian peninsula in the expulsion of 139 BCE does not change the fact that these were essentially localized measures, intended for the capital and the surrounding regions alone. Furthermore, it seems likely that measures against divination, and the expulsion of diviners and other private practitioners in particular, were intended to combat civic unrest within the city. The fact that all three of these measures took place in times when Rome was in turmoil may tentatively be considered to be of importance in this context: in 213 BCE, Rome was under threat due to the Second Punic War, while 139 and 33 BCE found the city threatened by internal conflicts, all of which may have contributed to a situation in which the authorities were particularly concerned with public order. The fact that neither the measure from 139 BCE nor that of 33 BCE—as they have been transmitted to us at least—deals with individual diviners, but rather with the expulsion of these practitioners as a group, is particularly telling in this regard. The same holds true for the fact that no one appears to have been punished during the 213 BCE intervention, when inhabitants of the city were only required to stop practising foreign rites in public and hand in any material that could help in their spread. This course of action seems to indicate that the authorities did not consider these divinatory practices to be a criminal offence as such, but were instead concerned with the disruptive effect diviners as a group could have on the general population by attempting to profit from their art.

2.5 Augustan Measures: A Precedent?

More than perhaps any other Roman ruler, Augustus has become deeply associated with divination. As exemplified by the anecdotes referenced at the very beginning of this chapter, stories about portents, omens, and divinatory signs of various other kinds contributed immensely to the almost legendary status of the first emperor even years after the end of his reign, and during his lifetime divination likewise came to play an important part in his self-representation.[89]

[89] See Wildfang (2000) for a discussion of a number of Augustus' so-called *omina imperii*, as well as the argument that they were carefully crafted to appeal to specific demographics and fit within the wider scope of his propaganda campaign. For the plurality and complexity of Augustus'

Figure 2 Reverse of an aureus displaying Capricorn, with the upper body of a horned goat and the lower body of a fish, alongside the words *signis receptis*. The coin was found in Pergamum and is dated 19–18 BCE.

Image courtesy of the American Numismatic Society. Permalink: http://numismatics.org/collection/1944.100.39177.

The constellation of Capricorn, which became closely connected to the emperor, was even displayed on coinage, thus broadcasting what is often assumed to have been an essential part of the imperial horoscope for all to see (see Figure 2).[90] It therefore comes as no surprise that Augustus' government soon attempted to define, as well as safeguard, the limits of acceptable divination.

2.5.1 The Sibylline books and the destruction of oracular texts

A prime example of this attitude may be found in Augustus' involvement in the creation of an officially sanctioned version of the Sibylline books in 12 BCE (Appendix 1.4). According to our sources, this process involved the destruction of texts that were considered to be less authoritative, and very likely also the subsequent restriction of access to the approved material. Suetonius links this measure to the emperor's adoption of the position of *pontifex maximus* after the death of Marcus Aemilius Lepidus, and claims that Augustus had all oracular texts whose authors were either unknown or unauthoritative, whether written in Greek or

self-representation, see Hekster (2011), 112–14. While not directly related to the person of the new emperor, the so-called *sidus Iulium*, the famous comet said to have appeared shortly after Caesar's death, may likewise be seen as part of the Augustan astrological and imperial programme. The *sidus* was interpreted as a sign of the deification of Augustus' adoptive father Julius Caesar, thus allowing the emperor to adopt the title *divi filius* and to present himself as the heir of a (divine) dynasty. The story of the comet is recounted—though in very different contexts—by Ovid, *Metamorphoses* 15.745ff. and Suetonius, *De vita Caesarum: Iulius* 88, and was likewise referenced on coinage. Pliny the Elder, *Naturalis Historia* 2.23 (93–4) reports that the comet was subsequently worshipped as part of Caesar's cult. For the argument that Augustus' personal influence on this mythologizing of the *sidus Iulium* was not so great as is often assumed, see Pandey (2013), contradicting e.g. Zanker (1988), 34.

[90] The exact position of Capricorn in Augustus' horoscope is still subject to debate. See Barton (1995), 37–44, which gives an elaborate discussion of the emperor's horoscope, as well as an attempt to cast it. See also Green (2014), 97–100; Santangelo (2013), 240–66; Zanker (1988), 47–8.

Latin (*quidquid fatidicorum librorum Graeci Latinique generis nullis vel parum idoneis auctoribus*), consigned to the flames.[91] The measure was likely a local one, as Tacitus notes that unsanctioned texts had to be handed over to the *praetor urbanus* within a certain number of days, which inhabitants of the provinces, and even large parts of Italy, would almost certainly have been unable to comply with.[92] The Sibylline books were in any case exempted from destruction,[93] although both Suetonius and Tacitus state that Augustus made efforts to determine which parts of these famous writings could be considered authoritative before officially sanctioning them, and subsequently destroyed the rest.[94] Both versions of the story make it plain that the emperor took the initiative for the proceedings, and that he had a remarkable degree of influence over the process as well as over the oracles themselves. Suetonius' account, in particular, emphasizes that the approved books were stored under the pedestal of the statue of Apollo Palatinus, whose temple had not only been dedicated by Augustus but is also said to have been directly connected to the emperor's residence.[95] As a result, divination in the capital became, at the very least symbolically, an imperial prerogative: for the time being, it was Augustus' government that decided which prophecies were considered authentic, and it was that same government that took away other citizens' access to these and other oracles, thereby also restricting access to the knowledge these texts contained.[96] Once again, then, maintaining public order and governmental authority was a central reason for measures attempting to regulate divinatory practices.

[91] Suetonius, *De vita Caesarum: Augustus* 31.1. The assertion made in Tacitus, *Annales* 6.12 that Augustus ordered the *multa vana sub nomine celebri* that circulated in the city to be handed over likely refers to the same event.

[92] Suetonius' account furthermore mentions that two thousand works were confiscated. It is difficult to determine whether this number is realistic, as one must take into account not only the question of literacy in the Roman world but also issues of distribution and ownership of the relevant works. As a result, Suetonius' figure cannot be used to determine the scope of the Augustan measure. For the relevance of texts in ancient divination, see Beerden (2013), 139–69.

[93] For an exploration on the origins, character and importance of the Sibylline books, see Buitenwerf (2003), 92–123; Orlin (1997), 76–115; and Parke (1988).

[94] Suetonius, *De vita Caesarum: Augustus* 31.1 and Tacitus, *Annales*, 6.12.

[95] Zanker (1988), 121 places these events in the context of increased centralized (imperial) control on Rome's priestly colleges. For a more elaborate discussion of the motivations for building the temple of Apollo next to Augustus' own residence, see Hekster and Rich (2006). For some critical remarks on the positioning of the temple in relation to the residence of Augustus, although based on literary rather than archaeological sources, see Wiseman (2012), especially 383–6.

[96] A similar attempt to regulate the Sibylline books is ascribed to Tiberius by Cassius Dio, *Historiae Romanae* 57.18.4–5 and again in Tacitus, *Annales* 6.12. For the claim that this repetition of Augustus' earlier efforts shows the ineffectiveness of the original measure, see Parke (1988), 142 and Wendt (2016), 46. These events will be discussed in more detail in section 2.6.1. See Rüpke (2016^{b}), 90 for the argument that divination was prominently targeted by various emperors precisely because it allowed private individuals to access knowledge that was believed to be dangerous in the hands of anyone except the proper (imperial) authorities.

2.5.2 Limiting divinatory enquiries?

The destruction of unsanctioned oracular texts, however, is not the only measure dealing with divination associated with Augustus. In the later years of his reign, the emperor is reported to have issued an edict that is widely regarded as the single most important attempt to regulate divination ever to be implemented in the Roman world, and as the precedent for many of the legal interactions that were to follow. The edict in question was reportedly issued in 11 CE (Appendix 1.5), and is referenced only once, in the works of Cassius Dio.[97] The historian's description of the law is very brief, and mentions simply that Augustus banned diviners (*μάντεις*) from practising their art without the presence of witnesses, or from answering divinatory enquiries about any person's death,[98] even if they took place in a public setting where everyone could see.[99]

Dio's account, however, contains a number of peculiar elements, and in part due to its brevity leaves us with more questions than answers. If the author's description is to be believed, the Augustan edict was noticeably different in scope and content than the overwhelming majority of known measures dealing with divination. Unlike almost all other cases in our corpus, no mention is made of limiting access to divinatory texts and tools, or of targeting individuals or groups involved in the practice. Instead, the edict as Dio presents it sought to restrict the specific questions that could be asked and the circumstances under which consultations were permitted to take place—notably without any reference to the measure being restricted to a particular geographical area. However, no record of any trials that can be directly linked to the original issuing of the Augustan edict is available to provide further context, and since our source likewise omits

[97] A similar measure is ascribed to Tiberius in Suetonius, *De vita Caesarum: Tiberius* 63.1, although the circumstances under which it occurred appear to have been different in a number of important ways. This case will be discussed in section 2.6.1.

[98] Dio is quick to add that the emperor did not take these measures to benefit his own interests. Instead, he made his own horoscope public, possibly in an attempt to convince the population that he was very much secure in his power and had no reason to fear enquiries regarding his personal health. The connection between this measure and the publication of Augustus' horoscope is disputed. It has been argued that the emperor published his horoscope many years before his famous edict, and that no connection between the two can therefore have existed. See Grothoff (2016), 358 n. 668 and Potter (1994), 256 n. 4.

[99] Cassius Dio, *Historiae Romanae* 56.25.5–6: *τοῖς μάντεσιν ἀπηγορεύθη μήτε κατὰ μόνας τινὶ μήτε περὶ θανάτου, μηδ' ἂν ἄλλοι συμπαρῶσίν οἱ, χρᾶν*. For the Greek text of the passage, alongside an Italian translation, see Cresci Marrone, Stroppa, and Rohr Vio (1998). This measure is generally referred to as an *edictum* in scholarship, and for brevity's sake this term will continue to be used in this analysis. It should be noted, however, that no equivalent term is used in the original Greek, and that the lack of context makes it impossible to establish what type of measure was originally issued. If we are indeed dealing with an *edictum*, however, the law was likely made on Augustus' own initiative and not in response to a particular case or enquiry brought before him. In addition, it is possible that Augustus meant for this law to be applied for a longer period of time, although it is uncertain whether it was meant to extend beyond his own death. See Jolowicz and Nicholas (1972), 367, as well as sections 1.2 and 1.4.2 of this study. For the claim that the measure 'no doubt' derived from a senate decree, see Swan (2004), 280.

mention of both the causes and the consequences of the measure,[100] modern historians are left to fill in the gaps. One of the most influential interpretations of this edict originates in the work of Frederick Cramer, who has maintained that the application of this measure underwent a swift development that caused it to become the legal foundation for a wide range of trials involving divinatory enquiries about the welfare of the emperor himself or, from the reign of Claudius onwards, that of the entirety of the imperial family.[101] The Augustan edict, it is argued, was initially used alongside other accusations to facilitate charges of *maiestas* against members of the Roman elite, but even before the middle of the first century CE evolved to allow divination about the welfare of members of the imperial family to be treated as sufficient evidence of treason without any additional charges.[102] The 11 CE edict is likewise often believed to have remained 'on the books' for cases that did not involve the imperial family. It is said to have had a remarkably wide reach in both capacities, and has come to be regarded as a long-lasting, empire-wide law that was enforced with some frequency—and therefore stands in contrast to the more temporary and localized measures dating from the republican period.[103]

There are, however, important reasons to doubt this interpretation, and while the details of this edict's presumed legal afterlife are best discussed in the context of the different trials for which it is believed to have formed the basis, a number of factors stand out when taking the available evidence into consideration. Most significantly, the claim that Augustus' 11 CE edict had an empire-wide impact finds little support in our sources, and concrete evidence for enforcement of the edict in the provinces is noticeably limited.[104] Even if the various known trials against those accused of having made divinatory enquiries about the welfare of the emperor did find their legal basis in this particular edict, the fact remains that the vast majority of these cases took place in Rome, while only a select few appear to

[100] Dio's description of the edict is included in a list of miscellaneous measures taken by the emperor, none of which gives any indication of the intentions the emperor might have had by issuing this edict. For the interesting, although ultimately unprovable, view that Augustus took this measure in response to requests 'from below', possibly the local officials of the capital, see Dickie (2001), 154.

[101] Cramer (1954), 259.

[102] Cramer (1954), 249–75, followed by Barton (1994[a]), 50–1; Desanti (1990), 80–1; and Raschle (2020), 102–3. For the inclusion of crimes against the emperor in charges of *maiestas*, see Balsdon and Lintott (2016); Santalucia (1994), 212; and Williamson (2016), 337–9.

[103] Cramer (1954), 249–75. The idea of the Augustan edict being empire-wide and long-lasting is followed in whole or in part by e.g. Beard, North, and Price (1998), 232; Green (2014), 104–5; Mace (2018), 436–7; and Sogno (2005) 171, but rejected by Grothoff (2016), 413–20 and Potter (1994), 174. Wendt (2015[a]), 188–9 sees legal action against private diviners, and other types of experts, as a frequently reoccurring phenomenon throughout the Roman world, but does not mention the 11 CE edict in this context.

[104] This much is admitted even by Cramer (1954), 251, who notes the scarcity of the sources from the provinces but nonetheless remarks that 'such violations of the law were undoubtedly prosecuted throughout the empire'.

have originated in the provinces.[105] References to cases that do not involve the emperor are similarly lacking. Not a single clear-cut mention of diviners being punished for enquiries about private individuals, or indeed for divination without the presence of witnesses, has been transmitted to us, either from Rome or from other parts of the empire,[106] and while it is of course possible that such cases simply escape our notice due to a lack of interest among ancient historians, it would nonetheless be unwise to assume wide-ranging and long-lasting enforcement of the edict on such a narrow basis. The Roman authorities are unlikely to have been proactive in seeking out cases of this kind, while likely being much more vigilant in seeking out those who predicted the emperor's imminent death and could therefore cause significant disruptions to public order. Although cases dealing with predictions about private individuals may certainly have been brought forward by those who believed that they or their relations had been victimized, such cases remain largely hypothetical, and it is simply impossible to determine what their legal basis might have been.[107]

A second reason to be careful in our approach of the 11 CE edict concerns the reliability of the available source material. While it would perhaps go too far to describe Cassius Dio's description of the Augustan edict as being completely unfounded in reality, the fact remains that he is our only source for this particular legal measure and furthermore composed his work almost two centuries after the fact—making the Augustan edict a less than ideal anchoring point for a potential chain of legal precedents.[108] The only other reference to a measure with similar characteristics may be found in Suetonius' account of Tiberius' reign. As a result, it has been suggested that Dio was simply mistaken in dating the law to the time of Augustus,[109] which—while certainly possible—does not by itself explain why

[105] See Appendix 1 for an overview. Two of these cases may in fact refer to the same incident and will be discussed in sections 2.7.1 and 2.8.3, respectively. The diviners leading popular uprisings referenced by Wendt (2015[a]), 188 n. 31 are unlikely to have been tried under the Augustan edict, or indeed specifically because of their divinatory practices, but would more probably have been targeted with military means instead.

[106] The only possible example of someone being punished for divination against a private individual may be found in *Digesta* 47.10.15.13. This passage is attributed to Ulpian and suggests that astrologers could be punished for falsely accusing someone of being a thief. However, since such an accusation did not concern death and was almost certainly made in front of witnesses—given the fact the diviner in question is being asked to help solve a crime—this passage cannot be said to relate to the Augustan edict. For a more detailed discussion of this passage, see section 2.10.

[107] It is unclear, for instance, whether cases that took place in Rome would have been covered by the praetorian edict or would have taken the form of a *cognitio* trial—if this was an option at the time. Similarly, we do not know if cases from the provinces would have been tried under the jurisdiction of a local official or a Roman magistrate. In the case of the latter, a *cognitio* procedure is likely, but it remains unclear whether the Augustan edict would have been well known enough to be brought forward in such a context. For the workings of different trial proceedings, see section 1.3.

[108] It should be noted that Sánchez-Moreno Ellart (2009), 213 mistakenly cites CIL XII.25 n. 147 and Valerius Maximus, *Facta et Dicta Memorabilia* 1.3.3 as additional sources. Neither makes reference to the Augustan edict.

[109] Grothoff (2016), 418–19 and Ripat (2011), 131. For the argument that Cassius Dio used Suetonius as a source, see Millar (2005), 33.

Dio also mentions a ban on enquiries regarding the death of individuals, whereas Suetonius' description of the Tiberian measure only mentions the outlawing of divination without the presence of witnesses.[110] Another difference between the two accounts may be found in the geographical scope of their intended application (as will be discussed in more detail in section 2.6.1), which combined with the difference in content makes it clear that the two sources are unlikely to refer to the same event. However, passages that show closer similarities to Dio's account do occur in the writings of two jurists from the third century: a ban on divination about anyone's welfare, but particularly the emperor, is mentioned in pseudo-Paul's *Sententiae*, as well as in Ulpian's *De Officio Proconsulis*, the latter of which was likely written around the same time as Dio's *Historiae Romanae*.[111] It is notable, however, that neither author ascribes this ban to Augustus, or indeed to any other emperor in particular. Enquiries about the death of the emperor were seen as highly suspect throughout the imperial period, as becomes evident from Ulpian's assertion that this is a very old ban that has been reiterated many times,[112] but this does not necessarily mean that the original measure was issued by Augustus in the form of an *edictum*—or indeed that it was enforced throughout the empire for a significant period of time. In fact, Ulpian's reference to multiple emperors attempting to regulate divination suggests that the various iterations of the measure were in use for shorter periods of time alone. It seems likely, therefore, that Ulpian (like the author of the *Sententiae*) retroactively created a cohesion between individual ad hoc cases that did not originally exist.[113] Dio's view on

[110] Suetonius, *De Vita Caesarum: Tiberius* 63.1.

[111] See pseudo-Paul, *Sententiae* 5.21.3–4 and Ulpian, *De Officio Proconsulis* 7 in *Leg. Mos. et Rom. Coll.* 15.2.3, respectively. The *Sententiae* were likely not written by Paul himself and appear to date from the late third century—see n. 40 of this chapter. It has been suggested by Fögen (1993), 63–74 that the relevant passage attributed to Ulpian likewise belongs to the late third century CE and is not the work of the jurist himself, but instead of an author from the time of Diocletian. Fögen's argument, however, is primarily based on the presumed uniqueness of this passage's phrasing, particularly the term *vaticinatores*. She also argues that no earlier jurist can be shown to have discussed the topic of divination, using the sixth-century *Digesta* as her primary point of comparison to substantiate both claims. This analysis, however, does not take into account the highly selective nature of the *Digesta*. It has been suggested, among others by Honoré (2010), 9, that only approximately 5 per cent of the legal texts available in the sixth century made its way into this new corpus. On this basis, the authorship of the Ulpian passage and its dating to the early third century cannot be sufficiently disproven, and the majority of it is very likely authentic. For the idea that the text as preserved in the *collatio* may be considered authentic, see Frakes (2011), 301; Liebs (1987), 172–3; and Nogrady (2006), 187–98. For the more conservative dating of *De Officio Proconsulis* in general to the first quarter of the third century CE, see Honoré (2002), 181–2.

[112] Ulpian, *De Officio Proconsulis* 7 in *Leg. Mos. et Rom. Coll.* 15.2.3. It should be noted that, in *Leg. Mos. Et Rom. Coll.* 15.2.1., Ulpian explicitly cites the expulsion of diviners from the time of Tiberius to prove how old the tradition of legal measures against diviners actually is. If an earlier law regulating divination existed, especially if it was created under Augustus, a mention of this fact might be expected.

[113] A similar idea may be found in Rives (2011[a]), 97–8 and Wendt (2016), 53. For the suggestion that trials regarding divination may well have taken place in the context of imperial *cognitio* proceedings, and that later jurists may have ignored this in order to create cohesion, see Sánchez-Moreno Ellart (2009), 211. The deduction of a general regulation from various individual cases may serve as

religion, meanwhile, appears to have been strongly shaped by Roman administrative practices of his day,[114] and since it is very likely that he used Ulpian as a source in other cases,[115] we cannot therefore exclude the possibility that a similar inspiration was at play here.[116] Dio may well have used Ulpian's conclusions, or those of other jurists, in his description of the time of Augustus, and he even appears to have generalized further by diminishing the focus on the person of the emperor that is so prominently present in the third-century sources, making it unlikely that we can distil the original edict from the description he provides.[117]

The suggestion that Cassius Dio's description of the 11 CE edict was shaped by a later view on the legal status of (certain kinds of) divination is made all the more plausible if we take into account the fact that the author uses Augustus as a vehicle for his personal views on the relationship between the imperial state and religion in similar ways elsewhere in his work. In a famous passage, Dio describes a discussion between Agrippa, Augustus, and Maecenas, in which the latter advises the new emperor to maintain the religious customs of his ancestors and to ensure that others do the same. As a part of this programme of religious conservatism, he recommends that divination should remain firmly in the hands of the government, since private diviners could trick the general population into open rebellion.[118] While this passage is unlikely to reflect the historical situation of the early principate, let alone accurately represent a conversation between the *princeps* and his advisors,[119] it does provide an insight into Dio's personal views on religion in general, and divination in particular.[120] It is likely, therefore, that Dio's perspective, which was moulded by the legal and political issues of his time, influenced his description of the edict he ascribes to Augustus. While this, again, does not fully discount the possibility that Augustus did indeed make an attempt to regulate divinatory practices, the available evidence thus does not seem to support the idea that subsequent trials involving divination may be connected to Dio's version

an example for the thesis found in Harries (1999), 86 that repetitions of a particular measure served to strengthen the general precedent, which also finds support in the claim in Tacitus, *Historiae* 1.22, which claims that diviners 'will always be forbidden in our state, yet will always be retained'. It should be noted, however, that this passage can hardly be seen as evidence for a 'standing' law against divination: instead, Tacitus' use of the future tense suggests the need for constant repetition.

114 Dickie (2010), 93–5. For the argument that the same may hold true for Dio's description of Augustus' judicial activities, see Tuori (2016), 89–92 and 112.

115 Simons (2009), 300; Urso (2011), 42–4.

116 A similar argument is made by Grothoff (2016), 413–20 and Fögen (1993), 135–6. The later author bases her argument on Dio's description of the debate between Augustus, Maecenas, and Agrippa discussed later in this section.

117 Pseudo-Paul, *Sententiae* 5.21.3–4 mentions enquiries about the health of the emperor or the state, as well as enquiries made by slaves about their masters. Ulpian, *De Officio Proconsulis* 7 in *Leg. Mos. et Rom. Coll.* 15.2.3 also mentions enquiries about the health of other individuals, including the questioner himself, but emphasizes that consultations about the emperor would be punished more severely.

118 Cassius Dio, *Historiae Romanae* 52.36.

119 Santangelo (2013), 267.

120 Millar (1964), 108. See also Grothoff (2016), 419–20 for the argument that Dio's views on this issue were strongly influenced by the growing presence of 'foreign' cults in his own time.

of the Augustan edict—or, as we shall see, the measure against divination in a private setting that emerged under Tiberius.

2.6 Divination and Conspiracy under Tiberius

Given the significant number of legal measures on divination dated to the time of Tiberius, it is no surprise that the emperor himself appears to have shown a particular interest in the practice. This fascination is reflected not just in his attempts to regulate and repress certain divinatory practices but also in his personal involvement with diviners: a number of ancient sources report that Tiberius counted the astrologer Thrasyllus among his close personal friends, and trusted in the diviner's abilities to protect him from those who sought to do him harm.[121] While these two aspects of Tiberius' preoccupation with divination have on occasion been seen as contradictory, possibly to the point of hypocrisy, or have instead been referred to as a sign of the emperor's paranoia, what stands out most is the significant power divination was thought to hold—either for good or for ill.[122]

2.6.1 Repeating Augustan measures?

Among the notable measures on divination taken by Tiberius, an important number are said to have been reiterations of earlier regulations implemented by his predecessor Augustus. This includes the aforementioned ban on the consultation of diviners without the presence of witnesses (*haruspices secreto ac sine testibus consuli vetuit*; Appendix 1.10),[123] which as mentioned has repeatedly been described as a repetition of Augustus' 11 CE edict (see section 2.5.2).[124] While this measure was likely taken later in the new emperor's reign,[125] discussing it in close connection with the Augustan measure allows for an easier comparison, and a more thorough understanding of the possible connections between the two.

[121] Cassius Dio, Historiae Romanae 55.11 and 57.15.7; Suetonius, *De vita Caesarum: Tiberius* 14 and 62; Tacitus, *Annales* 6.20–1.

[122] Wendt (2016), 46–7. See Cramer (1954), 233 and Desanti (1990), *passim*, but especially 121–9 for the argument that imperial measures about divination were caused by true belief in its power and fear of its disruptive potential, and Shannon-Henderson (2019), 224–9 for an analysis of Tacitus' account of Tiberius' interest in divination. For an interesting parallel between the exemption from expulsion of diviners working with the upper echelons of Roman society and philosophers who did the same, see Raschle (2020), 101.

[123] Suetonius, *De vita Caesarum: Tiberius* 63.1.

[124] Cramer (1954), 250; Kippenberg (1997), 154; MacMullen (1966), 129. See Grothoff (2016), 419 and Ripat (2011), 131 for the suggestion that one of the two edicts, likely the Augustan one, was mistakenly attributed. It is noteworthy that the Augustan edict of 11 CE has been almost universally accepted as an important precedent in legislation regarding divination, whereas this measure by Tiberius is often only briefly referred to, if it is mentioned at all.

[125] Kippenberg (1997), 154 gives the date of 19 CE, although without much explanation.

While it has been suggested that the Tiberian measure was meant to supplement its predecessor by clarifying that *haruspices* were also included,[126] it seems implausible that it would have taken the imperial authorities several years to recognize the practical limitations of an edict that, in its presumed original iteration, already appears to have been generally phrased, and furthermore was by all appearances rarely enforced. If we are indeed dealing with a repetition, it would therefore make more sense to see this measure as an attempt to revive the original edict, which may have fallen into disuse in the intervening years.[127] However, Tiberius' measure does not appear to repeat the ban on divination regarding anyone's death, but instead focuses exclusively on divination without the presence of witnesses. According to Suetonius' account, this regulation was part of a series of measures implemented by the emperor to placate his growing paranoia, and a repeated ban on predictions about an individual's death would thus have made sense if such a precedent had still been at the forefront of both his and other people's minds. One might even have expected a more specific measure that forbade enquiries about the death of the imperial family, but no such measure is mentioned. Instead, Tiberius' ban on divination without witnesses is included in a brief enumeration of various measures that serve to illustrate Tiberius' anxiety about divination (and life in general) at this point in his reign. These regulations included a failed attempt to close down oracles in the area around the city, as well as Tiberius' insistence that various newly appointed governors were not allowed to leave for their provinces but instead had to remain in the capital, firmly under his personal control.[128] This suggests that, rather than with an outright repetition of the 11 CE edict, we are instead dealing with a separate measure, intended to regulate public order and maintain a grasp on imperial power.

The idea that the authorities were apprehensive of divination is also confirmed by a disturbance caused by the introduction of new predictions ascribed to the Sibyl, which on at least one occasion caused Tiberius to begin an investigation into books containing oracular texts and to discard those he believed to be fraudulent (Appendices 1.11 and 1.14).[129] In this case, we almost certainly are dealing

[126] Cramer (1954), 250. [127] For a similar argument, see Grothoff (2016), 418.

[128] Suetonius, *De vita Caesarum: Tiberius* 63. Tiberius' unwillingness to let governors leave Rome is also mentioned in Tacitus, *Annales* 1.80.

[129] It is unclear whether such an event took place once or twice. Tacitus, *Annales* 6.12 mentions an incident in 32 CE, in which a young people's tribune introduced a new Sibylline book to the senate and attempted to have it included in the official collection without the approval of the relevant institutions. Tiberius reprimanded those involved, explicitly referencing Augustus' earlier measure. Cassius Dio, *Historiae Romanae* 57.18.4–5 mentions a similar event said to have taken place in 19 CE, in which Tiberius started a wider investigation after the senate had been shaken by a dire prediction, also said to have been ascribed to the Sibyl. Although these two passages are often taken to refer to separate measures, as in Parke (1988), 142–3 and Wendt (2016), 46, since Tiberius is said in Tacitus' account to have rebuked the tribune only gently, stating that he may not have been aware of ancient procedures due to his youth, it seems more likely that Tiberius was repeating the earlier Augustan enquiry, rather than one he had himself issued only a few years earlier. For the argument that Tacitus'

with a repetition of Augustus' previous actions to the same effect (section 2.5.1),[130] and Tiberius' efforts therefore show just how temporary measures against divination could be. Indeed, this new act demonstrates that Augustus' earlier attempts to regulate oracular texts had not produced lasting results, and that new situations could emerge in which the authorities believed intervention to be required.[131] It also shows Tiberius' willingness to restrict access to unsanctioned divination in an attempt to prevent further socio-political unrest. Tiberius' measures, then, appear to have been implemented to deal with the particular anxieties of his time, and their geographical scope likewise appears to have been limited. The other measures Suetonius uses to illustrate Tiberius' growing paranoia are all described as attempts to control the emperor's immediate surroundings, either by removing potentially dangerous institutions from the area around the capital or by keeping those he saw as a threat confined to that region, where they could be more easily supervised. It is thus very well possible that the same was true for his attempt to regulate private divination, and that this measure likewise applied primarily to the city of Rome. In addition to restricting the scope of Tiberius' measures, it may furthermore be argued that the general air of paranoia that surrounded his regulation limited its ultimate durability and made it a less viable precedent for future emperors. It is notable that the ban on divination in private is not mentioned in the surviving analyses of either pseudo-Paul or Ulpian, which suggests that legal actions against people who consulted diviners in private were hardly as prevalent as measures against those who enquired about potential (imperial) deaths appear to have been.[132]

2.6.2 The trial of M. Scribonius Libo Drusus

In spite of the fact, then, that Tiberius' ban against divination in private likely saw limited use, his reign still witnessed a number of trials that have traditionally

account, despite being milder in its phrasing than Dio's version of events, nevertheless reflects the instability of the period, see Shannon-Henderson (2019), 222–3.

130 According to Tacitus, *Annales* 6.12 Tiberius himself explicitly made this connection.

131 See Parke (1988), 142–3 and Wendt (2016), 46. Ripat (2011), 131 n. 91 suggests Dio may have confused Tiberius with Augustus.

132 While being absent from the surviving legal texts, the risks of divination in private are mentioned by the astrologer Firmicus Maternus, who was active during the reign of Constantine. Maternus advises those who are looking to practise divination against answering questions without the presence of witnesses and suggests that they speak loudly enough for bystanders to hear when answering enquiries. However, this is very much framed as a safeguard against accusations of having answered certain illegal questions, which is also a primary concern in the analyses of pseudo-Paul and Ulpian. Maternus' remarks, then, once again suggest that Tiberius' measure had by this point in time fallen into disuse, which would fit well with the argument made in Sogno (2005), 172 that Maternus was likely responding to the much more recent measures against divination instituted by Diocletian and Constantine. For an argument to the contrary, see Mace (2018), 444–6. Firmicus Maternus' remarks may be found in *Mathesis* 2.30.3–7. For the relevant Latin text, see the Budé edition of Monat (1992), 140–2.

been linked to suspicious divinatory practices—and that are often assumed to have been based on Augustus' 11 CE edict. These proceedings therefore serve as excellent case studies that allow us to trace how legal measures against diviners and those who consulted them took shape. The first relevant trial took place in the early years of Tiberius' time as emperor, likely before his ban on divination in private had been issued (Appendix 1.6). In 16 CE, a young man by the name of Marcus Scribonius Libo Drusus was accused of fomenting revolution (*res novae*) against the emperor and was tried accordingly. Libo's trial is remarkable, because it was apparently significant enough to be mentioned in a substantial number of ancient sources, more than any other trial in our corpus. While the details of the respective accounts vary, collectively they thus nonetheless present an interesting image of the course of events and the nature of the charges levelled against the accused.

The most elaborate (and most cited) version of the story comes from Tacitus, who describes Libo as a naïve young man who was persuaded by a close friend, the senator Firmius Catus, to consult all kinds of diviners (*chaldaei*, *magi*, *somniorum interpretes*) in order to investigate whether his illustrious ancestral credentials would lead to him achieving political success himself.[133] Catus, however, had malicious intentions for reminding his young friend of his exalted status: as soon as he believed that he had gathered sufficient evidence, he approached the emperor via an intermediary to inform him of the supposedly imminent danger of a political coup, likely hoping to gain favour for himself in the process.[134] While Tiberius initially refused to listen, the case was eventually brought before the members of the senate, who were told that they were to pass judgement on 'an enormous and horrifying matter'.[135] According to Tacitus, Libo was accused of having asked the diviners several, in themselves harmless, questions on issues like his possible future wealth, and he hastens to add that these enquiries were pitiable at most, if regarded with some leniency.[136] There was, however, an additional document, which contained the name of the emperor and various prominent senators, along with 'symbols of a terrible or mysterious nature'.[137] Libo denied that the document was his, but when his slaves were tortured to find out if they recognized his handwriting, he committed suicide without waiting for the outcome of his trial. The senate continued its enquiry and declared the late accused guilty, although Tiberius swore that he would have spared Libo's life, had he lived to see the verdict pronounced.[138]

[133] Tacitus, *Annales* 2.27. The reference to the conjuring of *infernas umbras* through *carminibus* in Tacitus, *Annales* 2.28 may likewise be a reference to divination with the help of *magi*.

[134] Catus did indeed profit from his accusation: he received part of Libo's possessions after the young man's death. See Tacitus, *Annales* 2.32. For the prevalence of *delatores* like Catus in Roman literature, see Robinson (2007).

[135] *Et vocantur patres, addito consultandum super re magna et atroci*; Tacitus, *Annales* 2.28.

[136] Tacitus, *Annales* 2.30. [137] Tacitus, *Annales* 2.30. [138] Tacitus, *Annales* 2.30–1.

Judging by Tacitus' account, it is understandable that this trial has often been considered an example of the application of Augustus' 11 CE edict to facilitate a charge of *maiestas* and possibly attempted usurpation. However, the role of divination in the trial appears to have been rather complex and deserves to be examined in more detail. Firstly, it is noteworthy that Tacitus is the only source to include suspicious divinatory practices as a key element of the proceedings: while Libo's trial, as mentioned, was referenced by a significant number of other authors, none of them makes a similar connection. The other available sources, which include Seneca, Suetonius, Cassius Dio, and an inscription, mention only Libo's attempts to gain imperial power, using such terms as *scelerata consilia*,[139] *res novae*,[140] and *nefaria consilia* against the well-being of Tiberius, his children, and other leading figures.[141] In part, this discrepancy could be explained by the fact that Tacitus, as a member of the priestly college of the *quindecimviri sacris faciundis*, was particularly interested in religious and divinatory matters, and therefore chose to include details that were considered to be less relevant by others.[142] However, the fact that divination goes entirely unmentioned in the overwhelming majority of the available sources nevertheless makes it unlikely that the Augustan edict formed a central part of the accusers' legal strategy, and instead suggests that the trial was based on accusations of *maiestas* in a more general sense.[143] Indeed, it is telling that Libo's divinatory practices were at this stage insufficient to conclusively prove that he had been involved in treason,[144] and Tacitus' aforementioned reference to a document containing 'symbols of a terrible or mysterious nature' serves to further confirm that Libo's conviction instead hinged on his alleged attempts to actively harm members of the Roman elite. While these symbols have been interpreted by some as an indication that the people mentioned on Libo's list had been the subject of 'forbidden divinatory or magical consultations',[145] the idea that the two can be conflated in this context, or even that the symbols were distinctly divinatory in nature, does not necessarily find clear support in the text itself. The use of the words *atrox* and *occultus* suggests nefarious intent that was rather more practical and direct than an enquiry about the fate of several prominent members of Roman society—possibly a curse of some kind.[146] The term *atrox*, in particular, carries connotations of horror and

[139] Velleius Paterculus, *Historia Romana* 2.130.3. Seneca, *Epistulae* 70.10 alludes to similar plans by suggesting that Libo 'hoped for greater things' (*maiora sperantis*) than anyone in that era could reasonably expect.

[140] Suetonius, *De vita Caesarum: Tiberius* 25.1. Cf. Cassius Dio, Historiae Romanae 57.15.4, who opts for *νεωτερίζειν*.

[141] *Fasti Amiternini*, CIL 1_2, p. 244.

[142] Dickie (2010), 82–3.

[143] It has been argued that Tacitus' reference to a change in regulations that allowed Libo's slaves to be tortured likewise points in the direction of a *maiestas* accusation in a more general sense. See Sánchez-Moreno Ellart (2009), 210–11.

[144] As acknowledged by Cramer (1954), 254.

[145] Cramer (1954), 255. See also Rives (2006), 62 and Shotter (1972), 91.

[146] For an argument to the contrary, see Rives (2006), 62, who describes Libo's trial as the cause of the later expulsions of diviners from Rome, and therefore argues that the accusations against Libo

violence that suggest that the symbols had directly harmful implications for the people to whose names they were attached.[147] This interpretation would also allow us to more closely reconcile Tacitus' account with the version of events presented in other relevant sources, in which Libo is accused of actively seeking to harm members of the Roman elite, including the imperial family, rather than of attempting to obtain knowledge about their fates.

This, however, means that the role of divination in this trial has to be reconsidered. Whichever version of events we follow, the primary accusation against Libo was that he conspired to perpetrate violence against a number of high-ranking individuals, either by magical or natural means, which does not align with the stipulations of the Augustan edict as we know it. Since it cannot be sufficiently proven that Libo consulted diviners about the death of the people on his list, his offence against the 11 CE edict would have amounted to divination without the presence of witnesses at the very most, which against the backdrop of a primary accusation as severe as *maiestas* seems more like a setback for the defence than a fully fledged secondary charge. While Tacitus may well be right in claiming that Libo's alleged attempts to obtain knowledge about his own future were brought up during the trial, this does not appear to have occurred in the form of a formal accusation on the basis of the Augustan edict, but rather as evidence to illustrate the character of the accused.[148] The trial itself, then, was very likely fundamentally based on a charge of *maiestas*, or perhaps took the shape of a more ad hoc *cognitio* proceeding, as the central involvement of both the emperor and the senate seems to suggest.[149]

2.6.3 Expulsion(s) from Rome

Soon after Libo's trial, a far more obvious attempt to regulate divination occurred. Tiberius had the senate issue a *senatus consultum* (Appendices 1.7 and 1.8), the

must have been related to divination. This line of thinking, however, has not proved to be beyond dispute, as will be discussed in section 2.6.3. Rives's assertion that the trial did not find its legal basis in the *Lex Cornelia de Sicariis et Veneficiis*, however, is very likely correct.

[147] See Lewis and Short (1975) and Glare (1982), *ad loc.* The suggestion that the content of the writings, rather than their purpose, was *atrox* cannot be reconciled with the fact that these writings are also called *occultus*: if they were indeed secret and unclear, how can the nature of their meaning be known? For the aggravating connotations of *atrox* in a legal context, see Berger (1991), *ad loc.* For a similar point of view, based on the words *magorum sacra* earlier in the Tacitus passage, see Dickie (2010), 97 and Ripat (2011), 119.

[148] Cramer (1954), 255 agrees that illicit divination was not the primary issue at stake during this trial, but nevertheless firmly adheres to the idea that the violation of the Augustan edict was one of the formal accusations. See Shotter (1972), 92 for the suggestion that Libo's enquiries about his own fortunes may have created an atmosphere in which the ominous list of names had a more substantial impact.

[149] For the highly plausible suggestion that this may have been a *cognitio* trial, see Sánchez-Moreno Ellart (2009), 211. For the idea that the greater role of the emperor and the senate in *maiestas* cases are indicative of the gradual transition to *cognitio* proceedings, see Williamson (2016), 340.

essence of which is fairly well established, although a number of important discrepancies between the various available accounts exist. All sources report that the senate ordered diviners to be expelled from Rome and Italy,[150] although some add that foreigners who were caught practising divinatory arts were executed rather than banished.[151] Furthermore, this measure does not appear to have been directed at astrologers specifically, and the terminology used in the various sources is notably diverse. Ulpian's *De Officio Proconsulis* mentions that the *senatus consultum* applied to *mathematici, chaldaei, arioli et ceteri*, and Tacitus likewise claims the expulsion targeted both *mathematici* and *magi*, which makes it more likely that the measure was aimed at a wider range of diviners, possibly in connection with other private religious practitioners.[152]

Our sources also suggest that, however severely the expulsion order may have been phrased, its application was rather more limited in practice. A number of sources mention that those targeted by the measure could obtain a pardon with relative ease, if they only recanted, obeyed the orders issued by the authorities, and promised to abandon their art (*ars*) in the future—a notable parallel to the treatment of Christians, as will be discussed in more detail in Chapter 4.[153] It is similarly very likely that Tiberius' expulsion measures were not meant to be enforced long term.[154] Although certain diviners are said to have been executed (Appendix 1.9), which suggests that harsher treatment was also possible,[155]

[150] Tacitus, *Annales* 2.32; Cassius Dio, *Historiae Romanae* 57.15.8; Suetonius, *De vita Caesarum: Tiberius* 36; Ulpian, *De Officio Proconsulis 7* in *Leg. Mos. et Rom. Coll.* 15.2.1. It is generally acknowledged that Ulpian's lack of reference to a specific region did not in any way mean that this was an empire-wide proclamation. See Cramer (1954), 238 and Goodyear (1981), 285 n. 2.

[151] Cassius Dio, *Historiae Romanae* 57.15.8; Ulpian, *De Officio Proconsulis 7* in *Leg. Mos. et Rom. Coll.* 15.2.1. The reason for this distinction between Roman citizens and foreigners is far from clear, but it may be connected to the idea that exile was traditionally reserved for the former. See Kelly (2006), 8. This may also be in keeping with Tacitus' reports of executions of astrologers during the same period, see Tacitus, *Annales* 2.32, who likewise reports that astrologers were killed, but does not mention citizenship as a factor.

[152] It is likely that the *magi* can also be taken to refer to divinatory practitioners, given the fact that Tacitus uses the word to refer to divination during the Libo trial. For the idea that 'joint expulsions are best understood not as actions against separate groups, but rather as attempts to be comprehensive', see Ripat (2011), 132–3. A similar argument is made by Wendt (2016), 47, who nevertheless mistakenly includes diviners in a later expulsion of Jewish and Egyptian worshippers. The Suetonius passage she mentions does include a reference to all three groups, but these appear in the context of Tiberius' general approach to religion, and the expulsion of diviners is presented separately from the banishment of the other two groups.

[153] Cassius Dio, *Historiae Romanae* 57.15.8; Suetonius, *De vita Caesarum: Tiberius* 36. Notably, no reference is made to the presence of witnesses or the nature of the questions being asked to ensure that diviners had truly recanted.

[154] Potter (1994), 174–5; Sánchez-Moreno Ellart (2009), 217. For a contradictory view, see Santangelo (2013), 254, who does add that there is no proof for systematic repression of divination, and that its practitioners were only infrequently expelled.

[155] Tacitus, *Annales* 2.32. Tacitus calls these diviners L. Pituanius and P. Marcius. The latter name appears to have been closely associated with divination, since a number of other soothsayers are reported to have shared it. See Cicero, *De Divinatione* 1.40.89, 1.50.115 and 2.55.113 and Livy, *Ab Urbe Condita* 25.12. Cassius Dio, *Historiae Romanae* 57.15.8 and Ulpian, *De Officio Proconsulis 7* in *Leg. Mos. et Rom. Coll.* 15.2.1 claim that Tiberius made a distinction between expulsion for those who

Suetonius mentions that the expulsion order was soon lifted altogether after various diviners had asked for leniency,[156] and the fact that various later emperors felt the need to issue similar expulsion orders furthermore suggests a lack of permanence. It is therefore likely that these expulsion measures were not substantially enforced between various iterations—possibly because diviners were not seen as a continuous threat, or because the support of the wider population, on whom enforcement may well have depended, was lacking.[157] The idea that Tiberius' measures were not universally popular, and were subject to debate, may be supported by Cassius Dio, who mentions that the senate, at least, was in favour of pardoning all accused citizens, not just those who had given up their divinatory practices, but that this attempt to negotiate for a more lenient approach was ultimately thwarted.[158] It is also likely that diviners as a group simply lacked distinct, fixed characteristics, which allowed them to shed their identity when it was convenient to do so—even if they did so only temporarily.[159] In any case, both this apparent lack of durability and the possibility for recantation suggest that the expulsion was not intended to systematically punish private practitioners for any particular criminal behaviours, but rather as a temporary measure meant to restore public order in the city of Rome by removing an element that was seen as disruptive.

Other aspects of the measure, however, are less straightforward, and remain hotly debated. Firstly, sources seem divided on the question of whether a single *senatus consultum* was issued or whether a second version existed, possibly because the first version was considered to be incomplete or unsuccessful. The only direct mention of two separate *consulta* may be found in the account of Cassius Dio,[160] which may be reinforced by Tacitus' use of the plural when referring

were Roman citizens, and execution for those who were not. This, however, does not fully explain Tacitus' claim that one of the diviners was thrown from the Tarpeian Rock, while the other was executed outside the Esquiline Gate, the specificity of which shows that additional distinguishing factors must have been at play. See Shotter (1989), 159 for the argument that Tacitus' P. Marcius can be conflated with the unnamed diviner who is executed in Cassius Dio, *Historiae Romanae* 57.15.7 because he had tried to deceive Tiberius into giving him money by sending him a dream.

[156] Suetonius, *De vita Caesarum: Tiberius* 36.

[157] For the idea that banishments were often temporary measures during the imperial period, see Kelly (2006), 66–7. See Ripat (2011), 144 for the idea that diviners were not always seen as a threat. Wendt (2016), 6 suggests that private practitioners like diviners were not as marginalized as is often assumed, and argues on p. 59 that the support of the population would have been needed to enforce measures of this kind.

[158] Cassius Dio, *Historiae Romanae* 57.15.9.

[159] Ripat (2011), 128–41. See Wendt (2015[a]), 186 for the argument that private practitioners, including diviners, were often ethnically coded, but that (186 n. 14) this connection could very well be based on association rather than fact.

[160] For the suggestion that Dio's *τὸ πρότερον δόγμα δι' οὗ ἀπηγόρευτο μηδὲν τοιοῦτον ἐν τῇ πόλει μεταχειρίζεσθαι* (*Historiae Romanae* 57.15.8) is meant to refer to the Augustan edict, see Swan (2004), 280. It is overwhelmingly assumed, however, that two expulsion orders were issued in quick succession—at least in part because the Augustan edict as previously presented by Dio makes no mention of a ban on divination in general. See e.g. Cramer (1954), 237; Barton (1994[a]), 44; Beard, North, and Price (1998), 231; Goodyear (1981), 284–5; Ripat (2011), 132–3 and 136.

to the event—although the latter does not make any explicit distinction between the two iterations of the order. At the very least, this discrepancy makes it unlikely that the two orders were aimed at different types of diviners: the word order of Tacitus' remark *facta et de mathematicis magisque Italia pellendis senatus consulta* presents both *mathematici* and *magi* as the subject of both *consulta*, and the next sentence in the passage refers to both groups collectively (*quorum e numero*).[161] It has also been suggested that the second *senatus consultum* imposed harsher penalties than its predecessor,[162] possibly because the first version had proved to be ineffective. This view may well be confirmed by Cassius Dio's reference to certain diviners still being active after the first ruling, and it is certainly more likely that the difference between the two expulsion orders lay not in their contents but rather in their severity.[163] In this context, the fact that Ulpian makes mention of a single expulsion likewise suggests that the first version was considered to be insufficient, and was therefore essentially replaced by the second, more authoritative order that was ultimately cited by the jurist.[164] It thus appears to be more likely that, rather than issuing one expulsion measure, the senate issued two in quick succession.

A second point of contention regarding Tiberius' expulsions lies in their exact date. The accounts of Tacitus and Cassius Dio place the *senatus consulta* in 16 CE, and this is certainly the more common assumption.[165] Ulpian, by contrast, mentions Pomponius and Rufus as the consuls who were in office when the expulsion order was issued, which would result in a possible alternative dating of 17 CE—and given Ulpian's lack of an obvious agenda, this may be the most likely option.[166] However, a historical oddity has caused an additional complication. Ulpian refers to each of the relevant consuls by only a single name, and, as coincidence would have it, these might just as well refer to the suffect consuls of 16 CE, who went by the very same names.[167] Since *senatus consulta* from the early principate generally favoured the names of the *consules ordinarii*, 17 CE still seems to be the most likely option,[168] but ultimately we cannot be completely certain. This

[161] Goodyear (1981), 284. [162] Cramer (1954), 238.

[163] Cassius Dio, *Historiae Romanae* 57.15.8. For the view that Tiberius' first measure was aimed exclusively at foreigners, whereas the second focused on Roman citizens, see Cramer (1954), 239. This interpretation is understandable, as the reference to a previous measure is linked to the treatment of citizens in particular, but does not appear to be completely correct, since Dio claims that divination in the city had been previously banned in more general terms. Although Ulpian, *De Officio Proconsulis* 7 in *Leg. Mos. et Rom. Coll.* 15.2.1 does distinguish between citizens and foreigners, both groups are said to have been included in a single proclamation. The argument made by Harries (1999), 87 that the repetition of regulation was not necessarily the result of disobedience thus does not seem to hold up in this particular case.

[164] Goodyear (1981), 284–5.

[165] Barton (1994[a]), 44; Cramer (1954), 234; Potter (1994), 174.

[166] Goodyear (1981), 284–5; Ripat (2011), 119–20.

[167] Rogers (1931), 203–4; Syme (1981), 189.

[168] For the various ways in which consular names could be used to date official documents, see Eck (1991), especially p. 26, where the author suggests that the consuls mentioned by Ulpian are indeed the *consules ordinarii* of 17 CE.

uncertainty regarding the date of the expulsion is particularly galling as it makes determining whether the *senatus consulta* can reasonably be said to have been issued in direct response to the trial against Libo Drusus particularly difficult. Such a link has generally been assumed on the basis of the close temporal proximity of these events, as well as the connection made between them by Tacitus, and we therefore cannot fully rule out the possibility that there was some connection between the two.[169] However, this line of thinking has not proved to be beyond dispute. While Tacitus' account is certainly the most authoritative, the absence of divination in the majority of sources regarding Libo's trial remains an important factor to consider: how can an expulsion of diviners be seen as a direct consequence of legal proceedings in which they played only a supporting part?[170] Furthermore, Suetonius makes no mention of a connection between Libo's trial and the expulsion, and instead mentions the expulsion separately in a list of measures intended to restore public morality.[171] We know from other sources that the emperor also made an attempt to expel actors, as well as their spectators, in a similar attempt to restore public order, and that an expulsion of Rome's Jewish and Egyptian communities took place only a few years later (section 3.9; Appendix 2.45).[172] The fact that divinatory practitioners were given the option to obtain a pardon likewise speaks against the possibility that they were directly linked to conspiracies of any kind, which would surely have resulted in harsher treatment. All this suggests that the connection between Libo's trial and the subsequent expulsion orders may have been rather more indirect: the conspiracy may well have led Tiberius to become less secure in his position as emperor, especially given the fact that it took place early in his reign. This insecurity, combined with the fact that the eyes of the senate were now drawn towards the dangers private diviners could pose, in turn became the inspiration for measures that were meant to benefit public order, and thus reinforced the emperor's position. While Libo's trial may not have been the direct cause for the *senatus consulta* of 16/17 CE, it is therefore very likely that it contributed to it indirectly. Even at this stage, the connection between private divination and public disruption appears to have been a strong one in the mind of the Roman authorities, and expulsions (or the

[169] Tacitus, *Annales* 2.32. See also, among others, Cramer (1954), 238; Green (2014), 105–6; Potter (1994), 174; Shotter (1972), 92. Rives (2006), 62 argues that Cassius Dio, *Historiae Romanae* 57.15.8, in which the measure is described, directly follows Dio's description of the Libo trial, which likewise suggests a connection between the two. It should be noted, however, that the two accounts are separated by a reference to Tiberius' notably mild attitude towards Vibius Rufus, which concludes a discussion of the emperor's inconsistency.

[170] Ripat (2011), 119–20. Ripat also assumes that the expulsion orders were issued in 17 CE, and states that such a temporal difference would make a connection with the Libo trial unlikely. However, as we have seen, it is not certain that this dating is, in fact, correct.

[171] Suetonius, *De vita Caesarum: Tiberius* 33–7. See also Kelly (2007), 158.

[172] See Tacitus, *Annales* 1.77 for the banishment of the audience in 15 CE, and Tacitus, *Annales* 4.14.3 for that of the actors themselves in 23 CE. See Kneppe (1988), 167–9 for expulsions of actors in general. For a similar point of view, see Ripat (2011), 144. Tacoma (2016), 92–104 makes the argument that expulsions are best seen as an attempt to rid Rome of unwanted elements.

threat thereof) were likely seen as an important tool in, for the time being at least, getting a troublesome group under control.

2.6.4 Later trials under Tiberius

In the years that followed the Libo scandal and the subsequent expulsion measures, a number of other trials occurred that have traditionally been linked to Augustus' 11 CE ban on death-related divinatory enquiries and are said to have established the idea that violations of this edict constituted direct evidence of *maiestas* when they involved the emperor or his family.[173] Once again, however, the connection between these different events and the Augustan edict has to be carefully considered. The most historically reliable case is the trial of Aemilia Lepida, which took place before the senate in 20 CE (Appendix 1.12). Tacitus once again presents the most elaborate version of events and states that the first charge against Lepida concerned an alleged attempt to pass off her child as the offspring of a wealthy and childless member of the Roman nobility, presumably in an attempt to gain access to his inheritance. A number of different accusations were subsequently added, including adultery and attempted poisoning, both in connection to the disputed paternity of Lepida's child, as well as consulting astrologers (*chaldaei*) about the welfare of the imperial family, which Tacitus' use of the phrase *in domum Caesaris* suggests was alleged to have had hostile intent.[174] This last charge, however, was swiftly dropped on the orders of Tiberius, and the rest of the trial dealt primarily with the alleged poisoning—which is the only charge mentioned by Suetonius.[175] While Lepida's suspicious divinatory consultations are referred to under the heading of *maiestas* later in Tacitus' account,[176] the accusation thus almost seems like an afterthought, and given Suetonius' claim that this trial was part of Tiberius' attempts to rob Rome's noble families of their possessions, we cannot rule out the possibility that it was indeed added by the accusers in order to gain imperial favour and attention. The idea that this trial was political in nature is further reinforced by Tacitus' claim that Tiberius behaved ambivalently during the proceedings.[177] Since the accusation of improper divination was dropped despite the availability of evidence, however, it would seem that such an accusation, while certainly not favourable, was not considered

[173] Cramer (1954), 251. [174] Tacitus, *Annales* 3.22.

[175] Tacitus, *Annales* 3.22–3; Suetonius, *De vita Caesarum: Tiberius* 49.1. See Cramer (1954), 256 for the idea that this trial constituted a failed first attempt to 'base a *maiestas* charge solely on a violation of the edict of A.D. 11'.

[176] Tacitus, *Annales* 3.22. No other accusations that could possibly be described as *maiestas* are mentioned, see also Cramer (1954), 255.

[177] Tacitus, *Annales* 3.22.

to be especially damning either—a suggestion further supported, it bears repeating, by the fact that Suetonius does not mention divination at all. It seems that accusations of irregular divination were, once again, added to place the accused in a negative light.

Judging by the available sources, the connections between the next three trials widely linked to Augustus' edict and divination are likewise more tenuous than often assumed. In 26 CE, Claudia Pulchra was accused of unchaste behaviour (Appendix 1.13), as well as having made attempts on the emperor's life with poison and sorcery, which does not amount to a charge of illicit divination but rather to one of outright attempted murder,[178] and neither Augustus' 11 CE edict nor Tiberius' ban on divination without witnesses therefore seems to be relevant to this particular case. A similar pattern emerges in the next two cases. Mamercus Aemilius Scaurus, who was brought to trial twice, in 32 and 34 (Appendix 1.15), likewise does not appear to have been accused of any improper divination. The first charge against him was likely one of *maiestas*, and no further details are mentioned, except that he was apparently part of a group of like-minded individuals—which seems to suggest an attempt at conspiracy.[179] The second charge, however, is slightly more complicated: both Tacitus and Cassius Dio share the assumption that the primary basis for the trial was a combination of alleged adultery with a member of the imperial family and a play that supposedly painted Tiberius as tyrannical.[180] Tacitus also remarks that Scaurus was accused of performing magical rites (*magorum sacra*), and mentions certain *artes*, which could refer to either of the latter two charges but most likely the suspected magical rites.[181] There is little to suggest, however, that these included divinatory practices in any way, and it thus seems highly implausible that this trial meant that 'henceforth forbidden inquiries about the emperor [...] would be treated as *prima facie* evidence of *maiestas*', let alone that they were designated as such on the basis of the Augustan edict.[182]

Judging by the legal interactions about divination that took place under Tiberius, it would therefore seem that the Augustan edict of 11 CE was not as influential in legal practice as it is often assumed to have been. This is suggested not only by the lack of evidence proving that this measure was enforced throughout

[178] Tacitus, *Annales* 4.52. Cassius Dio, *Historiae Romanae* 59.19–20.1, who discusses the aftermath of the trial, mentions no charge at all. Cramer (1954), 256–7 concedes that 'no violation of the edict of A.D. 11 was officially charged', but nevertheless maintains that this was a trial that involved divination.

[179] Seneca Maior, *Suasoriae* 2.22; Tacitus, *Annales* 6.9. The latter mentions Scaurus as part of a group of alleged conspirators.

[180] Cassius Dio, *Historiae Romanae* 58.24.4–5; Tacitus, *Annales* 6.29.

[181] Rogers (1935), 152 identifies these *artes* as 'traffic with astrologers', but neglects to give any further explanation.

[182] Cramer (1954), 259. It should be noted that the charge of *maiestas* is not mentioned in connection to Scaurus' second trial.

the empire, but also by the fact that suspicious or potentially subversive divinatory enquiries have so far appeared only as evidence, or at the very most ancillary accusations, for more concrete and often better proven crimes. Notably, the known trials that took place under Tiberius all occurred place in Rome itself and involved members of the Roman elite: the accused were said to have consulted diviners about high-profile public matters, namely the lives of the imperial family and, in the case of Libo Drusus, other members of the aristocracy. However, no records of trials involving divinatory enquiries about private affairs remain. In addition, it should be noted that neither Libo Drusus' conviction nor that of Aemilia Lepida was ultimately based on illicit divination, and while Lepida was originally charged with having made subversive divinatory enquiries, this accusation appears to have been introduced specifically to incur imperial favour—or attention at the very least. Our sources indicate that alleged attempts to actively harm other individuals were generally the primary ground for conviction, and the same holds true for Claudia Pulchra and Mamercus Aemilius Scaurus, whose cases have erroneously been included in the list of those who were tried for their divinatory practices. It may therefore be argued that during this period accusations of improper divination appear to have been used to supplement other, formal charges, and generally acted as character evidence that was brought forward to cast further suspicion on the accused.

It furthermore bears repeating that Tiberius' ban on divination without witnesses, if it was indeed a repetition of Augustus' 11 CE edict, primarily serves to demonstrate that the original measure had fallen into disuse in the years since it was allegedly issued, and that there is furthermore little to suggest that this new version would have fared better, as references to the possible application of this measure, too, are noticeably limited. Tiberius' expulsion orders and attempts to regulate divinatory texts likewise appear to have been limited in scope, and in this regard follow a pattern similar to that of earlier, republican measures of the same kind. In the early imperial period, too, legal measures were created in response to local events, primarily those within the city of Rome itself, and generally appear to have been temporary in nature. Expulsion orders in particular were intended to maintain, or establish, public order in the region by removing a group of practitioners that was regarded as disruptive. Generally, there does not appear to have been a connection to a concrete criminal act, and the diverse ways in which private diviners were treated, which included the possibility for recantation, furthermore suggests that the treatment of individual practitioners was frequently up for negotiation. In addition, the implementation of such measures so far appears to have been both sporadic and inconsistent: the repetition of specific measures, even within the reign of the same emperor, makes clear that measures were not systematically enforced, but that they were instead the result of temporal and local circumstances.

2.7 Trials and Expulsions under the Later Julio-Claudians

Descriptions of legal interactions with diviners are less frequent in accounts about the later emperors of the Julio-Claudian dynasty, and our sources are likewise generally less elaborate than similar reports from the time of Tiberius.[183] Nevertheless, the surviving accounts provide a fascinating insight into the legal position of divination in this period, and are furthermore highly significant in tracing developments in the treatment of the practice.

2.7.1 Caligula: divination in Egypt

The only known case from the reign of Caligula concerns a diviner by the name of Apollonius (Appendix 1.16), who is said to have been active in Egypt, and thus represents a rare example of an accused diviner hailing from the provinces. According to Cassius Dio, the man made predictions about the imminent death of Caligula and was subsequently arrested and brought to Rome.[184] The story goes that Apollonius was condemned to death, but since Caligula died before the execution could be carried out, he apparently survived his ordeal.[185] While this story suggests that Roman authorities in the provinces could indeed be on the lookout for disruptive divinatory activity, especially when it involved public order and the stability of the empire, the reliability of this particular account is in doubt. As will be discussed later, Dio and others recount a story that is notably similar in their discussion of the reign of Domitian (section 2.8.3),[186] which allows for the possibility that we are dealing with a literary trope, or at least a mistaken repetition, rather than with an accurate description of historical events. On the other hand, this particular report of divinatory anxiety may find some support in the account of Suetonius, who describes a number of omens thought to predict Caligula's death in the final months of his life, including an reference to a *mathematicus* by the name of Sulla, who announced Caligula's imminent death after the emperor had requested to be told his fortune.[187] While there is no mention of Caligula harming the diviner in this particular case, such reports do suggest that

[183] Most of these accounts may be found in the works of Tacitus. For the importance of religious elements in Tacitus' work, see Shannon-Henderson (2019).

[184] The specific type of divination used by the man in question is not mentioned. Instead, only the verb προλέγω is used to indicate his predictions. The account contains no indication that the diviner's words were prompted by the enquiry of a client.

[185] Cassius Dio, *Historiae Romanae* 59.29.4.

[186] Cassius Dio, *Historiae Romanae* ep.67.16.2. See also Suetonius, *De vita Caesarum: Domitianus* 16.1.

[187] Suetonius, *De vita Caesarum: Caligula* 57.2.

stern action against those who predicted the emperor's death outside of the context of the imperial court was not completely out of the question.[188]

If we consider, however tentatively, the story about Apollonius' arrest to be true (even if the same cannot be said for the circumstances of his execution), the role of the *praefectus Aegypti* in the legal proceedings must be taken into account. Since the diviner was arrested in his homeland and only thereafter transferred to Rome, we must assume that the initial procedure took place under the jurisdiction of the local governor, Gaius Vitrasius Pollio, whose province was notably troublesome during the period. Some years before, under his predecessor Aulus Avilius Flaccus, the city of Alexandria had erupted in riots, in which the position and authority of Caligula as emperor, as well as the worship of his person, played a notable part.[189] His perceived mishandling of the 38 CE disturbances had caused Flaccus to be disgraced and ultimately executed,[190] and these tense circumstances may well have inspired his successor to be especially careful in how he handled the still unstable situation. Given the barely concealed hostilities in the city, predictions about the emperor's death might well have been seen as an attempt to incite renewed riots, or even rebellion. Pollio may thus have regarded his predecessor's fate as a warning, and may therefore have decided to involve his emperor directly in order to prevent potential charges of lax governance. If we accept this possible interpretation of events, it would be more reasonable to assume that Apollonius was arrested because he threatened the stability of the region by contributing to political unrest, rather than specifically because of his divinatory activities.[191] Divination in itself would have been only a minor accusation in comparison, which governors were furthermore perfectly able to deal with themselves—as will be demonstrated later in this chapter (section 2.9).

2.7.2 Claudius: trials and expulsion

The reign of Claudius once again witnessed a number of trials against members of the Roman elite who were accused of consulting diviners of various kinds. The first of these took place in 47 CE and has often been overlooked in studies dealing with the legal position of divination. The case involved two brothers from an equestrian family who shared the *cognomen* Petra, who had become embroiled in a rivalry of unknown origin between Empress Messalina and Poppaea Sabina

[188] It should be noted that the emperor had enquired about his birth horoscope (*de genitura*), which means that Sulla's pronouncement was not necessarily a reply to the emperor's question. A violent response might thus have been expected.

[189] Philo of Alexandria, *Legatio ad Gaium* 132–4 and *In Flaccum* 42–3. See also Avidov (2009), 156–7. The Alexandrian riots will be discussed in more detail in Chapter 3, sections 3.10–3.11.1.

[190] Philo of Alexandria, *In Flaccum* 108ff.

[191] Cramer (1954), 271–2 likewise makes the connection between Apollonius' arrest and the events in Alexandria, but nevertheless attributes the diviner's arrest to a breach of the 11 CE edict.

Maior by allowing the latter to meet her lover, the actor Mnester, in their house (Appendix 1.17).[192] While Tacitus maintains that this association with Poppaea was the real reason for the brothers' indictment, he also suggests that the formal accusation was instead based on the fact that one of them had had a dream with high-stakes political implications.[193] Tacitus is unsure of the exact contents of the dream and gives two possible versions. According to the first, Petra had seen Claudius crowned with wheat with the ears turned towards the ground, which he had subsequently interpreted as an omen for meagre harvests. The second version of the story holds that he instead saw the emperor wearing a crown of white leaves, which he took to mean that Claudius would die by the end of autumn. Tacitus does not state which, if any, of these accounts he believes to be true,[194] but in both cases the politically charged nature of the dream is clear. Predicting the death of the emperor was, as we have seen, considered to be disruptive behaviour, and predictions about the grain supply could be similarly dangerous. It has rightly been remarked that grain shortages were a major contributing factor to social unrest, the prevention of which was furthermore considered to be the emperor's personal responsibility.[195] We need not, then, take Tacitus completely seriously when he emphasizes the perceived unfairness of the situation by arguing that the Petra brothers were convicted purely 'on the basis of some dream' (*qualicumque insomnio*).[196] The politically charged nature of the predictions is very likely to have been considered inflammatory—as is the fact that the brother who had the dream is said to have come up with these interpretations himself, and may likewise have spread the story around. Once again, then, divination appears to have been used as evidence for disruptive behaviour, which may also explain why both brothers, and not just the dreamer, were executed.[197]

The second known trial from the reign of Claudius took place in 49 CE and involved a certain Lollia Paulina, who was accused of approaching *chaldaei* and *magi*, as well as the oracle of Apollo of Clarus, to ask questions about the state of

[192] Tacitus, *Annales* 11.4. The surviving narrative of the rivalry between Poppaea Sabina and Messalina begins abruptly in *Annales* 11.1, where it is assumed to be familiar to the reader. It is likely that the matter was more fully introduced in Tacitus' now lost account of the emperorship of Caligula, or the early reign of Claudius.

[193] This reading is inverted in Migdał (2020), 149, who suggests that the dream was the real reason for the trial, while the involvement in Poppaea's affair was only a pretext. Tacitus' use of legal terminology in the context of the dream, however, suggests that this was the official legal charge. For the idea that the brothers had not, in fact, opened their house to Poppaea and her lover, see Fenechiu (2011), 203–4.

[194] For the lack of certainty in Tacitus' account, see Fenechiu (2011), 204 and Shannon-Henderson (2019), 241–2.

[195] Ripat (2011), 145 n. 165. For a possible alternative interpretation of the corn-ear crown, see Shannon-Henderson (2019), 241–2.

[196] For the idea that Tacitus uses this story to highlight the perversions of justice under the imperial regime, see Fenechiu (2011), 204 and Shannon-Henderson (2019), 242.

[197] This idea is tentatively referenced in Shannon-Henderson (2019), 242, based on Furneaux (1891), *ad loc.*

the marriage between Claudius and his last wife Agrippina (Appendix 1.18). According to Tacitus, Lollia was falsely accused at the behest of the new empress herself,[198] and the fact that she enquired about the relationship between members of the imperial family, rather than their deaths, immediately stands out. It has therefore been suggested that this trial marks the final stage in the development of Augustus' 11 CE law, which meant that not only those who asked questions about the health of the emperor were susceptible to a charge of *maiestas*, but that the same went for whoever enquired about members of his family.[199] The fact remains, however, that death in general apparently went unmentioned: Lollia might just as well have been asking about the possibility of a divorce, rather than the death of the empress.[200] It should also be noted that her consultation with Apollo, at the very least, is unlikely to have occurred without the presence of witnesses: the oracle at Clarus, like many other similar sanctuaries, heavily relied on the involvement of its priests.[201] It can therefore hardly be seen as a secretive, clandestine operation, unless we assume that she consulted a statue of Apollo she had in her own home with the help of the aforementioned magicians, as some have suggested.[202] While this certainly explains why Tacitus would mention a *simulacrum* of the god specifically, the magicians and the statue are clearly referred to as separate divinatory entities, which makes this interpretation of the text unconvincing. Whether Lollia consulted diviners in private or not, Claudius seemingly bypassed the issue of divination altogether, and instead declared before the senate that she harboured *perniciosa in rem pubicam consilia* (destructive plans against the state), before ultimately sending her into exile with only a relatively small portion of her reportedly vast wealth—a common punishment for members of the Roman elite. While Tacitus' account does not tell us about the exact nature of her plotting, this phrasing does suggest that Lollia's divinatory practices were considered to be strongly linked to accusations of more concrete nefarious designs on her part and were primarily used as evidence for her plans. The fact that Claudius himself was responsible for the ultimate verdict, and proclaimed it before the senate, furthermore suggests that we are dealing with an example of imperial *cognitio* proceedings,[203] as well as highlighting the political importance that was attached to the matter.

198 Tacitus, *Annales* 12.22. Cassius Dio, *Historiae Romanae* ep.61.32.4 likewise mentions that Lollia was killed on the orders of Agrippina, but makes no reference to divination of any kind.

199 Cramer (1954), 259.

200 Given the fact that Lollia was at one point considered a possible marriage candidate for Claudius, it is hardly surprising that she would have been interested in the state of his marriage to Agrippina. See Suetonius, *De Vita Caesarum: Claudius* 26.3 and Tacitus, *Annales* 12.1.

201 For the workings of the oracle, see Parke (1985), 137.

202 Parke (1985), 141.

203 Sánchez-Moreno Ellart (2009), 211 suggests that trials of this kind may well have taken place in the context of the *cognitio* procedure. See Santalucia (1994), 220 for the senate's criminal jurisdiction in *crimina maiestatis*, as well as the emperor's right to intervene in all stages of this process. For the argument that the *quaestio perpetua* on *maiestas* disappears from the record after the time of Tiberius, see Robinson (1995), 7.

While there is little to suggest that Lollia indeed used divination to further her nefarious political plans, the accusations brought forward in the next known trial appear to have rested on firmer ground. In 52 CE (Appendix 1.19), Furius Camillus Scribonianus was banished from Rome, along with his mother Vibia,[204] because he had allegedly asked astrologers (*chaldaei*) about the emperor's death. While no other accusation, nor any additional details, are mentioned, Tacitus does indicate that Vibia held a deeply rooted hatred towards the imperial family. According to his account, she had already been sent into exile once before, ten years earlier, when her husband, and Scribonianus' father, Camillus had incited an armed revolt against Claudius in his province of Dalmatia.[205] Tacitus' mention of this earlier rebellion may suggest that Scribonianus' trial, too, had larger-scale political implications, or that his family connections made him a suspected cause of future unrest, which seems to be confirmed by the fact that he died soon after his trial, after which rumours of poisoning are said to have abounded.[206] While Scribonianus and Vibia may have been formally punished for their divinatory practices, it is therefore once again likely that the political circumstances of the case were the deciding factor in settling the verdict.

As had been the case after the trial of his ancestor Scribonius Libo Drusus (section 2.6.2),[207] the verdict against Scribonianus was followed by an expulsion of astrologers (*mathematici*) from Italy by way of a *senatus consultum* (Appendix 1.20).[208] Once again, Tacitus is the one to connect both events by mentioning them in direct succession,[209] although Cassius Dio briefly references the same measure without expanding on it, or in fact mentioning Scribonianus at all. Instead, he adds only that those who consorted with diviners were punished alongside those they had consulted.[210] Indeed, Tacitus does not explicitly link the trial and the expulsion, and he furthermore makes no mention of Rome's diviners having been directly accused of any particular crime. It has therefore been suggested that the connection between the trial and the expulsion was more complicated than it at first appears. The argument goes that astrologers were the ones responsible for spreading the story that Scribonianus had been poisoned, and that Claudius saw this as a threat to his reputation and position, especially given the grain riots that had taken place in Rome the year before, which were commonly seen as a bad

[204] While Vibia is the preferred reading in most editions, Scribonianus' mother may also have been called Iunia or Vinia. See Furneaux (1891), *ad loc.*

[205] Tacitus, *Annales* 12.52.

[206] Tacitus, *Annales* 12.52. For a more elaborate discussion of the possible danger Scribonianus presented, as well as the view that Agrippina saw him as a possible rival to Nero, see Groag (1910), 351.

[207] Grothoff (2016), 404 n. 711.

[208] We might make something of the fact that Tacitus alternates between *chaldaei* and *mathematici* within the same paragraph, but the interpretation of this curiosity is far from clear. It might support the thesis posed in Ripat (2011), 145 that the trial of Scribonianus and the expulsion were only loosely connected, but it may be equally possible that Tacitus simply uses different words for the same group of people as a form of literary *variatio*.

[209] Tacitus, *Annales* 12.52.

[210] Cassius Dio, *Historiae Romanae* ep.61.33.1.

omen.[211] The connection made between the expulsion and popular unrest in Rome is certainly a convincing one, and we cannot fully exclude the possibility that the perceived poisoning of Scribonianus may have aggravated these troubles—although concrete evidence for the involvement of diviners in spreading this particular rumour is lacking. However, the expulsion of the Jewish community from Rome in the same period (Appendix 2.52) does appear to have been at least partially the result of internal disturbances within that group that threatened to cause larger-scale unrests in the city (see section 3.11.3), and thus serves to demonstrate how religious outsiders could be seen as a threat to public order. Whatever its cause, our sources tell us that the expulsion was both fierce (*atrox*) and thoroughly ineffective (*inritum*).[212] It thus seems likely that this expulsion was as limited in temporal scope as it was in its geographical application, and it is furthermore probable that this measure, like its predecessors, was deeply linked to fears of political unrest.

The later years of Claudius' reign saw two more trials that have been connected to a charge of illicit divination,[213] although substantive evidence is lacking in both instances. The first case dates from 53 CE (Appendix 1.21), and deals with Titus Statilius Taurus, who was accused of *magicas supersititiones*, as well as a minor charge of extortion. Tacitus claims that the accusation in question was false, arguing that it was instigated by Agrippina, who wanted to lay claim to the accused's gardens.[214] There is nothing to indicate, however, what the exact nature of Taurus' alleged magical practices was, and there is therefore no real reason to assume that divination must have been involved. The second trial, against Domitia Lepida, took place in 54 CE, shortly before the ascension of the accused's nephew Nero to the imperial throne (Appendix 1.22).[215] The case is mentioned by both Tacitus and Suetonius,[216] the second of whom neglects to mention any charge at all. Tacitus, however, states that Lepida was convicted because she had made sacrifices (*devotiones*) intended to invoke a curse on Agrippina, and because she had lost control of her slaves in Calabria, who now threatened the peace in Italy. Once again, then, we are dealing with an alleged attempt to actively harm a member of the imperial family, rather than an enquiry about their health and welfare, which was further aggravated by the fact that Lepida's alleged negligence had led the stability of Italy as a whole to become threatened. Despite the fact, then, that these two trials have a number of things in common with the trials that did clearly involve divination (namely the fact that they took place in the city of Rome, dealt

[211] Ripat (2011), 145. For the grain riots, see Tacitus, *Annales* 12.43 and Suetonius, *De vita Caesarum: Claudius* 19.

[212] Tacitus, *Annales* 12.52. For the argument that the Roman authorities would have needed the help of the Roman populace to enforce such measures, see Wendt (2016), 59.

[213] Cramer (1954), 262–4.

[214] Tacitus, *Annales* 12.59.

[215] Despite the similarity in name, she was only very distantly related to the Aemilia Lepida discussed in section 2.6.4.

[216] Tacitus, *Annales* 12.65 and Suetonius, *De vita Caesarum: Nero* 7.1.

with members of the Roman elite, and centred on charges related to threatening the peace and stability of the empire) they should not be included in the corpus of divination-related legal measures.

2.7.3 Nero: trials—and expulsion?

The idea that measures against divination were often prompted by socio-political unrest is further confirmed by two additional trials, which took place in 66 CE under the rule of Nero. The first case is particularly interesting, because it allows us to take a rare glimpse at the fate of a diviner after his banishment. This man, a certain Pammenes, had been sent away from Rome for an unknown reason, although we may assume it was related to his knowledge of the *ars chaldaeorum*, for which Tacitus claims he was renowned (Appendix 1.23).[217] Rather than giving up his divinatory practices, however, Pammenes continued to practise his profession in exile. He apparently did so without any real hindrance, since he is noted to have received great numbers of visitors and messages, and although he evidently stayed away from Rome, this still serves to reinforce the idea that expulsions of diviners were primarily intended to safeguard public order. This is not to say, however, that their predictions could no longer have an impact. One of Pammenes' fellow exiles, a Roman politician called Antistius Sosianus,[218] saw the diviner's continued activity as an opportunity to improve his own situation and managed to steal a number of compromising predictions, which had apparently been transcribed. These predictions related to Publius Anteius and Ostorius Scapula, both members of noble Roman families, who had independently asked Pammenes about their horoscopes and future careers. Sosianus, interpreting this as an attempt at subversive activity, wrote to the emperor to warn him that he was in danger—but apparently withheld the details until a reversal of his own punishment had been secured. The two alleged conspirators were subsequently found guilty without a trial (Appendix 1.24), likely by the emperor himself, and both committed suicide.[219] It does not seem likely, however, that their consultations with Pammenes were the primary reason these men were convicted. According to Tacitus, who is our source on the matter, Sosianus made the claim that the two had enquired not only about their own well-being but also about the future of the emperor. The historian implies that this accusation was not necessarily corroborated by the documentary evidence he had collected but was instead added to draw the emperor's attention. The language of the account, then, suggests that Sosianus was attempting to prove conspiracy and intended usurpation, for which

[217] Tacitus, *Annales* 16.14.
[218] Tacitus is likely referring to the same Antistius in *Annales* 14.48.
[219] Tacitus, *Annales* 16.14–15.

the papers and horoscopes he delivered were merely supposed to provide the proof. Sosianus' primary claim was apparently that Anteius and Scapula were 'threatening the empire' (*imminere rebus*), and that his warning would greatly contribute to Nero's personal safety (*incolumnitas*). Tacitus' later remark that Nero had been made fearful by the conspiracy (*coniuratio*) against him that had recently been discovered further confirms that he expected Publius Anteius and Ostorius Scapula to actually take action.[220] Once again, then, divinatory enquiries were connected to, and seen as evidence for, more concretely malicious intentions and subversive behaviour.[221]

The second case dated to the reign of Nero is centred around the prominent senator Barea Soranus, who was also proconsul of Asia, and his daughter Servilia (Appendix 1.25). According to Tacitus, the senator had repeatedly resisted Nero's more corrupt pursuits, and had therefore incurred the emperor's hatred. He was ultimately brought to trial because of his friendship with Rubellius Plautus (who himself had been exiled and executed on charges of rebellion some years earlier), as well as his alleged attempts to stir up revolt in his province.[222] During the legal proceedings, an additional charge was brought forward against his daughter Servilia, which alleged that she had asked certain magicians (*magi*) to perform a rite that might harm the emperor.[223] She herself, however, firmly denied these charges. Instead, she claimed that, while she had indeed consulted sorcerers, she had only done so to enquire about the safety of her father.[224] She added that she had not attempted to use enchantments (*devotiones*), and had not even mentioned the emperor *nisi inter numina*, 'except as one of the divine powers'.[225] While it has been argued that 'forbidden consultations and the suspected use of black magic combined to ruin her',[226] the short speeches that according to Tacitus were delivered by both father and daughter in their attempts to save each other tell a markedly different story. Servilia is said to have hesitantly claimed that, even if her behaviour constituted a crime, she alone was guilty of it (*si crimen est, sola deliqui*).[227] Her father, by contrast, argued that her enquiries about his welfare made her guilty of nothing more than being overly loyal to her father (*nimiae tantum pietatis ream*).[228] Since Servilia had previously denied any attempts on the emperor's life, it would thus seem that neither of the accused was familiar with the idea that associating with diviners, or indeed specific consultations she

[220] Tacitus, *Annales* 16.15.

[221] The fate of Pammenes is not recorded. This may suggest that he was not personally involved in the trial, which may strengthen the suggestion that divination was not the primary accusation.

[222] Tacitus, *Annales* 16.23. For Rubellius Plautus see *Annales* 14.57–9.

[223] Tacitus, *Annales* 16.30–1; Cassius Dio, *Historiae Romanae* ep.62.26.3 reports that the father was accused of practising some form of magic via his daughter.

[224] Tacitus, *Annales* 16.30. Servilia claimed that 'both their names and the arts they practice' had been unknown to her before she consulted them. See *Annales* 16.31.

[225] Tacitus, *Annales* 16.31.

[226] Cramer (1954), 265.

[227] Tacitus, *Annales* 16.31.

[228] Tacitus, *Annales* 16.32.

might have made, constituted crimes in themselves. While it must be remembered that the *ipsissima verba* of these speeches are almost certainly a literary construct, and should therefore be ascribed to Tacitus rather than to the relevant historical figures, it is nonetheless telling that the author presents Servilia's claims that she was merely enquiring about her father's welfare as a solid legal defence against the charge of seeking to harm the emperor by magical means, rather than as a statement that may have constituted incriminating evidence in a case of illicit divination. This suggests that Tacitus, at the very least, did not recognize enquiries about the well-being of oneself or one's family to be a valid ground for legal accusations, which speaks against the idea that the Augustan edict (or, as the case may be, Tiberius' ban on divination without witnesses) was a familiar, well-established legal measure that was frequently enforced at his time of writing. There is likewise little indication that divinatory enquiries about the person of the emperor were seen as either the father's or the daughter's primary offence as no such charge is mentioned in the available accounts, and even an accusation of divination about the current political situation in general in itself does not appear to have been seen as a ground for conviction on the basis of some pre-existing regulation.[229] At the same time, however, the passage shows that divinatory practices—as benign and well-meaning as their usage may have been in reality—could easily be confused with more actively harmful behaviours, and furthermore could serve as evidence for accusations of harbouring politically subversive designs, with which they had come to be closely associated. It was for this reason that both accused were ultimately declared guilty and were ordered to commit suicide.

Despite the fact that multiple trials from Nero's time are linked to divination, the existence of a potential expulsion edict during his reign is mentioned by only a single source—and an unreliable one at that. This singular reference may be found in a tenth-century manuscript that was discovered in Paris, and contains a collection of testimonials about astrologers in Rome that were copied down by an anonymous Byzantine author.[230] In his brief description of the later days of Nero's reign, the author mentions that the emperor, for unknown reasons, became particularly perturbed by the magicians and astrologers (γόητες; ἀστρολόγοι) of Rome, and ordered them to leave Italy by a specified day (Appendix 1.26). This provoked a reaction from the diviners, who as a form of revenge for their treatment published a prediction that the emperor would die within that same established timeframe, which reportedly did indeed occur. It has long since been argued, however, that the anonymous author of the manuscript made a mistake,

[229] Cramer (1954), 264–5 makes the argument that Servilia's enquiries were political in nature, and had thus become a capital violation of the 11 CE edict 'long ago'—while acknowledging that the case was not exclusively based on a charge of what he sees as illicit divination.

[230] The manuscript is generally referred to as Cod. Paris. suppl. gr. 607A. Its text may be found in Boudreaux (1921), 100.

and that this anecdote is simply a displaced reference to a remarkably similar event dated to the reign of Vitellius by Cassius Dio and several other more reliable authors (see section 2.8.1).[231] Dio's account likewise includes an imperial attempt to banish Rome's astrologers (though the magicians are omitted), and their subsequent bid to retaliate by correctly predicting the date of their oppressor's death. It thus seems likely that our tenth-century author was simply mistaken in his dating of the measure, and that no expulsion measure occurred during the Neronian period.

Throughout the Julio-Claudian period, a distinctive pattern in the legal interactions between the Roman authorities and divinatory practices began to emerge. What stands out most is the fact that pre-existing bans on divination, whether implemented by Augustus or Tiberius, appear to have been less far reaching and significant than is often assumed. Not only did some trials that have traditionally been said to derive from such a ban not involve divination at all, in cases where divination is in fact mentioned, the primary charge overwhelmingly appears to have amounted to rebellion or active attempts to harm a member of the imperial family, rather than illicit divination. This holds true even for the sole legal interaction from the provinces we have encountered so far, in which case the diviner's trial may well have been connected to the fragile political situation in the region. It thus becomes likely that the known trials against individuals, whether diviners themselves or those who consulted them, primarily centred around the accused's involvement in and knowledge of public affairs. Trials in which divination played a part therefore often appear to have been strongly politicized, and could even be described as show trials. Nevertheless, the association between diviners and threats to the security of the state has been shown to have been a particularly powerful one, as is demonstrated by the fact that allegedly subversive divinatory practices were frequently presented as evidence for such accusations, as well as by the expulsions of diviners that occurred in this period.

2.8 The Year of the Four Emperors and the Flavians

After Nero's death, the lack of an obvious, natural heir led to a politically chaotic situation that has famously become known as the Year of the Four Emperors. This period was characterized by profound uncertainty, and it is therefore little wonder that attempts to predict the unpredictable play an important role in the historical narrative. Reports of omens, whether favourable or not, abound in many of the

[231] Cramer (1954), 242. Potter (1994), 175 incorrectly cites Cramer as suggesting that Nero did, in fact, order an expulsion of astrologers. While Cramer does include this episode in his list of expulsions, he later explains that the source cannot be trusted. For the events from the reign of Vitellius, see Cassius Dio, *Historiae Romanae* ep.64.1.4.

available accounts of the period, and the impact of some of these predictions on the swift rise and fall of the period's many emperors appears to have been significant—as was the perceived importance of the divinatory practitioners who made them.[232]

2.8.1 Otho and Vitellius: diviners in times of crisis

One of the most influential diviners said to have been active in the period is a man who is referred to as Seleucus by Suetonius,[233] as Ptolemy by Plutarch and Tacitus,[234] and as Ptolemy Seleucus by most of modern scholarship.[235] Whatever the man's actual name was, he is repeatedly described as having been a member of Otho's entourage, which he likely joined even before the later emperor's time as governor of Hispania Lusitania.[236] The available sources also consistently make note of his prediction that Otho would certainly survive the reign of Nero, and they claim that, when this in fact came true, he used his growing influence to push Otho into taking action against Galba and claiming the imperial throne for himself.[237] Despite Ptolemy Seleucus' clear connection to politically disruptive activities, however, these accounts give no indication that he was ever involved in legal interactions with the Roman authorities, and in fact his connection to Otho seems to suggest the continued prevalence and popularity of diviners.[238] His influence certainly appears to have been considerable, but we find no clear references to him ever coming into contact with the law. The sole exception to this is a brief passage in Juvenal's sixth satire, which may indicate otherwise (Appendix 1.27):

Praecipuus tamen est horum, qui saepius exul,
cuius amicitia conducendaque tabella

[232] For a remarkable modern example of this, see Wellesley (2000), 1, who opens his book on the Year of the Four Emperors by emphasizing the divinatory status of the beginning of the new year, and mentions prophecy and divination with some frequency throughout his introduction. See Morgan (2000) for the importance of omens in Tacitus' account of the period. For a critical analysis of the most significant academic studies on the period, see Morgan (2006), 1–10.

[233] Suetonius, *De vita Caesarum: Otho* 4.1 and 6.1. The same name is used in Tacitus, *Historiae* 2.78 to refer to an astrologer employed by Vespasian. This has led Chilver (1979), 84–5 and Murison (1992), 102 to argue that Suetonius is simply mistaken in the name, while others, like Barton (1994ᵃ), 66, assume that the same person was first employed by Otho and later by Vespasian.

[234] Plutarch, *Galba* 23.4; Tacitus, *Historiae* 1.22.

[235] Barton (1994ᵃ), 66; Cramer (1954), 272–3; Ripat (2011), 127 and 130.

[236] See Morgan (2006), 37–8 for Ptolemy's role during this stage of Otho's career.

[237] Tacitus, *Historiae* 1.22 and Suetonius, *De vita Caesarum: Otho* 4.1. Plutarch, *Galba* 23.4 seems to imply that both predictions were originally made around the same time, but nonetheless implies a long-lasting relationship between the two men.

[238] For a rejection of the idea that private divinatory practitioners were always relegated to the societal margins, see Wendt (2016), 6. In this, diviners find an interesting parallel in philosophers, who could likewise hold positions of great authority. See MacMullen (1966), 62.

magnus civis obit et formidatus Othoni.
inde fides artis, sonuit si dextera ferro
laevaque, si longe castrorum in carcere mansit.
Nemo mathematicus genium indemnatus habebit [...].[239]

He who is exiled most is first among [astrologers],
he, through whose friendship and horoscope-for-hire
the great citizen [Galba] died, who made Otho quake with fear.
From this trust in his art is derived: if his right hand clanks with iron,
as does his left, if he has long remained in a military jail.
No astrologer who has not been convicted has any talent [...].

If this reading of Juvenal's text is correct, the poet seems to suggest that Ptolemy Seleucus did in fact run afoul of the authorities, and that he was banished multiple times—possibly more than any other diviner. This, however, does not appear to have been entirely negative: Ptolemy apparently derived special prestige from his many banishments, which allowed him to influence political players of his day. However, the second and third lines of the cited passage are often, rightly, regarded as an interpolation, which disrupts what is otherwise a fairly general, if scathing, critique of diviners and their practices with a reference to a particular individual.[240] The value of the passage as a source about Ptolemy Seleucus and his supposed many exiles is therefore uncertain at best, although it should be noted that it is significant even under these circumstances. Juvenal's insistence that arrest and exile only increased a diviner's standing not only suggests that measures dealing with divination did not succeed in curtailing the practice, but also provides an additional explanation for why expulsions were so frequently repeated: it is possible that diviners who had been banished were regarded as especially trustworthy, precisely because they were apparently dangerous enough to be expelled. Paradoxically, this made expulsion beneficial, rather than detrimental, to those who were targeted by it, and these measures thus failed to deter practitioners from publicly proclaiming their expertise.[241]

Vitellius' 69 CE edict intended to expel astrologers does not appear to have been an exception in this regard (Appendix 1.28), although it remains interesting for other reasons. The measure is fairly well attested in multiple sources, and is the first of its kind that can reliably be claimed to have been issued directly by the

[239] Juvenal, *Saturae* 6.557–62.

[240] Braund (2004), *ad loc.*; Courtney (2013), 291–2; and Grothoff (2016), 330 n. 624. Courtney makes the suggestion that the interpolated lines are derived from another ancient poem, although it is impossible to interpret them without their original context, which is now lost. For the argument that lines 558 and 559 should not be removed, but rather that we should assume the existence of a lacuna between lines 557 and 558, which would facilitate a more logical transition, see Nadeau (2011), 292.

[241] Ripat (2011), 149. For the idea that expulsion may have been similarly beneficial for philosophers, see Wendt (2015[a]), 188–9.

emperor in the form of an imperial edict, rather than relying on the more indirect construction of a *senatus consultum*.[242] Tacitus presents just the briefest of accounts, mentioning only that 'astrologers [were] expelled from Italy'.[243] Suetonius, on the other hand, offers a slightly longer version of the story. He starts out by mentioning that Vitellius held a particular hatred for astrologers (*mathematici*),[244] and executed them without so much as a trial whenever they were brought before him (*ut quisque deferretur*).[245] According to Suetonius, this aversion found its origin in Vitellius' attempt to issue an order that commanded astrologers to leave Rome and Italy before the first of October, which only resulted in them publishing a pamphlet that stated that the emperor would not live to see the day mentioned in his own edict—a prediction that would not, in fact, come true.[246]

The cause of the expulsion, however, does not immediately become clear from any of the surviving accounts. The available sources do nothing to suggest that the expulsion was connected to specific conspiracies,[247] although some have argued that Vespasian's burgeoning influence may have been at play—a statement for which there is, ultimately, little to no evidence.[248] Nonetheless, it is not difficult to see how Vitellius' measures may have been linked to the general sociopolitical unrest that plagued Rome during his exceptionally brief time in power. Since control of the capital would have been vital during the Year of the Four Emperors,[249] an attempt to expel disruptive elements in order to increase his hold on power, possibly before the new emperor himself even reached the city, may well be seen as a sensible move on Vitellius' part.[250] As in the case of his predecessor Otho, various authors mention Vitellius' particularly strong belief in

242 Barton (1994ª), 50. This may be seen as a sign of decreased importance of the senate as an institution. Both Augustus and Tiberius are said to have issued edicts against divinatory practices, but neither of these were expulsion measures. The argument made by Grothoff (2016), 421, however, that edicts from now on became the 'standard form of enacting banishments and other forms of punishment of astrologers and diviners' is belied by the references to later measures in the form of rescripts by Ulpian. The fact that Vespasian is said to have issued a similar edict soon after likewise speaks against Grothoff's argument that Vitellius' edict 'endured long in popular memory'.

243 Tacitus, *Historiae* 2.62. For the argument that Tacitus presents this expulsion as a sign of Vitellius' moderation (albeit mockingly), see Morgan (2006), 152.

244 For the wider context of this aversion, see Morgan (2006), 76–7.

245 Suetonius, *De vita Caesarum: Vitellius* 14.4.

246 Cramer (1954), 244 correctly remarks that Suetonius exposes the astrologers' prediction as being incorrect—Vitellius did not die until December 69 CE. Cassius Dio, *Historiae Romanae* ep.64.1.4 tells more or less the same story, although with fewer details and more reverence for the astrologers' predictions, which he claims to have been correct. His version of events appears to have been followed by the twelfth-century Byzantine historian Zonaras, who likely copied parts of Dio's account. Notably, however, Zonaras' version mentions the existence of two edicts, one against astrologers and the other against sorcerers. However, the reliability of this account must be strongly questioned due to its later date, and it is therefore best to assume the existence of a single edict.

247 Ripat (2011), 120.

248 Potter (1994), 175 insinuates that the false prediction about Vitellius' death was a sign of 'Vespasian's prophetic underground in the capital'. Even if this was true, however, it can hardly have been the cause of the expulsion, since the prediction was made only when Vitellius' edict had already been issued.

249 Ripat (2011), 144.

250 Cramer (1954), 243–4.

the accuracy of oracles and other predictions, and it is therefore plausible that an expulsion of potentially disruptive divinatory practitioners would appeal to these sensibilities.[251] The fact that Suetonius' account also mentions the authors of invectives (*vernaculi*) as being targeted by the executions, although not the expulsions, serves to further demonstrate how concerned the emperor was with maintaining public order, as well as his personal authority, in an environment in which both were under constant strain.[252] This desire to prevent public disorder may also explain Vitellius' alleged turn towards executing diviners after his previous, more measured, expulsion order was met with public mockery. Once again, the coexistence of different types of measures serves to demonstrate that at this point in time there was no fixed, established way to deal with divinatory practices that were deemed improper or subversive, but that the legal treatment of the perpetrators could be adapted when this was believed to be appropriate. In this context, we also get a tantalizing glimpse at the involvement of the general population in legal measures against divination: by remarking that Vitellius condemned diviners whenever charges against them were brought before him (*ut quisque deferretur*), Suetonius' account suggests that private individuals could, and did, make complaints against these practitioners.[253] This, in turn, seems to indicate that Vitellius' concerns for the effect of private diviners on public order may have been more widely shared than is immediately apparent, or at least that such accusations were considered to be beneficial by those who made them.

2.8.2 Vespasian: expulsion

Vitellius' concern for public order appears to have been shared by his successor Vespasian, whose ascent to power is simply riddled with prophecy.[254] While it is difficult to determine if all authors who reference these alleged *omina imperii* took them completely seriously, or believed that they did indeed predict Vespasian's rise to power,[255] there is little to suggest that their accounts are entirely

[251] Suetonius, *De vita Caesarum: Vitellius* 14.5 mentions a rumour that the emperor killed his own mother because he was promised a long, secure reign if he survived her. Zonaras calls him φιλόμαντις.

[252] The term *vernaculi* in a literal sense refers to slaves born within a household. It has been suggested that such slaves were particularly favoured and were thus raised to be witty and impertinent, hence the common translation of 'jesters'. For this idea, see Shotter (1993), *ad loc.* In this context, the word may be taken to refer to the sharp phrasing of the anonymous pamphleteers, as is the case in Martial, *Epigrams* 10.3.1. This interpretation is also followed by Ripat (2011), 139.

[253] The assertion in Cramer (1954), 251 that 'the Roman government must have relied chiefly on devious methods in obtaining evidence of forbidden astrological consultations' does not take into account the widely acknowledged importance of such private accusers within Roman legal proceedings.

[254] Stories about the role of divination in Vespasian's ascent to power are told in Cassius Dio, *Historiae Romanae* ep.65.1.2–4; Flavius Josephus, *Bellum Iudaicum* 6.5.4 (312–14); Suetonius, *De vita Caesarum: Vespasianus* 4.5–5; and Tacitus, *Historiae* 2.78 and 5.13.

[255] Morgan (2000), 29–31.

made up. Prophecy appears to have played an important part in the new emperor's political strategy, establishing him as a ruler with divine approval.[256] While Vespasian, then, appears to have been eager to use prophecy for his own ends, and his response to its use by others is described in less extreme terms than that of his predecessor, there is still some evidence that he, too, issued an edict banishing astrologers (ἀστρολόγοι) from Rome—according to Cassius Dio while he himself was still en route to the capital (Appendix 1.29).[257]

The comparatively short span of time that passed between the issuing of Vespasian's edict and the aforementioned expulsion by Vitellius may suggest that the latter had not been particularly successful, but other than that, no particular cause for the expulsion is mentioned.[258] Dio's account, however, does provide some insight into what the new emperor's motivations may have been, especially in his assertion that Vespasian expelled astrologers from Rome, despite making use of their services himself.[259] This suggests a desire to control and limit the group's divinatory practices, as well as widespread access to them, and it is therefore likely that we are once again dealing with a targeted attempt to maintain public order and to re-establish a form of imperial authority during a time of political unrest.[260] It is also interesting that Dio's brief reference to the expulsion is preceded by a mention of another of Vespasian's proclamations, in which he pardoned all those who had been condemned for *maiestas* under previous emperors, and forbade the application of that charge in the future. This seems to be intended to demonstrate that, in Dio's view, an era of imperial overreach and fickleness was at an end, which appears to be confirmed by Vespasian's apparent refusal to take action against those who appeared to have an imperial horoscope.[261] This last episode is particularly telling for two reasons. On the one hand, it once again supports the idea that the divinatory practices of private individuals could be used to support accusations of conspiracy or otherwise subversive behaviour. On the other hand, Dio's account also suggests that the handling of such accusations, like accusations of *maiestas*, could differ substantially depending on the emperor who was currently in charge. This once seems to contradict the existence of a long-standing measure that served as a clear precedent banning divination about the position of the emperor, as the Augustan edict of 11 CE is

[256] Potter (1994), 173. [257] Cassius Dio, *Historiae Romanae* ep.65.9.2.

[258] Ripat (2011), 120.

[259] See Ripat (2011), 122 for the remark that Vespasian would hardly have targeted his own son Titus, who is said to have been able to calculate astrological predictions, with his edict.

[260] Potter (1994), 175 and Ripat (2011), 144. In this regard, it is telling that Vespasian is also said to have expelled philosophers that offered explicit opposition to his rule—see Cassius Dio, *Historiae Romanae* ep.65.13ff. and Suetonius, *De vita Caesarum: Vespasianus* 13 and 15.

[261] See Suetonius, *De vita Caesarum: Vespasianus* 14 and Cassius Dio, *Historiae Romanae* ep.67.12.3 for the story that Vespasian refused to act against Mettius Pompusianus, whose involvement with Domitian will be discussed later in this section.

ultimately said to have done, and instead serves to support the idea that such trials instead took place in the form of the more flexible *cognitio* proceeding.[262]

2.8.3 Divination under Domitian

The importance of a particular emperor's personal attitude becomes even more clear in the later years of the Flavian period. While Vespasian and his successor Titus both gained a reputation for their comparatively mild style of governance, the same cannot be said for Domitian. The difference in the reputation of these respective emperors is visible not only in the tone of the narratives about their individual reigns in the available sources but also in the legal interactions with diviners attributed to them. While there are no reports of trials involving divination from the reigns of the first two Flavians, Domitian, by contrast, is said to have taken a different approach, and various sources report that he took (allegedly draconian) measures against the practice. This difference may once again serve as an indication that the treatment of divination by the Roman authorities was dependent not solely on the precedent set by previous measures, but also on the attitude of the relevant authorities and the circumstances in which legal interactions occurred.[263]

The first case dated to Domitian's reign (Appendix 1.30) involved a single person called Mettius Pompusianus, whose imperial horoscope apparently incurred the emperor's wrath—despite the notable fact that Vespasian had previously ignored similar charges against him.[264] Although we are not told if the predictions about Pompusianus' future had been made at his own request,[265] both Suetonius and Cassius Dio report that his ultimate execution was due not just to his involvement in divination, but also to the fact that he was alleged to show signs of more concrete imperial aspirations. According to the accusations levied against him, he had maps of the world in his possession (either on parchment or

[262] Cramer (1954), 249–51. See Sánchez-Moreno Ellart (2009), 211 for the suggestion that trials involving divination often took place in the form of a *cognitio* proceeding.

[263] See Suetonius, *De vita Caeasarum: Domitianus* 14.1–2 for Domitian's particular interest in divination.

[264] Pompusianus is mentioned in both Suetonius, *De vita Caesarum: Vespasianus* 14 and *Domitian* 10. Cassius Dio, *Historiae Romanae* ep.67.12.2–4 first mentions an unnamed man who was condemned to death for associating with astrologers, before mentioning Pompusianus as an example of the 'many who perished' during Domitian's reign. It is thus unclear whether he did indeed see astrology as the primary cause of Pompusianus' execution, or if we are dealing with two separate cases. Interestingly, Dio also reports that Pompusianus was first banished to Corsica, and was condemned to death only at a later date. For the idea that Domitian was in the habit of targeting people who had an imperial horoscope, even if they did not seek out imperial power, see Cassius Dio, *Historiae Romanae* 67.15.6.

[265] Both accounts seem to suggest that Pompusianus' imperial horoscope was a popular rumour (*Οὐεσπασιανὸς μαθὼν ἐκ φήμης τινὸς ὅτι μοναρχήσει*; *volgo crederetur*, and *vulgo ferebatur*) rather than something he had actively sought out.

painted on the walls of his bedroom), frequently read passages from Livy's *Ab Urbe Condita* that contained speeches of kings and other great leaders from Roman history, and owned two slaves named after the famous Carthaginian generals Mago and Hannibal. The maps may well have been construed as a sign of his wish to claim dominion over the depicted regions,[266] while the speeches may have been seen as preparation for leadership, and the names of the two slaves as a sign of anti-Roman sentiments. In this context, then, the alleged imperial horoscope became one of many pieces of evidence for Pompusianus' apparently subversive plans. It is furthermore noteworthy that both authors present the charges against Pompusianus as highly contrived, and include their narrative about his execution in short lists of other trumped up, unreasonable charges intended to demonstrate the severity of Domitian's rule. Among the emperor's other alleged victims were a woman who supposedly undressed in front of a statue of the emperor, a sophist who made a detrimental remark about tyrants in a practice speech,[267] and a legate of Britain who had been confident enough to allow a new type of lance to be named after himself. It is telling that a conviction based on subversive divinatory practices is referenced among other events that are clearly meant to suggest that Domitian was both cruel and paranoid. This is further underscored by the fact that Pompusianus was condemned to death, while an important number of earlier trials involving divination ended in exile—the more traditional punishment for those who, like Pompusianus, were members of the higher classes. The attitude of the emperor, then, did not just determine whether cases involving divination were taken up in the first place—it could have an effect on the level of punishment as well. While this description must certainly be seen as part of both authors' political programme, it is unlikely that they would have referenced the case of Pompusianus in this context if such trials were a well-established, familiar part of the Roman legal landscape.[268] Instead, the accusation of subversive divination once again appears alongside other allegations that helped to facilitate charges of suspected treason or disloyalty.

In addition to the aforementioned legal interaction with Mettius Pompusianus, it has also been suggested that Domitian attempted to take more far-reaching measures against diviners as a group. However, while an expulsion of philosophers during his reign is well attested in a significant number of sources,[269] the

[266] For the idea that the maps were in fact astrological charts, see Geus (2019). However, given the fact that both our sources explicitly refer to maps of the earth (τὴν οἰκουμένην and *orbem terrae*) rather than the sky, this theory seems unlikely.

[267] Such speeches, in which students were expected to praise the virtues of famous individuals or decry their vices, were an important part of Roman education—see Quintilian, *Institutio Oratoria* 2.4.20.

[268] For the contrary view, see Cramer (1954), 267.

[269] Cassius Dio, *Historiae Romanae* ep.67.13.3; Philostratus, *Vita Apollonii* 7.4; Pliny the Younger, *Epistulae* 3.11; and Suetonius, *De vita Caesarum: Domitianus* 10.3. The expulsion of philosophers provides an interesting parallel for similar measures against diviners. The possible overlap between the two groups under the heading of 'freelance experts' is discussed by Wendt (2016), 17–30, and both

same cannot be said for similar the actions against astrologers (*mathematici*) he is said to have taken not just once, but possibly even twice (Appendix 1.31 and 1.32). The only source for these events is the church father Jerome's *Chronicon* (late fourth century CE), which contains an expanded translation of the church historian Eusebius' earlier work of the same name.[270] The *Chronicon* provides us with only the briefest of references, stating that Domitian expelled astrologers and philosophers from Rome in 89/90 CE (*Domitianus mathematicos et philosophos Romana urbe pepulit*), and that he did so again by edict in 93 CE (*Domitianus rursum philosophos et mathematicos Roma per edictum extrudit*). While the details of the account are very much in accordance with earlier expulsions, including the measure's focus on the city of Rome and the use of an imperial *edictum*, the fact that no other, earlier source mentions astrologers as being involved in any way remains difficult to explain. In particular, the fact that Suetonius was a contemporary of the expulsion lends additional credence to his assertion that only philosophers were expelled. The suggestion that Domitian expelled diviners from the city in response to the large-scale political difficulties he faced at the time therefore seems to be based less on concrete, reliable evidence than on a dubious connection between reports about the expulsion of philosophers on the one hand, and Domitian's personal interest in divination on the other.[271] While it is almost certain, then, that Domitian ordered expulsions of some kind, which were likely intended to safeguard public order, it is at the same time unlikely diviners were their target.[272]

The last year of Domitian's reign is said to have been dominated by a remarkable number of politically motivated executions, two of which have been linked

their sporadic and local character, and the underlying mechanisms of their legal treatment do indeed appear to be analogous. It is very likely that philosophers were likewise targeted because they were perceived as causing political unrest, or provided political opposition to the Roman authorities, as argued by MacMullen (1966), 62; Raschle (2020), 101 n. 62; Ripat (2011), 127. For the related argument that these measures were caused by a discomfort with organized groups that fell beyond the grasp of those in power, see Nippel (1995), 87 n. 2. Another notable parallel between the two groups may be found in the fact that they both held an ambivalent position in Roman society, and that both philosophers and diviners who worked with members of the elite could on occasion, although likely not always, be targeted in different ways—see MacMullen (1966), 62; Raschle (2020), 101; Ripat (2011), 127. Finally, Wendt (2015[a]), 188–9 notes that frequent banishment became a mark of distinction for philosophers as much as for diviners.

[270] Eusebius' Greek original has not survived, although an incomplete translation in Armenian has been transmitted. However, the differences between the Armenian edition and Jerome's Latin translation are often so significant that it is impossible to determine which version better approaches Eusebius' original. See Burgess (1999), 22. The passage of the *Suda* on Domitian mentions a single expulsion of astrologers, but likely used Jerome as a source. See Grothoff (2016), 256 n. 285.

[271] The alleged date of Domitian's second expulsion has been linked to both the uprising of prefect Lucius Antonius in Germania Superior in the late 80s of the first century, and a series of high-profile executions in 93 CE. See Cramer (1954), 245–6; Potter (1994), 175–6.

[272] Wendt (2016), 44 regards both philosophers and diviners as different forms of freelance experts, and sees both groups as related legal categories for this reason. While this is certainly a valid connection, the inclusion of diviners in this particular expulsion is not clearly borne out by the available sources, and this case is thus beyond the scope of this particular study.

to some form of divination. The first of these involved the diviner Ascletario (Appendix 1.33),[273] who appears to have been quite famous in his day.[274] The story is told by multiple sources,[275] but the most reliable account seems to be that of Suetonius, who presents the events as follows:

> *Nulla tamen re perinde commotus est, quam responso casuque Ascletarionis mathematici. Hunc delatum nec infitiantem, iactasse se quae providisset ex arte, sciscitatus est, quis ipsum maneret exitus; et affirmantem fore ut brevi laceraretur a canibus, interfici quidem sine mora, sed ad coarguendam temeritatem artis sepeliri quoque accuratissime imperavit. Quod cum fieret, evenit ut, repentina tempestate deiecto funere, semiustum cadaver discerperent canes, idque ei cenanti a mimo Latino, qui praeteriens forte animadverterat, inter ceteras diei fabulas referretur.*[276]
>
> But [Domitian] was by nothing so strongly affected as by the response and the end of Ascletario the astrologer. This man was accused, and did not deny that he had proclaimed certain things that he had foreseen by his art. He was asked what manner of death would befall him, and when he answered that he would shortly be torn apart by dogs, Domitian ordered that he should be executed immediately, but also buried with the utmost care, in order to prove the uselessness of his art. When this was about to happen, it occurred that a sudden downpour extinguished the pyre, and dogs tore apart the half-burned body. The emperor was told about this at dinner by the actor Latinus, who happened to have seen it in passing, among the other news of the day.

Although this story is likely heavily embellished in order to appear more spectacular, it nonetheless contains a number of revealing details. Firstly, the phrasing of the passage, especially the use of verbs like *deferre* and *infitiari*, suggests a formal legal charge brought forward by a private accuser, which suggests that the Roman authorities were (at least to an extent), reliant on the help of the wider population in suppressing unwanted divinatory activities.[277] Furthermore, Domitian does not appear to have intended Ascletario's execution exclusively as a punishment for his divinatory practices. Instead, his goal appears to have been in large part to prove the diviner wrong in a brutal (as well as public) fashion, presumably in an attempt to dispel rumours of his own imminent death.[278] This idea

[273] This is the name used by Suetonius. Other sources refer to him as Asclepion, Asclation, or Asclepius—see Cramer (1954), 273.

[274] Cramer (1954), 273.

[275] Cassius Dio, *Historiae Romanae* ep.67.16.3 and Suetonius, *De vita Caesarum: Domitianus* 15.3. The account in the tenth-century manuscript Cod. Paris. suppl. gr. 607A, as printed in Boudreaux (1921), 101, may be based on Cassius Dio. See Cramer (1954), 273.

[276] Suetonius, *De vita Caesarum: Domitianus* 15.3.

[277] Wendt (2016), 59.

[278] The relevant passage of Dio's account only survives as a summary and does not mention the emperor's intentions. The tenth-century manuscript Cod. Paris. suppl. gr. 607A, which is possibly

is supported by the fact that Suetonius includes this story in a list of dire oracles that troubled Domitian in the later days of his reign, most of which were of divine, rather than human, origin. Ascletario's prediction, then, was the only one that Domitian could feasibly prove wrong: he could hardly argue with Fortuna and Minerva, but he could attempt to restore some of his authority by proving the man who had predicted his death to be a fraud. When seen in this light, Ascletario's execution becomes less of a punitive measure for divinatory practices that were considered improper than an attempt to remove a stain on Domitian's authority—and the individual who had caused it in the process.

A similar desire to prove subversive diviners wrong appears to have been at play in the case of Larginus Proculus (Appendix 1.34), who was brought before the emperor around the same time as Ascletario and was allegedly sent to Rome by the governor of Germania because he had publicly predicted that Domitian's death was imminent.[279] Upon his arrival in the capital he was convicted, but, if Cassius Dio is to be believed, it was determined that the execution would only be carried out after the emperor's hour of danger had passed—once again confirming the idea that Domitian had a vested interest in proving those who predicted his death to be frauds in order to reaffirm his own authority. According to the story, however, Proculus ultimately escaped death: Domitian died right at the appointed hour and the diviner's life was spared. This, however, is not the most significant part of the story. What is more interesting is the fact that the governor's involvement provides another rare hint that divination was a matter of public order in the provinces as well and was therefore a point of concern for the local authorities. Furthermore, it is remarkable that Proculus does not appear to have been punished in any way by Domitian's successor Nerva. If we are to believe Dio's account, he even received a substantial monetary reward, which may serve as an indication that the personal attitude of the relevant authorities was of great importance in shaping the legal treatment of divinatory practices. However, given the sensationalist nature of the account it is difficult to be fully certain.

The events from the Year of the Four Emperors and the Flavian dynasty, then, serve to reaffirm the connection between measures against divination and attempts to maintain public order, including the stability of imperial rule. This is especially clear in the case of the two expulsions accredited to Vitellius and Vespasian, which are best contextualized by the still unstable positions of their

based on Dio's original, more complete version, does mention that Domitian intended to prove the diviner wrong. For the argument that punishment and an attempt to prove the diviner wrong were inextricably linked in this case, see Barton (1994[a]), 48. For the suggestion that Ascletario may have made his prediction *ex nihilo* as a form of self-advertisement, see Ripat (2011), 137.

[279] Cassius Dio, *Historiae Romanae* ep.67.16.2; Suetonius, *De vita Caesarum: Domitianus* 16.1; Cod. Paris. suppl. gr. 607A. This story bears a striking resemblance to the case of the Egyptian diviner Apollonius, who was said to have predicted the death of Caligula—see section 2.7.1. Since that event is only mentioned by Dio, however, it seems to be the less reliable instance of the two.

respective reigns. Furthermore, the events from the reign of Domitian further emphasize just how politically charged trials against individuals who were involved in divination could be, as well as the great significance of the specific attitudes of the relevant authorities and the socio-political and administrative context in which such interactions took place. Although references to trials about divinatory practices, or the lack thereof, are often used as part of a conscious historiographical programme to paint an image of the respective emperors' characters, such differing accounts do suggest that the legal status of divination was not perceived as a constant or well established.

2.9 Later Incidents: Completing the Picture

While the number of known interactions between diviners and the Roman authorities becomes noticeably more limited after the end of the Flavian dynasty, the surviving examples are nonetheless interestingly diverse in character, provenance, and outcome. They therefore provide a fascinating insight into continued attempts to regulate divinatory practices, not just within the city of Rome but also in the provinces, from which more concrete examples begin to emerge in the available sources. The first case often connected to the period dates from 137 or 138 CE,[280] when a young man by the name of Pedanius Fuscus was executed at the command of Emperor Hadrian (Appendix 1.35). By all accounts, Fuscus was barely 18 years old, but, from what Cassius Dio tells us, he was already strongly involved in political life. Both he and his grandfather apparently argued against the ailing Hadrian's choice of Lucius Commodus as his successor,[281] and the notoriously dubious source known as the *Historia Augusta* even claims that Fuscus was persuaded by certain predictions to envision himself as the next emperor (*imperium praesagiis et ostentis agitatus speraret*).[282] While further

[280] 137 CE is the date given by Potter (1994), 161. Cramer (1954), 268 suggests 138 CE. The former option is more likely, given Cassius Dio's claim that Pedanius Fuscus and his father were executed because they rejected the adoption of Lucius Commodus as heir-presumptive, who died before his adoptive father very early in 138 CE.

[281] Cassius Dio, *Historiae Romanae* ep.69.17.1. Notably, Lucius Commodus' son, Lucius Verus, would be adopted by Hadrian's alternative heir, Antoninus Pius.

[282] Scriptor Historiae Augustae, *Hadrianus* 23.3. For a relatively recent version of the text, see the Teubner edition of Samberger, Seyfarth, and Hohl (1997). The many problems with the *Historia Augusta* as a source, of which the date and the number of authors involved are the most prominent, are summarized in Johne (2006). It is generally considered likely that the work dates to the last years of the fourth century CE, as for instance by Honoré (1987), 159–65 and Syme (1968), 72–9. Likewise, the argument for a single author is widely considered persuasive. For this, see Johne (2006); Honoré (1987), 156 n. 8; Syme (1968), 176–81. The reliability of the work is in any case a thorny issue. Johne (2006) suggests that Hadrian's *vita* contains reliable information, and Honoré (1987), 176 likewise suggests that the author of the *Historia* is 'not as careless of the historical truth as is supposed'. He does, however, note that the work contains parts that are not meant to be believed, and suggests that it may be seen as covert commentary on the author's own time. Syme (1968), 218–19 recommends

details are scarce, both sources clearly indicate that Fuscus' downfall was primarily related to his attempts to gain political influence, whether he saw himself as Hadrian's successor or not, and the involvement of divination in the case is much less firmly established. While prophecy may have been the catalyst for his ambitions, it is notable that this element goes entirely unmentioned in Cassius Dio's account as it survives today,[283] and appears only in the *Historia Augusta*—although the idea that divination played a role in the proceedings might find some support in the fact that Fuscus' horoscope appears to have been published soon after his death. The relevant predictions, which have survived independently from our other sources about the case, appear to have been intended to clear Hadrian of any blame,[284] and suggest that Fuscus was fundamentally unsuitable for leadership—which could tentatively be seen as a response to previous claims of an imperial horoscope. All in all, however, there is little to suggest that Fuscus' consultation with diviners was a central charge during his trial, and at the very most such accusations may have contributed to painting him as politically subversive.

In addition to such reports of trials against those involved in divination, accounts of the period also include a number of brief references to various types of measures intended to regulate the practice in a more general sense, about which we otherwise know very little. In his *First Apology*, Justin Martyr fleetingly mentions a ban on divinatory texts (Appendix 1.36), which he claims prescribed the death penalty for anyone who read 'the books of Hystaspes, the Sibyl, or of the prophets'.[285] Due to the brevity of the remark, it remains unclear which exact measure Justin is referencing here, to which geographical area it applied,[286] or even if he believed that the ban was still in use during his lifetime.[287] The only

extreme caution and points out the work's frequent fabrications, while Rohrbacher (2015), 11–14 points out the author's tendency to heavily distort his sources.

[283] It should be noted that the relevant passage survives only as an epitome.

[284] See Potter (1994), 161. The Greek text of the horoscope can be found in Ruelle (1911), 85–6, and an English translation in Neugebauer and van Hoesen (1959), 108–9.

[285] Justin Martyr, *1 Apology* 44.12. Hystaspes is a prophet from the Zoroastrian tradition, whose alleged works became popular in the Roman world in the first century CE. The 'books of the Sibyl' are likely the so-called Sibylline Oracles, which became popular in Jewish and Christian circles, see Parke (1988), 157–8. The prophets he refers to are also very likely to derive from a Jewish context. See Minns and Parvis (2009), 197 n. 2 and Wartelle (1987), 278.

[286] Given the fact that many of the texts mentioned by Justin were popular in Jewish communities, and the author's familial roots in Judea, we may speculate that he is referring to a regional measure repressing potentially disruptive divinatory texts after the Bar Kokhba Revolt. For a similar argument, see Wartelle (1987), 278. This argument is rejected by Minns and Parvis (2009), 197 n. 2, who claim that Jewish communities were not prevented from reading their sacred texts.

[287] Wartelle (1987), 278 is unable to find a particular known measure that fits the profile. Minns and Parvis (2009), 197 n. 2 express some doubt as to whether Justin believed the decree he mentions to still be in use. Parke (1988), 158 believes that Justin meant to imply that the measure was a thing of the past, and argues that the death penalty would not have been pronounced in any case. Wendt (2016), 50–1 takes this reference to mean that books of prophecies were widely banned by the middle of the second century, but does not specify whether this was because of a new measure or an existing one.

other measure on divination that is known to have been issued around the same time is a rescript sent to governor Pacatus of Gallia Lugdunensis by Antoninus Pius (Appendix 1.37),[288] but this measure appears to have had a strictly local application, and although its exact contents are otherwise altogether unknown to us, the context of the reference strongly suggests that it in some way dealt with the treatment of diviners themselves, rather than their written works.[289] At most, Justin's reference thus serves to support the idea that divinatory texts, like divinatory practices, continued to be regarded with some suspicion by the Roman authorities—even if we cannot be fully certain if, and under which circumstances, the possession of such works was actively punished.

That divinatory practices in general could still be a cause of concern is made clear by an additional measure that is reported to have been implemented during the reign of Marcus Aurelius (Appendix 1.38). While a short reference to the banishment of *mathematici* by the contemporary Christian apologist Tertullian may suggest that this measure involved the expulsion of diviners as a group, this can hardly be considered conclusive evidence due to the lack of concrete information about the date of the measure it provides.[290] Ulpian, by contrast, mentions only that the emperor banished a single astrologer to one of the Greek islands, apparently because he made dangerous predictions during a time of political unrest,[291] while a portion of the *Digesta* attributed to Modestinus claims that Marcus Aurelius issued a more expansive rescript ordering anyone who caused general terror by superstitious remarks should be banished to an island (*si quis aliquid fecerit, quo leves hominum animi superstitione numinis terrentur, divus Marcus huiusmodi homines in insulam relegari rescripsit*).[292] Despite the impersonal phrasing, both the shared reference to the diviner's feigned supernatural powers and the similarity in punishment (namely *relegatio in insulam*) suggest that this is an indirect reference to the same diviner that is mentioned by Ulpian. Interestingly, this measure by Marcus Aurelius is described as a rescript, which suggests that he was responding to a particular legal question posed to him, likely

[288] See Ulpian, *De Officio Proconsulis* 7 in *Leg. Mos. et Rom. Coll.* 15.2.4, where the measure is referred to as both a decree and a rescript. For the argument that the latter term is correct, see Nogrady (2006), 196 n. 950. In any case, the measure would have been a response to a very specific case.

[289] For the idea that the governor had captured a druid and was asking the emperor for advice on the correct procedure, see Frakes (2011), 301.

[290] *Expelluntur mathematici, sicut angeli eorum; urbs et Italia interdicitur mathematicis, sicut caelum et angelis eorum*, Tertullian, *De Idolatria* 9.2. Cramer (1954), 247 suggests that this passage does indeed refer to an expulsion of astrologers as a group during the time of Marcus Aurelius but admits that the evidence for this is hardly air-tight. See also Grothoff (2016), 256 n. 485, who is rightly critical of Cramer's line of thinking. For the argument that Tertullian was instead referring to various earlier police measures, see Sánchez-Moreno Ellart (2009), 217. Tertullian's Latin text may be found in Waszink and van Winden (1987).

[291] *Denique divus Marcus eum, qui motu Cassiano vaticinatus erat et multa quasi instinctu deorum dixerat, in insulam Syrum relegavit.* Ulpian, *De Officio Proconsulis* 7 in *Leg. Mos. et Rom. Coll.* 15.2.5.

[292] *Digesta* 48.19.30.

by a provincial governor.[293] The banishment of this particular diviner thus appears to have been strongly linked to the particular circumstances of his case and to the political unrest to which his predictions were said to have contributed.[294]

Another interesting, although ultimately unreliable, example of a trial against an individual who allegedly consulted diviners is said to have taken place a few years later during the reign of Commodus (Appendix 1.39). Notably, the accused in this particular case was the future emperor, Septimius Severus, who had apparently received a horoscope predicting that he would one day achieve imperial power,[295] and allegedly attempted to increase his changes by marrying a woman who had been told that she was destined to become the wife of a ruler.[296] According to the *Historia Augusta*, however, Severus was ultimately arrested and tried *quasi de imperio vel vates vel chaldaeos consuluisset*, 'as though he had consulted either seers or astrologers about the imperial throne'.[297] The trial is said to have taken place under the jurisdiction of the praetorian prefect,[298] who allegedly acquitted him because Commodus was becoming increasingly unpopular. Instead, he condemned Severus' accuser (*calumniator*) to death. Our source provides us with no additional information, but heavily implies that the accusation was both false and politically motivated, possibly in an attempt to cast Severus in a more favourable light. As interesting as it may be to see a future emperor represented as a defendant, however, it remains notoriously difficult to mine the *Historia Augusta* for reliable information, and the story is not confirmed by any earlier sources. Although Cassius Dio reports a great number of omens that allegedly predicted Severus' reign,[299] this is no more than an unremarkable parallel to the similar stories told about previous emperors like Augustus and Vespasian, and Dio's account as we know it makes no mention of the trial. Ultimately, then, while the passage at first glance seems to suggest that accusations of divinatory

[293] Nogrady (2006), 197. In Scriptor Historiae Augustae, *Marcus Aurelius* 13.6 we find an account of Marcus Aurelius pardoning a man who went about making predictions about the imminent end of the world in an attempt to gain access to the city of Rome and plunder it. Although the man is described as a charlatan, this story may tentatively serve as an indication that divinatory practices were not punished consistently, and that the general expulsion of diviners implicitly referred to by Tertullian did not, in fact, take place. It should be noted, however, that the reliability of the *Historia Augusta* remains doubtful—although the suggestion in Honoré (1987), 167–8 that the author may well have worked in the urban prefecture, and was likely familiar with Ulpian's work, is interesting in this regard.

[294] It is unclear if the diviner in question was directly involved in the rebellion of Avidius Cassius, or simply made disruptive predictions during this period. Given the fact that he was punished with exile, the latter seems more likely.

[295] Scriptor Historiae Augustae, *Septimius Severus* 2.8–9.

[296] Scriptor Historiae Augustae, *Septimius Severus* 3.9.

[297] Scriptor Historiae Augustae, *Septimius Severus* 4.3.

[298] The office of the praetorian prefect was afforded increasing judicial responsibilities from at least the time of Hadrian onwards, although the available information about its exact jurisdiction is unfortunately limited. See Lintott (2015), 323.

[299] Cassius Dio, *Historiae Romanae* ep.75.3.

enquiries about the imperial throne continued to occur on occasion and were still likely to be made by private individuals, the source ultimately provides little reliable evidence.

Once Septimius Severus ascended to the imperial throne, we hear of two more cases in which he played a part, although not as an alleged consultor of diviners but as the ruling emperor. The first of these (Appendix 1.40) is perhaps the single most fascinating legal interaction between diviners and Roman officials, not only because it was transmitted on a relatively complete papyrus but also because it is one of the very few examples of legal measures dealing with divination that can without a doubt be shown to have applied to the provinces, rather than to the city of Rome. While the exact provenance of the papyrus is unknown,[300] the text allows us to determine that we are dealing with a letter about a proclamation by the *praefectus Aegypti*, Q. Aemilius Saturninus from 199 CE.[301] In his missive, the prefect attempts to put an end to the unbridled practice of divination in his province. While it has been suggested that this proclamation was issued in response to an imperial visit of Septimius Severus and Caracalla to the province, and may thus have reflected the emperors' personal wishes,[302] it is ultimately difficult to determine whether the dates match up satisfactorily.[303] Furthermore, the first lines of the missive suggest that Saturninus was responding to complaints made by the inhabitants of the region, who had found themselves deceived by unscrupulous divinatory practitioners.[304] While his decision to take action may have been prompted by a desire to restore public order before the imperial visit, it is therefore unlikely that this course of action was directly proscribed by his superiors—an idea that is reinforced by the fact that no mention of imperial authority is made in the text itself.

Saturninus' letter also contains a number of remarks about the enforcement of his ban: he orders local officials to put up a copy of his missive in every settlement under their control and to closely monitor the situation afterwards, demanding that anyone who does not comply with this order should be sent to his court to be executed. However, the measure does not appear to have been intended as a

[300] The papyrus, known as both P.Yale Inv. 299 and P.Coll.Youtie 1.30, was bought in 1931 from an unknown private individual in Paris. Under such circumstances, the exact provenance of an artefact is often lost. See Parássoglou (1976), 261.

[301] The name of the prefect is not mentioned in the letter itself but can be deduced from the date mentioned at the end of the proclamation.

[302] Frankfurter (2012), 326; Parássoglou (1976), 264–5; Potter (1994), 176. According to Cassius Dio, *Historiae Romanae* ep.76.13.2, Severus confiscated all books containing secret knowledge (*βιβλία πάντα τὰ ἀπόρρητόν τι ἔχοντα*) from the sanctuaries he visited in Egypt, but this is presented as a sign of his personal curiosity, not as a ban on divination—if this was indeed the subject of the books in question.

[303] Rea (1977), 156.

[304] The reading of the first two lines of the papyrus is not completely clear, but this interpretation is supported by most commentators. See Dickie (2001), 157–8; Parássoglou (1976), 266; Rea (1977), 151.

punishment for past behaviour, and it seems likely that diviners who gave up their art after the proclamation had been published were able to escape punishment, as becomes clear from the fact that the governor specifically directs his threats of execution at those who were still practising when the local authorities came to investigate (*τις* [...] *παραμένων*).[305] Saturninus strongly insists that he expects utmost vigilance, even threatening lax officials with the same punishment as the criminals they have neglected to report.[306] What is especially interesting, however, is the fact that he lists a number of specific types of divination that are included in the ban, presumably in an attempt to clarify its scope and alert his officials to the various methods that were being employed. Among these types of divination is one, indicated simply with the term *κωμασίας*, processions,[307] that seemed '*prima facie* [...] wrong' to the first editor of the text, who subsequently suggested that the phrase must have been a synonym for *μαγεία*.[308] Later commentators have rejected this suggestion, arguing that Saturninus is instead referring to a traditional Egyptian type of soothsaying that attempted to find divinatory signs in the movements cult images of the gods made as they were carried through the town in procession.[309] At first sight, this may seem like an insignificant detail, but it does serve to demonstrate that Saturninus made notable attempts to tailor his measure to the particular circumstances in his province, not only by responding to complaints made by the locals but also by specifically referring to Egyptian traditions. This fact serves to reinforce the idea that the prefect was acting on his own authority, and that his measure applied to his own province in particular.[310]

Some years later, in 205 CE, Septimius Severus himself showed some signs of being concerned about divination, which appears to have led to the execution of Popilius Pedo Apronianus, who was *proconsul* of Asia at the time (Appendix 1.41).[311] The accusation against Apronianus appears to have been based on two points, namely the rumour that his nurse had once had a dream that predicted that he would one day be emperor,[312] as well as his own attempts to gain access to

[305] Statements to this effect are made in both P.Yale Inv. 299.10–12 and 16–18. The use of the present participles in [*τις*] *παραμένων* and [*τινα*] *πράσσοντα* to refer to those who should be arrested and executed is particularly telling in this regard, and further confirms that such investigations were aimed at present rather than past behaviour.

[306] P.Yale Inv. 299.12–23. [307] P.Yale Inv. 299.6. [308] Parássoglou (1976), 269–70.

[309] Rea (1977), 154–5. See also Frankfurter (2005), 236 and (2012), 326.

[310] For a similar view, see Ritner (1995), 3355.

[311] Cassius Dio, *Historiae Romanae* ep.77.8.1. For a discussion of the titles of the various governors of the region under Septimius Severus, see Demougin (1996).

[312] 'Nurse' is the most common translation, although the word *τήθη* can also mean grandmother. Since there is no further indication of the relationship between Apronianus and this otherwise unnamed woman, I have chosen to follow common practice. It should, however, be noted that a nurse would likely have had this dream during Apronianus' infancy, since that is when she would have been in his proximity, which would make a delayed conviction on the grounds of divination alone unlikely.

the highest office by magical means (μαγεία).[313] Of these two charges, the second one certainly appears to have been the primary accusation, since it hardly seems likely that the case against Apronianus would have rested entirely on a dream another person had had. Once again, however, the divinatory practices of the accused appear to have been seen as significant evidence for seditious plans, to the extent that the members of the senate, when they handled the case, appear to have been primarily concerned with who else might possess knowledge that could undermine the position of the emperor. When it was reported that 'a certain bald senator' had peeped into the room when the prophecy was first related, the other members of the senate became so afraid that they themselves might be accused of having been this unknown senator that they allegedly executed one of their number as a scapegoat before the emperor could even be notified.[314] This individual, a certain Baebius Marcellinus, does not appear to have been involved in the prediction in any way, save for the fact that his knowledge of it, if indeed he had any, may have made him a viable candidate for involvement in rebellion. It is therefore unlikely that either he or Apronianus was convicted because of behaviour that would constitute illegal divination under a pre-existing regulation—instead, it seems to have been their perceived attempts to actually make the nurse's prediction come true that provided the primary basis for their sentence.[315]

2.10 The Jurists: Creating Coherence

The events discussed in this chapter so far represent over two centuries of legal interaction between the Roman authorities and divinatory practices. While the intensity and character of the various legal measures are noticeably diverse, and intervention by the authorities occurred at irregular intervals, many of these cases nevertheless also show important similarities, and even in antiquity itself they appear to have been seen as part of the same legal tradition. In the third century CE, the jurists Ulpian (Appendix 1.42) and pseudo-Paul (Appendix 1.44) each attempted to present a systematic, coherent analysis of how Roman officials were to deal with legal matters related to divination in the future, in which Ulpian in particular makes extensive use of a collection of precedents with which he was

[313] Notably, Liebs sees this as a trial about dark magic, rather than divination. See Liebs (2012), 22–3.

[314] Cassius Dio, *Historiae Romanae* ep.77.8.2–77.9.2.

[315] If we believe the author of the *Historia Augusta*, Severus also executed a notable number of others due to their alleged consultations with diviners (*chaldaeos aut vates*) about his death. The author notes that he was particularly concerned with those whose own horoscope qualified them for imperial power, since his own sons were still young and could thus easily be set aside. Once again, then, the focus appears to have been on types of divinatory enquiries that could be linked to both politically disruptive behaviour and outright nefarious actions in the eyes of the presiding authorities. See Scriptor Historiae Augustae, *Septimius Severus* 15.5.

familiar.[316] The fact that both jurists saw the need for such an analysis is interesting in itself: it suggests that no single well-established rule for dealing with the practice was in place, and indeed the fact that Ulpian mentions repeated measures against divination by a variety of emperors indicates that he did not believe that a single measure lay at the basis of all later interactions.[317] The writings of these jurists on the subject thus provide a fascinating insight into the legal landscape in which they operated, and both address a number of different points, including the expulsion of diviners, consultations about the death of an individual (particularly the emperor), and the legality of divinatory practices in general. Although pseudo-Paul omits the explicit references to specific legal precedents that are so prominently present in Ulpian's text, the two jurists come to largely the same conclusions, which on the one hand allows us to get an idea of the legal consensus at their time of writing, while on the other hand making the slight differences in their accounts all the more telling.

In their respective analyses, both jurists are quick to mention that diviners of various kinds pose a substantial risk to society and are therefore not to be tolerated. Throughout, they similarly both adopt a universalizing approach. Despite the fact that the known expulsions, as we have seen, were historically limited to the city of Rome and the Italian peninsula, pseudo-Paul omits any mention of this. Instead, he refers to expulsion from the *civitas*, without making explicit which specific community is meant,[318] while Ulpian uses the traditional phrase *aquae et ignis interdictio* (denial of water and fire) to indicate banishment from general society as well as a loss of citizenship. He, too, makes no reference to any specific region—although the focus on exclusion from of a particular community in both passages may be taken to suggest that both jurists expected such expulsions to be enforced on a local level.[319] It should be noted, however, that their opinions about the other punishments that should apply to these practitioners differ on a number of interesting points. Pseudo-Paul addresses the issue of repeat offenders by saying that diviners who persist in practising their art despite having been beaten and driven from the city should be kept in chained captivity or sent into exile. Ulpian, on the other hand, makes no specific provisions for those who refused to give up their art, but instead suggests different types of punishments according to the social class of the offender. Although we find little indication that such a distinction was consistently made during the expulsions of which we are

[316] It should once again be noted that the *Sententiae* were likely not authored by Paul himself, but by another author who was active later in the third century. See n. 40 of this chapter. Wendt (2016), 53 sees these texts as evidence for the idea that previous measures 'stemmed from an underlying concern about these religious actors', and similarly argues that the jurists were attempting to create coherence between individual previous measures.

[317] Ulpian, *De Officio Proconsulis* 7 in *Leg. Mos. et Rom. Coll.* 15.2.3.

[318] Pseudo-Paul, *Sententiae* 5.21.1.

[319] Ulpian, *De Officio Proconsulis* 7 in *Leg. Mos. et Rom. Coll.* 15.2.1. The idea that expulsions of diviners were a local practice has been widely recognized, see e.g. Cramer (1954), 233 and 238.

aware, the jurist reserves banishment and the confiscation of property as a punishment for those diviners who were citizens,[320] while proscribing death for any foreigner who did the same (*externarum gentium quis*), apparently on the basis of a *senatus consultum* from the time of Tiberius.[321] Thus, while both jurists share the opinion that diviners of various kinds should be expelled, the specific details of the procedure vary, which indicates that they may have drawn slightly different conclusions from similar sources, and that full consensus had not yet been achieved.

A similar pattern emerges in the case of the respective jurists' analysis of the appropriate response to harmful divinatory consultations, where both show a similar concern with determining which exact types of enquiries should be banned—although they each do so in their own way. Both authors are quite clear in their assertion that consulting diviners about the health of the emperor (*de salute principis*) is an offence punishable by death,[322] but they once again add different elements to this general rule. Pseudo-Paul supplements that both diviner and questioner are to be executed, and remarks that a similar rule should be applied to slaves consulting about the welfare of their master.[323] Ulpian, by contrast, makes no reference to either regulation but seems to expand the ban by stating that consulting parties should also be punished for making enquiries about themselves or their family (*de sua suorumque*), albeit less severely (*levius*).[324] This, once again, suggests a lack of legal consensus regarding which enquiries ought to be punished and how. Both authors furthermore seem not just to diverge from each other but also to leave out part of the pattern that emerged in this chapter: as we have seen in a number of cases, consultations about one's own future career historically on occasion proved to be just as fatal as direct consultations *de salute principis* if they were perceived to be connected to excessive political ambition, but no mention of this specific context is made. In addition, it should be noted that none of the cases known to us makes any mention of slaves being punished for consultations about their master's health. Nevertheless, this regulation is prominently present in pseudo-Paul's writings. While it is very likely

[320] The forfeiture of the banished party's possession was traditionally associated with the *aqua et igni interdictio*. See Berger (1991), 507.

[321] The expulsion order of 16/17 CE has been discussed in more detail in section 2.6.3.

[322] Pseudo-Paul, *Sententiae* 5.21.3; Ulpian, *De Officio Proconsulis* 7 in *Leg. Mos. et Rom. Coll.* 15.2.3. Desanti (1990), 119 draws a parallel with Tertullian, *Apologeticus pro Christianis* 35, where the apologist likewise points out the inherently suspicious character of enquiries about the welfare of the emperor.

[323] Pseudo-Paul, *Sententiae* 5.21.3–4.

[324] Ulpian, *De Officio Proconsulis* 7 in *Leg. Mos. et Rom. Coll.* 15.2.3. The term *levius* stands in contrast to the assertion that those who enquire about the welfare of the emperor are to be punished *capite* [...] *vel qua alia poena graviore*. For the argument that the term *gravior* is here meant to refer to slower punishments like crucifixion, see Frakes (2011), 301. Whatever the case, the diversity in the proposed punishments suggests that the responsible magistrate retained some personal influence over the proceedings, and that no fixed procedure existed.

that Roman historians simply did not include such cases in their narratives due to their perceived lack of relevance for larger-scale political events, the apparent omission of a similar legal category by Ulpian at least allows for the possibility that we are dealing with an extrapolation from the apparently better-established ban on consulting about the death of the emperor, rather than a reference to a specific previously established regulation or precedent. It is not too much of a stretch to see the master of a household as paralleling the status of the emperor on a micro-level, making consultations on his health indicative of rebellion against the foremost authority in the questioner's life.

Having discussed expulsions and attempts to regulate specific divinatory questions, both jurists finally reflect on the extent to which divination in its totality could be considered to be a punishable offence. While Ulpian opens his analysis by confidently arguing that private divination, including the type practised by the *mathematici*, had long since been forbidden (*interdictum*), he later references a long-standing legal debate about whether this ban should apply only to the practice of the art (*exercitio*, *professio*), or to knowledge (*scientia*, *notitia*) about it as well.[325] Ulpian seems to settle on the latter, although not without mentioning that different opinions on the matter emerged over time (*postea variatum*).[326] In his own analysis, pseudo-Paul uses the even more careful phrasing *non tantum divinatione quis, sed ipsa scientia eiusque libris melius fecerit abstinere*, 'one would act better by abstaining not only from [the practice] of divination, but also from the field of knowledge in itself and from books about it'.[327] While it is clear, then, that both jurists are inclined to see both the practice and knowledge of divination in general as legally dubious, pseudo-Paul's lack of conviction regarding the

[325] Ulpian, *De Officio Proconsulis* 7 in *Leg. Mos. et Rom. Coll.* 15.2.2. For a similar debate among Roman jurists about the knowledge and practice of magic, although with a more decisive conclusion, see pseudo-Paul, *Sententiae* 5.23.18. It has been suggested by Fögen (1993), 64–, whose analysis was largely followed by Sánchez-Moreno Ellart (2009), that this passage may be an interpolation from the time of Diocletian or slightly after, in part because of the idea that the transition between the first and third paragraph of the analysis attributed to Ulpian becomes more logical when the second is seen as a gloss, and because the style of the passage seems dissimilar to the passages of *De Officio Proconsulis* contained in the *Digesta*. As a result, it is not unwise to treat this passage with caution. However, it seems implausible that a substantial point of discussion was interpolated in a text that sought to create more coherence, especially at a time in which divination had been made more fully illegal than ever before. It is likewise unlikely that the author of the *collatio* invented the passage, as the goal of that text appears to be to showcase the substantial overlap between Roman and biblical law, from which the passage seems to detract. See Liebs (1987), 170. The authenticity of the passage, and paragraph two in particular, is acknowledged by Frakes (2011), 301; Liebs (1987), 172–3; Nogrady (2006), 187–98. For a more elaborate discussion on why Fögen's argument that the entire text may have a later date does not, in the end, hold up, see n. 111 of this chapter.

[326] Desanti (1990), 90–1 and Nogrady (2006) 192–4 rightly argue that Ulpian does not assume the existence of a clear ban on the *scientia* of divination, with the latter noting that all specific examples cited by the jurist contain restrictions on the practice alone, and suggest that he leaves the ultimate decision regarding the treatment of mere knowledge up to the governor. Cramer (1954), 278 argues that Ulpian considered the *scientia* of divination to have always been legal.

[327] Pseudo-Paul, *Sententiae* 5.21.4.

illegality of divinatory knowledge suggests that debate continued to exist, or had at the very least been an important feature in the work of previous jurists.[328]

When considering the earlier cases discussed in this chapter, it is hardly surprising that such questions about the exact legal basis of measures involving divination should emerge. Even within the surviving corpus, the diversity of the various cases stands out, and it is therefore perhaps unsurprising that neither jurist appears to refer to a single type of diviner in particular, instead choosing to cover as much ground as possible by referring to *mathematici, harioli, haruspices, vaticinatores* and *mathematici, chaldaei, harioli et ceteri*, respectively.[329] For both authors, then, determining who was being targeted by measures against divination in general proved to be difficult, and this complication would have been further aggravated by the fact that there appears to have been no real precedent for attempts to consistently define who was supposed to be included in expulsion measures in particular. Although trials about particular disruptive enquiries were likewise diverse, and generally included divination in a wider array of treasonous and disruptive behaviours, these cases at least revolved around the specific questions divination was used to answer, and involved specific individuals who could be tried and, if found guilty, punished. Had the jurists only been dealing with these trials, it would therefore have been relatively easy to determine which types of divination had historically been marked as problematic, and why this was the case. When it came to expulsions, however, determining who was included in these measures appears to have been difficult even when they were first issued, and our sources continuously suggest that these orders could target not only those who were specifically involved in subversive dangerous consultations, but also everyone who was perceived to have divinatory knowledge, or defined themselves as such.[330] The idea that divinatory knowledge in general had a substantial disruptive power, and could thus pose a considerable risk to public order,[331]

[328] For the argument that no imperial pronouncement on the matter existed, and that this was left entirely to legal scholars, see Nogrady (2006), 192–3.

[329] Pseudo-Paul, *Sententiae* 5.21.3; Ulpian, *De Officio Proconsulis* 7 in *Leg. Mos. et Rom. Coll.* 15.2.1. The fact that both jurists reference multiple types of divination as a collective in the known passages ascribed to them speaks against the suggestion in Nogrady (2006), 198 that *vaticinatores* were treated with more leniency than *mathematici*: the distinction hardly seems to have been so clear-cut, or indeed binary, and is furthermore untraceable in any of the earlier legal interactions between diviners and the Roman authorities. It should also be noted that no definition is provided, as might have been expected if the jurists were truly referring to separate legal categories.

[330] See Ripat (2011), 128–41 for the argument that astrologers, at least, were largely self-selecting and could shed their identity with relative ease, which made them difficult to target. While this is certainly an important factor in the frequent repetitions of expulsion edicts, the possibility remains that those who were perceived as private diviners, without necessarily defining themselves as such, may also have faced punishment.

[331] The jurists both emphasize divination's potentially disruptive power. Pseudo-Paul, *Sententiae* 5.21.1. remarks that diviners should be expelled *ne humana credulitate publici mores ad spem alicuius rei corrumperentur, vel certe ex eo populares animi turbarentur*. Likewise, Ulpian, *De Officio Proconsulis* 7 in *Leg. Mos. et Rom. Coll.* 15.2.3 states that diviners practise their arts *contra publicam quietem imperiumque populi Romani*.

would furthermore have found its share of support in known historical attempts to confiscate divinatory texts—a type of measure that seems to be referenced by pseudo-Paul's recommendation to abstain from consulting books on the subject. It is therefore little wonder that the line between banned knowledge and banned practice became hard to draw, and that debate on the matter continued to exist—although it seems very clear that both were seen as fundamentally suspicious, as well as inextricably linked, in the eyes of the jurists.

Despite the fundamental suspicion towards divination present in the writings of the jurists, there are clear indications that private divination not only very much remained in popular demand,[332] but also to an extent continued to be tolerated by the Roman authorities throughout the imperial period. A possible material remnant of the established nature of private divination may be found in the so-called Owl of Thoms (Figure 1), which likely acted as a shop sign for a private diviner. The fact that a statue of this kind was apparently created specifically for public display, and given its use of marble was likely intended to be a fairly permanent fixture, suggests that diviners could afford to be visible and even make investments to this end. The subject of divination furthermore occurs one final time in the works of the Roman jurists, in a passage derived from Ulpian's *Ad Edictum* that was later incorporated in the *Digesta* (Appendix 1.43). Although the text as we know must be treated with some caution due to the fact that it was likely edited to contain a reference to the imperial *constitutiones* rather than a rescript dealing with a single particular case,[333] a number of telling elements nonetheless remain. In the passage, Ulpian discusses the appropriate way to deal with diviners who made false accusations of theft, and argues that they should not be tried in a civil case under an *actio iniuriarum*,[334] but instead according to some other regulation—likely the aforementioned rescript, which has since been lost, but may well have facilitated a criminal procedure. This passage is interesting for two reasons: not only does it provide a rare glimpse at cases in which diviners could be punished for making pronouncements about the lives and behaviours of ordinary individuals, but it also suggests that private divination was not considered to be fully illegal at this stage. Instead, Ulpian's discussion of the issue refers to the fact that false accusations made by diviners could do substantial damage to the reputation of the accused, and therefore seems to suggest that the testimonies they provided continued to carry at least some weight in a

[332] For the continued importance of divination, even in a Christian context, see Barton (1994[a]), 64–85; Frankfurter (2005); and Klingshirn (2005).

[333] Ulpian, *Ad Edictum* 77 in *Digesta* 47.10.15.13. For the theory that the passage was edited, see Sánchez-Moreno Ellart (2009), 207–8 and 221–2. The imperial *constitutiones* in question are likely those in the *Codex Iustiniani* 9.18, the relevant passages of which all derive from a later date than Ulpian's original text. See Desanti (1990), 44–6 and Sánchez-Moreno Ellart (2009), 197 for the argument that the reference to *illicitam divinationem* in *Ad Edictum* is likewise an interpolation.

[334] See Sánchez-Moreno Ellart (2009), 221 for an analysis of the meaning of this charge in Ulpian's time.

legal context, possibly even within the context of a formal trial.[335] If private divination had indeed become fully illegal by this period, such a clarification of how a specific divinatory behaviour could be legally addressed would hardly have been necessary. Notably, Ulpian is exclusively concerned with diviners whose accusations proved to be false, rather than with their practice in general, and he furthermore discusses the matter in the context of a dispute between private individuals. This suggests that diviners were in practice only brought to trial if their predictions were perceived to have caused some measure of concrete harm (in this case to the accuser's reputation), and whether or not this occurred therefore heavily depended on the circumstances under which such predictions had been made. Despite the attempts made by jurists like Ulpian and pseudo-Paul, then, to systematically discuss and analyse the legal treatment of divination in the Roman Empire,[336] it remains likely that the frequency and character of legal interactions between diviners and the Roman authorities to a large extent continued to depend on the individuals involved, and the circumstances in which they found themselves.

2.11 Conclusion

Throughout this chapter, we have discussed a wide variety of legal interactions between the Roman authorities and those involved in divination, including trials against individual practitioners and those who consulted them, attempts to regulate divinatory texts, and expulsion measures aimed at diviners as a group. While some references to these events may be found in the works of the Roman jurists, the overwhelming majority has been described by historians like Tacitus, Suetonius, and Cassius Dio, and it is therefore very likely that the cases that are known to us represent only a limited selection of the interactions that historically took place. Nevertheless, the size of the available corpus allows us to draw a number of important conclusions regarding the legal treatment of divination in the Roman world, including the origins, content, and enforcement of the relevant legal measures. Furthermore, it is clear that attempts to regulate divination were highly diverse in character, and that the practice was of significant interest both to the inhabitants of the empire, and to Roman magistrates—including the emperors.

[335] The text gives no indication of the context in which the diviner would have made his accusations, but given Ulpian's focus on the falseness of the accusation, it seems plausible that diviners may have been brought forward as witnesses during formal legal proceedings.

[336] The fact that Ulpian's analysis is said to have been included in his *De Officio Proconsulis* suggests that he intended his work to have an empire-wide application. It bears repeating, however, that this need not have been the original intent of the precedents he cites. For the argument that the Roman authorities' concerns about divination increased in the third century CE, at least in part due to political instability, see Rüpke (2016[b]), 83.

What stands out most about the legal interactions between diviners and the Roman authorities, is that the cases known to us are overwhelmingly reported to have taken place within the city of Rome and the Italian peninsula, while events that took place in the provinces are referenced only on rare occasions and were furthermore noticeably reactive. Although this relative scarcity of accounts dealing with other parts of the empire is likely due to the preoccupations and biases of the available sources, and should therefore not be taken to mean that divination was a concern only for those inhabiting the capital, the limited scope of such measures does suggest that they were strongly embedded in the geographical and temporal circumstances in which they occurred. This pattern is perhaps most clearly visible in the case of trials against individuals who were said to have consulted private diviners. Although the number of relevant cases is smaller than is often assumed, it is notable that the accused in the majority of known trials were specifically members of the Roman elite, whose alleged enquiries about high-profile public matters (including the welfare of the emperor and their own chances of obtaining a prominent position in the governance of the empire) served to paint them as politically disruptive and possibly treasonous.

While the 11 CE edict ascribed to Augustus by Cassius Dio is often seen as an essential part of the legal foundation for such trials, particularly those that involved alleged consultations about the death of the emperor, the evidence for this claim is ultimately hardly conclusive. As central as the edict has become to the debate about the legal status of divination in the Roman world, this connection is tenuous even for the first known case in which it is said to have played a part, and any proposed development in the edict's application that would have allowed certain divinatory enquiries to be seen as treasonous without any additional charges, is hardly as linear, or as final, as it is sometimes claimed to have been. Cassius Dio's account of the edict is furthermore not corroborated by any other source and is instead very similar to the legal analyses on divination written by the jurists of his day, which makes it plausible that his description shows a sense of (retroactive) cohesion that is more suited to his own time than the one he is describing. The assertion that the Augustan edict formed the basis for an empire-wide, long-lasting ban on both divination without the presence of witnesses and on enquiries about the death of an individual therefore rests on shaky ground. While it is true that divination is often linked to treasonous behaviour (*maiestas*) in the available sources, it must be remarked that even later cases hardly ever rest on the accused's divinatory practices alone. Instead, accusations of improper or subversive divination frequently appear in combination with allegations of more concrete, actively treasonous, or destabilizing behaviour. If Augustus' edict as we know it did indeed exist, it is therefore unlikely that it was as influential as is often assumed. As we have seen, it is even unlikely that Tiberius' ban on divination without witnesses was a reiteration of the Augustan measure, or that it had a long life of its own. The presence of a third-party witness to a divinatory enquiry is only ever mentioned again as a recommended way to prevent accusations of treasonous behaviour, and the absence of such witnesses is never described as a possible charge in itself.

As far as we can tell from the available sources, then, it is unlikely that accusations of subversive divinatory enquiries about one's own possible fortunes or the welfare of the imperial family were based on a single measure intended to ban such practices. Instead, these allegations generally appear to have been brought forward to serve as evidence in trials in which the primary charge was one of *maiestas* or a similar offence—or that took place in the context of more flexible *cognitio* proceedings, as some sources seem to suggest. The fact that the analysis of later jurists references the existence of repeated individual cases, rather than a single underlying measure, furthermore strongly suggests that the cohesion between these various trials was only formally recognized at a later date, and the assumed existence of a pre-existing, wide-ranging legal measure is simply unnecessary to explain the emerging pattern that closely associated divinatory enquiries with resistance against the established authorities. Similar concerns regarding the disruptive power of divination likewise become visible in the known trials against individual diviners themselves, whose activities appear to have been strongly associated with disturbances of the public order of various kinds. Concerns about divinatory practitioners disrupting the socio-political stability of their communities appear in the stories about certain diviners from the provinces who were perceived to be the cause of unrest and rebellions, and even in the rare known reference to legal proceedings dealing with divinatory enquiries about private individuals. In particular, Ulpian's discussion of diviners being tried for false accusations of theft suggests that these practitioners, like their colleagues involved in more high-profile cases, were on at least some occasions targeted for the potential harm their pronouncements could cause to those around them. While a lack of available sources does not allow us to determine to what extent non-experts were charged for enquiring about another private person's welfare, the omnipresence of divination, as well as the apparently prevalent belief that divinatory consultations may well be linked to concrete harmful action, tentatively suggests that such trials may have taken place.

It should furthermore be noted that trials against those who were actively or passively involved in divination (whether it concerned members of the imperial family or less prominent individuals, under whichever immediate charges) appear to have been overwhelmingly instigated by private accusers. This lack of initiative on the part of the Roman authorities, while not in itself a notable departure from normal trial proceedings of the period, is nonetheless telling. A reliance on private initiative may serve to explain why the available sources rarely present subversive divination as the sole charge, and why such accusations were often connected to allegations of more concrete attempts to harm the welfare of particular individuals, or indeed the state: pointing towards the accused's divinatory practices as evidence for their apparent ambitions may well have served to convince the relevant officials of the importance of the case, and increased the accuser's chance of success.

While larger scale measures like the expulsion of diviners seem to have required more initiative on the part of the Roman authorities, it should be emphasized that these measures, too, appear to have found their origins in local circumstances, and almost certainly applied to specific regions. Once again, most known sources refer to Rome and Italy in particular, but the fact that attempts to regulate divination in the provinces repeatedly took the form of imperial rescripts suggests that these measures were the result of particular difficulties about which the governor of the region had asked the emperor's advice. Even the only known measure of a provincial governor on the subject, although it orders the execution rather than exile of divinatory practitioners, appears to have been strongly localized and specifically tailored for the Egyptian context in which it was created, and is therefore unlikely to have held much sway elsewhere in the empire. The fact that these measures applied to relatively limited geographical areas, however, should not be taken to mean that they were implemented in response to the actions of specific diviners, for which a much larger group was then blamed. Although trials against individual diviners or their clients were sometimes closely followed by an expulsion, it has been demonstrated that no clear, consistent connection between these two types of measures existed. In addition, diviners as a group generally do not appear to have been targeted for any suspected involvement in concrete disruptive behaviour, unlike individuals whose divinatory practices became the subject of legal proceedings. Instead, expulsions may best be seen as ad hoc attempts to maintain public order, often in times of more widespread socio-political unrest. This tendency is most obviously visible in the expulsions ordered by Vitellius and Vespasian, but the pattern can be observed even in early measures dating from the republican period. This serves to indicate that divination and those involved in it were perceived to have a strongly disruptive potential even when no concrete actions to this effect could be pointed out—as is further demonstrated by the known attempts to regulate divinatory texts, which might likewise provide access to destabilizing information.

The coexistence of these different kinds of legal interactions between the Roman authorities and diviners, then, makes it difficult to establish a singular legal basis for measures against divination. Roman jurists disagreed on whether the knowledge or practice of divination should be punished, and throughout the principate this question does not necessarily appear to have had a clear-cut answer. Trials against individuals, whether diviners or those who consulted them, were quite clearly overwhelmingly directed at people whose particular divinatory practices or enquiries were considered to be inappropriate, which likely contributed to the idea that divination could be put to dangerous use, and to a general sense of suspicion regarding private practitioners and their clients. As mentioned, it is this idea of divination as a potentially disruptive force, even in the absence of concrete behaviours that disrupted public order, that underpinned both expulsions and attempts to regulate divinatory writings, both of which may have led jurists to consider that both the practice and the knowledge of divination should be punished. However, the authorities appear to have made little effort to define who was to be included in such measures. The perceived disruptive potential of divination does not appear to have been linked specifically to any particular divinatory method, and in legal and administrative practice such distinctions between different types of divinatory practitioners are likely to have been of little value, and often impossible to draw. Expulsions in particular appear to have been aimed at a wide variety of people who were recognized as private diviners or identified themselves as such. As a result, the scope of these measures likely depended not only on the guidelines of the Roman authorities but also the visibility (whether intentional or not) of diviners themselves, and possibly even on the cooperation of the general population.

Like the targets of legal measures involving divination, the types of punishment that were implemented likewise appear to have been diverse, in spite of Ulpian's reference to the common idea that citizens should be punished with banishment, while non-citizens should be executed. While members of the Roman elite who were tried for allegedly consulting diviners about the welfare of the emperor and his family were indeed generally banished, in practice this punishment does not appear to have been exclusively reserved for citizens, as becomes clear from the case of the diviner Pammenes, and especially from the repeated expulsions of diviners as a group. Furthermore, expulsions and executions notably appear to have occurred concurrently on a number of occasions, once again suggesting that legal measures against divination were tailored to the particular circumstances under which they occurred. This apparent flexibility can once again be used to argue against the existence of a specific edict from the early years of the first century CE onwards, which would likely have specified a punishment. In this context, it also bears mentioning that the goal of measures against divination were not necessarily aimed at punishing previous behaviour, but rather at restoring order: on at least one occasion, during the expulsions ordered by Tiberius, we hear that diviners who were being targeted by these measures received the official promise that they would be shown leniency in return for giving up their art. On other occasions a similar possibility to escape punishment may well have existed informally, as is suggested by the measure of the *praefectus Aegypti* Q. Aemilius Saturninus, who limits punishment to those who were still practising when his ban went into effect. In a number of other cases, we hear about specific individuals, both diviners and their clients, who were pardoned despite having been involved in disruptive activities, which suggests that the precise treatment the accused received was up for negotiation, and is likely to have depended on the attitude of the relevant authorities towards the accused.

While the lack of available sources from the provinces makes it difficult to determine to what extent legal measures involving divination were implemented uniformly throughout the empire, the strongly localized origins and character of the known cases make it very unlikely that attempts were made to implement similar, contemporaneous actions throughout the Roman territories, and certainly expulsion orders, at the very least, were simply too focused on Rome and Italy to reflect a wide-ranging policy. It should furthermore be noted that the temporal scope of the measures that targeted groups or diviners, or indeed divinatory texts, likewise appears to have been limited. The frequent repetition of expulsion measures was remarked upon even in antiquity itself by authors like Tacitus and Ulpian, and we find a number of reports of multiple expulsion orders being issued in quick succession, sometimes even by the same emperor. Measures against diviners thus do not appear to have been systematically enforced, and were furthermore likely at least partially ineffective. Despite the fact that divination frequently appears to have been regarded with suspicion when practised by private individuals, the prevalence of and popular demand for the practice likely made it difficult, and possibly even undesirable, to treat diviners as a continuous threat, while diviners' lack of distinct, fixed characteristics by which they could be recognized likely made them difficult to target. Legal measures against divination in the first two centuries CE can therefore be considered to have been ad hoc, localized, and subject to frequent renegotiation, targeting only particular events and circumstances. Only by the early third century CE do we find attempts at a systematic legal analysis of the subject, and even then elements of debate and flexibility remain visible.

Although diviners were a less distinct and recognizable entity than the Jewish and Christian communities, whose interactions with the Roman authorities will be discussed in following chapters, the treatment of this group nevertheless serves to illustrate the general principles and mechanisms according to which Roman legal measures dealing with perceived religious outsiders were formed. Despite the fact that involvement in divination was not just commonly accepted but even widely popular throughout the Mediterranean world, those who participated in the practice could—and evidently did—become the target of legal measures. The treatment of diviners shows that concerns regarding public order or the stability of Roman rule provided a primary catalyst for legal action against religious groups and practices that were regarded as deviating from societal norms. While such deviations are often highly concrete in trials involving the divinatory practices of particular individuals, the previous analysis has shown that matters were not always so clear-cut. Instead, we have seen that larger religious groups on occasion became closely associated with social disruption and potential danger in both popular and legal consciousness, to the point that the group in question could come to be seen as a viable target for legal measures even when no such concrete actions that posed a threat to public order could be pointed out.

At the same time, it should be emphasized that such an association does not, as a rule, appear to have resulted in measures that were systematic in nature. The various known interactions between diviners and the Roman authorities serve to demonstrate that measures against perceived religious outsiders, despite their apparent similarities, emerged from a plurality of contexts, were overwhelmingly both temporary and local in nature, and depended heavily on the initiative of private individuals. More general, coherent rules attempting to regulate religious groups emerged only gradually, and as we have seen coherence was ultimately created by the analyses and deductions of the Roman jurists, rather than the decisions of practising magistrates. Furthermore, it has become clear that even the existence of repeated measures against a particular religious group did not constitute full illegality, either by design or by default. As the legal treatment of diviners has shown, the Roman authorities' overriding concern for maintaining the stability of both city and empire did not in the first instance express itself in punishing previous involvement with suspect religious practices, at least for those who did not become actively involved in treasonous plots against the state or the imperial family. Rather, the fact that diviners were allowed to give up their profession, or to return to the city after being expelled, shows that restoration of public order was seen as centrally important, and that forgiveness for past behaviours could be used to achieve this—if the situation allowed.

Marginalized Religion and the Law in the Roman Empire. K. P. S. Janssen, Oxford University Press.
 DOI: 10.1093/9780191946400.003.0003

3
Judaism in Roman Legal Measures

3.1 Introduction

While interactions between diviners and the Roman authorities provide an insight into the repression of religious groups that were seen as potentially socially and politically disruptive, divination as a practice could otherwise be fairly comfortably integrated in the 'traditional' Roman religious experience. The treatment of the various Jewish communities of the empire, on the other hand, allows us to investigate the legal position of a group whose exclusive belief in a single supernatural power made them a notable anomaly within the Roman world—and who therefore experienced its own particular set of challenges. Certainly, the distinctive character of Jewish religious beliefs and practices frequently captured the attention of Roman authors. A central example of this may be found at the very beginning of the fifth book of Tacitus' *Historiae*, where the historian discusses the involvement of the Flavian dynasty in the conflict that is most commonly known as the Jewish War and announces his intention to discuss the origins of the city of Jerusalem before moving on to its imminent destruction.[1] What follows is one of the most elaborate known descriptions of ancient Judaism from an outsider's point of view, but Tacitus' portrayal is far from favourable. He describes Jews as a *genus hominum* [...] *invisum deis* (a 'race of men hated by the gods') and repeats the apparently widely held belief that the very presence of a Jewish community in Egypt had caused a disfiguring plague.[2] He then moves on Jewish religious rites, claiming that:

> *Profana illic omnia quae apud nos sacra, rursum concessa apud illos quae nobis incesta.*[3]
>
> There all that we hold sacred is unholy, and by contrast everything that we consider impure for them is permitted.

To further emphasize the perceived otherness of the Jewish people from the other inhabitants of the Mediterranean world, Tacitus continues his diatribe by arguing that Jewish beliefs are only defensible because of their antiquity but have no other

[1] Tacitus, *Historiae* 5.1–2. For the Latin text of the passage, see Fisher (1911).
[2] Tacitus, *Historiae* 5.3. [3] Tacitus, *Historiae* 5.4.

redeeming qualities. He argues that Jews present themselves as an entirely distinct group and isolate themselves even further by demanding that converts abandon not only their ancestral religion but also their fatherland and even their families. The Jewish ban on images, says Tacitus, even makes proper reverence for both their own kings and the Roman emperors impossible.[4]

Tacitus' deeply hostile description of Judaism is perhaps the most famous of its kind, and his perspective has therefore often been taken to be representative of the prevailing Roman opinion.[5] Indeed, the forceful assertion of a Roman senator that Jews were fundamentally 'other' and un-Roman in every conceivable way has led many scholars to assume that the author's hostility must have been widely shared among the Roman elite. Some have argued that the Roman authorities came to see Judaism as a threat to the so-called *Pax Deorum*, and thus believed that the marginalization (and possibly destruction) of this anomalous group was necessary for the continued well-being of Rome.[6] Similarly, the attitude of the Roman state towards Judaism has been described in terms of profound hostility,[7] Judeophobia,[8] and the assertion that Jews were, in Roman eyes, 'not reckoned among nations'.[9]

To argue that Tacitus' view of Judaism as a contemptible, alien superstition represents the prevailing attitude within Roman government would, however, be strongly misleading. While it is certainly true that relationships with Jewish groups could be contentious, as is demonstrated by the repeated occurrence of Jewish uprisings against Roman authority, as well as by the fact that the Jewish community of the empire's capital was repeatedly expelled, this was by no means the full extent of Rome's interactions with the Jewish communities within its sphere of influence. Even before Roman rule extended to the eastern Mediterranean, the Roman state forged multiple allegiances with the Jewish leaders of Judea, and in later periods Roman attitudes were likewise not simply repressive, or even unequivocally negative. Instead, we are dealing with a broad spectrum of different measures, both positive and negative, dating from both the republican and the imperial periods. The interactions that have been transmitted to us deal with a wide range of issues and occurred in various parts of the Roman Empire. This corpus is furthermore remarkably well documented. Thanks in large part to the works of contemporary authors like Flavius Josephus and Philo of Alexandria, both of whom wrote at least partially within a Jewish context, we have access to more Roman legal interactions with Jewish communities than with any other

[4] Tacitus, *Historiae* 5.5.

[5] See Schäfer (1997), 185, who refers to the Tacitus passage as 'the grand synthesis of the Roman attitude towards the Jews'. For the suggestion that a degree of irony is present in Tacitus' account, see Gruen (2011), 186–96. For a compilation of remarks on Judaism by Greek and Roman authors, see Stern (1974–84).

[6] Avidov (2009), 3–6 and 169.

[7] Schwartz (2014), *passim*.

[8] Schäfer (1997).

[9] Avidov (2009).

religious group in the empire. While we should certainly be mindful of these respective authors' intentions and agenda, their accounts are furthermore supplemented by papyrological evidence, or by ancient authors who adopt different perspectives, on a number of crucial occasions.[10] Texts like the so-called *Acta Alexandrinorum*, as well as Claudius' famous letter to the Alexandrians and other documentary papyri, all provide complementary, and sometimes contrasting, points of view on the causes and effects of Roman legal measures related to Judaism, and therefore serve as a useful addition to Jewish reports of the same events.[11]

Like most aspects of Jewish life in the Roman Empire, the political and legal position of Jewish communities has attracted a significant amount of attention over the years. Traditionally, however, much of existing scholarship has tended to draw a generalized picture of Roman policy, while the particular characteristics of individual legal interactions have been comparatively neglected. Although local and regional circumstances have become increasingly important in our understanding of the workings of the Roman provincial administration, as has been discussed in Chapter 1, this idea has received relatively little attention in scholarship on the legal treatment of Judaism in the Roman world. Instead, it has been widely assumed that the experiences of Jewish communities throughout the empire were shaped by either predominantly positive or overwhelmingly negative attitudes on the part of the Roman authorities, which remained in place for significant periods of time. The exact manner in and extent to which this occurred, however, remains a point of debate. As has been remarked, some have argued that the Roman state ultimately saw Judaism as a substantial threat that had to be held in check,[12] or that 'the Romans' tendency to statism and to interventionism made life complicated for people who had competing loyalties',[13] which assumes the presence of a strong, centralized Roman policy aimed at repressing the perceived deviance of Jewish communities. On the other side of the spectrum, there are those who believe the Roman government to have adopted a more supportive, although ultimately largely indifferent, approach towards its Jewish subjects.[14] In this view, the official policy would have been one of toleration, even if genuine approval of Jewish religious beliefs and practices was lacking.[15] The most influential example of this line of thinking may be found in the seminal work of Jean Juster, who famously argued for the existence of a comprehensive corpus of Roman legislation safeguarding the rights of the empire's Jewish

[10] The reliability of the legal measures cited by Flavius Josephus in particular will be discussed in more detail in section 3.5.2.

[11] The *Acta Alexandrinorum*, which are also known as the *Acts of the Pagan Martyrs*, have been collected and published in Musurillo (1954). The letter of Emperor Claudius to the Alexandrians is also known as P.Lond. 6.1912.

[12] See Avidov (2009), 3–6 and 101–93 for the idea that the Romans originally attempted to integrate Jews into the empire and only took a more aggressive approach in the wake of the Jewish War. Schäfer (1997), 180–95 suggests that Judaism was seen as a substantial threat by the Romans, despite (or perhaps because of) a degree of sympathy for its followers on the part of the Roman authorities.

[13] Schwartz (2014), 79. [14] Gruen (2011), 181. [15] Garnsey (1984), 10.

population, which he called 'une véritable *Magna Charta* [*sic*]'.[16] Juster's ideas remained highly influential long after their publication, and were taken up by, among others, Alfredo Rabello in 1980.[17] A more recent version of this approach may be found in the work of Amnon Linder, who has argued that Judaism fell 'within the boundaries of the accepted deviance', and that the Roman authorities implemented what he calls a 'special law instituted by the host society'. This special law, while consisting of multiple legal measures that were both general and local in nature, ultimately recognized Jews throughout the Roman Empire as a distinct entity and granted them the right to live according to their ancestral customs, as well as a degree of legal autonomy.[18]

However, the idea that the legal status of Jewish communities in the Roman Empire was determined by a strong, centralized Roman legal framework has increasingly come to be rejected. Perhaps most prominent among its detractors is Tessa Rajak, who has championed a more localized approach. According to this line of thinking, Roman legal measures involving Judaism often applied to smaller areas, largely located in the Diaspora,[19] and the so-called 'charter concerning the Jews' did not, in fact, exist.[20] Instead, it has been suggested that local conflicts between Jewish communities and their non-Jewish neighbours were of far greater significance than any form of centralized Roman policy.[21] This localized approach, however, has so far been adopted only fragmentarily, and has overwhelmingly been applied to specific periods of Judeo-Roman interaction or to specific historical corpora,[22] while comparatively little attention has been paid to long-term developments in the legal position of Judaism in the Roman world, the potential differences between various regions, and the particular local circumstances under which legal measures came into existence. By combining the detail-oriented methodology of the localized approach and the broader scope of the generalizing approaches, then, it should be possible to present a more comprehensive and nuanced analysis of the legal position of Jewish communities in the Roman world.

3.2 Terminology and Definitions

Unlike the almost overwhelmingly wide variety of terminology related to divination, which has been discussed extensively in Chapter 2, the Roman legal (and, in fact,

[16] Juster (1914), 1.217. In using this term, Juster has followed Niese (1876), 488.
[17] Rabello (1980). See also Guterman (1951), 158 and Smallwood (1976), 124.
[18] See Linder (2006), 130 and 136–44; as well as Linder (2011), 150–9.
[19] Rives (2007), 195.
[20] Rajak (1985) and (2002^{b}). For the view that some rights were only granted to the Jewish communities of specific cities, whereas other privileges were valid throughout the Roman Empire, see Pucci Ben Zeev (1998), 409–50.
[21] Schuol (2007), 331. See also Barclay (2004), 3 for the idea that Diaspora communities are often faced with issues of contested power and tradition within the so-called 'host community'.
[22] The thorough investigation of Schuol (2007) is focused on the Augustan age, while the similarly impressive work of Pucci Ben Zeev (1998) focuses on an important number of legal texts quoted by Flavius Josephus in his *Antiquitates Iudaicae*.

general) vocabulary surrounding Jewish communities appears to have been more straightforward, with members of these communities consistently being described as *Iudaei* or its Greek equivalent *Ἰουδαῖοι* (see Appendix 2). For the modern reader, it may seem self-evident that the Graeco-Roman authors who used these terms were referring to a religious group whose unifying beliefs and way of life can be succinctly summarized under the moniker of 'Judaism'. In reality, however, these terms are not so easily translated, and their historical meaning has proved to be far from clear cut.[23] Some modern authors, Steve Mason prominently among them, have argued that—in Roman eyes at least—the term *Iudaei* and its cognates had ethnic, rather than religious, connotations. According to this line of thinking, the term 'Judaism' derives from a modern perception of religion and is therefore without clear parallels in the ancient world. The only possible Graeco-Roman candidate for a phrase expressing such ideas is the Greek *Ἰουδαϊσμός*, which may be seen as the direct predecessor of the modern 'Judaism'. However, this term occurs in ancient sources only sparingly, primarily in 2 and 4 Maccabees and two inscriptions dating from the third century CE.[24] The word furthermore makes use of the Greek suffix *-ίζω*, which tends to evoke an action rather than a system of belief and is often attached to the name of an ethnic group to demonstrate that an individual is behaving according to the customs of that group—thereby deserting their own ancestral way of life.[25] Little in this description suggests the emphasis on religious beliefs that has become so essential to modern understanding of the term 'Judaism'. Mason further suggests that the concept of religion as we know it may not even have existed in Roman times, referencing the similar discrepancy between the Latin word *religio* and the modern 'religion'.[26] Instead, Mason argues, beliefs and actions surrounding the supernatural were often bound up in one's ethnicity, or *ἔθνος*, in important ways.[27] He therefore claims that the suspicion those who wished to join the *Iudaei* encountered throughout the Mediterranean world, and in the Roman Empire in particular, was overwhelmingly framed in terms of politics and ethnicity, and therefore did not necessarily stem from any hostile reaction to a change in religious beliefs, or conversion, per se.[28] According to Mason, however, the same categorization also allowed Jews (or, in his words, Judeans) to be understood as one *ἔθνος* among many, which rendered their adherence to their own ancestral customs and laws both familiar and expected—even if the adoption of those customs by

[23] For an elaborate analysis of scholarship on this subject, see Miller (2010), (2012), and (2014), in which the author summarizes the most important arguments, and presents a thorough overview of the different lines of thinking.

[24] Mason (2007), 460–1.

[25] Mason (2007), 461–3. See also Liddell, Scott, and Jones (1968), *Ἰουδαΐζω*, *Ἑλληνίζω*, and *Μηδίζω* for specific examples. This argument is rejected by Miller (2014), 250–1.

[26] Mason (2007), 480–2. A similar argument is made in Nongbri (2013).

[27] Mason (2007), 483–8.

[28] Mason (2007), 505–10.

outsiders was seen as problematic.[29] This applied even to Jewish communities in the Diaspora, since (according to Mason), ethnicity was not strictly linked to geography.[30]

The common ancient qualification of Jews as an ἔθνος has likewise been remarked upon by Benedikt Eckhardt, who has suggested that the distinction between ethnicity and religion was essentially meaningless in the Roman period, because these two concepts were so heavily intertwined as to be indistinguishable from one another in practice. However, it has been argued, both by Eckhardt and a number of others, that this perception of Jews as an ethnic group among many others gradually began to change. When exactly this change occurred remains the subject of some debate. Eckhardt suggests that the distinction between religion and ethnicity became more centrally important after the introduction of the Jewish Tax, which made the issue of who exactly was liable to pay this new fee acutely relevant.[31] He argues that the tax raised questions about who could be considered Jewish in the eyes of the Roman authorities, and what was to be done with people whose ethnic background and beliefs regarding the supernatural did not straightforwardly overlap. However, the divergence between religion and ethnicity has been dated earlier by Shaye Cohen, who argues that the first non-ethnic usage of terminology related to Jewishness may be found as early as the second century BCE, at which point he believes Jewish communities started defining themselves in religious terms.[32]

These terminological difficulties, however, do not appear to be limited to the modern era, and even in antiquity itself the character of Jewish communities appears to have been subject to discussion. It is difficult to deny that the word *Iudaei* and its equivalents were often used to evoke a group with a shared ethnic background both by those within the community and those without, which would have made its members more distinctive than either diviners or Christians in Roman eyes.[33] Likewise, the right to maintain and uphold ancestral customs was granted not just to Jewish communities but also to various cities in the empire, which suggests that the two were seen as roughly equivalent. However, there are some important indications that Jews were in some ways regarded differently than members of other ἔθνη, and indeed the specific customs that are evoked in relation to this privilege are connected to religious practices on an

[29] Mason (2007), 489–512. For this perspective, see also Linder (2011), 152–3.

[30] Mason (2007), 504. For an opposing view, see Guterman (1951), 77, who argues that Judaism became a 'purely religious community' when it first settled in the city of Rome. The issue of geography, and particularly the connection of Jewish communities in the Diaspora to Jerusalem, is an oft-discussed subject in the works of both ancient and modern authors. For an interesting analysis of Philo of Alexandria's view on this subject, see Pearce (2004). In his discussion of the Jewish community in Alexandria, Avidov (2009), 172 suggests that the ethnic distinctions in that city were introduced by the Roman authorities for fiscal purposes.

[31] Eckhardt (2017), 49–52. For the argument that Jewish communities were still seen as ethnically based in the time of Augustus, see Eckhardt (2018[b]), 65.

[32] Cohen (1999), 70 and 78–81.

[33] Barclay (1996), 405–8.

important number of occasions. In some cases, the treatment of Jewish communities even appears to have been notably distinct from that of the empire's various other ethnic groups. There is, for example, little convincing evidence for any other community, whether ethnic or religious, being exempt from attending the law courts on particular days, as was the case in certain cities for Jews whose desire to observe the Sabbath prevented them from participating in public affairs on that day.[34] Likewise, the exemption from military service that was granted to certain members of the Jewish community in Ephesus is not paralleled by any known privilege granted to a specific ethnic group, city, or people, with similar provisions only made for members of various priesthoods.[35] Distinctly religious issues like the involvement of communities from the Jewish Diaspora with the Temple in Jerusalem, circumcision, and ritual purity also feature prominently in legal interactions between the Roman authorities and Jewish groups throughout the empire.[36] Finally, the fact that the Jews of Rome were expelled from the city alongside other religious groups on a number of occasions has also been named as a clear indication that cult, rather than ethnicity, was the primary issue at stake in orchestrating these banishments.[37]

The known Roman legal interactions with the Jewish population, then, overwhelmingly dealt with the religious aspects of people's lives, which suggests that this part of the group's identity was seen as a, if not the, primary distinguishing feature. This idea appears to be confirmed by the remarks of ancient authors, who dwell extensively on religious issues, while making little to no mention of factors like clothing, speech, and occupation.[38] Participation in Jewish religious rites, as well as intensive social interaction and integration with others who did the same, would therefore have served as the surest and easiest way to determine who was considered part of a Jewish community.[39] To an extent, this could include people who were not born into Jewish families but nonetheless adopted a Jewish

[34] Eckhardt (2017), 24. [35] Eckhardt (2017) 25–6.

[36] For an overview of the various interactions between the Roman authorities and Jewish communities that will be discussed in this chapter, see Appendix 2.

[37] Eckhardt (2017), 41–4. Eckhardt argues against Avidov (2009), 177, who claims that Jews were expelled on ethnic grounds.

[38] Cohen (1999), 28–37. A significant number of the relevant themes presented by Karl Leo Noethlichs in his discussion of the perceptions of Jews in the Roman Empire among non-Jewish and non-Christian authors likewise have to do with religious behaviour. These include the Jewish conception of god, circumcision, cult, the Sabbath, and proselytes. See Noethlichs (1996), 45–75. While circumcision has on occasion been mentioned as an important distinguishing feature of members of Jewish communities, it should be noted that this practice was (and is) both fraught with religious significance and of limited relevance in an everyday context. As is argued by Cohen (1999), 37–49, the result of the procedure would not normally be publicly visible, nor would Jewish women be recognizable in the same way. The fact that circumcision was also linked to other inhabitants of the eastern Mediterranean likewise serves to further limit the everyday importance of circumcision in determining who was seen as Jewish, and who was not.

[39] Cohen (1999), 67–8. For a similar argument, see Wendt (2015^{b}), 120, who nevertheless perceives ethnic distinctions to be highly relevant.

way of life—and the reverse also appears to have been possible.[40] While some have framed the issue of non-Jews making the transition to a more Jewish way of life in terms of ethnicity,[41] it should be noted that such a shift was widely regarded to include a change in religious behaviour.[42] As discussed, Tacitus explicitly referenced the idea that inclusion in a Jewish community meant the rejection of one's former gods, and the anti-Jewish polemicist Apion likewise framed the perceived difference between Jews and his own Alexandrian community in religious terms, asking how Jews could possibly be citizens of Alexandria if they do not worship the Alexandrian gods.[43] While the link to ethnicity (or at least citizenship) is still present in the version of Apion's work transmitted to us by Josephus, it is notable that Apion sees religion as a deciding factor in determining Jewish 'otherness'. When, on the other hand, *Iudaei* took on a Graeco-Roman way of life, for instance by exercising in the gymnasium, this does not necessarily appear to have impeded their inclusion in the Jewish community, unless their behaviour came into conflict with Jewish religious law.[44]

Religion, then, was at the very least a highly significant part of Jewish identity, and it was likely often recognized as such by outsiders. This does not invalidate the argument that the term *Iudaei* could carry ethnic connotations, but it does suggest that members of this community were at times, for all intents and purposes, a 'religious' group, even if they were not unified by religion exclusively. While some have referred to Jewishness as an 'ethno-religion' in order to do justice to both lines of thinking, thereby suggesting that ethnic identity was supplemented by a more religion-based sense of community,[45] others argue for observing a similar middle ground without adopting a particular alternative terminology.[46] In any case, the fact that religion played at least some part in distinguishing Jewish communities from their non-Jewish neighbours has proved almost indisputable, even for those who otherwise favour the model of ethnicity to study the concept of Jewishness in the ancient world,[47] and it must therefore be acknowledged that it likewise played an important role in the legal interactions between this group

[40] See Barclay (1996), 403–4 for an example of someone born in a Jewish family abandoning their ancestral customs, which is at least in part described in religious terms.

[41] Mason (2007), 491.

[42] See Cohen (1999), 140–74 for the various ways in which this could occur.

[43] Flavius Josephus, *Contra Apionem* 2.6 (65). The text of *Contra Apionem* may be found in the Loeb edition of Thackeray (1926). For a more recent translation and commentary of the text, see Barclay (2007). This volume is part of the Brill series of Mason (1999–2022), which at the time of writing remains incomplete.

[44] For the example of Jewish priests using the gymnasium in the city of Jerusalem, see 2 Maccabees 4.13–16. Although the text portrays such behaviour in a negative light, there is nothing to suggest that it led to the removal of these priests from the Jewish community. As will be discussed in more detail in section 3.11.1, the Jewish community of Alexandria likely engaged in similar practices.

[45] Cohen (1999), 137.

[46] Miller (2014), 255. In arguing that the term κατὰ τὰ πάτρια was on occasion used to emphasize ethnic differences in religious terms, Rüpke (2014), 205 seems to imply a similar overlap.

[47] Miller (2014), 255.

and the Roman authorities. In order to succinctly express these ideas and behaviours, the terms 'Jewish' and (on occasion) 'Judaism' will therefore be applied throughout this study, although with the necessary caveat that Judaism in the ancient world should not be taken to be wholly identical to its modern counterpart.[48]

3.3 Outline and Central Questions

Over the course of this chapter, the known legal interactions between the Roman authorities and the various Jewish communities of the empire will once again be systematically analysed in chronological order as much as possible. It should be noted that this approach, which throughout this study is central to our understanding of legal precedent and the possible disappearance or re-emergence of certain types of legal measures, is doubly valuable in the case of the present corpus. In a number of important cases, the available source material allows us to trace the creation of new measures in remarkable detail, and even to investigate how various parties involved in the same case responded to each other's actions. In addition, different types of legal measures (e.g. fiscal issues, cases involving Jewish ancestral customs, expulsions, etc.) can on occasion be connected to the same event or historical period, which adds to the benefit of ordering the known legal interactions by date rather than content. A full overview of all relevant cases may be found in Appendix 2 for reference.[49]

Throughout, due consideration will once again be given to all stages of the legal process, including the origin, contents, and enforcement of each legal measure. In addition to this established framework, however, a number of factors that are particularly relevant to the legal position of Jewish communities in the Roman world stand out, and therefore deserve special attention. When it comes to the origins of legal measures, it is firstly especially important to consider which actors played a part in the legal process: was the initiative for specific measures taken by the Roman authorities or was their involvement a response to requests made by local administrators, the local population, or possibly even unrests in a specific region? In connection to the aforementioned debate surrounding the existence of a 'Jewish Magna Carta', we must also consider which levels of government played

[48] See Miller (2014), 255–9 for a discussion on what the best translation for *Iudaei* might be. Miller here argues that distinguishing between 'Jews' and 'Judeans' may give the reader a false sense of precision.

[49] Although this list also includes a number of important political interactions between the Roman state and the rulers of Judea for the sake of comprehensiveness, it must be remarked that these events will play a part in our analysis only occasionally: while the political relations between Rome and Judea are a fascinating subject, they will be discussed here only to contextualize the legal interactions that are the main focus of this chapter, or whenever they are related to the treatment of Jewish communities and their religious customs in general.

a part in the proceedings, and to which regions particular regulations applied.[50] Furthermore, the extent and way in which previous measures were used as legal precedent may well provide us with essential information about the motives that played a role in the creation of legal measures, as well as the wider socio-political context in which these legal interactions took place.

When considering the contents of the various legal measures under discussion, it is likewise important to take into account whether specific regulations were aimed at protecting Jewish communities, or whether they instead favoured more repressive or exclusionary attitudes. This question is especially relevant because it ties into the idea that Judaism enjoyed a special status within the Roman world and was even granted the special status of '*religio licita*'.[51] While this is by no means a technical legal term, and is exclusively derived from the work of the Christian apologist Tertullian, who uses it to distinguish between the treatment of Jews and his own Christian community, the idea that Jewish religious practices held this special legal status has nevertheless proved historically significant enough to warrant attention.[52]

A final point that deserves our consideration is the extent to which legal measures were enforced for longer periods of time, and especially if they were reiterated on later occasions. If certain measures were indeed repeated after their original creation, it is important to investigate under which circumstances this occurred: why was a repetition deemed necessary, and which parties were involved in the process? In this regard, we must also consider which role the various levels of Roman administration played, and whether the way in which certain legal measures were enforced led to traceable differences between various regions of the empire.

Throughout this chapter, the negotiations that repeatedly took place between the various levels of Roman administration, including the inhabitants of the provinces (whether Jewish or non-Jewish), will be a prominent point of discussion. In this regard, the various organizational structures of Jewish communities, both political and social, are particularly deserving of our attention. At least in some part due to their antiquity, many Jewish communities throughout the Diaspora not only maintained recognizable institutions of their own but also established contacts with other communities, particularly the Temple in Jerusalem, which in

[50] See section 3.1. For the argument that such a charter for Jews in the Roman world existed, see Juster (1914); Linder (2006) and (2011); and Rabello (1980).

[51] The idea that Jewish communities were explicitly exempt from participating in the imperial cult has historically played an important part in this discussion—see Smallwood (1976), 137 and 345. Given the fact that a measure of this kind is not explicitly attested anywhere, and that participation in the imperial cult was in any case likely never officially required, such a formal exemption is unlikely to have occurred. For a more elaborate discussion of the relationship between Judaism and the imperial cult, see McLaren (2005). The idea that emperor worship was shaped by an interplay between local and central impulses is discussed in Price (1984), 53–77.

[52] Tertullian, *Apologeticus pro Christianis* 21.1. See, for instance, Avidov (2009), 170–1 and Hasselhoff and Strothmann (2017), both of whom argue against the historical validity of the term.

turn had significant political standing up to its destruction in 70 CE. It is especially interesting to consider how these frameworks influenced the position of Judaism in the Roman world, both in a positive and a negative sense, especially when comparing Jewish communities to their Christian contemporaries. While these communities shared a number of important characteristics, Christian communities initially lacked similarly well-established and familiar institutions.

Finally, a few notes on the temporal and geographical scope of this chapter should be made. While a significant portion of the available corpus dates to the imperial period, an important number of pivotal interactions between Jewish communities and Roman authorities date from the republican period. Since these events are essential for our understanding of the later imperial measures that form the primary focus of this study, they will be discussed in detail. Particular attention will be paid to the cases dating from the later years of the republic, from Julius Caesar onwards, but a few earlier events will be discussed as well. From a geographical perspective, the majority of Roman legal measures related to Judaism originated in the eastern Mediterranean, particularly in Jerusalem, the cities of Asia Minor, and the great Jewish community of Alexandria. While less material from the western Mediterranean is available, a number of crucial cases from the city of Rome also appear in the available sources and will thus receive due consideration.

3.4 Early Points of Contact: Judea and Rome

The first known interactions between Jewish communities and the Roman state took the shape of military allegiances and occurred before Rome had even gained a firm foothold in the eastern Mediterranean. By 161 BCE a substantial part of the Jewish population of that region fell directly or indirectly under the authority of the Seleucid Empire, which had controlled the community's sacred capital of Jerusalem since the beginning of the second century BCE. The new Seleucid king, Demetrius I, had recently ascended to the throne, and his relationship with the Jewish inhabitants of his realm appears to have been complex from the very beginning. While a certain faction of the Jewish population, led by newly appointed high priest Alcimus, supported Demetrius' rule, others were staunchly anti-Seleucid—among them a priestly family from the rural town of Mode'in, most commonly known as the Maccabees, who would later gain power as the Hasmonean dynasty. The anti-Seleucid faction attempted to strengthen its position by sending an embassy to Rome (Appendix 2.1),[53] which was considered to be a power on the rise and was beginning to become involved in military engagements

[53] Seeman and Marshak (2012), 42–3.

with both Macedonia and the Seleucid Empire itself. Judas, leader of the Maccabees, may have expected his delegates to obtain some form of direct military support, but it is equally possible that the propagandistic aspects of a foreign treaty with an emerging power like Rome appealed to his political and dynastic ambitions.[54] Whatever his motives were, the Roman senate granted Judas' emissaries an audience, and agreed to back the Maccabees in their resistance against Demetrius—at least in spirit.[55] Both known versions of the treaty stipulate that neither party should help the other's enemies with weapons, money, ships, or provisions and promise military assistance to whichever party was attacked first.[56] However, each version also allowed both parties to interpret this promise of armed support as best suited their political needs, stating that they should act 'as circumstances dictate them' (ὡς ἂν αὐτοῖς ὁ καιρὸς ὑπογράφῃ),[57] or 'as they are able' (κατὰ τὸ δυνατόν).[58] Thus, while both parties clearly stood to gain from entering into this agreement, it is not particularly surprising that the treaty did not lead to concrete military action against the Seleucid Empire on the part of the Romans at this point in time.[59]

[54] Baltrusch (2002), 93 and 97; Gera (1998), 314; Seeman and Marshak (2012), 43. Some support for this interpretation may be offered by Flavius Josephus, *Antiquitates Iudaicae* 12.10.6 (414), who states that Judas sent a delegation to Rome because he had heard about Rome's power in the East (ἀκούσας περὶ τῆς Ῥωμαίων δυνάμεως). This is likely an exaggeration, since Rome (for all its growing influence) was arguably not a very significant force in the eastern Mediterranean at the time. See Eck (2007), 5. The author of 1 Maccabees 8.18 states merely that Judas wanted to rid his country of Seleucid oppression (ἆραι τὸν ζυγὸν ἀπ' αὐτῶν).

[55] Some, like Sherwin-White (1984), 70–9, have argued that the allegiance never existed and that the negotiations and their results are nothing more than an invention on the part of the author of 1 Maccabees. This argument is based on the lack of influence Rome held in the East at the time of the Maccabean revolt, the lack of material aid the Jewish troops actually received, and the assumption that a weakening in Seleucid rule was not in Roman interests. However, it is ultimately unlikely that the agreement is a complete fiction, for a number of reasons. Firstly, the Roman senate supported a number of other factions that posed a threat to Demetrius' rule in the first few years of his kingship, as argued by Gera (1998), 303. In addition, the text of the treaty as transmitted in 1 Maccabees mirrors the structure and phrasing commonly used in treaties (or *foedera*) dated to the second century BCE, as is pointed out in Gera (1998), 305. We may also ask ourselves what might motivate the author of 1 Maccabees to invent a treaty with the Roman Republic to begin with: it seems unlikely that an author who elsewhere displays strong anti-foreign tendencies would depict Judas Maccabee and his followers as supplicants to an external power when no such embassy had ever taken place. It may be true that the original text of the treaty presented in 1 Maccabees regarded both parties as being on a fairly equal level, as argued in Gera (1998), 307, but the author does explicitly mention that Judas took the initiative to request Roman friendship and allegiance (1 Maccabees 8.17–20). It has also been suggested that the conditions of the treaty were not completely equal and seemed to favour the Romans. See Schäfer (1995), 50. For the theory that bronze tablets set up in Rome to commemorate the treaty survived well into the medieval period, see Zollschan (2012).

[56] 1 Maccabees 8.25–8 and Flavius Josephus, *Antiquitates Iudaicae* 12.10.6 (417). The full texts of the treaty may be found in 1 Maccabees 8.23–32 and Flavius Josephus, *Antiquitates Iudaicae* 12.10.6. A detailed comparison of Josephus and 1 Maccabees, while exceedingly interesting, is beyond the scope of this study.

[57] 1 Maccabees 8.25 and 8.27.

[58] Flavius Josephus, *Antiquitates Iudaicae* 12.10.6 (418).

[59] It has even been argued that this lack of support did not constitute a breach of treaty, based on the 'escape clause' incorporated in the agreement. See Gera (1998), 313. See also Baltrusch (2002), 98 for the idea that concrete military action was not necessarily even expected by either party.

Despite the fact that the treaty of 161 BCE did not lead to tangible results in the field, our sources indicate that it was renewed repeatedly in the years that followed (Appendices 2.3 and 2.5),[60] and was possibly even recognized by other powers in the region (Appendices 2.2 and 2.6).[61] The Maccabees continued to seek the legitimacy and recognition that bonds of friendship with Rome afforded them, and sent delegations whenever the need for a renewal of relations arose.[62] These treaties of allegiance with the Maccabees, however, do not appear to have resulted in a positive attitude towards the Jewish community residing in Rome itself, although it may have led to the idea that the Roman authorities now had the right to interfere in its affairs. In 139 BCE, the *praetor peregrinus* Cn. Cornelius Hispalus issued an edict that not only banished the *Chaldaei* (section 2.4.2; Appendix 1.2)[63] but also ordered Jews to depart from the city (Appendix 2.4).[64] The edict is briefly referenced by Valerius Maximus in his *Facta et Dicta Memorabilia*, but the existence of two different textual traditions raises complications in determining the exact course of events. According to the older version of the text, attributed to Iulius Paris, Jews were ordered to go back to their homeland because they 'had attempted to infect the Roman way of life with the cult of Jupiter Sabazius' (*idem Iudaeos, qui Sabazii Iovis cultu Romanos inficere mores conati erant, repetere domos suas coegit*).[65] The later version, ascribed to Ianuarius Nepotianus, likewise accuses Jews of attempting to spread their religion to Rome, but makes no mention of the particular god they worshipped. However, this version does add that Hispalus ordered Jewish altars to be removed from public places (*Iudaeos quoque, qui Romanis tradere sacra sua conati erant, idem Hispalus urbe exterminavit arasque privatas e publicis locis abiecit*). While Paris' version of Valerius Maximus' text is generally considered to be the more reliable one across

[60] A complete overview of the various treaties may be found in Baltrusch (2002), 90–113. See 1 Maccabees 12.1–4 and Flavius Josephus, *Antiquitates Iudaicae* 13.5.8 (163–5 and 169–70) for a renewal in the time of Jonathan Apphus, and Flavius Josephus, *Antiquitates Iudaicae* 13.9.2 (259–66) for a similar renewal in the time of Hyrcanus I.

[61] For a missive of the consul Gaius Fannius to the magistrates of Cos, see Flavius Josephus, *Antiquitates Iudaicae* 14.10.15 (233). Josephus wrongly dates this letter to 49–44 BCE. According to Gera (1998), 310, the name of the consul suggests a dating of 161 BCE. Sherwin-White (1984), 73–4, however, sees the abundance of consular Fannii in the historical record as a complicating factor, and is inclined to accept a later date—possibly that of 122 or shortly before 48 BCE. For an example of Roman attitudes towards Judea being copied by other (local) governments, see Flavius Josephus, *Antiquitates Iudaicae* 14.10.22 (247–55). Here, the city of Pergamum, which had recently been incorporated into the Roman Empire, declares its intention to follow the Roman example and enter into a league of friendship with Judea. This measure was issued by the Pergamene βουλή. It is certain that the local Pergamene institution is meant here and not the Roman senate, to which Josephus continuously refers as σύγκλητος, both in this context and elsewhere. While Josephus includes this source in his account of the rule of Hyrcanus II, it likely dates from the time of Hyrcanus I. See Rajak (2002[b]), 308.

[62] Gera (1998), 314.

[63] For a discussion of this expulsion, and the textual traditions of the relevant text, see section 2.4.2.

[64] Valerius Maximus, *Facta et Dicta Memorabilia* 1.3 (*De Superstitionibus*).3.

[65] For the Latin edition of both epitomes, see Briscoe (1998), 30–1 and Stern (1974), 358.

the board,[66] his reference to Jupiter Sabazius has given rise to suspicion.[67] Some have argued that the use of this particular phrasing constitutes evidence for Jewish syncretism in this period,[68] but the overwhelming consensus is that the term is either the result of Roman confusion upon encountering the Jewish deity Yahweh Sabaoth,[69] or of a similar mistake on the part of a later copyist.[70] The claim made by Nepotianus that Jewish altars were removed from public spaces is similarly problematic: Jewish communities in the Diaspora did not normally erect altars as such, and it is unlikely that this passage is meant to be a reference to synagogues, which could hardly have been confused with altars.[71] Despite these complications, however, it is hard to discount the essence of Valerius Maximus' report:[72] both versions of the text plainly assert that Jews were banished from Rome because they involved Romans in their religious practices. Whether these charges were exaggerated or not,[73] the episode certainly suggests that the Jewish community present in Rome during this period was seen as a potentially disruptive foreign entity that posed a risk to public order—an idea emphasized by the fact that the *praetor peregrinus* was responsible for issuing the edict of expulsion.[74]

[66] Stern (1974), 357; Wardle (1998), 18–19.

[67] For a valuable overview and analysis of the debate, see Stern (1974), 359.

[68] Feldman (1993), 93; Hengel (1973), 478–9; Simon (1976), 52–6.

[69] Barclay (1996), 285; Castritius (2006), 280; Scurlock (2000), 143; Stern (1974), 359; Wardle (1998), 150–1.

[70] Barclay (1996) 285; Cappelletti (2006), 35; Lane (1979).

[71] Gruen (2002), 17; Wardle (1998), 151. The synagogue hypothesis is tentatively presented as an option by Stern (1974), 358. See also Wendt (2015^b), 106–8, who cautions against using a 'normative definition of Judaism', and suggests that the *arae* could include a wider range of monuments or structures involved in religious practices.

[72] While Alessandri (1968) argues that this expulsion is an invention by Valerius Maximus, the fact that no other source mentions these events is hardly enough evidence to support this claim. His argument that the Roman authorities would hardly have expelled Jews from Rome when diplomatic relationships with the Maccabees were favourable likewise does not necessarily hold water. As Gruen (2002), 261 n. 13 rightly remarks, there need not necessarily be a connection between foreign policy and attitudes towards immigrants in Rome itself, as shall also become clear in the case of later expulsions. For a similar argument, see Cappelletti (2006), 39 and Stern (1974), 359–60, the latter of whom is sceptical about a connection between the expulsion and Hasmonean delegations in general. Wendt (2015^b), 109 argues that the delegation's visit may have contributed to an increased interest in 'Judean cultural practices'. See Schuol (2007), 247 for the idea that the internal contradictions in Roman interactions with Jewish groups in this period (allegiances on the one hand versus expulsion on the other) are representative of Roman attitudes towards Judaism in later periods as well.

[73] For the suggestion that the proselytism of Romans was at the heart of the issue, see Baltrusch (2002), 116–18; Castritius (2006), 280; Feldman (1993), 93; Smallwood (1976), 205. See Stern (1974), 358 for the suggestion that the altars mentioned in the Nepotianus-version may refer to altars built by non-Jews to honour the Jewish God. For the idea that this was an overblown accusation, see Gruen (2002), 19. Cappelletti (2006), 42–3 suggests that no charge was originally mentioned, and that the issue of proselytism was added by the two epitomizers.

[74] Cappelletti (2006), 43; Gruen (2002), 18–19; Schäfer (1997), 106–7. Cappelletti (2006), 39–41 notes that the expulsion edict may have been aimed at a group of Jewish merchants simply passing through Rome, rather than an established community living there on a permanent basis, although this is uncertain. In any case, it is unlikely that the Jews who were expelled were part of an embassy sent by the Hasmoneans, which does not seem to fit with the chronology of events. See Gruen (2002), 17; Stern (1974), 359–60; Wardle (1998), 150.

3.5 Judaism under Rome: Early Legal Measures

After the expulsion of 139 BCE, the Jewish community of Rome disappears from the historical record for a significant number of years, and while political interactions between the Roman Republic and the Hasmoneans (as the Maccabees soon came to be called) continued during this time, they contributed little to Hasmonean success. No Roman troops were ever sent to come to the aid of their Jewish allies, and no other form of direct assistance was ever provided.[75] Instead, the treaties that had been established between Rome and Judea initially remained largely symbolic. In the years that followed, however, Roman power in the eastern Mediterranean steadily increased, and the number of Jewish communities within Rome's sphere of influence grew along with its borders. In Judea, the Hasmoneans struggled with almost continuous unrest and civil war for almost a century: they were faced both with rival factions and with internal dynastic struggles between various possible successors. It was one of these conflicts, namely the struggle for royal power between Hyrcanus II and Aristobulus II, that would lead to the direct presence of Rome in the region. In 63 BCE both parties petitioned for the support of Pompey Magnus, who sided with Hyrcanus and besieged Jerusalem in an attempt to defeat Aristobulus and his supporters.[76] This first direct Roman intervention in the region resulted not only in Pompey's famous desecration of the Jewish Temple but also in increased Roman involvement in the lives of Jewish communities, not only in Judea but in the Diaspora as well.[77]

3.5.1 Lucius Valerius Flaccus and the Jewish communities of Asia

This increase in Judeo-Roman interaction did not always lead to positive results, however, and the interests of Roman magistrates and local Jewish communities could at times clash significantly. One example of this may be found in Cicero's *Pro Flacco*, in which Cicero defends his client Lucius Valerius Flaccus against charges of financial misconduct, which he allegedly committed during his time as governor of Asia in 62 BCE. As a part of his defence, Cicero discusses Flaccus' ban on the export of gold from Asia (Appendix 2.7). This measure directly affected the Jewish community of that province, which found itself unable to send the

[75] That some form of assistance was indeed asked for becomes clear from a Jewish request to the Roman senate for a committee to assess the damage done to Hasmonean territories in a previous war, mentioned in Flavius Josephus, *Antiquitates Iudaicae* 13.9.2 (263). It is unlikely, however, that this request was granted, as the delegation is never mentioned again and the senate did not grant the requests made by the embassy out of hand, but rather indicated the need to deliberate further.

[76] Flavius Josephus, *Bellum Iudaicum* 1.6.4–1.7.7 (131–58). For the suggestion that Rome saw its intervention in the region as legitimate because of the 161 BCE treaty, see Baltrusch (2002), 83, 89–90, and 105.

[77] For Pompey's desecration of the Temple, see Flavius Josephus, *Bellum Iudaicum* 1.7.6 (152–3).

customary Temple Tax to Jerusalem. It seems that both the Jewish community in Flaccus' province and that of Rome itself were enraged as a result,[78] and according to Cicero the latter made its dismay publicly heard.[79] It is uncertain, however, if the edict was truly intended as a direct attack on the Jewish communities of Asia, and Flaccus may instead have simply been concerned with stabilizing the province's struggling finances, thereby safeguarding Rome's taxes.[80] In this, he likely had legal precedent on his side: the Roman senate repeatedly passed resolutions banning the export of gold and silver, including most recently in 63 BCE. Although we are not told to which region these *senatus consulta* applied, Cicero certainly uses these measures to suggest that Flaccus was simply following an established procedure.[81] The fact that Asia's cities were in grave financial difficulty at the time may even have meant that Flaccus' measure was generally met with approval, although it is not clear whether his intervention was requested by the inhabitants of his province.[82] In any case, the interests of Asia's Jewish communities took a back seat in the face of a crisis in public finances: their religious scruples likely meant very little compared to a measure for which there was not only precedent but possibly also an important amount of public and political support among their non-Jewish neighbours.

3.5.2 Flavius Josephus: collecting legal interactions

Not all interactions with the Roman authorities, however, were so fraught. On a significant number of occasions, the involvement of Roman officials could prove to be beneficial to Jewish communities—especially those of Asia Minor, who had so recently clashed with Flaccus. Our most important source for these events is Flavius Josephus' *Antiquitates Iudaicae*, in which the author at multiple points quotes impressive collections of documents that he claims played a direct part in Judeo-Roman interactions. This material has become extremely important for our understanding of the legal position of Jewish communities in the Roman world—although it is not without its share of difficulties.[83] The documents on occasion contain puzzling corruptions, particularly in the names of Roman magistrates and other individuals, and their dating can prove equally troublesome. Furthermore, they are presented fragmentarily, and the order in which they are cited does not

[78] Gruen (2002), 20. [79] Cicero, *Pro Flacco* 66–7. [80] Marshall (1975), 152.

[81] See Cicero, *Pro Flacco* 67 and Marshall (1975), 145.

[82] For a similar argument, see Marshall (1975), 148–9.

[83] Most of Josephus' citations of legal sources may be found in books 14 and 16 of the *Antiquitates*, which at the time of writing have not yet been covered by the Brill series of Mason (1999–2022). The Greek text found in the Loeb series of Feldman, Marcus, Thackeray, and Wikgren (1930–65) continues to be frequently used.

appear to follow any discernible logic.[84] The authenticity of these texts has therefore been challenged by some, most prominently by Horst R. Moehring, who argues that both Flavius Josephus and modern historians are guilty of apologetic tendencies and that the documents should therefore be treated with great scepticism.[85] However, the style and language of the relevant passages has been found to closely match the proper characteristics of the types of documents Josephus claims to cite,[86] and a number of reasonable explanations for the textual corruptions that are present can be given.[87] Josephus' corpus is thus overwhelmingly considered to be authentic,[88] but an uncritical approach nonetheless carries significant risks. The difficulties in determining the dates of certain documents and the distorted names of many of the referenced magistrates certainly present an obstacle to the reader, but it is especially important to consider that Josephus cites these documents in a very specific context. While Moehring likely goes too far in dismissing the contents of these passages as altogether unreliable, he is by no means wrong in pointing out the importance of Josephus' apologetic programme. The author starts his enumeration of documents by explicitly stating that he cites them:

> [...] ἵνα μὴ λανθάνῃ τοὺς ἄλλους ἅπαντας, ὅτι καὶ οἱ τῆς Ἀσίας καὶ οἱ τῆς Εὐρώπης βασιλεῖς διὰ σπουδῆς ἔσχον ἡμᾶς τήν τε ἀνδρείαν ἡμῶν καὶ τὴν πίστιν ἀγαπήσαντες.[89]
>
> [...] so that all the others may not forget that the kings of Asia and Europe have held us in great esteem, having come to admire our bravery and loyalty.

The fact that Josephus is open about his rhetorical goals in presenting these documents, however, need not deter us from taking the material itself seriously. As Tessa Rajak has astutely argued, Josephus' rhetorical strategy almost certainly depended on the overall tone of the material he presented rather than the particular details of each individual text, and it is very likely that the whole of the cited measures was, in their collector's eyes at least, infinitely greater than the

[84] For a more elaborate overview of the most important objections to the sources presented by Josephus, as well as the ultimate, though tentative, conclusion that they are likely genuine, see Pucci Ben Zeev (1998), 357–68.

[85] Moehring (1975), especially 149 and 155–8.

[86] Rajak (2002^b), 305 and, more elaborately, Pucci Ben Zeev (1998), 357–9. In addition to the formal aspects of the documents, the fact that Josephus presents a large collection of measures with an often limited and repetitive subject matter is hardly indicative of a forgery. If Josephus wanted to make a grand statement about the good relationship between Jews and Romans, one, or even several, more extensive regulations might have served him better.

[87] It must, for instance, be noted that Josephus often quotes his edicts fragmentarily, as argued in Pucci Ben Zeev (1998), 357, which would resolve the objection found in Moehring (1975), 144 that the formal mark of approval given by the senate is consistently missing. For the idea that many of the corruptions in the text are due to 'common phonetic phenomena', see Pucci Ben Zeev (1998), 360.

[88] See also Trebilco (1991), 7 and Schuol (2007), 66–75.

[89] Flavius Josephus, *Antiquitates Iudaicae* 14.10.1 (186).

sum of its parts.[90] Thus, while we should remain cautious in our use of names and dates, and should keep in mind that Josephus was undoubtedly selective in his citations, the general contents of the documents are likely to be reliable.

3.5.3 Dispensation from military duties: a collection

The oldest set of legal documents in Josephus' collection that references Jewish ancestral customs and their protection by the Roman authorities dates from the years 49 and (possibly) 48 BCE.[91] The issue at stake in this sub-collection is a dispensation from military service, which would protect certain members of Jewish communities from having to join the Roman army. In itself, it is not surprising that this issue caused conflicting obligations to come to the forefront, as adhering to central Jewish religious customs like observance of the Sabbath and dietary laws would have been extremely difficult within the strict discipline of the Roman army. While the relevant documents are not cited together, and instead appear at peculiar intervals,[92] they can nevertheless be connected by their shared references to the responsible magistrate, the consul Lucius Lentulus whose own missive is the first one in the collection to be cited (Appendix 2.8):

> *Λεύκιος δὲ Λέντλος ὕπατος εἶπεν· πολίτας Ῥωμαίων Ἰουδαίους ἱερὰ Ἰουδαϊκὰ ἔχοντας καὶ ποιοῦντας ἐν Ἐφέσῳ πρὸ τοῦ βήματος δεισιδαιμονίας ἕνεκα στρατείας ἀπέλυσα πρὸ δώδεκα καλανδῶν Ὀκτωβρίων Λευκίῳ Λέντλῳ Γαΐῳ Μαρκέλλῳ ὑπάτοις. Παρῆσαν* [...].[93]
>
> Lucius Lentulus the consul decreed: 'On account of their religious scruples, I have at my tribunal released Jews who are Roman citizens, who observe Jewish rites and practice them in Ephesus, from military service. I did so on the twelfth day before the Kalends of October, when Lucius Lentulus and Gaius Marcellus were consuls. Those present were: [list of members of the tribunal follows].'

[90] Rajak (2007), 178 and 186. See also Trebilco (1991), 1 for the suggestion that Josephus cites these documents, which mainly concern Asia Minor, specifically because he considered them to be relevant for the rest of the Diaspora. It is telling that Josephus himself describes his corpus of edicts as pertaining to *τὸ ἔθνος ἡμῶν*, the entirety of the Jewish people, twice in short succession. See Flavius Josephus, *Antiquitates Iudaicae* 14.10.1 (186) and 14.10.1 (189).

[91] Flavius Josephus, *Antiquitates Iudaicae* 14.10.13–14 (228–32),14.10.16 (234), and 14.10.18–19 (236–40). For the dating of these documents, see Pucci Ben Zeev (1998), *ad loc.* References to Jewish religious practices, which are often indicated by the words *δεισιδαιμονίας ἕνεκα*, 'on account of their superstition', occur frequently in this dossier. Throughout, the term *δεισιδαιμονία* appears to be used in a technical, rather than a derogatory sense.

[92] The collection is broken up at Flavius Josephus, *Antiquitates Iudaicae* 14.10.15 (233) and 14.10.17 (235). For the idea that Jewish dietary restrictions played a role in creating relatively isolated communities, as well as the contrasting Roman preference for pork, see Kraemer (2018).

[93] Flavius Josephus, *Antiquitates Iudaicae* 14.10.13 (228).

While Lentulus' measure in itself seems fairly understanding of the difficulties inherent in reconciling military service with Jewish religious obligations, it should be noted that this exemption did not apply to all Jews who lived within Roman territories and served in the Roman army. The text instead refers specifically to a much smaller area, namely the city of Ephesus, and Lentulus furthermore limited his exemption not only to the observant Jewish population of that city but also to those members of the community who were Roman citizens—of which there would at this stage have been few. It therefore seems unlikely the group to which this measure applied would have been significant in size, which in turn would have made Lentulus' decision relatively risk free: the smaller the exemption, the less likely it was that other groups would demand the same privilege. In addition, the cost to Roman manpower of such a limited measure would have been almost negligible,[94] which would have further enabled Lentulus to be obliging.

Interestingly, Lentulus' measure occurs twice more in Josephus' collection, with some small differences in phrasing but none in content (Appendices 2.11 and 2.14).[95] The existence of multiple versions of what is essentially the same missive likely suggests that the consul's decision was passed on by lower magistrates until it reached the city of Ephesus, for which it was originally intended. There are some indications, however, that matters did not end there, and that Ephesus instead functioned as an example to other cities, possibly due to its status as the provincial capital of Asia.[96] The idea that Jews who held Roman citizenship should be exempt from Roman military service also appears in a ruling from Delos and Sardis (Appendix 2.10), the former of which is notably located outside the province of Asia.[97] While this particular document explicitly mentions Lentulus' ruling as a precedent, it leaves out the qualification that only observant Jews should be dismissed from military service (instead referring to *Ἰουδαῖοι* in general), while retaining the clause limiting the measure's applicability to Jews who are Roman citizens. The text also mentions that the measure was issued by the local magistrates at the behest of the Roman legate Marcus Piso, whose explicit efforts to forbid the harassment of members of Delos' Jewish community suggests that he took action precisely because their lack of participation in the army made them a target for such behaviour (*ἵνα εἴ τινές εἰσιν Ἰουδαῖοι πολῖται Ῥωμαίων τούτοις μηδεὶς ἐνοχλῇ περὶ στρατείας*). This may indicate that Piso responded to complaints made by the local Jewish population, although more concrete clues to this effect are sadly lacking in this particular document. It is clear, however, that he subsequently decided to involve the local institutions, who in turn issued proclamations of their own to comply with Piso's order. Even in

94 Gruen (2002), 87.

95 See Flavius Josephus, *Antiquitates Iudaicae* 14.10.16 (234) and 14.10.19 (237–40).

96 For the suggestion that the measure was originally accompanied by a letter indicating that it applied to the entire province, see Pucci Ben Zeev (1998), 161 and 166.

97 Flavius Josephus, *Antiquitates Iudaicae* 14.10.14 (231–32).

cases dealing with military matters, which would naturally incur more centralized oversight, then, the Roman authorities are still shown to have depended heavily on the implementation of their orders by the local authorities.

In addition to providing us with information about the local implementation of Lentulus' measure, Josephus also cites two documents that offer fascinating details about the context of its inception. The two relevant passages suggest that the initiative for this measure was indeed taken by local Jewish communities, or even by specific Jewish individuals, who found themselves unable to combine their religious and military obligations, and therefore began negotiations with various Roman authorities in order to find a solution. Indeed, one of these two documents appears to be a testimonial by a number of otherwise unknown Romans, who recount having approached Lentulus (here mistakenly addressed as proconsul) in order to convince him to dismiss Jewish citizens from the Roman army (Appendix 2.13).[98] They claim to have done so at the request of one Dositheos, son of Cleopatrides, of Alexandria, whose name has been seen as an indication that he was Jewish himself.[99] This Dositheos was apparently able to exert some influence in Rome, and his involvement suggests that active negotiation was required to spur the Roman authorities into action. The idea to ask for dismissal from military service appears to have originated with local Jews, who in turn requested the help of members of other Jewish communities, as well as a number of non-Jewish Romans, in order to see their problems resolved. These non-Jews apparently included not only the unknown figures whose testimonial is cited by Josephus but also one Titus Ampius Balbus, legate and propraetor, who is the apparent author of another relevant document from Josephus' collection that sheds even more light on the situation (Appendix 2.9).[100] In his letter to the magistrates, council, and people of Ephesus, Balbus claims to have interceded on behalf of the Jewish communities of Asia not only with Lentulus but also with two other Roman officials (a propraetor and proquaestor). He is not above boasting about his influence with the consul, claiming that Lentulus granted the privileges requested by the Jewish community specifically because of his personal interference. In spite of this, however, the letter suggests that Balbus, like the other Roman officials involved in the case, did not act on his own initiative, and that Ephesian Jews may have made complaints because they were being harassed.[101]

[98] Flavius Josephus, *Antiquitates Iudaicae* 14.10.18 (236–7).

[99] Pucci Ben Zeev (1998), 183. As will be discussed in sections 3.10 and 3.11, Jews from Alexandria had a significant interest in positive Roman legislation concerning Jewish communities, which may also have been Dositheos' reason to speak out.

[100] Flavius Josephus, *Antiquitates Iudaicae* 14.10.13 (230). Balbus' version of the measure is reasonably faithful to Lentulus' original, although he does neglect to mention that only Jews who were Roman citizens would be exempt from military service. It is unclear whether this is a later corruption or a mistake on his part. See Pucci Ben Zeev (1998), 164.

[101] For the suggestion that local Greeks had played an active part in forcing the enlistment of Jews, see Pucci Ben Zeev (1998), 166.

As had been the case for the Delians, the population of Ephesus is explicitly warned to make sure that Lentulus' measure is enforced, with the insistence that they should take care *ἵνα μή τις αὐτοῖς διενοχλῇ*, 'so that no-one harasses [the city's Jews]'. The fact that Balbus saw the need to personally write to Ephesus about Lentulus' decision furthermore suggests that he was not only involved in presenting the petition but also contributed to enforcing the resulting ruling. The picture that results from this collection of documents, then, is one of extensive negotiation between (members of) the Jewish communities of Asia, their representatives in Rome, and various levels of Roman government.

A similar pattern appears in a letter by Lucius Antonius, proquaestor and propraetor, to the magistrates, council, and people of the city of Sardis, which has been dated to 49 BCE (Appendix 2.12), and deals with a different request made by a local Jewish community:[102]

> *Λούκιος Ἀντώνιος Μάρκου υἱὸς ἀντιταμίας καὶ ἀντιστράτηγος Σαρδιανῶν ἄρχουσι βουλῇ δήμῳ χαίρειν. Ἰουδαῖοι πολῖται ἡμέτεροι προσελθόντες μοι ἐπέδειξαν αὐτοὺς σύνοδον ἔχειν ἰδίαν κατὰ τοὺς πατρίους νόμους ἀπ' ἀρχῆς καὶ τόπον ἴδιον, ἐν ᾧ τά τε πράγματα καὶ τὰς πρὸς ἀλλήλους ἀντιλογίας κρίνουσιν, τοῦτό τε αἰτησαμένοις ἵν' ἐξῇ ποιεῖν αὐτοῖς τηρῆσαι καὶ ἐπιτρέψαι ἔκρινα.*[103]
>
> Lucius Antonius, son of Marcus, proquaestor and propraetor, to the magistrates, council, and people of the Sardians: greetings. When our Jewish citizens came to me, they demonstrated that according to the laws of their fathers they had an assembly of their own from the earliest times, as well as a place to meet, where they judged their affairs and their disputes with each other, and after they requested that it would be allowed for them to do these things, I judged that this should be maintained and granted.

As becomes clear from Antonius' letter, the Jewish population took the initiative to send a delegation to the Roman magistrate in order to obtain the right to hold their own assemblies in a *σύνοδος* and to manage their own internal affairs.[104] This request is granted in the letter, but the privilege appears to have been highly localized and was furthermore based on existing precedent: according to the members of the Jewish delegation, the rights they requested were not new but rather existed *ἀπ' ἀρχῆς*, 'from the very beginning'. Thus, while this document in particular deals with the political rights of Jewish communities rather than with the right to observe their religious customs,[105] it does provide an interesting

[102] Pucci Ben Zeev (1998), 176. [103] Flavius Josephus, *Antiquitates Iudaicae* 14.10.17 (235).

[104] A *σύνοδος* was a council for a particular social group that was generally seen as a part of the city's administration. See Dmitriev (2005), 131.

[105] That the two could become strongly entangled will become clear during our discussion of the events in Alexandria in section 3.10.

example of how tradition and precedent could be used in the negotiation for privileges: Roman authorities were often strongly inclined to follow pre-existing regulations,[106] and presenting evidence of this kind could therefore be highly beneficial.

3.6 Jewish Communities under Julius Caesar

In the years that followed, the series of civil wars in which Rome had been entangled for the majority of the first century BCE began to play a significant, although sometimes indirect, part in the interactions between Jewish communities and the Roman authorities. The later years of this conflict in particular turned the eastern Mediterranean into a battleground where competing Roman generals all attempted to gain support, and local communities of all kinds stood to gain significant privileges by aiding the winning side. One of these possible rewards was the highly coveted right to maintain one's own laws and institutions.[107] This privilege is referenced in contemporary inscriptions, which often use the phrase *πάτριοι νόμοι* (ancestral laws) to refer to existing traditions—a term that may be used to refer to a number of areas of life, including religion.[108] This principle is best illustrated, however, by the window of opportunity the period provided for the Hasmonean ruler Hyrcanus II. A number of documents dated to the time of Julius Caesar (47–44 BCE) are concerned with legitimizing Hyrcanus' power, naming him and his successors the Jewish ethnarch and high priests until the end of time, with all the rights that traditionally entailed, and granting Judea specific financial and territorial privileges (Appendices 2.15, 2.17–2.20, 2.26, and 2.27).[109]

[106] See section 1.4.1. This line of thinking is also followed by Pucci Ben Zeev (1998), 179.

[107] The dubious story told in Flavius Josephus, *Antiquitates Iudaicae* 14.10.1 (188) may also be seen as an example of this. In this passage, Josephus claims that Caesar (or possibly Augustus) granted the Jewish community of Alexandria citizenship of that city (Appendix 2.16). The question to what extent Jews could and did hold Alexandrian citizenship is a hotly debated issue that will be discussed in more detail in section 3.10.

[108] Schröder (1996), 200–6. Schröder remarks that it was often the less powerful party who made a request in these terms. See Pucci Ben Zeev (1998), 415–18 for a discussion of the terms *νόμος* and *ἔθος*, and why these terms would have been virtually interchangeable in a Jewish context, although the latter is used more frequently. Pucci Ben Zeev also makes the argument that Caesar simply used 'well established Roman policy' by allowing Jews the continued use of their ancestral customs. For the use of *κατὰ τὰ πάτρια* in a non-Jewish context to denote the importance of a practice that is being challenged, see Guettel Cole (2008), 58.

[109] The proclamations regarding Hyrcanus II may be found in Flavius Josephus, *Antiquitates Iudaicae* 14.10.1–7 (185–212). The measures cited in 14.10.2 (190–5) and 14.10.3 (196–8) appear to be interconnected. They both emphasize Caesar's friendship with Hyrcanus and the latter's position as ethnarch, but the first missive is addressed to the magistrates, council, and people of Sidon, whereas the second contains a directive to display the agreement in several cities and send it to an unnamed number of others. Hyrcanus is named high priest in 14.10.2 (194–5) and 14.10.4 (199), while taxation is referenced in 14.10.2 (195), 14.10.5 (201), and 14.10.6 (202–10). The latter passage also mentions a grant of lands. The document cited in 14.10.7 (211–12) discusses Caesar's view that Hyrcanus should be formally thanked by the senate for his services. It is important to remark that this first selection of

These measures have at times been seen as evidence that Caesar granted Jews 'official permission to use their own law',[110] and a number of excerpts from the documents concerning Hyrcanus have been cited to support this. In one passage, Caesar appears to appoint Hyrcanus as his first point of contact 'whenever in the meantime an inquiry about the Jewish way of life should arise' (*ἄν τε μεταξύ γένηταί τις ζήτησις περί τῆς Ἰουδαίων ἀγωγῆς, ἀρέσκει μοι κρίσιν γίνεσθαι παρ' αὐτοῖς*).[111] In another document, Hyrcanus is appointed as defender of 'the Jews who are treated unjustly' ([...] *τῶν Ἰουδαίων προϊστῆται τῶν ἀδικουμένων*).[112] While it is unclear what these statements meant in practice, and debate about the concrete validity of Caesar's honours remains,[113] it should be noted that these mentions of Jewish ancestral law are overwhelmingly connected to the privileges of the high priest and his authority over the *Ἰουδαῖοι*.[114] This does not amount to a formal grant of Jewish religious liberty valid throughout the empire, but rather constitutes a guarantee that the authority of Hyrcanus as high priest would be safeguarded in his own territories. This is not to say, however, that Caesar's support of Hyrcanus' position could not contribute to the rights of Jewish communities elsewhere in the empire in more indirect ways. Josephus' collection of documents contains a number of passages that suggest that Hyrcanus played an important part in acquiring privileges for Jewish communities, not only within Judea but also in the Diaspora—even if he did so by using his negotiating power rather than his formal jurisdiction.

The first example of this appears in a letter by the magistrates of the city of Laodicea to the proconsul Gaius Rabirius (Appendix 2.22). The letter is dated to 47 or 46 BCE,[115] and offers fascinating glimpses into the process of negotiation about Jewish religious rights:

measures is preceded by the remark that Hyrcanus himself sent an embassy to Caesar to request confirmation of a pre-existing treaty of friendship and allegiance, see Flavius Josephus, *Antiquitates Iudaicae* 14.10.1 (185). This pre-existing treaty may be the first measure cited in Josephus' catalogue, 14.10.2 (190–5), as argued by Pucci Ben Zeev (1998), 26. Whatever the case, the Judeo-Roman agreement appears to have been on uncertain footing, and its validity depended on whatever Roman faction happened to be in power at the time.

[110] Pucci Ben Zeev (1995), particularly p. 36.

[111] Flavius Josephus, *Antiquitates Iudaicae* 14.10.2 (195).

[112] Flavius Josephus, *Antiquitates Iudaicae* 14.10.3 (196–7).

[113] Pucci Ben Zeev (1998), 412–19 argues that Caesar followed well-established Roman practice by granting Jews the right to use their ancestral customs but adds that this privilege was far from stable. She goes into more detail about the legal status of Caesar's grants in Pucci Ben Zeev (1995). Rajak (2002[b]), 319 sees these claims as an exaggeration that suited Hyrcanus' claim to power. It should be noted that Caesar's orders cited in Flavius Josephus, *Antiquitates Iudaicae* 14.10.2–3 (190–8) contain instructions to set up bronze plaques proclaiming the two leaders' friendship on the Roman Capitol, as well as in Sidon, Tyre, and Ascalon, in both Greek and Latin. This is, in itself, not remarkable, since we are here dealing with political events, the symbolic meaning of which was significant.

[114] See Flavius Josephus, *Antiquitates Iudaicae* 14.10.2 (194) and 14.10.6 (207–8) in particular.

[115] Pucci Ben Zeev (1998), 192.

> *Σώπατρος Ὑρκανοῦ τοῦ ἀρχιερέως πρεσβευτὴς ἀπέδωκεν ἡμῖν τὴν παρὰ σοῦ ἐπιστολήν, δι᾽ ἧς ἐδήλου ἡμῖν παρὰ Ὑρκανοῦ τοῦ Ἰουδαίων ἀρχιερέως ἐληλυθότας τινὰς γράμματα κομίσαι περὶ τοῦ ἔθνους αὐτῶν γεγραμμένα, ἵνα τά τε σάββατα αὐτοῖς ἐξῇ ἄγειν καὶ τὰ λοιπὰ ἱερὰ ἐπιτελεῖν κατὰ τοὺς πατρίους νόμους, ὅπως τε μηδεὶς αὐτοῖς ἐπιτάσσῃ διὰ τὸ φίλους αὐτοὺς ἡμετέρους εἶναι καὶ συμμάχους, ἀδικήσῃ τε μηδὲ εἷς αὐτοὺς ἐν τῇ ἡμετέρᾳ ἐπαρχίᾳ, ὡς Τραλλιανῶν τε ἀντειπόντων κατὰ πρόσωπον μὴ ἀρέσκεσθαι τοῖς περὶ αὐτῶν δεδογμένοις ἐπέταξας ταῦτα οὕτως γίνεσθαι. παρακεκλῆσθαι δέ σε, ὥστε καὶ ἡμῖν γράψαι περὶ αὐτῶν. ἡμεῖς οὖν κατακολουθοῦντες τοῖς ἐπεσταλμένοις ὑπὸ σοῦ* [...].[116]
>
> Sopatrus, the ambassador of high priest Hyrcanus brought us your letter, with which you made clear to us that some representatives of the Jewish high priest Hyrcanus came to you bringing letters written about their people, stating that they should be allowed to observe their Sabbaths and to perform their other sacred rites according to their ancestral laws, and that no-one shall order them around, because they are our friends and allies, or do them injury in our province; and since the people of Tralles objected in your presence that they were unsatisfied with your decisions about them, you ordered that these things had to be done accordingly, adding that you have been called on to write to us about them. Therefore, we, obeying your commands, [...].

In this passage, it becomes clear that Hyrcanus was at times called upon to represent Jewish communities in the Diaspora, in this case Asia Minor, and that he invoked previous Roman measures as precedent to make his case with the responsible governor.[117] This included not only his own status as ally of the Romans but also, it would seem, specific documents that referenced Jewish rights to observe the Sabbath and other religious rites. It is important to note, however, that the Roman governor, not Hyrcanus, was ultimately responsible for the final decision, and that Hyrcanus and the Jews of Asia Minor were not the only parties whose wishes had to be taken into account. A number of representatives from the town of

[116] Flavius Josephus, *Antiquitates Iudaicae* 14.10.20 (241–3).

[117] Pucci Ben Zeev (1998), 197. For the argument that Hyrcanus' involvement serves to demonstrate that the Roman authorities were inclined to see Jewish communities as 'members of a single body', which would distinguish their position from that of 'other locally defined groups', see Rives (2009), 106–11. Rives also notes, however, that Hyrcanus is unlikely to have been involved in an official capacity, and it remains telling that his interaction with the Roman authorities in this case specifically dealt with the Jewish community of Asia, while no other regions appear to have been involved. While it is certainly notable, then, that an ambassador from a different region was so actively involved in bringing this case before a Roman governor, Rives notes that Rome's 'tendency to deal with the Judaeans as a single geographically dispersed people', while present, should not be overestimated. Instead, it seems more likely that the Roman authorities of this period were certainly aware of such transregional connections between Jewish communities, and acknowledged their validity and significance, but otherwise overwhelmingly continued to make decisions on a local level. It may therefore be suggested that Hyrcanus' involvement was not entirely dissimilar to the activities of Roman senators whose help was invoked by the Greek cities for whom they served as patrons, as was still common during this period. See Eilers (2002), 85–95.

Tralles were also present in the governor's tribunal (as indicated by the phrase κατὰ πρόσωπον), and raised objections to his decisions favouring the Jewish communities.[118] While they appear to have been quickly overruled by the magistrate, this short passage does demonstrate that Roman decisions regarding Jewish rites were by no means uncontested and furthermore heavily relied on local enforcement: the Jewish communities pleading their case to the governor apparently feared that his decisions would amount to very little if they were not also sent to the various cities involved, and were entered in the local public records there.[119] The fact that references to these difficulties survive even in Josephus' compilation has led to the suggestion that at least some now unknown Jewish appeals to the Roman authorities must have been rejected at some stage during this process.[120] The documentary evidence for such unsuccessful encounters, however, would not have been transmitted in a Jewish context, whereas favourable rulings would have been passed on to other communities who could, in turn, use them as legal precedents to improve their own positions if the situation allowed.[121]

The letter from the magistrates of Laodicea, while brief, thus serves to indicate how complex these negotiations between various interested parties could be, and how effective a precedent and a recognized negotiating partner like Hyrcanus could be in achieving one's objective. It also suggests that the delegations sent to the Roman authorities by Jewish communities often found their origins in problems encountered on a local level. While this is certainly a particularly rich and complex example, it is hardly unique. In a ruling from the people of Halicarnassus (ψήφισμα; Appendix 2.23), we once again find a reference to Roman intervention on behalf of the local Jewish community, although in this instance no mention of concrete difficulties is made.[122] It is notable that the city takes care to point out its own good relationship with Rome, which is praised as the εὐεργέτης, or benefactor, of all mankind. This sense of alliance with Rome is explicitly presented as Halicarnassus' primary reason for granting their Jewish community the right to observe its ancestral customs, as well as a location to build their synagogue. The decision by the local officials to comply with Rome's wishes, then, appears to have been facilitated by previous Roman benefactions.

A similar measure from the people of Sardis (Appendix 2.24) provides a more elaborate description of the events that preceded its creation, and in addition makes mention of a Jewish delegation appearing before the city's own βουλή,

[118] This passage seems to provide a counter-argument to the observation made by Harries (1999), 87 that repetitions of legal measures were not generally caused by disobedience.

[119] See Flavius Josephus, *Antiquitates Iudaicae* 14.10.20 (243), where the magistrates of Laodicea let the governor know that they will, indeed, confirm his measures.

[120] Trebilco (1991), 12. [121] Rajak (2002[b]), 324–5.

[122] Flavius Josephus, *Antiquitates Iudaicae* 14.10.23 (256–8). It is notable that this document references a fine imposed on anyone preventing Jews from adhering to their ancestral customs.

rather than before representatives of the Roman administration.[123] According to the text presented by Josephus, the Jewish delegation referenced both local and Roman precedents for the privileges they requested, and were thus granted the right to meet in order to observe their religious obligations, as well as the guarantee that the market officials would provide food suitable for their community. It has been suggested that the 'laws and freedom' restored by the Roman senate and people mentioned in this document are a reference to the rights granted to Hyrcanus II and his children by Julius Caesar,[124] but if this is indeed the case, the precedent appears to have been used with some flexibility. As mentioned, Caesar's measures were likely primarily concerned with the political status of Hyrcanus, rather than with the position of Jewish communities in the Diaspora. In addition, it is notable that no direct Roman involvement appears to have been necessary in this particular case, and that Jewish delegations could also address the local authorities directly—which could apparently have considerable effect. While this is a rare occurrence in Josephus' catalogue, it does suggest that direct Roman intervention was not, strictly speaking, a legal necessity: Jewish communities could at times obtain the rights they desired by directly negotiating with local governments instead.

This course of action does not, however, appear to have been available for the Jewish community of Miletus, which found itself compelled to ask for Roman intervention in order to maintain its rights (Appendix 2.25).[125] According to the document cited by Josephus, which is a letter from governor Publius Servilius Galba, Jews in that city had previously been granted the right to observe the Sabbath and uphold their ancestral ways of worship but had recently encountered resistance.[126] A certain Prytanis complained of this to the governor, who after hearing the arguments of both parties (*διακούσας* [...] *λόγων ἐξ ἀντικαταστάσεως γενομένων*) decided the matter in favour of the Jewish community.[127] Once again, then, we find an example of Jewish communities asking for help from the Roman authorities because they had encountered difficulties in the cities they inhabited, and once again we find evidence that the local authorities made their own contrasting arguments. While the exact contents of these arguments go unmentioned, the fact that Roman magistrates saw the need to listen to both parties nonetheless

[123] Flavius Josephus, *Antiquitates Iudaicae* 14.10.24 (259–61). While this measure may be connected to the earlier document cited in Flavius Josephus, *Antiquitates Iudaicae* 14.10.17 (235), which likewise deals with the Jewish community of Sardis (Appendix 2.12), it is uncertain if the two are related—see Pucci Ben Zeev (1998), 223. However, both the difference in their respective stipulations and the reference to a Jewish delegation appearing before the local assembly in this later document suggest that this pronouncement is not directly responding to Lucius Antonius' message.

[124] Flavius Josephus, *Antiquitates Iudaicae* 14.10.2 (190–5). See Pucci Ben Zeev (1998), 225.

[125] Flavius Josephus, *Antiquitates Iudaicae* 14.10.21 (244–6).

[126] This included the right to manage *καρπούς*, the exact meaning of which is unclear. For a more detailed exploration of the subject, see Pucci Ben Zeev (1998), 201–3.

[127] In this context, Prytanis is used as a personal name, rather than the title of a magistrate.

remains highly significant, as does the fact that the responsible Roman official once again ruled in the Jewish community's favour.

The last known case of legal interaction between Jewish communities and the Roman authorities from the time of Julius Caesar took place in Rome, rather than in the eastern Mediterranean (Appendix 2.21). Although the evidence for this particular measure contains some interpretative difficulties, it nevertheless suggests that the city's Jewish community was exempted from a measure by Caesar that was, according to Suetonius, intended to dissolve all Roman *collegia*, with the exception of those that had particularly ancient origins (*cuncta collegia praeter antiquitus constituta distraxit*).[128] Suetonius' account does not provide any further details about the specific *collegia* that were excluded from the ban, but a tangential reference to these events in one of the documents cited by Josephus (which will be discussed in more detail in section 3.7) connects this measure to Rome's Jewish community, and claims that it was the only association that was allowed to continue to exist.[129] Despite the obvious implausibility of this statement, it is likely that the passage still contains a kernel of truth, and it has rightly been suggested that Josephus' account may best be described as a reference that is simply not verbatim, and therefore possibly misleading.[130] Roman Jews, then, were likely not the sole exception to Caesar's ban on *collegia*, but rather one of a variety of groups who escaped it.[131] Still, the very fact that they were considered exempt is nonetheless telling: it suggests that Jewish communities could be seen as fitting within frameworks that were familiar to the Roman authorities,[132] and that this,

[128] Suetonius, *De vita Caesarum: Iulius* 42.3.

[129] For the inclusion of Jewish communities within the framework of the *collegia*, see Eckhardt (2018[b]). Cappelletti (2006), 8 mistakenly suggests that Josephus' text references an exemption to a similar ban on *collegia* for the Jews of Parium. The *πόλις* referred to in Flavius Josephus, *Antiquitates Iudaicae* 14.10.8 (215) is clearly Rome, however, since this is the last city mentioned in the passage. Smallwood (1976), 134 suggests that the ban on *collegia* applied to the entire empire, as does Baumann (1983), 252, arguing: 'Diese Bestimming [i.e. Caesar's exemption of Jewish communities from the ban on *collegia*] galt, da keinerlei Grund vorlag, bei der Behandlung von Diasporagemeinden irgenwelche Unterschiede zu machen, im ganzen Reich.' However, this seems unlikely, both because Suetonius places the ban in the context of Caesar's measures to restore order in Rome and because the document cited by Josephus limits its applicability to that city alone. See Rajak (2002[b]), 312. This, of course, does not mean that the measure applied to Rome could not be seen as precedent elsewhere. See Eckhardt (2018[a]), 36–9 for the many complexities of this issue.

[130] Gruen (2002), 26.

[131] For the idea that Jews were exempt from the ban because they were not involved in the internal Roman struggles for power that characterized the period, see Pucci Ben Zeev (1998), 112. For the suggestion that this exemption occurred only because Rome's Jewish community specifically requested it, see Rocca (2022), 82. The term *διάταγμα* used in the document cited by Josephus, however, is generally used in a technical sense to refer to an *edictum* rather than a *decretum*. See Pucci Ben Zeev (1998), 62 and 112.

[132] Eckhardt (2018[b]), 91. For a more elaborate discussion of the extent to which Jewish communities actually fit within the framework of private associations, see Eckhardt (2020); Eckhardt and Leonhard (2018); and Rocca (2022), 91–5, who argue that the similarities between the two types of groups should not blind us to their differences, and that Jewish communities did not fit the familiar framework of Graeco-Roman associations entirely comfortably.

along with their antiquity and established character, may on occasion have been to their advantage.

3.7 Legal Measures between Caesar and Augustus

After Caesar's death, it soon became clear that many of his measures held little permanent value, and the position of Hyrcanus II had to be reaffirmed both by Mark Antony and the Roman senate,[133] once again on the king's own initiative (Appendices 2.28 and 2.33–2.36). Lucius Lentulus' decisions regarding the dismissal of certain Jews from the Roman army appear to have suffered a similar fate: in 43 BCE,[134] Hyrcanus II once again came to the aid of Diaspora communities (Appendices 2.29 and 2.30) and contacted Publius Cornelius Dolabella, who is described as governor of Asia in the surviving source material.[135] Hyrcanus' aim, it would seem, was primarily to reaffirm the previously existing exemption from military service, although there is some indication that he may have asked for permission for the adherence to Jewish customs outside of a military context as well.[136] In any case, Dolabella's response was favourable, and he sent a missive to Ephesus granting Hyrcanus' request and ordering his missive to be passed on to the other cities of the province, thus once again showing the reliance of Roman officials on local administrators. In itself, this order seems relatively straightforward. It is significant, however, that less than a decade had passed between Lentulus' original order and Dolabella's repetition of it. Dolabella may have been eager to comply with Hyrcanus' request, but it seems clear that the original order was under threat of falling into disuse to the extent that re-issuing the measure became necessary. This suggests that Roman measures, as valuable as they might have been to the communities that requested them, were a relatively unstable factor, and thus required frequent renegotiation.[137] Signs of this negotiation are visible even in Dolabella's reply: not only does he mention the fact that Hyrcanus'

[133] See Flavius Josephus, *Antiquitates Iudaicae* 14.10.10 (219–2), 14.12.3 (306–13), 14.12.4 (314–18), 14.12.5 (319–22), and 14.12.6 (323).

[134] Pucci Ben Zeev (1998), 139.

[135] Flavius Josephus, *Antiquitates Iudaicae* 14.10.11–12 (223–7). The application of this title by Josephus is not, strictly speaking, correct. Dolabella was in fact governor of Syria but would nevertheless have had some influence in the province of Asia due to his close connection to the *triumvir* Mark Antony. For Dolabella's official title, see Pucci Ben Zeev (1998), 138. Rives (2009), 107–8 argues that it is notable that Hyrcanus, as ruler of Judea, was seen as an appropriate representative for the Jewish communities of Asia, and suggests that this may be indicative of a Roman tendency to see Jewish communities from various regions as belonging to the same group. He adds, however, that this is unlikely to have occurred in an official capacity. For a more in-depth discussion of this argument, see n. 117 in this chapter.

[136] Notably, freedom from military service and permission to hold religious congregations are presented as separate decisions by Dolabella.

[137] For the idea that the relationship between Jewish and non-Jewish communities was frequently unstable and up for renegotiation, see likewise Linder (2006), 128–9.

delegation explained Jewish customs to him, but his insistence that he was following the lead of previous governors may furthermore indicate that the ambassadors reminded him of the existence of this particular precedent. On one crucial point, however, Dolabella may have diverted from his predecessors' attitude: he neglected to limit dispensation from military service to Jews who were Roman citizens, which may have meant that all Jews of Asia, including non-citizens, were now exempt from military service in the auxiliary forces, and perhaps even in the legions, which in this period appear to have enlisted recruits without citizenship due to the increased military demands of the civil war.[138] However, since a similar omission occurs in one of the versions of Lentulus' measure transmitted by Josephus (Appendix 2.9), we ultimately cannot be certain if Dolabella did indeed expand the existing regulation.

On other occasions, the effect of the available precedents was far more straightforward. In the year 42 BCE,[139] the people of Ephesus issued a measure granting the Jewish community of the city the right to maintain their ancestral customs and keep their own laws (Appendix 2.31).[140] The text of the grant is particularly interesting because it includes references to a number of different stages of the negotiation process. It is very likely that members of the Jewish community of Ephesus were at some point prevented from observing the Sabbath by their non-Jewish neighbours and were possibly even fined for maintaining the custom, since both are explicitly mentioned as examples of behaviours now relegated to the past (*μηδένα κωλύεσθαι παρατηρεῖν τὴν τῶν σαββάτων ἡμέραν μηδὲ πράττεσθαι ἐπιτίμιον*). Given the mention of fines, this harassment may have been an official policy by the magistrates of the city, which might explain why the Jewish community made a direct appeal to the Roman governor,[141] rather than attempting to resolve the issue with the local authorities. The text furthermore suggests that this was a strictly local measure, and that these events only involved Ephesian Jews, referred to as *οἱ ἐν τῇ πόλει Ἰουδαῖοι*, which makes it more likely that the petitioners responded to specific events in their city. The delegation was apparently successful and the council of Ephesus proceeded to ratify the governor's decision.

Something similar appears to have occurred in the case of the final measure from the republican period known to us,[142] which has been tentatively dated to 42 or 41

[138] For the idea that the exemption included service in both the legions and the auxiliary forces, see Smallwood (1976), 137, who also adds (somewhat implausibly) that the exemption now applied across the Roman Empire. For the idea that the measure had a more limited scope, see Pucci Ben Zeev (1998), 148 and 440–1. For the inclusion of non-citizens in the Roman legions during the civil war, see Goldsworthy (1996), 37 and Southern (2007), 99.

[139] Pucci Ben Zeev (1998), 226.

[140] Flavius Josephus, *Antiquitates Iudaicae* 14.10.25 (262–4).

[141] The governor in this case may well have been the famous Marcus Junius Brutus. For a more elaborate discussion of the presiding magistrate's name, see Pucci Ben Zeev (1998), 228.

[142] Flavius Josephus, *Antiquitates Iudaicae* 14.10.8 (213–16).

BCE, and could potentially have involved Gaius Octavian (Appendix 2.32).[143] Much about this document remains unclear, including its intended destination,[144] but what does stand out is that we are once again dealing with a Roman response to complaints made by a Jewish delegation.[145] The Jews of Delos and the surrounding islands turned to the Roman authorities after a regulation had been issued that banned them from observing their 'ancestral customs and sacred rites', which likely included the contribution of money for communal meals. The Roman magistrate involved strongly expresses his disapproval of this course of events and makes mention of the fact that the Jews of Rome were allowed to continue their religious practices even under Julius Caesar's aforementioned ban on *collegia* (Appendix 2.21). As has been discussed, the capital's Jewish community was likely not the only association that continued to exist under Caesar's measures, despite the author's assertions to the contrary, and a similar measure from the time of Augustus likewise exempted multiple associations from being disbanded.[146] It is significant, however, that a measure that originally applied to the city of Rome in particular is here used as a precedent for a region in the eastern Mediterranean. For this reason, the letter has been seen as evidence for a wider acknowledgement of Jewish religious liberties, but we should be careful not to overstate this point: Caesar's original measure applied to Rome specifically,[147] just as this document refers to Delos and the surrounding islands alone. The application of these measures, then, was still very local. It also bears repeating that the Roman authorities did not intervene on the Delian Jews' behalf of their own accord. Instead, they were prompted to do so by a local delegation that had encountered difficulties in its hometown. Therefore, while it remains significant that previous measures could be used as precedent in areas of the empire other than the ones for which they were originally intended, it is difficult to see this missive as evidence for the so-called Jewish *Magna Carta*. Instead, this episode demonstrates not only the importance of local initiative and negotiation between local groups and the Roman authorities but also the latter's reliance on procedures and regulations with which they were already familiar. The fact that Jewish communities could be recognized as fitting within the established framework of legitimate associations or *collegia* by Roman officials, even if they were not

[143] Pucci Ben Zeev (1998), 109, 114–15. The fact that a similar measure is ascribed to Augustus in Philo of Alexandria, *Legatio ad Gaium* 311–12 may suggest that this ruling was indeed of his making.

[144] The island of Paros seems most likely, since this would explain the mention of nearby Delos in the text. However, it has often been assumed that Parium, located near the Hellespont, was meant instead. See Eckhardt (2018[b]), 64–5; Pucci Ben Zeev (1998), 110.

[145] Eckhardt (2018[b]), 65.

[146] Suetonius, *De vita Caesarum: Augustus* 32.1. The measures cited by Suetonius in this passage once again seem to be focused on the city of Rome. An inscription referring to the approved *collegium symphoniacorum*, CIL VI 4416, was likewise found in the capital. For the idea that the renewal of Caesar's measure was inspired by the fact that new *collegia* had sprung up in the meantime, see Eckhardt (2018[a]), 28.

[147] Rajak (2002[b]), 312.

perceived as such on a local level, in this case seems to have significantly aided the Jewish delegation's argument and apparently overruled the opposition in the eyes of the Roman magistrate.[148]

While the various cases discussed so far in this chapter may seem disparate in nature, it is nevertheless possible to discern a pattern that had emerged in the interactions between Jewish communities and the Roman authorities by the end of the republican period. The origins of the known cases from this period can overwhelmingly be found in local affairs from the various cities of the empire, and seldom, if ever, on a centralized level. This holds true even for the political alliances between the Roman state and the various rulers of Judea, which were often instigated by the latter, but the pattern of local initiative is particularly clear in those cases that deal with the right to uphold Jewish ancestral customs. Time after time, we see that local Jewish communities took action in response to specific problems they encountered in their own cities, and attempted to resolve them either by approaching the local authorities,[149] or, as is more frequently attested in our sources, by asking for Roman assistance—in some cases with the help of powerful external representatives from Judea like Hyrcanus II.[150] In most cases, these communities requested the right to maintain Jewish ancestral customs, which could include the right to observe the Sabbath, a location to meet, or access to food that met Jewish dietary restrictions. An interesting number of cases, as we have seen, also dealt with dispensation from military service, which was seen as being incompatible with upholding these customs.

While the examples of Roman intervention transmitted to us seem to have primarily favoured the wishes of Jewish communities over those of their non-Jewish neighbours, at least in the documents that have survived, it should be noted that these responses, like the associated petitions, are overwhelmingly local in nature, often referring to single cities, or the province of Asia at the very most. This, as Tessa Rajak has rightly noted, would serve to contradict the notion that these measures amounted to a universal guarantee of Jewish rights.[151] The implementation of Roman decisions, likewise, frequently occurred on a local level, and we find repeated references to the administrators of various cities confirming such

[148] It remains notable that the Roman authorities apparently made the connection between the Jewish communities of different regions. For the argument these translocal connections between Jewish communities, especially after 70 CE, marks them out as different from other associations in the Graeco-Roman world, see Eckhardt and Leonhard (2018), 336. The reference in Flavius Josephus, *Antiquitates Iudaicae* 14.10.8 (213–16) to emissaries from the region addressed in the letter being present may suggest that the Jewish delegation was met with some opposition, as also happened in other cases—see Appendices 2.22 and 2.25.

[149] As in the rare case of the measure from Sardis presented in Flavius Josephus, *Antiquitates Iudaicae* 14.10.24 (259–61).

[150] As in Flavius Josephus, *Antiquitates Iudaicae* 14.10.20 (241–3) and 14.10.11–12 (223–7). For the argument that this was fairly exceptional both within the wider context of Roman administration and of interactions between Jewish communities and the Roman authorities, see Rives (2009), 106–11.

[151] Rajak (2002^{b}), 312.

verdicts in order to enter them in the city archives. However, not all local officials appear to have been enthusiastic about following the Roman lead. As we have seen in the cases of Laodicea and Miletus,[152] non-Jewish delegations from these cities on occasion attempted to object and pleaded their own case before the Roman authorities in order to maintain their own policies. In addition, many measures appear to have only been effective for relatively short periods of time: on a number of notable occasions, we see Jewish communities asking for confirmation of rights that they had already been granted before only a few years previously, possibly because they had once again been confronted with local hostilities.

Despite the importance of both local initiative and local implementation, however, we should not underestimate the importance of Roman intervention. The Roman authorities may have mostly limited their involvement to individual cases, but it becomes clear throughout the available sources that they could exercise significant power, and that Roman measures concerning certain cities could even be used as precedents by communities that were not originally included in their stipulations.[153] Precedents, whether Roman or local, could be extremely valuable for Jewish communities who wished to uphold their rights, even if—or especially because—they frequently had to renegotiate in order to achieve this. This is not to say, however, that Roman attitudes were unambiguously positive. We have to take into account the strong possibility that our overview of Roman legal measures regarding Jewish communities is incomplete, and that Jewish petitions may well have been rejected in cases that are now lost to us. Certainly, both the expulsion of 161 BCE and Lucius Valerius Flaccus' attempt to prevent Asia's Jewish communities from sending money to the Temple in Jerusalem suggest that Jewish rights were not always indisputably at the forefront of Roman officials' minds—and in this regard, they likely fared no worse than other communities in the Mediterranean world.

3.8 Augustan Measures: Precedented Benevolence

The emergence of a new, imperial form of government in the wake of the Roman civil wars added a new layer to interactions between Jewish communities and the Roman authorities. In addition to provincial governors and the senate, the latter of which at least theoretically retained its important position, Rome was now headed by the *princeps*, who as a result of his position of supreme authority became the focus of petitions and delegations from all parts of the empire.

[152] Flavius Josephus, *Antiquitates Iudaicae* 14.10.20 (241–3) and 14.10.21 (244–6).

[153] See Trebilco (1991), 1 for the assertion that Josephus himself saw the documents he cited as precedents that could be relevant for Jewish communities throughout the Diaspora.

It is little wonder, then, that Augustus became highly influential in the lives of various Jewish communities after his ascension to power.[154] His influence was felt not only in Judea, where he became heavily involved in the reigns of King Herod and his successors,[155] but also in Asia Minor and the cities of northern Africa—and, of course, Rome. No less than six measures from the time of Augustus appear in our sources, particularly in the works of Flavius Josephus and Philo of Alexandria.[156] These measures are especially fascinating because they demonstrate a stronger coherence and interdependence than even the measures from the republican period discussed in this chapter so far.

3.8.1 Delegations from Asia Minor and Cyrene

Josephus introduces his collection of Augustan documents by offering his personal perspective on the circumstances under which they were composed. He claims that Jewish communities had acquired equal rights and privileges to the other inhabitants of the cities in which they lived under the reigns of the Hellenistic kings,[157] before arguing that 'the Greeks' had subsequently tried to limit these liberties, particularly the right to send money to Jerusalem. According to Josephus, events of this kind occurred throughout the eastern territories of the Roman Empire, and prompted Jews from Asia Minor and Cyrene to send embassies to Augustus requesting his help in resolving their difficulties.[158] This story once again confirms that the initiative of specific Jewish communities was essential for the creation of legal measures protecting their liberties, although it remains unclear how the delegations from the two regions connected to this particular case related to each other. Certainly, the missives directed at Asia and Cyrene quoted by Josephus grant very similar (although notably not identical) protections, which may suggest that the two worked together to bring about a measure that applied to a larger geographical area than any previous ruling. Contact between Jewish communities was not, in itself unusual, and mutual assistance and joint embassies for different cities, at least, did occur on occasion during the republican period.[159] However, the suggestion that Jewish communities from different provinces could likewise work together remains speculative at best.

[154] A similar argument is made by Schuol (2007), 63.

[155] Seeman and Marshak (2012), 51–3.

[156] Flavius Josephus, *Antiquitates Iudaicae* 16.6.1–7 (160–73) and Philo of Alexandria, *Legatio ad Gaium* 158 and 311–17.

[157] It is notable that none of the documents cited by Josephus actually mentions equal rights (ἰσονομία) for Greek and Jewish citizens. See Pucci Ben Zeev (1998), 234 and Schuol (2007), 123.

[158] Flavius Josephus, *Antiquitates Iudaicae* 16.6.1 (160–1).

[159] Schuol (2007), 106–24 discusses the complaints brought forward by the Jewish communities of Asia Minor separately. For the difficulties in determining where exactly Agrippa received the delegation, see Schuol (2007), 107.

It is interesting, for instance, that Josephus makes mention of similar difficulties in various cities (explicitly indicated by the plural πόλεις), rather than provinces. In addition, Asia and Cyrene are never mentioned together in the actual cited documents, which may suggest that the embassy was not, in fact, transregional. It is therefore possible that the documents were instead grouped together by Josephus because of their similar dates and subject matter. Still, whether formal cooperation occurred or not, these missives do suggest that different Jewish communities could be faced with very similar problems, which could in turn result in similar measures being applied to a larger geographic area.

The earliest two documents connected to these measures are ascribed to Augustus' close advisor Marcus Agrippa, and are both commonly dated to 14 BCE.[160] The first letter in the collection is addressed to the magistrates, council, and people of Ephesus (Appendix 2.37),[161] whereas the second was directed towards the same authorities in Cyrene (Appendix 2.38).[162] While both letters are primarily concerned with the right of the respective Jewish communities to send money to the Temple in Jerusalem, a number of interesting differences suggest that each missive was, in fact, intended as a response to differing local circumstances. The letter to Ephesus grants Jews the right to send money to Jerusalem and proclaims that anyone who violates this right is to be punished according to a pre-existing law on temple robbery. In addition, Agrippa makes mention of a letter he has sent to praetor Silanus demanding that Jews could no longer be compelled to appear in court during the Sabbath. Neither the comparison with temple robbery nor the issue of court cases occurring during the Sabbath appears in the letter to Cyrene.[163] The localized character of the measure is further enhanced by the surrounding narrative provided by Josephus. The historian describes the delegation to Agrippa from the province of Asia on two separate occasions, and in both cases we learn that he questioned both a Jewish and a non-Jewish party, before ultimately siding with the former.[164] This decision appears to have been based at least in part on precedents provided by the representative of the Jewish delegation, Herod's chief diplomat Nicolas of Damascus, who argued that the Romans had previously allowed the Jews of Asia to observe their own customs—perhaps referring to the exemption from military service first granted by Lucius Lentulus.[165] This argument seems to have appealed to Agrippa, who according to Josephus clearly expressed his inability to override existing rights and privileges

[160] Pucci Ben Zeev (1998), 270 and 275–6.
[161] Flavius Josephus, *Antiquitates Iudaicae* 16.6.4 (167–8).
[162] Flavius Josephus, *Antiquitates Iudaicae* 16.6.5 (169–70).
[163] Flavius Josephus, *Antiquitates Iudaicae* 16.6.5 (169–70).
[164] The relevant passages may be found in Flavius Josephus, *Antiquitates Iudaicae* 12.3.2 (125–8) and 16.2.3–5 (27–65).
[165] Flavius Josephus, *Antiquitates Iudaicae* 12.3.2 (126) and 16.2.3 (28).

(καινίζειν).[166] The presence of King Herod, who accompanied Agrippa on his journey through the province, likewise seems to have played an important part. According to one of Josephus' versions of the story, Agrippa declared that he would grant the requests of the Jewish delegation 'because of Herod's goodwill and friendship towards him' (διὰ μὲν τὴν Ἡρώδου πρὸς αὐτὸν εὔνοιάν τε καὶ φιλίαν ἕτοιμος εἶναι πᾶν ὁτιοῦν χαρίζεσθαι Ἰουδαίοις).[167] The opposing delegation, by contrast, appears to have focused on painting the Jewish community as a troublesome force that did not belong in their cities, arguing that they had no right to citizenship because they did not worship the same gods as their non-Jewish neighbours and claiming that Jewish presence was in itself disruptive.[168] These arguments, however, appear to have been less compelling. According to Josephus' account, then, Agrippa's letter to Ephesus was once again the result of elaborate negotiations,[169] and dealt specifically with issues related to the province of Asia.

Agrippa's letter to Cyrene likewise appears to have dealt with local circumstances, although his conclusions are largely similar. As mentioned, no provision exempting Jews from appearing in court on the Sabbath is present, and those who have confiscated money earmarked for Jerusalem are simply required to make amends with the Jewish community (ταῦτα διορθώσασθαι τοῖς ἐκεῖ Ἰουδαίοις κελεύω) but are not punished as temple robbers.[170] The issue of precedent, however, does reoccur, albeit in a different form. In this case, the Jewish delegation appears to have referred to an earlier letter by Augustus allowing their community to send money to Jerusalem. This Augustan measure is otherwise unknown to us,[171] but according to the Jewish delegation the Cyrenians wilfully disobeyed it, harassing the city's Jews and confiscating the money ἐν προφάσει τελῶν μὴ ὀφειλομένων, 'under the pretence of taxes that were not owed'. This highly evocative phrase gives an important indication of the problems that lay at the root of these disputes between Jews and their neighbours in Cyrene. It may be suggested

[166] Flavius Josephus, *Antiquitates Iudaicae* 12.3.2 (126). Since Josephus is paraphrasing here, we should perhaps not take his assertion that Agrippa was unable to make changes (μηδὲν αὐτῷ καινίζειν ἐξεῖναι) too literally.

[167] Flavius Josephus, *Antiquitates Iudaicae* 16.2.5 (60). For Herod's involvement in convincing Agrippa to listen to the Jewish delegation, see Flavius Josephus, *Antiquitates Iudaicae* 16.2.3 (29). For more details on Herod's central role in the negotiations between Jewish communities and Rome, see Schuol (2007), 124–35. The importance of a personal connection to the Roman authorities for ambassadors in general is emphasized by Rives (2009), 106–15.

[168] Flavius Josephus, *Antiquitates Iudaicae* 12.3.2 (125–6) and 16.2.5 (59). The idea that at least some Jews in the province of Asia held citizenship is confirmed by Lentulus' exemption from military service for this exact group. See Flavius Josephus, *Antiquitates Iudaicae* 14.10.13 (228–9). The argument that citizenship could only be held by those who worshipped the local gods is notably paralleled by a similar remark from the anti-Jewish polemist Apion about the situation in Alexandria, which will be discussed in section 3.10. See Flavius Josephus, *Contra Apionem* 2.6 (65).

[169] Schuol (2007), 123.

[170] Flavius Josephus, *Antiquitates Iudaicae* 16.6.5 (169–70).

[171] Pucci Ben Zeev (1998), 234 sees this letter as conclusive evidence for Josephus' claim that Augustus interfered on behalf of the region's Jewish community in *Antiquitates Iudaicae* 16.6.1 (160–1).

that local administrators in the region, and possibly the general population as well, were displeased with the fact that significant amounts of money left the province.[172] These financial considerations were then disguised as concerns about fiscal malversations and used to set aside Augustus' wishes. Agrippa's letter to Cyrene therefore shows not only another example of local aggression laying at the root of Jewish requests for Roman intervention but also the potentially fleeting nature of Roman legal measures, dependent as they were on implementation by the local authorities.

3.8.2 Temple Tax in Asia Minor: passing on the message

The next three measures presented in Josephus' Augustan corpus are likewise focused on the issue of the Temple Tax, and can likely be dated to the year 12 BCE.[173] The first of these documents is the longest (Appendix 2.39), and concerns the rights of the Jewish communities of the province of Asia as granted by Emperor Augustus.[174] These rights once again include not only permission to send money to Jerusalem but also an exemption from having to appear in court during the Sabbath and punishment for those who steal the Jewish community's consecrated money. In content, then, this proclamation is strongly similar to Agrippa's earlier letter to Ephesus, although the reason for this potential repetition is unclear.[175] However, the letter is slightly more explicit about Augustus' motivations for his display of benevolence and states that Jews had been allies of the Romans since the time of his adoptive father Julius Caesar. Furthermore, the brief reference to a Jewish honorary decree offered to Augustus (*ὅ τε ψήφισμα τὸ δοθέν μοι ὑπ' αὐτῶν ὑπὲρ τῆς ἐμῆς εὐσεβείας ἧς ἔχω πρὸς πάντας ἀνθρώπους*) may lead to the tentative suggestion that the granting of these rights was once again the result of requests made by a Jewish delegation, and tantalizingly suggests that flattery of the

[172] See Barclay (1996), 268–9, who also refers to the story told in the speech by Nicolas of Damascus presented in Flavius Josephus, *Antiquitates Iudaicae* 16.2.4 (31–57).

[173] Pucci Ben Zeev (1998), 252, 259–61, and 283.

[174] Flavius Josephus, *Antiquitates Iudaicae* 16.6.2 (162–5). The text as transmitted by Josephus omits an addressee, but in the final paragraph Augustus demands that his decision, along with the testimonial of the Jewish delegation, be inscribed on the temple of Augustus and Roma in Ancyra. See Flavius Josephus, *Antiquitates Iudaicae* 16.6.2 (165). The fact that only the temple of Augustus and Roma in the province of Asia is mentioned may very well indicate that this measure was meant for this region specifically. Moreover, there is no indication, either in the introduction by Josephus or in the letter itself, that Augustus' missive was sent anywhere else. For the argument that this interaction involved an unusual degree of collective activity on the part of the Jewish communities of Asia, see Rives (2009), 109–10. Since the same letter also references the collective activities of the *κοινόν* of Asia, however, it does not seem unexpected that the various Jewish communities in the province would have had similar connections.

[175] Philo of Alexandria, *Legatio ad Gaium* 313 reports similar measures and also adds the provision that Jews could not be prevented from meeting.

emperor could be a useful tool in achieving success in obtaining the desired result. The letter and two other documents from the same collection, furthermore, provide a fascinating insight into the way in which Augustus' orders were meant to reach their intended audience. While the first letter includes instruction to have a plaque inscribed with these grants set up in the temple of Augustus and Roma in Ancyra, Josephus then proceeds to cite a message from Augustus to the governor Norbanus Flaccus of Asia (Appendix 2.40),[176] and Flaccus' subsequent letter to the magistrates and council of Sardis (Appendix 2.41),[177] both of which suggest that the ruling was also spread via lower Roman and local officials. In Philo of Alexandria's *Legatio ad Gaium*, furthermore, we find a citation of a very similar letter addressed to the magistrates of Ephesus.[178] All these passages serve to further demonstrate that Augustus' orders were primarily implemented on a local level, and that the regional administrative infrastructure was essential in ensuring that the emperor's proclamation reached its intended goal.

This, however, is not the end of the collection presented by Josephus. A final letter dealing with the issue of the Temple Tax survives, which likely dates from 4 BCE and was once again prompted by a Jewish embassy from the province of Asia (Appendix 2.42).[179] This delegation turned to the new governor Julius Antonius, claiming that they had been granted the right to adhere to their own religious customs and to send offerings to Jerusalem without hindrance.[180] In order to support this argument, they referred to the proclamations by Agrippa and Augustus, thus allowing us to combine all the documents discussed in this section into a single dossier. However, rather than simply showing continuous Roman support for Jewish ancestral customs, these documents also show that these regulations intended to protect Jewish religious practices had fallen into disuse within ten years of their original issuing, and that the Jewish communities of Asia were once again confronted with hostilities in the cities they inhabited. The exact circumstances of these requests for repeated confirmation of previous orders are not transmitted in the letter, but the document does show how important the preservation of precedents could be for Jewish communities: by using them, they could hold on to their rights, even if doing so could prove to be a frequent struggle. Even an imperial missive, it would seem, was no guarantee for a permanent change in the attitude or behaviour of the local populations Jewish communities had to live with.

[176] Flavius Josephus, *Antiquitates Iudaicae* 16.6.3 (166).
[177] Flavius Josephus, *Antiquitates Iudaicae* 16.6.6 (171).
[178] Philo of Alexandria, *Legatio ad Gaium* 314–15.
[179] Flavius Josephus, *Antiquitates Iudaicae* 16.6.7 (172–3). For the dating of the letter, see Pucci Ben Zeev (1998), 289–90.
[180] For the suggestion that these offerings were the Temple Tax, see Pucci Ben Zeev (1998), 287.

3.8.3 Augustan measures in Alexandria and Rome

This is not to say, however, that Roman measures could not at times make tangible differences for both the political and religious lives of Jewish communities, as is demonstrated by a number of additional measures from the time of Augustus. According to Philo of Alexandria, Augustus granted the Jewish community of his home town the right to a degree of self-governance in the form of a *γερουσία* (Appendix 2.44).[181] Information about this episode is scant, but it has been argued that Augustus' intervention was requested because the Alexandrian Jewish community feared instability in the wake of their ethnarch's recent death.[182] Another example of Augustus' positive interventions is, once again, briefly referred to by Philo, who positively compares Augustus to the later emperor Caligula by mentioning an undated measure that improved the accessibility of the grain dole for Rome's Jewish community (Appendix 2.43).[183] According to Philo, at least some Jews were eligible for the monthly distributions of grain or money used to feed designated Roman citizens living in the city,[184] and while this was in itself a significant advantage, it could cause unforeseen problems when the distribution of these gifts took place during the Sabbath, when observant Jews would be unable to attend. Philo alleges that Augustus therefore granted the Jews of Rome special permission to pick up their allotted portion on the following day, thus preventing their exclusion. While this measure has been referred to as a 'striking concession',[185] its scope was likely more limited than at first seems apparent. It should be noted that this measure only applied to Jews in the capital, and had little relevance for those living outside the city.[186] It has even been suggested that the Jewish community of the city was responsible for the measure, and had petitioned Augustus for its implementation when they encountered problems.[187] In general, however,

[181] Philo of Alexandria, *In Flaccum* 74. [182] Gruen (2002), 72.

[183] Philo of Alexandria, *Legatio ad Gaium* 158. For the contrast between Augustus and Caligula in Philo's works, see Schuol (2007), 291.

[184] This passage clearly indicates that at least some Jews were Roman citizens at the time, since there is little doubt that only citizens were entitled to the dole, thus Tacoma (2016), 84. It may also suggest that these Jews had been living in the city for some time, since it has been argued that recent migrants were excluded, see Bernard (2016). For Augustus' attempts to limit the number of people eligible for such grain distributions, see Garnsey (1988), 236–8.

[185] Barclay (1996), 292–3.

[186] Pucci Ben Zeev (1998), 439. The author does mention that a similar measure may have applied to Alexandria, citing an oblique reference in Flavius Josephus, *Contra Apionem* 2.5 (63)—by which she (rightly) does not seem entirely convinced.

[187] Gruen (2002), 29. The likelihood of this course of events is enhanced by Suetonius, *De vita Caesarum: Augustus* 40.2, which reports that the population of the city could indeed have an influence on the time the dole was handed out. In this passage, Suetonius relates how Augustus originally wanted to distribute corn only three times a year, providing supplies for four months at a time, but was prevented from doing so by objections made by the general population. Both the measure reported by Philo and the one mentioned by Suetonius are said to have been the result of imperial concerns about the intended recipients' physical presence at the distribution of the dole, see Tacoma (2016), 85.

it is likely that Augustus, while he certainly seems to have taken a benevolent attitude towards the Jewish community in his capital, did not go out of his way to be considerate. It has been rightly remarked that this is the only overtly positive measure mentioned by Philo, who otherwise only gives examples of suppressive measures the emperor might have taken, but didn't—like expulsion, removal of citizenship, or suppression of the synagogues.[188] Nevertheless, a ruler who was not, in principle, ill-disposed towards members of the Jewish community could make their lives significantly easier.

3.9 Expulsion under Tiberius

As would become clear under Augustus' successor Tiberius, however, the opposite attitude could have equally significant effects. In 19 CE another expulsion of Jews took place in Rome (Appendix 2.45), and while the event has been recorded by a remarkable number of ancient authors, much about its circumstances remains the subject of debate. The bare bones of what transpired, however, are very similar in most versions of the story: Tiberius expelled the Jewish community from Rome, and in the process likely singled out a significant number of young men to be conscripted into military service and sent to highly dangerous areas.[189] Most sources also connect the expulsion to similar measures against devotees of Egyptian rites, who were met with repressive actions at the same time.[190] While these facts are rarely, if ever, contested,[191] at first glance the available accounts about the underlying motivations of the imperial authorities seem to differ strongly. The version offered by Flavius Josephus alleges that the measure originated in a single incident of a high-ranking Roman matron being scammed out of her money by no fewer than four nefarious figures who used her newfound Jewish faith to their advantage. Given the scope of the resulting expulsion, however, this claim is likely to be exaggerated at the very least, and seems intended to exonerate the Jewish community as a whole.[192] Philo appears to attempt something similar by stating that the Jewish community was falsely

[188] Gruen (2002), 28. See also Philo of Alexandria, *Legatio ad Gaium* 157.

[189] Flavius Josephus, *Antiquitates Iudaicae* 18.3.5 (83–4); Suetonius, *De vita Caesarum: Tiberius* 36; Tacitus, *Annales* 2.85. By contrast, Cassius Dio, *Historiae Romanae* 57.18.5a mentions only the expulsion, not the forced military service, whereas Seneca, *Epistulae* 108.22 only alludes to these events without naming any specifics. The philosopher mentions only that a number of foreign cults were persecuted in this period, without mentioning either the cults or the nature of the persecution explicitly. Suetonius also mentions that religious clothing and attributes had to be burned. The conscription of young Jewish men suggests that the exemption from military service that had been granted to Jews in the province of Asia was hardly universal, or had at the very least been abandoned.

[190] Flavius Josephus, *Antiquitates Iudaicae* 18.3.4 (65–80); Suetonius, *De vita Caesarum: Tiberius* 36; Tacitus, *Annales* 2.85. For the argument that Tacitus is wrong in suggesting that devotees of Egyptian cults were likewise banished, see Williams (1989), 772.

[191] Williams (1989), 765. [192] Wendt (2015^{b}), 114.

accused by Tiberius' right-hand man Sejanus—although he never mentions of what crime, and the details of the passage are generally suspect.[193] The Roman authors who discussed the matter, however, evidently omit such attempts at self-defence, and while neither Suetonius nor Tacitus explicitly mentions any alternative reasons for the expulsion, Cassius Dio claims that the Jews of Rome were expelled because they were actively attempting to spread their religion. It is primarily this last account that has led many to believe that proselytism must have been the primary cause of the expulsion.[194] Although this connection is not directly confirmed by the other sources, they too seem to suggest that the apparent attraction Judaism held for non-Jews may have caused the presence of Jewish communities in the city to be perceived as problematic. Flavius Josephus, as we have seen, focusss strongly on the conversion of a single Roman matron, while Suetonius explicitly includes converts among the Jews who were expelled, and Tacitus makes mention of those who were 'infected by that superstition' (*ea superstitione infecta*), which could likewise be interpreted as a reference to conversion.[195] It seems likely, then, that anxieties about the expansion of Rome's Jewish community played at least some part in the creation of the measure. It should be noted, however, that converts were not the only ones being targeted, and that the available sources instead suggest a more expansive measure. A similar objection may be made to the otherwise compelling argument that the expulsion order was directed not at converts themselves, but at the private religious practitioners who converted them.[196] The scope of the expulsion as described by the various authors, as well as their references to the Jewish community and its religious practices in general, ultimately suggests that they cannot have been the only target. Instead, it seems that a wider net was cast, and that the measure was aimed at those who were seen to be involved in Jewish life in general, rather than at a specific sub-group.[197]

[193] This story is not repeated by any other source and is included by Philo in a passage specifically meant to demonstrate that Caligula's predecessors had generally been quite benevolent towards the Jewish community—an argument that can only be made by blaming not Tiberius himself but rather his nefarious advisors for the expulsion. Caligula had already been born when these events took place and could thus conceivably have remembered it even if Philo had chosen to omit the story. For the idea that Sejanus was likely not yet a major political actor in 19 CE, and that his accusations against the Jewish community may therefore have occurred at a later date, see Gruen (2002), 35. The claim made in Philo of Alexandria, *Legatio ad Gaium* 161 that Tiberius granted Jews throughout the empire their religious liberties in any case resembles fiction more than fact.

[194] Barclay (1996), 298–300; Cappelletti (2006), 58–66; Smallwood (1976), 208. Cappelletti suggests that the issue was not necessarily Judaism itself, but rather the spread of that religion to the higher ranks of Roman society—a suggestion that may find confirmation in the fact that Egyptian cults were also targeted.

[195] An argument referenced by Williams (1989), 770.

[196] See Wendt (2015^b), 109–16 and 120, who does acknowledge that non-experts were very likely also swept up in such measures.

[197] One might here draw a comparison to the argument made in Ripat (2011), 132, who suggests that measures against diviners included not just astrologers but instead a wider array of practitioners in an attempt to be comprehensive. Targeting converts or so-called freelance religious experts

The available sources thus suggest an increased hostility towards the Jewish community in 19 CE, and the wider societal circumstances of the period may well help to further explain why the expulsion took place. While it has been suggested that the Jewish community was actively causing disturbances, possibly due to food shortages,[198] others more plausibly connect the expulsion to the political unrest caused by the death of Germanicus in the same year.[199] The mysterious circumstances under which the designated heir passed away likely led to elevated tensions, particularly in the capital, and therefore may well have led to increased suspicion towards religious practices that were seen as 'deviating from the norm'. Indeed, this state of heightened socio-political anxiety may well explain the emphasis on conversion in the available sources, since converts could be seen as abandoning their ancestral religious customs and may therefore have been considered especially disruptive. The idea that the authorities became particularly concerned with upholding public order is further confirmed by Tacitus, who claims that banishment could be avoided by those who gave up their religious rites. This suggests that the authorities were more concerned with restoring the status quo than with punishing any perceived criminal activity, for which a similar escape would not have been available.[200] The expulsion measure, then, serves to demonstrate that Jewish communities could indeed be targeted by the Roman authorities on the basis of their religious practices,[201] but that this was likely not due to any particular acts in which they were involved. Instead, they were counted among a variety of different religious groups that could be seen as a threat to public order, which did not 'belong', and could therefore be considered disruptive. This included the aforementioned Egyptian cults, with whom Judaism is continuously juxtaposed in the available accounts, as well as diviners, who were likewise expelled from Rome only a few years earlier (section 2.6.3; Appendices 1.7 and 1.8), and who were notably also allowed to escape punishment if they recanted.[202] It seems likely, then, that we are dealing with a wider range of measures against groups that were perceived as being somehow alien or disruptive. These measures were once again strongly localized, and in the long run likely ineffective.

specifically, and even distinguishing them from other people involved in Jewish religious practices, is likely to have been very difficult for the Roman authorities. For a similar argument, see Wendt (2015[b]), 120.

198 Rutgers (1998), 104–5; Williams (1989), 781–3. The latter author suggests that economic causes may have been central but admits that this cannot be proven.

199 Goodman (2007[a]), 369; Gruen (2002), 33.

200 Tacitus, *Annales* 2.85. Cf. Williams (1989), 770.

201 While Rutgers (1998), 104 suggests that '[Jewish] civic or religious liberty was not otherwise impeded', Flavius Josephus, *Antiquitates Iudaicae* 18.3.5 (84) reports that Jews who refused military service because they were afraid to break their ancestral laws (*πάτριοι νόμοι*) were punished. This suggests that the measure may have been seen as an infringement of religious liberty, even if we (perhaps overly generously) assume that it was not intended as such. Furthermore, expulsion on account of one's religious beliefs can hardly be seen as maintaining one's religious liberty.

202 For similar suggestions, see Rutgers (1998), 100–1.

Only a few years after the expulsion, Rome's Jewish community seems to have recovered,[203] and once again appears to have reached its former size—in spite of the harsh punishment of slavery that, according to Suetonius, initially threatened Jews who refused to leave the city.[204] The limited temporal and geographical scope of the measure, then, lends additional credence to the idea that this was a measure aimed at restoring public order during a time of heightened social tensions.

3.10 Riots in Alexandria: The Question of 'Belonging'

As succinct as the available accounts about Tiberius' expulsion are, they are in this sense representative of most references to the difficulties Jewish communities encountered in the respective cities they inhabited. The documents cited by Flavius Josephus, as we have seen, frequently mention conflict between Jewish and Greek inhabitants of Asia Minor, but detailed accounts of the course of events are consistently lacking. The same cannot be said, however, for the violent clashes that took place in the city of Alexandria between *c.* 38 and 41 BCE.[205] The circumstances of these riots are described or referenced in a diverse number of sources, including Flavius Josephus' *Contra Apionem* and two accounts written by Philo of Alexandria. Philo in particular is a remarkable source: he was not only an eyewitness of the turmoil that engulfed his home town, but he was also directly involved in attempts by the various parties to request imperial intervention, recording his experiences with in writings known as *In Flaccum* and *Legatio ad Gaium.*[206] While this personal involvement, and his focus on theology rather than history,[207] means that Philo's accounts should be treated with caution, his treatises are nonetheless invaluable sources on what happened both in Alexandria

[203] Barclay (1996), 300; Goodman (2007[a]), 369; Gruen (2002), 32.

[204] Suetonius, *De vita Caesarum: Tiberius* 36.

[205] These clashes have, at times, been referred to as the 'first pogrom', for instance by Barclay (1996), 51; Gruen (2002), 54; and particularly Van der Horst (2002). A more indirect reference is made by Feldman (1993), 116. Due to the fact that this term evokes connections with later historical events, as has been rightly remarked by Gambetti (2009), 11, this terminology has been avoided in this discussion. See Bremmer (2021), 245–7 for a more elaborate discussion of the appropriateness of the term, which he ultimately concludes is only partially useful for our understanding of the events of 38 CE.

[206] See Van der Horst (2003) for a relatively recent translation and commentary on *In Flaccum*. The Greek text of the treatise may be found in the Loeb edition of Colson (1941). For the edition of *Legatio* in the same series, see Colson (1962). A comparison between the account of Philo and that of Josephus may be found in Schwartz (2012).

[207] Alston (1997), 173; Van der Horst (2002), 469–70. Schwartz (2000), 212 sees Philo's angle in both treatises as philosophical rather than theological. See Bilde (2009) for a discussion of Philo as a politician and polemist. Van der Horst's assertion that Philo's texts are problematic because he does not describe the causes of the riots is nevertheless not completely correct, as will be discussed in more detail throughout section 3.10.

and in Rome—at least in the author's memory.[208] Thus, while we should be mindful of potential exaggerations, it is nonetheless likely that the core of Philo's description is correct, and the value of an eyewitness testimony certainly cannot be discounted.

In addition to these reports by Philo and Josephus, our knowledge of the Alexandrian riots is to an extent supplemented by the opposing faction's perspective: both authors on occasion cite or paraphrase the arguments made by non-Jewish inhabitants of Alexandria, which allows us to get at the very least a general sense of what they considered to be the central issues that contributed to the outbreak of the riots. The perspective of Greek Alexandrians is likewise represented by a number of papyrological texts from a corpus that has collectively become known as the *Acta Alexandrinorum*. This group of texts consists of highly polemic (and often extremely fragmentary) accounts of interactions between Greek Alexandrians and a variety of Roman emperors in which the emperor is presented as siding with the Jewish community and Alexandrian nobles die after heroically attempting to defend their position in the city. The narratives presented in the *Acta* are often profoundly anti-Jewish in tone,[209] and are generally considered to be at least partially fictionalized.[210] This combative, almost courtroom drama-like angle, as well as the late date of transcription,[211] make these texts notably tenuous sources, although they may nonetheless provide us with insights about the literary afterlife of the events of 38 CE, as well as a Greek perspective on the Jewish presence in Alexandria. A final piece of invaluable, and in this case contemporary, evidence may be found in a single papyrus document, which appears to contain a letter by Emperor Claudius to the Greek inhabitants of Alexandria.[212] Although it has been argued that the text as we know it does not constitute the entire letter, but instead contains only an excerpt of the original made by an individual favouring the side of the Greek Alexandrians,[213] the contents of

[208] It is very likely that Philo wrote his accounts after the death of Caligula in January 41 CE, given his harsh portrayal of that emperor in *Legatio ad Gaium*. It is remarkable, however, that the author does not mention Claudius' later intervention in the matter. For the argument that Philo almost certainly invented his descriptions of Flaccus' emotional state but could not divert too far from the historical truth in his descriptions of the events in Alexandria themselves, see Van der Horst (2003), 11–12. Petersen (2009) points out that our sources about Jewish life in Alexandria in general derive from the Jewish elite and thus offer a limited perspective.

[209] For the suggestion that the *Acta* are in fact against all things non-Greek, and not specifically anti-Jewish, see Harker (2008), 175. A critical edition of the relevant texts may be found in Musurillo (1954).

[210] It has been argued that the basis for these accounts can be found in the transcripts of actual historical trials. See Harker (2008), 1 and 96–8.

[211] The texts as we know them were likely transcribed in the late second to early third century CE. See Harker (2008), 2.

[212] This letter is commonly known as P.Lond. 6.1912.

[213] Harker (2008), 25–6. Harker does not argue, however, that the letter as we know it is an outright falsification, arguing instead that it is selective in the passages it cites. Even from the available excerpt, however, it becomes obvious that Claudius gave both sides reasons to be satisfied, and reasons not to be, as will be discussed in more detail in section 3.11.1.

the letter are generally considered to be mostly reliable. The number of sources about the Alexandrian riots, then, can seem almost overwhelming, but it should be noted that all of them are to some degree biased, and that certain crucial elements of the narrative appear to have been so obvious to the various authors describing these events that they simply neglected to mention them—which leaves the modern reader with several tantalizing gaps. Nevertheless, the abundance of available material does allow for the investigation of the Alexandrian riots from various angles. This in turn enables us to paint a reasonably nuanced, if regrettably incomplete, picture of what transpired, and to determine which issues both parties saw as central to the conflict.

3.10.1 Alexandria's Jewish community: position and privileges

Before discussing the events of 38 CE in more detail, it is important to first consider the history of the Jewish population of Alexandria. It is likely that a Jewish community was present in the city from its early days onwards,[214] but its exact status has been much disputed, both in antiquity and in modern scholarship. According to Flavius Josephus, Jews had been present in Alexandria from the very moment of its foundation, and had even obtained political privileges equal to those of the Macedonian settlers of the region (*ἴσης παρὰ τοῖς Μακεδόσι τιμῆς ἐπέτυχον*), of which citizenship was most important.[215] While the reliability of this claim has been strongly doubted,[216] Josephus' insistence on the matter does indicate that the legal position of Alexandrian Jews was considered to be of importance, as well as a point of disagreement: if *ἰσονομία* was indeed granted in Macedonian times, this would have set a very strong precedent, all but guaranteeing the status of the Jewish community in Josephus' own time.[217] This may well be the reason why Josephus addresses the issue not just once but on multiple occasions, and cites a Roman precedent on top of its Macedonian predecessor, which was allegedly inscribed on a bronze pillar and confirmed that Jews were citizens of Alexandria (*ὅτι Ἀλεξανδρέων πολῖταί εἰσιν*; Appendix 2.16). However, this Roman measure likewise seems to rest on shaky historical grounds: it is unclear whether it was issued by Caesar or Augustus,[218] and its exact meaning remains

[214] See, among others, Zangenberg (2013), 96–7.

[215] Flavius Josephus, *Contra Apionem* 2.4 (35). A similar statement is made in *Bellum Iudaicum* 2.18.7 (487).

[216] See, among others, Gambetti (2009), 23 and Gruen (2002), 71. For the argument that Alexandrian Jews of the Ptolemaic period did have 'a certain degree of political freedom as well as distinct religious autonomy', see Petersen (2009), 132.

[217] The Greek terminology regarding this issue is not entirely consistent in the relevant literature. Alongside *ἰσονομία*, *ἰσοτιμία*, and *ἰσοπολιτεία* are also used.

[218] In Flavius Josephus, *Antiquitates Iudaicae* 14.10.1 (188) the author of the edict is described as *Καῖσαρ Ἰούλιος*, which may refer to both men, as shown in Pucci Ben Zeev (1998), 27–8. In *Contra Apionem* 2.4 (37), however, the phrasing *Καῖσαρ ὁ μέγας* is used, which would be more consistent

equally opaque. In particular, the terminology of citizenship used in this passage is hardly as clear cut as it may at first appear: while the term *πολίτης* most commonly refers to a citizen in the legal sense of the word, it also occasionally appears to have been used to indicate residents of a city in general, especially by Jewish authors.[219] It has therefore been suggested that Josephus, whether deliberately or accidentally, used this ambiguity to support his argument that the Roman authorities had lent support to Jewish communities throughout the empire and granted them substantial rights and privileges.[220] In this context, it is particularly remarkable that Josephus' other reference to the pillar on which the grant was apparently inscribed only mentions certain ordinances (*δικαιώματα*), but does not explicitly refer to citizenship.[221] This at the very least constitutes a peculiar discrepancy, and suggests that the inscribed text instead referred to a more limited set of privileges.

Whether Alexandrian Jews did indeed have citizenship equal to that of Greek Alexandrians thus remains very much in doubt, and the idea that Jews were full citizens of Alexandria by default has overwhelmingly been abandoned by recent scholarship.[222] It seems equally unlikely that the Jewish community intended to obtain full citizenship for all its members: since the Jewish community likely numbered in the tens of thousands,[223] such an attempt would be extravagant at best. Nevertheless, it remains likely that at least some members of the Jewish elite (some of whom we know by name) were considered to be Alexandrian citizens, and that others attempted to gain access to this institution—as is also evidenced by the frequent discussions of the extent to which Jews qualified for citizenship in the available sources.[224] The position of citizen is likely to have been appealing, not only because it entailed significant social status but also because it—in the

with Augustus. If Caesar did indeed issue a command of this nature, it is possible that Augustus repeated it, as is suggested in Claudius' letter to the Alexandrians, P.Lond. 6.1912.87, where the Jewish community's right to uphold its own customs is specifically linked to the Augustan period.

[219] Barclay (1996), 62 and Pucci Ben Zeev (1998), 27–30. See, for instance, Flavius Josephus, *Antiquitates Iudaicae* 14.10.24 (259–61). See Delia (1991), 23–8 for the argument that the term *Ἀλεξανδρεύς* could be used in a similarly ambiguous way—as may be seen in Flavius Josephus, *Contra Apionem* 2.4 (39–40).

[220] Harker (2008), 214; Pucci Ben Zeev (1998), 29–30.

[221] Flavius Josephus, *Contra Apionem* 2.4 (37).

[222] e.g. by Barclay (1996), 63; Collins (2005), 91; Harker (2008), 214; Zangenberg (2013), 101–3.

[223] Zangenberg (2013), 98 gives the figure of between 120,000 and 180,000 Jewish residents. Delia (1988) sees this estimate as too high, since it would have amounted to about a third of the general population of Alexandria. Bremmer (2021), 248 cites an estimate of 10–20 per cent of the Alexandrian population, which would amount to 50,000–100,000 people.

[224] See, non-exhaustively, Barclay (1996), 66–9; Bremmer (2021), 248; Collins (2005), 91–2; Delia (1991), 27; Van der Horst (2003), 23–4; Ritter (2015), 89–100; Tcherikover (1959), 327 and 515 n. 90; Zangenberg (2013), 103; *contra* Gruen (2002), 75–8. See especially Flavius Josephus, *Contra Apionem* 2.6 (65–72), where it becomes clear that the anti-Jewish Apion actively argued against Jewish citizenship, which the author rebuts by pointing out that Egyptians were never granted Alexandrian citizenship, while Jews were. The use of the present indicative in the construction *si sunt cives* that is attributed to Apion is particularly interesting and suggests that Jewish claims of citizenship were at least not presented as absolutely untrue or impossible. For this, the use of a subjunctive (in the Latin) or a past tense (in the original Greek) might have been expected. Kasher (1985) and Smallwood (1976), 227–30 argue against the idea that Jewish Alexandrians held citizenship of the Greek *πόλις* but

case of Alexandria—came with important financial benefits: full Alexandrian citizens had been exempt from the Roman poll tax in the time of Augustus,[225] and indeed the fact that the majority of the city's Jewish community was very likely liable for taxation may well have been a cause for dissatisfaction.[226] The general consensus, though it has been phrased and framed in a variety of ways, is that Alexandrian Jews, rather than being citizens by default, were primarily organized in a semi-political, semi-ethnic governing body of their own, which in scholarship is often referred to as a *πολίτευμα*.[227] While this did not amount to full citizenship, it did come with several important privileges, including a degree of self-governance in the form of a *γερουσία* and the right to adhere to the ancestral Jewish customs.[228] Furthermore, it served to set the Jewish community apart from the Egyptian class of the city's population, which enjoyed far fewer rights and was frequently regarded with derision.

3.10.2 The origins and progression of the riots

It should be noted, however, that the political status of Alexandria's Jewish community was almost certainly controversial and unclear even in the first century CE. Throughout the available sources, both the question of citizenship and the

claim that they did hold civic rights as members of the Jewish *πολίτευμα*. See Petersen (2009), 134 for the argument that Jews at least 'conceived of themselves in terms of Alexandrian citizenship'.

225 Bremmer (2021), 249; Delia (1991), 30; Harker (2008), 212; Schäfer (1997), 136.

226 Harker (2008), 217–18 argues that Jews were exempt from the poll tax, while Barclay (1996), 49–50 maintains that the rate at which members of the Jewish community were taxed depended on their citizenship status. Schäfer (1997), 136 claims the same. That taxation was considered by the later tradition to have played some part in the conflict may be surmised from the *Acta Isidori*, recension C, line 29–30. See Musurillo (1954), 18–26. For the recent argument that the Roman reforms during the reign of Augustus may have caused many Jews to lose the more favourable tax rate they had enjoyed under the Ptolemies, see Czajkowski (2019[a]), 85 and Honigman (2021), 136–7.

227 Van der Horst (2002), 475; Kasher (1985), 356; Smallwood (1976), 225; Zangenberg (2013), 98–103. Barclay (1996), 65–6; Gruen (2002), 74–5; and Harker (2008), 213–14 discuss the debate surrounding the applicability of the term *πολίτευμα*, but ultimately agree that Jews formed their own semi-political group with specific privileges. For the argument that the existence of a Jewish *πολίτευμα* in Herakleopolis from the second century BCE onwards makes the existence of an Alexandrian Jewish *πολίτευμα* more probable, see Czajkowski (2019[a]), 82; Gruen (2002), 74–5; Harker (2012), 278 and Zangenberg (2013), 100.

228 Barclay (1996), 66; Harker (2008), 216–17; Petersen (2009), 132–4; Zangenberg (2013), 100–1. Petersen (2009), 134 poses the intriguing question whether all Alexandrian Jews, regardless of status, were members of the *πολίτευμα*, and argues that we ultimately cannot be certain, due to the fact that the available sources say very little about Jews who did not belong to the elite. Harker (2008), 213–14 and Zangenberg (2013), 100 suggest that the *πολίτευμα* did not, in fact, include all members of the Jewish community, as does Czajkowski (2019[a]), 85–6, who argues that it should be understood as a private association that was disconnected from political or religious self-governance, and was in fact not awarded any special privileges at all. Whether or not the self-governance of the Jewish community was linked to the *πολίτευμα*, the fact remains that privileges of this kind are repeatedly mentioned by the available sources. See Appendices 2.16 and 2.44, as well as Flavius Josephus, *Antiquitates Iudaicae* 14.7.2 (117), who mentions the significant authority of the ethnarch who preceded the *γερουσία*. See also Harker (2012), 278.

issue of religion repeatedly reappear, and these factors historically combined into not only strong debate but also violent outbursts.[229] While it has been argued that the riots that broke out in 38 CE were an extremely rare occurrence for Alexandria (and possibly the rest of the Roman world),[230] Philo's account suggests that tensions in the city had been building for some time,[231] and furthermore references a number of factors that contributed to their eventual eruption. On the one hand, he claims that Caligula became hostile towards the Jewish communities of his empire due to their refusal to acknowledge him as a god, and argues that the Greek Alexandrians therefore perceived the new emperor's ascension as the ideal opportunity to take action against a group against whom they already bore a grudge.[232] According to Philo, representatives of the city's Greek elite subsequently approached the Roman governor Aulus Avilius Flaccus and were apparently successful in convincing him to turn against the local Jewish community. It has been suggested that Flaccus was willing to go along with this because he feared that his less than friendly relationship with the new emperor might not just mean the end of his career but also put his life at risk.[233] This uncertainty made Flaccus particularly dependent on the leaders of the Greek faction, who were therefore able to persuade him that it was in his best interest to take their side: if they interceded with the emperor on his behalf, they might be able to strengthen his position. On the other hand, any complaint they might have made was very likely to have the opposite effect and prove to be the final nail in Flaccus' proverbial coffin. This threat appears to have been effective, and Philo claims that Flaccus proved unwilling to grant a fair hearing to Jews involved in legal disputes from this moment onward.[234]

The situation finally erupted into open violence when Agrippa I, King of Judea, visited Alexandria,[235] which seems to have been particularly aggravating to Greek Alexandrians for a number of reasons.[236] Firstly, as Philo himself points out, the presence of a Jewish king reminded the Alexandrians that the status of their city, the former royal capital of the Ptolemies, had been greatly diminished under Roman rule, whereas a group of people they saw as intruders appeared to

[229] For the suggestion that this confusion was at least in part due to a new Roman method of classifying the various inhabitants of Alexandria, see Avidov (2009), 172–4.

[230] Collins (2005), 87, who refers to Gruen (2002), 67–8.

[231] Philo of Alexandria, *Legatio ad Gaium* 120.

[232] Philo of Alexandria, *Legatio ad Gaium* 116–20.

[233] Feldman (1993), 114; Gruen (2002), 55; Smallwood (1976), 236.

[234] Philo of Alexandria, *In Flaccum* 20–4. While not related to religious affairs, this episode provides an interesting example of the effect negotiation by local power players could have on Roman administration.

[235] Philo of Alexandria, *In Flaccum* 25–43.

[236] For the suggestion that a large part of the anti-Jewish movement consisted of Egyptians, see Gruen (2002), 63–5 and Schäfer (1997), 144–5. See Bremmer (2021), 257 for the idea that mobs often contained members of the higher social classes and that these particular riots were likely instigated by members of the Alexandrian elite.

prosper.[237] These hostile feelings were very likely aggravated by the debate surrounding the civic status of members of the Jewish community: on the one hand, Alexandria no longer had a governing body of its own after its *βουλή* had been disbanded, presumably by Augustus,[238] while the Jews were allowed to maintain both a *γερουσία* and a degree of self-governance.[239] Even the various associations of the city, which were likely similar to Roman *collegia*, had been disbanded by Flaccus before he aligned himself with the Graeco-Alexandrian cause—although it is possible that the Jewish synagogues escaped this ban in one way or the other, given their prominent presence later in Philo's account.[240] Greek Alexandrians may therefore have believed that the Jewish community not only laid claim to privileges to which it had no right by asserting citizenship, but that they even surpassed the Greek elite of the city in status. In this context, the presence of Agrippa I only served to escalate tensions. Although Jewish rulers like Hyrcanus II and Herod may have come to the aid of Diaspora communities in other cases, in this instance Agrippa functioned not as a negotiator but as an involuntary incendiary. Non-Jewish Alexandrians viewed his visit as a provocation and as a manifestation of illegitimate Jewish claims. The royal procession through the city therefore quickly became the first target of the mob: they publicly insulted and derided the king by dressing a local man who was known for his mental disability in royal insignia, and by addressing him with the Aramaic word for 'lord'.[241] According to Philo, Flaccus failed to stop this mockery, which caused a further escalation of violence (although he likely exaggerates the governor's disinterest,

[237] Philo of Alexandria, *In Flaccum* 29. According to Josephus' citation, the anti-Jewish polemicist Apion made an interestingly opposing claim, which can be found in Flavius Josephus, *Contra Apionem* 2.11 (125) See also Smallwood (1976), 238.

[238] Barclay (1996), 49; Gambetti (2009), 57; Harker (2008), 218; Zangenberg (2013), 101. For the argument that the *βουλή* was abolished in the Ptolemaic period, see Czajkowski (2019[a]), 79. The reference to the *βουλή* in Claudius' letter to the Alexandrians (P.Lond. 6.1912.66–72) provides no conclusive evidence on the matter, but it does state clearly that Alexandria had no *βουλή* under any previous emperor. If any similar requests for reinstatement had already been made at an earlier stage, it is thus likely that they were denied—which is likely to have contributed to existing frustrations regarding the perceived preferential treatment of the Jewish community.

[239] For the argument that the Alexandrians had likewise maintained their *γερουσία*, although it had no political or administrative role, see Czajkowski (2019[a]), 80 n. 13. The request for a *βουλή* in P.Lond. 6.1912.66–72 further suggests that whichever degree of self-governance the Alexandrians had, it was not considered to be sufficient.

[240] Philo of Alexandria, *In Flaccum* 4. It should be noted that the term 'synagogue' is in this case anachronistic, and that our sources on the Alexandrian situation instead tend to refer to *προσευχαί*, or houses of prayer. These buildings would become the target of attacks during the 38 CE riots. See Czajkowski (2020), who further cautions against applying information about Jewish community buildings in Alexandria to other parts of the Diaspora. For Philo's attitudes on the non-Jewish associations in the city, see Seland (1996). For the possibility that Jewish groups could be recognized as associations by the Roman authorities and could thus be included in Flaccus' ban, see Czajkowski (2019[a]), who makes the argument that Philo was actively arguing for the legitimacy of Jewish organizations and suggests that he used Roman legal language to do so. Importantly, Claudius' insistence that the religious rites and customs of the Jewish community should be respected suggests that he, at least, did not consider these aspects of Jewish community life to be included in the measure. See P.Lond. 6.1912.82–8.

[241] Philo of Alexandria, *In Flaccum* 36–40.

see section 3.10.3). The attention of the mob now turned to the synagogues, which they desecrated by decorating them with statues of the emperor, and in some cases destroyed them completely.[242] Philo describes these events as an attack on Jewish ancestral customs, and adds that things went even further: within a few days after the attacks on the synagogues, Flaccus issued an order stripping Jews of their legal protection and political rights, declaring them to be *ξένοι καὶ ἐπήλυδες*, foreigners and aliens.[243] According to the author, this led to a final increase in violence: the Jewish community was driven together into a single district of the city,[244] Jewish houses and shops were plundered,[245] and people were tortured and killed.[246] In some cases, the torments described by Philo seem to be related to the issue of citizenship: members of the Jewish *γερουσία*, he claims, were punished 'as if they were Egyptians', rather than as 'free men and citizens'.[247] In other cases, however, the actions of the mob appear to have been more religiously motivated, and we find stories of women being forced to eat pork to see if they were Jewish.[248]

Judging by Philo's account of the events of 38 CE, then, the causes of the Alexandrian riots appear to have been both complex and multifaceted. While it has been argued that there is 'no evidence, allusion, external hint, or context of any kind' to support the view that the issue of citizenship played a part in the violence,[249] its terminology, ambiguous as it may be, occurs too often in the various available sources to be otherwise explained. This is true not only in Philo's version of events[250] but also in the works of Josephus, who repeatedly cites hostile accusations that Jews gained their position in Alexandria by unlawful means,[251] and makes a great point of refuting his adversary Apion's own claim to citizenship of the city.[252] Even setting aside the issue of full Alexandrian citizenship, however, it is clear that the origin of the riots was strongly linked to disputes about political status.

242 Philo of Alexandria, *In Flaccum* 41–53 and *Legatio ad Gaium* 132–7.

243 Philo of Alexandria, *In Flaccum* 53–4. Gambetti (2009) makes the argument that only Jews who lived outside the city's overwhelmingly Jewish district Δ were deprived of their legal status (which in her mind included tax benefits) and were declared foreigners, according to a precedent provided by Caligula in 37 CE. This line of thinking is strongly dependent on the interpretation of one of the *Acta Alexandrinorum*, which is known as the *Gerousia Acta* or P.Yale 2.107, and while such a theory does explain why Jews were driven to a single district, the highly fragmentary text simply does not contain enough evidence to prove that the events described by Gambetti actually took place. The text of the *Gerousia Acta* may be found in Gambetti (2009), 94–101.

244 Philo of Alexandria, *In Flaccum* 55 and *Legatio ad Gaium* 124.

245 Philo of Alexandria, *In Flaccum* 56–60.

246 Philo of Alexandria, *In Flaccum* 65–96.

247 Philo of Alexandria, *In Flaccum* 80.

248 For this notable parallel to the sacrifice tests used in trials against Christians, see Philo of Alexandria, *In Flaccum* 96. The argument that this event belongs not to the immediate context of the show trials in which it is described, but rather to the preceding riots, is made in Bremmer (2021), 256 and Van der Horst (2003), 185. See Van der Horst (2003), 186 for other references to similar 'tests' in being applied to Jews in the context of the Maccabean revolt.

249 Gambetti (2009), 248–9.

250 Philo even alludes to the issue of citizenship in the *Legatio ad Gaium* 194, which is otherwise rather unclear about the circumstances that prompted the riots.

251 Flavius Josephus, *Contra Apionem* 2.4 (33 and 38) and 2.6 (65).

252 Flavius Josephus, *Contra Apionem* 2.3 (29–32).

The comparatively large degree of self-governance and status afforded to members of the Jewish community, as we have seen, likely inspired hostility, and thus contributed to the outbreak of the violence. The socio-political status of the Jewish community, however, also became heavily entwined with issues of religious identity. Participating in the proper cults in the appropriate way became a clear symbol of being a 'true' Alexandrian, and a distinguishing feature in determining who 'belonged' and who did not. The answer to this question was certainly partially political and involved visible signs of loyalty to Rome in the form of participation in emperor worship,[253] but it was also distinctly religious, as is demonstrated by the aggression of non-Jewish Alexandrians towards the synagogues of the city. The link between civic status and religion is, however, most concisely presented in a passage ascribed to the anti-Jewish polemicist Apion (see also section 3.2), who asks the question:

> [...], *quomodo ergo, inquit, si sunt cives, eosdem deos quos Alexandrini non colunt?*[254]
>
> [...] so why, [Apion] says, if [Jews] are citizens, do they not worship the same gods as the Alexandrians?

The causes of the 38 CE riots, then, were firmly embedded in Alexandrian conceptions of both socio-political relations and religion,[255] and it is important to consider the strongly localized nature of the conflict when discussing the measures taken by the various Roman authorities in response.

3.10.3 The role of the Roman authorities

When reading Philo's account of the Alexandrian riots, it is easy to see the Roman governor Aulus Avilius Flaccus as the great villain of the story, who went along

[253] See McLaren (2005), 275. It must be noted that emperor worship, in itself, combines aspects of the religious and the political. While this is not the place to discuss Roman attitudes towards the so-called imperial cult in detail, a few brief remarks about Caligula's attitude towards the practice must be made. As we have seen, Philo cites Caligula's self-deification as one of the causes for the Alexandrian riots in Philo of Alexandria, *Legatio ad Gaium* 116–20. While Philo presents this as an act of unparalleled madness, one might tentatively point towards the Hellenistic origins of the Roman ruler cult, as discussed in Rives (2007), 149, which meant that, like many cities in the eastern parts of the Empire, Alexandria had a tradition of worshipping its leaders. For this reason, Caligula's endorsement of his personal cult, which was likely more explicit than that of his predecessors, may have fallen on especially fertile ground in this part of Roman world, and could potentially have been seen as an indication that traditional Alexandrian religious practices were viewed favourably by the Roman authorities. The fact that Claudius later felt the need to reject divine honours (see P.Lond. 6.1912, 48–51) may also point in this direction, and supports the idea that the issue of emperor worship did indeed play a part in the disturbances in Alexandria. It is especially telling that Claudius rejects the proposed cult because he does not wish to be 'offensive towards [his] contemporaries'.

[254] Flavius Josephus, *Contra Apionem* 2.6 (65).

[255] For the idea that it was precisely the dual identity of certain members of the Jewish community that caused offence, see Barclay (2007), 204–5.

with Alexandrian anti-Jewish sentiments in order to protect his own interests and safeguard his position.[256] Despite the viciousness of Philo's invective, however, it becomes clear even in *In Flaccum* that the governor's attitude was chiefly reactive and likely aimed at maintaining peace and quiet in his province, where he found himself increasingly under strain. As established, the safeguarding of public order was considered to be the primary task of a Roman governor for the duration of his appointment, and while Flaccus certainly seems to have failed, this is unlikely to have been for lack of trying.[257] Flaccus' efforts to disband the clubs and associations of Alexandria in his early years in the city should likely be seen as an attempt to prevent further disturbances after a period of unrest,[258] which shows that he was at some point aware of the potential dangers and willing to take unpopular decisions in an attempt to keep the peace. During the riots of 38 CE, he likewise seems to have taken measures that, even when seen through the hostile lens of Philo's writings, could be seen as conciliatory, or at least protective. In a brief aside, Philo remarks that the governor at some point during the riots invited the leaders of the various factions and made attempts to resolve the matter through negotiation.[259] The fact that Flaccus gave orders to search Jewish homes for weapons may likewise be interpreted as a safety measure, intended to prevent increasingly violent clashes.[260] Some of Flaccus' other measures, however, are less easy to interpret. While Philo accuses Flaccus of failing to react to the insults aimed at Agrippa I during his visit to the city, it has been argued that the measure that declared Jews to be 'foreigners and aliens' was originally meant as an expulsion order intended to remove unwanted, disruptive elements from the city—which was hardly an uncommon response to rioting and unrest, as the repeated expulsions of diviners from Rome has shown. This measure may then have been misinterpreted by the Greek faction, who used it as an excuse to turn on the Jewish community.[261] It is also possible that this measure should be seen as a concession to the wishes of the Greek Alexandrians, and while the decision ultimately

[256] For the argument that the existence of this pact is difficult to prove, see Harker (2008), 12.

[257] Harker (2008), 13.

[258] Philo of Alexandria, *In Flaccum* 4. See also Smallwood 236 n. 64 for the suggestion that the disbanding of the *collegia* was the direct result of earlier unrest caused by Isidorus, one of the leaders of the 38 CE riots, and his followers.

[259] Philo of Alexandria, *In Flaccum* 76. The importance of this passage has been astutely remarked upon by Gruen (2002), 59.

[260] Philo of Alexandria, *In Flaccum* 86–90.

[261] Harker (2008), 13. Barclay (1996), 54 and 66 makes the argument that Flaccus' order did in fact target the political status of the Jewish community, but likewise suggests that this was taken as a sign that the it was no longer protected by the Roman authorities. However, it has been argued that it was not within the governor's powers to change the status and privileges of specific groups without imperial approval, for which see Gambetti (2009), 176–80. If the measure was indeed intended as a retraction of Jewish rights, it is therefore possible that Caligula played some role in the affair, although it seems unlikely that he took the initiative. It should also be noted that Philo's description of these events is far from clear, and therefore makes it difficult to understand the exact status of the measure and the intention behind it. See Bremmer (2021), 254.

sparked more violence, it might originally have been intended to prevent further escalation—albeit to the clear disadvantage of the Jewish community. The corporal punishment of several members of the Jewish *γερουσία* has at times been interpreted in a similar way.[262] In neither case, however, can Flaccus be seen as a clear co-instigator of the riots, in spite of any speculation about his anti-Jewish sentiments.[263] Instead, it is likely that the governor made at least some effort to react to the circumstances in his city and prevent the violence from becoming unmanageable. Ultimately, however, his attempts at pacification failed, and it is likely that Caligula ordered his arrest for this very reason.[264]

Due to these escalating hostilities, it had become unlikely that the conflict between Greek and Jewish inhabitants of Alexandria would be resolved locally, and so the matter was referred to Rome (Appendix 2.46).[265] According to Philo, this was not the first time that the Jewish community had attempted to obtain imperial assistance, as he reports that they had sent a written petition with Agrippa I only shortly before.[266] Agrippa's influence, however, in this case proved of little use. After a seemingly positive first meeting, Caligula kept the delegations waiting while he himself travelled,[267] and before a second meeting could take place, an incident occurred in the city of Jamnia that put the mission of the Jewish delegation from Alexandria in jeopardy: the local Greek population had erected various statues in Caligula's honour, which the local Jewish community had subsequently destroyed.[268] Caligula then ordered that an enormous statue of himself should be placed in the Temple in Jerusalem (Appendix 2.47), possibly as a punishment for what he saw as an act of profound hostility, and perhaps even rebellion.[269] This imperial order in turn led to deep anxiety among Jewish communities throughout the eastern Mediterranean, and a flurry of hasty negotiations followed. At the request of various Jewish delegations, Caligula's representative Petronius, as well as Agrippa I and his brother Aristobulus, attempted to

[262] Gruen (2002), 59.

[263] It is unclear whether the description in Philo of Alexandria, *De Somniis* 2.18 (123–32) of a Roman governor attempting to force the Jewish community to abandon their religious customs refers to Flaccus. It has not been interpreted as such by Feldman (1993), 95, and in any case the passage is too vague to allow for speculation about any potential legal measures.

[264] Gruen (2002), 57 and Harker (2008), 13.

[265] The exact date of the two delegations remains in doubt. See Harker (2008), 14 for the suggestion that they left Alexandria in the winter of 38 CE.

[266] Philo of Alexandria, *Legatio ad Gaium* 179.

[267] Philo of Alexandria, *Legatio ad Gaium* 181. See Harker (2008), 17–18 for the suggestion that Caligula was planning to visit Alexandria himself.

[268] Flavius Josephus, *Antiquitates Iudaicae* 18.8.1–9 (257–309); Philo of Alexandria, *Legatio ad Gaium* 200–348. For the possible role of the Roman procurator Herennius Capito in these events, see Eck (2011), 66–8.

[269] McLaren (2005), 265. For the argument that Caligula was simply ignorant of Jewish religious practices, see Gruen (2012), 144. Given the close relationship between Caligula and Agrippa I, one might ask if this interpretation is truly likely.

dissuade the emperor from this course of action. In the end, however, the construction of the statue is said to have been prevented only by Caligula's death.[270]

These tensions certainly did not make for a pleasant atmosphere when Caligula finally received the respective Alexandrian delegations. According to Philo, the emperor mocked and insulted the Jewish emissaries at every turn, but despite these ominous signs nothing came of his evident hostility: Caligula was murdered before he could reach a verdict or take concrete action to resolve the crisis in Alexandria to the advantage of either party.[271] According to the available accounts of the Alexandrian delegations, then, Caligula ultimately contributed little (if anything) to the resolution of the violence, and very likely became involved only after local attempts proved ineffective. While it has been suggested that Flaccus would not have had the authority the change the legal status of the Jewish community without imperial approval, as he appears to have done when he declared Jews to be 'foreigners and aliens',[272] this is ultimately not sufficient to prove the alternative argument that the emperor became involved at an earlier stage, and that Flaccus was simply following his orders. This theory, which has been championed by Sandra Gambetti, holds that Caligula himself had at an earlier date issued a decree that determined that the privileges of the Jewish community would henceforth be limited to those who lived in the city's traditionally Jewish district Δ, and that everyone who lived outside of this quarter would lose their right of residence,[273] thereby making the rights of the Jewish community 'territorial and not personal'.[274] Notably, however, such a measure goes entirely unmentioned by Philo: Caligula may serve as the primary antagonist of the *Legatio* (as is to be expected in a work dealing primarily with the two delegations to Rome rather than the origins of the Alexandrian riots), but even then the author never insists on his personal intervention before the outbreak of the riots, as we might have expected him to do if he was at this point in time indeed finally 'free to openly accuse' the emperor.[275] Likewise, his claims that the Alexandrian mob responded

[270] This version of the story is told in Flavius Josephus, *Antiquitates Iudaicae* 18.8.9 (305–9) and *Bellum Iudaicum* 2.10.5 (199–203). See Gruen (2012), 137–8 for the suggestion that this course of events seems all too convenient.

[271] Philo of Alexandria, *Legatio ad Gaium* 349–73. See also Flavius Josephus, *Antiquitates Iudaicae* 18.8.1 (257–60), who claims that Caligula became incredibly angry upon meeting the Jewish delegation, refused to listen to their version of events in full, and promised to punish them at a later date. This promised punishment apparently never took place. See Harker (2008), 18 for the suggestion that Caligula ruled in favour of the Greek Alexandrians. A possible reference to this may be found in the historically dubious P.Giss.Lit. 4.7 iii.27–35, the relevant part of which may be read in Tcherikover and Fuks (1960), 64–6 (no. 155). If Caligula did indeed rule in favour of the Greek Alexandrians, however, nothing appears to have come of this ruling.

[272] Gambetti (2009), 176–80. See also Bremmer (2021), 254 and, implicitly, Zangenberg (2013), 105.

[273] Gambetti (2009), 149; 172–82.

[274] Gambetti (2009), 243.

[275] See Gambetti (2009), 6, where the author also makes the argument that Philo's account of the riots in *In Flaccum* has been unfairly privileged over that in the *Legatio ad Gaium* and suggests that the latter text places the blame for the events in Alexandria squarely on Caligula.

to what they perceived as a favourable political climate in no way imply that any direct incentive to do so was given by the central authorities. Rather than being based on Philo's contemporary accounts, then, the idea that Flaccus was simply enforcing Caligula's orders finds its foundation in the so-called *Gerousia Acta* (also known as P.Yale 2.107), which is commonly considered to be part of the *Acta Alexandrinorum*.[276] This text is thought to depict a trial between Greek and Jewish Alexandrians before Caligula, in which the Jewish delegation's loss ultimately formed the legal basis for the (geographical) restriction of the Jewish community's rights.[277] As a source, however, P.Yale 2.107 is highly problematic, and the text is not only extremely fragmentary but also contains various serious anachronisms that severely limit its credibility.[278] In addition, we might ask ourselves why Caligula would ultimately order Flaccus' arrest if there was no serious animosity between the two and the governor had done nothing more than enforce imperial orders.[279] By contrast, if Flaccus made his declaration that Jews were 'foreigners and aliens' without imperial approval, this may have further contributed to the accusations of maladministration levied against him.

Up to this point in time, then, it is likely that the involvement of both central and local authorities in the Alexandrian riots was primarily reactive and strongly rooted in local events and concerns. In particular, disagreements about various rights and privileges and the question of who 'belonged' in both a socio-political and religious sense played an important role. The circumstances surrounding the Alexandrian riots also demonstrate, however, that connections between various Jewish communities were not always employed to such positive effect as our sources from the republican and early imperial periods suggest. While it is true that Agrippa I served as a negotiator in the case of Caligula's intended desecration of the Temple, and various Jewish communities requested the help of the emperor's representative to prevent this measure from being carried out, Philo repeatedly expresses fear that trouble in one city (be it Alexandria, Jerusalem, Rome, or Jamnia) could lead to difficulties for other Jewish communities as well.[280] If positive precedent could be disseminated between the Jewish communities of various cities, the same thing could happen to measures that were detrimental to their well-being.

[276] See Harker (2008), 195–6 under 'P.Giss.lit. 4.7' for the history of this text and the various names by which it is referenced in scholarship. The text may be found in Gambetti (2009), 94–101, with an older version in Musurillo (1954), 8–17.

[277] Gambetti (2009), 136 and 149.

[278] Harker (2008), 35–7.

[279] Seland (2010). For Flaccus' arrest and trial, see Philo of Alexandria, *In Flaccum* 108 and further. Philo's phrasing in this instance is interesting. He claims that Flaccus was arrested *ἕνεκά* [...] *τῶν Ἰουδαίων*, 'because of the Jews'. See *In Flaccum* 116.

[280] See, for instance, Philo of Alexandria, *In Flaccum* 47 and *Legatio ad Gaium* 120; 188–206 and 370.

3.11 The Reign of Claudius: Limited Support

When Caligula was assassinated in 41 CE, the troubles in Alexandria were far from resolved, and violence in the city even erupted again soon after his death.[281] This meant that Claudius, as the new emperor, was confronted with the competing Alexandrian factions almost immediately after his ascension.[282] Claudius appears to have seen the urgency of the situation, and promptly responded to the requests made by both delegations (Appendix 2.48). Two separate versions of his ruling are known to us,[283] one of which is presented in Flavius Josephus' *Antiquitates Iudaicae*,[284] while the other survives as part of the papyrological record.[285] Both versions of the text are plainly responding to an embassy,[286] but otherwise they contain a number of significant differences in their presentation of Claudius' decisions.

3.11.1 Claudius' letter to the Alexandrians

The text of Claudius' letter as presented by Josephus seems to exhibit a benevolent attitude towards the Alexandrian Jewish faction, placing the blame of the riots almost entirely on the shoulders of the Greek Alexandrians. The text emphasizes that the Jewish community had been present in Alexandria since the earliest days of the city's existence, and that its members held citizenship equal to Greek Alexandrians. The letter concludes by stating that the privileges the community had held before 38 CE should be restored, and that both parties should take care to prevent further disturbances:

[281] Flavius Josephus, *Antiquitates Iudaicae* 19.5.2 (278). See Harker (2008), 18 for the suggestion that this new outbreak of violence may have been a reaction to Caligula ruling against Alexandria's Jewish community.

[282] It is unclear whether the two delegations sent to Caligula were still in Rome at this time, or whether new embassies were dispatched. Gruen (2002), 78–9 argues for the former, but adds that the Alexandrian Jews likely sent another delegation. A similar view is held by Harker (2008), 18–19. Claudius' letter to the Alexandrians, P.Lond. 6.1912.90–1 suggests that two Jewish embassies, likely with competing views, were present. See Gambetti (2009), 224 n. 38 for an overview of the various theories on this subject, and Schäfer (1997), 151 for the view that one Jewish embassy was more radical, whereas the other was more moderate. See Harker (2008), 26 for the idea that the text of Claudius' letter was summarized by a copyist and is therefore now more obscure on this point than was originally the case.

[283] For the suggestion that Josephus' version in fact reflects an earlier pronouncement made by Claudius that was subsequently revoked, possibly due to the fact that violence in Alexandria had once again broken out, see Pucci Ben Zeev (1998), 309–13. This, however, seems unlikely due to time constraints, and does not resolve several problematic aspects of the letter. See Gruen (2002), 82; Harker (2008), 19.

[284] Flavius Josephus, *Antiquitates Iudaicae* 19.5.2 (279–85).

[285] P.Lond. 6.1912, more commonly known as *Claudius' letter to the Alexandrians*.

[286] The Josephus-version of the letter claims that the petition was made by the kings Agrippa and Herod, while the papyrus makes mention of the various delegations from Alexandria itself.

βούλομαι μηδὲν διὰ τὴν Γαΐου παραφροσύνην τῶν δικαίων τῷ Ἰουδαίων ἔθνει παραπεπτωκέναι, φυλάσσεσθαι δ᾽ αὐτοῖς καὶ τὰ πρότερον δικαιώματα ἐμμένουσι τοῖς ἰδίοις ἔθεσιν, ἀμφοτέροις τε διακελεύομαι τοῖς μέρεσι πλείστην ποιήσασθαι πρόνοιαν, ὅπως μηδεμία ταραχὴ γένηται μετὰ τὸ προτεθῆναί μου τὸ διάταγμα.[287]

It is therefore my wish that none of the rights of the Jewish people fall away because of Gaius' [Caligula's] madness, and that the rights which they previously held be preserved for them, including the right to abide by their own customs. And I order both parties to apply great caution, so that no disturbance occurs after the issuing of my order.

The authenticity of this version of Claudius' letter has often been doubted, and with good reason. The fact that the letter elsewhere appears to confirm general Jewish citizenship of Alexandria is generally considered to be not just dubious, but even a likely falsification on the part of either Josephus himself or one of his sources.[288] Likewise, it is highly implausible that Claudius would openly refer to his predecessor as insane in an official missive.[289] This is not to say, however, that Josephus' version of Claudius' ruling should be dismissed out of hand. It has been astutely remarked that only the cited portion of the letter actually seems to contain Claudius' concrete orders, as is indicated by the customary *βούλομαι*. Everything before that, including the reference to full Jewish citizenship, may be interpreted as a summary of the arguments brought forth by the Jewish delegation.[290] This would support the idea that Claudius in fact only restored the rights the Jewish community had held before 38 CE, including the use of their own religious customs, but did not grant the entire Jewish community full Alexandrian citizenship.

However, while the gist of Josephus' version of Claudius' letter may not have been too far from the truth, it remains likely that it is ultimately a heavily abbreviated and edited version of the emperor's real reply.[291] The text as presented on the papyrus known as P.Lond. 6.1912, while it is very likely abbreviated as well,[292] almost certainly approaches the original missive more closely. It not only addresses the conflict between Greek and Jewish Alexandrians, but it also deals with other issues relevant to the well-being of the city, such as questions about Claudius' personal cult and the possible re-institution of the Alexandrian *βουλή*.[293]

287 Flavius Josephus, *Antiquitates Iudaicae* 19.5.2 (285).

288 Gruen (2002), 82; Harker (2008), 27; Schäfer (1997), 149; Tcherikover and Fuks (1957), 70 n. 45; Tcherikover (1959), 411–12.

289 Harker (2008), 27; Schwartz (1990), 103–4.

290 Schwartz (1990), 101–2. See also Pucci Ben Zeev (1998), 316–18.

291 Harker (2008), 26; Schwartz (1990), 99–106; Tcherikover and Fuks (1957), 70 n. 45. For the idea that we are instead dealing with two separate communications by Claudius, see Pucci Ben Zeev (1998), 305–26.

292 Harker (2008), 25–6.

293 P.Lond. 6.1912.48–51 and 66–72. The request for a personal cult in Claudius' honour was denied because the emperor did not believe it to be appropriate for a mortal man to claim honours that were normally reserved for the gods. In the case of the *βουλή*, Claudius made no formal

While these issues may appear to be entirely separate from the 38 CE riots, as we have seen they both played a part in the outbreak of the violence. The papyrus letter thus goes beyond reprimanding both parties for their behaviour, instead addressing the fundamental causes of dissatisfaction in Alexandria. Even the passage that deals directly with the Alexandrian Jewish community exhibits little of the blatant favouritism that seems to be present in Josephus' version of the letter. Instead, Claudius appears to blame both parties in equal measure:

> *Τῆς δὲ πρὸς Ἰουδαίους ταραχῆς καὶ στάσεως, μᾶλλον δ' εἰ χρὴ τὸ ἀληθὲς εἰπεῖν τοῦ πολέμου, πότεροι μὲν αἴτιοι κατέστησαν [...] ὅμως οὐκ ἐβουλήθην ἀκριβῶς ἐξελένξαι, ταμιευόμενος ἐμ̣αυτῶι κατὰ τῶν πάλειν ἀρξαμένων ὀργὴν ἀμεταμέλητον· ἁπλῶς δὲ προσαγορεύωι ὅτι ἂν μὴ καταπαύσηται τὴν ὀλέθριον ὀργὴν ταύτην κατ' ἀλλήλων αὐθάδιον ἐγβιασθήσομαι δῖξαι ὗον ἐστιν ἡγεμὼν φιλάνθροπος εἰς ὀργὴν δικαίαν μεταβεβλημένος.*[294]
>
> Regarding the trouble and strife, or rather, if it is necessary to tell the truth, the war, with the Jews, I was unwilling to establish exactly which party was responsible for it, [...] though I keep within myself an unrelenting anger against whosoever starts the conflict again: and I tell you plainly that if you do not stop with this deadly and stubborn strife against each other, I will be forced to show how a loving princeps responds when driven to righteous anger.

After reprimanding both sides of the argument and insisting on their peaceful behaviour in the future, Claudius acknowledges that the Jewish community has been present in Alexandria for a long time. He tells the Alexandrians that he, like Augustus, has formally allowed Jews to practise their ancestral customs, and charges them not to disrupt these rites in any way.[295] Claudius here not only refers to his use of precedent, but also to the fact that he came to his decision *διακούσας ἀμφοτέρων*, after having heard both sides—a clear allusion to his conversation with the various delegations.[296]

So far, the contents of P.Lond. 6.1912 are very similar to Claudius' pronouncements as represented by Josephus, even if the tone is markedly different.[297] In a clear departure from Josephus' account, however, Claudius continues by reprimanding Alexandria's Jewish community, telling them to 'bargain for nothing more than they previously had' (*μηδὲν πλήωι ὧν πρότερον ἔσχον περιεργάζεσθαι*).[298]

pronouncement but instead promised an investigation. In the end, the *βουλή* was only reinstated in the Severan period. See Czajkowski (2019[a]), 79.

[294] P.Lond. 6.1912.73–82. For a critical edition of this passage, see Tcherikover and Fuks (1960), 41 (no. 153).

[295] P.Lond. 6.1912.83–7.

[296] P.Lond. 6.1912.87–8.

[297] See Gambetti (2009), 233 for the contrasting view that the papyrus text and Josephus' version are diametrically opposed to each other.

[298] P.Lond. 6.1912.89–90.

He then encourages them not to infringe on the games presided over by the gymnasiarchs or kosmetes (μηδὲ ἐπισπαίειν γυμνασιαρχικοῖς ἢ κοσμητικοῖς ἀγῶσει), before reminding them that they should be content to enjoy their privileges ἐν ἀλλοτρίᾳ πόλει, in a city not their own.[299] The meaning of this passage has proved to be a source of debate, particularly due to disagreements regarding the interpretation of the verb ἐπισπαίειν (to intrude). While this has widely been taken to mean that Claudius banned Jewish participation in these games to prevent Jewish youths from entering the ἐφηβεία, and thereby from gaining Alexandrian citizenship,[300] others have instead suggested that Claudius' remark was instead intended to prevent Jews from attending the games *en masse* in order to provoke a riot.[301] This interpretation, however, does not take the immediate context of the phrase into account: why would Claudius incorporate an instruction to stay away from public festivals right in the middle of his assertion that members of the Jewish community should be satisfied with the rights they already had if there was no connection between these remarks?[302] Claudius' insistence that the Jews of Alexandria were living in 'a city not their own' furthermore implies a separation between the Jewish community and the city of Alexandria, which once again seems to be related to the issue of citizenship.[303] This passage of Claudius' letter therefore confirms that the issue of Jewish citizenship likely played a part in the origin of the 38 CE riots, but some details of his ruling nevertheless remain unclear: certainly, Alexandrian Jews who had not enjoyed citizenship before 38 CE were now banned from obtaining this status, but Claudius' insistence that the Jewish community was to maintain the privileges it had previously enjoyed leaves open the possibility that those who already had Alexandrian citizenship were allowed to keep it.[304]

In his letter, then, Claudius gave both parties reasons to be satisfied, and reasons not to be.[305] He promised the Greek Alexandrians an investigation into

[299] P.Lond. 6.1912.92–5.

[300] Barclay (1996), 71; Bremmer (2021), 252; Harker (2008), 22 and 185–6; Smallwood (1976), 234; Tcherikover and Fuks (1960), 53 (no. 153); Zangenberg (2013), 103 and 106. Another reference to a Jewish Alexandrian participating in the ephebate may be found in Tcherikover and Fuks (1960), 29–33 (no. 151). For the nature of the ephebate, see Laes and Strubbe (2014), 104. Delia (1991), 71–88 argues that the ephebate was not in itself a requirement for Alexandrian citizenship, although it was of great social significance, and Egyptians were specifically excluded from participation.

[301] Gruen (2002), 80–1; Kasher (1985), 314–21. Kasher's analysis rejects the reading ἐπισπαίειν and is instead based on the older ἐπισπαίρειν (to be alarmed). In doing so, however, he seems to unduly stretch the meaning of the verb, which is in any case exceedingly rare.

[302] P.Lond. 6.1912.89–90 and 94–5. See also Schäfer (1997), 151.

[303] Kasher (1985), 325–6 takes this phrase to mean that Claudius regarded Alexandria as his personal property, over which he should have the final say. This interpretation, however, seems ill suited to the preceding lines, which all appear to deal with the position of the Jewish community within the city. If we follow this reading, the remark would furthermore hold equally true for Greek Alexandrians, which makes it difficult to explain why Claudius' comment is specifically directed at the Alexandrian Jews.

[304] *Contra* Barclay (1996), 59–60.

[305] For a similar argument, see Harker (2008), 21–2. An indication that non-Jewish Alexandrians were dissatisfied with Claudius' judgement may be found in the *Acta Isidori*, one of the *Acta*

the possible re-institution of their *βουλή*, which would in the end not have the desired result,[306] and accepted a number of the honours they offered him and his family—although he notably declined a personal cult in his honour. All this had the added benefit of preventing further violent behaviour towards the Jewish community being perpetrated in his name. Alexandrian Jews, on the other hand, were given the right to adhere to their ancestral customs and the promise of imperial protection for their religious rites, but they could not expand their claim to citizenship and were banned from bringing in their compatriots from either Egypt or Syria to support their cause.[307] Claudius' efforts to restore law and order in Alexandria, then, are much more substantial than a simple order to cease hostilities: they address many of the fundamental political and religious causes of the 38 CE riots, and are founded in pre-existing laws and privileges, thereby increasing their perceived legitimacy. The emperor thus presented a potential solution that was firmly rooted both in local circumstances and in the wishes of the different parties involved.

3.11.2 To the entire world?

Claudius' reference to Jews from Egypt and Syria, however, also demonstrates his awareness of the connections between various Diaspora communities, and of the ease with which conflicts like the one in Alexandria could spread. The existence of these transregional ties was in all likelihood already familiar to the Roman authorities due to the earlier interventions of the rulers of Judea on behalf of Diaspora communities,[308] and the scope of their potential significance had certainly become obvious from Caligula's attempt to have his effigy placed in the Jerusalem Temple and the widespread outrage that followed. According to Josephus' account of the Alexandrian riots, Claudius therefore issued a second proclamation closely related to his first, this time directed *εἰς τὴν ἄλλην οἰκουμένην*, to the rest of the inhabited world (Appendix 2.49).[309] The missive granted Jewish communities throughout the empire the same rights that had previously been confirmed for the Alexandrian Jews: they would be allowed to

Alexandrinorum. The text may be found in Musurillo (1954), 18–26, and contains a description of the emperor being remarkably pro-Jewish (possibly even Jewish himself) and of him having had one of the Alexandrian delegates executed.

[306] The Alexandrian *βουλή* would not be reinstated until the Severan period. See Czajkowski (2019[a]), 79.

[307] P.Lond. 6.1912.96–8. This may be the reason why Josephus' version of the letter is said to have been addressed to both Alexandria and Syria, as argued by Pucci Ben Zeev (1998), 313. Syria may have also been included because of the disturbances surrounding the construction of Caligula's statue in the Temple in that region, in which Petronius as legate of Syria played a major part.

[308] Compare Rives (2009), 106–11.

[309] Flavius Josephus, *Antiquitates Iudaicae* 19.5.3 (286–91).

maintain their πάτρια ἔθη without hindrance,[310] so long as they treated their non-Jewish neighbours with respect—a clear sign that the emperor may have feared another outbreak of riots like the ones that had plagued Alexandria.[311] Claudius' motivations for this decision once again appear to have been rooted in negotiation and precedent. Not only does he indicate that his decision was prompted by a request made by Herod II and Agrippa I, both of whom had also played a part in preventing the desecration of the Temple under the rule of Caligula, he also expresses his unwillingness to change the policies previously established by Augustus, not just in the case of Jewish communities but also for the Greek cities of the eastern Mediterranean. The contents of this missive at first glance seem so far-reaching that they have been considered inauthentic by a number of authors, but ultimately the document is mostly accepted as genuine.[312] We should be careful, however, not to ascribe a landmark-status to Claudius' proclamation out of hand. It has been rightly remarked that this measure was not entirely innovative, but rather collects the decisions that had previously been made on a city-to-city basis by Augustus in one coherent proclamation.[313] In addition, Paul Trebilco is very likely correct in suggesting that Claudius' measure in practice probably amounted to nothing more than a general statement of goodwill: there is no mention of concrete behaviours that are allowed (or forbidden), and no punishment for those who went against the emperor's will appears to have been established.[314]

While Claudius' measure was certainly of great value to Jewish communities as a possible precedent, it proved far from effective in practice. Soon after Claudius had issued his confirmation of Jewish rights,[315] the Greek inhabitants of the city of Dora placed a statue of the emperor in the local Jewish synagogue.[316] According to Josephus' account, King Agrippa I was incensed by what he saw as a violation of his ancestral laws, and approached the Roman governor of Syria Publius Petronius with his complaint—apparently citing Claudius' missives to Alexandria in the process.[317] Petronius then sternly rebuked the perpetrators, likewise referring to Claudius' previous orders and confirming that everyone should practise their own religion (ἑκάστους τὰ ἴδια ἔθη θρησκεύειν; Appendix 2.51).[318] He also warned lower magistrates that they should take strong action if any similar events

[310] Later in the same passage, the phrase τοὺς ἰδίους δὲ νόμους is used.

[311] Smallwood (1976), 247 argues that this was the main objective of this proclamation.

[312] For an overview, see Pucci Ben Zeev (1998), 333.

[313] Rajak (2002^b), 316. For a similar argument, see Pucci Ben Zeev (1998), 342. Rives (2009), 110 instead describes this measure as a climax of the Roman tendency to treat various Jewish communities as 'a single geographically dispersed people'.

[314] Trebilco (1991), 10. A similar argument is made by Rajak (2002^b), 317, who calls the proclamation 'a fine-sounding verbal gesture'.

[315] For the date of these events, see Pucci Ben Zeev (1998), 344 and 347.

[316] Flavius Josephus, *Antiquitates Iudaicae* 19.6.3 (300–11).

[317] Exactly which letters are meant is unclear—see Pucci Ben Zeev (1998), 354.

[318] It is unlikely that Petronius is referring to Jewish citizenship of Dora. See Pucci Ben Zeev (1998), 354–5.

occurred again, lest it be thought that they had consented to the local population going against the emperor's orders. The Jewish community of Dora was likewise warned not to retaliate, again with a reference to Claudius' letters to Alexandria. The governor's missive cited by Josephus thus once again contains the familiar elements of appealing to precedent and negotiations between various levels of government, but it is most significant for what it says about the enforcement of Roman legal measures: the ink of Claudius' proclamation was barely dry when Jewish religious practices were once again violated, notably in a way that was extremely similar way to the anti-Jewish actions in Alexandria. Given the hostility faced by Jewish communities in a number of cities, even more wide-ranging statements of Jewish religious liberty like the one made by Claudius could hardly be considered effective. The frequent need for the repetition of legal measures, as well as their dependence on local magistrates for enforcement, may not detract from the intended scope of Claudius' declaration of goodwill, but they do severely limit the practical significance of an imperial missive that was supposedly addressed to the entirety of the Roman world.

3.11.3 Expulsion under Claudius

The importance of Claudius' empire-wide proclamation regarding Jewish rights is likewise diminished by the expulsion of the Jewish community from the city of Rome that allegedly took place during the emperor's own reign. Despite the confusing, and at times potentially suspect, nature of the source material, it is generally accepted that Claudius took action against the Jewish community in his capital at some point during his time in power, or at the very least attempted to do so (Appendices 2.50 and 2.52). Both Suetonius and the biblical book of Acts seem to suggest that Claudius ordered all Jews to leave Rome,[319] whereas the later account by Cassius Dio claims that the size of the Jewish community prevented him from doing so. Dio suggests that the emperor instead banned the Jewish community from holding meetings, but otherwise allowed them to continue practising their ancestral religion (*τῷ δὲ δὴ πατρίῳ βίῳ χρωμένους ἐκέλευσε μὴ συναθροίζεσθαι*).[320] This discrepancy has led to the now commonly accepted argument that we are dealing with separate events that took place at different times during Claudius' reign: the ban on Jewish meetings is widely believed to have taken place in 41 CE, while the expulsion is assumed to have occurred only

[319] Acts 18.1–3; Suetonius, *De vita Caesarum: Claudius* 25.4.

[320] Cassius Dio, *Historiae Romanae* 60.6.6. This reading of the phrase is most commonly accepted. For a discussion of an alternative interpretation, which suggests that Claudius may also have banned the Roman Jews from practising their ancestral religion, see Gruen (2002), 37–8.

around 49 CE.[321] The occurrence of two separate measures in such close proximity in itself speaks volumes about the temporary nature of this type of proclamation, and it is in any case likely that both measures were taken with public order in mind: Dio's account juxtaposes the ban on Jewish meetings with Claudius' general ban on *collegia*, and even taverns, while Suetonius mentions that the expulsion took place because the Jewish community became involved in notable disturbances.[322]

The exact nature of these disturbances, however, remains the subject of much debate. While it has been suggested that Claudius' measures were not aimed at particular behaviours exhibited by the Jewish community, but should instead be seen as an attempt to increase general political stability,[323] a common explanation draws on Suetonius' reference to a mysterious figure called Chrestus, who was apparently responsible for the unrest among Rome's Jewish population. As will be discussed in more detail in the following chapter (section 4.4.3), this has at times been taken to mean that the Jewish community became divided over the best way to deal with the emerging Christian movement, which then supposedly led to the violent outbursts in the city that were described by Suetonius as having originated *impulsore Chresto*, at the instigation of Chrestus.[324] It should be noted, however, that Suetonius' phrasing is far from straightforward, and that even the link between Christians and the text's *Chrestus* is hardly guaranteed. The name Chrestus was a common one during the period, and Suetonius' phrasing does seem to imply that this person was in Rome at the time of the unrests.[325] It is thus likely that we are not dealing with an oblique reference to the emergence of Roman Christianity, but instead with a more commonplace instigator of unrest.[326] Whatever the case, all available sources indicate that the Jewish community was the primary target of the expulsion order, and it is unlikely that the cause of the unrest mattered much from Claudius' perspective—what mattered was being able

321 Barclay (1996), 305–6; Botermann (1996), 134–5; Cappelletti (2006), 87–8; Gruen (2002), 37–8 and 270 n. 146; Smallwood (1976), 212–16.

322 Barclay (1996), 305–6; Cappelletti (2006), 89; Goodman (2007ᵃ), 370; Rutgers (1998), 106; Smallwood (1976), 216.

323 Gruen (2002), 37–41 argues that Claudius' attempts to restore traditional religion may have played a part in the expulsion and rejects the idea that the Jewish community of Rome may have been a genuine threat to the public order. Some confirmation of this may be found in the fact that Suetonius includes the measure in a list of Claudius' dealings with foreigners, and foreign rites in particular.

324 Barclay (1996), 306; Botermann (1996), 98–102; Cappelletti (2006), 73–89; Smallwood (1976), 215–16. For the argument that Claudius was attempting to target the early Christian movement specifically, rather than Rome's Jewish community, see Dibelius (1971), 78. For the manuscript tradition on the correct reading of the name, see Boman (2011).

325 Goodman (2007ᵃ), 370; Gruen (2002), 39.

326 For the idea that the expulsion was the result of a conflict among private religious practitioners, or 'freelance experts', see Wendt (2015ᵇ), 119. It is notable that the brief reference to this expulsion in Acts 18.1–3 states only that Jews were compelled to leave Rome by the emperor's orders, without making any mention of disputes about the emerging Christian movement. It seems likely that the author of Acts would have mentioned such conflicts, especially given the fact that he otherwise frequently emphasizes the rejection of early Christians by the existing Jewish authorities.

to end it. Despite the claims made in Acts 18.1–3, however, it is unlikely that the entire Jewish community was expelled. As evidenced by the repeated expulsions of diviners, this would likely have proved difficult, not to mention beyond the authorities' intention, and it is therefore more plausible that only part of the community was forced to leave the city—quite possibly only for a relatively short amount of time, as was frequently the case for diviners.[327] This, it should be noted, is not to discount the importance of either of Claudius' measures. Even if Jews were initially allowed to practise their own religion after 41 CE, so long as they did not hold meetings to do it, and even if the actual scope of the later expulsion was relatively small, these events still suggest that Claudius was willing to act against the Jewish community of his capital when he considered it necessary to do so, and that Jews could still be seen as potentially disruptive outsiders. Such a course of action was clearly not unthinkable even in the light of his verbal support of Jewish customs elsewhere, and Claudius was willing to use it when he believed public order to be in danger.

In many ways, then, the early imperial period saw a consolidation of the pattern in Judeo-Roman interactions that had emerged in republican times. Almost all of the interventions of the Roman state on behalf of Jewish communities were still prompted by a request made by those communities themselves, frequently in response to difficulties they encountered on a local level—particularly in Diaspora cities with a mixed population and significant legal diversity. The use of precedent and negotiation remained an important factor in this regard, and both were used regularly to obtain a favourable outcome in the available sources. Whether these negotiations were conducted with the help of recognized rulers like Herod and Agrippa I, or (more frequently) by embassies sent by specific towns or regions, it is notable that the vast majority of measures continued to be prompted by local circumstances, and therefore remained relatively small in scope, both in a temporal and in a geographical sense. Requests for repeated confirmation of previously granted rights continued to emerge with some regularity, sometimes even within a few years after the original ruling. The 38 CE riots and the subsequent interactions with various Roman authorities in many ways exemplify this pattern: not only were they in all likelihood caused by strongly localized religious and socio-political factors, but attempts to resolve the conflict also heavily involved references to precedent by both parties, as well as delegations to Rome when matters could not be resolved on a local level.

However, the aftermath of these riots also demonstrates that the various Diaspora communities were far from isolated, and that not only beneficial

[327] Barclay (1996), 306; Cappelletti (2006). 88–9; Smallwood (1976), 216. For the idea that those who were expelled returned to Rome relatively quickly, see Barclay (1996), 306 and Smallwood (1976), 216. See Romans 16.3 for a mention of Aquila and Prescilla as members of the Roman Christian community.

precedents could spread. This becomes particularly evident in the case of Caligula's attempt to erect a statue of himself in the Jerusalem Temple, which may well have started out as a response to a local conflict in Jamnia, but ultimately affected Jewish communities throughout the Diaspora, and especially in Alexandria. It may well have been a desire to prevent similar disturbances that led Caligula's successor Claudius to issue the first known measure aimed at Jewish communities throughout the Roman Empire. It bears repeating, however, that Claudius did little more than collectively confirm privileges that had previously been granted on a city-by-city basis, and that his edict still depended heavily on local enforcement. The measure also appears to have done little to resolve existing tensions, as is demonstrated by the fact that renewed conflict broke out in Dora soon after it had been issued. A final aspect of Judeo-Roman relations that should be addressed is the expulsions of the Jewish community from the city of Rome that occurred both under Tiberius and under Claudius. These expulsions were very likely attempts to maintain public order and possibly political stability, and also serve to demonstrate that—despite available precedent—Jewish communities and their religious practices were far from untouchable. Even after Claudius issued his confirmation of Jewish ancestral customs 'to the rest of the world', he himself undertook action against the Jewish community of his own capital, thus demonstrating that its members were still seen as potentially disruptive outsiders. The privileges of these communities, then, could be revoked whenever Roman administrators considered it necessary to do so.

3.12 The Time of Nero: The Road to War

While Alexandria may well have been the city most central to Judeo-Roman relations in the early imperial period, that changed during the reign of Nero. The focal point would instead move towards the province of Judea, where a series of events not dissimilar to the ones preceding the Alexandrian riots would form the basis not just for legal measures but also for outright military intervention. The causes of the conflict that has become known as the Great Revolt—or the 'Jewish War', to follow the terminology used by Josephus—are described by a number of ancient authors. The Roman accounts of Tacitus and Suetonius provide a rather simplified version of events, and ascribe the cause of the revolt to an oracle that was thought to predict the overthrow of Rome and the independence of Judea.[328] This focus on Judean independence suggests that both authors saw the revolt as a

[328] Suetonius, *De vita Caesarum: Vespasianus* 4.5; Tacitus, *Historiae* 5.13. Interestingly, this oracle is also mentioned in Flavius Josephus, *Bellum Iudaicum* 6.5.4 (312–13), where it is included in a list of portents warning the Jewish rebels about their ultimate defeat. Josephus, too, appears to think that the incorrect interpretation of this oracle fanned the flames of the rebellion, although it is far from the only cause he mentions.

strictly regional conflict focused on Jerusalem and the surrounding cities, and this interpretation seems to be confirmed by the fact that neither author makes mention of simultaneous acts of rebellion by Jewish communities in other provinces of the empire. Still, references to any substantial grievance with Roman rule on the part of the rebels or the deeper causes of the uprising are notably omitted.

As may be expected, however, Flavius Josephus devotes a significant amount of attention to the context of the revolt, discussing the worsening relations within the region that preceded the immediate outbreak of the conflict in some detail.[329] According to Josephus, troubles started under Ventidius Cumanus, who was procurator in Judea between 48 and *c.* 52 CE, during the celebration of Passover. While a military presence was not, in itself, unusual on such occasions, in this case one of the soldiers sent by the procurator (possibly a non-Jewish inhabitant of the region), supposedly antagonized the festival-goers by exposing himself and shouting insults.[330] A number of young men then retaliated by throwing stones at the soldiers, and Cumanus attempted to regain control by calling in reinforcements to drive the worshippers from the Temple sanctuary. While the severity of this episode was likely aggravated by the very fact that it occurred during an important religious festival in a major city, which would likely have resulted in safety concerns regardless of what happened, tensions also came to the forefront in far less strained situations. On another occasion, for instance, Josephus describes how a soldier tore and burned a copy of the Torah after confiscating it from some robbers and was subsequently punished by Cumanus to prevent further escalation.[331]

Although Josephus' description of events should not necessarily be taken at face value,[332] his account does suggest that (from his perspective at least) Jewish religious practices could easily become a source of conflict, and that the region was rife with strong underlying tensions that were ready to erupt into the open.[333] This appears to have been the case not just in Jerusalem itself but also in Caesarea, where Jewish and non-Jewish inhabitants of the town came to blows and even requested Emperor Nero's intervention (Appendix 2.53).[334] Josephus suggests

[329] Only part of the commentary on Josephus' *Bellum* has appeared in the Brill series of Mason (1999–2022) at the time of writing. For the full text of the account, see the Loeb edition of Thackeray (1927–8).

[330] Flavius Josephus, *Bellum Iudaicum* 2.12.1 (224–7). Josephus mentions the prevalence of military presence during festivals in the same passage. See also *Bellum Iudaicum* 2.13.7 (268) for the claim that the garrison in Caesarea, at least, was mostly Syrian, which may suggest that this provocative soldier was a non-Jewish local as well. For the animosity that the presence of Roman soldiers could generate, see Fuhrmann (2012), 187–9.

[331] Flavius Josephus, *Bellum Iudaicum* 2.12.2 (229–31).

[332] See Mason (2011) for an elaborate discussion of the reliability of Josephus as a historical source for the Great Revolt.

[333] For the suggestion that violent outbreaks initially tended to occur in response to specific incidents, see Goodman (2007[a]), 386. For the importance of underlying regional ethnic tensions, see Mason (2014), 205.

[334] Josephus tells this story twice. For the first version, see Flavius Josephus, *Antiquitates Iudaicae* 20.8.7 (173–8) and 20.8.9 (183–4), and for the second *Bellum Iudaicum* 2.13.7 (266–70) and 2.14.4–5 (284–92).

that citizenship of the city was at the heart of the dispute and claims that the then-procurator Felix handled the situation so badly that the Jewish community of the town eventually sent a delegation to Rome to make a complaint.[335] The Greek population,[336] however, also sent a delegation of its own to ask for Jewish citizenship to be denied, and when Nero granted this request, apparently due to the influence of a number of his most important advisors, violence erupted once again. The nature of the riots shows that tensions were not just political or ethnic but also religious in nature: according to Josephus, Greek inhabitants of the city purchased lands surrounding the local synagogue and built new structures on it that actively prevented the Jewish community from gaining access to the premises. The new procurator, Gessius Florus, was asked for help, and according to the story he was even paid for his assistance, but he left the city without intervening in any way. Matters only worsened when non-Jewish Caesareans allegedly performed a mock-sacrifice near the entrance of the synagogue during the Sabbath, thus polluting the property. While the administrative details of this episode are exceedingly scant, it is not difficult to see echoes of the Alexandrian riots that took place several years earlier. Once again, we see an intermingling of religious and political issues, claims of 'belonging' in a city to the exclusion of other parties, the reference to existing precedents from both sides, and negotiations between various layers of government, including the central Roman administration.[337] The fact that Nero ruled in favour of the Greek inhabitants of Caesarea is significant, and despite the fact that Josephus attributes the emperor's ruling to his advisors, it still demonstrates that not all encounters between Jewish communities and the Roman authorities ended in the confirmation of Jewish rights.

In addition to these conflicts between Jews and non-Jews in Caesarea and the rest of Judea, the Roman administrators who governed the region furthermore had to deal with a variety of factions within the Jewish community itself, which made it particularly difficult to satisfy all parties without causing offence.[338]

[335] For the idea that Felix himself encouraged the two parties to take their dispute to Rome, see Flavius Josephus, *Bellum Iudaicum* 2.13.7 (270).

[336] The second party in this dispute is referred to as Greeks in *Bellum Iudaicum*, but as Syrians in *Antiquitates Iudaicae*.

[337] The Jewish community of Caesarea was not the only group to appeal directly to the emperor. According to Josephus, procurator Cumanus was banished by Claudius after a complaint about his handling of a conflict between Galilean Jews and Samaritans was made by a Jewish embassy, as shown in Flavius Josephus, *Bellum Iudaicum* 2.12.3–7 (232–46). One of his successors, Gessius Florus, was apparently so hated by the population that they begged the governor of Syria to help them get rid of him, see Flavius Josephus, *Bellum Iudaicum* 2.14.3 (280).

[338] To fully explore the various factions in the revolt, as well as their motivations, would be well beyond the scope of this study. It deserves mention, however, that groups like the *Sicarii* were not only anti-Roman, but that they also aimed their assassination attempts at members of the Jewish priestly elite, as may be seen in Flavius Josephus, *Antiquitates Iudaicae* 20.8.5 (164). For the disagreements between various groups on the best way to interact with the Romans, see Smallwood (1976), 274 and 277–8, and particularly Wilker (2012). For a more elaborate discussion of the causes of the war as portrayed in Josephus compared to its portrayal in other sources, see McLaren (2011). For the

According to Josephus' narrative, however, several of Judea's procurators actively worked to make the situation worse—a suggestion that may well be confirmed by Tacitus' version of events.[339] After violence had once again broken out in Caesarea, and attempts by local Roman authorities to prevent further disturbances had failed, a Jewish delegation followed Florus to Jerusalem in order to once again request his intervention.[340] The procurator responded by confiscating money from the Temple, claiming that he did so on imperial orders. This behaviour was seen as a provocation and was met with both outrage and mockery. According to Josephus, some ridiculed the procurator's apparent greed by publicly pretending to beg on his behalf, which in turn inspired Florus to march on Jerusalem.[341] Subsequent attempts at restoring the peace, both by factions among the population of Jerusalem and by Queen Berenice and King Agrippa II, ultimately failed.[342] Eventually, high priest Eleazar even decided to cease the offering of sacrifices for the well-being of the emperor in the Temple, which had thus far functioned as a symbolic act of loyalty to Rome.[343] If Josephus is to be believed, this was as good as a declaration of war.[344] Violence soon escalated, and after some initial successes by the rebels in 66 CE, Emperor Nero gave Vespasian command over significant military forces in order to end the rebellion.

3.13 The Early Flavians: Taxation and Intervention

Vespasian would emerge from his command in Judea as emperor of Rome, and it is therefore little wonder that the war is often considered to have been the foundation of the Flavian dynasty's claim to power,[345] as well as a turning point in the relationship between the Roman authorities and the Jewish communities of the

economic difficulties that may well have formed the background of the revolt, see Freyne (2002), 50–4; Goodman (1987), 51–75; and Smallwood (1976), 282.

[339] See Tacitus, *Historiae* 5.9–10, in which the historian casts a particularly harsh judgement on procurator Felix, and states that *duravit tamen patientia Iudaeis usque ad Gessium Florum procuratorem.* The term *patientia* indicates that he has at least some regard for the restraint of the Jewish inhabitants of the province and casts a rather dim view not only on Felix but also on his successor Gessius Florus, under whose authority the war broke out. For the profound influence of local Roman administrators on the situation, see Mason (2016), 278, who suggests that the revolt was not so much aimed at the central Roman authorities but rather against their local representatives. A less critical view of the Roman procurators may be found in Eck (2011).

[340] Flavius Josephus, *Bellum Iudaicum* 2.14.5 (291–2).

[341] Flavius Josephus, *Bellum Iudaicum* 2.14.6 (295–6).

[342] Flavius Josephus, *Bellum Iudaicum* 2.14.7–2.17.1 (297–407).

[343] Flavius Josephus, *Bellum Iudaicum* 2.17.2–3 (408–16). See McLaren (2005), 271–3 for a brief exploration of the sacrifices offered on behalf of the Roman authorities.

[344] For the important role sacrifice played in the political relations of the Roman world, see Rives (2014), who notes that this was initially a point of similarity between Jewish and Roman religious practices, and adds that the Roman authorities would therefore likely have attached similar importance to the fact that these sacrifices had come to an end.

[345] As argued by, among others, Overman (2002) and Zangenberg (2016), 1437–49.

empire.[346] From a Jewish perspective, it is easy to see why this may have been the case, since the Temple in Jerusalem had been destroyed by Titus' troops during the later stages of the revolt, and loot from the sanctuary played a significant part in the Flavian triumph.[347] In addition, the early years of the Flavian dynasty saw the institution of the so-called Jewish Tax, which was collected by a special treasury known as the *Fiscus Iudaicus*.[348] The tax is commonly regarded as a replacement for the traditional Jewish Temple Tax after the destruction of the Temple in Jerusalem,[349] and like its predecessor amounted to two *drachmae*, or its Roman equivalent of two *denarii*, being imposed on Jews throughout the Roman Empire. The wide application of the tax has often been seen as a clear sign that the Roman authorities held the entire Jewish population of the empire responsible for the recent revolt.[350] Perhaps most comprehensively, however, the Jewish Tax has been described as 'a dramatic signifier of new loyalty', indicating that it served both to permanently remind Jewish communities of what they had lost and as a warning against future rebellions.[351]

3.13.1 Intervention in Antioch

To characterize the attitudes of Vespasian and Titus as altogether anti-Jewish, however, would not do justice to the full scope of their measures. That much, at least, becomes clear from the new emperor's responses to certain outbursts of violence that took place outside Judea in the aftermath of the Great Revolt. One particularly notable example occurred in Antioch, where the legal status of the

[346] See, for instance, Schwartz (2014), 86–9. See also Goodman (2007[a]), 3: 'Over the following centuries [after 70 CE] Jews were pushed to the margins of Roman society. Rome came to be viewed by Jews as the epitome of evil power.' See Ando (2007), 7 for some criticism of Goodman's decision to open his exploration of the relationship between Jerusalem and Rome by discussing the revolt.

[347] Despite Josephus' claims to the contrary, it is likely that the Temple was destroyed on purpose. See Rives (2005), 145–54.

[348] I have chosen to clearly distinguish between the Jewish Tax and the *Fiscus Iudaicus* because the date of the latter's creation remains in doubt. For the idea that the tax implemented after the revolt was merged with a pre-existing provincial coffer for Judea, see Alpers (1995), 301–2, who is followed by Zangenberg (2016), 1440. This idea is firmly rejected by Günther (2017), 176–8, and more cautiously by Heemstra (2010), 12. See Günther (2017), 179 for the argument that the *Fiscus Iudaicus* was established specifically to collect the Jewish Tax.

[349] Flavius Josephus, *Bellum Iudaicum* 7.6.6 (218). The tax is also mentioned by Cassius Dio, *Historiae Romanae* ep.65.7.2, as well as Appianus, *Syriaca* 50.251–3 and Origen, *Epistula ad Africanum* 14.

[350] For the idea that the Jewish Tax was linked to the humiliation of the Jewish people, see not only Appianus, *Syriaca* 50.251–3 but also Avidov (2009), 4. Pucci Ben Zeev (2005), 124–5 refers to the tax as a 'frustrating humiliation'. A similar sentiment is expressed by Schwartz (2014), 89. See Goodman (1992), 31 for the argument that the expansive character of the tax was in part due to the ambiguity of the term *Iudaeus* and Goodman (2005), 170 for the suggestion that 'the state appeared opposed to Judaism wherever its practitioners might be'.

[351] Gruen (2002), 246.

Jewish community had been a point of contention for a long time, possibly from the very foundation of the city onwards.[352] However, little is known about existing tensions before the outbreak of the revolt in Judea,[353] and Josephus even mentions that the Jewish community in Antioch was among the few that escaped the wave of anti-Jewish violence that gripped the province of Syria in 66 CE.[354] Barely a year later, however, the situation was radically different.[355]

Shortly after the outbreak of the revolt, an accusation of conspiracy to commit arson was levied against the local Jewish community. This resulted in violent anti-Jewish outbursts, and those who were suspected of being Jewish were forced to sacrifice 'according to Greek custom' on penalty of death. This test was intended to 'prove' that the accused was not, in fact, Jewish—and therefore apparently innocent of involvement in the alleged plot. As would later become the case in trials against Christians, then, a willingness to participate in the 'accepted' religious customs was seen as a way to distance oneself from a group of potentially threatening outsiders. As a further measure, Roman troops were even enlisted to prevent the Jewish community from celebrating the Sabbath. While it has been suggested that this could only happen because the Roman authorities were simply too preoccupied with the situation in Judea to pay much attention to this violation of Jewish rights,[356] it is more likely that this measure was intended to prevent meetings that could result in organized resistance from taking place, and thus preserve public order in a time of war. This theory is supported both by the fact that the Jewish community apparently retained its right to buy its own oils without non-Jewish interference even during the revolt (Appendix 2.54),[357] and by Titus' response to a renewed outbreak of violent riots when he visited the city in 70 CE (Appendix 2.55). In a notable similarity to the events of several years earlier, this time a fire had actually broken out in the city and the temporary governor of Syria could only barely restrain the furious Greek inhabitants, who were once again intent on blaming the Jewish community.[358] When Titus arrived, he was met with requests to expel Jews from the city, and—when he chose to deny that petition—to remove the bronze tablets on which Jewish privileges were

[352] Smallwood (1976), 359–60.

[353] According to some reports, conflicts erupted in Antioch alongside the 38 CE riots in Alexandria, but these accounts are provided by the sixth-century author John Malalas, and the incident goes unmentioned by Josephus. While we need not dismiss these accounts in full, the evidence is ultimately too sparse to draw any substantial conclusions. See Smallwood (1976), 360–1.

[354] Flavius Josephus, *Bellum Iudaicum* 2.18.5 (479). It is unclear why this would have been the case. The theory presented by Smallwood (1976), 361 that the presence of the Roman legate must have prevented the outbreak of violence is interesting but ultimately cannot be proven.

[355] Flavius Josephus, *Bellum Iudaicum* 7.3.3 (46–53).

[356] Smallwood (1976), 362.

[357] Flavius Josephus, *Antiquitates Iudaicae* 12.3.1 (120). This passage is dated to the time of the revolt by Barclay (1996), 256 n. 63.

[358] Flavius Josephus, *Bellum Iudaicum* 7.3.4 (54–62). Note the parallel to the treatment Christians are, according to Tacitus at least, said to have received in the aftermath of the Great Fire (Appendix 3.6).

displayed.[359] This appeal, too, was rejected, as was a request made by Greek Alexandrians to the same effect.[360]

While details on the administrative procedures surrounding these decisions are scant, it thus seems very likely that the Flavians were willing to protect the rights and privileges of Jewish communities that had not been directly involved in the recent uprising, which suggests that they were not considered to be complicit. The violence against these communities, then, was once again largely instigated by their immediate neighbours. In the absence of such overt attacks, measures by the Roman authorities likewise disappear from the historical record. The Jewish community in Rome itself, for instance, which in spite of its lack of involvement in the revolt might have been expected to bear the brunt of any imperial repercussions that may have emerged, does not appear to have faced any formal consequences that can be detected—with the important exception of the Jewish Tax.[361] The unrests that are reported to have occurred in Syria (and later, as will be discussed in section 3.13.3, in North Africa) tended to be at least in part inspired by local tensions and conflicts, the outcome of which was largely dependent on local Roman officials. The Flavians themselves, however, do not appear to have been willing to impose wide-ranging regulations limiting the rights of the Jewish population of their empire.

3.13.2 The Jewish Tax

If the Flavian response to the revolt was overwhelmingly local, however, why then was the Jewish Tax in particular so widely imposed (Appendix 2.56)? In order to better understand the interconnecting motivations that likely contributed to this new regulation, it is important to first consider the wider fiscal policy of the Flavian dynasty. When the Jewish Tax was implemented, presumably around 71 CE, the Roman Empire was attempting to recover from severe financial and political difficulties.[362] The Year of the Four Emperors in 68–9 CE had caused not only substantial chaos throughout the empire but also a significant loss of resources.[363] Rome had suffered the destruction of one of its principal sanctuaries,

[359] Flavius Josephus, *Bellum Iudaicum* 7.5.2 (100–11).

[360] Flavius Josephus, *Antiquitates Iudaicae* 12.3.1 (121–4). Next to nothing is known about the exact nature of the events in Alexandria that led to this petition. While both passages deal prominently with Jewish political rights, the nature of the violent outbursts in 67 CE and the mention of specific oils used by the Jewish community suggest that religious privileges also played a significant part. Rajak (2017), 48 argues that these two instances may be reflective of a wider pattern in the Diaspora.

[361] Barclay (1996), 310; Gruen (2002), 42; Smallwood (1976), 356–7. See Bendlin (2020) for the important argument that, while physical violence may have been absent, Jewish communities throughout the Diaspora are likely to have been treated with hostility.

[362] For a discussion of the starting date of the Jewish Tax, see Heemstra (2010), 10–11.

[363] Alpers (1995), 198; Griffin (2008), 26. These financial difficulties are mentioned in Tacitus, *Historiae* 4.9.

the temple of Jupiter on the Capitoline hill, and the restoration of this highly symbolic building alone would require vast amounts of funding, for which the new tax levied on the Jewish inhabitants of the empire became the designated source.[364] Furthermore, the recent power vacuum made the speedy establishment of a stable new government absolutely imperative. In a number of ways, the empire was in dire need of a renovation,[365] and Vespasian, who had a reputation for being a competent administrator, needed financial means to achieve this. The new emperor increased existing taxes by a substantial amount,[366] while also reviving old levies that had fallen into disuse and implementing new ones in the form of the Jewish Tax—and possibly the taxes collected by the *Fiscus Asiaticus* and the *Fiscus Alexandrinus* as well.[367] While it is not clear if the latter two *fisci* were indeed first created under the Flavians,[368] Vespasian's willingness to be inventive in order to increase his government's revenue is generally well attested.[369] He reduced the percentage of silver in the imperial coinage,[370] and reincorporated a number of regions that had previously enjoyed a degree of independence into the administrative structure of the Roman provinces—thereby making them subject to central taxation.[371]

Under such circumstances, the Jewish Tax, in Roman eyes, may well have seemed like a rather logical expansion of existing practices. It was not unusual to tax recently defeated peoples in an attempt to acquire perceived compensation for the costs of war, and this practice had certainly been common in the time of the republic.[372] Normally, such taxation would have been limited to a specific geographic territory, but in this case the well-organized, long-standing system of the Temple Tax, in which Jewish communities throughout the empire were

[364] The connection between the temple of Jupiter and the Jewish Tax is made both in Cassius Dio, *Historiae Romanae* ep.65.7.2 and Flavius Josephus, *Bellum Iudaicum* 7.6.6 (218).

[365] See also Suetonius, *De vita Caesarum: Vespasianus* 8.1.

[366] Eck (2000), 283.

[367] Cassius Dio, *Historiae Romanae* ep.65.8.3–4 claims that Vespasian created a number of new taxes and revived some others that had fallen into disuse. Notably, he mentions the Jewish Tax separately. For the parallel between the *Fiscus Iudaicus* and the other two *fisci*, see also Castritius (2006), 284 n. 27; Griffin (2008), 27; Günther (2017), 178; Feldman (1993), 492 n. 43; Mrozewicz (2010), 27–8. Griffin expresses some hesitation about the significance of the *Fiscus Alexandrinus*, but does not explain why.

[368] Procurators for all three *fisci* are first recorded in Flavian times. See Heemstra (2010), 12 n. 8. As Alpers (1995), 278 n. 961 rightly notes, however, this does not necessarily mean that they were first established during this period.

[369] Vespasian's dedication to the collection of taxes has become almost proverbial, as demonstrated by the famous maxim *pecunia non olet* (Suetonius, *De vita Caesarum: Vespasianus* 23.3), which he supposedly coined.

[370] Griffin (2008), 26.

[371] Griffin (2008), 27–8 and 39 states that taxation need not have been the sole reason for re-annexation, but that increased revenue was certainly the result. Suetonius, *De vita Caesarum: Vespasianus* 8.4 mentions that Vespasian withdrew the liberties of Achaea, Rhodes, Samos, Byzantium, and Lycia that had been granted to them by Nero. Mrozewicz (2010), 28 interprets this as a reinstitution of taxes.

[372] Gambash (2015), 159. Zangenberg (2016), 1441 emphasizes that Vespasian did not consider the revenues of the Jewish Tax personal spoils, but instead treated them as public money.

known to take part, may have suggested to the Roman authorities that Jews throughout the empire could be seen as a single fiscal unit—even if many of them had not been directly involved in the revolt.[373] Vespasian's attempts to increase the yield of the tax may likewise be detected in the fact that he expanded the age range of the original Temple Tax and applied it to both men and women, as well as children and slaves.[374] This flexible use of a pre-existing transregional fiscal infrastructure not only allowed Vespasian to tap into a potentially vast source of revenue,[375] but it also had the added benefit of preventing further unrest. If the money of the empire's Jewish communities was redirected to Rome, instead of continuing to make its way to Jerusalem, it could not be used to restore the Temple,[376] which had been so centrally important during the revolt and could furthermore pose a risk to societal stability beyond the province of Judea because of its claim to the loyalty of the Jewish inhabitants of the Diaspora. These loyalties would now, in a financial sense at least, be redirected towards the temple of Capitoline Jupiter, and the Roman state in general.[377] In addition to being financially profitable, then, the tax was symbolically representative of Jewish defeat and newly enforced loyalty to Rome, and therefore played an integral part in upholding Flavian authority.

3.13.3 The aftermath of the revolt in Alexandria and Cyrene

Vespasian's focus on re-stabilizing the empire likewise becomes clear from the events that took place in Alexandria during the aftermath of the revolt. Hostilities in the city had once again broken out in 66 CE,[378] presumably in response to Rome's perceived anti-Jewish sentiments and residual resentments from the 38 CE

[373] For the idea that the Romans often adapted pre-existing taxes, see Weikert (2017), 163. Bruce (1964) likewise suggests that Vespasian simply adapted the pre-existing Temple Tax due to financial considerations, but he contradicts himself by continuing to argue that the Jewish Tax was only ever imposed on the eastern provinces of the empire. For the idea that the Jewish Tax was meant to address the perceived threat of the interconnectivity between Jewish communities both within the Roman Empire and outside of it, and their shared alliance to Jerusalem, see Gross (2023), 500–1.

[374] See Heemstra (2010), 9 and 13–14. Non-Jewish slaves of Jewish owners were almost certainly included in the tax. It is not completely clear if Jewish slaves of non-Jewish masters were liable for taxation as well. If so, their owners would likely have been required to pay, which would reinforce the idea that Vespasian's motives were financial rather than punitive. See Smallwood (1976), 373 n. 62. Tcherikover and Fuks (1960), 114 make a good argument for the idea that Jewish slaves of non-Jewish owners were not included.

[375] For the idea that the Jewish Tax amounted to 5–6 per cent of the total tax revenue, see Mrozewicz (2010), 28. For the return of *c.* 10 to 12 million *denarii* per year, see Smallwood (1976), 374.

[376] For the heavy financial burden the tax must have imposed on the Jewish population of the empire, see Bendlin (2020), 163.

[377] Rives (2005), 153 and 162; Zangenberg (2016), 1441–2. For the idea that the Jewish Tax demonstrated Rome's toleration of Judaism, see Horbury (2014), 117 and Keresztes (1979), 258, whose view may be supported by a number of Christian authors. See Origen, *Epistula ad Africanum* 14 and Tertullian, *Apologeticus pro Christianis* 18.8.

[378] Flavius Josephus, *Bellum Iudaicum* 2.19.7 (490–2).

riots,[379] and despite intervention by the Roman authorities, tensions persisted for a number of years.[380] The influx of *Sicarii* from Judea after the end of the revolt subsequently led to great consternation among Alexandria's Jewish elite, who wanted to have nothing to do with any form of resistance against the Romans and accordingly attempted to resist the rebels—thus demonstrating that, as far as we can tell from Josephus' description at least, Jewish support for the revolt was far from universal.[381] Lupus, the new governor of Alexandria, reported these unrests to Vespasian, who in response ordered him to demolish the so-called Temple of Onias in Leontopolis—an alternative temple which had been built by an exiled high priest during the reign of Antiochos IV centuries earlier (Appendix 2.57).[382] According to Josephus, the emperor feared that the temple might be used as a rallying point for a new revolt, and this idea was not in itself far-fetched. While it has been argued that the Temple of Onias held little attraction for the Alexandrian Jewish community, and therefore was unlikely to have become the focus of further rebellion from those quarters,[383] this does not preclude the possibility that non-Alexandrian Jews may have viewed matters rather differently, and that Vespasian may therefore have ordered the temple to be destroyed to prevent it from becoming a replacement for the Temple in Jerusalem that could form a focal point for further unrest.[384]

There were, however, certain lines that Vespasian would not cross, as becomes clear from an event that took place in Cyrene only a short time after the disturbances in Alexandria.[385] Here, too, the *Sicarii* played a significant part in causing disturbances, presumably aided by severe local socio-economic tensions.[386] This movement primarily attracted Jews from the lower classes, who hoped that their new leader—a man called Jonathan—would help them to escape their financial difficulties. Despite the fact that no violence appears to have been used, this greatly concerned the members of the local Jewish elite, who asked Catullus, then governor of Cyrenaica, to intervene. When Jonathan was subsequently arrested, he accused the Jewish elite of having secretly been involved in his plans.

[379] Smallwood (1976), 365.

[380] See Flavius Josephus, *Bellum Iudaicum* 2.18.9 (494–8) for the intervention of the Roman governor Tiberius Alexander. For Titus' refusal to dissolve Jewish privileges, which has been discussed in section 3.13.1, see *Antiquitates Iudaicae* 12.3.1 (121).

[381] Flavius Josephus, *Bellum Iudaicum* 7.10.1 (409–16). The discussion about the reasons for Alexandrian Jewish support for the *Sicarii* in Smallwood (1976), 367 postulates the introduction of the Jewish Tax as the primary reason for anti-Roman sentiments in Alexandria, but notably does not take the almost continuous Alexandrian conflicts into account. While it is certainly true that Titus had just confirmed Jewish rights, this does not mean that the animosities had been in any way resolved. Thus, non-elite Jews may have seen the *Sicarii* as help in their dispute with Greek Alexandrians, rather than a chance to revolt against the Romans.

[382] Flavius Josephus, *Bellum Iudaicum* 7.10.2–4 (420–36).

[383] Smallwood (1976), 367–8.

[384] Rives (2005), 153–4.

[385] Flavius Josephus, *Bellum Iudaicum* 7.11.1–2 (437–46). Barclay (1996), 239 suggests a dating of 73 CE for these events.

[386] Applebaum (1979), 220 and 223.

This accusation was readily accepted by Catullus, who proceeded to kill the accused and seize their property, thus using their earlier request for his help in de-escalating a potentially dangerous situation to his own advantage (Appendix 2.58). Up to this point, the governor's behaviour went unopposed, likely because, according to Josephus, at least part of the confiscated property benefited the imperial coffers,[387] or potentially because removing a powerful governor at this stage could have dangerously weakened the Flavian powerbase.[388] Whatever the case, Catullus was never formally punished for his actions but only received a reprimand. However, the accusations he levied against several prominent members of the Jewish communities in Alexandria and Rome, including Josephus himself, were not taken seriously, and went unheeded:[389] the emperor, it seems, saw no evidence for a widespread conspiracy against his rule and was furthermore unwilling to contribute to the further spread of existing unrest.

3.13.4 After the revolt

All things considered, then, the early Flavians proved willing to uphold the rights of Jewish communities that faced hostile attacks in the aftermath of the revolt. They likewise appear to have refrained from implementing overtly retaliatory measures against Jews living in the Diaspora, for instance in the form of expulsion orders like those issued under their predecessors.

The only concrete measure from this period that affected Jewish communities throughout the Roman territories was the Jewish Tax, which, as we have seen, was motivated by various interconnecting factors. On the one hand, it certainly seems likely that the tax was at least in part inspired by traditional Roman ways to financially retaliate against recently subjugated peoples, and that the suppression of the Great Revolt by whatever means necessary, taxation included, played a significant part in legitimizing Flavian authority.[390] However, fiscal considerations

[387] Flavius Josephus, *Bellum Iudaicum* 7.11.2 (446). [388] Applebaum (1979), 222–3.

[389] Flavius Josephus, *Bellum Iudaicum* 7.11.3–4 (447–53). Another reference to these events may be found in his *Vita* 76 (424–25), although the governor's involvement there remains obscure.

[390] The slogan *IUDAEA CAPTA* features prominently on Flavian coinage and painted Vespasian and his successors as conquerors of foreign territories, rather than generals who had put down a rebellion in a Roman province. A unique and apparently very early gold coin with the legend *IUDAEA RECEPTA* in the collection of the Israel Museum in Jerusalem suggests that this framing was not present from the very start of the Flavian period—see Gambash, Gitler, and Cotton (2013). Zollschan (2019) makes the contrasting argument that the coin's legend refers to the surrender of Judea, not to its reconquest. The coin may be viewed via 'Unique coin of "Recaptured Judea"', The Israel Museum, Jerusalem, 4 July 2015, https://www.imj.org.il/en/exhibitions/unique-coin-recaptured-judea#:~:text=The%20debut%20presentation%20of%20a,province%2C%20precisely%20what%20one%20would. The lack of a dynastic tradition in large part explains the Flavian focus on military victories to demonstrate that they were the ones to restore Rome to its former glory after the recent civil war. See Goodman (2005), 171 and Rives (2005), 156. The building programme that underscored this focus on restoration included the destroyed temple of

likewise appear to have played a role in the implementation of the tax, as did concerns for the stability of the empire and the desire to prevent further unrest. These mechanisms were not necessarily unique to Rome's interaction with Jewish communities,[391] but the particular shape this measure took was likely influenced by the fact that the Temple Tax was available as a precedent. This adaptation of a pre-existing system of taxation was likely at least in part intended to maximize the government's revenue in a time when it was desperately needed. Nevertheless, its financial and symbolic effects were also undoubtedly severely felt by Jewish communities, whose religious sensibilities would have been outraged both by the destruction of the Temple and the redirection of its funds to the temple of Jupiter Capitolinus.

While it is very likely, then, that Jewish communities throughout the Roman world faced both symbolic humiliation and social exclusion in addition to the overt violence Jews from cities like Antioch and Alexandria experienced,[392] the tax should not be seen as a sign that Jewish communities would henceforth be faced with empire-wide vindictive and repressive policies. The violent outbursts in both Alexandria and Antioch were instigated by the local population on the basis of specific circumstances, and likely pre-existing grievances, while Vespasian proved unwilling to believe accusations about a widespread attempt by members of the Jewish elite to destabilize his rule and did not implement blanket measures beyond the Jewish Tax. Flavian attitudes, then, did not necessarily correspond entirely with public opinion in the cities of the empire. Roman officials by and large seem to have been concerned with maintaining peace, and—setting exceptions like Catullus in Cyrene aside—they were generally unwilling to turn the Judean revolt into a war against all Jews throughout the empire. Differences in the treatment of Jewish communities in various parts of the empire, then, likely continued to exist. Indications of this may even be found in the collection of the Jewish Tax. It is likely that officials of the *Fiscus Iudaicus* frequently used local synagogues to determine who was part of the Jewish community of a particular town and was thus liable to be taxed.[393] This, indeed, could account for Cassius Dio's claim that only observant Jews were required to pay, although this may also

Jupiter Optimus Maximus and a temple of Pax. See Rocca (2022), 258–66 and Zangenberg (2016), 1437–45 for the visibility of the war in the city of Rome.

[391] See, for instance, Augustus' treatment of Egypt, which contains a number of parallels, including the use of the phrase *AEGYPTO CAPTA* on coinage. See Zangenberg (2016), 1430–3. For the suggestion that Augustus converted pre-existing Egyptian taxes into tribute to Rome, see Rathbone (1993).

[392] See Bendlin (2020) for the importance of acknowledging structural and cultural violence, rather than focusing exclusively on physical violence. The often derogatory remarks of authors like Juvenal, Quintilian, and Tacitus, all of whom were active during the time of Domitian, may be an indication of the hostility Jewish communities faced under the Flavian emperors. See Stern (1974), 512–14 and (1980), 1–107. See however Rocca (2022), 271–5 for the suggestions that Roman attitudes towards Jews did not necessarily change for the worse.

[393] Heemstra (2010), 23. Eckhardt (2020), 319 more generally attributes this role to Jewish organizations that were recognized as associations by the Roman authorities.

be an anachronism on his part, as will be discussed in section 3.14.2.[394] Moreover, there are some tentative indications that regional differences in the formal characteristics of the tax existed. Egypt in particular seems to have used a different type of coinage than the rest of the empire, and members of the Jewish community there likely paid two obols extra to cover the exchange rate.[395] In addition, it has been suggested that the age limits for taxation in Egypt may have differed from those in other parts of the empire, possibly to correlate with the poll tax in that region.[396]

3.14 Domitian and Nerva: Changes in the Jewish Tax

Despite the fact that the Jewish Tax was instituted by Vespasian, his second son Domitian has become most closely associated with the measure. Suetonius tells us that the emperor once again faced the financial difficulties his father and brother had attempted to resolve, primarily due to growing military expenses and ambitious building projects.[397] In an attempt to balance his budget, Domitian resorted not only to the devaluation of his coins,[398] but also to a wide variety of measures that ancient authors describe as tyrannical and unjust.[399]

3.14.1 Domitian: harsh enforcement

According to Suetonius, the harsh enforcement of the Jewish Tax (Appendix 2.59) was an important part of Domitian's financial programme.[400] The exact nature of his measures, however, continues to be the subject of intense debate, and Suetonius' phrasing is hardly helpful in this regard:

> *Praeter ceteros Iudaicus fiscus acerbissime actus est, ad quem* [sc. fiscum Iudaicum] *deferebantur, qui vel improfessi Iudaicam viverent vitam, vel dissimulata origine imposita genti tributa non pependissent. Interfuisse me adulescentulum memini, cum a procuratore frequentissimoque consilio inspiceretur nonagenarius senex an circumsectus esset.*[401]

[394] Cassius Dio, *Historiae Romanae* ep.65.7.2.
[395] Cappelletti (2006),106–9; Heemstra (2010), 15; Weikert (2017), 164.
[396] Cappelletti (2006), 114–15 and 117.
[397] Suetonius, *De vita Caesarum: Domitianus* 12.1.
[398] Griffin (2008), 69–76; Heemstra (2010), 25–6.
[399] Griffin (2008), 76. See also Suetonius, *De vita Caesarum: Domitianus* 12. For the idea that Domitian convicted members of the Roman elite in order to confiscate their property, see Cassius Dio, *Historiae Romanae* ep.67.14.
[400] This passage notably contains one of the earliest references to the term *Fiscus Iudaicus* and furthermore implies that the collection of other taxes was strictly enforced as well.
[401] Suetonius, *De vita Caesarum: Domitianus* 12.2.

> Among other [taxes] the *Fiscus Iudaicus* was administered with extreme severity, on account of which accusations were brought forward both against those who lived a Jewish life without declaring themselves, and against those who did not pay the tax imposed on their people because they had hidden their origin. I [i.e. Suetonius] recall being present as a youngster, when an old man in his nineties was inspected by the procurator—and an exceedingly crowded court—to see if he had been circumcised.

According to Suetonius, then, there were two separate groups who were accused of evading the Jewish Tax: those who lived a Jewish life, but nevertheless did not declare themselves to be Jewish, and those who avoided paying the tax by hiding their Jewish origins. Although this description has proved to be frustratingly opaque, the debate about the interpretation of the second category (people who hid their Jewishness to avoid taxation) has at least resulted in a degree of consensus: it is mostly accepted that this group included not only practising Jews who were unwilling to pay but also Jewish apostates and possibly Jews who sympathized with Christianity.[402] It remains unclear, however, who was included in Suetonius' first group (those who lived a Jewish life without declaring themselves). There is little doubt that these were people who were not part of a Jewish community from birth, but who were nevertheless perceived to sympathize with Judaism in some way. However, the question remains as to what level of involvement in a Jewish community was required to be included in this category. While some have suggested that this group primarily included full converts, arguing that Suetonius' description of the old man's humiliating ordeal seems to suggest that circumcision was a criterion for inclusion in both groups mentioned by the author,[403] others have noted that circumcised converts would hardly have been *improfessi*, and they therefore include only sympathizers with Judaism (θεοσεβεῖς).[404] Others, again, think that these 'people who lived a Jewish life' may have included a more diverse range of people, including individuals who were attracted to Judaism but had not become full members of the community by circumcision, as well as gentile Christians, who were believed to be Jewish because of their similarly monotheistic views.[405]

402 See e.g. Barclay (1996), 311; Cappelletti (2006), 126–7; Heemstra (2010), 54–63; Schäfer (1997), 114.

403 See e.g. Schäfer (1997), 115. Williams (1990), 199 expresses a similar view, and emphasizes that Domitian did not include any new groups in the tax but simply strictly upheld the existing rules. Goodman (2005), 173 and (2007ª), 445 claims that few pagans would have converted to Judaism after the destruction of the Temple. While the number of converts may have been small, it is impossible to prove that no one was converted at all. Juvenal's *Saturae*, at least, seem to suggest that enough people were drawn to Jewish religious practices to be remarked upon by non-Jewish Roman commentators. See Stern (1980), 94–107.

404 See e.g. Smallwood (1976), 376–7. Keresztes (1973) 4–5 includes both sympathizers with Judaism and full proselytes.

405 Heemstra (2010), 32–54 and (2014).

The interpretive problem, it seems, arises from the confusing connection between the two groups that, according to Suetonius, were denounced to the *Fiscus Iudaicus*, and the circumcision test described later in the same passage. On closer examination, however, these two elements of Suetonius' account seem to refer to separate phases in the legal process. The two groups described by the author were not those convicted of having evaded the Jewish Tax, but rather those who were likely to be denounced for having done so by private accusers, as is implied by the verb *deferebantur*.[406] However, while such accusations would likely be encouraged by Domitian, who sought to increase the revenue of the Jewish Tax as much as possible, it would be unwise to see these groups as distinct legal categories.[407] The circumcision test, on the other hand, seems to have been used at a later stage by at least some officials to determine the truth of the charges in a formal legal setting. If this is correct, both actual converts and so-called 'Judaizers' may well have been included among those who were accused of living a Jewish life without admitting to it, while circumcision became a possible piece of evidence that was used to determine who was actually required to pay the Jewish tax—whether they were still active members of the Jewish community or not.[408] This course of action likely increased the number of taxpayers, since those who had drifted away from Judaism would likely not have been included in the lists supplied by synagogues.[409] Both this humiliating practice and the use of anonymous accusations—the employment of which Trajan would later condemn in the context of trials against Christians—therefore may well have been responsible for the inclusion of the Jewish Tax in Suetonius' list of fiscal abuses.[410]

The question remains, then, what became of those who were found not to be circumcised, despite having been accused of evading the Jewish Tax on account of their alleged affinity with Judaism. It should be noted that Suetonius specifically describes the circumcision test as something he witnessed himself, and it is therefore unknown whether his description actually reflects the full extent of the legal proceedings that took place or whether other Roman officials could also accept different forms of evidence for the accused's alleged Jewish beliefs. However, it seems unlikely that standard procedure, if indeed it existed at all, was limited to checking for circumcision: the Jewish identity of women could not

406 See Lewis and Short (1975) *ad loc.* II.B.2.b.

407 The contrary view is held by Günther (2017), 182, who describes the behaviour of both categories as legal offences.

408 A similar view is held by Heemstra (2010), 64–5. For the view that apostates were more likely to be resentful of this policy than practising Jews, see Goodman (1992), 32. Weikert (2017), 171 suggests that confusion existed about who was supposed to pay the Jewish Tax, since some would have left the Jewish community after the revolt, whereas others would have converted to Judaism.

409 Cappelletti (2006), 127. For the suggestion that Jewish organizations that were recognized as associations by the Roman authorities filled this role, see Eckhardt (2020), 319.

410 Barclay (1996), 311; Cappelletti (2006), 124–5; Williams (1990), 200–2. The argument made by Bruce (1964) that Domitian was the first to impose the Jewish Tax on Jews living in Italy, who had previously been exempt, has little to recommend it.

have been determined in the same way, and it is thus by no means inconceivable that some of the accused were subjected to alternative tests on the basis of dietary practices and observance of the Sabbath, and were held liable for the Jewish Tax on this basis.[411] An alternative suggestion, made largely on the basis of the account of Cassius Dio, is that people who were believed to sympathize with Judaism but 'passed' the circumcision test were subsequently met with another, second charge and were potentially even executed on this basis.[412] According to the relevant passage, Domitian ordered the execution of consul Flavius Clemens and his wife on the basis of their atheism, ὑφ' ἧς καὶ ἄλλοι ἐς τὰ τῶν Ἰουδαίων ἤθη ἐξοκέλλοντες πολλοὶ κατεδικάσθησαν, 'on account of which many others who drifted towards the Jewish customs, too, were convicted' (Appendix 2.60).[413] For this reason, it has been argued that Jewish communities under Domitian's rule faced active persecution on a significant scale because they refused to venerate the emperor as *dominus et deus noster*, 'our lord and god'—behaviour that would allegedly have amounted not only to atheism but to outright treason, and therefore would have warranted execution.[414] It has even been suggested that a second test, similar to the sacrifices often prescribed in trials against Christians, followed the check for circumcision precisely to prove such accusations.[415]

Ultimately, however, there is little evidence for this. It is uncertain if Domitian ever presented himself as divine to such an unprecedented extent,[416] and it is likewise notable that Suetonius does not mention any trials on the basis of atheism at all, and instead describes the execution of Flavius Clemens as having been based on trumped up political charges against members of the political elite that Domitian saw as a threat to his authority.[417] No reports of people from the lower classes being executed on account of their Jewish sympathies survive, in spite of complaints about the frequency of conversion in Juvenal's *Saturae*,[418] and it is therefore likely that most members of this group were not being targeted in this way. Cassius Dio's use of the word πολλοί to refer to the victims of Domitian's alleged atheism trials at a substantially later date can hardly be seen as conclusive evidence for a larger-scale persecution of proselytes outside the city Rome. In fact,

[411] For this argument, see Zangenberg (2016), 1443.

[412] See Goodman (1992), 32 and especially Heemstra (2010), 64–6. Pucci Ben Zeev (2005), 125 argues that Domitian attempted to launch a persecution against the Jewish population of his empire, or would have done so if he had lived longer.

[413] Cassius Dio, *Historiae Romanae* ep.67.14.1–2. The same people are sometimes considered to have been among those who are said to have been exiled on account of their Christianity in Eusebius, *Historia Ecclesiastica* 3.18. For a more thorough exploration of these events in relation to the treatment of early Christianity, see section 4.6.

[414] Smallwood (1976), 379. A similar view is expressed by Cappelletti (2006), 133–6. For the phrase *dominus et deus noster*, see Suetonius, *De vita Caesarum: Domitianus* 13. It should be noted that this phrase is not attested in any official inscriptions from the time of Domitian. See Spinelli and Gregori (2019), 255–8.

[415] Heemstra (2010), 29–30.

[416] Jones (1992), 108–9.

[417] Suetonius, *De vita Caesarum: Domitianus* 15.1.

[418] Stern (1980), 94–107.

Dio's mention of political exiles being recalled to the city after Domitian's death may well suggest that these events only occurred in the capital.[419] It is more likely, therefore, that we are instead dealing with a charge of *maiestas* that is very similar to the ones used against members of the Roman elite who were linked to illicit divination throughout the imperial period.[420] Suspicions of Jewish sympathies among members of Domitian's inner circle, whether real or alleged,[421] may even have been particularly dangerous during this period, since the emperor's hold on power was still strongly based on his father's and brother's victory in the Jewish War.[422]

3.14.2 Nerva: restoring order

Domitian's death in 96 CE did not put an end to the Jewish Tax, although his direct successor Nerva did change the Roman government's way of dealing with the institution (Appendix 2.61). Evidence for this may be found not only in Cassius Dio's assertion that the new emperor put an end to malicious accusations of *maiestas* and a Jewish way of life but famously also on coins dated to the time of Nerva, which proudly proclaim *FISCI IUDAICI CALUMNIA SUBLATA* (see Figure 3).[423] However, the theory that Nerva abolished the Jewish Tax altogether, even if only

Figure 3 Reverse of a sestertius (Münzkabinett, Staatliche Museen zu Berlin, 1820025231) displaying a palm tree, the abbreviation *S[enatus] C[onsultum]*, and the words *fisci iudaici calumnia sublata*. The coin is dated 97 CE and was minted in Rome.
Images courtesy of the Münzkabinett, Staatliche Museen zu Berlin. Photographs by Lutz-Jürgen Lübke (Lübke und Wiedemann). Permalink: https://ikmk.smb.museum/object?id=18200252.

[419] Cassius Dio, *Historiae Romanae* ep.68.1.2.
[420] See Schäfer (1997), 116 and Weikert (2017), 172 for the connection between the trial of Flavius Clemens and *maiestas*. Griffin (2008), 76 and Williams (1990), 206–11 argue that charges of atheism were only levied against members of the higher classes.
[421] See Goodman (2005), 174.
[422] Goodman (2005), 171. See also Zangenberg (2016), 1446–9.
[423] Cassius Dio, *Historiae Romanae* ep.68.1.2. The claim by Heemstra (2010), 70 that only slaves and freedmen were no longer allowed to make this accusation is based on an incorrect citation of Stern (1980), 384–5.

for a short time, is ultimately unfounded.[424] Nerva's reign was too short for the absence of documentary evidence to be considered statistically significant, and the tax continued to be paid for decades, and possibly even centuries, afterwards.[425] It is more likely that Nerva's measures instead put an end to the malicious accusations that had fuelled the atmosphere of paranoia that characterized the later years of Domitian's reign.[426] The fact that all available sources focus strongly on the end to judicial overreach and renewed adherence to proper procedure is a strong argument in this theory's favour: the word *calumnia* ('false accusations') is prominently present on Nerva's coinage, and Cassius Dio includes his reference to Judaism in an account of Nerva's attempts to restore those who had been falsely accused by Domitian to their previous positions. It is therefore very well possible that this rejection of unbridled accusations on the subject of the Jewish Tax, and the possible appointment of a specialized praetor to deal with disputes,[427] benefited those who had moved away from Judaism, which may explain Cassius Dio's earlier claim that only observant Jews were obliged to pay the tax.[428] It has also been argued, however, that Nerva's attempts to distance himself from Domitian's policy, including the reference to the abuse of the Jewish Tax on his coinage, should above all be seen as an attempt to restore relations with the Roman senatorial elite.[429] These two possibilities, of course, need not exclude each other: even if Nerva's attempts to restore proper legal procedure were aimed at the higher classes, this change in attitude may very well still have affected the lives of people on the lower end of the social scale. However, the use of coinage in Nerva's self-representation does suggest that his message can hardly have been intended exclusively for Jewish communities, and his relaxation of Domitian's policy should therefore not necessarily be seen as an act of benevolence towards Judaism. It is more likely that he intended to signal the start of a new era, in which there was no room for abuse of imperial power or a tyranny of the courts, and where public order would once again be restored.

[424] For this theory, see Goodman (2007[b]), as well as Goodman (2005), 176 and Goodman (2003), 25–7, the latter of whom argues that Nerva substantially relaxed the Flavian policy on Judaism until his adoption of Trajan. Bruce (1964) suggests that Nerva restored the tax-exempt status of Jews living in Italy that Domitian had abolished.

[425] Heemstra (2010), 19–21.

[426] Griffin (2008), 74; Keresztes (1973), 6; Williams (1990), 200; Zangenberg (2016), 1443.

[427] Heemstra (2010), 71.

[428] Cassius Dio, *Historiae Romanae* ep.65.7.2. For this point of view see Goodman (1992), 33 and Heemstra (2010), 10. For the argument that Nerva once again limited the scope of the tax after it had been expanded by Domitian, see Keresztes (1979), 260. See Heemstra (2014) for the argument that Flavius Josephus' *Antiquitates Iudaicae* may have contributed to this renewed focus on Jews who adhered to their ancestral customs.

[429] Günther (2017), 186–8. For the notion that Nerva's coinage referencing the Jewish Tax was only distributed in Rome, which would support the idea that the Roman elite was the intended audience, see Goodman (2007[a]), 447. The suggestion made in Rocca (2022), 269 that non-Jews who owned Jewish slaves were the most noticeable targets of Domitian's harsh enforcement of the Jewish tax may likewise serve as an explanation for this numismatical reference to the tax.

3.15 Trajan and Hadrian: The Causes and Consequences of Revolt

Nerva's departure from Domitian's policies may have been lauded in Rome, but it would not prove sufficient to prevent the outbreak of a series of revolts by Jewish groups in various provinces under the reign of his successor Trajan. While, as discussed, similar eruptions of violence had occurred in Alexandria and Cyrene in the wake of the destruction of the Temple, these riots hardly put an end to anti-Roman sentiments.

3.15.1 The Diaspora revolt

Starting in 115 or 116 CE, Jewish groups in Libya, Egypt, and Cyprus, and possibly Babylonia and Judea as well,[430] took up arms against the Roman authorities, almost certainly in an attempt to capitalize on the army's preoccupation with Trajan's campaign against Parthia.[431] The causes of these revolts remain the source of much speculation, but it is likely that anti-Roman sentiments caused by the destruction of the Temple and the financial strain of the Jewish Tax,[432] continuing hostilities between Jewish and Greek residents of various cities,[433] and religious motivations each played a part.[434] However, the exact combination of and interaction between these elements is assumed to have varied from region to region, or even from city to city.[435] Whatever the causes of the revolt (or revolts) were, the scale of the devastation appears to have been vast. Cassius Dio reports enormous casualties among the non-Jewish population of the relevant provinces, and even claims that the rebels resorted to cannibalism.[436] In Cyrene, temples

[430] Goodman (1992), 34 and Smallwood (1976), 415–21. While the connection to Trajan's campaign in Parthia is beyond dispute, the archaeological evidence for the revolt in Mesopotamia is rather scant, see Applebaum (1979), 299–300. The extent of the unrest in Judea remains debated. For the argument that it was less severe than the conflicts in the Diaspora, see Applebaum (1979), 322–3 and Smallwood (1976), 421–7. See Horbury (2014), 257–64 for the argument that the so-called War of Quietus amounted to serious difficulties in Judea.

[431] Horbury (2014), 195; Pucci Ben Zeev (2005), 142.

[432] Pucci Ben Zeev (2005), 123–5.

[433] Goodman (1992), 34; Horbury (2014), 166; Pucci Ben Zeev (2005), 125–6. This idea is supported by one of the *Acta Alexandrinorum*, the *Acta Hermaisci*, which is set early in Trajan's reign and describes a Greek embassy sent to the emperor, presumably in the aftermath of another conflict in Alexandria. Interestingly, Trajan is depicted as greatly favouring the Jewish community, despite the later conflict. For the text of the *Acta*, see Musurillo (1954), 44–8. For a more elaborate discussion of the events in Alexandria, see Pucci Ben Zeev (2005), 133–41.

[434] See Goodman (1992), 34–5 for the theory that Jewish rebels deliberately attacked pagan sanctuaries. See Pucci Ben Zeev (2005), 141 and Smallwood (1976), 397 for the possible Messianic inclinations of the rebels.

[435] Pucci Ben Zeev (2005), 125–41 and 264.

[436] Cassius Dio, *Historiae Romanae* ep.68.32. Eusebius, *Historia Ecclesiastica* 4.2 reports significant casualties on the Jewish side.

appear to have been destroyed.[437] The Roman response to these events was correspondingly harsh, especially due to the fact the rebellion in northern Africa threatened Rome's grain supply.[438]

After the revolt, evidence for Jewish communities in Egypt and Cyrene disappears for a significant period of time,[439] Trajan's recent conquests in Mesopotamia were swiftly abandoned,[440] and according to Cassius Dio Jews were even banned from ever setting foot on Cyprus again.[441] No such ban is reported for any of the other regions involved in the revolt, which may lead us to tentatively conclude that some differences in the handling of the revolt in the various provinces existed. Due to lack of evidence, however, this remains nothing more than speculation. For the most part, Rome's response to the revolt was a show of military rather than legislative force, and there is no evidence that Jewish communities like those of Italy and Asia Minor, which did not participate in the uprisings, suffered any consequences.[442] In this regard, the famous Babatha archive is particularly interesting. The archive was found in a region that became part of the Roman province of Arabia in 106 CE and contains documents dating up to 132 CE. Although the exact balance between local Jewish law and Roman legal practices displayed in the relevant texts remains a matter of debate,[443] it does seem clear that Jewish law and tradition still played a notable role, and that Jewish inhabitants of the empire actively (and by all appearances safely) sought out the Roman courts during this period. This suggests that the relationship between Jews and the Roman authorities was not purely antagonistic during this period, and that Roman courts could be expected to provide an acceptable resolution to cases in which members of the Jewish community were involved.[444]

3.15.2 The Bar Kokhba Revolt

In 132 CE, less than twenty years after the end of the uprisings under Trajan, another revolt broke out in Judea. This conflict is generally called the Bar Kokhba

437 Applebaum (1979), 272–85. 438 Smallwood (1976), 403.

439 Applebaum (1979), 342–3; Pucci Ben Zeev (2005), 264; Seeman and Marshak (2012), 65.

440 Goodman (1992), 35; Pucci Ben Zeev (2005), 264–5; Smallwood (1976), 421.

441 Cassius Dio, *Historiae Romanae* ep.68.32.

442 Goodman (1992), 36; Seeman and Marshak (2012), 65.

443 For a more elaborate analysis of this fascinating archive, see Schuol (2007), 224–36, but particularly Czajkowski (2017) and Oudshoorn (2007), the latter of whom makes the argument that certain documents in this archive display use of Roman procedural law combined with what is referred to as Jewish substantial law. See Cotton (1993) for the contrasting argument that the application of Jewish law in the portion of the archive written in Greek, at least, was very limited, and that Roman legal practices instead played a far more substantial role. In Cotton (1994) she furthermore argues that Jewish marriage contracts, for example, strongly resembled non-Jewish contracts from the same period, and thus reflect mixed local traditions. The suggestion that 'Jewish law' was still highly diverse and in flux in this period is confirmed by Czajkowski (2017), 204–5. For the argument that Jewish law nevertheless existed before the Mishnah, see Oudshoorn (2007), 44–50.

444 Cotton (1999), 234–5.

Revolt in reference to its leader and is often considered to have been a continuation of the previous revolts in the Diaspora.[445] Despite this possible connection, the violence appears to have been limited to a relatively small region, but the causes of the conflict are in no way easier to determine. Ancient sources offer rather contradictory accounts, none of which is entirely satisfactory. According to Cassius Dio, the revolt broke out because Hadrian founded a new city, known as Aelia Capitolina, in place of Jerusalem, and used the former location of the Jewish Temple to build a temple for Jupiter (Appendix 2.62).[446] The *Historia Augusta*, however, claim that the rebels were incensed *quod vetabantur mutilare genitalia*, 'because they were forbidden to mutilate their genitals'.[447] Of these two theories, the former seems closer to the truth, although the sequence of events remains the subject of debate. This is in part due to the fact that Eusebius' account contradicts Cassius Dio by describing the foundation of Aelia Capitolina as a punishment for the revolt, rather than its cause.[448] The archaeological evidence, however, seems to side with Dio: the legend 'For the Freedom of Jerusalem' on coins struck by the rebels lends some credence to the theory that Roman intervention in the city had, at the very least, been announced before the start of the rebellion,[449] while the paving of the Roman city's main street seems to have begun well before the start of the revolt.[450] Whether the name of Aelia Capitolina was already attached to this intervention before the revolt remains unclear, but it is very possible that the building project was only finished after it had been suppressed, which may explain Eusebius' confusing statement.[451] This, however, raises the question of Hadrian's motivation in re-founding the city under a Roman name, the answer to which likewise remains speculative. Some authors are inclined to see the rebuilding of the city as a punishment for perceived Jewish offences predating the Bar Kokhba Revolt, or at the very least as an attempt to ensure Roman control over the region.[452] Others, by contrast, have argued that Hadrian's intentions were by no

[445] Applebaum (1979), 342; Goodman (1992), 35; Smallwood (1976), 426.

[446] Cassius Dio, *Historiae Romanae* ep.69.12.1.

[447] Scriptor Historiae Augustae, *Hadrianus* 14.2.

[448] Eusebius, *Historia Ecclesiastica* 4.6.4.

[449] Cotton Paltiel and Ecker (2019), 691; Eshel (2006), 107 and 115. For the idea that the foundation of Aelia Capitolina had at least been announced before the revolt, see also Horbury (2014), 308–11. Goodman (2003), 28–9 sees the founding of Aelia Capitolina as a punishment for the revolt under Trajan, rather than the Bar Kokhba Revolt.

[450] See Cotton Paltiel and Ecker (2019) and Weksler-Bdolah (2020), 51–60 for a thorough analysis of the archaeological material pertaining to the founding date of Aelia Capitolina.

[451] Smallwood (1976), 433; Tsafrir (2003), 32. Tsafrir (2003), 34–6 suggests that the renaming of Jerusalem may have been intended as punishment, but that the founding of the new Roman colony nevertheless predated the revolt. In doing so, he rejects a hoard of coins containing both Bar Kokhba coinage and coins referencing Aelia as unreliable: according to Tsafrir, these coins need not have been deposited at the same time. For the idea that the name Aelia Capitolina did indeed predate the revolt, see Meshorer (1989). See Eck (2014), 242 for the suggestion that the change of the region's name from *Iudaea* to *Syria Palaestina* was a response to the revolt, possibly requested by non-Jewish inhabitants of the region.

[452] Goodman (2003), 28–9.

means anti-Jewish, and that he instead intended the measure as a response to requests for formal civic institutions by Roman veterans,[453] or more generally as an honour, a part of the emperor's famously elaborate programme of building and restoring cities that backfired spectacularly.[454] It remains uncertain, however, whether any additional factors may have been at play, and indeed the lack of participation by Jewish communities in the Diaspora suggests that the founding of Aelia Capitolina interacted with more localized circumstances to trigger the revolt.[455] A similar lack of response may likewise be observed in the case of Hadrian's reported attempt to banish all Jews from his new city in the aftermath of the revolt (Appendix 2.63),[456] which notably goes unmentioned in Jewish sources.[457] It has therefore been suggested that no such measure was ever issued, and that devout Jews may have instead left the city of their own volition. From a Roman perspective, the argument goes, it would have made little sense to deprive the inhabitants of the emperor's new city of a local workforce.[458] It should also be noted that Jerusalem had primarily become a military settlement in the period between the destruction of the Temple and the Bar Kokhba Revolt, which means that its Jewish population may well have been small to begin with.[459] If, however, the measure did exist, it was certainly not permanent, and a Jewish presence in the city is once more reported at the end of the second century CE.[460]

A final measure that has often been connected to the Bar Kokhba Revolt is Hadrian's supposed ban on circumcision (Appendix 2.64). This regulation is indicated as the primary cause of the revolt by the *Historia Augusta*,[461] but the veracity of this claim has frequently been doubted.[462] Aside from the fact that the source is often considered to be unreliable, an empire-wide ban of this kind makes the lack of an attested response outside Judea difficult to explain.[463] However, the fact that a ban on circumcision and other Jewish practices does appear prominently in the Rabbinic tradition has led to the suggestion that we are instead dealing with a punitive measure issued for Judea (possibly by local officials) either during

453 Cotton Paltiel and Ecker (2019).

454 Rizzi (2010), 13–14; Tsafrir (2003), 33.

455 Isaac (2003), 37.

456 Eusebius, *Historia Ecclesiastica* 4.6.3; Justin Martyr, *1 Apology* 47.4–6; Justin Martyr, *Dialogue with Trypho* 16.

457 See Horbury (2014), 405, who nevertheless believes that Eusebius' account reflects an older measure.

458 Goodman (2007ᵃ), 478.

459 Cotton Paltiel and Ecker (2019), 682. See also Weksler-Bdolah (2020), 204–5 who remarks on the disappearance of archaeological evidence for Jewish religious practice after 70 CE, but connects this to a deliberate expulsion of the Jewish population.

460 Horbury (2014), 405; Schäfer (1995), 164.

461 Scriptor Historiae Augustae, *Hadrianus* 14.2.

462 Abusch (2003), 73; Isaac (2003), 38; Oppenheimer (2003), 55–6. For claims to the contrary, see Linder (2006), 138.

463 Oppenheimer (2003), 68–9.

or after the revolt.[464] Another possible explanation, for which evidence is more solid, is that Hadrian issued an unrelated regulation that, while not aimed at Jews in particular, could nevertheless be interpreted as limiting their ancestral practices. The *Digesta* indeed cites a rescript attributed to Hadrian in which the emperor includes castration among the behaviours that are banned by the much earlier *Lex Cornelia de Sicariis et Veneficiis*,[465] but even setting aside the fact that the measure appears to have been formulated in response to a particular query, no specific reference to circumcision is ever made. That is not to say, however, that it was not taken as such.[466] The *Digesta* likewise cites a rescript issued by Antoninus Pius in which it is clearly stated that Jewish inhabitants of the empire are permitted to circumcise their own sons—but no one else (Appendix 2.65).[467] Notably, the text of the rescript specifies that anyone who broke this command should be prosecuted according to the existing ban on castration. This suggests that Hadrian's previous proclamation did not specifically mention circumcision and that Pius was instead attempting to resolve lingering uncertainties about its interpretation, likely at the request of Jewish petitioners.[468] In doing so, he both formally protected the Jewish custom of circumcision and limited its application, although it would be unwise to assume that the law was widely enforced: the Roman government was strongly dependent on self-reporting, and we may ask ourselves how much of a barrier this law actually was to those with a sincere desire to convert. Furthermore, it bears repeating that this measure is contained in a rescript and may thus have derived from a more specific temporal and geographic context than is suggested by the passage's later inclusion in the *Digesta*. It is little wonder, therefore, that reports about circumcisions during this period do not describe the practice as a particularly remarkable occurrence.[469] Whatever the case, Antoninus' rescript shows that uncertainty about the correct interpretation of Hadrian's ban on castration existed during his reign. If such obscurity existed not only in Pius' own time but also in Judea prior to the Bar Kokhba Revolt, it may have given local officials too much room to come to an anti-Jewish interpretation. As a result, the measure may have contributed to anti-Roman sentiments and led to the idea that a ban on circumcision had been the cause of the rebellion.

[464] Horbury (2014), 314–16; Oppenheimer (2003); Smallwood (1976), 429–31. Isaac (2003), 38 claims that Hadrian did not ban circumcision by Jews, but instead continued a long-standing ban on conversion. For the tentative suggestion that these measures were issued by local officials, see Abusch (2003), 83–4.

[465] *Digesta* 48.8.4.2.

[466] Nogrady (2006), 181–2.

[467] *Digesta* 48.8.11. Cappelletti (2006), 136 and Isaac (2003) see this as an implicit ban on conversion to Judaism. However, see Feldman (1993), 385 for the idea that a ban on circumcision would not prevent women from converting. Although Pius' name is not mentioned, this may also be the measure referenced in pseudo-Paul, *Sententiae* 5.22.4.

[468] Abusch (2003), 88; Horbury (2014), 314; Noethlichs (1996), 77. Schäfer (1997), 104 likewise agrees that Antoninus Pius' rescript does not imply the existence of a ban of circumcision under the heading of castration in the time of Hadrian.

[469] Justin Martyr, *Dialogue with Trypho* 8.4, 23.3–5, 123.1, as referenced by Feldman (1993), 385–6.

3.16 The Late Second and Early Third Centuries: Completing the Picture

After the end of the Bar Kokhba Revolt, a final number of interactions between the Roman authorities and Jewish communities are said to have taken place, which date from the late second and early third centuries CE. The first of these is a measure by Septimius Severus, who according to the *Historia Augusta* forbade conversion to either Judaism or Christianity, proscribing heavy penalties for anyone who disobeyed (Appendix 2.66).[470] This measure has often been seen as a more explicit reiteration of Antonius Pius' rescript forbidding circumcision by non-Jews, possibly because that previous proclamation once again resulted in similar misunderstandings.[471] If we accept this interpretation, the law may represent a shift in the Roman legal treatment of Judaism, for the first time explicitly 'policing the boundaries of the Jewish community'.[472] It should be noted, however, that our source for this measure is dubious at best,[473] and that any potential ban on proselytism does not appear to have been rigorously enforced: mentions of conversion continue to appear, without any mention of negative consequences.[474] In any case, even if a ban on conversion to Judaism was indeed issued, this almost certainly did not amount to Jewish practices being suppressed altogether: Septimius Severus and Caracalla allowed Jews (*qui Iudaicam superstitionem sequuntur*) to obtain local public office (*honores*; Appendix 2.67).[475] While various explanations for this measure exist,[476] its most remarkable and significant aspect is the fact that Jews are explicitly exempt from duties that would compel them to violate their ancestral customs (*sed et necessitates eis imposuerunt, qui superstitionem eorum non laederent*). This amounts to a formal recognition of the particular difficulties members of various Jewish communities could face when holding public office, and it is likely that the measure made it easier for members of Jewish communities to be accepted as negotiating partners by Roman officials.[477]

[470] Scriptor Historiae Augustae, *Septimius Severus* 17.1. A similar measure may be found in pseudo-Paul, *Sententiae* 5.22.3. An argument may be made, however, that pseudo-Paul's text reflects a later period. See Feldman (1993), 386.

[471] Abusch (2003), 90; Stern (1980), 625.

[472] Abusch (2003), 90.

[473] Feldman (1993), 386; Honoré (1987), 164; Syme (1968), 218–19.

[474] Feldman (1993), 386; Isaac (2003), 51. It should be noted that the passage in Eusebius, *Historia Ecclesiastica* 6.12.1 cited by Feldman describes a conversion from Christianity to Judaism going unpunished. Such a conversion may have been of significantly less concern to the Roman authorities than a conversion that involved a former adherent of traditional Roman practices.

[475] *Digesta* 50.2.3.3.

[476] Feldman (1993), 101 sees this as a reversal of a previous ban on Jews holding public office issued after the Bar Kokhba Revolt (for which no evidence exists), while Smallwood (1976), 513 sees it as having been akin to a punishment, due to the heavy burden public office represented in the period. Trebilco (1991), 47 and 174 sees this measure as a practical move to increase the number of people who could hold office, but also acknowledges that it was an honourable position that may have benefited the status of members of the Jewish elite. See Harker (2012), 286 for the offhand suggestion that this may have been a ratification of a previously existing measure.

[477] For the way in which rabbis, in particular, came to be embedded in Roman provincial life and administration, see Lapin (2012).

However, the consequences of this measure likely varied from city to city, and relations between Jews and their non-Jewish neighbours could remain ambivalent even within individual communities.[478] While it is therefore unlikely that the hostilities so prominently present in accounts from earlier periods disappeared entirely,[479] there are nonetheless some notable hints that Jewish communities continued to be integrated in the Roman legal system. Although the references contained in the *Historia Augusta* to various Severan emperors regarding Jewish customs with respect, or even admiration, are of doubtful authenticity,[480] more firm evidence for the attitude of the imperial authorities towards Jewish communities during the period may be found in Caracalla's rescript regarding a bequest left to the Jewish community of Antioch (Appendix 2.68).[481] Although Caracalla ultimately declared that the legacy could not be claimed by the community for which it was intended, this likely did not occur on the basis of anti-Jewish sentiments, and the very existence of the rescript serves as an indication that Jews continued to be able to plead their case with the emperor and that arguments related to Jewish law could furthermore be brought forward in legal negotiations of the period.[482] Indeed, this process may well have been made easier by the introduction of the *Constitutio Antoniniana* in 212 CE, which included Jews in Caracalla's grant of universal Roman citizenship,[483] without necessarily affecting the extent to which Jewish communities could continue to use their own laws and customs.[484] Like the archaeological and epigraphic record, then, the legal

[478] For an exploration of this topic in the case of the city of Sardis, see Rajak (2002[a]).

[479] Rajak (2017), 41. It is notable that the literature of the *Acta Alexandrinorum* continued to be widely read and transmitted until the second and early third centuries, as argued by Harker (2008), 2, and that even an emperor like Trajan is depicted as greatly favouring the Jewish inhabitants of the empire (see the *Acta Hermaisci*, also known as P.Oxy. 10.1242). The last emperor mentioned in one of the *Acta* is Caracalla. This indicates not only that anti-Jewish sentiments continued to exist but also that Jews should not be seen as a completely marginalized group in this period.

[480] For an overview, see Feldman (1993), 101–2. For the idea that the attitude of the *Historia*'s author towards Judaism may well be influenced by attitudes from his own time, see Rocca (2022), 46. For the author's dubious handling of his sources, see Rohrbacher (2015), 11–14.

[481] *Codex Iustiniani* 1.9.1.

[482] Yaron (1964). For this particular rescript, see pp. 284–6, where the author makes the argument that the bequest was left to *incertae personae* and could thus not be collected under Roman law. Under Jewish law, however, such a claim does appear to have been possible. This argument is expanded upon by Humfress (2011), 42, who like Yaron does not interpret the reference to the *universitas Iudaeorum* in the rescript as referring to a formally recognized entity, but rather to unspecified individuals. The contrary view is held by Eckhardt (2019), 146 n. 121. The addressee of this rescript is very likely the same Claudius Triphoninus who was one of the period's most important jurists, and whose work is repeatedly cited in the *Digesta*. This may suggest that the issue was being treated as a legal test case after the implementation of the *Constitutio Antoniniana*.

[483] Linder (2006), 135.

[484] Linder (2006), 135–6 and 139. For the idea that local sources of law to some extent continued to exist, and continued to be used, after the implementation of the *Constitutio Antoniniana*, see Alonso (2016), 65–6 and (2020); Amelotti (1999); Czajkowski (2019[b]), 110–11; Czajkowski and Eckhardt (2020), 4; Garnsey (2004), 140; Humfress (2013), 90–4; Tuori (2007), 51.

interactions of the period after the Bar Kokhba Revolt suggest that Jewish communities, and their customs, continued to exist—and in some cases even thrive.[485]

3.17 Conclusion

Throughout this chapter, I have discussed the wide range of legal interactions between Jewish communities and the Roman authorities that occurred until the middle of the third century CE. While it bears repeating that the surviving corpus may well be selective, and that the available sources sometimes lack important details or context, the list of known legal interactions is both long and diverse. Our sources include both reports about specific events or measures by members of the various Jewish communities of the Roman Empire, documents from the Roman authorities, and accounts by non-Jewish individuals. The available sources about the legal position of Judaism in the Roman world therefore allow us to form an overall picture and to detect the general trends and mechanisms that governed the relevant interactions. Geographically, most known cases took place in the eastern Mediterranean, primarily Alexandria and the cities of Asia Minor, although an important number of measures applied to the city of Rome itself. Both the temporal and local contexts of these events have been crucial to our discussion.

The known interactions between Jewish communities and the Roman authorities dealt with an impressive number of topics, the most centrally important of which was likely the right to uphold Jewish ancestral customs. This issue, it seems, took many different forms, depending on the specific community that requested Roman intervention and the period in which the request was made. In some cases, references to Jewish custom are abstract and include few details, but in others we find more specific reports of the various concerns Jewish communities living in the Diaspora could have. The right to send money to Jerusalem frequently reoccurs in the available sources (although these cases naturally all date to the period before 70 CE), as do measures allowing Jews to observe the Sabbath, which take the form of exemptions from both military service and from public duties on that particular day. Jewish communities also frequently appear to have requested the right to hold meetings to perform their devotions or made complaints when the synagogues in which such meetings were held were violated. In the second century CE, the legality of circumcision (and by association conversion to Judaism)

[485] Ameling (2004), *passim*. See pp. 46–51, 179–86, 204–6, and 224–97 for inscriptions concerning synagogues in various towns in Asia Minor, the first of which uses the style of a polis decree. See pp. 162–7 for a dedication to a presumably non-Jewish woman who was honoured for her favour towards the Jewish community. See pp. 168–74 for the allocation of theatre seats to Jews, which demonstrates a degree of integration of the Jewish community into local public life. For the idea that Jewish communities were allowed to exist by the Antonines due to their importance for tax revenue, see Goodman (2016).

appears to have become a more central issue, but in this period, too, more wide-ranging references to Jewish communities being allowed to maintain their customs continue to occur, which suggests that this was still very much in people's minds.

Overwhelmingly, however, no real punishments appear to have been established for those who hindered Jewish religious practices. Only in two scant cases do we hear that those who attempted to confiscate Jewish sacred money were to be treated as if they had robbed a temple—an interesting use of non-Jewish precedent in a Jewish context—and in one case the city of Halicarnassus established a fine for anyone preventing Jews from practising their customs. Otherwise, however, a stern rebuke appears to have been the sole expression of Rome's displeasure. Even after the Alexandrian riots, Claudius' retribution appears to have gone no further than a vague, if threatening, warning to both parties involved in the conflict. Nevertheless, the available sources suggest a strong willingness to judge Jewish requests favourably on the part of the Roman authorities. It should be noted, however, that our principal source on the matter is hardly unbiased: it is very likely that Flavius Josephus tailored the selection of documents he presents to the reader precisely to suggest continuously good relations between Jewish communities and Roman authorities. It remains possible, therefore, that Jewish requests for protection of their ancestral customs were at times rejected.

Indeed, there are important indications that the attitudes of Roman officials could at times be decidedly less than favourable: the Jewish community was expelled from Rome on a number of occasions, Domitian appears to have viewed sympathy for Judaism in his inner circle with suspicion, and neither Caligula nor Nero appears to have been particularly open to Jewish requests for protection. It seems unlikely, therefore, that Judaism was formally considered to be a '*religio licita*', even during the early imperial period. A similar combination of favourable and unfavourable measures appears to have persisted after the perceived watershed of the Great Revolt. With the sole (though highly significant) exception of the Jewish Tax, which was likely implemented for a number of different reasons, there is no solid evidence that any Roman measures adversely affected Jewish communities throughout the empire: Jewish communities in regions that did not participate in the revolt, or subsequent unrests in later decades, do not seem to have been systematically targeted by the Roman authorities. In fact, the customs of the Jewish communities in Antioch and Alexandria were protected by the early Flavians, and while those who attempted to evade the new tax were aggressively sought out under Domitian's rule, accounts of people being executed because of their Jewish beliefs are likely strongly exaggerated. While Hadrian's supposed ban on circumcision has often been seen as an explicitly anti-Jewish measure, there is some evidence to suggest that it was not intended as such. A later rescript by Antoninus Pius on the same subject may well have been created to clarify to whom exactly the ruling applied, and while this ambiguity may have been locally used to prevent Jews from practising their ancestral customs, this does not appear to have been an empire-wide policy. The official attitudes of the Roman authorities towards Judaism, then, appear to have been neither universally favourable nor universally negative—whatever their personal views might have been. Instead, much seems to have depended on the particular circumstances in which each interaction occurred.

It has furthermore been demonstrated that the initiative of particular local communities, both Jewish and non-Jewish, played a central part in the origins of Roman legal interactions with Judaism. This was the case not only for the early political treaties between the Maccabean rulers and the Roman senate but especially for the attempts to maintain Jewish ancestral customs that dominate the record of the republican and early imperial periods. On many occasions, Jewish communities themselves requested Roman assistance. In a significant number of cases, we furthermore find reports of such requests for intervention occurring in the context of disputes and conflicts with non-Jewish neighbours, showing that these communities tended to have very concrete reasons for drawing the attention of the authorities to their problems. According to the evidence transmitted to us, such conflicts were often related to non-Jews attempting to hinder Jewish communities in practising their ancestral customs, although socio-political circumstances appear to have played an important part in a number of significant events, including the conflicts in Alexandria, Caesarea, and Antioch. In such cases, the question of who 'belonged' in a particular city in both a political and in a religious sense appears to have been at the forefront of the respective disputes. On occasion, this sense of 'belonging' even appears to have been tested by the local population, who used a number of different methods to determine whether certain individuals were Jewish. During Domitian's strict enforcement of the Jewish Tax, Jewishness was ascertained by determining whether a person had been circumcised, while the consumption of pork was demanded during the Alexandrian riots, and sacrifice according to Greek customs was employed in Antioch. However, not all interactions were prompted by the deliberate hindering of Jewish ancestral practices by the local population. In certain other cases, Jewish communities simply seem to have encountered difficulties in adhering to existing procedures and made the Roman authorities aware of this fact, as for instance in the case of Augustus' decision to allow the Jewish community of Rome to pick up grain rations on a different day when the appointed date coincided with the Sabbath. The same may have been true for the ruling on circumcision made by Antoninus Pius, which was likely an emendation of a previous Hadrianic ruling on castration that, whether intentionally or not, appears to have negatively impacted at least some Jewish inhabitants of the empire.

The procedures followed by Jewish communities, however, could also be employed by the non-Jewish inhabitants of the cities of the empire. We repeatedly find evidence of opposing delegations being heard by various Roman authorities, and of debates or negotiations about the appropriate course of action taking place. The most famous and explicit example of this are the Alexandrian riots of 38 CE, but one might just as well refer to Titus' intervention in Antioch during the aftermath of the Great Revolt or to examples from Laodicea and Miletus, both of which date to the late republican period and make reference to non-Jewish delegations pleading their case in opposition to their Jewish neighbours. Both Marcus Agrippa's intervention on behalf of the Jewish communities of Asia and Nero's involvement in the disturbances in Caesarea preceding the Great Revolt may also be seen as part of this pattern, as could the charges brought forward against Jews accused of attempting to evade the Jewish Tax in the time of Domitian—although in the latter case we appear to be dealing with charges made by and against individuals rather than entire communities.

It is furthermore notable that complaints brought forward by either party during the republican and early imperial periods were usually initially presented to local or regional Roman officials, or sometimes even to the city authorities. Setting aside cases brought to the attention of an emperor or another high Roman official during his presence in a particular city, whether in Rome or elsewhere, the central authorities generally appear to have been the primary respondent only in cases dealing with the political status of certain groups or in the response to larger-scale military matters—as for instance in the case of the Jewish Tax. Local Roman officials were usually the ones who initially dealt with conflicts and, sometimes by request, referred a matter to higher-ranking magistrates or the central authorities for advice or approval when necessary. This pattern seems to have changed during the second century CE, when more centralized efforts are mentioned, although this is likely due to the nature of the available sources, which generally pay less attention to the procedures that resulted in a particular ruling than the material available from earlier periods.

In this process of negotiation with various authorities, a number of factors appear to have been crucially important in determining the resulting decision, first among which is the ability to employ existing, recognized institutions and structures. In the late republican and early imperial periods, Jewish communities at times called in the help of the various rulers of Judea, whose political status and sometimes personal connections to Roman dignitaries could prove to be highly instrumental in maintaining Jewish ancestral customs. On other occasions, the fact that Jewish communities could be seen as similar to the familiar Roman associations known as *collegia* may have worked to their advantage, as did the fact that Jewish communities in many cities had established elite representatives that could become part of embassies when necessary. The availability of precedent likewise played a significant role in negotiations with the Roman government, and likely continued to do so throughout the first two centuries CE. On the one hand, the frequent use of terms like *πάτριοι νόμοι* in itself demonstrates the sense of importance that was attached to existing traditions, and suggests that Jewish communities often referred to the established characters of their beliefs and practices when dealing with the Roman authorities. On the other hand, positive pre-existing Roman rulings could also be used to encourage another, similar decision. Roman authorities were frequently inclined to leave existing regulations in place or make use of known precedent—although it should be noted that this did not always work to the advantage of Jewish communities, as demonstrated by Claudius' demand that the Jewish inhabitants of Alexandria should not ask for more rights than they already had. Finally, the desire to preserve public order and prevent unrest frequently emerges as a prominent concern on the part of various Roman officials. Particularly clear examples of this may be found in the various expulsions of the Jewish community from Rome, particularly in Tiberius' attempt to restore the status quo by exempting those who gave up their Jewish religious practices from banishment. However, we also see this consideration reflected in Aulus Avilius Flaccus' alleged attempts to placate the Greek Alexandrian elite, and the efforts made in Claudius' later letter to the Alexandrians to satisfy both parties in the conflict. Even Domitian's actions against members of the Roman elite that he perceived to be sympathizing with Judaism could be seen in this context, given the importance of his family's victory in Judea for his claim to power.

For the majority of the first century BCE and the first century CE, Roman measures on Judaism were directed at a single city, or a specified area that was often no larger than a province in practice, and were initially applied in the area that had originally prompted the intervention of the Roman authorities. It should be noted, however, that the various Jewish communities of the Mediterranean world were hardly isolated: the very existence of Flavius Josephus' elaborate corpus of Roman rulings suggests that precedents from one city were considered to be potentially relevant in another, and references to regulations applying to other cities occur on a number of occasions in the available sources. In addition, the aforementioned interventions by rulers of Judea on behalf of Diaspora communities suggests that the validity and significance of these transregional relationships were on occasion acknowledged by Roman officials. The same, however, held true in the case of less favourable interactions. Caligula's attempt to place his statue in the Temple in Jerusalem, for instance, while inspired by local disturbances in Jamnia, had a substantial effect on Jewish communities elsewhere in the Diaspora, particularly in Alexandria. However, the concrete effect of the Roman authorities' awareness of such connections between Jewish communities on actual legal intervention generally appears to have been limited. The rare known examples of larger-scale measures mostly emerged in relation to extensive conflict or the threat thereof, and their scope furthermore appears to have been shaped by mechanisms strongly similar to those that influenced the outcome of smaller scale interactions. The most impactful of these wide-ranging measures was the implementation of the Jewish Tax, which could well be regarded as a case in which both the recognized connections between various Jewish communities and the established nature of the Temple Tax played a detrimental, rather than beneficial, part. The other is Claudius' edict addressed 'to all the world', which appears to have been prompted not only by the threat the disturbances in Alexandria spreading to other parts of the empire but also by the intervention of kings Agrippa and Herod—thus highlighting the importance of negotiation and the use of power structures recognizable to the Roman authorities therein. After the end of the Great Revolt, it becomes difficult to determine if the existing pattern of legal rulings applying to specific regions continued, although the fact that repercussions for the next two revolts appear to have fallen specifically to the communities that participated in them suggests that it likely did to some extent. While it is possible that the measures dating from the period after the Bar Kokhba Revolt had a wider application, it should be noted that the measures from both Hadrian and Antoninus Pius are contained in rescripts and thus were at least prompted by local requests for imperial guidance.

As becomes clear from the source material, especially in those cases dating from the republican and early imperial periods, Roman legal measures not only frequently found their origins in local circumstances but were also locally enforced. On a number of occasions, for instance, local Roman officials were ordered to make sure that new regulations were published in the area under their jurisdiction. It also becomes clear that the effectiveness of such measures was often limited, and that Jewish communities frequently had to make repeated requests to Roman officials because earlier regulations had fallen into disuse. The series of documents dealing with the Temple Tax dating from the Augustan period is a particularly good example of this phenomenon in action. The limited duration of many measures likewise becomes clear from the lacking effectiveness of the known expulsions of the Jewish community from the city of Rome, and indeed of Claudius' sweeping edict 'to all the world'. The legal measures from the second century CE limiting or banning conversion to Judaism, too, appear to have had a very limited effect in practice. The only notable exception in this regard is once again the Jewish Tax, but even in that case, the exact level of enforcement seems to have varied according to time, and possibly also place. It thus becomes clear that the creation, content, and enforcement of measures relating to Judaism are simply too often too deeply rooted in local and temporal circumstances for a single, unified policy (whether in the form of a charter or otherwise) to have existed. Throughout the first two centuries CE, the legal position of Jewish communities in the Roman Empire was subjected to repeated renegotiation, and while the results of such negotiations frequently appear to have been favourable for Jewish communities, this was certainly not universally the case.

The known legal measures involving Jewish communities, then, serve to illuminate the significant extent to which negotiations between various levels of government and the inhabitants of the provinces could, and did, influence the treatment of religious communities by the Roman authorities. Whether the outcome of specific legal interactions was favourable or repressive in nature, it remains important to note that such measures did not emerge from straightforward top-down policies, but rather from a variety of factors and from the arguments presented by the parties involved. The availability of relevant precedents could be a particularly useful tool for communities seeking to uphold their ancestral religious practices: as we have seen on a number of occasions, a favourable ruling, once made, could be repeated and reinforced, even in different regions from the ones from which they originally emerged. The presence of established organizational structures and recognizable political representatives likewise proved to be particularly useful: a community with a recognizable leader, as well as long-standing institutions, could be incorporated in the Roman administrative system with greater ease, which in turn could significantly aid the negotiating process. It should be noted, however, that even for religious groups who were well established in this way, the question of 'who belonged', and who could by contrast be seen as a religious outsider, continued to be exceedingly relevant, as becomes evident from the frequent hostilities Jewish communities faced in the cities in which they lived. Furthermore, the existence of various types of tests to determine who was Jewish and who was not, as well as the option to recant one's beliefs offered in the time of Tiberius, suggest a concern for determining who could be considered a religious outsider, and furthermore implies a desire to pressure these perceived outsiders to conform to general religious norms. While Jewish communities, then, were on many occasions able to find the support of the Roman authorities, they likewise shared many of the difficulties that would also be faced by their Christian counterparts.

Marginalized Religion and the Law in the Roman Empire. K. P. S. Janssen, Oxford University Press.
 DOI: 10.1093/9780191946400.003.0004

4
Early Christianity in Roman Legal Measures

4.1 Introduction

From very early on, the legal power of Rome played an important role in the collective consciousness of the empire's Christian communities. To an extent, this was almost unavoidable: those who saw themselves as followers of Jesus of Nazareth could hardly have been unaware that the object of their devotion had been tried and executed in a Roman court, under the jurisdiction of a Roman prefect. Whatever the road to Jesus' execution may have looked like, it was Pontius Pilate whose name would become synonymous with the legal proceedings surrounding the crucifixion, in spite of his portrayal as a reluctant participant in the accounts of the story that would come to be considered canonical.[1] It is clear, then, that even the foundational narrative of Christianity established interactions with the Roman authorities as fraught, as well as potentially dangerous, and the idea that Roman courts were an arena in which members of the emerging Christian community could expect little sympathy has strongly persisted ever since. It features prominently in many early Christian writings, particularly in the literary genre of the Martyr Acts, which tend to focus on the trial and execution of Christians, often by Roman officials.[2] Even the earliest Roman sources on Christianity, like Tacitus, Suetonius, and Pliny the Younger, frequently highlight the fraught nature of interactions between members of Christian communities and the Roman authorities. As mentioned in the Introduction, similar narratives continue to be visible today in artworks the world over and in the religious practices and experiences of many members of various Christian denominations, which continue to venerate martyrs from classical antiquity.

[1] This portrayal of Pontius Pilate was very likely influenced by Christian self-representation and apologetics and was meant to show that the crucifixion was unjust even in Roman eyes. In contrast to the four canonical gospels, in which Pilate is reluctant to order Jesus' execution and suggests that he should instead be released, the prefect is described as a harsh and deeply (possibly deliberately) unpopular administrator in Flavius Josephus, *Antiquitates Iudaicae* 18.3.1–2 (55–62), as well as Philo of Alexandria, *Legatio ad Gaium* 299–305. For Pilate's attitude in the gospels, see Matthew 27.15–26; Mark 15.6–15; Luke 23.13–25; and John 19.4–16. Pilate is also mentioned in connection to the crucifixion in Tacitus, *Annales* 15.44, although it has been suggested that this passage may contain substantial interpolations by later Christian copyists. See Carrier (2014), 274–6.

[2] For the connection between early Christian descriptions and practices of martyrdom and the trial of Jesus, see Moss (2010^{b}).

It is little wonder, then, that scholarly interest in the legal position of Christianity in the Roman world has likewise proved enduring, and that field is correspondingly vast to the point of intimidation. Nevertheless, it is possible to distinguish between three principal schools of thought, all of which continue to be of importance despite a degree of overlap.[3] The first of these, which may be referred to as the 'general law' theory, holds that the Roman authorities at some point in time issued a measure that explicitly banned Christianity throughout the Roman territories.[4] Differing opinions regarding the exact date and character of such a law continue to exist, but the time of Nero has widely proved to be a popular choice. This is in large part due to a well-known remark by the Christian apologist Tertullian, who in his *Ad Nationes* suggested that the persecution of Christians was an *institutum Neronianum*.[5] Although this claim finds some support in the fact that both Tacitus and Suetonius likewise attribute the earliest measures against Christians to Nero,[6] the concept of a general anti-Christian law has received substantial amounts of criticism, and has widely fallen out of favour for a number of reasons. The most important of these is the notable lack of evidence for either general legislation or a continuous, empire-wide persecution in the first two centuries CE, which one might have reasonably expected if such a measure had indeed been taken.[7] In this regard, it should also be noted that our perspective on events from the first and second centuries CE has likely been skewed by the available sources, which overwhelmingly mention only cases in which Christians came into open conflict with the Roman administration, while

[3] For the origins of this framework, see the selected bibliography in Rives (2011^b), 203 n. 7, who on pp. 204–10 also provides an overview of scholarship on the issue. Rives rightly remarks that strict adherence to these three categories 'obscures agreements between and differences within the three schools of thought'.

[4] Allard (1911), 170–4; as well as Callewaert (1901), (1902), and (1911), are often regarded as the foundational authors of this theory. For other early scholarship that represents this view, see the overview provided by Wlosok (1971), 276 n. 5 and 276 n. 6. Other analyses that follow this line of thinking may be found in Keresztes (1979); Molthagen (1970) and (1991); Sordi (1983); Zeiller (1951) and (1955).

[5] Tertullian, *Ad Nationes* 1.7.9. A similar point is made by Wlosok (1971), 277. For the idea that Tertullian was not referring to an actual law, but rather a custom established under Nero, see Borleffs (1971); Rives (2007), 198; Ste Croix (1974^a), 223. An early example of the idea that Trajan, rather than Nero, was the creator of the foundational piece of anti-Christian legislation may be found in Aubé (1875), 225. Anderson (1986), 293 likewise dates the legal basis for the treatment of Christians to the time of Trajan, but argues that it established proper procedure, rather than a general, empire-wide pronouncement declaring Christianity to be illegal. For the idea that Christians could be punished for being political dissidents since the execution of Jesus and that this formed the basis for the Neronian persecution, see Vittinghoff (1984), 339–43. For the attitude of Christian apologists towards the Roman authorities in general, see Odahl (2015).

[6] Suetonius, *De vita Caesarum: Nero* 16; Tacitus, *Annales* 15.44. The accounts of both authors differ substantially on a number of important points, as will be discussed in more detail in section 4.5.

[7] Barnes (1968^a); Borleffs (1971), 218; Crake (1965) 62–70; Lane Fox (1986), 423; Last (1954), 1220–4; Rives (2011^b), 206; Sherwin-White (1952), 201–2; Smuts (1965), 72–3; Vogt (1954), 1170; Walsh and Gottlieb (1992), 9; Wlosok (1971), 290–1. See Ste Croix (1974^a), 223–4 for the argument that Lactantius, *Divinae Institutiones* 5.11.19 references imperial rescripts, rather than *edicta* or *mandata*, and therefore likely suggests that emperors had not implemented a general law.

periods of more peaceful coexistence, by contrast, are marked only by silence, and are therefore more easily overlooked. The 'general law' theory therefore fails to account for the possibility that the available examples of repressive measures, however numerous they may be, are not necessarily representative of the typical experiences of Christian inhabitants of the empire nor of dominant attitudes among the relevant authorities.

At least in partial response to such criticisms, the representatives of the second school of thought have suggested that Christians were not targeted on the basis of a general law aimed at them specifically, but rather because they came into conflict with pre-existing Roman legislation on other issues. However, no consensus has been reached regarding the specific law that could have been used for this purpose, and a number of authors that support this theory have presented multiple possible options. The possibilities offered range from the well-known accusations of cannibalism and incest already referred to by Christian apologists to the idea that Christian gatherings had become illegal after a ban on *collegia*, charges of arson (often attributed to the time of Nero), crimes against the emperor or state, and various religious offences like atheism or a refusal to participate in the official cults of the empire.[8] It has been rightly remarked, however, that this approach is likewise not without its limitations.[9] Firstly, many of the accusations that were levied against Christians do not appear to have constituted crimes for which there would have been a formally recognized legal remedy, while frequent references to attempts to make Christians recant in the available sources seem to disprove the idea that they were believed to have done something that was considered worthy of punitive measures.[10] In addition, the charge of 'being Christian' appears in our sources on a number of occasions, and seems to stick even after potential evidence for other criminal actions has been found wanting and was subsequently rejected.[11] In an attempt to resolve this issue, it has been suggested that Christians were in such cases not ultimately punished for any of the

[8] Le Blant (1866), who focuses on accusations of *maiestas* and *sacrilegium*, is often referred to as one of the earliest proponents of this theory, along with Conrat (1897). See also Boni (2014), 142; Borleffs (1971), 226; Frend (1965), 165–8; Guterman (1951), 45–53; Merrill (1924), 52–66; and Smuts (1965). Frend (2000), 821 refers to crimes associated with Christianity as a 'secondary charge'. Wlosok (1971), 300 argues that Christians were condemned for more general crimes only until the time of Trajan, and were thereafter targeted simply for 'being Christian'. See Baudy (2006), 106–9 for the idea that Christian communities were seen as illegal *collegia*, and that measures against them, like those against other illegal associations, were inspired by a general fear of conspiracy on the part of the Roman authorities. A similar parallel is drawn by Beard, North, and Price (1998), 230 and Nippel (1995), 29–30. For the suggestion that *collegia* were not strictly defined in a legal context, see Rüpke (2016[b]), 66. Eckhardt (2018[c]) argues that Christian communities were not seen as *collegia*, or indeed associations more generally, by authors from the pre-Constantinian period.

[9] For a more elaborate discussion, see Rives (2011[b]), 205–6, who cites Last (1954), 1215–19; Sherwin-White (1952), 206; Ste Croix (1974[a]), 214–17.

[10] This curiosity was already discussed by Tertullian, *Apologeticus pro Christianis* 2.10. See Ste Croix (1974[a]), 232 for the argument that this could originally be considered a privilege, which he connects to the idea that the Roman authorities intended to 'make apostates, not martyrs'.

[11] See, for example, Pliny the Younger, *Epistulae* 10.96.7–8.

aforementioned crimes, but because of their *contumacia*—the obstinate refusal to obey a Roman magistrate's orders.[12] This idea has famously led to extensive debate between the theory's primary representative, A. N. Sherwin-White, and G. E. M. de Ste Croix,[13] the latter of whom has argued, among his other points of criticism, that Christians could hardly have been accused of having been obstinate in the face of a magistrate before having been brought before that magistrate under some other charge in the first place. While the persistence attributed to many Christians by some of the available sources may have been a source of substantial irritation for the Roman authorities,[14] this is unlikely to have been the legal basis for trials against them.

The third of the major theories seeks the legal basis for the treatment of Christians not in any particular law, whether aimed specifically at Christianity or not, but rather in the administrative and judicial authority of the Roman governor. This school of thought finds its basis in the idea that Christians were punished on the basis of *coercitio*, which gave magistrates with *imperium*, like governors, the authority to intervene directly when they believed public order to be in danger.[15] According to Theodor Mommsen, who was the first to advocate this theory, Christians came to be seen as a fundamental threat to the stability of the empire due to what he called their *Religionsfrevel*: the crime of perceived disloyalty to traditional Roman religion—and by extension to the Roman state.[16] While this theory has attracted its fair share of support, in particular due to its ability to explain the fragmentary and local nature of early Roman interactions with Christian communities,[17] objections have also been raised. On the one hand, it has been argued that the treatment of Christians was too consistent to be the result of the will of various individual governors. In addition, Mommsen's explanation of the reasons these magistrates may have had to apply *coercitio* has since proved to be unsatisfactory.[18] On the other hand, a more recent reworking of

[12] Sherwin-White (1952), 210–11 and (1974). Similar suggestions are made by Crake (1965), 62; as well as Walsh and Gottlieb (1992), 9 and Wilken (1984), 23, the former of whom suggest that this accusation was an artificial excuse devised by Pliny, who was looking for a reason to execute the Christians who had been denounced to him.

[13] See Ste Croix (1974[a]), 229–32 and (1974[b]), as well as Sherwin-White (1974). While these articles were initially published in subsequent issues of *Past & Present* in 1963 and 1964, they were later jointly reprinted in the cited edition. For the justified observation that both Sherwin-White and Ste Croix found common ground in their understanding of Roman legal procedure, see Streeter (2006), 14–15.

[14] Walsh and Gottlieb (1992), 27–9.

[15] The workings of this principle, particularly in the republican period, are discussed in Jolowicz and Nicholas (1972), 305–17. See also Nippel (1995), 5, who notes that the term is a modern one.

[16] Mommsen (1890). See Rives (2011[b]), 205 for the remark that Mommsen has much in common with those who focus on pre-existing laws in this regard. This is confirmed by Streeter (2006), 14, who notes that the two theories suffer from very similar pitfalls.

[17] Cook (2010); Last (1954), 1221–3; Sherwin-White (1952); Walsh and Gottlieb (1992), 11.

[18] For a more elaborate discussion of these objections, and possible counter-arguments, see Rives (2011[b]), 207–8.

Mommsen's theory by G. E. M. de Ste Croix[19] seems to avoid some of these pitfalls by finding the basis of Roman trials against Christians not in 'pure *coercitio* in the narrower sense', but rather in governors' usage of their legal authority in the context of *cognitio* procedure.[20] In the view of Ste Croix, the frequent application of this procedure in trials against Christians gave governors a significant amount of freedom to decide which cases to hear, and which charges to accept as legally valid—which means that they were the ones to decide if 'being Christian' was sufficient basis for a trial. For this reason, the theory also places more weight on the participation of the inhabitants of the governor's province, since they were the ones who would originally have brought charges against their Christian neighbours to the attention of the governor.[21] Certainly, this theory goes a long way towards explaining the legal treatment of Christians in the Roman world, and would serve to more closely align the treatment of Christians with that of diviners and Jewish communities, both of which as we have seen were closely linked to the circumstances from which the relevant interactions emerged.[22] However, a number of important questions remain. Why, for instance, are the accusations of various crimes levied against Christian communities referenced so frequently in the works of both Christian and Roman authors if they were 'essentially appendages of some more real [i.e. religiously motivated] complaint'?[23] It has also been remarked that Ste Croix's analysis does not provide a full explanation for one of the most significant of the aforementioned criticisms of the *coercitio* theory, namely the ostensibly strong coherence and similarity between the known trials against Christians. This resemblance remains difficult to explain if we accept the idea that such measures were the result of the personal administrative decisions of a variety of different governors.[24] The debate, then, has hardly been resolved.

[19] For an in-depth discussion of Ste Croix's wider scholarly context and his influence on later scholarship, see Streeter (2006).

[20] Ste Croix (1974[a]), 217–28, specifically 219. This idea is supported by Crake (1965), 61–2; Rives (2011[b]), 208–9; and Wilken (1984), 23. For more details on the nature of the *cognitio* procedure, see section 1.3. It should be noted that Ste Croix later acknowledged that the term *cognitio extra ordinem* is not a technical one. See Streeter (2006), 14.

[21] This view is followed by Lane Fox (1986), 422–3 and 450. For the importance of the introduction of this element to the debate, see Rives (2011[b]), 209. Very recently, Corke-Webster (2023) has drawn new attention to the importance of local, social tensions and has suggested that Christians were most often denounced by the those closest to them—including other Christians.

[22] See Wendt (2015[a]) for the argument that measures against Christians are best explained by connecting them to the wider 'unofficial pattern' of measures against freelance religious experts. The question remains, however, whether her focus on individuals is indeed supported by the available sources.

[23] For the view that religious complaints were the true foundation of trials against Christians, see Ste Croix (1974[a]), 233.

[24] Rives (2011[b]), 208.

4.2 Terminology and Definitions

When discussing the legal position of Christianity in the ancient world, it is important to first consider when its followers came to be seen as a distinctive movement, and what characteristics contributed to making them a recognizable entity within the contemporary religious landscape. This question is complicated by a number of factors, perhaps the most significant of which concerns the cultural context from which this group emerged. Christianity may have taken its name from Jesus of Nazareth,[25] but it would be altogether inadequate to claim that it was his direct, explicit intention to found the larger-scale movement that would emerge in later years.[26] In fact, rather than claiming that Jesus set out to create a distinctively novel religious movement, the available narratives about his activities repeatedly show signs of being set in a predominantly Jewish context, rather than a new Christian one. Jewish customs, festivals, and religious institutions appear with notable frequency, and if the various descriptions of Jesus' trial in the canonical gospels are to be believed, at least part of his final conflict was not with the Romans but with the Jewish authorities.[27] While Jesus' relationship with contemporary Judaism was hardly uncomplicated, it may nevertheless be argued that his trial should not be seen as the first example of legal action against a member of the Christian community, but rather as a dispute between different Jewish groups.[28] The distinction between the nascent Christian movement and the Jewish communities from which it originated gradually became more obvious as the years went on, and some members of the community came to see the figure of Jesus as central to their religious experience. However, this process does not appear to have been clear cut, and much debate about the approximate date of the separation, or the 'parting of the ways', continues to exist.[29]

[25] The Latin suffix *-iani* is often used to denote followers of an authority figure, often in a political context, as is the case with, e.g. *Pompeiani* and *Caesariani*. See Bickerman (1949), 116–18 and Lund (2008), 255.

[26] The person of Jesus of Nazareth, his background, and his ideas have all been interpreted in a wide variety of ways, which need not be discussed in detail here. For a very select number of examples in an extensive and diverse field, see Dunn (2003); Ehrman (1999); and Evans (2011).

[27] It bears mentioning that the canonical gospels can hardly be said to represent unbiased historical fact, and that their descriptions of events likely diminished the role of the Roman authorities. However, if it is indeed true that the terminology of 'King of the Jews' played a part in the legal proceedings surrounding the crucifixion, this may serve as an indication that the Roman authorities did indeed see Jesus in a Jewish context—and as a potential rebel.

[28] Due to the fact that the Roman authorities appear to have viewed this as a political matter, the trial against Jesus has not been included in Chapter 3. Nevertheless, it may be argued that the legal proceedings as we know them seem to fit with that chapter's conclusion that the Roman authorities were often inclined to allow Jewish communities to use their ancestral rights and customs, and that Roman intervention was requested by those communities with some frequency. The importance of access to established institutions is also a notable feature of the narrative.

[29] For the suggestion that gentile Christians in Rome may have been part of the city's Jewish synagogues in the early days of the community, see Lampe (1989) 53 and (2003), 69–70. See also Hengel and Barrett (1999) for the emergence of Christianity from Judaism, as well as Dunn (1992) and

While the author of the book of Acts suggests that the term *Christiani* first emerged in reference to the Christian community of Antioch in the time of Paul,[30] it is particularly difficult to determine to what extent this apparent separation from the local Jewish community was understood, or even visible, from the outside. The Roman authorities very likely had little interest in what they, at least for some time, continued to see as an internal legal and theological dispute,[31] and due to a severe lack of first-century Roman sources on the subject it is almost impossible to determine when the authorities began to see Jews and Christians as separate entities. The first Roman accounts in which 'Christians' are explicitly mentioned did not emerge until the early second century CE, when the term appears in the writings of Tacitus, Suetonius, and Pliny the Younger.[32] The first two authors describe the involvement of Christians in earlier historical events from the time of Nero, which seems to imply that the emergence of Christianity as a distinct group had already occurred at that point in time. It has been argued, however, that these accounts are instead anachronistic projections on the part of the authors, who lived in a time when the Christian community had become much more recognizable, and therefore referenced Christians where historically there were none. The matter is certainly not helped by the co-existence of the spelling *Chrestiani* in Tacitus' *Annales*, and the more familiar alternative *Christiani* used by Suetonius.[33] The spelling used in the Tacitus passage has caused some to connect this account with Suetonius' reference to a person named Chrestus, who allegedly caused a disturbance in the city of Rome in the time of Claudius, but whose actions are said to have been the cause of legal measures against the Jewish community of the city, rather than against emerging Christian

Streeter (2006), 33 for a variety of perspectives on the subject. See Heemstra (2010) for the idea that the Jewish Tax played an important role in this process of separation.

[30] Acts 11.26. It may be significant that this detail appears in the context of 'Paul's' assertion that his community should include not just those who followed Jewish law and were therefore circumcised, but also those who were not. The significance of this passage is underscored by Jones (2017), 148–9.

[31] As, for instance in Acts 18.14–15, where the Roman governor Gallio refuses to hear a charge against the apostle Paul brought forward by the Jewish community of Corinth, stating that they should resolve disputes about Jewish Law themselves. A similar argument is made by Streeter (2006), 33–4. For a discussion of the idea that the expulsion of the Jewish community from the city of Rome under Claudius was the result of a similar conflict between Jews and Christians, see section 3.11.3.

[32] At a later date, the term also appears in Lucianus, *De morte Peregrini*. For some reflections on the origins of the term 'Christians', see Bickerman (1949). For the argument that Christians only started referring to themselves as *Christiani* in the late second century, see Lund (2008), 255, who argues that the term was a Roman slur before that point in time. However, the fact that the author of Acts 11.26 picked up on the phrase, and chose to repeat it without any apparent reservations, seems to contradict this idea. An overview of the available ancient sources for early Christianity may be found in Whittaker (1984), 133–91.

[33] Tacitus, *Annales* 15.44 and Suetonius, *De vita Caesarum: Nero* 16. The exact text of the Tacitus passage continues to be the subject of much debate, as will be discussed in section 4.5.1. Fisher (1906), *ad loc.* prints *Christiani*, but Carrier (2014), 273 and Shaw (2015), 84, among many others, take the alternative reading.

groups.[34] The similarity in names is therefore said to have led to confusion between Christians and these Jewish rioters, who were likely still well known in the time of Nero.[35] This confusion could then, in turn, indicate that Jews and Christians were still seen as closely related groups—if not in the time of the two historians, then at least in the period they describe.

This hypothesis, however, fails to account for a number of important factors. The fact remains that both Tacitus and Suetonius are quite capable of directly referring to Jewish groups when this was their intent elsewhere in their works, and that they nevertheless chose to use terminology related to Christianity in their discussion of the state of affairs under Nero.[36] This is particularly notable because their respective accounts of the relevant events otherwise differ significantly, which makes it more difficult to dismiss both references to Christians as one author copying the mistake of the other, or as intentionally or accidentally unreliable.[37] If both Suetonius and Tacitus came to the conclusion that a group that they recognized as Christians had been active during the Neronian period and had been subjected to some form of legal intervention, despite their apparently independent investigations, it becomes likely that the cause for this similarity may be found in the earlier sources used by both historians.[38] Their accounts are thus at the very least likely to be indicative of an emerging Roman awareness of Christianity in the 60s CE, even if Christians may not yet have been seen as a fully distinct community.

By the time Tacitus and Suetonius composed their works, that awareness had certainly grown, possibly due to Domitian's harsh enforcement of the Jewish Tax.[39] It is clear that Christianity was now recognized as a distinct group, indicated quite consistently as *Christiani*, or the Greek *Χριστιανοί* (see Appendix 3),

[34] Suetonius, *De vita Caesarum: Claudius* 25.4. A more elaborate analysis of this passage in the context of measures against Jewish communities may be found in section 3.11.3. See also Acts 18.1–3.

[35] For this connection and the likelihood of confusion in the time of Nero, see Fuchs (1950), 69–72. Fuchs also points out Tacitus' notable claim that Christians were called *Chrestini* by the *vulgus*—the common people—in particular, which may suggest that the author was to some extent aware of the misspelling. A similar argument is made by van Voorst (2000), 43–4, who sees Tacitus' use of *Christus* later in the same passage as a subtle correction of 'vulgar' terminology. Carrier (2014), 273–7 and Shaw (2015), 84 also connect the events under Nero and Claudius. This idea is rejected by Cook (2010), 49.

[36] For the related argument that Suetonius is quite capable of distinguishing between Chrestus (and therefore *Chrestiani*) and *Christiani*, see Botermann (1996), 86. Benko (1984), 16 and Lund (2008), 256 argue that Tacitus made no distinction between Jews and Christians in this passage, overlooking the fact that Tacitus elsewhere refers to *Iudaei* directly.

[37] See Carrier (2014); Hansen (2023[a]) and (2023[b]); and Shaw (2015) for elaborate discussions of this argument. Shaw (2015), 84 acknowledges Suetonius' account likely contains a reliable core, but dismisses the idea that his reference to Christians in this context could be based on sources contemporary to the events without elaborating on his reasons.

[38] See Power (2014) for a rejection of the common assumption that Suetonius was strongly inspired by Tacitus and used his work as one of his most significant points of reference.

[39] For the suggestion that Domitian's actions played a significant part in the emerging distinction between Christianity and Judaism, see Heemstra (2010). For a more elaborate discussion of these events, see section 3.14.1.

in texts discussing their legal interactions with the Roman authorities.[40] If any memory of the movement's Jewish heritage remained, this appears to have been rarely referenced in the first two centuries CE, and certainly not within the context of legal proceedings.[41] It must be stressed, however, that the relative simplicity of the terminology used to describe Christianity from a Roman perspective should not be taken to mean that its followers were at this stage in any way monolithic in their beliefs and practices. Instead, the lack of an extensive and sophisticated Roman jargon on the subject should simply be taken to mean that such differences likely did not attract the eye of the non-Christian inhabitants of the empire, or were not considered to be relevant in a legal context.[42] For this reason, the term 'Christians' will be used throughout this chapter to indicate the wide variety of groups referred to as such in the first and second centuries CE, whatever their differences may have been. Whenever possible, the other groups that are relevant to our discussion, such as Romans and members of the empire's Jewish communities, will also be referred to by the terms used in our source material. To prevent us from taking on an overtly Christian perspective, however, terms like 'pagan' will be avoided outside of the context of direct citation.

4.3 Outline and Central Questions

In the remainder of this chapter, the legal interactions between various representatives of the Roman authorities and the emerging Christian movement will be analysed in detail. Once again, we will follow a chronological sequence as much as possible in order to better trace the development of the applied procedures, as well as the availability of potential precedents. In the case of Christianity, this adherence to chronology is slightly more straightforward than it was in previous chapters: while the corpus of legal measures dealing with diviners and Jewish communities included a number of different types of legal interactions, the majority of sources dealing with early Christianity refer to specific trials, either against individual Christians or larger groups. Nevertheless, we will occasionally encounter measures that were intended to offer regulations for these legal proceedings, Trajan's famous reply to his governor Pliny's letter chief among them. An overview of all relevant cases may be found in Appendix 3.

[40] A potential reference to Christians as 'Galileans' occurs in Epictetus, *Dissertationes* 4.7.6. without any references to legal proceedings.

[41] See Barclay (2014). Shaw (2015), 86 makes the argument that the information about Christianity ascribed to Tacitus places special emphasis on its origins in Judea. It is notable, however, that both Tacitus and Lucianus, *De morte Peregrini* 11 describe Jesus as having introduced a new cult, despite also mentioning the movement's origins in Palestine.

[42] For a similar argument, see Streeter (2006), 33–4.

As was the case in previous chapters, only interactions dated before the middle of the third century CE will be considered in our analysis. In addition to the large-scale political developments already discussed in the Introduction, Decius' edict of universal sacrifice in the year 249/250 has widely been regarded as a significant turning point in the Roman state's approach to Christianity, and for this reason this date is a particularly apt endpoint.[43] In order to present an overview that is as complete as possible, however, this analysis will include a brief look at the various legal conflicts referenced in the biblical book of Acts on the other side of our timeline. Although it is highly doubtful that the individuals involved in these proceedings were at this stage recognized as Christians by the relevant authorities, as discussed in section 4.2, such a discussion may nevertheless greatly aid our understanding of the historical background from which later events emerged. While G. E. M. de Ste Croix is right to remark that we know of 'no persecution by the Roman government until 64 [i.e. when Nero is said to have taken actions against the Christian community of Rome]',[44] this should not prevent us from discussing earlier events. The way in which the local populations of various cities responded to the emerging Christian movement in its early days may well provide us with much-needed context for the mechanisms, considerations, concerns, and beliefs that would contribute to later cases under the auspices of the Roman authorities, especially when combined with our earlier discussion of the treatment of diviners and members of Jewish communities.

The number of Roman sources that deal with the legal treatment of Christians is relatively limited, consisting mostly of brief references by both Tacitus and Suetonius, as well as the famous Pliny–Trajan correspondence and a select number of other missives ascribed to Roman officials. For this reason, accounts of martyrdom by Christian authors are one of the most prominent, and at the same time one of the most complex, sources for the legal treatment of early Christianity.[45] Such narratives come in many forms, but their descriptions of the lives and deaths of early Christians often include references to the legal proceedings in which their subjects became involved. On some occasions, we are given only brief references to the death of important figures from the early days of the church, without significant details about charges or procedures.[46] At other times,

[43] See (among many others), Leppin (2007), 100; Rives (2007), 199; and Ste Croix (1974ª), 211. Keresztes (1979), 308 is less exact in his distinction between phases in the treatment of Christians, but nevertheless sees Decius as part of a broader transition to a 'new era'. For the idea that Decius' edict was not aimed at Christians in particular, but may still be seen as an indication of shifting political structures, see Leppin (2007), 100–1 and particularly Rives (1999).

[44] Ste Croix (1974ª), 211.

[45] The number of official legal or administrative documents on the subject is exceedingly limited, which necessitates the inclusion of more literary materials. See for instance the collection of legal documents in Coleman-Norton (1966), the overwhelming majority of which dates to the time of Constantine or later.

[46] Many such stories may be found in the earlier books of Eusebius, *Historia Ecclesiastica*. While Keresztes (1979) briefly includes a number of these references in his analysis of the legal treatment of Christians in the imperial period, they ultimately lack sufficient detail to be truly useful.

however, the accounts are more substantial, and may even provide elaborate descriptions of trials that provide useful additional information. The extent to which such narratives may be seen as viable historical sources, however, continues to be the subject of much debate, and certainly not all accounts are created equal in this regard. The date of composition of these texts in particular has traditionally played an important role in scholarly attempts to determine their trustworthiness. As the reasoning goes, narratives that were composed significantly later than the events they describe may well reflect experiences that differ vastly from what originally occurred, particularly if they were written after 250 CE. The number of accounts that can be considered to fit this definition of historical reliability has dwindled significantly over the years,[47] and of the many martyr narratives that are known to us, fewer than ten now appear with some regularity in lists of texts that are said to have been written before the time of Decius, or at the very least contain a core of material that can be dated to that period. The texts that are most commonly included in such overviews are:

(1) the Martyrdom of Polycarp;
(2) the Martyrdom of Ptolemaeus and Lucius;[48]
(3) the Acts of Justin Martyr and his companions;[49]
(4) the letter of the Christian communities of Lyon and Vienne;
(5) the Acts of the Scillitan Martyrs;
(6) the Martyrdom of Apollonius;
(7) the Martyrdom of Perpetua and Felicitas.[50]

Such lists have been compiled by a variety of different authors, each of whom used different criteria to decide on the inclusion and exclusion of certain

[47] Rebillard (2017), 1–21 provides a historical overview of this development, before suggesting an alternative standard that is not based in attempts to determine the authenticity of the various martyr narratives on the basis of internal criteria, but instead results in a list that includes only those texts whose dating to the period before *c.* 260 CE is supported by external evidence—primarily Eusebius and Augustine. More recently, the author has argued that the concept of 'authenticity' should not be applied to Martyr Acts, which he instead regards as living, literary texts. See Rebillard (2020).

[48] This account is tentatively included in Barnes (1968[b]) but omitted without comment in Barnes (2010). Rebillard (2017) also omits this account, presumably due to the fact that it only occurs in the works of Justin Martyr, and therefore does not fit his criterion of the presence of external evidence. Since it is likely, however, that the composition of Justin's *Second Apology* also predated the time of Decius, it will nevertheless be included in our discussion. For the date of the *Second Apology*, see Marcovich (1994), 11. The *Martyrdom of Potamiaena and Basilides* is similarly excluded by both Barnes (2010) and Rebillard (2017), despite its likewise tentative inclusion in Barnes (1968[b]). However, since this narrative is only discussed by Eusebius in his *Historia Ecclesiastica* 6.5 and cannot therefore reliably be dated to the pre-Decian period, it will be omitted here.

[49] This account is excluded in Rebillard (2017). This is further explained in Rebillard (2019): because of the differences between the account of the *Acta Iustini* and the version of the story presented by Eusebius, the latter can no longer serve as external evidence for the date of the former.

[50] Not included in the selection of Bisbee (1988), 82.

accounts.[51] In order to avoid omitting potentially valuable material a priori, the widest possible range of material about which a degree of consensus exists has been included in this chapter—pending further consideration. While the martyrdoms of Carpus, Papylus and Agathonicê, and Pionius and his companions, have also been on occasion been accepted due to the date ascribed to these events by Eusebius, they have since been dated to the time of Decius by scholarly opinion, and will therefore not be included.[52]

It should be noted, however, that even this relatively limited selection includes texts that, despite their often very different characters, are often distinctly literary in nature, and that none of them should be treated without due caution. While it has long been argued that certain accounts of martyrdom were based on Roman court records, the so-called *commentarii*, this assumption has since been challenged in important ways, and according to G. A. Bisbee, none of the remaining passages in which potential martyrs are interrogated by Roman officials can be said to fully conform to the style of such formal transcripts as we know it from other, documentary sources.[53] While this makes it unlikely that the martyr narratives as we know them are direct copies of official documents, this does not mean that they must therefore be discarded without further consideration. It remains possible that Christians were present at the trials of members of their community, and that their accounts were later recorded in a style that was both familiar and considered appropriate for the occasion. In addition, court records often appear to have been publicly displayed for a short period of time, which could have given interested parties the opportunity to copy excerpts that were of particular relevance to them.[54] It thus remains possible that court records formed the basis for some of the accounts transmitted to us, although in analysing them we should be no less aware of potential biases and later alterations than in the case of texts whose literary bent is more overt. In recent years, this cautious and critical attitude has gained a more prominent position in scholarship dealing with martyr narratives,[55] and while the observation that many (if not all) early Christian texts

[51] For various selections of these texts, see Barnes (1968[b]); Barnes (2010), 356–9; Bisbee (1988), 82; Delehaye (1966); Knopf (1913); Moss (2013), 92; Musurillo (1972); Rebillard (2017).

[52] Rebillard (2017), 35 and 47. Rebillard (2020), 85 also includes the *Life and Passion of Cyprian*, the *Passion of Lucius and Montanus*, and the *Passion of Marian and James* in his overview of early accounts, all of which describe events that are said to have taken place in the late 250s CE.

[53] Bisbee (1988), especially 81–90. See also Rebillard (2017), 15–17 for the argument that it would have been difficult for anyone not involved in a particular trial to gain access to transcripts of such trials before the reign of Gallienus. Rebillard (2020) argues that the use of this format should instead be seen as a literary choice, tailored to produce an effect on the audience and serve an agenda—although the nature of that agenda could vary by time and place.

[54] Rebillard (2017), 17.

[55] This stance is strongly represented in the works of Candida Moss, particularly Moss (2013). See also Ehrman (2013), which focuses on the idea that many early Christian texts have been falsely attributed to well-known individuals, while at the same time acknowledging that such an incorrect authorial attribution was 'widely considered a form of literary deceit', for which see specifically p. 529. For Christian martyrdom in the wider context of the *topos* of heroic death in the ancient world, see

were emended and edited is certainly warranted, we must be careful not to dismiss these texts as potential sources of historical information by default. To do so would be to discount the fact that every text is ultimately bears the mark of its author(s), regardless of what that author's religious beliefs might have been, and that even fictionalized texts would have been made to appear verisimilitudinous and recognizable, even if they are not in the strictest sense 'true'.[56] To swing from a general acceptance of all martyr narratives to an equally comprehensive dismissal is therefore simply not the most productive course of action. Instead, each text must be considered on its own merits, contextualized with the help of other sources on the same or similar events, and be used or discounted on that basis.

In discussing the various stages of the relevant legal interactions, a number of central questions related to the treatment of Christians in the Roman world are deserving of particular attention. The temporal and geographical context in which such measures originated will of course be taken into account, and will in this case include a discussion of the number of Christians that became involved in each particular event: especially in the case of trials, measures aimed at specific individuals may well have been motivated by different circumstances than cases affecting larger groups of Christians. The way in which earlier legal measures shaped specific interactions with members of the Christian community should furthermore be examined with particular care. A number of measures against Christians have been named as potential precedents or landmark decisions, of which those ascribed to Nero and Trajan are the primary candidates. These will therefore be subject to special consideration. In addition, while scholarship has mostly limited itself to precedents involving Christians in particular,[57] it remains important to consider whether measures originally intended for other religious groups may indeed have served a similar function, as has been most prominently suggested by Heidi Wendt.[58]

van Henten and Avemarie (2002). For an exploration of the balance between realism and exaggeration in the setting of Christian trials as described in martyr narratives, see Aubert (2010), while Dinkler (2016) offers a discussion of the importance of genre.

[56] For the idea that the institutional framework presented in martyr narratives can be seen as coherent and realistic, see Aubert (2010). The idea that martyr narratives were fundamentally shaped by (fear of) the legal proceedings Christians could be forced to undergo has been explored from a variety of angles. See Bryen (2014[a]) for the idea that martyr narratives attempted to make sense of a legal system that was perceived as chaotic and illogical, and therefore represent a strongly provincial perspective on Roman government. Shaw (2003) argues that Christian memory was fundamentally shaped by this experience. For the idea that this approximation of historical realism must be considered an important literary device in martyr narratives, see Rebillard (2020), who does however dismiss these accounts from the consideration of historians interested in the legal treatment of Christians.

[57] See, for instance, Rives (2011[b]), 199 and Ste Croix (1974[a]), 242 for the idea that the legal treatment of Christianity was without precedent in the Roman world.

[58] See Wendt (2015[a]) and (2016) for the argument that measures against Christians are best explained by connecting them to the wider 'unofficial pattern' of measures against freelance religious

With regards to the contents of the relevant legal interactions, it pays to reinvestigate a question that Pliny the Younger notably already posed in his correspondence with Emperor Trajan—whether Christians were being punished simply because they were Christians (i.e. because of the *nomen ipsum*), or because they were accused of certain *flagitia* (specific immoral or criminal actions) connected to their beliefs.[59] The idea that Christians were punished simply for their beliefs, rather than any criminal behaviour, gave rise to the argument that the treatment of Christians was unique in the Roman world even in antiquity itself.[60] A claim of this magnitude should, in itself, be enough to warrant suspicion, and we should therefore carefully examine to what extent this was indeed the case. Furthermore, this question is strongly related to the ongoing debate on the legal basis for trials against Christians discussed in the introduction to this chapter and may thus help us in analysing the types of accusations Christians were faced with. In this regard, we should also consider the usage of the so-called sacrifice test, which appears to have been used with some frequency to determine whether the accused was truly Christian. The issue of punishment is also of particular importance. Although we should always remember that our source material likely represents only part of the trials that historically took place, it remains essential to consider whether a proven accusation of Christianity always led to punishment and, if so, what this punishment was, especially given the common perception that Christians were inevitably faced with execution. On a number of occasions, we should also consider the possibility that the accuser could likewise be faced with significant repercussions if his claims proved false and were rejected. Finally, the question to what extent an established procedure for trials involving Christianity existed in the first place, and whether Christianity can truly be considered to have been an 'illegal religion'—either intentionally or by default—should remain central to our analysis.

Throughout this discussion, it will be especially important to consider the involvement of all levels of the Roman administration. This includes not only the centralized imperial authorities and the provincial administration under the leadership of the governor, both of whom have often been the primary focus of scholarly enquiries into the legal treatment of early Christianity,[61] but also local authorities, such as city councils, and the general populations of the regions or cities in which legal interactions with the early Christian movement took place.

experts. Also of note is Beard, North, and Price (1998), 236–8. It bears repeating, however, that such comparisons are relatively rare.

[59] Pliny the Younger, *Epistulae* 10.96.2. See Shaw (2018), 240 n. 27 for the astute observation that term *flagitia* should not necessarily be taken to refer to formal criminal charges but rather to moral judgements. This is not to say, however, that the two could not conceivably overlap in some cases.

[60] Tertullian, *Apologeticus pro Christianis* 2–6.

[61] Opinions about the respective importance of emperor and governor differ vastly. See e.g. Barnes (1985), 149–58 for the argument that the attitude of the emperor was rarely, if ever, truly relevant for the treatment of Christians before the time of Decius.

We will consider how these various levels of government interacted with each other, at which point each of them became involved in the proceedings, and how they made their voices heard—which allows for a more systematic approach. This is especially important when it comes to the role of the general populace. While it is true that the role of this group in instigating trials against Christians has been emphasized on a number of occasions,[62] few analyses make direct reference to 'ordinary' inhabitants of the empire after charges against Christians had been brought before the relevant Roman authorities.[63] It thus remains important to consider not only at what stage the various actors, including Christians themselves, became involved in the legal process but also which methods they used to influence the proceedings and how they were involved in enforcing the ultimate verdict.

4.4 Before the *Institutum Neronianum*: Early Interactions

Although it is unlikely that the Roman authorities recognized Christianity as a distinctive movement in the early years after the execution of Jesus of Nazareth, a number of legal interactions involving his earliest followers are nevertheless referenced in our sources. The first measure dealing with Christians is said to have been created in Rome within mere months after the crucifixion and serves as an interesting example of the way in which measures ascribed to the Roman authorities, and particularly emperors, could be employed by Christian apologists to make their case. In the fifth chapter of his *Apologeticus pro Christianis*, the Christian author Tertullian references a curious incident that, according to his account, occurred during the reign of Tiberius (Appendix 3.1). The story goes that someone, presumably a member of the Roman administration in Judea, had sent an account of recent events in his province to the emperor, on whom the missive allegedly had such a profound impact that he apparently became convinced of the divinity of Christ and attempted to formally include him in the Roman pantheon.[64] However, the acceptance of new deities had traditionally been a privilege reserved for the senate, which subsequently rejected the emperor's suggestion. Angered by this course of events, Tiberius then allegedly swore to punish anyone who attempted to act against the Christians, thereby in effect granting them special protected status.

While the story of Tiberius' supposedly favourable view of Christianity is truly fascinating, and would later be repeated by the fourth-century church historian

[62] See for instance Lane Fox (1986), 422–3 and 450; Rives (2011[b]), 211; Ste Croix (1974[a]), 225–6.

[63] See e.g. Ste Croix (1974[a]), 210 and 238–48.

[64] Tertullian, *Apologeticus pro Christianis* 5.2.

Eusebius,[65] it is almost certainly not based on historical fact.[66] Eusebius explicitly cites Tertullian as his only source for these events, and no other record of Tiberius' remarkable course of actions exists. In fact, the existence of formal legal actions that influenced the lives of members of early Christian communities is doubtful even on the basis of the sources we do have. Tertullian does not explicitly state that Tiberius ever made his allegedly pro-Christian attitudes into law, whether in the form of an imperial edict or otherwise, and even the senate's refusal to include Christ in the Roman pantheon, if it ever occurred, need not have resulted in an alternative ruling that was openly hostile towards Christians—it simply meant that Tiberius' initial proposal was rejected. Furthermore, any imperial or senatorial measure of that kind would certainly have had a greater influence on the events that would transpire under later emperors, and we may therefore have expected it to be mentioned outside the context of Tertullian's *Apology* as well.[67] It is therefore more likely that the author is simply presenting the argument, embellished as it may be, that the central Roman authorities were not involved in legal measures against Christians until the time of Nero, and that he uses this fact to suggest that those who were in office during his own time should therefore likewise refrain from repressive action.[68]

4.4.1 Paul in the eastern Mediterranean: legal interaction in Acts

This is not to say, however, that the early decades of the Christian community were completely uneventful. According to the biblical book of Acts, some of the first members of the movement repeatedly ran into difficulties during their travels through the eastern Mediterranean, and the account of their experiences provides us with interesting insights into the type of reception perceived religious outsiders could encounter during the period (Appendix 3.2).[69] It should be noted, however, that these accounts must be treated cautiously: although the authorship of Acts has traditionally been ascribed to a member of Paul's inner circle who witnessed the events he describes in person, the account is now more commonly

[65] Eusebius, *Historia Ecclesiastica* 2.2. See also Jerome's version of Eusebius' *Chronicon*, AD 35. The account in Orosius, *Historiae adversus Paganos* 7.4.6 is likely based on that of Eusebius. See Barnes (1968a), 33 n. 8.

[66] This episode is seen as at least partially historical by Sordi (1983), 18–20, who argues that Tiberius' measure applied to Judea specifically.

[67] Barnes (1968a), 33 likewise remarks that Tertullian simply makes note of the senate's refusal to incorporate Jesus in the Roman pantheon but does not mention any official legal measure. See also Crake (1965), 61.

[68] This episode may thus parallel Tertullian's reference to what he called the *institutum Neronianum*. See Tertullian, *Ad Nationes* 1.7.9.

[69] See the fascinating analysis of Wendt (2016), 146–89, who sees the apostle Paul in particular as a representative of what she calls the 'religion of freelance experts'.

dated to the end of the first, or possibly the beginning of the second, century CE.[70] Nevertheless, Acts remains one of the most significant sources for Christianity's early development, in large part because of its unique insight into the period in question.[71] In addition, it has been argued that the legal procedures described by the author, while diverse, are nevertheless largely historically accurate.[72]

While the account in Acts concludes with Paul's arrival in Rome, where he had been sent by Roman magistrates to make his appeal before the emperor against charges brought against him in Judea,[73] the overwhelming majority of the legal interactions described in the text notably do not involve Roman officials at all. Most difficulties Paul and his travel companions encountered in the various cities of the eastern Mediterranean had a strongly local character, and although it would go too far to describe all these turbulent interactions in detail, a number of illustrative examples may nonetheless be given. According to Acts, Paul and his companions were met with mixed responses by the Jewish communities they visited both in Antioch in Pisidia and in the city of Iconium.[74] If the account as we know it is indeed accurate, a pattern soon emerged in which the men were initially met with enthusiasm, before relations quickly turned sour. In the case of Antioch, the author of Acts reports that certain members of the Jewish community were offended by Paul's attempts to preach not only to them but also to their non-Jewish neighbours, and they turned to the city's most pre-eminent citizens in an attempt to have Paul and his companions expelled.[75] While the story told in Acts is relatively brief, and seems to be strongly representative of the author's complicated relationship with Judaism,[76] some have suggested that the suspicions against Paul were not entirely unwarranted or unmotivated. The Jewish community was fairly well established in the city, as is demonstrated both by their apparently good relationship with the local authorities and the fact that the female

[70] Molthagen (1991), 44. See also Billings (2017), 11–14 for a critical analysis of the existing consensus and the debate surrounding it. Much of the dating of Acts depends on possible references to the fall of the Temple in Jerusalem, and especially on one's views on the author's use of external sources, particularly the works of Josephus and Paul's letters. If Acts does indeed make reference to either of these works, which are assumed to have been in circulation since the early second century CE, a later dating becomes more likely.

[71] The question of the sources used by the author of Acts remains difficult to answer. Josephus and the Pauline letters both feature prominently in the debate, as mentioned in the previous note, but Molthagen (1991), 44–5 suggests that there may also have been many other (possibly oral) traditions on which the author could rely. For the argument that Paul's interactions with the Roman authorities were essential for creating a formal distinction between Jewish and Christian communities, see Lane Fox (1986), 432.

[72] Sherwin-White (1963), 48–119 disputes the idea that the course of events as described in Acts is historically problematic, focusing especially on the account of Paul's trials with Roman officials.

[73] For Paul's appeal (which he notably requested before the governor had given his verdict), see Acts 25.11. A brief, open-ended description of his stay in Rome is given in 28.17–28.

[74] See Acts 13.42–50 and 14.1–6, respectively.

[75] Acts 13.50. For the idea that the *duoviri* of the city were involved in this matter, see Molthagen (1991), 47 and Vittinghoff (1984), 337.

[76] Dunn (2016), *ad loc.*; Harvey (2004), 434–5.

sympathizers with Judaism (σεβόμεναι) mentioned in the text are said to have been members of the local elite.[77] It is thus very possible that certain members of the Jewish community were concerned that the arrival of the newcomers would cause a disruption of the existing equilibrium. They may therefore have attempted to prevent any potential disturbances by enlisting the help of the local authorities and driving Paul and his companions away from the city.[78]

This course of events was repeated in Iconium, where the town's non-Jewish magistrates (ἄρχοντες) are once again said to have been involved.[79] When the group later arrived in Lystra, a similar pattern once again emerged, and the population of the city again attempted to remove Paul and his companions from their territories.[80] All three cities seem to have been only briefly successful in their attempts, since the company is reported to have retraced their steps only a short time later.[81] The short duration of their removal from the city makes it even more likely that the actions of the various city authorities described in Acts should be seen as attempts to maintain public order and not as an attempt to systematically oppress the movement spearheaded by Paul and his companions. The events in the Greek city of Thessalonica that are described later in Acts present a similar picture: once again, Paul and his followers are said to have been initially successful, but their efforts were then thwarted by what the author calls the jealousy of the local Jewish community.[82] In this case, however, the ending of the story is slightly different: instead of Paul and his companions, who appear to have disappeared at some point during the commotion, it was a local man called Jason who was brought before the city authorities (πολιτάρχοι) along with his brothers, likely because he had offered the visitors a place to stay. The reasons the crowd gave for Jason's arrest confirm that a fear for disturbances of the peace played a significant role in shaping their attitude towards Paul and his companions: they accused the group of 'having brought the whole world into an uproar' and followed this up by saying that these dangerous individuals had now come to their own doorstep.[83] In addition, they claimed that Paul and his followers have broken

[77] The word σεβόμενοι may be a reference to the so-called god-fearers, a term that is commonly used to denote Greeks and Romans who sympathized with Judaism without fully converting.

[78] Dunn (2016), *ad loc.* See also Hare (1967), 1–18 for the various underlying reasons for conflict between Jewish communities and early Christians.

[79] Acts 14.5.

[80] Acts 14.19–20. In this passage, the author claims that members of the Jewish communities from Antioch and Iconium arrived to spur on the locals. This course of events is doubted by Molthagen (1991), 49; while Dunn (2016), *ad loc.* calls it 'surprising, but not incredible', before pointing out a number of curious inconsistencies in the passage.

[81] Acts 14.21. [82] Acts 17.1–13.

[83] Acts 17.6–7: *Οἱ τὴν οἰκουμένην ἀναστατώσαντες οὗτοι καὶ ἐνθάδε πάρεισιν, οὓς ὑποδέδεκται Ἰάσων.* One might tentatively suggest that the phrasing of this passage, with its quick, repetitive references to Paul and his followers, and its direct juxtaposition of turmoil in the rest of the world and turmoil at home, indicates distress on the part of the populace. Harvey (2004), 449 has suggested that this may be a reference to Claudius' letter to the Alexandrians, in which the emperor accuses the Jewish community of that city of stirring up trouble in similar terms. While such a direct link cannot be proven,

with imperial commands by 'saying that there is another king', thus showing that they saw the Jesus-followers not only as a threat to local public order but also as a potential rebellious entity that could seriously endanger their relationship with the imperial authorities.[84] Ultimately, Jason and his brothers were released on bail, likely on the condition that they ensured their guests' good behaviour—or alternatively their departure—and thereby restored public order in the city.[85]

On other occasions, the reception the Jesus-followers received in the various cities they visited seems to have been at least partially influenced by additional economic motivations. When describing the arrival of Paul in the Macedonian city of Philippi, the author of Acts mentions an encounter with an enslaved woman, whose prophetic gifts were apparently highly profitable for her owners.[86] However, when Paul subsequently performed an exorcism, the woman's divinatory abilities (and therefore her masters' source of income) are said to have quickly disappeared. Enraged by this course of events, the inhabitants of the town brought Paul and his companion Silas before the local authorities (*ἄρχοντες*; *στρατηγοί*), arguing that the men were Jews who caused disturbances in the city, and in addition proclaimed customs which the inhabitants, as Roman citizens, were not allowed to follow.[87] While it is true that the citizens of Philippi had a special status due to the city's position as a Roman colony,[88] it nevertheless remains unclear what exactly they meant by this. The accusation of subversive behaviour is clear enough and fits the established pattern of Paul's treatment in various other cities discussed in this section, but the second complaint raises questions. Some have seen this particular accusation as a sign that Paul's accusers were aware of Emperor Claudius' alleged attempts to limit the spread of Judaism (section 3.11.3).[89] However, the more convincing interpretation is that we may not be dealing with a formal ban on conversion as such, but rather with an appeal to

the word *ἀναστατώσαντες* in particular likely does reference a common fear of escalating unrests in many cities of the ancient Mediterranean.

[84] This accusation is a clear reference to the trial of Jesus himself. Despite the obvious parallel, both Dunn (2016), *ad loc.* and Harvey (2004), 450 assume that these were the actual accusations made by the inhabitants of Thessalonica. It is of course possible that even those not directly involved with Paul and his followers had picked up on this narrative from public speeches, or even rumours, but caution is nevertheless warranted. Whatever the case, the gist of the accusation—namely disturbance of the peace and potential attempts to stir up political unrest—remains unaltered.

[85] Dunn (2016), *ad loc.*; Harvey (2004), 450.

[86] Acts 16.16–40.

[87] It should be noted that Paul and his companions were seen as Jewish, which places this passage in the context of the popular hostility against various Jewish communities discussed in the previous chapter. In this case, however, we are not dealing with a Jewish community from within a specific city but rather a group of travelling outsiders, who furthermore would likely have been unwilling to reference precedents allowing Jewish communities to practise their ancestral customs.

[88] Molthagen (1991), 49. While Sherwin-White (1963), 101 calls this the first time Paul is brought before a Roman tribunal, the officials appear to have been those of the city itself, without direct connection to a Roman governor. See Harvey (2004), 446–7.

[89] See Sherwin-White (1963), 81, who in this context mentions Claudius' expulsion of Jews from Rome.

the Roman identity of this *colonia* in Greek territory.[90] It is therefore likely that Paul and Silas' trial was based on a variety of factors, which were both economic, religious, and political in nature. In the end, however, the consequences of the charge were limited: Paul and Silas were initially beaten and brought to prison, but when it became known that they were Roman citizens, they were quickly released.[91] The fact that they were still asked to leave the city afterwards serves only to confirm that public order had once again been a primary concern. The events that occurred during Paul's stay in Ephesus show a similar combination of different types of concerns: a local silversmith famously instigated a riot against both Paul's companions and the local Jewish community out of fear for his livelihood, by complaining that they presented a threat to the status of the city's world-famous sanctuary of the goddess Artemis.[92] According to the author of Acts, this accusation led to an uproar in the city's assembly, which only calmed down when the city scribe (*γραμματεύς*) reminded the population that they should make formal accusations before the governor if they felt that they had grounds to do so, lest they themselves be accused of instigating a riot.[93] The account does not mention if such charges were actually filed,[94] but nevertheless demonstrates the complex web of economic, religious, and social anxieties and motivations that could lead people to argue for legal measures against religious groups perceived as outsiders.

4.4.2 Roman officials in Acts

While the idea of Roman intervention is present in the background of the Ephesian narrative, Roman officials themselves appear in Acts only rarely—and when they do, they are not always eager participants. During his long-term stay in Corinth,[95] Paul was brought before the proconsul Gallio by members of the

[90] Harvey (2004), 447 n. 25; Sherwin-White (1963), 82. See also Dunn (2016), *ad loc.* and Molthagen (1991), 50–2 against the argument that this trial was based on a formal ban on proselytism. The ambiguous use of the verb [*οὐκ*] *ἔξεστιν*, which may indicate religious incompatibility as well as legal prohibition, is particularly interesting in this regard.

[91] Acts 16.37–40.

[92] Acts 19.23–41. For a more elaborate analysis of this passage, see Brinks (2009). For the argument that Paul himself may not have been involved in these events, see Molthagen (1991), 68–70, who nevertheless does not dispute that something similar to the events described in Acts did, in fact, take place.

[93] For the correctness of the recommended procedure, see Harvey (2004), 462–3; Sherwin-White (1963), 83–4. Harvey (2004), 462 also argues that the Roman authorities could well have seen such a spontaneous assembly as an abuse of the city's political privileges.

[94] The reference to 'combat with beasts' in 1 Corinthians 15.32 should not be taken to mean that Paul was actually condemned to the arena. Instead, it is more likely that the phrase is meant as a metaphor for conflict with worshippers of Artemis, who was associated with wild animals. See Hooker (2013).

[95] It is interesting to note that the author of Acts claims that Paul lived in Corinth for a year and a half. While it is unclear at what stage the Jewish community of the city decided to turn against him

Jewish community, who accused him of encouraging people to worship god in ways contrary to the law (*λέγοντες ὅτι παρὰ τὸν νόμον ἀναπείθει οὗτος τοὺς ἀνθρώπους σέβεσθαι τὸν θεόν*).[96] This complaint is notably ambiguous, and it remains unclear whether the phrase is referring to Roman or Jewish law. It has been remarked that the text makes no mention of Jews specifically, but that Paul was instead accused of trying to convert a larger group described only as *ἄνθρωποι*.[97] For this reason, the argument goes, it may be possible that the Jewish community of Corinth was trying to attract the governor's attention by suggesting that Paul was trying to divert Romans from their traditional practices, thereby allegedly breaking Roman law.[98] Even if this was their intent, however, proconsul Gallio appears to have interpreted their words rather differently:

> *Μέλλοντος δὲ τοῦ Παύλου ἀνοίγειν τὸ στόμα εἶπεν ὁ Γαλλίων πρὸς τοὺς Ἰουδαίους, Εἰ μὲν ἦν ἀδίκημά τι ἢ ῥᾳδιούργημα πονηρόν, ὦ Ἰουδαῖοι, κατὰ λόγον ἂν ἀνεσχόμην ὑμῶν· εἰ δὲ ζητήματά ἐστιν περὶ λόγου καὶ ὀνομάτων καὶ νόμου τοῦ καθ' ὑμᾶς, ὄψεσθε αὐτοί· κριτὴς ἐγὼ τούτων οὐ βούλομαι εἶναι.*[99]
>
> Just when Paul wanted to open his mouth, Gallio said to the Jews: 'If there were some injustice, or a base misdeed, Jews, I would of course bear with you: but if the dispute is about a word, or names, or that law of yours, then see to it yourselves: I do not want to be the judge of that.'

Gallio, then, clearly saw the complaints made against Paul as an internal dispute between different members of the Jewish community, and therefore believed that he had no reason to judge the matter. According to Gallio, there was no foundation for a trial before a Roman court and he outright refused to hear the case, thereby showing the importance of the governor's role in accepting or rejecting specific charges even at this early point in time.

The same consideration would once again play an important part after Paul's return to Jerusalem, where he was likewise accused of encouraging his followers to break with Jewish law.[100] According to the author of Acts, this accusation caused a substantial riot, which in turn forced the Roman authorities (in this case

and his followers, the phrasing of the passage suggests that this did not occur at the very beginning of his stay. Further context is, however, omitted.

[96] Acts 18.12–17. [97] Sherwin-White (1963), 101.

[98] See Sherwin-White (1963), 101–2, where Sherwin-White also draws a parallel to the events in Philippi and Thessalonica discussed in section 4.4.1. See also Dunn (2016), *ad loc.* and Harvey (2004), 456, both of whom point out the ambiguity. Sherwin-White (1963), 102–3 adds the suggestion that the Jewish community was referring to Claudius' decision that Jews in the Diaspora should be allowed to maintain their own customs (Appendix 2.49). Measures of this kind, however, usually seem to have offered protection against local authorities targeting a Jewish community, and it is unlikely that they would have been employed against a fringe group that may not have differed greatly from the city's Jews in Roman eyes, and whose alleged suppression of Jewish *mores* might therefore have been difficult to prove before a Roman judge.

[99] Acts 18.14–15. [100] For the accusations levied against Paul, see Acts 21.20–9.

the χιλίαρχος) to intervene. The accusations levied at Paul were at first lost in the turmoil, and the commander showed his concern with public order by trying to determine if Paul could be identified as a certain notorious Egyptian who had recently fled the city with an armed group of *Sicarii* at his side.[101] When this turned out not to be the case, the commander made preparations for Paul's interrogation under torture, but was promptly dissuaded from this when his captive announced that he was a Roman citizen, and he decided to make further enquiries of the high priests and the Sanhedrin instead.[102] This meeting did not, however, prove fruitful, and the author of Acts alleges that the commander received word about a conspiracy against Paul's life shortly after. Whether or not such a conspiracy did indeed exist, it is likely that the commander now considered matters to have escalated beyond his jurisdiction. He contacted Felix, the governor, who was at the time residing in Caesarea, and asked him to judge the matter as he thought best—with the additional remark that he himself had not been able to find any ground for punishment, and that the matter appeared to him to be nothing more than an internal dispute about Jewish law.[103]

Once again, then, we are dealing with a Roman official who was reluctant to judge a case in which he felt no crime had been committed, but on this occasion, considerations for public order seem to have carried more weight—especially given the particularly sensitive nature of disputes surrounding the Jewish temple. In the procedures that followed, both under Felix and his successor Festus, the question of charges seems to have remained of primary importance. According to the account, neither the two governors nor King Agrippa I, who was apparently allowed to personally question Paul, were able find anything that warranted a trial,[104] and at Paul's request the case was ultimately referred to Rome. While Acts does not provide us with a description of the subsequent trial in Rome, or even an indication of the imperial authorities' ultimate verdict, it has been argued that its description of Paul's dealings with the Roman authorities in Judea is at least partially reliable.[105] Throughout Acts, it thus becomes clear that the legal problems faced by the early Jesus-followers tended to emerge from the particular towns and cities they visited, and that the trials that involved them were particularly concerned with upholding public order in the face of concerns about religious nonconformity and, on occasion, the economic and socio-political prosperity of people living in these communities. Such complaints were usually

[101] Acts 21.31–40. [102] Acts 22.22–30.

[103] Acts 23.26–30. Dunn (2016), *ad loc.* sees a parallel with Pliny's consultation of Trajan when he perceived events in his province to have grown beyond his control.

[104] This point is made on a number of occasions. See Acts 25.5, 25.20, 25.27, 26.31–2. Dunn (2016), *ad loc.* argues for the historical accuracy of this account, which also remains unquestioned by Sherwin-White (1963), 51.

[105] Molthagen (1991), 71; and Sherwin-White (1963), 48–70. The latter argues that the legal procedures followed in the text are a good example of the *cognitio* procedure and is supported in this view by Shaw (2015), 78.

handled by local officials, and when Roman authorities did become involved, they appear to have been more concerned with proper procedures than with the religious beliefs of the people brought before them, which they appear to have considered an internal matter of Jewish communities.

4.4.3 Claudius' expulsion: Christian involvement?

A potential parallel to the events described in Acts may be found in Emperor Claudius' attempt to expel the Jewish community from the city of Rome (Appendix 3.3). While it is unlikely that this measure was intended to target Christians in particular, as has been discussed in sections 3.11.3 and 4.2,[106] Suetonius' use of the phrase *impulsore Chresto* has led some scholars to believe that the expulsion found its origins in disturbances caused by disputes between Jesus-followers and other parts of Rome's Jewish community—and that Christians were therefore *de facto* included in the measure.[107] On the one hand, it is unlikely that the distinction between various sub-groups of the Jewish community was particularly relevant from a Roman perspective, and the fact remains that the terminology used in the various sources that describe the event is exclusively focused on Jewish groups. On the other hand, parallels with the numerous conflicts described in Acts stand out even from the exceedingly brief references to Claudius' expulsion available to us.[108] The focus of the authorities on maintaining public order is particularly noticeable, even at first glance: disputes within a religious group, or between that group and the rest of the city's inhabitants, could clearly lead to substantial unrests, and Acts establishes the expulsion of the perceived offenders as a standard response to such situations. A reference to Claudius' measure in Acts itself even claims that two of those expelled became members of Paul's circle in Corinth soon after his arrival there,[109] suggesting that they felt affinity with his ideas. All of this, however, does not provide us with concrete evidence that early Christians were indeed involved in Claudius' expulsion of the Jewish community from Rome: our sources notably refer to the Jews of the city as a single group, rather than multiple factions, and Suetonius' mention of an individual known as Chrestus is ultimately inconclusive.[110]

[106] For an argument to the contrary, see Dibelius (1971), 78.

[107] See Botermann (1996), 98; Dunn (2016), 241; Harvey (2004), 455. For a discussion of the manuscript tradition of the phrase *impulsore Chresto*, see Boman (2011).

[108] Acts 18.1–3; Suetonius, *De vita Caesarum: Claudius* 25.4. Another reference to measures against the Jewish community of Rome under Claudius may be found in Cassius Dio, *Historiae Romanae* 60.6.6.

[109] Acts 18.1–3.

[110] For the view that Chrestus was almost certainly a living individual, and that the name was indeed a very common one during the period, see Koestermann (1967), 460.

Yet, it is likewise impossible to fully rule out the possibility that Christians were indeed swept up in the expulsion—or indeed contributed to it. The fact that Roman officials like Gallio, Felix, and Festus showed little interest in the particulars of what they saw as internal Jewish disputes, but nevertheless attempted to deal with such disturbances in their own ways, makes the idea that similar conflicts lay at the basis of the disturbances in Rome more likely. Indeed, it may be argued that this measure paralleled the expulsions of diviners discussed in Chapter 2, which likewise appear to have made little to no attempt to distinguish between different types of diviners. For those who believe that Jesus-followers were indeed involved in the events in Rome, a similar attitude on the part of Claudius or his administrators in the city may in fact explain the lack of direct, unambiguous references to the presence of Christians in Roman sources on the subject. Such considerations, however, likely go beyond the intentions that ultimately underpinned Claudius' expulsion as a legal measure. It must be acknowledged that both in the case of the events described in Acts and in that of Claudius' expulsion, Roman officials were attempting to take administrative decisions they believed to be appropriate for protecting public order, and that they did so while using terminology related to Judaism. The expulsion, then, cannot be seen as a measure aimed at Christians specifically, and if they did become involved in its enforcement, it was because they were seen as members of a group that allegedly threatened law and order.

4.4.4 Peter and Paul in Rome?

Traditionally, two final legal interactions have been dated to the period before, or surrounding, Emperor Nero's measure against Christians as a group. The deaths of the apostles Peter and Paul have remained of particular importance for Christian collective memory, but the exact circumstances of these events remain difficult to determine. In part, this is due to their almost legendary nature, and the available accounts may well have distorted the historical facts beyond all recognition. In addition, most references to the events are brief and provide little additional information about the legal proceedings that may have preceded the men's final moments. This becomes particularly clear in the various accounts discussing the death of Peter (Appendix 3.4). While the tradition of his martyrdom is significant, and likely dates back to a relatively early period,[111] the majority of

[111] For an elaborate discussion of the various sources dealing with Peter's martyrdom, see Bauckham (1992). For the idea that Peter was not martyred but died peacefully in Judea, see Goulder (2004). Zwierlein (2009) and (2013) follow a similar line of thinking. Both arguments are taken up by Shaw (2015), who also argues strongly against any possible connection between the martyrdoms of Peter and Paul and the Great Fire of 64 CE. For an elaborate discussion of the archaeological evidence for Peter's presence in Rome, see Weber (2011).

sources tell us little about the nature of any potential charges brought against him nor about the procedures that were followed. Even the method of execution, which is traditionally said to have been crucifixion—although famously upside-down—occurs only in a single source that can be dated before the third century, and in opaque terms at that.[112] The first epistle of Clement mentions that Peter became the victim of jealousy, but makes no attempt to further expand on the issue or to present details about the nature of his 'many tribulations'.[113] The so-called Acts of Peter provide more information, and claim that Peter's death was due to the animosity of several members of the Roman elite, who held Peter responsible for the fact that their wives and mistresses had left them, and therefore demanded his crucifixion on the charge of godlessness (*ἐπ' αἰτίᾳ ἀθεότητος*).[114] The historical reliability of this account, however, has widely been doubted.[115] Finally, both Tertullian and Lactantius link the deaths of Peter and Paul to the alleged Neronian persecution in the wake of the Great Fire, but once again little additional information is provided, and their accounts have likewise come to be regarded with suspicion.[116] Thus, while the extensiveness of the tradition regarding Peter's martyrdom makes it difficult to fully dismiss the possibility that he was condemned to death, possibly at the behest of the Roman authorities, the variety and brevity of the available accounts make it altogether impossible to reach any definitive conclusion as to its nature and circumstances. We simply do not know for certain what Peter may have been charged with, or what events may have contributed to the potential verdict.

The tradition of Paul's martyrdom (Appendix 3.5) rests on firmer historical grounds, in large part due to the fact that his arrest and treatment by Roman officials in Judea is described in great detail by the author of Acts 28.11–30. While this account, as remarked, breaks off during Paul's extended stay in the city of Rome, it at least provides us with a plausible explanation for the idea that his case came to the attention of the central Roman authorities. However, it is unclear whether Paul was ultimately executed on the basis of the accusations referred to in Acts, if new allegations were brought forward during his stay in the capital, or even if he left Rome and subsequently travelled elsewhere.[117] The substantial duration of his stay in itself need not be seen as evidence against the continuation of the procedures started in Jerusalem. It is possible that the imperial authorities simply took a long time to process the diverse range of cases brought before them, or that the delay was increased by the travel times between Jerusalem and Rome that Paul's

[112] John 21.18–19. [113] 1 Clement 5.4.

[114] Acts of Peter 33–6.

[115] Shaw (2015), 75 rejects this source, and suggests a fourth- or fifth-century dating. Bauckham (1992), 578–80 favours a second-century date and is generally less critical regarding the tradition of Peter's martyrdom, but nevertheless likewise draws attention to various factors that may complicate a historical reading of the text.

[116] Especially by Shaw (2015).

[117] Harrill (2012), 70–2 emphasizes the diversity of the accounts of Paul's later days.

accusers had to contend with.[118] It thus remains possible that Paul was indeed executed in Rome, and the repeated occurrence of this idea in Christian tradition does seem to point in that direction.[119] However, we are once again faced with a lack of information regarding the nature of the procedures that would have led to this verdict. Paul's execution, like that of Peter, has been connected to the events surrounding the Great Fire of 64 CE, but this idea has in recent years increasingly come to be seen as unlikely.[120] As far as we can tell, each of the legal proceedings Paul went through was the result of disputes within particular cities in the eastern provinces of the empire. It is therefore most prudent to assume that these or similar events may have led to his ultimate execution without assuming an active intervention on the part of the central authorities. Unfortunately, this means that we are left with no other option than to omit any definitive conclusions about the end of the legal proceedings described in Acts due to lack of evidence. It is certainly possible that the accusations of disturbing public order that had followed Paul from Jerusalem were ultimately seen as credible and that he was punished on this basis, but we simply cannot be certain.

4.5 Christians under Nero: Smoke and Fire?

The reign of Emperor Nero has also become inextricably associated with the first larger-scale suppression of Christianity by the imperial authorities. In itself, this is not unwarranted: both Tacitus and Suetonius report that Nero took action against Christians living in the city of Rome (Appendix 3.6), and this idea is likewise prominently present in the Christian tradition.[121] Tacitus' account of the events surrounding Nero's measures, with its vivid and comparatively elaborate descriptions, has understandably become most famous, and it is here that we first find the connection between Christians and the devastating fire that razed large parts of Rome in the summer of 64 CE:

[118] Harvey (2004), 484; Sherwin-White (1963), 118–19.

[119] See Acts of Paul; Eusebius, *Historia Ecclesiastica* 2.25.5–8 and 3.1.2–3; Jerome, *De Viris Illustribus* 5; and Tertullian, *Scorpiace* 15. Many others, including 1 Clement 5.4; Ignatius of Antioch, *Letter to the Ephesians* 12; and Lactantius, *De Mortibus Persecutorum* 2 mention Paul's martyrdom, and at times even link it to Nero, but do not make specific mention of its location. The idea that Paul, as a Roman citizen, would have been beheaded emerges in the Acts of Paul and in Tertullian, *De Praescriptione Hereticorum* 36.

[120] Shaw (2015), 76–8. Zwierlein (2013), 146 goes further by arguing that there is no real evidence that Paul died in Rome or was martyred.

[121] See especially Tertullian's claim that the persecution of Christians was an *institutum Neronianum* in Tertullian, *Ad Nationes* 1.7.8–9. The importance of this tradition is emphasized by Jones (2017), 147. For the two non-Christians accounts, see Suetonius, *De vita Caesarum: Nero* 16; Tacitus, *Annales* 15.44. While Lund (2008), 256 is right in remarking that we are dealing with Tacitus' etic perspective rather than the internal, emic perspective of the Christian community, his reference to Christianity nevertheless remains significant. The story of Nero 'fiddling while Rome burned' has likewise become the stuff of legend. For this issue, see Scheda (1967).

> *Sed non ope humana, non largitionibus principis aut deum placamentis decedebat infamia quin iussum incendium crederetur. Ergo abolendo rumori Nero subdidit reos et quaesitissimis poenis adfecit quos per flagitia invisos vulgus Chrestianos appellabat.*[122]
>
> But neither human ability, nor the largesse of the emperor or means of appeasing the gods could do away with the ugly rumour that held that the fire had been the result of an order. Therefore, to do away with the gossip, Nero supplied as the offenders those who, hated for their crimes, were called *Chrestiani* by the populace, and afflicted them with special punishments.

After offering a brief explanation of who these Christians were and where they came from,[123] Tacitus then proceeds to discuss the legal treatment of this group under Nero. This passage has proved to be highly controversial, in large part due to a number of important textual problems, the various resolutions of which have been used to support an equally diverse number of interpretations of what occurred during the period. On the one hand, we find those who argue that Christians were targeted specifically for their religious beliefs, either on the basis of a general law or in a more ad hoc fashion—a distinction that to some extent depends on one's interpretation of Tertullian's reference to the almost proverbial *institutum Neronianum*.[124] On the other hand, there is the school of thought that finds the legal basis for the execution of Christians under Nero in the charge of arson—as well as a smaller group that believes that Christians were not targeted at all and that Nero's measure was instead aimed at members of the Jewish

[122] Tacitus, *Annales* 15.44. The edition used is that of the Oxford Classical Text by Fisher (1906), with the exception of *Chrestianos*, for which Fisher prints *Christianos* without reference to alternative readings. The debate about the correct reading of this particular phrase is a long one, even by the standards of this highly contentious passage, and need not be exhaustively discussed here. It should be noted, however, that scholarly opinion remains divided. Ash (2018), 205 prints *Christianos* without further comment, as does the Loeb edition of Jackson (1937), 282. Koestermann (1968), 254 holds that the oldest surviving version of the passage in the second *Codex Mediceus* (11th century CE) originally read *Chrestianos* but was changed to reference *Christianos* by a later hand. In this, he is followed by Boman (2011), 355 n. 2 and the Teubner edition of Heubner (1983), 369. Given Tacitus' apparent juxtaposition of the vulgar term for the movement and his own explanation of its origins in what follows, *Chrestiani* should be preferred. This reading provides the necessary contrast with *Christus* in the next sentence, as has been observed by van Voorst (2000), 43–4, and without it the reference to the Roman *vulgus* makes little sense. Even on a practical level, a correction from *Chrestianos* to *Christianos* is substantially more likely than the reverse.

[123] This part of the passage has proved to be particularly susceptible to the argument that Tacitus' account as we know it was the result of later (Christian) interpolations, as for instance in Carrier (2014). However, as Koestermann (1968), 254–5 rightly remarks, the passage is strongly integrated in the rest of Tacitus' narrative, and Tacitus' membership of the *quindecimviri sacris faciundis* furthermore suggests that he would indeed have had more knowledge of Christianity than the average Roman. For a similar argument, see van Voorst (2000), 49–52. Shaw (2015), 79–81 likewise rejects the idea of a Christian interpolation in this passage.

[124] For a variety of arguments on this spectrum, see Dibelius (1971), 81; Fuchs (1950), 77–87; Frend (2006), 504; Keresztes (1979), 248–57; Sordi (1983), 24–35; Ste Croix (1974[a]), 213; Vogt (1954), 1167; Williams (2012), 179 and 218–19; Zeiller (1951) and (1955).

community.[125] As discussed in the context of the time of Claudius (section 4.4.3), this last option is made unlikely by Suetonius' independent reference to Neronian measures against Christians,[126] and the fact that both authors were otherwise quite capable of naming the Jewish community by name when this was their intent.[127]

4.5.1 Tacitus on Christians and the Great Fire

Even the Tacitean passage itself, however, provides ample cause for speculation about Nero's reasons for targeting the Christians, and has proved to be dense almost past the point of comprehension:[128]

> *Igitur primum correpti qui fatebantur, deinde indicio eorum multitudo ingens haud proinde in crimine incendii quam odio humani generis convicti sunt.*[129]
>
> Therefore, first those who confessed were arrested, and thereafter—on the basis of their information—a great multitude was convicted, not so much because of the charge of arson, but rather on the basis of the[ir?] hatred of the human race.

This section, brief as it is, contains three significant textual problems, which in turn result in an even larger number of interpretive difficulties. The first of these concerns the initial phase of the proceedings, the chronology of which is notably odd. The text seems to suggest that the accused were only arrested after they had already confessed (*primum correpti qui fatebantur*), which has been considered unlikely in the context of legal proceedings.[130] This apparent discrepancy has led

[125] For the former, see e.g. Barnes (1968ª), 34–5; Borleffs (1971), 217 and 226–7; Getty (1966); Last (1954), 1211. Benko (1984), 24; and Lund (2008), 259 hold an intermediate position, arguing that Christians were punished both for being Christian and for the fact that they were associated with crimes. For the idea that Christians were not the target of Nero's measure, see Carrier (2014), 277–83; Koestermann (1967), 464–6 and (1968), 256; and Shaw (2015). Wlosok (1971) expresses similar doubts. For the idea that the more orthodox Jewish community instead instigated Nero's anti-Christian measures, see Frend (1965), 164–5, which is firmly rejected by Corke-Webster (2023), 20–4.

[126] Shaw (2015), 83–4 is certainly right in pointing out that Suetonius' reference is very brief and is furthermore not in complete agreement with Tacitus' account, as will be discussed in more detail in section 4.5.2. In spite of (or rather because of) this, the fact that both authors mention a Neronian measure against Christians remains telling.

[127] The extent to which Christians had become a distinct, recognizable group in the time of Nero is the subject of some debate between Brent Shaw and Christopher Jones. See Jones (2017) and Shaw (2015) and (2018). Jones primarily emphasizes the extensive references to Christians as an independent community within the city of Rome in Acts and the Epistle to the Romans.

[128] For a similar view see Fuchs (1950), 78, who declares: 'so muß allerdings zugegeben werden, daß Tacitus sich mit einer Knappheit ausgesprochen hat, die dicht bis an die Grenze der Mißverständlichkeit reicht'. Likewise, Petersen (2019), 38–9 calls the passage a 'durch wiederholte Ellipsen mehrdeutiger Satz'.

[129] Tacitus, *Annales* 15.44.

[130] Ash (2018), 206; Getty (1966), 287–8; Koestermann (1968), 256.

to the suggestion that we should read *quidam* rather than *qui* ('some who were arrested confessed'), and while this idea would admittedly solve the chronological problems present in the phrase, it is not based on any of the available manuscripts and has not been universally accepted.[131] Others have suggested that the verb *fateor* should be taken to refer to an earlier, public profession of Christian faith, which would have led to the arrest of prominent members of the community during the aftermath of the Great Fire.[132] However, the idea that Tacitus is simply describing Christians who had at some unspecified point in time openly declared their religious beliefs, and had admitted to nothing else, is made unlikely by the fact that he nowhere uses *fateor* in a similarly religious context.[133] Another explanation for the order of events as presented in the text must therefore be found. While it is impossible to do so with absolute certainty, the lack of an explanation for this apparent oddity in Tacitus' narrative and the brevity of his description may indicate that the author attempted to make a point that was more straightforward than is generally assumed by his highly detail-oriented modern-day readers. It may thus be suggested that we are *not* dealing with an oblique reference to Christian declarations of faith, but rather with a deliberate attempt by Tacitus to paint the image of an all-out search for possible culprits that was fuelled by escalating public disorder and anxiety and was therefore fundamentally flawed. This idea is underscored by Tacitus' repeated emphasis on the unfavourable reputation Christians had with the general population of Rome, which suggests that pre-existing tension may well have escalated under these extraordinary circumstances. In this context, it becomes possible that the first people to confess (to use *fateor* in a more literal sense) did so because they had been pressured in some way by the general population, possibly with the help of the police forces of the city of Rome or more informally organized groups attempting to uphold public order.[134] This very likely substantial pressure comes to the forefront even more prominently in the next part of the passage, in which Tacitus claims that the number of accused was vastly expanded because those who had previously been arrested started implicating others in their alleged crimes—a mechanism strongly

[131] This suggestion was made by Getty (1966), 287–8, who is followed in this by Ash (2018), 206 and Corke-Webster (2023), 19 n. 64. This idea is rejected by Shaw (2015), 81, who argues that due process could not be guaranteed in the aftermath of the Great Fire, but unfortunately does not expand on this idea. In this context, it is interesting to compare this passage to Tacitus, *Historiae* 4.45, where the author describes a trial that he says took place according to ancient custom by using a very similar brief phrasing, but places events in a logical chronological order.

[132] Fuchs (1950), 78 makes the argument that those who were initially arrested only confessed to Christianity. He bases this idea on the fact that Tacitus apparently believed the accused to have been innocent, which neglects the possibility that false confessions were extracted under torture. For a similar argument, see Keresztes (1979), 251. Koestermann (1968), 256 raises the suggestion that Tacitus may have been referring to false confessions by agents of Nero meant to implicate Christians, which would then have led to further, more vigorous actions.

[133] Getty (1966), 286.

[134] See Petersen (2019), 38–9 for the argument that the passage can only be understood by filling in the public denunciations that no doubt occurred.

reminiscent of literal and metaphorical witch hunts the world over.[135] It therefore seems likely that the chronological inversion in the text should be seen as an attempt by Tacitus to highlight the irregularity of the proceedings by implying that the initial confessions were not made under the jurisdiction of the appointed magistrate during a formal line of questioning, but rather were extracted at an earlier stage through violence, or at the very least the threat thereof.

The question of the exact nature of the charges against the arrested Christians comes up once more in the next part of the passage, and disagreement once again abounds. This is at least in part due to a dispute about the correct reading of the penultimate word of the passage: while the earliest manuscript reads *coniuncti* rather than the *convicti* offered by later versions, scholarly consensus has since overwhelmingly settled on the latter version, which fits well with the ubiquitous legal terminology of the passage.[136] However, the essence of the phrase ultimately remains discernible whatever the correct reading might be: in either case, we are dealing with a reference to the charges underlying the proceedings. The more significant issue, then, lies in the reasons for arrest and conviction presented by Tacitus. The author claims that the fate of those who were ultimately arrested was due not so much to a formal charge of arson (*crimen incendii*), but rather because the Christians were seen as generally suspect due to *odium humani generis*. The latter phrase has proved particularly vexing, and opinions vary on whether we are dealing with a subjective or objective genitive—that is: were Christians convicted (or added to the list of suspects) because they were hated by humankind or because they were accused of hating humankind themselves?[137] The latter interpretation of the two is more likely, and finds support in the fact that a similar accusation was also occasionally levied against members of the Jewish community.[138] However, it goes too far to suggest, as some have done, that the official charge against Rome's Christians was not arson but rather something akin to *μισανθρωπία*.[139] No record of such an accusation being accepted and employed as

[135] The number of those arrested remains unknown, but it is likely that Tacitus' use of the phrase *multitudo ingens* is to some extent hyperbolic. See Ash (2018), 207; Carrier (2014), 283; and Koestermann (1968), 256. Corke-Webster (2023), 26–7 is right in pointing out that accusing others may have been a route to immunity, but perhaps underestimates the psychological pressure inherent to such scenarios by suggesting that these accusations may have been made willingly.

[136] See, among others, Ash (2018), 207; Fisher (1906); Heubner (1983), 369; Jackson (1937), 284; Koestermann (1968), 256. Getty (1966), 289 rejects this idea, while also rearranging the interpunction of the passage, and Keresztes (1979), 251–2 leans in the same direction when it comes to his acceptance of *coniuncti*. It has been argued, among others by Getty (1966), 288, that the singular *multitudo* cannot be combined with the plural of the verb. This argument is rejected by Ash (2018), 207.

[137] Ash (2018), 207; Frend (2006), 504; Fuchs (1950), 82–7; Koestermann (1968), 257; Lund (2008), 259; and Shaw (2015), 81 favour the objective genitive. Carrier (2014), 272; Getty (1966), 290–1; and Keresztes (1979), 255 lean towards a subjective use of the genitive.

[138] See especially Flavius Josephus, *Contra Apionem* 2.14 (148).

[139] For the idea that Christians were tried for their perceived misanthropy, see Dibelius (1971), 81; Keresztes (1979), 252–4; Molthagen (1970), 23–4; Williams (2012), 219; Zeiller (1955), 397.

a viable charge exists, and it should in any case be noted that *odio humani generis* is not, like *incendii*, dependent on *crimine*, which speaks against the idea that Tacitus meant to describe the Christians' perceived hatred of all mankind as a formal legal basis for the proceedings. Instead, the phrase fits Tacitus' generally disparaging description of the course of events by suggesting that it was not the formal accusation of arson levied against the Christians that ultimately determined the outcome of the proceedings, as should have been the case, but rather vague accusations and fearful rumours about the status of Christians as potentially dangerous and subversive outsiders.

The fact that a number of the arrested Christians are subsequently described as having been burned, however, may well point to the continued importance of the charge of arson, and suggests that a deliberate connection between crime and punishment was made.[140] It also bears repeating that Tacitus' account is very firmly rooted in the narrative of the Great Fire, and starts out with an attempt to find someone to blame for that dreadful event.[141] His description of the legal proceedings is not only heavily abbreviated but also suggests duplicity on the part of the imperial authorities, and—even more significantly—a sense of continuous escalation of the accusations due to the highly pressurized socio-political environment that gripped the city after the disaster. While Tacitus undoubtedly connects the accused to Christianity, as is also demonstrated by his assertion that Christians were generally 'hated for their crimes', his account of events remains fundamentally tied to the immediate context of the Great Fire, in which the accusations of arson would have been more fundamentally at the forefront of everyone's mind. Thus, while 'being Christian' is indeed presented as a related allegation, Tacitus' account suggests that such claims did not form the appropriate legal basis for the proceedings and would furthermore not have carried the same weight without the setting in which he presents them. That is, without the Great Fire and accusations of arson, the actions of Tacitus' Nero against the Roman Christians would have lacked an impetus. Whatever reading of the text we choose to accept, the course of events as it is presented to us simply cannot be adequately explained by accusations of Christianity alone. The context in which such claims became relevant must therefore remain of central importance for any analysis of the legal treatment of Christians under Nero.

[140] Ash (2018), 208; Lampe (1989), 65; and Lund (2008), 259–60. Keresztes (1979), 255 rejects this argument. Lund argues that the Christians who were thrown to the dogs wrapped in animal skins suffered this fate because they were considered to be in some way 'beastly'. Ash (2018), 207 and Benko (1984), 129–30 draw attention to a parallel with the punishment for *magi* described in pseudo-Paul, *Sententiae* 5.23.17, which also mentions crucifixion, burning, and the accused being thrown to wild beasts. For the symbolic meaning of the punishments referred to in 1 Clement 6.2, which might describe the same period, see Schmitt (2012). The fact that Tacitus describes these different methods of execution as *ludibria* seems to underscore the idea that he disapproved of the procedural irregularities.

[141] For a similar argument, see Getty (1966), 292.

4.5.2 Christians under Nero according to Suetonius

Tacitus' description of events, however, is not the only account by a Roman author to make mention of interactions between Christians and the Roman authorities during this period: Suetonius likewise references a measure against the Christians (*Christiani*) of Rome. However, he in no way connects this event to his account of the Great Fire,[142] and this discrepancy between the two accounts has understandably raised questions about the historical accuracy of both versions—but especially the one by Tacitus.[143] Nevertheless, it remains important to compare the two and to investigate whether they have any common ground, since similarities between two accounts that otherwise differ considerably are likely more significant than those elements that are unique to either. What, then, does Suetonius have to say about Nero's attitude towards the Christian community?

> *Multa sub eo et animadversa severe et coercita nec minus instituta:* [...] *affecti suppliciis Christiani, genus hominum superstitionis novae ac maleficae* [...].[144]

[142] The fact that Tacitus is the only Roman author to directly link Nero's measures against Christians to the Great Fire has been widely noted. See Shaw (2015), 82–3; Vogt (1954), 1165; Williams (2012), 218; Wlosok (1971), 283. See Shaw (2015), 83 for the argument that later Christian sources are very likely dependent on Tacitus.

[143] The two most important recent arguments against the historical reliability of Tacitus' account as we know it may be found in Carrier (2014) and Shaw (2015), both of whom assume Suetonius' account to have been authentic, if anachronistic in his reference to Christians. The claim made by Dando-Collins (2010), 6 that Suetonius' remark about Christians appears out of context, and could therefore easily have been the work of a later Christian copyist, need not necessarily be seen as a solid argument against the phrase's authenticity: Suetonius on multiple occasions includes passages in which he briefly references multiple measures taken by a specific emperor, and the remark is therefore hardly out of character. In addition, the description of Christianity as a *superstitio nova et malefica* hardly seems like the work of a Christian scribe. In Hansen (2023ᵃ), 8–11 and (2023ᵇ), the author suggests that both Tacitus and Suetonius may have based their accounts on Pliny the Younger's reports of his interrogations of Christians in Bithynia-Pontus, and thus reflect a mythologized narrative of persecution provided by these Christians rather than historical reality. However, the account provided in Pliny the Younger, *Epistulae* 10.96 provides no concrete evidence that Pliny had specific knowledge of a Christian tradition regarding persecution under Nero, and Hansen (2023ᵃ), 6 even argues that the letter cannot be used as proof for the existence of earlier trials against Christians. The suggestion in Hansen (2023ᵃ), 12 n. 38 that Pliny is simply 'not letting on as much as he knows' thus seems too tenuous to explain the discrepancies between the three authors' accounts. The argument that Pliny obscured his knowledge of this tradition in his official correspondence because he wanted to 'whitewash' the Christians, cited in Hansen (2023ᵇ), 72, becomes particularly puzzling when taking into account Pliny's assertion that unrepented Christians should indeed be executed, but that no evidence for criminal behaviour could be found.

[144] Suetonius, *De vita Caesarum: Nero* 16. Boman (2011), 355 n. 2 holds that *Christiani* is indeed very likely to be the most reliable reading in Suetonius' text. The case for *affecti* over *afflicti* is made by Bradley (1972) on the basis of a suggested emendation in the Parisian edition of Robertus Stephanus, which finds a parallel in the work of Orosius, who often is remarkably accurate in his use of Suetonius as a source. His suggestion has been taken up by a number of editions, including Kaster (2016ᵃ), 294 and (2016ᵇ), 208; Kierdorf (1992), 53; and Warmington (1999), 6 and 43. The Teubner edition of Ihm (1908), 231 and Rolfe (1997), 106 both adhere to *afflicti*.

> Many things came to be severely punished and repressed during his reign, and no fewer new measures were instituted: [...] The Christians, a group of people holding a new and nefarious superstition, were visited with punishments.

This short passage is included in a list of various legal measures taken by Nero,[145] all of which are likely to have applied specifically to the city of Rome, as is indicated by a reference to Nero's building projects in the region made in the same paragraph. The reasons behind the emperor's measures against the city's Christian community, however, are less easily discernible. It has been suggested that Suetonius' use of the term *maleficus* to describe the Christian *superstitio* is intended to imply that Christians were perceived to have used dark magic,[146] which is an interesting thought, but not otherwise supported or expanded upon within the text. Others have argued that *superstitio* [...] *malefica* is meant to suggest that Christians were targeted because of their religious beliefs, since it is their *superstitio* itself that is referred to as malicious—or even potentially criminal.[147] It seems more likely, however, that the adjective in this context serves as an explanation of the perceived nature of Christianity for the reader, rather than as a remark on the legal basis for measures against it.[148]

A more productive point of entry into Nero's possible motivations may be found in the other measures Suetonius references in the passage, all of which were in some way intended to maintain public order. The inventory starts out by mentioning a new sumptuary law, followed by bans on public banquets that went beyond point of simply distributing food, a ban on the sale of elaborate foods in taverns, and—after its reference to Christians—continues by mentioning measures against other groups that were seen as a threat to law and order in the city, namely charioteers, as well as actors and their fans. The charioteers are explicitly accused of cheating and robbing the populace, while the expulsion of actors is also mentioned by Tacitus, and is connected there to accusations of causing general disorder.[149] The fact that Suetonius references Christians in such company very likely indicates that he saw Nero's measure against them (whatever its nature may have been) as a police measure meant to maintain peace and quiet in the city.

What, then, do the combined accounts of Tacitus and Suetonius tell us about the legal treatment of Christians under Nero? Most importantly, both authors agree with later Christian tradition that some form of legal interaction took place, and that people that they recognized as Christians were in some way involved. Both authors furthermore hold that these events took place in Rome itself and

[145] Shaw (2015), 83 not unreasonably refers to this passage as a 'legal potpourri'.

[146] Frend (2006), 504.

[147] Liebs (2012), 119; Molthagen (1970), 25; Ste Croix (1974[b]), 258.

[148] Shaw (2015), 83–4.

[149] Tacitus, *Annales* 13.25. The riots that could result from theatre performances are also referenced in Suetonius, *De vita Caesarum: Nero* 26.

make no mention of any effects beyond that geographical area.[150] While some have considered it peculiar that no similar actions were taken in the provinces,[151] this is in fact hardly surprising if we consider the context in which both authors present the measure. It is true that Tacitus stands alone in connecting Nero's measures against the Christians with the aftermath of the Great Fire, but both authors' accounts nevertheless seem to suggest that measures against the Christians occurred in response to some perceived disruption of the social order—although Tacitus' version of events is admittedly far more severe. Neither account gives us sufficient grounds to assume that Christians were simply punished for being Christian, but both instead suggest that Christians were considered to be socially—and potentially criminally—disruptive. Given the discrepancies between the available sources, this minimalist reading is all that can be reasonably hoped for, but its parallels to the measures against diviners and the Jewish community of Rome described in previous chapters are nonetheless illuminating and suggest a similar association between membership of a particular religious group and accusations of suspicious behaviour.

4.6 Pliny and Trajan: The First Trial?

After the time of Nero, the Christian communities of the Roman Empire disappear from the written record for some time, only reliably re-emerging during the reign of Emperor Trajan. While Christians may have been caught up in Domitian's rigorous enforcement of the Jewish Tax, and may indeed have been included among those who were denounced to the authorities for allegedly trying to evade it, no explicit reference to their involvement is made.[152] Nevertheless, the idea that Domitian was one of the emperors who targeted Christians for their religious beliefs is mentioned repeatedly in the works of authors who were themselves members of the Christian community (Appendix 3.7). Tertullian compares Domitian to Nero and calls both emperors exceptionally cruel, but ultimately remarks that Domitian's measures were only temporary.[153] Eusebius of Caesarea connects Domitian's alleged anti-Christian attitude to his numerous trials against members of the Roman elite, and claims that Flavia Domitilla, the niece of consul Flavius Clemens, was exiled for being Christian.[154] Other sources do confirm that Clemens himself was a victim of Domitian's policies, but they either omit

[150] A similar point is made by Sherwin-White (1952), 202.

[151] Frend (2006), 504–5.

[152] Suetonius, *De vita Caesarum: Domitianus* 12.1–2. For a more elaborate discussion of the subject, see section 3.14.1.

[153] Tertullian, *Apologeticus pro Christianis* 5.4. 1 Clement 1.1 makes mention of difficulties faced by the church in the city of Rome specifically, but due to the letter's uncertain date its usefulness is limited. See Williams (2012), 213–15.

[154] Eusebius, *Historia Ecclesiastica* 3.18.4.

religious motivations entirely or hold that the consul was targeted for his Jewish sympathies, which appear to have given rise to accusations of atheism.[155] According to the latter view, Clemens' wife Flavia Domitilla was banished for similar reasons, and given their identical names it is very well possible that she is the one who inspired Eusebius' reference to Clemens' Christian niece.[156]

Given these conflicting accounts, the extent and nature of Domitian's interactions with Christian communities remains obscure. While it has been argued that Domitian used a Neronian precedent to continue his predecessor's repressive policies,[157] solid evidence for this claim is ultimately lacking. For this reason, many have maintained a sceptical attitude, and have focused instead on the treatment of Jewish communities, for which more reliable sources exist.[158] It should also be noted that the people explicitly connected to Domitian's alleged anti-Christian measures all appear to have been members of the Roman elite, and part of the emperor's inner circle, who may therefore have been more susceptible to scrutiny of their loyalties—religious or otherwise.[159] It is therefore likely that only a very limited group was ever faced with accusations of atheism, whatever their religious sympathies may have been in practice. While we cannot, of course, fully exclude the possibility that Christians became involved either in these events, or in the trials surrounding the Jewish Tax, or indeed that they were faced with repressive actions by local communities, it would go beyond all available evidence to state that they were explicitly and intentionally targeted by the emperor himself.[160]

4.6.1 Letters from the province

By contrast, there can be little debate about the fact that legal interactions between Christians and the Roman authorities occurred during the reign of Trajan. A number of martyrdoms, including those of prominent figures within the early church like Pope Clement I and Ignatius of Antioch, are said to have taken place during this period, although the available accounts of these events can generally

[155] Cassius Dio, *Historiae Romanae* ep.67.14.1–2; Suetonius, *De vita Caesarum: Domitianus* 15.1. The link to atheism is made by Dio.

[156] See Lampe (1989), 167–8 for the idea that both are the same person.

[157] Williams (2012), 217; Zeiller (1951), 523 and 526 and (1955), 395.

[158] Barnes (1985), 150; Cook (2010), 117; Molthagen (1970), 22 n. 50.

[159] For a more elaborate discussion of this theory, see section 3.14.1.

[160] For the idea that a persecution did indeed take place, see Lane Fox (1986), 433. It has been remarked, among others by Cook (2010), 135–6 and Vogt (1954), 1168–9, that the former Christians who told Pliny the Younger that they had given up their faith some time ago may have done so during the reign of Domitian. However, the circumstances under which they did so are never mentioned and need not have been related to imperial policy of any kind. Against the argument that Pliny based his treatment of Christians on earlier measures dating back to the time of Domitian, see Reichert (2002), 245–8.

be considered (semi-)legendary rather than historical. The same cannot be said, however, of the single most famous trial involving members of the Christian community, in which the emperor himself would in time become involved. This trial took place under the jurisdiction of Pliny the Younger during his time as governor of the province Bithynia et Pontus (*c.* 110–13 CE),[161] and it remains one of the most extensively and reliably documented cases available to those interested in the legal treatment of Christians in the Roman world. Pliny has become deservedly famous for his extensive corpus of letters, the tenth book of which is focused on his official correspondence with the emperor during his tenure as governor. This series of letters is the only large-scale collection of Roman administrative correspondence belonging to a single official left to us,[162] and it has become invaluable due to the fact that it provides a fascinating insight into the wide variety of issues that governors had to contend with. In addition to the famous exchange about the legal treatment of Christians,[163] these letters include questions on the correct way to deal with foster children, burials, and protection against fires.[164]

Traditionally, the collection contained in book ten has been seen as a more or less distinct entity within Pliny's *Epistulae*: while books one through nine are generally considered to be highly literary in character, and are strongly focused on Pliny's self-representation,[165] it was long believed that book ten was published not by Pliny himself, but posthumously by his heirs or friends,[166] and that it shows 'no sign of literary revision'.[167] This idea, however, has come under scrutiny in recent years: book ten has come to be seen as a continuation, and in fact as the ultimate conclusion, of the programme of self-representation set up by Pliny in the previous nine books.[168] In addition, it has been remarked that the letters lack the customary opening and closing salutations, and that each letter deals with only a single subject, both of which suggest that at least some editing took place.[169]

[161] The exact dates of Pliny's appointment are uncertain. Sherwin-White (1966), 80–1 suggests a starting date of 109 CE, while Gibson and Morello (2012), 11 and 269 present both 109 and 110 CE as possibilities.

[162] While Sherwin-White (1966), 533–5 argues that the collection of letters is largely complete, it is notable that Trajan's responses are often absent, as are exchanges for which the emperor took the initiative. See Öhler (2021), 273. Sherwin-White's commentary on Pliny's letters remains indispensable for those interested in their social and historical background.

[163] Pliny the Younger, *Epistulae* 10.96 and 10.97. These letters appear to have been well known among Christians at a relatively early date. See Corke-Webster (2017ª).

[164] Pliny the Younger, *Epistulae* 10.65 and 10.66; 10.68 and 10.69; and 10.33 and 10.34, respectively.

[165] Gibson and Morello (2012), 234–64. For the strong focus on Pliny's self-representation in modern scholarship, see Häger (2015), 564–6. For the distinct position of book ten, see Bodel (2015), 21–2 and Häger (2015), 570. The former both points to the fact that book ten is the only part of Pliny's *Epistulae* to contain letters to just two correspondents, one of which is (notably) Pliny himself, and argues that the early transmission of book ten appears to have looked rather different than that of the first nine books.

[166] See, among others, Syme (1958), 660.

[167] Sherwin-White (1966), 12.

[168] Gibson and Morello (2012), 251–3. See also the works of Noreña (2007); Stadter (2006); and Woolf (2006), 101–4.

[169] For an overview of the various arguments, see Öhler (2021), 272–3. For the argument that the chronology of the letters has been altered to place Pliny's letters directly alongside Trajan's

Nevertheless, there is little to dispute that the letters in book ten are indeed largely authentic at their core, and served a practical purpose during Pliny's time as governor.[170] The language used by both Trajan and Pliny himself contains little of the literary style applied in the other books, but instead closely matches the bureaucratic idiom of the period.[171] The famous correspondence about the Christian presence in Bithynia-Pontus between Pliny and Emperor Trajan, then, continues to stand out as both the earliest and one of the most direct sources for legal interactions between Christians and the Roman authorities, and its value is further enhanced by the rare fact that they are written from the perspective of the latter.

4.6.2 Christians in Bithynia-Pontus

At its very core, then, Pliny's letter about the emerging Christian movement of his province is part of his administrative correspondence. Despite the fact that it is among the longest missives in the collection, it follows a pattern that is largely similar to that of many other letters in the tenth book of the *Epistulae*, which open by presenting Emperor Trajan with the necessary information about Pliny's activities as governor, and then proceed to ask for advice or approval—and in some cases both.[172] Letter 96 opens in a similar fashion: Pliny declares himself to be utterly dependent on Trajan's advice (*quis enim potest melius vel cunctationem meam regere vel ignorantiam instruere?*), and then quickly proceeds by introducing the subject of trials against Christians (Appendix 3.8). He claims to have never attended any of the earlier proceedings against them, and indicates that he is therefore unaware of common practice (*ideo nescio quid et quatenus aut puniri soleat aut quaeri*).[173] He then asks a number of question about the correct way to

corresponding replies, see Millar (2004), 40. Lavan (2018) is critical of the idea that the individual letters were substantially edited and suggest that Pliny's letters are notably similar to other surviving correspondence between emperors and governors in form and content.

[170] See for example Noreña (2007), 239; Öhler (2021), 270–3; Sherwin-White (1966), 12; Stadter (2006), 69 and 75; Syme (1958), 660. This much is generally acknowledged even by those who view book ten in the context of Pliny's self-representation.

[171] Coleman (2012), 233–5. For a similar argument, see Noreña (2007), 267 and Öhler (2021), 270 and 273, the latter of whom adds that the known text of book ten contains no traces of deleted passages. For the differences (and similarities) in Pliny's use of personal names in the different books of the *Epistulae*, see Jones (1991), 149–53.

[172] A similar point is made by Öhler (2021), 276. For an exploration of the delicate nature of communication between governor and emperor, see Mazzoli (2003). For the idea that Pliny's frequent messages to Trajan show his lack of competence—or at the very least his indecisiveness, see Sherwin-White (1966), 547. A similar argument may be found in Coleman (2012), 233, but it is notable that Pliny seems to make his own suggestions on a number of occasions, as will be discussed in section 4.6.3.

[173] Some authors consider Pliny's claim of ignorance to be an exaggeration, if not blatantly untrue. See for example Liebs (2012), 130–1; Ste Croix (1974[b]), 257; Williams (2012), 204. This argument is rejected by Walsh and Gottlieb (1992), 6–10.

deal with these Christians, during which he famously distinguishes between the Christian 'name itself' and crimes associated with that name as the basis for punishment (*nomen ipsum* [...] *an flagitia cohaerentia nomini puniantur*), before describing the procedure he has thus far followed:

> *Interim, in iis qui ad me tamquam Christiani deferebantur, hunc sum secutus modum. Interrogavi ipsos an essent Christiani. Confitentes iterum ac tertio interrogavi supplicium minatus: perseverantes duci iussi. Neque enim dubitabam, qualecumque esset quod faterentur, pertinaciam certe et inflexibilem obstinationem debere puniri. Fuerunt alii similis amentiae, quos, quia cives Romani erant, adnotavi in urbem remittendos.*[174]
>
> In the meantime, I have employed the following procedure regarding those who were denounced to me as Christians. I have asked them if they were Christians. If they confessed, I asked them a second and third time after threatening punishment. If they persisted, I ordered them to be taken away for execution. For I did not doubt that, whatever it was they confessed, certainly their stubbornness and inflexible obstinacy demanded punishment. There were others of similar madness, who I marked for transportation to the capital because they were Roman citizens.

Initially, then, Pliny does not appear to have seen the events he describes as particularly problematic or deserving of the emperor's attention. This changed, however, when the number of accused started to grow. Pliny states that he received an anonymous list of accusations (*propositus est libellus sine auctore multorum nomina continens*), on which he felt compelled to act. As he had done previously, he released those who denied ever having been Christians (*qui negabant esse se Christianos aut fuisse*) and could prove this assertion by offering sacrifices. However, he was also confronted with a group of people who admitted to having been Christians at some point in the past but claimed that they had since left the community—often years ago. Pliny then proceeded to investigate further, first confirming that these people were indeed no longer Christians, and then further examining the practices Christians engaged in. Although he characterizes Christianity as a *superstitio prava et immodica* later in the letter, he found no evidence of actual wrongdoing: both former and current Christians swore that they had made a vow to avoid all criminal activity,[175] ate only normal food, and had even ceased to meet after Pliny had banned *collegia* on Trajan's orders.[176] At this

174 Pliny the Younger, *Epistulae* 10.96.2–4. The edition used is that of Mynors (1963).

175 In this context, the term *sacramentum* is used. For the usage of this term, see Sordi (2003).

176 This ban is also referenced in Pliny the Younger, *Epistulae* 10.33 and 10.34, as well as 10.92 and 10.93. Eckhardt (2018[c]), 301 rightly remarks that Pliny in no way suggests that the Christians actually formed *collegia*, or indeed associations of any other kind. Instead, this phrase seems to indicate that Christians were keen to avoid all appearances of suspicious behaviour. Indeed, while the behaviour of

point, Pliny decided that he needed Trajan's advice: he saw the growing number of accused as particularly problematic (*maxime propter periclitantium numerum*) and was therefore hesitant to proceed as he had done before. However, he also concluded that his actions had apparently had the desired effect: temples were once again being visited, rituals were being taken up again, and sacrificial meats were once again being sold.

Pliny's letter, then, provides us with a wealth of information about all stages of the legal proceedings against the Christians in his province. It should first be noted that this was a strongly localized event that has widely been recognized to have found its origins in complaints made by the local population of Bithynia-Pontus.[177] Pliny describes the accused as 'those who were denounced to me as Christians', and later makes reference to an anonymous *libellus* containing yet more names. At least some of the inhabitants of the province, then, appear to have presented 'being Christian' as a valid reason for denouncing their neighbours to the Roman authorities,[178] and Pliny himself seems to have agreed—at least initially and to a certain extent. His interrogation of the accused, including both straightforward repeated questions during the initial proceedings and the use of the well-known sacrifice test during the later stages of his enquiries, focused primarily on whether or not the accused were indeed Christians. It is furthermore especially notable that he convicted confessed Christians without feeling the need to consult the emperor during the first round of accusations. This indicates that he saw the case brought forward by the accusers as essentially persuasive and was therefore willing to use his authority as governor to accept it as a valid reason for prosecution.[179]

Pliny's reasons for taking up the case are not made explicit, but the letter nevertheless gives a number of indications as to what they may, or may not, have been. On the one hand, it is very unlikely that Pliny based his actions on a concrete, pre-existing law aimed at Christians; as we have seen, there is no evidence that such a law existed, and the uncertainty Pliny expresses at the beginning of the letter likewise seems a strike against this idea. Pliny elsewhere frequently cites

Christian communities and that of Graeco-Roman associations share some broad similarities, it is unlikely that Christians fit within the established framework of private associations. See Eckhardt and Leonhard (2018). Still, it remains possible that this accusation was levied against the Bithynian Christians by their accusers, although it is very unlikely that this applied to other trials against Christians as well. Not only is the accusation noticeably absent from other accounts, but Trajan's ban was also specifically aimed at reducing tensions in Bithynia-Pontus and thus did not apply to other parts of the empire.

177 See, for instance, Sherwin-White (1966), 697; Ste Croix (1974ᵃ), 215; Walsh and Gottlieb (1992), 5.

178 Ste Croix (1974ᵃ), 215 holds that the locals were just trying out the accusation to see if it would work. Reichert (2002), 244 is critical of this point and holds that this letter can only be used to prove that Pliny took Christianity to be the sole charge, not that it was intended as such. For the idea that social tensions were more important than religious concerns, see Corke-Webster (2023).

179 For the idea that it was up to the governor's personal discretion to accept and reject cases, and that he had significant liberty in proceeding as he saw fit, see Ste Croix (1974ᵃ), 218–20.

earlier legal measures when he is able to find them, and the fact that he omits one here is therefore telling.[180] This does not mean, however, that Pliny was going into the trials without any previous knowledge whatsoever. He appears to have at least known about earlier trials involving Christians, even if he claims to be unaware of all the details. While some have dismissed this argument for the idea that Pliny was making use of existing precedent as invalid,[181] it is nevertheless very likely that he was at least generally aware that Christians could potentially be subject to punishment, or had been so in the past. He saw no need to explain who these Christians were, seeming to assume some general knowledge on the part of the emperor, as well as any other potential readers. Furthermore, he suggests the existence of a customary treatment of such cases by his use of the verb *soleat*, thus confirming that similar trials likely took place at some point in the past—even if these previous cases remain decidedly undated, and we, like Pliny, have no reliable information about what they may have looked like.[182]

In addition to this abstract awareness of precedent, it is very likely that accusations of particular crimes likewise played a part in Pliny's decision: although these allegations would later be disproven, the very fact that Pliny felt the need to investigate potential criminal behaviour after receiving the anonymous *libellus* suggests that such claims had been made and were considered to be relevant to the proceedings.[183] That is not to say that these *flagitia cohaerentia nomini*, as Pliny calls them, ultimately formed the legal basis for conviction. It has repeatedly, and rightly, been remarked that this can at the very least hardly have been true for the second group of Christians, during whose trial the accusations were investigated and subsequently dismissed—which seems to rule out a conviction on the basis of any pre-existing law against cannibalism, incest, or indeed illegal associations.[184] Nevertheless, it would be unwise to fully dismiss the potential importance of the fact that a connection between membership of the Christian community and criminal behaviour had once again been made, and that Pliny felt compelled to investigate it. While it is impossible to establish the sincerity of such claims,[185] the fact remains that they were used to establish Christians as a

[180] Williams (2012), 203.

[181] Reichert (2002), 243–4 sees the reference as too vague to be conclusive. In response to a similar argument, Williams (2012), 204 n. 63 argues that Pliny would likely have pointed out the general lack of precedent, had there been one. Instead, he attributes his ignorance to the fact that he has not been present at any trials against Christians—an important, if nuanced, distinction.

[182] Reichert (2002) is certainly right in pointing out that these previous trials cannot be straightforwardly dated to the time of Domitian, but in my opinion goes too far by seeing Pliny's treatment of the Christians in his province as a complete innovation.

[183] For the suggestion that Pliny was initially primarily concerned with Christian gatherings, see Corke-Webster (2017[b]), 381, who suggests that this was likely not the official charge, but nevertheless an important motivation for Pliny's attempts to take action.

[184] See, for instance, Lane Fox (1986), 427; Keresztes (1979), 284; Rives (2011[a]), 202 and 206; Ste Croix (1974[b]), 259–60; Walsh and Gottlieb (1992), 13.

[185] Benko (1984), repeatedly argues that the various accusations levied against Christians were sincerely believed, and at times even found their basis in fact. For a thorough exploration of the origins of the accusations of cannibalism, see Bremmer (2013).

potential threat and to place them outside the boundaries of civilized society. As a result, Christians could be seen as a danger to the social and political order of the region, and this may well have been an argument to which Pliny was particularly receptive. In part, his concerns appear to have been religious in nature, as is demonstrated by the final paragraph of his letter, in which he describes the significant decline of the traditional religious practices of Bithynia-Pontus before the Christians had been brought to his attention.[186] There is even some indication that this diminished traditional piety may have had economic consequences for certain parts of the population, as had been the case during Paul's confrontation with the inhabitants of Antioch—if Pliny is to be believed, the sale of sacrificial meat had come almost to a complete standstill. These may have been worrying signs under the best of circumstances, but they would have been particularly disconcerting in Bithynia-Pontus. The province had been plagued by economic difficulties and social unrest before Pliny's tenure as governor even began, and two of his predecessors had been formally accused of administrative malpractice by its inhabitants.[187] This, indeed, had been the reason behind Trajan's ban on *collegia* for that particular province.[188] Any disturbances of the peace, then, were to be strictly avoided, which may have made Pliny all the more inclined to take complaints brought forward by the locals, as well as potential threats to his authority, particularly seriously.[189]

4.6.3 Seeking and shaping imperial guidance

While Pliny's initial actions against the Christians of Bithynia-Pontus were thus firmly rooted in the local circumstances of his province, these were not the only factors he had to contend with. As becomes clear from the very existence of his letter, he eventually felt compelled to consult the emperor and to ask for his superior's approval for his actions. This decision was very likely prompted by the fact that matters were escalating. Pliny himself reports that that many more cases appeared *diffundente se crimine*, as the charge became more widespread, and later cites his concern about the number of accused as his primary reason for involving the emperor (*visa est enim mihi res digna consultatione, maxime propter*

[186] Pliny the Younger, *Epistulae* 10.96.10: *Certe satis constat prope iam desolata templa coepisse celebrari, et sacra sollemnia diu intermissa repeti passimque venire carnem victimarum, cuius adhuc rarissimus emptor inveniebatur*. Pliny also refers to Christianity as a *superstitio prava et immodica* in 10.96.8. The importance of religious motivations on the part of both Pliny himself and the general population of his province is rejected outright by Nixey (2017), 68–70.

[187] Corke-Webster (2017^b), 378–9 and 389; Gibson (2020), 197–9; Williams (2012), 201. See also Pliny the Younger, *Epistulae* 10.32.

[188] See Pliny the Younger, *Epistulae* 10.33 and 10.34, as well as 10.92 and 10.93. For the argument that the Roman authorities pronounced bans on *collegia* while at the same time allowing the practice to thrive, and even encouraging it, in an attempt to exert social and political control, see Perry (2016).

[189] For a similar point of view, see Nixey (2017), 77.

periclitantium numerum). In attempting to deal with the ever-increasing number of cases, Pliny appears to have discovered that matters were more complicated than originally thought.[190] On the one hand, the diverse backgrounds of the accused appear to have caused some consternation,[191] and the governor was furthermore confronted with people who freely admitted to having been Christians in the past but denied their continued involvement. By now, the question was therefore no longer simply whether people were Christian (a question that could be answered with a simple yes or no), but whether having been so in the past in itself provided sufficient basis for a legal charge to be brought forward, even if this past behaviour had apparently not had any lasting adverse effects.[192] Pliny now had to determine to what extent he was willing to go along with the accusers, and whether further escalation could lead to a dangerous destabilization of his province. It is therefore little wonder that he found it necessary to consult the emperor. However, Pliny's letter to Trajan ultimately contained far more than a simple request for guidance. Instead, the governor appears to have made significant efforts to convince the emperor of the appropriateness of his previous and proposed actions, using various types of arguments to achieve this.[193]

The first group of arguments Pliny employed is primarily procedural: the governor repeatedly attempts to show that he did his due diligence, and this display of thoroughness and careful consideration is even further emphasized by the elaborate nature of the letter itself. When discussing the first stage of events, Pliny makes sure to explain that he gave the Christians brought before him multiple chances to withdraw their confessions, and furthermore justifies their execution by drawing attention to what he calls their *pertinacia* [...] *et inflexibilis obstinatio*. While this aspect of the accused's behaviour is unlikely to have been the formal charge that led to their conviction, as some have argued,[194] it does help Pliny to

[190] Ste Croix (1974^a), 215 suggests that Pliny may have had 'second thoughts', but does not discuss why this may have been.

[191] See Walsh and Gottlieb (1992), 18–19 for the idea that Pliny was particularly concerned with the fact that entire *familiae*, including women and children, might become involved in the proceedings.

[192] For the idea that Pliny's recent discovery that no actual crimes had been committed contributed significantly to his unwillingness to let the escalation continue, see Corke-Webster (2017^b), 381–9.

[193] The idea that Pliny is attempting to argue his case for a specific legal treatment of Christians, or is trying to defend his own actions, has been raised by Barnes (1968^a), 36 n. 49, and has gained more support in recent years. Reichert (2002), 241 argues that Pliny is suggesting very specific, innovative measures, which include both the idea that Christians should be punished and the possibility for release. A similar point is made in Öhler (2021), 291. For the potentially innovative nature of the sacrifice test, see Millar (1977), 558. Corke-Webster (2017^b) is more inclined to believe that Pliny attempted to defend his previous conduct to prevent being reprimanded.

[194] See, famously, Sherwin-White (1952), 210 and again (1974), 253–4, who sees this as a charge of *contumacia*. In the same vein, Corke-Webster (2017^b), 382 argues that Pliny did not punish Christians 'for their creed in the first instance', citing the governor's reference to Christian obstinacy immediately after. Reichert (2002), 236 suggests that Pliny gave this reason for conviction to shield himself from potential criticism. The idea that obstinacy formed the legal basis for conviction is vigorously countered by Ste Croix (1974^a), 228–30, who among other criticisms of the theory argues that Christians could hardly have been charged with *contumacia* when they had not yet had a chance to resist the governor's authority before the trial had begun.

demonstrate that these people could potentially have undermined his authority if he had not decisively acted against them. Since his primary task as governor was to maintain peace and quiet in his province, this may well have seemed like a valid argument. However, Pliny also shows himself to be aware of the limits of his power: he is quick to note that he did not judge Roman citizens who became involved in the case himself, but instead formally marked them down for transportation to Rome, where they would be judged by the appropriate authorities.[195] In his description of the second phase of the proceedings, Pliny furthermore elaborately discusses his attempts at truth-finding. These included both the sacrifice test, which was intended to prove beyond a doubt that those who recanted had indeed left Christianity and (it is implied) the potentially disruptive behaviours associated with it behind,[196] as well as his investigations of the wider Christian community, which notably involved the torture of two *ancillae* to prove that no actual crimes had been committed.[197] Pliny, it may be concluded, has done everything he possibly could to ensure that the case, for which he believed there to be precedent but no established procedure, was properly handled.

The second type of reasoning Pliny uses to explain his conduct is based on the local circumstances in which he found himself. He notes that his initial decision to take action was based on accusations brought forward by the locals, which, while not necessarily surprising within the context of Roman administration, was nevertheless essential for Trajan's understanding of the situation. When combined with the steadily increasing number of accused, this aspect of the proceedings paints a clear picture of the amount of pressure to take action Pliny experienced, while at the same time demonstrating that there was a significant danger of escalation, which necessitated restraint. The same also holds true for Pliny's reference to the state of traditional religious practices in Bithynia-Pontus at the end of the letter, and his assertion that the problem appears to be spreading. He points out that the number of suspects (*periclitantes*) is growing rather numerous, that people of all ages, ranks, and genders are being accused, and that the *superstitionis istius contagio* has infected both town and countryside.[198]

[195] Sherwin-White (1966), 700 notes that *adnotavi* is a technical administrative and judicial term, thus underscoring the idea that Pliny attempted to show his adherence to proper procedures.

[196] Smuts (1965) suggests that Christians' failure to pass this test may have led Pliny to associate them with *maiestas*, which in turn would have compelled him to act. Since this test was only introduced later in the proceedings, however, it can hardly serve to explain why the trials were initiated. Furthermore, Pliny specifically brings up the test in the context of people being released—not of them being convicted.

[197] Pliny the Younger, *Epistulae* 10.96.8. Corke-Webster (2017[b]), 387 sees the torture of these two women as an assertion of Roman authority, which was subsequently undermined when it produced an unexpected result. Within the context of the letter, however, it is more likely that Pliny referenced the torture to further prove that he had indeed made every effort to ascertain the truth of the matter, and to thereby show himself to have been a diligent administrator.

[198] See Cook (2010), 250–1 for the idea that Pliny and Trajan were primarily concerned with Christianity's deviation from traditional Roman religious practices. For the extent to which Christianity had spread in Pliny's province, see Öhler (2021).

On the one hand, then, this passage serves to demonstrate the need for legal measures against the Christians, but on the other Pliny also shows that overly severe measures could have a dangerously destabilizing effect on an already unruly province, and directly links the recent restoration of the religious order to his more lenient attitude, arguing that a significant number of people could very well change their ways if given a *locus paenitentiae*.

4.6.4 Imperial response

Pliny's letter, then, strikes a delicate balance between various considerations. On the one hand, he attempts to combine the decisive action against steadfast Christians he on some level believed to be necessary (especially during the early stages of his interactions with the community) with the more lenient approach he has come to see as more beneficial over the course of the proceedings. On the other hand, he is confronted with the necessity to take into account not just precedent, established procedures, and the will of the emperor but also the local circumstances in the province and his own knowledge of the situation—both of which, it should be noted, Trajan had repeatedly encouraged him to apply throughout his tenure as governor.[199] In the end, his arguments appear to have been effective: Trajan's reply is comparably short (Appendix 3.9), and largely serves to confirm the suggestions Pliny had made:

> *Actum quem debuisti, mi Secunde, in excutiendis causis eorum, qui Christiani ad te delati fuerant, secutus es. Neque enim in universum aliquid, quod quasi certam formam habeat, constitui potest. Conquirendi non sunt; si deferantur et arguantur, puniendi sunt, ita tamen ut, qui negaverit se Christianum esse idque re ipsa manifestum fecerit, id est supplicando dis nostris, quamvis suspectus in praeteritum, veniam ex paenitentia impetret. Sine auctore vero propositi libelli in nullo crimine locum habere debent. Nam et pessimi exempli nec nostri saeculi est.*[200]
>
> You have followed the correct procedure, my dear Pliny, in investigating the cases of those who were denounced to you as Christians. It is after all impossible to make any general pronouncement that could act as a clear guideline. They are not to be sought out; if they are denounced and found guilty they should be punished, yet in such a way that whoever denies that he is a Christian, and in

[199] Trajan's insistence that Pliny himself should judge matters 'on the ground' and make use of local circumstances plays a part in a significant number of letters in their correspondence. See Pliny the Younger, *Epistulae* 10.20, 10.40, 10.42, 10.50, 10.55, 10.62, 10.69, 10.76, 10.84, 10.93, 10.109, 10.113, and 10.117, all of which consist of Trajan's responses. For another example of a letter that contains substantial evidence that Pliny attempted to persuade Trajan of his preferred course of action, see 10.41.

[200] Pliny the Younger, *Epistulae* 10.97.

fact makes this plain (that is, by worshipping our gods) may obtain a pardon by repentance, even if he was suspected in the past. Anonymous pamphlets should not have a place in any trial. For this is both a terrible precedent, and ill-suited to our times.

In his letter, Trajan confirms that 'being Christian' could indeed be seen as a viable charge, but only if the accusation was brought forward by inhabitants of the province themselves within the confines of proper procedure. He shows himself to be primarily concerned with the potential for unnecessary escalation that might result from abandoning these protocols: it is for this reason that he sees no benefit in the Roman authorities seeking Christians out (*conquirendi non sunt*), and—in a deviation from the procedure Pliny had followed—strongly rejects the use of anonymous accusations, which he calls a *pessimum exemplum*. Trajan's approval of the sacrifice test applied by Pliny should likewise be seen in this context: he seems to regard this test as a potential argument for the defence, and includes its proper application in a series of references to the formal stages of the trial, including denunciation and verdict (*si deferantur et arguantur*).[201] In no way, however, does Trajan indicate that this procedure will henceforth be applied throughout the empire. Indeed, he not only fails to establish a fixed punishment but also explicitly states that it is impossible to formulate a general guideline (*neque enim in universum aliquid, quod quasi certam formam habeat, constitui potest*), which indicates not only that subsequent cases in Pliny's own province might warrant a different treatment, but by extension also that events in other provinces are not automatically covered by his *rescriptum*.[202] Both Pliny and Trajan, then, are attempting to deal with an unexpected series of events in one particular province of the empire, and are considering the interest of all parties, including the general population of Bithynia-Pontus, in their attempts to resolve the issue. Trajan's response may ultimately imply that the *nomen ipsum* can indeed be seen as a valid charge, but this decision is firmly rooted in Pliny's account of the various accusations made by the locals, as well as his argument

[201] Sherwin-White (1966), 711–12 likewise sees Trajan's use of the term *defero* as an indication that the normal procedure of the *cognitio* trial is to be followed. The verb *arguo* can be used to indicate both an accusation in a more general sense (which would make Trajan's use of the term an approximate repetition of *defero*), and the process of providing proof for that accusation and subsequently guilty verdict. It is likely that the latter is meant in this context, although there is some indication that the term was ambiguous even in antiquity itself, as Ulpian saw fit to explain it in his *Ad Edictum*. See *Digesta* 50.16.197, which contains the jurist's assertion that *'indicasse' est detulisse; 'arguisse' accusasse et convicisse.*

[202] Throughout their correspondence, Trajan repeatedly tells Pliny that precedents from one province do not necessarily apply to another. See especially Pliny the Younger, *Epistulae* 10.65 and 10.66, but also 10.34 and 10.69. Another notable parallel may be found in 10.113, in which Trajan once again notes that nothing can be determined *in universum*. For a similar line of thinking, see Corke-Webster (2017^{b}), 397–404. Here, and in (2017^{a}), he particularly delves into later Christian uses of the Pliny–Trajan correspondence.

that a more lenient approach may help to alleviate the threat of disturbances in his province. We are therefore hardly dealing with a premeditated regulation, but instead with a series of negotiations and practical measures that was, in all likelihood, taking place within the boundaries of Pliny's normal administrative practice.[203] While many have seen the Pliny–Trajan correspondence as a 'landmark decision' in the Roman legal treatment of Christians,[204] it therefore nevertheless remains unlikely that it was ever intended to function as such—as is confirmed by the fact that the measure is never explicitly cited by later Roman authors.[205]

4.7 Hadrian and Minucius Fundanus: An Obscured View

Indeed, whatever precedent was set by Trajan's rescript, whether deliberate or not, it soon appears to have fallen from active use. Within two decades of the Pliny–Trajan correspondence, questions regarding the legal treatment of Christians once again arose—this time in the province of Asia under the governorship of one Granianus, who appears to have written to Emperor Hadrian for help.[206] While Granianus himself did not receive a reply before the end of his tenure as governor, the imperial administration did eventually send out a response to his successor, Minucius Fundanus (Appendix 3.10), who was governor in 122 and 123 CE, and by whose name the rescript is most commonly known.[207] The text of the letter in question has been exclusively transmitted by Christian sources,[208] but may nonetheless be largely considered reliable.[209]

203 It is notable that Pliny's letter describes the growing number of accusations as something that commonly happens (*ut fieri solet*) when a specific legal charge gains traction among the population. This assertion is not specifically linked to Christians in any way, but instead seems to indicate that Pliny sees this escalation of local tensions as problematic, but nothing unusual.

204 See, among others, Barnes (2010), 10–11; Cook (2010), 251; Frend (2006), 508; Öhler (2021), 291; Reichert (2002), 241–2; Ste Croix (1974ª), 223–5; and Vogt (1954), 1171. Against this point of view, see Corke-Webster (2017ᵇ), 397–404 and Lane Fox (1986), 424.

205 Corke-Webster (2017ᵇ), 399.

206 According to the manuscript tradition, the governor's name was Serenius or Serennius Granianus. This is likely to be a reference to Q. Licinius Silvanus Granianus, who was suffect-consul in 106 CE and could therefore have become proconsul of Asia during the reign of Hadrian. 'Serenius' is thus likely a corruption of either 'Licinius' or 'Silvanus'. See Minns and Parvis (2009), 265 n. 6 and Minns (2007), 38.

207 For the dating of Fundanus' governorship, see Eck (1983), 155–7.

208 See Justin Martyr, *1 Apology* 68.5–68.10 and Eusebius, *Historia Ecclesiastica* 4.9. Eusebius claims that his Greek text is a translation of the Latin offered by Justin, but the available manuscripts of both works now offer the same Greek text. A Latin version does survive in the translation of the *Historia Ecclesiastica* made by Rufinus, who likely did not have access to Justin's original and therefore only provides translation twice removed. Various critical editions of Justin's First Apology are available, including Marcovich (1994); Minns and Parvis (2009); and Wartelle (1987). For the usefulness of Rufinus' translation in approaching the original Latin of the rescript see Minns (2007). Eusebius, *Historia Ecclesiastica* 4.26.10 also cites a reference to the rescript by Melito of Sardis, who apparently knew of its existence but as far as we know did not cite it.

209 Minns (2007) offers an elaborate and useful overview of the debate surrounding the origins of the text as it survives in Justin's *Apology*, but ultimately sees the available version as a reliable

This does not mean, however, that the contents of the rescript are immediately clear: on this occasion, we are not granted the luxury of being able to investigate both the governor's question and the emperor's response, as we were in the case of Pliny's correspondence with Trajan, which means that our knowledge of the rescript's context is far less complete. Nevertheless, the text provides some valuable insights regarding the origins of Hadrian's measure in its own way. The repeated references to petitions (*ἀξιώσεις*) seem to indicate that Fundanus' predecessor, like Pliny, had been approached by inhabitants of province who demanded some form of legal action against the Christians in their region.[210] Although it is impossible to determine the exact nature of their request, we may deduce from the phrasing of the letter that the proposed measures went further than a straightforward legal case against one or more members of the Christian community: Hadrian negatively compares the petitions and demands of the people to the formal trials (*πρὸ βήματος*) he does approve of, which strongly suggests that what was being demanded went beyond the limits of accepted legal procedure. The emperor's declaration of concern at the start of the letter as we know it furthermore suggests that these appeals had been accompanied by unrests: Hadrian feels he cannot leave the matter unexamined and worries that the people might become agitated (*ἵνα μήτε οἱ ἄνθρωποι ταράττωνται*).[211] His reference to the 'shouts' (*βοαί*) of the people later in the letter serves to further emphasize that the emperor considered the way in which the locals attempted to make their demands known to be inappropriate at the very least. The primary focus of the emperor's response, then, appears to have been adherence to proper—and peaceful—procedure: he speaks of the potential for false accusations under the current circumstances with dismay, firmly insisting that the inhabitants of Fundanus' province take any grievances they might have to court, instead of resorting to other, less regulated means. He in turn encourages his governor to hear such cases and to judge them accordingly *εἴ τις οὖν* [...] *δείκνυσίν τι παρὰ τοὺς νόμους πράττοντας*—if someone proves that the Christians have done anything contrary to the laws.

approximation of the original missive. See also Cook (2010), 279–80 and Williams (2012), 208 n. 75. Millar (1977), 559 argues that the rescript seems to be largely similar to Hadrian's other known letters and considers it to be unlikely that Justin would forge a letter by the immediate predecessor of the emperor he is addressing. By contrast, Corke-Webster (2017[b]), 400 holds that 'there is little to recommend [the rescript] as authentic' and takes particular issue with the fact that the text is only preserved in Christian sources, which in his view has caused accounts of other, similar rescripts to be dismissed. In this, however, he does not consider the more significant problems regarding both contents and transmission attached to these other passages, which will be discussed in sections 4.8.2 and 4.9.3.

210 Barnes (1968[a]), 37. For the suggestion that the governor had simply passed the petition on without undertaking anything, see Keresztes (1979), 292. While it has been argued that the petition was offered by the *κοινόν* of Asia, this notion has been rejected by Cook (2010), 263–5.

211 For the suggestion that the opening passage of the letter as presented by Justin contains a lacuna, see Minns (2007), 42–3.

It is this last phrase that has made the exact implications of Hadrian's rescript especially difficult to determine. Some, Justin Martyr likely first among them,[212] have argued that this measure protected Christians from being prosecuted solely on the basis of their religious beliefs, and instead created a situation in which they could only be punished if they were found guilty of particular crimes.[213] If this is indeed true, it would mean that Hadrian did not consider the *nomen ipsum* to be a sufficient ground for prosecution, and told his governor not to allow trials on this basis. This idea, however, is overwhelmingly rejected, and some have suggested that Hadrian was more concerned about false accusations being made without the formal context of legal proceedings—which may parallel Nerva's objections to trials related to the Jewish Tax.[214] Indeed, this interpretation certainly seems to fit the preoccupations of the letter more closely: Hadrian mentions the formalities of the trial throughout his rescript, whereas he references Christians by name only once. Furthermore, he does not voice any objection against the fact that people want to bring forward charges against the Christians in itself, but only seeks to limit the ways in which they can do so, even arguing that those who were found to be making false accusations for the sake of slander (*συκοφαντίας χάριν*) should be punished for this behaviour. This measure was very likely intended to deter people from making careless allegations, and thus to reduce the number of charges that were brought forward. In addition, it is notable that Hadrian does not specify exactly to which laws he is referring. The phrase

[212] Frend (2006), 508; Minns (2007), 42. Keresztes (1967[a]) argues against the idea that Justin interpreted Hadrian's rescript in this way, and repeats this point in (1967[b]) and (1979), 290–2. Instead, he argues that the apologist saw this measure as an issue of procedure: a ban on using confessions of Christianity as a default admission of guilt in cases where the actual charge had been one of crimes associated with Christianity. Keresztes furthermore believes Justin to have been completely correct in this interpretation. It should be noted, however, that Justin begins his *Apology* by claiming that Christians are currently found guilty simply for bearing the name of Christian, which he considers to be unjust (Justin Martyr, *1 Apology* 4). He then proceeds to explain why Christians cannot be guilty of the crimes often attributed to them, some of which (particularly atheism under the Roman definition) he does not believe to be crimes at all. While it is certainly true that he argues for an individual trial about the actions of each accused Christian (*1 Apology* 7), and leaves open the possibility that some (false) Christians may have committed acts that he himself agrees are immoral, the main goal of both such an investigation and his own *Apology* (which seems to function as a legal defence in its own right) therefore appears to be to re-define what constitutes criminal behaviour, and thereby to disconnect the name of Christianity from that particular label. Justin's insistence on a proper trial, which Keresztes sees as his primary objective, therefore takes a back seat to this more fundamental point. Since Justin describes Hadrian's rescript as being in complete accordance with his own views (*1 Apology* 68), it stands to reason that he interpreted the measure in a similar way: Christians should only be convicted if the accusation that they had acted 'against the laws' could be proven in a proper trial and should not be found guilty on the basis of their Christianity alone. Notably, Eusebius' description of the rescript in *Historia Ecclesiastica* 4.8.6 seems more focused on proper procedure and the right to a trial than on redefining the charge.

[213] See especially Sordi (1983), 66–7. For others, see Williams (2012), 208 n. 77.

[214] Barnes (1985), 145–6; Cook (2010), 270–80; Frend (2006), 508; Minns (2007), 42; Wilken (1984), 68; Williams (2012), 209.

παρὰ τοὺς νόμους is decidedly vague,[215] and leaves open the possibility that 'being Christian' was among the accusations that could be considered viable, providing that the case was appropriately made.[216] However, Hadrian himself does not appear to make any clear-cut pronouncements on this point. Instead, he leaves his governor with significant liberty to act as he sees fit. It is left up to Fundanus not only to determine if something contrary to the laws has in fact happened but also to decide how grave the offence was and what the appropriate punishment should be.[217] It therefore seems unlikely that Hadrian is making a general pronouncement on how Christians should be treated. Instead, he gives the governor the tools to deal with a potentially volatile situation in an appropriate way and encourages him to take the particular circumstances of each case into account. It should be noted, however, that our sources do not provide any information on the exact nature of Fundanus' later actions, and that we therefore do not know which accusations he accepted and which he rejected. It therefore remains possible that Hadrian's rescript did improve the lives of members of Asia's Christian community, which would indeed explain why later Christian apologists saw it as a potentially useful precedent and attempted to use it as such—although the value they attached to the rescript may just as well be the result of the same vagueness that makes it so difficult to interpret.

Much has been made of the apparent similarities between Hadrian's rescript and the letter Trajan wrote several years earlier: it has been argued that both missives are strongly focused on regulating the legal process and seek to limit the ways in which accusations against Christians can be brought forward. This has led many to see Hadrian's measure as a simple confirmation of his predecessor's regulations, with at most some very minor innovations.[218] To adhere to this idea, however, is to overlook a number of crucial aspects of the proceedings. Firstly, it has been noted that Hadrian makes no reference to Trajan's precedent and that their focus is at times noticeably different: unlike Trajan, for instance, Hadrian deliberates explicitly on the appropriate punishment for those who are convicted. In a departure from Trajan's tacit confirmation of Pliny's decision to execute Christians because they refused to abandon their religious beliefs, Hadrian's assertion that the punishment should depend on the nature of the crime suggests that he believed there to be multiple grounds on which Christians could be

[215] Minns (2007), 42; Minns and Parvis (2009), 267 n. 6. The claim made in Keresztes (1979), 290–2 that Christians were charged with atheism and disloyalty to the emperor finds its origin in Justin's *Apology*, not in the rescript itself.

[216] Minns (2007), 42; Williams (2012), 209.

[217] The repeated use of imperative verbs in the final lines of the rescript, as well as the assertion that the governor himself should judge the cases people may want to make (τοῦτό <u>σε</u> διαγινώσκειν; emphasis mine), are especially notable in this context, and underscore Fundanus' personal responsibility.

[218] Barnes (1968[a]), 37; Cook (2010), 270–9; Frend (2000), 822 and (2006), 508; Ste Croix (1974[a]), 223; Wilken (1984), 68. See Minns (2007), 42 for the idea that Hadrian further specifies Trajan's ban on anonymous accusations.

convicted. The possibility of convictions based on the '*nomen ipsum*' is therefore not excluded—but neither is this charge presented as the only option. The same goes for the verdict of execution: while this is the only punishment considered by Pliny and Trajan, Hadrian suggests that Christians could be punished in a number of different ways. Furthermore, his insistence that false accusations should be met with repercussions is wholly unparalleled in Trajan's proclamation.[219] These differences, then, suggest that we are dealing with a new legal measure, rather than a straightforward confirmation of existing procedure. Indeed, the very fact that the governor of Asia once again asked for imperial guidance on the same subject so quickly after Trajan had issued his verdict suggests that the precedent, such as it was, was hardly set in stone. Not only does Hadrian not appear to have known about Trajan's measure but, as far as we can tell, neither did Granianus. This lack of knowledge is especially notable because of the geographical proximity of the provinces of Asia and Bithynia-Pontus: if Trajan's rescript had gained the force of accepted law in Pliny's former province, it is not completely inconceivable that the governor of a neighbouring territory could have used it as a basis for his own measures, even if no official collection of precedents appears to have existed at this point in time. Instead, this new interaction between Christians and the Roman authorities once more required negotiation between the various parties involved,[220] and the imperial administration again appears to have been primarily concerned with upholding public order in one particular province.[221] The repeated need to consider how Christians should be treated is, in this case, almost more interesting than the contents of the rescript: it serves to indicate that the correct legal treatment of this group was, in this period, far from immediately obvious.

4.8 Antoninus Pius: Dubious Accounts

The material from the reigns of Trajan and Hadrian suggest that Christians were becoming increasingly visible by the early second century CE, and this pattern

[219] Corke-Webster (2017b), 400; Minns (2007), 41. For the interpretation of *duci* in Pliny the Younger, *Epistulae* 10.96.3 as a reference to execution, likely by the sword, see Sherwin-White (1966), 698.

[220] There are some indications that Christians themselves may also have attempted to sway the course of events. The emergence of Christian apologetics under Hadrian is mentioned by Eusebius, *Historia Ecclesiastica* 4.3, who references Quadratus and Aristides. The work of the latter author survives but makes mention of the legal treatment of Christians only in general terms, stating that they are being harassed. For the idea that Hadrian's policies contributed significantly to Christianity's 'external projection', see Rizzi (2010), 18–19, who also notes that Christians of the period defined themselves both in ethnic and in philosophical terms in order to gain legitimacy.

[221] Interestingly, we hear of local repressive measures against Christians in Judea during the Bar Kokhba Revolt. Since the Roman authorities do not appear to have been involved in this, however, these events will not be considered here. See Eusebius, *Historia Ecclesiastica* 4.8.4 and Justin Martyr, *1 Apology* 31.6.

continued under Hadrian's successor Antoninus Pius, whose reign likewise appears to have been the backdrop for a number of legal interactions between Christians and the Roman authorities. Judging by established tradition, it seems almost beyond dispute that at least some Christian communities in the empire were faced with significant difficulties during this period—but the accounts about these events are hardly straightforward.

4.8.1 The trial of Polycarp

This is especially true for the well-known text known as the Martyrdom of Polycarp (Appendix 3.11), which has been the subject of substantial amounts of debate.[222] The account purports to be a letter from the Christian community of Smyrna in Asia Minor to their acquaintances in Philomelium, a city located further inland in the same region, and claims to describe events that allegedly occurred at some point during the reign of Antoninus Pius.[223] The date of the text itself, however, is heavily contested. Traditionally, it is said to have been composed within a year of Polycarp's death, as is suggested by the author's remark that the community has yet to celebrate the anniversary of the martyr's death.[224] This apparently remarkably early date has enshrined the text as one of the more reliable accounts of Christian martyrdom, and it has been highly valued for this very reason.[225] It has been noted, however, that the anniversary referred to in the

[222] The account of Polycarp's death has been transmitted both in Eusebius, *Historia Ecclesiastica* 4.15 and in a separate *Martyrium Polycarpi*, of which various Greek manuscripts exist. It has long been thought that Eusebius' account differs significantly from the manuscript traditions and is therefore independent of them, but it is now commonly believed that these differences are due to the fact that Eusebius cites some portions of the text, while summarizing others. For this argument, and the various versions of the *Martyrium Polycarpi* that likely predate Eusebius, see Rebillard (2017), 81–143, especially p. 82. See also Dehandschutter (1993), 487 and Musurillo (1972), xiv. Another edition of the text may be found in Bastiaensen (1987), 6–31.

[223] Eusebius, *Historia Ecclesiastica* 4.15.1 attributes these events to the reign of Marcus Aurelius, but the various details given in *Martyrium Polycarpi* 21 seem to suggest an earlier date. However, the interpretation of the passage is far from clear, and much has been said about the date of the martyrdom, as is shown in the overview of the relevant scholarship presented by Dehandschutter (1993), 497–501. Bastiaensen (1987), 4 settles on a general date of 156–67 CE, whereas Bisbee (1988), 121 adheres to 155–8 CE. The more recent analysis of Barnes (2010), 368–73 settles on a more precise date of 157 CE, which is the one adhered to here. However, it should be noted that no imperial involvement is actually mentioned in the text, which may serve to remove some of the urgency behind the debate.

[224] *Martyrium Polycarpi* 18.3. See Dehandschutter (1993), 497 for the remark that 'the date of MPol is obviously dependent on the moment of Polycarp's death', and Bastiaensen (1987), 4 for a similar argument. Dehandschutter ultimately argues that the text may firmly be considered to predate the year 177 CE, see Dehandschutter (1993), 501–2. Parvis (2006) settles on a date no later than 156 CE.

[225] Barnes (1968[b]), 510–14 accepts the first twenty paragraphs of the text as we know it as a contemporary letter. Dehandschutter (1993), 492–7 rejects the possibility that substantial interpolation may have taken place, but he is rightly cautious in seeing the text as deriving from an earlier account of Polycarp's martyrdom that originally provided nothing more than a direct, straightforward recounting of events. Nevertheless, he still sees the text as largely historically reliable. Buschmann (1994), 321 and 327 accepts the text as a genuine early letter, while rejecting the possibility that it contains a core of reliable *acta* on pp. 1–2.

text need not necessarily have been the first commemoration of Polycarp's death,[226] and that the account was, for this reason among others, likely composed in a later period.[227] As it is furthermore highly unlikely that the text known to us was based on official Roman records,[228] the account should therefore be treated carefully—especially given the explicit parallels between Polycarp's martyrdom and the execution of Jesus that emerge over the course of the narrative.[229] Nevertheless, the text can still be regarded as fairly early, and therefore provides valuable insights into the way in which trials of this kind were perceived and described by members of Christian communities.

When the narrative of Polycarp's martyrdom opens, it immediately becomes clear that he is not the first member of Smyrna's Christian community to be targeted. After a brief opening paragraph, the narrative begins its description of events in the city *in medias res*, and the first few passages deal with the torture and executions of various martyrs.[230] The presence of the governor (ἀνθύπατος) is mentioned, but we are given few details about his previous actions or the legal proceedings that led to this treatment. Instead, we are only told that some, though not all, of the twelve accused had originally turned themselves in (a concept of which the author of the text strongly disapproves), and later recanted by offering sacrifice, as the governor had encouraged them to do.[231] We also learn that Polycarp himself was not originally involved, and that he was only brought before the governor because 'the mob' (τὸ πλῆθος) had demanded it, possibly because they recognized him as a leader of the Christian community. In this context, it becomes clear that the objections against the Christians voiced by the inhabitants of Smyrna were at least partially religious in nature: according to the account, they encouraged each other to 'seize the atheists' (αἶρε τοὺς ἀθέους!)[232] and later

[226] Rebillard (2017), 84.

[227] Moss (2010[a]) tentatively suggests a date in the first half of the third century CE, while Rebillard (2017), 85 is even more cautious and argues for Eusebius as the only possible *terminus ante quem*. Rebillard (2020), 70–2 argues that the narrative makes little use of the supposed epistolary format, and suggests that the paragraphs that immediately follow the 'letter', in which its alleged transmission is discussed in great detail, further confirm that the *Martyrium* should be seen part of a narrative tradition that quoted supposed documentary texts in order to enhance the narrative's authenticity.

[228] Bisbee (1988), 130–2.

[229] See Aubert (2010), 302–7; Moss (2013), 98–9. The author of the martyr act remarks on these parallels in *Martyrium Polycarpi* 1 and 6. For the rhetorical purpose of the text, see Bryen (2014[a]), 257–9.

[230] *Martyrium Polycarpi* 2–3.

[231] *Martyrium Polycarpi* 4. The number of martyrs is referred to in *Martyrium Polycarpi* 19. This issue of voluntary martyrdom, its frequency, and the way in which it was viewed by early Christian communities, has been the subject of some debate, which cannot be sufficiently addressed here. See for instance Butterweck (1995); Buck (2012); and Moss (2012[b]). See Frend (1974) for the idea that the willingness of Christians to die for their beliefs contributed to what he calls the 'failure of the persecutions', and Nixey (2017), 70–1 for the argument that Christians were far more eager to die than Roman officials were to convict.

[232] *Martyrium Polycarpi* 3. See also paragraph 9, where the governor asks Polycarp to take up this chant as a proof of his innocence. Interestingly, Polycarp then turns the accusation on its head, and accuses the other inhabitants of the city of being atheists themselves.

claimed that Polycarp has destroyed their gods by encouraging people not to worship them.[233] This may indicate that he was specifically targeted because of his especially vocal derision of traditional religious practices, and it is certainly telling that Polycarp's death is said to have put an end to the troubles faced by the Christian community of the city.[234] The text also indicates that, once again, the interactions between Christians and the Roman authorities were instigated by the local population. In this context, it is notable that it was a local peacekeeper, known as the εἰρήναρχος, who arrested Polycarp when he attempted to flee the city, along with his διωγμῖται, or 'chasers',[235] and that we find no indication that the governor gave any orders to this effect. The arrest of Polycarp is thus framed as having been heavily embedded in Smyrna's local administration, and it is certainly possible that the same was true for the Christians who had previously been convicted.

After his capture, Polycarp was allegedly brought to Smyrna's stadium,[236] where the governor finally became involved. Notably, he did not ask if Polycarp was a Christian, but rather if he was indeed the man the people thought he was—which emphasizes both that specific Christians, rather than the entire community, were being targeted, and that it was not the governor himself who took the initiative for the arrest. He then attempted to persuade Polycarp to recant, encouraging him, among other things, to 'swear by the *genius* of the emperor' and to curse Christ.[237] Polycarp refused, admitted that he was a Christian, and asked the governor if he could have some time to explain his faith. The governor told him to 'convince the people',[238] once again indicating that he was under significant public pressure. The governor then proceeded to threaten Polycarp with various forms of execution, but eventually had his herald announce to the people that 'three times Polycarp has confessed to being a Christian'.[239] This particular detail has

[233] *Martyrium Polycarpi* 12. This course of events may serve to align Polycarp with Heidi Wendt's category of freelance religious experts. See Wendt (2015[a]) and (2016).

[234] *Martyrium Polycarpi* 1.

[235] The name of the official in question, Herod, is likely an invention, as has been argued by Moss (2013), 98–9, who makes much of this detail in her rejection of the text as a reliable source. While she is certainly right in pointing out that the text contains important literary parallels to the narrative of Jesus' crucifixion and that it should be treated cautiously for this reason, it has also been argued that this Herod's actions in the narrative are plausible for his office. For this argument, and more details on what his work entailed, see Fuhrmann (2012), 66–9. It should also be noted that the terminology of this office was specific to Asia Minor, which again suggests that these events were highly localized, and confirms the text's origins, if not its date.

[236] While occasionally referred to as an amphitheatre in scholarship, the venue in which Polycarp's trial took place is called a στάδιον in the original Greek. The fact that the proceedings took place in such a location is seen as suspicious by Aubert (2010), 303; Moss (2010[a]), 549 and (2013), 97; and Parvis (2006), 109; among others. By contrast, Williams (2012), 192–3 argues that the practice is far from unattested.

[237] *Martyrium Polycarpi* 9.

[238] *Martyrium Polycarpi* 10.

[239] *Martyrium Polycarpi* 12. It is unclear whether Polycarp himself swore three times or if this qualification applies to the herald's announcement. Musurillo (1972), 11 assumes the latter, as does Bastiaensen (1987), 18. Den Boeft and Bremmer (1985), 111–13 and Rebillard (2017), 99 apply τρίς to Polycarp's confession.

been seen as evidence that the governor in Smyrna used the procedure established by Pliny as a precedent, although it is also noted that the number three was generally significant in the ancient world and therefore need not refer to any specific example.[240] As a result, we need not necessarily assume that the governor was intent on following Pliny's example, especially because the various ways to recant he suggests are rather more diverse than the sacrifice test ultimately recommended by Trajan: he makes no mention of sacrificing to the Roman gods, but rather urges Polycarp to offer sacrifice to the emperor's *genius*, to repeat the mob's slogan of 'seize the atheists', and to curse Christ. The goal is the same in both cases, but the methods are noticeably different.

Given the nature of Polycarp's confession, the narrative seems to suggest that the accusation on which the trial centred was once again that of 'being Christian'. In this regard, however, two remarks should be made, which may serve to nuance the apparent simplicity of the allegation. First, within the context of the events in Smyrna, the accusation of Christianity seems to have been combined not only with accusations of atheism and destroying traditional religion, as has been mentioned, but also with concerns about potential political disloyalty towards the emperor—as is suggest both by the fact that Polycarp is encouraged to sacrifice to the *genius* of the emperor and by the fact that the *εἰρήναρχος* encouraged Polycarp to acknowledge the emperor as his lord (*κύριος*).[241] This gives us some indication of the arguments the inhabitants of Smyrna may have presented to the governor, and furthermore demonstrates that the charge of 'being Christian' was not an isolated accusation. Second, it should be noted that no formal charge, or formal verdict, is ever mentioned in the text:[242] Polycarp confesses and is then executed almost immediately. Notably, this is said to have occurred not at the order of the relevant officials (Roman or otherwise) but at the hands of the mob—although it is unclear whether anything of this kind would have been allowed to occur.[243]

The rhetorical and literary nature of the *Martyrium Polycarpi* makes it difficult to determine to what extent this course of events reflects historical reality: we are dealing with a text that is focused more on the actions and suffering of the martyrs than on the legal procedures they underwent. While it is unclear, then, whether a specific trial against Polycarp did indeed take place as described, a number of things about the way in which events of this kind are represented nevertheless stand out. The number of accused appears to have been relatively small, and those who became involved were likely specifically targeted because of

[240] Den Boeft and Bremmer (1985), 112. [241] *Martyrium Polycarpi* 8.

[242] This curiosity has also been remarked upon by, among others, Bisbee (1988), 130; Moss (2010[a]), 548–50; Musurillo (1972), xiv; Parvis (2006), 109.

[243] *Martyrium Polycarpi* 12–16. Note that it was also the mob who ordered the *confector* to end Polycarp's life, and that the wider population likewise urged the governor to burn Polycarp's body rather than release it to the Christians, which might result in his veneration. Williams (2012), 190–2 denies that anything particularly unusual or contrary to established legal procedure happened.

their open disregard for traditional religious practices, which suggests that measures against Christians could be smaller in scale. In addition, the text seems to confirm that the initiative usually came from the local population, who apparently found the governor willing to cooperate—although it is unclear whether he shared the population's disdain for the Christians, or was simply overruled by what we might refer to as mob justice.[244] In any case, the emperor does not appear to have been consulted, which may tentatively indicate that this was not considered to be a standard part of trials against Christians. Instead, the *Martyrium Polycarpi* provides us with an example of a governor acting as he believed the situation demanded without reference to his superior—although he is hardly described as being similarly independent from his subjects.

4.8.2 A rescript to Asia?

While Antoninus Pius was not involved in the events in Smyrna, a number of other sources nevertheless mention him as the author of an interesting pronouncement regarding the appropriate legal treatment of Christians addressed to the province of Asia (Appendix 3.12). However, much about this measure remains unclear, and even its dating to the time of Antoninus Pius is far from straightforward: while he is indeed the emperor referenced by Eusebius in his introduction to the rescript in question, the cited text that follows mentions not Pius but Marcus Aurelius.[245] To further complicate matters, a version of the rescript that is connected to Justin's *First Apology* in the *Codex Parisianus* of that work, but does not appear to have been a part of the original text, contains an opening address referencing Pius as the author. While this version is ultimately considered to be less reliable,[246] the earlier date does appear to be supported by the fact that the rescript references a series of earthquakes that famously devastated the province of Asia during Pius' reign. In addition, Eusebius cites a passage from the apologist Melito of Sardis, who likewise believes Pius to have taken measures regarding the Christians, but—in another baffling inconsistency—believes the rescript to have

[244] The text does not provide us with a definitive answer to the issue. On the one hand, the governor barely participates in the proceedings: Polycarp is arrested by local magistrates rather than Roman troops, and his execution is even described as having been carried out by locals. On the other hand, the author of the text does assert that Polycarp 'overcame the unjust governor'—see *Martyrium Polycarpi* 19.

[245] Eusebius, *Historia Ecclesiastica* 4.12–13. Coleman-Norton (1966), 8 notes that Eusebius incorrectly refers to the text as an edict (διάταξις).

[246] Marcovich (1994) and Wartelle (1987) cite the rescript in an Appendix of their editions of Justin's *Apologiae* rather than as part of the apologies themselves, while Minns (2007), 38–9 outright rejects the possibility that the rescripts could have belonged to Justin's original. The edition of Minns and Parvis (2009) does not cite the rescript at all. The argument that the version connected to Justin is inferior to the one cited by Eusebius has been made since Harnack (1895), and more recently by Minns and Parvis (2009), 30 n. 84.

applied to various Greek cities in the provinces of Achaea and Macedonia, rather than to Asia.[247] The text is now generally dated to the reign of Antoninus Pius, but this has certainly not proved to be beyond dispute.[248] The contents of the rescript are likewise extremely contentious: ever since the seminal analysis of the rescript by Adolf Harnack, it has been widely acknowledged that the text contains substantial interpolations,[249] and while some maintain that an authentic core may nonetheless be discoverable,[250] many others have rejected the rescript as a potential source.[251] The emperor's assertion that the Christians remain faithful to their god while their accusers neglect their own deities is particularly suspect, as is the order to immediately punish anyone who accuses a Christian.[252]

Nevertheless, a few scant details shared by the different versions of the rescript could potentially be significant. Firstly, our sources seem to suggest that Antoninus' missive was prompted by a local request of some sort, although details of both the provenance and the exact nature of such a request escape us. The versions connected to both Eusebius and Justin link this measure to the series of earthquakes that devastated the province of Asia, which would seem to indicate that social and economic unrests once again played a part, and that these disasters fuelled concerns about divine anger prompted by Christian rejection of the traditional gods. Such a response to disruptions of the 'natural order' would indeed fit well with Tertullian's fervent claim that 'if the Tiber reaches the walls, if the Nile does not reach the fields, if the sky does not move, if the earth does move, if there is famine, if there is a plague, immediately the call goes: Christians to the lions!'[253] Some hints of similar disturbances are likewise present in Melito's version, which states that Antoninus forbade any *νεωτερίζειν* against the Christians—a verb that not only suggests innovation but also carries with it implications of violence.[254] All versions of the rescript furthermore seem to express a reluctance to take more wide-ranging measures than had so far been common—although it should be noted that the distinctly pro-Christian interpolations in the cited versions make it

[247] Eusebius, *Historia Ecclesiastica* 4.26.10. The cities referenced are Larissa, Thessaloniki, and Athens. Millar (1977), 560 believes that all sources refer to the same set of rescripts, while Keresztes (1971), 16 suggests that Melito may not have provided a complete list of the emperor's missives and may therefore have been referring to different proclamations.

[248] Coleman-Norton (1966), 8 argues for a dating to the time of Marcus Aurelius on the basis of the superiority of Eusebius' version.

[249] Harnack (1895).

[250] See especially Barnes (1985), 155; Frend (1965), 239–40; Keresztes (1971), 13–15; Keresztes (1979), 294–5.

[251] Barnes (1968[a]), 38; Millar (1977), 560; Williams (2012), 199 n. 55. Wartelle (1987), 220–1 refers to the passage as the 'faux rescript d'Antonin le Pieux'.

[252] For this last point, see Frend (1965), 239–40.

[253] *Si Tiberis ascendit in moenia, si Nilus non ascendit in arva, si caelum stetit, si terra movit, si fames, si lues, statim Christianos ad leonem!* Tertullian, *Apologeticus pro Christianis* 40.2.

[254] See Liddell, Scott, and Jones (1968), *ad loc.* 2.

difficult to determine the tone of the original rescript, if indeed it ever existed.[255] For this reason, our interpretation of the available sources must remain minimalist: it remains possible, although not certain, that Antoninus Pius was confronted with questions regarding the appropriate treatment of Christians by the population or magistrates of one or more specific provinces, which may have arisen during difficulties in that region. Furthermore, his response seems to have urged restraint and adherence to proper legal procedures. If these events did indeed take place, it would mean that this was the third time in three generations of emperors that such a warning was necessary. On the basis of the available sources, however, we simply cannot go any further.

4.8.3 The trial of Ptolemaeus and Lucius

The final episode dated to the reign of Antoninus Pius is a trial against two Christian men known as Ptolemaeus and Lucius (Appendix 3.13). The case is said to have taken place in Rome itself, and the only available account is part of Justin Martyr's *Second Apology*, which was written some time before the author's death in 165 CE.[256] The text therefore likely represents an almost contemporary description of events.[257] This is not to say, however, that the narrative can be taken completely at face value, or is without its problems. It has long been noted that Justin likely tailored his account, and especially the passages of direct speech present in the text, to suit his literary and apologetic purpose,[258] and that the text furthermore contains notable references to both Socrates and the Stoics that may well

[255] For the idea that this rescript amounts to nothing more than a repetition of established procedure, see Barnes (1968ᵃ), 37; Barnes (1985), 154; Frend (1965), 240; Keresztes (1979), 295; Keresztes (1971), 15; Molthagen (1970), 34.

[256] Justin Martyr, *2 Apology* 2. The text is also cited by Eusebius, *Historia Ecclesiastica* 4.17. The exact nature of the relationship between the texts known as the *First* and *Second Apology*, as well as their respective dates, remain the subject of substantial debate. That both are ultimately of Justin's hand, however, is rarely disputed, not even by Moss (2013), 66–8 and 105, who is otherwise highly critical of many martyr narratives. For the idea that the text we now know as the *Second Apology* was compiled from fragmentary, leftover passages of Justin's work after his death, see Parvis (2007). For the suggestion that the *Second Apology* was a later piece of writing by Justin that in some way depended on his own *First Apology*, see Minns (2007), 48. For a date of the early 150s CE for the martyrdom, which is at least partially based on the identification of the urban prefect in the narrative with Q. Lollius Urbicus, see Barnes (1968ᵇ), 515.

[257] It is presumably the origin of the account within the context of Justin's *Apology*, rather than any disputes about its contemporary nature, that has led to its omission from many collections of Martyr Acts, since these normally focus on independent texts dealing with a single martyr or a coherent group. See for instance Barnes (2010), 356–9 and Bastiaensen (1987). This motivation is made explicit by Rebillard (2017), 21. Here, the account has been included due to its close temporal proximity to the events it describes, following compilations such as those by Bisbee (1988), 82 and Musurillo (1972), 38–41.

[258] Barnes (1968ᵇ), 515 acknowledges that the account is very likely more or less contemporary but is still wary of the literary motives it contains. Musurillo (1972), xvi refers to the account as 'strange but moving', without specifying why he believes this to be the case.

have been intended to make Christianity more palatable to Roman readers.[259] Nevertheless, the account contains a number of interesting details that are worth investigating, especially those that relate to the setting and origins of the trial.

According to Justin, certain members of Rome's Christian community first attracted the attention of the city authorities because they became involved with a woman from the Roman elite, whose new-found Christian beliefs encouraged her to seek a divorce from her non-Christian husband.[260] Her husband then attempted to bring her to court for being Christian, but after a petition to the emperor she was allowed to first manage her financial affairs before answering the charges. This apparently delayed the proceedings substantially, and possibly indefinitely,[261] which in turn led the woman's ex-husband to bring charges against Ptolemaeus, who had been his former wife's teacher and was therefore held responsible for her change of heart. This does not, in itself, seem particularly unusual: Flavius Josephus likewise reports multiple occasions on which husbands undertook action against those they believed to have led their wives astray, and it is not inconceivable that something similar may have happened here.[262] It is much more notable that the woman in this situation was granted at least a temporary reprieve from her own trial. In this case, her new religious convictions do not appear to have been seen as a particularly serious transgression that warranted immediate attention—as could easily have been the case for a woman of her class, who may have been expected to conform more closely to traditional piety. In this case, however, her status and apparent access to the emperor seem to have protected her,[263] and we hear nothing about any further case against her.

[259] Moss (2012[a]) 86–8 and (2013), 66–8. A similar tendency to use philosophy in defence of Christianity may be observed in the *Legatio pro Christianis* by Athenagoras of Athens. A critical edition of this text may be found in Marcovich (1990).

[260] Justin never names the woman, either to protect her from the Roman authorities or to protect her past, which he describes as less than virtuous. See Minns and Parvis (2009), 273 n. 4. See Lampe (1989), 200–3 and (2003), 237–40 for a theory on the woman's name. Justin uses a Greek rendition of the technical Latin term *repudium* to indicate the idea of a divorce, which originally seems to have referred to a husband divorcing his wife but could also be used when the other partner took the initiative. See Minns and Parvis (2009), 275 n. 1.

[261] Justin Martyr, *2 Apology* 2.7–8. It has been argued that the husband accused his wife of being Christian to show that she had behaved improperly, which would have allowed him to retain part of her dowry after the divorce. However, when the emperor allowed her to put her affairs in order before answering the charge, this may have meant that the charge of Christianity could not be used in the divorce proceedings, and that the husband therefore had to choose between keeping part of the dowry or progressing the trial regarding his wife's Christianity, which could only take place when he had given up her money. For this theory, see Minns and Parvis (2009), 275 nn. 4 and 5. For the argument that such disputes about private affairs between Christians and non-Christians must have occurred with some frequency and were likely resolved 'behind closed doors', see Lane Fox (1986), 423–4.

[262] Flavius Josephus, *Antiquitates Iudaicae* 18.3.4–5 (65–84). For the pattern of various types of 'freelance religious experts' being targeted by the Roman authorities, see Wendt (2015[a]) and (2016). See Moss (2012[a]), 87 for the trope of the pious woman being mistreated by her husband.

[263] See Lampe (2003), 239 for the argument that the woman was spared because of her social status.

The charge of 'being Christian', which was levied both against the unnamed woman and her teacher Ptolemaeus, seems to have been much more effective in the case of the latter, whose trial before the *praefectus urbi* Urbicus is described in heavily abbreviated form. We are told that he was arrested by a centurion who was friendly with his pupil's former husband—which once again shows that social status could play an important part in trials against Christians—and was held captive until his hearing with the prefect. When this inquiry took place, Urbicus only asked Ptolemaeus if he was a Christian, to which he promptly confessed. Justin then claims that this confession elicited the support of another Christian named Lucius, who is then depicted as accusing the prefect of acting unreasonably and furthermore contrary to the wishes of both emperor and senate (presumably in Justin's words rather than his own).[264] Both Lucius and another, unnamed Christian were then also executed. Once again, the formal charge appears to have been that of 'being Christian', but it is important to remember this was not a large-scale measure aimed at the entire Christian community of the city: Ptolemaeus was targeted specifically because he was seen as the corruptor of a Roman matron, while Lucius and the other, unnamed Christian may well have been perceived to have directly challenged the authority of the prefect. The total number of accused was thus limited, and included only people who were by all appearances targeted for very specific reasons. The brevity of the proceedings as Justin describes them, as well as the highly limited number of questions, is thus likely at least partially exaggerated, and we might wonder if Lucius' claim that Urbicus acted contrary to the wishes of the emperor was indeed in accordance with the facts—assuming he actually made it. Justin's apology of Christianity at least in part relied on the claim that previous emperors had been willing to support Christians rather than repress them, and far-reaching claims of this nature should therefore be taken with a pinch of salt. Rather than being an example of illegal overreach, the trials of Ptolemaeus and Lucius should be seen as a fascinating example of the substantial effect personal grievances may at times have had on trials against Christians.[265]

4.9 Marcus Aurelius: Christians and the Philosopher-Emperor

The importance of private accusers, and their motivations, once again comes to the forefront during the reign of Antoninus' successor Marcus Aurelius. This period appears to have been one of significant difficulties for various Christian

[264] See Moss (2013), 109 for the suggestion that Justin himself is responsible for Lucius' last words. Bryen (2014[a]), 260–1 argues that Justin used this story to make the argument that legal procedures were only valid if there was room for what he saw as logical, reasonable dialogue.

[265] For the importance of such social tensions in instigating trials against Christians, see especially Corke-Webster (2023).

communities in the empire, and likely for this very reason witnessed a surge in Christian apologetics.[266] A primary example of this may be found in Melito of Sardis, who (among his many other writings) produced an apology of Christianity addressed to Marcus Aurelius himself. Although a list of Melito's works has been transmitted, it is unknown if this overview is complete. Little is known about his life, and the text of his *Apology* survives only in the form of selected passages cited by Eusebius, the original order of which is now difficult to determine.[267] Nevertheless, what remains of Melito's work is fascinating, especially because his *Apology* appears to have been notably explicit in addressing the particular circumstances to which it is responding. Where authors like Justin reference the plight of Christians in general, and at times discuss specific events from the past to illustrate their point, Melito seems to be asking for the emperor's help in resolving very concrete, and very current, circumstances.[268]

4.9.1 Anti-Christian actions in Asia

Melito's surviving description of events is brief, and in its current form likely more obscure than was originally the case. It is clear that he is referring to disturbances in his home province of Asia, and that he perceives the situation to be unprecedented. Melito states that no similar event has ever occurred (*οὐδεπώποτε γενόμενον*) before,[269] and furthermore adds that Christians in his province have become the victim of 'new decrees' (*καινά δόγματα*; Appendix 3.14) that encouraged false accusers to rob them. The origins of these new decrees, however, remain unclear. They have on different occasions been identified with a wide variety of measures that may or may not have been intended to target Christians specifically but are often assumed to have been used for that purpose

[266] For a brief overview of the various authors involved in apologetic writing in this period, see Norris (2004), 40–4. For the argument that many of these apologists, like Melito, attempted to adopt 'the standard forms of traditional diplomacy', see Rives (2009), 114.

[267] Eusebius, *Historia Ecclesiastica* 4.26.5–11. For the list of Melito's other works, see *Historia Ecclesiastica* 4.26.2.

[268] I would like to thank Dr Diederik Burgersdijk for drawing my attention to this aspect of Melito's work.

[269] It is unclear what this remark means. In this context, Melito may have meant to imply that Christians had never before been actively pursued, possibly to make a rhetorical point that might compel the emperor to take a desired course of action. Notably, Melito seems to have argued that only bad emperors like Nero and Domitian have acted against the Christians (a claim paralleled in Tertullian, *Apologeticus pro Christianis* 5.3), and although we do not know how the two cited passages relate to each other, he may be making a similar case in his description of events in Asia. See Eusebius, *Historia Ecclesiastica* 4.26.9. He certainly seems to have been aware that the Christian communities of Asia had faced difficulties in the past, as becomes clear in the passage cited in *Historia Ecclesiastica* 4.26.10. It is also possible that Melito is referring to the number of Christians involved, although this fits the phrasing rather less well.

throughout the empire.[270] This assumption, however, finds no clear confirmation in Melito's description of events as we know it. The author explicitly limits the outbreak of violence to Asia, which indicates that the relevant measures were issued on a regional level, although it remains unclear by whose authority. Melito questions if the emperor himself could indeed have given permission for these measures, which may indicate that their origin, as well the legality of their application, was in question. It is unlikely that Melito would have raised the question of Marcus Aurelius' approval in these terms if the 'new measures' were unambiguously directed against Christians and clearly issued in the emperor's name. Given the lack of context, however, the possibility remains that we are dealing with a more general imperial measure aimed at the province of Asia—although Melito's description suggests it was either not issued in any other regions or did not elicit the same effects there.

The exact contents of the measures likewise remain ambiguous, although Melito's account of them gives us some fascinating clues. It is notable that the author focuses heavily on the fact that Christians are being robbed (*ληστεύειν*; *διαρπάζειν*; *τοιαύτη δημώδει λεηλασία*). The possibility of execution is mentioned almost as an afterthought in the text as we know it,[271] and is used primarily to express the idea that both Melito and his community consider themselves to be completely subjected to the emperor's wishes. It thus seems very likely that the 'new decrees' were in some way financial in nature, which suggests that measures against Christians could at times take different forms than the trials ending in executions that feature so prominently in other accounts of interactions between Christians and the Roman authorities.

The way in which Melito's account has been tailored to convince Marcus Aurelius to take action is likewise fascinating.[272] As mentioned, Melito is writing to the emperor about a current and likely ongoing problem, and even in the brief passages available to us, it is clear that he makes significant attempts to portray the matter as highly urgent. His frequent references to 'robbery' imply that these new decrees did not serve to uphold the law but instead led to substantial criminal activity, and that they were furthermore used to target the innocent rather than the guilty. Melito, as a Christian, thus uses the language of instability and

[270] See especially Keresztes (1968), 335–6, who relates Melito's statement to the events in Lyon, which will be discussed in section 4.9.4. The remarks on the subject made in Williams (2012), 197 n. 50 imply a similar line of thinking. MacMullen (1966), 130 references a similar theory, which assumes that a rescript aimed at diviners was also used to target Christians, but ultimately rejects this possibility. This theory may be found in Sordi (1983), 68. This rescript is referred to in Ulpian, *De Officio Proconsulis* 7 in *Leg. Mos. et Rom. Coll.* 15.2.5 and *Digesta* 48.19.30. The view expressed in Nogrady (2006), 64–5, that Marcus Aurelius issued a *mandatum* that allowed governors to actively seek out not only *latrones* but all *mali homines*, does not sufficiently take into account the distinction between local and Roman authorities that plays a significant part in the known anti-Christian trials from the period.

[271] Eusebius, *Historia Ecclesiastica* 4.26.6.

[272] For Christian apologists working within the diplomatic framework favoured by the Roman authorities, see Millar (1977), 561–6 and Rives (2009).

unrest (which traditionally had been levied *against* the Christians) to appeal to the emperor's authority, suggesting that these things may be happening contrary to his wishes, and that he could therefore rectify the situation. He further reinforces this argument by supplying measures of Marcus Aurelius' predecessors as potentially valid precedents,[273] and by attempting to incorporate Christianity in the emperor's worldview by describing it as a philosophy and a *λόγος*.[274] Melito, then, used arguments he believed to be acceptable to the Roman authorities in order to alleviate the pressures faced by his community.

4.9.2 The trial of Justin Martyr

Whatever the result of Melito's petition may have been, reports of trials against Christians from other regions continue to appear. Of these, the text known as the *Acts of Justin Martyr*, which deals with the trial of the famous apologist and a number of his students, has often been considered to be of particular interest (Appendix 3.15). This is primarily due to the fact that the text is thought by many to have been based on the official record of the trial in question, which would make the account especially reliable.[275] However, the transmission of the text is far from straightforward: three versions of various lengths are known to us, and while the longest of these (commonly known as 'C') is generally considered to have been substantially edited, no general consensus has yet been reached on the relationship between the shortest version 'A' and medium-length version 'B'—although a slight preference for the former appears to have emerged.[276] The origins and sources of the text have likewise come under suspicion, and the aforementioned idea that the shortest version of the text (A), with the exceptions of

[273] Melito makes mention of the rescripts by Hadrian and Antoninus Pius discussed in sections 4.7 and 4.8.2. See Eusebius, *Historia Ecclesiastica* 4.26.10. Elsewhere, he likewise suggests that emperors from Augustus onwards left Christians well alone, and that this contributed to the flourishing of the empire—with the implication that this was due to the favour of the Christian God. See *Historia Ecclesiastica* 4.26.7.

[274] See Eusebius, *Historia Ecclesiastica* 4.26.7 and 8. Note that Melito explicitly describes Marcus Aurelius as a particularly philosophically minded emperor in *Historia Ecclesiastica* 4.26.11. For the argument that various Christian authors, including Tertullian, *Apologeticus pro Christianis* 30, also argued against the idea that Christians were a threat, often by underscoring their loyalty to the emperor, see Rives (2009), 117–18. Athenagoras' *Legatio pro Christianis* likewise repeatedly plays on the emperor's philosophical interests.

[275] For a discussion of the various authors who hold this view, see Bisbee (1988), 95–6. See especially Freudenberger (1968) for the view that the account was based on a Roman *commentarius*. For the view that the account is notably reliable, see Barnes (1968[b]), 527; Barnes (2010), 63; Freudenberger (1968); Moss (2013), 109–11.

[276] Barnes (1968[b]), 515–17; Bisbee (1988), 117; Moss (2012[a]), 89 and (2013), 110; Musurillo (1972), xviii. Musurillo (1972), 42–61 presents all three versions of the text, while Bastiaensen (1987), 52–7 offers only version A, and Knopf (1913), 16–19 prints only version B. For this discussion, version A has been used as a basis, with occasional references to version B. Due to the more substantial editing of C, this version has been excluded.

the first and sixth paragraphs, is essentially an authentic trial record has rightly been called into question.[277] Although the text does exhibit certain characteristics that are often associated with this type of document, factors like the lack of a proper introduction and conclusion, the peculiar style of questioning, and various other elements suggest that even the earliest known version of the text was edited—likely multiple times—between its original composition and the end of the third century, or even the fourth.[278] A historical core of some kind remains a strong possibility, but it would be unwise to take the text in its current form as a completely authentic document.

The trial of Justin and his companions is set in Rome itself, under the supervision of *praefectus urbi* Rusticus.[279] The author of the text makes mention of certain 'impious edicts of idolatry' (ἄνομα προστάγματα τῆς εἰδωλολατρίας), which version B later interpreted as a formal command compelling Christians—and them alone—to offer sacrifice.[280] It has been suggested by some that this is in fact a reference to an imperial edict ordering general sacrifice in a time of grave difficulties, for which no additional evidence exists.[281] Others have been more inclined to see this passage as a reference to the famous sacrifice test, the use of which is hardly exclusive to the reign of Marcus Aurelius.[282] This interpretation therefore comes with substantial problems of its own: the introduction of both versions A and B seems to indicate either that new measures were being issued or that older measures which were no longer in use had been recently renewed. Neither option seems to be particularly applicable to the sacrifice test, and it remains unclear whether the claim that the arrest of Justin and his followers was based on specific legal measures is based on historical fact. However, it need not be assumed that such measures, whatever they may have been, were aimed specifically at Christians, since no such claims are made by the earlier version A. The geographical scope of the measure may likewise very well have been much more limited than some have suggested.[283] The account of these events is set in Rome itself, where the relevant authorities may well have been especially concerned with upholding traditional piety. No empire-wide edict need therefore have been issued, and evidence for such a claim is indeed lacking.[284] Nevertheless, the concept of sacrifice appears to have played an important part in the prefect's

[277] Bisbee (1988), 117.

[278] Bisbee (1988), 117 believes that the last editing cannot have taken place later than the late third century. Freudenberger (1968), 24 believes the first and last paragraphs to have been fourth-century additions.

[279] This Rusticus is very likely Q. Iunius Rusticus, who had a close relationship with Marcus Aurelius and is referenced in his *Meditations* 1.7 and again in 1.17. Rusticus was urban prefect between 163 and 168 CE. See Musurillo (1972), 43 n. 1.

[280] See Bisbee (1988), 100 for the conclusion that version B has a later date than version A.

[281] Keresztes (1968), 329.

[282] Bisbee (1988), 97–100.

[283] For the claim that such a measure was issued throughout the empire, see Keresztes (1968), 329.

[284] See Rives (1999), 152 for the suggestion that such wide-ranging measures were pioneered by Decius several decades later.

considerations, as he cites the Christians' refusal to cooperate in this ritual as the primary reason for his ultimate verdict.[285] Whatever the cause of Justin's arrest, it therefore seems clear that his religious behaviours (or lack thereof) were what ultimately led him and his companions to be convicted.[286]

Notably, however, the issue of sacrifice plays little to no part in the description of the main part of the proceedings. Instead, Rusticus opens by asking Justin: 'What kind of life do you lead?'—a question that prompts a discussion of Christianity that is rather philosophical in nature.[287] The line of questioning then shifts, now focusing on the meeting place used by Justin and his followers. Justin argues that Christians commonly meet wherever is most convenient, and adds that he personally prefers his own living quarters, where anyone interested in his words knew to find him.[288] Justin thereby implies that his meetings are completely ordinary and transparent, rejecting the prefect's insinuation that Christian activities were illicit and potentially subversive. This implication is carried over into Rusticus' next series of questions, in which he asks Justin's followers if they are indeed Christians, before asking if Justin converted them (*Ἰουστῖνος ὑμᾶς ἐποίησε Χριστιανούς;*).[289] The answer is consistently negative: Justin's companions claim that they became Christian because of their parents, which safeguards their teacher against accusations of actively trying to recruit his followers. Christianity is established as a community one can be born into, rather than as a way of life one actively adopts, thereby deserting one's ancestral practices and possibly causing unrest.[290] In addition to his religious concerns, Rusticus' line of questioning therefore also shows his preoccupation with public order, and although the text as we know it suggests that he found nothing that was particularly incriminating, it is nonetheless telling that he chose to investigate.[291]

[285] *Acta Iustini* A 5.6; Version B 5.8 offers a more elaborate version, which makes the assumption that new imperial proclamations were at issue more explicit. Bisbee (1988), 116 once again confirms that B is likely the later version.

[286] Bisbee (1988), 116 suggests that version A's use of the verb *ἀπάγω* indicates that Justin and his companions were led away, possibly into captivity, but does not necessarily imply execution. The later reference to 'the customary spot' and an earlier mention of beheading, however, suggest otherwise.

[287] *Acta Iustini* A 2.1. See Moss (2012[a]), 89–93 for the philosophical tone of the discussion. For the suggestion that Rusticus was attempting to give Justin a chance to escape by claiming that he was a philosopher, see Barnes (1968[b]), 516.

[288] Bisbee (1988), 111–13 suggests that version A 3 has been corrupted, since the questions and answers do not logically follow each other, but that version B 3 has suffered no such corruption.

[289] *Acta Iustini* A 4. See also B 4.

[290] Version B repeats these points but adds a remarkable reference to Christ as the true father, and faith as the true mother of these Christians. See Bisbee (1988), 114–15 for parallels.

[291] This focus on active recruitment may serve to place Justin within the context of freelance religious experts. See Wendt (2015[a]) and (2016), as well as Corke-Webster (2023), 15–16, who suggests that Justin was likely met with competition from other Christian teachers, which may have led to tensions within the Christian community. The report by Eusebius, *Historia Ecclesiastica* 4.16, which claims that Justin was specifically targeted because he had insulted the philosopher Crescens, likewise suggests that the accusations against Justin may have included claims of nefarious behaviour. It should be noted that Rebillard (2019), in response to Bremmer (2019), sees the difference between the

4.9.3 Marcus Aurelius protecting Christians?

While the legal interactions described in the *Acts of Justin* are distinctly local and small scale, this is very much not the case for a peculiar measure ascribed to Emperor Marcus Aurelius himself, which was supposedly meant to protect Christians from precisely the sort of treatment that Justin and his companions had received (Appendix 3.16). The existence of such far-reaching, centralized protective efforts at this point in time is highly dubious to say the least, but remarkably the measure is mentioned in a notable number of sources.[292] In all versions of the story, the emperor's army was on campaign during the Marcomannic Wars when it was surrounded by the enemy and lost all access to water. When the soldiers were close to perishing of thirst, however, they were saved by an unexpected storm, which not only provided them with the water they needed but also allowed them to win the subsequent battle with the seemingly supernatural help of thunder and rain. This part of events is widely attested in ancient sources, and likely has at least some basis in historical fact.[293] Explanations for the supposed miracle, however, vary widely. On the one hand, Cassius Dio suggests that an Egyptian magician may have been responsible,[294] while Christian authors appear to have cast members of their own community as the army's rescuers relatively soon after the event.

One of the first examples of this may be found in the account of Apollinaris, which was likely composed during the reign of Marcus Aurelius himself but is now known only from a reference by Eusebius.[295] Tertullian likewise attributes the miracle to the power of Christian prayer, and adds that the emperor was so grateful that he protected Christians from any harm by punishing all those who brought accusations against them—although not by official law.[296] This version of

account of the *Acta Iustini* and the one in Eusebius as a reason not to include the *Acta* in his collection of martyr narratives, since this means that there is no external evidence for the date of *Acta*.

[292] Christian versions of the story may be found in Tertullian, *Apologeticus pro Christianis* 5.6–7 and *Ad Scapulam* 4.6; Eusebius, *Historia Ecclesiastica* 5.5.1–6; and, most notably, Justin Martyr, *1 Apology* (Appendix). An alternative account is presented in Cassius Dio, *Historiae Romanae* ep.72.8–10. This part of Dio's work survives only as summarized by the Byzantine scholar Xiphilinus, who adds his own notes in chapter 9 of the cited passage and claims that Marcus Aurelius' army was not saved by an Egyptian magician, as Dio had claimed, but by Christians.

[293] See Israelowich (2008), 86. The story is even depicted on the column of Marcus Aurelius, which was erected between 176 and 193 CE, and shows a divine intervention that is for all intents and purposes unprompted by humans. See Kovács (2009), 159. Some also claim to see references to the miracle in imperial coinage of the period, although Kovács (2009), 107–11 raises some significant doubts.

[294] Cassius Dio, *Historiae Romanae* ep.72.8.

[295] Eusebius, *Historia Ecclesiastica* 5.5.4. For the date of the account, see Israelowich (2008), 87–90 and Kovács (2009), 48.

[296] See especially Tertullian, *Apologeticus pro Christianis* 5.6. Tertullian likewise mentions the miracle in *Ad Scapulam* 4.6 but makes no mention of any legal protection in that context. Instead, he suggests that Christians used the name of Jupiter to pray to their own god. These two versions of the story seem to be incompatible, because how would Marcus Aurelius have known to protect the Christians if they did not explicitly present themselves as such?

the story was later repeated by Eusebius, who conveniently neglected to mention Tertullian's assertion that no official measure was ever taken,[297] and it also appears in a letter to the senate that is attached to Justin's *Apology* under the name of Marcus Aurelius.[298] This letter claims that the emperor issued a protective order for all Christians, condemned their accusers to be burned alive, and furthermore states that he ordered copies of his proclamation to be distributed throughout the empire. As demonstrated by the clear escalation of the various accounts, this last version of the story is almost certainly false, and its language, along with its use of Byzantine military terminology, suggests that it may be dated to the fourth or fifth century.[299] The earlier versions of the story, particularly that of Tertullian, have been considered by some to contain some measure of truth,[300] but even these must remain under suspicion: the available Roman sources seem to tell a rather different story, and the various actions against Christians dated to Marcus Aurelius' reign furthermore suggest that no protective measures were ever issued. It is therefore more likely that the Christian apologists used a popular story of the time to argue that, contrary to popular belief, Christians were highly loyal to the empire, and at times even responsible for its rescue.[301]

4.9.4 Anti-Christian actions in Lyon

Marcus Aurelius' supposed benevolence towards Christianity is also belied by an event dated to the later years of his reign, which appears to have been rather larger in scale than the trial against Justin and his companions.[302] At the very beginning of the fifth book of his *Historia Ecclesiastica*, Eusebius references a series of events that he considers to be representative of the position of Christians in the Roman world at the end of the second century CE.[303] Rather than describing the case himself, however, he quotes lengthy passages from a fascinating piece of writing that he believes is 'worthy of everlasting remembrance'. The document in question is a letter written by the Christian communities of Lyon and nearby Vienne to their brethren in Asia and Phrygia, which seems to contain an eyewitness account of the anti-Christian actions that took place in their region

[297] Eusebius, *Historia Ecclesiastica* 5.5.5–6.

[298] Justin Martyr, *1 Apology* (Appendix). The text is printed in Marcovich (1994), 165–8. This version was likely not based on Eusebius' account—see Kovács (2009), 119.

[299] For a more elaborate argument to this effect, see Kovács (2009), 119–20.

[300] Sordi (1983), 74.

[301] Israelowich (2008), 90.

[302] A version of this analysis was published as Janssen (2021[a]) with Vandenhoeck & Ruprecht Verlage. It is reproduced here with permission.

[303] Eusebius, *Historia Ecclesiastica* 5.pr.1 and 5.2.1. A number of editions of the relevant passage are available. Musurillo (1972), 62–85 provides both the Greek text and an English translation, as does Rebillard (2017), 145–73. The latter makes extensive use of the edition in Bastiaensen (1987). Another recent edition may be found in Seeliger and Wischmeyer (2015).

(Appendix 3.17). As in the case of the *Martyrium Polycarpi*, the authors are said to have directly witnessed the events they describe, and the letter as transmitted to us is still generally considered to be largely faithful to Eusebius' original source.[304] While some have suggested that the events discussed in the letter took place in Galatia, rather than Gaul,[305] this view has overwhelmingly been dismissed due to a lack of evidence.[306] The argument for relocating the events described by Eusebius to the eastern Mediterranean is primarily based on the fact that Lyon and Vienne were part of different provinces, namely Gallia Lugdunensis and Gallia Narbonensis, respectively. They would therefore have been part of different jurisdictions, but are nonetheless jointly described as the setting of the narrative in Eusebius' introduction to the letter.[307] However, the geographical proximity of the two towns—which were connected by both road and river—makes it likely that close relations between their respective Christian communities existed, and we might therefore ask ourselves if such a far-reaching solution to what is ultimately little more than a curiosity is warranted. It is likely that Lyon and Vienne fell under the authority of the same bishop, and that Sanctus, the deacon of Vienne, was arrested while he was visiting Lyon.[308] If this is indeed true, it seems more probable that the events described in the letter took place in Lyon, and that a number of Christians from Vienne became involved due to their presence in that city.[309] It has also been suggested that the author of the letter appears to have been familiar with the Latin translation of biblical texts, which makes a western origin of the account more likely.[310] The traditional date of 177 CE ascribed to the events in the letter is likewise widely considered to be at least approximately accurate, despite the fact that this dating is not included in the letter itself, but rather in Eusebius' introduction to it.[311] At times, the reputation of Marcus Aurelius as a moderate and not particularly anti-Christian emperor

[304] It should be emphasized that Eusebius presents only parts of the letter. However, he claims to have had access to the entirety of the document (see Eusebius, *Historia Ecclesiastica* 5.pr.2.) and indicates when passages have been omitted. See Rebillard (2017), 145. This seems to suggest a degree of faithfulness to the available sources on Eusebius' part. Moss (2012ª), 104–6 has likewise argued against the wholesale invention of the letter by Eusebius.

[305] Colin (1964), 59. [306] Barnes (1968ᵇ), 517. [307] Colin (1964), 20.

[308] Frend (1965), 2. While Moss (2012ª), 103 has drawn attention to the fact that the cities of Lyon and Vienne were historically at odds with each other, as is stated in Tacitus, *Historiae* 1.65, the same need not have held true for the Christian communities of the region.

[309] It may be tentatively noted that the descriptions of anti-Christian hostilities in the letter appear to refer to a single city, rather than multiple: Eusebius, *Historia Ecclesiastica* 5.1.8 mentions only a single city council and only a single prison. The emphasis on the role of the mob in the text may likewise suggest a single urban environment.

[310] This observation was originally made by Robinson (1891), 97–100. The connection between the author's apparent knowledge of Latin and the origin of the letter in the western empire is made by Barnes (1968ᵇ), 517. See Barnes (1978), 138 for the scarcity of accounts about the treatment of Christians from the western Mediterranean.

[311] Barnes (1968ᵇ), 518; Colin (1964), 12; Dehandschutter (2005), 6–8; Keresztes, (1967ᶜ), 75 and (1979), 299; Musurillo (1972), xx. Notably, Eusebius presents a date of 166–7 CE in his *Chronicon*. For the idea that the date in the *Historia Ecclesiastica* is a correction of an earlier mistake in the *Chronicon*, see Barnes (1978), 143.

has been used to argue that these events must have taken place at a significantly later date,[312] but the noted increase in apologetic Christian literature in the late second century CE seems to belie this argument.[313]

The time and place of the events described in the letter are thus fairly well established. This is not to say, however, that its text is to be regarded uncritically: in recent years, more attention has been paid to the literary aims of both Eusebius and the author(s) of the letter,[314] which has included an exploration of the idea that the original missive was edited at some point during its transmission. It should be noted, however, that the debate on this subject has generally been concerned with the descriptions of the martyrs in the letter, and the possible theological or ideological implications of that portrayal. By contrast, the legal proceedings referred to in the letter do not appear to have been the primary concern of any potential editor, and their description is considered to be largely historically accurate even by Winrich A. Löhr, whose analysis of the letter is still seen as foundational by many authors who take a more critical view of the text presented by Eusebius.[315] The overwhelming majority of scholarship thus continues to hold that the core of legal proceedings described in the missive is largely authentic.

The origins of the events in Lyon have been the subject of an extensive debate, and a significant number of researchers have approached these events with the assumption that they are somehow different from any anti-Christian actions that

312 Thompson (1912), 361. Thompson also argues that Marcus Aurelius would not have tolerated what he calls 'flagrant violations of Roman law'. See Thompson (1912), 379–80 and Thompson (1913), 252–4. Although a similar argument has recently been made by Corke-Webster (2013), 200–1, who holds that these violations may have been the result of Eusebius' editing, the idea that the governor in Lyon acted extrajudicially is by no means beyond dispute, as we shall see over the course of this analysis.

313 Keresztes (1979), 301–2. For a brief overview of the various authors involved in apologetic writing in this period, see Norris (2004), 40–4.

314 See, for instance, Corke-Webster (2013) and Dehandschutter (2005); as well as Moss (2012[a]), 100–16 and Moss (2010[b]), 90–4. The latter work provides interesting insights into the various sets of metaphors employed in the letter. For a brief examination of the ideas of martyrdom present in the text, see den Boeft and Bremmer (1991), 115–16. The similarities between the letter and Eusebius' *Martyrs of Palestine* noted by Corke-Webster (2013) occur only in the longer version of the latter text, which is now only extant in Syriac, and which Corke-Webster believes predates the *Historia Ecclesiastica*. According to Corke-Webster, Eusebius then removed the parallels when he included a shorter version of *Martyrs of Palestine* in the *Historia Ecclesiastica* in order to 'hide them from the reader'. If this is indeed true, and if Eusebius indeed originally intended the previously written *Martyrs of Palestine* to act as the eighth book of his *Historia*, it seems highly unlikely that that he would deliberately create parallels in book five, only to remove them from their primary location in *Martyrs* after it had been attached to book eight. It may therefore be possible that *Martyrs of Palestine* was based on the letter from Lyon and Vienne, which Eusebius may have had in his possession at this earlier date, but the reverse seems less probable. On this basis, we therefore need not assume that Eusebius edited the letter from Lyon and Vienne.

315 Löhr (1989), 138 and 143–4. Löhr rejects the descriptions in the letter on a number of smaller points, which will be discussed in more detail over the course of this analysis. Seeliger and Wischmeyer (2015), 80 n. 4 express some scepticism with regard to Löhr's acceptance of the legal course of events, but nevertheless continue to use the letter as a valid source for the social and religious context of Lyon's Christian community, as well as the imperial cult.

preceded them, offering various explanations as to why such a departure would have occurred.[316] Attention has primarily been directed at centralized legislation that could have contributed to a spike in popular violence against Christians, either in Gaul specifically or throughout the empire. The most popular suggestions include a law that allowed for the use of convicts as cheap gladiators,[317] an edict that prescribed universal sacrifice,[318] or a measure that was originally aimed at astrologers and other diviners but was nonetheless used to target Christians (Appendix 1.38).[319] In the latter two cases, however, we might ask ourselves to what extent Gaul would have been affected by these measures in practice. As discussed in Chapter 2, the known measures dealing with divination generally had a very limited scope, and the same appears to have been true of the specific measure attributed to Marcus Aurelius.[320] It should furthermore be noted that the text of this imperial rescript only refers to banishment, and thus does not explain the executions that took place in Lyon. Universal sacrifice likewise appears to be without substantial precedent until the time of Decius, and there is little conclusive evidence to suggest that such a measure was ever widely enforced by law before that time.[321] Others have concluded that the events in Lyon were simply the result of officials 'yielding to popular feeling',[322] and possibly even acting unlawfully in order to do so.[323]

A careful analysis of the letter, however, yields a rather more complex picture, with a number of highly illuminating details. At the very beginning of the document as cited by Eusebius, we find what may well be seen as a description of the social position of Christians in the city on the eve of the violent outbreaks. The author mentions that Christians were excluded from all public places, including 'houses, baths and the marketplace', before being banned from 'being seen in any place whatsoever'.[324] While it is easy to assume that this is an official policy,

[316] Orgels in Grégoire (1955–7), 303–4; Keresztes, (1967[c]), 86; Keresztes, (1979), 301; Moss (2012[a]), 106–7; Williams (2012), 198. Orgels even makes the suggestion that the events in Lyon were part of the first empire-wide persecution.

[317] Croteau (1992), 114–15; Grégoire (1955–7), 300–1; Frend (1965), 5; Keresztes (1979), 303; Moeller (1972); Moss (2012[a]), 106–7; Oliver and Palmer (1955), 324–7. Seeliger and Wischmeyer (2015), 83 reserve judgement on this theory.

[318] Croteau (1992), 114–15; Keresztes (1979), 300; Williams (2012), 198.

[319] Benko (1984), 43. This option is rejected by MacMullen (1966), 130.

[320] Ulpian, *De Officio Proconsulis* 7 in *Leg. Mos. et Rom. Coll.* 15.2.5 and *Digesta* 48.19.30. It is particularly interesting that this measure is described as a rescript addressing a very specific situation, which speaks against the idea that had significant influence on the events in Lyon. While an earlier rescript ascribed to Antoninus Pius was indeed sent to the governor of Gallia Lugdunensis (Appendix 1.37), in this case the temporal distance is a complicating factor. For a more elaborate discussion of both rescripts, see section 2.9.

[321] Rives (1999), 144–7.

[322] Musurillo (1972), xx.

[323] Coleman-Norton (1966), 1180; Colin (1964), 20; Harries (2007), 40–1; Keresztes (1967[c]), 75 and 80. As mentioned in n. 312 of this chapter, Thompson and Corke-Webster see the perceived illegality of the governor's action as a reason to reject the authenticity of the letter. See Thompson (1912), 379–80 and (1913), 252–4, as well as Corke-Webster (2013), 200–1.

[324] Eusebius, *Historia Ecclesiastica* 5.1.5.

possibly one instituted by the local authorities to isolate the city's Christians as a precursor to more violent actions, this suggestion does not, in the end, hold up: it is simply unlikely that any official would have the authority to ban Christians from other people's houses.[325] In addition, this paragraph is not yet part of the legal proceedings proper, but rather a passage describing the events to come as a struggle of the saints with the great adversary of the Christians and his servants. While the author of the letter uses this passage to briefly introduce the hostilities faced by the Christians of the city, and to predict a final struggle between the forces of good and evil, he does not yet make mention of physical violence. Therefore, this phrase is more likely to suggest a widespread sense of unease and hostility towards Lyon's Christians, thus providing the setting for what was to follow.

Although the direct cause for the city's eventual turn to violence is not made fully explicit in the text, it is nevertheless clear from the very beginning that the initiative was taken by Lyon's general population, with at the very least symbolic support of the town's city council:

> *καὶ πρῶτον μὲν τὰ ἀπὸ τοῦ ὄχλου πανδημεὶ σωρηδὸν ἐπιφερόμενα γενναίως ὑπέμενον, ἐπιβοήσεις καὶ πληγὰς καὶ συρμοὺς καὶ διαρπαγὰς καὶ λίθων βολὰς καὶ συγκλείσεις καὶ πάνθ' ὅσα ἠγριωμένῳ πλήθει ὡς πρὸς ἐχθροὺς καὶ πολεμίους φιλεῖ γίνεσθαι* [...].[326]
>
> First, they [sc. the Christians] nobly bore whatever the mob heaped on them, shouts and blows and dragging and robberies and stonings and imprisonment, and all those things an angry mob is wont to do to foes and enemies.

In this passage, and throughout the text of the letter, the author repeatedly refers to the perpetrators of the violence as 'the mob' (using the terms *ὄχλος* and *πλῆθος* alternately), and remarks that the actions of this mob were not at all uncommon for a population that was confronted with a perceived enemy. The behaviour of the crowd towards the Christians of Lyon, then, is initially characterized as mass violence towards people seen as hostile outsiders. These hostile feelings of Lyon's inhabitants towards the Christians in their midst were not, in themselves, particularly remarkable, especially given the close connection to Rome and the imperial family that Lyon had had since the early days of the principate. In

[325] Keresztes (1967[c]), 81 rejects the notion of an official exclusion order without giving further reasons. While a number of authors, including Moss (2012[a]) 106; Musurillo (1972), 63; Rebillard (2017), 153; and Williams (2012), 195 translate the term *οἰκία* as 'our houses' (i.e. the houses of the Christians themselves), the possessive pronoun is not present in the original Greek and there is little basis for this qualification. Furthermore, the various locations mentioned appear to be ranked in order of the increasing inconvenience Christians experienced due to their exclusion. It is thus more likely that the author of the letter is instead referring to the social isolation of Christians in Lyon.

[326] Eusebius, *Historia Ecclesiastica* 5.1.7.

12 BCE, the city became home to the sanctuary of the so-called *Tres Galliae*, the centre of the cult of the goddess Roma and Emperor Augustus in the three Gallic provinces Aquitania, Belgica, and Lugdunensis.[327] Every year, on the first of August, a festival to honour this cult was celebrated, and great importance was attached to the occasion.[328] Its priesthood was considered to be an office of significant status for members of the regional elite,[329] who would have been drawn to Lyon by its administrative and religious importance.[330] The cult was therefore not only religiously but also socially, economically, and politically significant for the city, as is demonstrated by Hadrian's investments in its infrastructure: this was the place where Gallo-Roman identity was forged, confirmed, and publicly demonstrated. Since the Christian inhabitants of Lyon could not in good conscience participate in this prominent aspect of provincial and city life, it is no wonder that they stood out, and their non-Christian neighbours may well have felt that they had good reason to regard them as potential enemies whose loyalty was in question.[331]

The first steps towards initiating these proceedings against Lyon's Christians, then, were almost certainly made by the local population, and there is no indication in the letter that any external factors, whether laws or administrators, contributed to inflaming anti-Christian sentiments. If such a thing had happened, it is likely that the letter would mention it. Any imperial command that may have formed the basis for anti-Christian violence would have to have been publicly proclaimed, as was part of the standard legislative procedure,[332] and any connection between an imperial missive and the events that followed would therefore almost certainly have drawn the attention of the local Christians.[333] Another element that suggests that the origins of the events in Lyon lay with the local population rather than the Roman authorities is the fact that the letter explicitly reports that the governor was not in Lyon when hostilities broke out.[334] In itself, this was not unusual: governors often travelled throughout their province, so it is very well possible that this unnamed official's itinerary had taken him elsewhere

[327] Fishwick (1978), 33–4. Originally, the cult was centred around an altar, but in the time of Hadrian a temple dedicated to the deified Roman emperors was erected, and the focus of the cult changed from the person of Augustus to a number of the new emperor's predecessors. For this, see Fishwick (1972). Under Septimius Severus, the focus of the cult would shift once again, this time to worship of the living emperor. In this period, the altar was once again the primary focus of the cult. See Fishwick (1973).

[328] Glay (1978), 20–9. [329] Drinkwater (1979), 94–5. [330] Rougé (1978), 48.

[331] Moss (2012[a]), 106 agrees with this assessment in general terms.

[332] For the mechanisms that played a part in the proclamation of a law, see Ando (2000), 96–117.

[333] In the case of Diocletian's 'Great Persecution', Eusebius does explicitly mention the connection between the proclamation of new legal measures and the outbreak of violence. See Eusebius, *Historia Ecclesiastica* 8.2.4. This difference in procedure seems to speak against the suggestion in Corke-Webster (2013) that Eusebius edited the letter in order to create parallels between the martyrs of his own time and those of the past.

[334] Eusebius, *Historia Ecclesiastica* 5.1.8.

at the time.[335] Despite the absence of the emperor's primary representative in the city, however, matters progressed according to what may well be described as a judicial procedure: those who were accused of being Christians were led to the marketplace by the tribune, who was the governor's second in command, and the local magistrates (*ὑπό τε τοῦ χιλιάρχου καὶ τῶν προστηκότων τῆς πόλεως ἐξουσιῶν*). Once they had arrived at their destination, the Christians were publicly questioned. After a confession had been extracted, the arrested Christians were incarcerated to await the return of the governor and a second trial under his jurisdiction. We are thus certainly dealing with an element of mob justice, but that does not mean that this course of events was, in itself, unlawful. Local courts continued to exist in many cities throughout the empire,[336] and while criminal cases generally fell under the jurisdiction of the governor, which means that, in all likelihood, no binding verdict could be pronounced without Roman involvement,[337] nothing of the sort appears to have actually been attempted. Instead, the presence of the local magistrates appears to have lent some authority to this part of the proceedings: this public, preliminary trial, combined with the confessions of the accused, would have been a clear signal to the governor that this was not an incident he could simply ignore. Lyon demanded his involvement, and the city was very clear about the direction his actions should take.[338]

This pressure in no way relented when the governor returned to the city. We do not know how long the accused Christians were imprisoned, only that they were at some point brought before the governor and once again questioned in public.[339] This public setting is central to what follows: although the author of the letters insists that the governor 'used all his cruelty against us', it becomes obvious soon after that he certainly did not act alone. During the public trial, a certain Vettius Epagathus asked to speak in defence of the Christians but was quickly shouted down by those who had gathered around the governor's tribunal before the governor himself had even had a chance to speak. The fact that, after such a reception, the governor only asked if Epagathus was himself a Christian may well show that he was influenced by the profound hostility of the general population

335 Fuhrmann (2012), 173. While the fact that Christians would later be brought into the arena may suggest a connection between these events and the festival of the *Tres Galliae*, the governor's absence suggests this first part of the proceedings, at least, did not take place during the main provincial festivities.

336 For the continued relevance of local institutions in Roman provincial administration, see Chapter 1.

337 The criminal jurisdiction of the governor is well established for the Severan period. See Galsterer (2000), 351. Galsterer also cites the earlier *Lex Irnitana*, which dates from the Flavian period and excludes the local *duoviri* from criminal jurisdiction.

338 For the role the local elites of this region could play in connecting the various levels of Roman administration, see Dondin-Payre (2004). In the case of the events in Lyon, the role of the city council appears to have been limited: after lending its symbolic support to legal actions against the Christians, it appears to have made no practical contribution.

339 Eusebius, *Historia Ecclesiastica* 5.1.9–10.

and the symbolic support of the city council, and believed it to be most beneficial to make example of those who had been accused—especially in the case of someone like Epagathus, who was apparently well known and seems to have incurred the special hostility of the population.[340]

The description of these two trials, one by the city council of Lyon and one by its governor, also gives some hints about the nature of the charges that were brought forward against the Christians. As mentioned, no indication is given that any 'new decree' was responsible for the outburst of hostility, as was apparently the case during the unrests in Asia described by Melito.[341] Even if, as some have suggested, a law allowing convicts to be used as cheap gladiators was to blame, this still does not explain why Christians would be convicted in the first place, as has rightly been remarked by Timothy Barnes.[342] The letter cited by Eusebius does, however, give us some indication of what the legal foundations for the trials of 177 CE were. In the first trial, it is made clear that the arrested Christians confessed after being questioned. This indicates that the formal charge was, once again, that of 'being Christian'. It is unlikely that these Christians would be described as confessing to a crime in any other sense of the word, especially because Epagathus later told the governor that there was 'nothing godless or impious' about them.[343] The governor, in turn, responded by asking Epagathus if he is a Christian himself, and his confession on this point resulted in his immediate arrest. This suggests that an admission of Christianity was, in itself, sufficient to be 'taken into the ranks of the martyrs', as the author of the letter calls it.[344]

After the first wave of arrests and trials, matters escalated rapidly. The governor publicly issued a command that all Christians were to be brought to trial (δημοσίᾳ ἐκέλευσεν ὁ ἡγεμὼν ἀναζητεῖσθαι πάντας ἡμᾶς).[345] While this has been seen as a notable departure from the course of action Trajan had prescribed for Pliny, the difference is not entirely unexpected.[346] Even disregarding the fact that Trajan's directive was aimed specifically at the situation in Bithynia-Pontus, and may furthermore well have fallen into disuse in the meantime, Pliny was dealing at least in

[340] For the idea that Epagathus was especially hated because of his significant status, which allowed his defence of the Christians to be perceived as betrayal of his city and his community, see den Boeft and Bremmer (1995), 154–5.

[341] As mentioned, Melito's account of the events in Asia is cited in Eusebius, *Historia Ecclesiastica* 4.26.5. For a more elaborate discussion, see section 4.9.1. The anti-Christian actions in Asia are linked to the events in Lyon by a number of authors, including Keresztes (1968), 335–6, on the basis that the 'new edicts' mentioned by Melito may have been empire-wide proclamations. However, as mentioned, Melito discusses Asia specifically, and he initially focuses on Christians being robbed and extorted by false accusers. The possibility of execution is only invoked later, and in the context of Christian submission to the emperor, rather than the difficulties Melito describes. It is thus far from certain that the events in Lyon and those in Asia were connected.

[342] Barnes (1968[a]), 44.

[343] Eusebius, *Historia Ecclesiastica* 5.1.9.

[344] Eusebius, *Historia Ecclesiastica* 5.1.10.

[345] Eusebius, *Historia Ecclesiastica* 5.1.14.

[346] Pliny the Younger, *Epistulae* 10.97.2. A similar observation is made by Bastiaensen (1987), 60; Croteau (1992), 56–7; Keresztes (1967[c]), 81; and Williams (2012), 197.

part with anonymous accusations. The governor in Lyon, by contrast, was directly faced with a screaming mob and the potential for escalating violence and may therefore have felt it prudent to conduct a more extensive investigation. With or without the governor's command, the masses continued their quest to remove the Christians from their city, and the author of the letter claims that new arrests were made every day.[347] It is notable, however, that these events seem to have taken place at least partially before the governor's order was issued, and that the magistrate's command is only explicitly connected to the arrest of a number of non-Christian servants. Although the overall effect of this order is indeed likely to have been the large-scale arrest of Christians, the primary goal of this particular action therefore appears to have been to acquire more information about their beliefs and practices.[348] The arrested slaves in turn contributed significantly to a final stage of escalation by accusing their Christian masters of 'Thyestean feasts and Oedipodean intercourse'; that is, cannibalism and incest.[349] The accusations were obviously extreme, but they appear to have been taken seriously nonetheless. Even those who had formerly supported or at the very least pitied the Christians now 'turned on [them] like beasts', indicating that these accusations were at least part of the reason for the treatment these people received, even if they only appeared during a later stage of the proceedings.[350] Above all, this passage presents an image of continuous escalation, in which the governor's soldiers and the people of the city cooperated in arresting as many Christians as possible.[351]

The letter indicates that the Christians were taken to prison after their arrest, where they were tortured to obtain further information about their identities and the nature of their crimes. According to the author, many remained steadfast in their beliefs, refusing to either recant or admit to the accusations of cannibalism and incest.[352] The letter claims that a great number of the accused were therefore either strangled or died in prison as a result of torture.[353] A select number of

[347] Eusebius, *Historia Ecclesiastica* 5.1.13–15.

[348] This may be seen as a parallel to the torture of the two *ancillae* referred to by Pliny, see Pliny the Younger, *Epistulae* 10.96.8. For the suggestion that these accusations may have been made not by pagan slaves but by arrested Christians, see Corke-Webster (2023), 43 n. 149, who references the passage to suggest that Christians were often accused by those close to them.

[349] Eusebius, *Historia Ecclesiastica* 5.1.14. For the suggestion that those who had previously disavowed their Christianity were now re-arrested, see Löhr (1989), 143. Similar accusations are among the scandalous rumours about Christians referenced in Athenagoras, *Legatio pro Christianis* 31–6 and Minucius Felix, *Octavius* 9.1–10.2. An attempt to refute them is made in paragraphs 28–31 of the latter work. For a more elaborate discussion, see Schubert (2014), *ad loc.*

[350] Eusebius, *Historia Ecclesiastica* 5.1.15.

[351] For the use of Roman soldiers as a police force, see Fuhrmann (2016), 303–5.

[352] Eusebius, *Historia Ecclesiastica* 5.1.19, 20, 26, and 30.

[353] Eusebius, *Historia Ecclesiastica* 5.1.27–8. Harries (2007), 40 suggests that this course of action would have been illegal based on *Digesta* 48.19.8.1, where it is stated that executions can only take place by the sword, and that governors were not free to select any other form (*quo alio modo*) of punishment. Since various alternative methods of punishment for specific groups of offenders are mentioned immediately after, however, it seems likely that this was not a general regulation, but instead applied to a specific group—possibly members of the higher classes. It cannot therefore be

Christians, notably those who are described by the author of the letter as being subject of 'all the fury of the mob, the governor and the soldiers' during an earlier stage of the proceedings,[354] are said to have been thrown to the wild animals during a public spectacle instead.[355] This course of action, if it indeed occurred, would likely have been well within the governor's rights as a holder of the *ius gladii*, the right to exert capital punishment over those who did not have Roman citizenship.[356] However, the governor in Lyon does appear to have proceeded with caution:

> *ὁ δὲ Ἄτταλος καὶ αὐτὸς μεγάλως ἐξαιτηθεὶς ὑπὸ τοῦ ὄχλου, καὶ γὰρ ἦν ὀνομαστός [...] καὶ περιαχθεὶς κύκλῳ τοῦ ἀμφιθεάτρου, πίνακος αὐτὸν προάγοντος ἐν ᾧ ἐγέγραπτο Ῥωμαϊστί· οὗτός ἐστιν Ἄτταλος ὁ Χριστιανός, καὶ τοῦ δήμου σφόδρα σφριγῶντος ἐπ' αὐτῷ, μαθὼν ὁ ἡγεμὼν ὅτι Ῥωμαῖός ἐστιν, ἐκέλευσεν αὐτὸν ἀναληφθῆναι μετὰ καὶ τῶν λοιπῶν τῶν ἐν τῇ εἱρκτῇ ὄντων, περὶ ὧν ἐπέστειλεν τῷ Καίσαρι καὶ περιέμενεν τὴν ἀπόφασιν τὴν ἀπ' ἐκείνου.*[357]
>
> Attalus himself was loudly called for by the mob, for he was well known. [...] He was led around the amphitheatre, and a sign was carried in front of him, on which was written in Latin: 'This is Attalus the Christian', and the people were very bitter towards him, but when the governor learned that he was a Roman citizen, he ordered him to be taken back to the others who were in prison, about whom he had written to the emperor and was awaiting a reply.

While some see the interruption of Attalus' execution as a literary fabrication, and not without reason,[358] it nonetheless remains telling that the governor had refrained from executing specific groups of prisoners in order to consult the emperor about their proper treatment. Those who remained in captivity very likely included Roman citizens like Attalus, who are once again referenced as a separate class later in the letter.[359] In itself, it is little wonder that this group

conclusively proven that the governor of Lyon acted outside the bounds of his jurisdiction. See Bauman (1996), 139 for the argument that prescribed punishments remained in flux until well into the Severan period.

[354] Eusebius, *Historia Ecclesiastica* 5.1.17 and 43.

[355] Eusebius, *Historia Ecclesiastica* 5.1.37. Lyon's amphitheatre was built under Tiberius but was significantly enlarged during the reign of Hadrian. It appears to have been part of the sanctuary of the *Tres Galliae*. See Audin (1979).

[356] Fuhrmann (2012), 171.

[357] Eusebius, *Historia Ecclesiastica* 5.1.43–4.

[358] Löhr (1989), 143 believes this passage to have been subjected to later editing, finding it unlikely that only some Christians were publicly executed while all others remained in prison to await the emperor's missive. This argument overlooks not only the earlier execution of other Christians in captivity, referred to in Eusebius, *Historia Ecclesiastica* 5.1.27, to which Löhr makes no objection, but also Pliny the Younger's reference to the execution of a number of steadfast Christians in his letter to Trajan, see Pliny the Younger, *Epistulae* 10.96.3. Both points contradict Löhr's suggestion that only one round of executions actually took place, although it does indeed remain strange that Attalus' Roman citizenship was not discovered at an earlier stage.

[359] Eusebius, *Historia Ecclesiatica* 5.1.47.

warranted special consideration,[360] but this course of action nonetheless shows that there were in fact limits to the amount of local pressure the governor was willing to comply with. Despite what the inhabitants of Lyon may have wanted, he apparently thought it necessary to consult the emperor in certain cases in which his jurisdiction was less straightforward, in order to ensure that his actions corresponded with his superior's wishes.

The emperor's answer, as it appears in the letter at least, was short: if the imprisoned Christians recanted, they would be free to go. If not, he authorized the governor to execute them (*ἐπιστείλαντος γὰρ τοῦ Καίσαρος τοὺς μὲν ἀποτυμπανισθῆναι, εἰ δέ τινες ἀρνοῖντο, τούτους ἀπολυθῆναι*).[361] No method of execution is specified in the available description of the emperor's letter, but the governor appears to have made is own decisions on the matter. As was traditional, the governor made a distinction between various groups of Christians by beheading those who were Roman citizens and sending those who were not to the arena—possibly as a part of the festivals connected to the cult of the *Tres Galliae*.[362] According to the letter as it has been transmitted to us, an exception was made for the aforementioned Attalus, who was once again sent to the wild animals 'to please the mob'.[363] While it has been argued that it was illegal to condemn Roman citizens to the arena, and that the governor therefore broke the law,[364] multiple references to Roman citizens being involved in a *damnatio ad bestias* may in fact be found from the early principate onwards, although this was generally considered to be a punishment reserved for those of low social status.[365] Whether Attalus himself was indeed sent to the arena or not, the governor's choice for this particular, highly public, method of execution may well be seen as an attempt to placate the inhabitants of Lyon: in this way, at least some of the hated Christians were forced to participate in the local public festivals, albeit in a particularly gruesome way.

The other less straightforward case about which the governor felt the need to defer judgement was that of the Christians who chose to recant. We know that at least some of them were originally re-arrested and imprisoned alongside Christians who refused to abandon their faith,[366] but after the emperor's response

[360] For a parallel, see Pliny the Younger, *Epistulae* 10.96.4.

[361] Eusebius, *Historia Ecclesiastica* 5.1.47.

[362] See Eusebius, *Historia Ecclesiastica* 5.1.47. It should be noted that the governor once again questioned these Christians, which shows a sense of due diligence on his part.

[363] Eusebius, *Historia Ecclesiastica* 5.1.50.

[364] Colin (1964), 20; Croteau (1992), 57.

[365] Bauman (1996), 124–9. The fact that Attalus is described as *ὀνομαστός* in Eusebius, *Historia Ecclesiastica* 5.1.43 does not necessarily give us a clear indication of his social status. In this, the term seems to differ subtly from the adjective *ἐπίσημος*, which was used to describe Vettius Epagathus—see n. 340 of this chapter.

[366] Eusebius, *Historia Ecclesiastica* 5.1.33. Croteau (1992), 57 suggests that these actions of the governor of Lyon towards Christians who recanted were unprecedented in the second century CE. This does not mean, however, that his actions were inexplicable or illegal. It seems that at least some Christians who recanted may have been rearrested and held for a longer period of time, likely due to

had reached Lyon, their situation appears to have changed.[367] The authorities once again questioned the Christians who had previously recanted, now in private, and the author of the letter emphasizes that this occurred 'with the intention of letting them go'. This suggests that the new round of interrogations was initially seen as redundant, if procedurally necessary, now that it was clear that those who abandoned their faith were to be released. While the author focuses on the renewed declaration of faith by these Christians, and the surprised reaction of the Roman authorities, it is equally important to note that even at this stage the general population of Lyon still appears to have been actively involved in the proceedings. It is later mentioned that they were furious that these former apostates retracted their previous statements,[368] and that they even attempted to make Christians swear by statues of the gods in an effort to make them renounce their faith once and for all—a practice that is notably absent in the narrative up to this point.[369] This combination of executions and attempts to encourage recantation—whether by sacrifice or through other means—shows strong parallels with the events described by Pliny the Younger several decades earlier, and thus suggests that both governors were struggling with very similar legal questions, the most important of which may well have been whether Christians who recanted should be released.[370] Although the emperor's response appears to have been the same in both cases, such similarities strongly suggest that no firmly established procedure for the treatment of Christians existed at this point in time, and that governors continued to feel a need for imperial guidance. In addition, both Pliny and Lyon's governor seem to have followed the imperial command as closely as possible, which once again speaks against the idea that the latter was acting illegally. Rome's influence only reached so far, however; according to the text of the letter as we know it, nothing could stop the locals from mutilating the bodies of the executed Christians. Some were fed to the dogs, but others were exposed to the elements for a number of days before being burned. The ashes were subsequently thrown into the river Rhône, according to the author of the letter, 'so that not a single trace of them remained on earth'.[371]

allegations of murder or the other crimes of which Christians had been accused—see Löhr (1989), 143. Others, however, may have retained their liberty, since they are reported to have returned to the governor's tribunal (possibly of their own volition) in order to confess their beliefs soon after the emperor's reply ordering the release of all Christians who had recanted arrived, as mentioned in Eusebius, *Historia Ecclesiastica* 5.1.45–6. The distinction between these two groups may have been the moment of their arrest, but details are sadly lacking. In any case, the emperor's reply suggests that the governor had asked a question regarding the treatment of lapsed Christians, and their continued captivity may thus have been the result of attempted diligence on the part of the authorities rather than unusual cruelty.

[367] Eusebius, *Historia Ecclesiastica* 5.1.48. [368] Eusebius, *Historia Ecclesiastica* 5.1.50.

[369] Eusebius, *Historia Ecclesiastica* 5.1.53–4.

[370] See Pliny the Younger, *Epistulae* 10.96.2 and 5–6. See also *Epistulae* 10.97.2 for Trajan's confirmation that lapsed Christians should, indeed, be released.

[371] Eusebius, *Historia Ecclesiastica* 5.1.57–63.

When analysing the events in Lyon, it becomes clear that the legal treatment of Christians in the city arose from negotiation between the various levels of government, which included not only the emperor and the Roman governor but also a strongly localized component. We have seen that the population of the region, including, significantly, Lyon's city council, was instrumental throughout. Inhabitants of the city arrested Christians and performed a preliminary trial even before the Roman governor arrived in the city, and their influence continued to be felt during the second trial under his supervision. In addition, it seems very likely that the local circumstances of these events found expression in the magistrate's selection of the methods of execution that would be used, even if we discount the idea that Christians who were particularly hated by the locals received more public, humiliating punishments than others. The condemnation of some Christians to a death in the arena may well be seen as an attempt by the governor to placate the local population and their magistrates by paying homage to Lyon's public festivals. It is likely, then, that the governor was under significant pressure, and that he thought it necessary to adhere to the wishes of the locals in order to prevent further escalation. That this was certainly a realistic risk is demonstrated by the frequent references to large, enraged mobs in the letter. Both the governor and the population of Lyon, however, had to contend with certain limits. We have seen that it was considered necessary to ask the emperor about the treatment of both Roman citizens and Christians who had renounced their faith. In the case of the latter, the emperor's remarks led to a significant change in the position of these individuals: whereas at first they were held captive despite their recantation, likely in anticipation of the emperor's response, the command to release them appears to have met with no opposition. At the same time, it must be remarked that the emperor's involvement was both brief and limited: the majority of the disturbances took place without any involvement on his part, and when that involvement finally came, it was in response to a question his governor had asked him. The emperor's orders appear to have been similar to Trajan's famous rescript, but the need for repetition is once again telling: the governor in Lyon clearly did not feel free to act on precedent, either because he did not know it, as seems likely, or because he felt that the particular situation he was faced with required special attention and did not want to rely on his personal discretion alone.

4.10 Commodus and the Severans: Diverse Approaches

Beginning with the reign of Marcus Aurelius' successor Commodus, a notably diverse image of the legal treatment of Christians in the provinces begins to emerge.[372] Where we were previously given only small hints that not all

[372] Commodus' personal attitude regarding Christianity is less relevant in this context, and little about it is known in any case. In Eusebius, *Historia Ecclesiastica* 5.21.1, the author reports that

confrontations between Christians and the Roman authorities ended in bloodshed, as for instance in Hadrian's rescript to Minucius Fundanus (Appendix 3.10), such indications now become more frequent, as well as more explicit. We find references to Christians being banished, rather than executed, in the works of Hippolytus of Rome, which suggests that a proven accusation of Christianity did not necessarily result in death, and thus indicates a wider possible array of attitudes and actions towards Christianity than is often assumed.[373]

4.10.1 The trial of the Scillitan Martyrs

Some hints of this diversity are also present in the first of two martyr narratives said to describe events from the reign of Commodus, a text known as the *Acts of the Scillitan Martyrs* that discusses the trial of a number of North African Christians (Appendix 3.18).[374] While the text has traditionally been seen as a reliable source, and according to some may even be a partial transcript of official records,[375] more recent analyses have concluded that the account has likely been substantially edited. This is especially evident in the verbal exchanges between the governor and the Christian leader Speratus, which contain a significant number of references to Christian scripture, as well as a number of literary devices.[376] The account must therefore be treated with caution, especially when it comes to the status of the Pauline texts mentioned by Speratus. However, a number of tentative remarks may nonetheless be made, especially since the legal core of the account likely had to be at least plausible for the text to be acceptable to its audience.

churches 'throughout the entire world' experienced a period of peace. By contrast, Cassius Dio, *Historiae Romanae* ep.73.4.7 reports that Commodus' mistress Marcia on occasion intervened on behalf of Christians, which suggests that such help was still necessary. Both accounts, however, are exceedingly brief and add little to our discussion of the individual cases dated to this period.

373 Hippolytus of Rome, *Refutatio Omnium Haeresium* 12.10–11. The account mentions that certain Christians were released from their imprisonment in Sardinia at the request of Commodus' mistress Marcia, with the emperor's approval. The fact that these Christian prisoners are referred to as *μάρτυρες* seems to indicate that they were banished on account of their religious beliefs rather than any other crimes, although no additional context is given. Hippolytus' work is also known under the titles *Elenchus* and *Philosophumena*, and no generally accepted numbering system of its paragraphs appears to exist. The edition referred to here is that of Marcovich (1986) and the relevant passage may be found on p. 352. For a similar argument, see Lane Fox (1986), 434.

374 The text itself provides a date of 17 July 180 CE, which is accepted by Bastiaensen (1987), 98; Moss (2012[a]), 125; and Musurillo (1972), xxii. For a more elaborate discussion, see Ruggiero (1991), 63–4. For the martyrs' place of origin, see Rebillard (2017), 357 n. 33. The text is presented alongside a translation by Bastiaensen (1987), 97–105; Musurillo (1972), 86–9; and Rebillard (2017), 356–9. Its most elaborate analysis may be found in Ruggiero (1991).

375 Barnes (1968[b]), 519–20; Keresztes (1979), 305; Musurillo (1972), xxii. For the view that the text is based on an eyewitness account, see Freudenberger (1973), 197.

376 See especially Moss (2012[a]), 125–9 and Rebillard (2017), 351–3, the latter of whom remarks that Tertullian does not appear to have known the text, which suggests a later date. For a dating to the fourth century, after Diocletian's 'Great Persecution', see Rebillard (2020), 10, 24, and 85.

Firstly, it is notable that the Roman official mentioned by the text has indeed been connected to legal proceedings involving Christians by other sources. The presiding magistrate in this trial was the proconsul Publius Vigellius Saturninus, whom Tertullian accused of being 'the first to wield the sword against us in these parts', thereby suggesting that legal actions against Christians were a relatively recent phenomenon in the region.[377] Another interesting detail is the fact that the trial is said to have taken place in the *secretarium*, which—while formally public—was part of the governor's residence and could therefore more easily be controlled.[378] Although this setting has been seen as an anachronism, and it may therefore be unwise to imbue this detail with too much meaning,[379] this more private backdrop to the proceedings could potentially indicate that the trial of the Scillitan Christians was the result of some disturbance in the region, which the governor attempted to contain by avoiding a public trial. This is far from certain, however, since the text as we know it omits any mention of the events that preceded the trial: we do not know how these Christians ended up in court, or even what they were initially charged with. The accused's insistence that they are Christians suggests that the charge that had been brought forward was related to 'being Christian',[380] but this proclamation was notably not made in direct response to a question asked by the governor, who initially seems to have been rather more focused on perceived loyalty to the emperor and the Roman state.[381] Furthermore, while the verdict is indeed focused on the accused's Christian beliefs, this is combined with their obstinate refusal to return *ad Romanorum morem*. While this is unlikely to have been the primary reason for the execution that followed, as some have argued,[382] the governor's words throughout the account do seem to suggest that he was just as much concerned with the Christians' potential disloyalty towards Roman institutions, and the emperor in particular, as with their religious practices. This may, at least in part, have been due to a final remarkable aspect of the text, namely the fact that the governor offers the Christians a period of thirty days to reconsider their stance.[383] This could be an attempt at leniency, in line with the governor's earlier offer of an

[377] *Qui primus hic gladium in nos egit*, Tertullian, *Ad Scapulam* 3.4. The number of martyrs in the *acta* is an oft-discussed difficulty that need not be resolved here: at the beginning of the text, the names of six martyrs are mentioned, whereas the herald's announcement in the text's penultimate paragraph makes mention of twelve. For possible solutions to this problem see Barnes (1968[b]), 519–20; Musurillo (1972), xxiii; and Rebillard (2017), 352–3, the latter of whom ultimately leaves the question open.

[378] Barnes (2010), 64; Moss (2012[a]), 125. For the argument that this private setting could potentially lead to an abuse of power due to a lack of transparency, see Aubert (2010), 286.

[379] For an exploration of this argument, see Barnes (1968[b]), 519; Rebillard (2020), 23–4; and Ruggiero (1991), 87. For the prevalence of the *secretarium* in the fourth century, see Slootjes (2006), 53–4.

[380] *Passio Martyrum Scilitanorum* 9–13.

[381] *Passio Martyrum Scilitanorum* 3–7.

[382] Frend (2006), 507, and of course primarily Sherwin-White (1952), 210 and (1974).

[383] *Passio Martyrum Scilitanorum* 11 and especially 13. For the argument that governors displayed a reluctance to execute Christians with some frequency, see Nixey (2017), 69 and 74–5.

imperial pardon if the Christians recanted.[384] While the stipulation that the recantation had to take place within a specific time frame was not without precedent, this is the first time we see it being applied to Christians.[385] If the text is to be believed, however, the offer was not accepted, and the Scillitan Christians were subsequently executed by beheading, despite their apparently low social status.[386]

4.10.2 Diverse proceedings in northern Africa

The second martyr narrative that has been dated to the time of Commodus is that of Apollonius, but the different versions of the story diverge so strongly, and contain such peculiar details, as to render it unusable for further analysis (Appendix 3.19).[387] The same, however, cannot be said for the various cases referenced by Tertullian in his *Ad Scapulam* (Appendix 3.20), which despite their brevity provide a number of valuable insights. *Ad Scapulam* itself is also quite concise,[388] and may best be seen as an attempt by its author to influence the attitude of the eponymous Scapula, who was proconsul of the province of Africa in 212/213 CE.[389] Throughout the text, Tertullian tries to dissuade Scapula from allowing any further trials against Christians by arguing that such procedures tended to end in disaster for the magistrates involved, that the proceedings in themselves made no

[384] *Passio Martyrum Scilitanorum* 1. For the offer of *indulgentia* in a wider legal context, see Freudenberger (1973), 199–202.

[385] See Freudenberger (1973), 211–12 for the legal context of the term *mora*, which appears to have been more commonly used in trials dealing with financial matters. The period of thirty days may come from the time frame in which an accuser could re-issue his accusation after the accused had been granted clemency in the context of an *abolitio publica*. Either procedure may well have been known to the governor, who in any case saw fit to expand existing precedent in this context.

[386] Barnes (1985), 148.

[387] The account presented by Eusebius, *Historia Ecclesiastica* 5.21 contains the unlikely assertion that the trial took place in the senate, and was supposedly—and implausibly—presided over by a magistrate of equestrian rank, as remarked by Barnes (2010), 46. Furthermore, the idea that both Apollonius and his accuser, one of his own slaves, were put to death seems highly improbable. The extant text of the *Acta Apollonii* survives in both a Greek and an Armenian version, which differ substantially from each other, as well as from the version presented by Eusebius, who appears to have known neither version. Even the location of events is unclear: Eusebius and the Armenian *Acta* set the trial in Rome, whereas the Greek version assumes Apollonius was called Apollos and was martyred in the province of Asia. The *Acta* are excluded by Bastiaensen (1987) and Moss (2012ᵃ), and regarded with strong suspicion by Barnes (1968ᵇ), 520–1 and (2010), 46, as well as Musurillo (1972), xxiii–xxv. Rebillard (2017), 31 includes a reference to the narrative, but does not cite any of the available texts of the *Acta* due to the fact that Eusebius cannot serve as an external source to confirm the existence of either version before the fourth century. Keresztes (1979), 306 is one of the few to accept the *Acta* as authentic, thereby ignoring the substantial problems listed by Barnes (1968ᵃ), 46–8.

[388] The text may be found in Bulhart and Borleffs (1957), 9–16, which remains one of the more recent editions of the work.

[389] For the date of Scapula's tenure, see Barnes (1985), 31. For the rhetorical purpose and structure of the work addressed to him, see Dunn (2002), who also provides an overview of the debate on this issue.

logical sense, and that they might result in punishment from the governor's superiors.[390]

Even at first glance, it is telling that Tertullian chose to address his argument to the governor: this is a clear indication that he considered his attitude to be a highly influential factor in determining the treatment of Christians in his province, and possibly even essentially responsible for it. This idea is further supported by the fact that Tertullian cites the behaviour of a number of Scapula's predecessors as precedent for a more lenient approach,[391] arguing that even those who were *constantiores et crudeliores* than Scapula himself regarded trials against Christians with some suspicion. The reader is then presented with a number of examples, all of which provide clear evidence of the fact that not all Roman governors accepted charges against Christians without question, and suggest that they instead responded to such accusations in a variety of ways.[392] The first of these officials is Cingius Severus, who according to Tertullian told those who were accused of being Christians how to respond to his questions in order to guarantee their release—apparently without punishment or consequences.[393] Vespronius Candidus similarly appears to have dismissed a Christian who had been brought before him,[394] while Gaius Iulius Asper is said to have used only

[390] For the idea that Scapula himself had been involved in trials against Christians, see Barnes (1985), 260–1. The divine punishments felt by those officials who mistreated the Christians are mentioned in Tertullian, *Ad Scapulam* 3, while the lack of concrete benefits derived from such trials are mentioned in chapter 2. The illogical nature of the proceedings is referenced in paragraph 4.1–2. For the idea that Tertullian brings up Christians' perceived willingness to die for their beliefs to support his argument, see Butterweck (1995), 49–50.

[391] The previous governors mentioned by Tertullian all appear to be historical figures, for whose existence and political career external sources are available, often in the form of inscriptions.

[392] For the argument that the governor's assize circuit was highly significant for shaping the distribution of trials against Christians, see Lane Fox (1986), 487.

[393] Tertullian, *Ad Scapulam* 4.3: [...] *Cincius* [*sic*] *Severus, qui Thysdri ipse dedit remedium, quomodo responderent Christiani, ut dimitti possent.* Cingius Severus was proconsul during the reign of Commodus, but the exact date of his tenure is unknown. See Thomasson (1960[b]), 89–90. For the methods employed in finding an approximate date, see Thomasson (1960[a]).

[394] Tertullian, *Ad Scapulam* 4.3: [...] *Vespronius Candidus, qui Christianum quasi tumultuosum civibus suis satisfacere dimisit.* The Latin of this phrase is particularly difficult to interpret. Given the context of Tertullian's argument, it is clear that Vespronius must have been fairly lenient towards the accused, although Barnes (1985), 144 strangely takes this phrase to mean that Vespronius sent the Christian in question back to his village to be punished there, which may well have resulted in his death. It is also possible that the governor punished this Christian under some lighter charge (possibly disturbance of the peace) before ultimately dismissing him, in order to show an apparently anti-Christian local population that at least some form of punishment was taking place, as suggested by Bryen (2014[a]), 263, and others. While this interpretation's focus on punishment does not comfortably fit the Latin, it does seem to be the best option, and—if correct—shows that the governor felt compelled to negotiate between his own wishes and those of the population. An alternative might be that the population was instead pro-Christian and would therefore have rejoiced in this lighter punishment. The exact date of Vespronius' tenure is unknown, but it likely took place during the reign of Commodus. See Thomasson (1960[b]), 90–1. The fact that Tertullian alternates between referring to groups of Christians and individuals may lend credibility to his account and suggests that more specific interpersonal tensions may have played a part. For the idea that social tensions may have been a more important motivation than religious concerns in bringing forward accusations against Christians, see Corke-Webster (2023).

moderate torture, and apparently did not even compel a recanting Christian to sacrifice. Tertullian furthermore claims that Asper had previously expressed his annoyance at having to deal with such a case at all, and apparently only agreed to do so because he was pressured into it.[395] The last governor to be referenced is Scapula's presumed direct predecessor Gaius Valerius Pudens, who apparently dismissed an accusation that he believed to have been made maliciously, tore up the relevant papers, and refused to hear the case without the presence of the accuser—all in accordance with the *mandata* he had received before his time in office.[396] Tertullian's accounts, then, suggest that governors could approach Christianity in a notably wide variety of ways, and that they could be (relatively) lenient when they believed this to be appropriate. This idea is furthermore confirmed by other sources, who at times reference Christians whose punishment consisted of imprisonment, rather than execution, or who even participated in wider society in relative comfort.[397]

4.10.3 The trial of Perpetua

Not all governors, however, shared such attitudes, and some dealt with trials against Christians with greater zeal. A primary example of this may be found in the famous piece of writing known as the *Passio Perpetuae et Felicitatis* (Appendix 3.21). This text has generally been taken to consist of two personal, first-hand accounts by Christians who were executed around 204 CE,[398] which were then

[395] Tertullian, *ad Scapulam* 4.3: [...] *Asper, qui modice vexatum hominem et statim deiectum nec sacrificium compulit facere, ante professus inter advocatos et assessores dolore se primum incidisse in hanc causam*. It should be noted that the text simply references this governor as Asper. For his tenure, see Thomasson (1960^{b}), 106–7. Barnes (1985), 162 makes much of the fact that this was apparently Asper's first interaction with Christians.

[396] Tertullian, *ad Scapulam* 4.4: *Pudens etiam missum ad se Christianum in elogio concussione eius intellecta dimisit scissoque eodem elogio sine accusatione negavit se auditurum hominem secundum mandatum*. While Bulhart and Borleffs (1957), 14 believe *mandatum* to refer to Hadrian's earlier proclamation (Appendix 3.10), this does not become clear from the text itself, and one might wonder if Tertullian could have assumed Scapula to have been aware of this particular precedent. It therefore seems more likely that the term is used in a technical sense, and that it refers not to a rescript originally directed at another province but rather to the general guidelines given to a governor by the emperor at the start of his time in office. It should be noted that Tertullian only refers to the governor in question as Pudens. For his tenure, see Thomasson (1960^{b}), 110–11.

[397] Barnes (1985), 148. See, for instance, Lucianus, *De Morte Peregrini* 14, and Eusebius, *Historia Ecclesiastica* 5.4.3 and 6.8.7, the latter of whom uses the term 'confessors' to denote these people. Imprisonment rarely appears to have been used as a punishment in the Roman world, but instead was often a prelude to trial and possible execution—see Harries (2007), 38. There are some indications, however, that magistrates could imprison those who disrupted public order, although this concept was likely not universally favourably regarded. See Bauman (1996), 30 and 170 n. 39. The fact that imprisonment is rejected under certain circumstances in *Digesta* 48.3.1 and 48.19.8.9, as well as *Codex Iustiniani* 9.47.6 merely serves to indicate that the practice did occur. For Christians holding public office in Egypt during this period, see the documentary evidence of P.Bas.2.43 in Huebner (2019), 19–21.

[398] For Perpetua's exceptional status as a female author, see Shaw (1993).

connected and expanded upon by the remarks of an unknown editor by 260 CE at the latest.[399] The text was therefore likely constructed unusually soon after the events it describes. At the same time, however, it is hardly a straightforward account of legal proceedings. The text's distinctly literary style, as well as its strong focus on visions and the perceived glories of martyrdom (which is present in both the two first-person accounts and the framing narrative) have relegated such details to the background, leaving us with very little concrete information to go on. What we do know, however, is that the trials were presided over by procurator Hilarianus,[400] who seems to have been rather more willing to have Christians executed than the various North African governors discussed by Tertullian.

While it is possible that the eventual outcome of the case was at least partially due to Hilarianus' strong personal religious convictions,[401] the text does not describe the circumstances under which the Christians were initially arrested in any great detail.[402] Concrete information about the trial's legal basis is likewise missing, although the direct interaction between the procurator and the accused suggests that 'being Christian' was indeed the primary complaint.[403] However, it does not appear to have been the only one, and we find a number of indications of more deeply rooted causes for hostility against the Christians. Once again, it seems that Christian beliefs were being perceived as a form of political disloyalty: Hilarianus does not simply order Christians to sacrifice, but instead demands that they do so *pro salute imperatorum*,[404] and the Christians were ultimately thrown to the beasts during a festival celebrated in honour of Emperor Geta's birthday, which suggests that they are being forced to participate in politically significant celebrations they would otherwise likely have avoided.[405] Fears about

[399] It has widely been acknowledged that the passages attributed to Perpetua and Saturus are indeed written in a style that is markedly different than the surrounding narrative, and these passages are generally seen as by-and-large authentic, as has been argued by Barnes (1968[b]), 521; Musurillo (1972), xxv–xxvii; and Rebillard (2017), 295–8 and (2020), 10. The latter author argues that Tertullian, *De Anima* 55 may have known the account attributed to Perpetua herself, but not necessarily the *Passio* as we know it today, adding that the references to the *Passio* in Pontius' *Vita Cypriani* suggest that the text was well known by the 260s CE. This suggests that both the full editorial text of the *Passio Perpetuae* and the older accounts embedded therein were written in relatively close proximity to the events they describe and can therefore be considered to provide an at least partially accurate account. It should be noted, however, that all aspects of the text display strong rhetorical and literary tendencies, as has rightly been remarked by Barnes (2010), 66. The martyrdoms described in the text have traditionally been dated to 203 CE, but more recently an argument for 204 CE has been made. See Barnes (1985), 267 and (2010), 304–7; as well as Rebillard (2017), 296.

[400] *Passio Perpetuae et Felicitatis* 6.3 makes mention of the fact that Hilarianus, while not formally governor, had assumed the powers of that office after the death of his superior, which Rives (1996), 4–5 considers to be plausible. Hilarianus may have formally become governor at a later date, since he is referred to as *praeses* in Tertullian, *Ad Scapulam* 3.1.

[401] For an exploration of Hilarianus' background and his personal convictions, see Rives (1996).

[402] We are simply told that people were arrested, see *Passio Perpetuae et Felicitatis* 2.1 and 3.1. The location of the arrest is discussed in den Boeft and Bremmer (2010), 49–51.

[403] *Passio Perpetuae et Felicitatis* 6.2–4.

[404] *Passio Perpetuae et Felicitatis* 6.3.

[405] *Passio Perpetuae et Felicitatis* 7.9. In this regard, it is notable that Perpetua is later said to have negotiated a better treatment for the Christians by claiming that they 'belonged to the emperor', see *Passio Perpetuae et Felicitatis* 16.3. Interestingly, the festival in question is said to have been a military

Christian hostility seem to have gone further, however; according to the narrator, the tribune who supervised the prisoners treated them especially harshly because he had been told that they might be able to escape with the help of some kind of magic (*incantationes aliquae magicae*).[406] One form of religious deviance is thus linked to another,[407] and it is therefore possible that the general population's fear for the Christians' potential power to cause harm contributed to their arrest.

In any case, it seems certain that the charges were seen as both valid and serious. Although the text omits any substantial details on the matter, Hilarianus appears to have convicted the Christians quickly, and his choice of punishment is particularly telling. The *damnatio ad bestias* was normally reserved for people of lower social standing, but Perpetua herself, at least, seems to have been distinctly upper class.[408] The fact that she was nevertheless condemned to the arena alongside the slaves Revocatus and Felicitas has been seen as an indication that Hilarianus took the matter particularly seriously, and potentially wanted to set an example.[409] However, the procurator was not the only one to influence the course of events. Certainly, the inhabitants of Hilarianus' province repeatedly made their opinions heard during the proceedings, and he appears to have been relatively willing to go along with their demands. This much becomes clear not only from the effect the aforementioned rumours about magical practices had on the treatment of the imprisoned Christians but also from the audience's recurring attempts to influence the type of punishment the accused should receive—apparently both for better and for worse, since they appear to have asked for both harsher and more lenient treatment at different points in the proceedings.[410]

It thus becomes likely that Hilarianus was at relative liberty to adjust the punishment as he thought best, although he does appear to have had to contend with certain limits. Soon after citing the two first-hand accounts, the narrator refers to Felicitas' fears that she would be unable to share in the martyrdom of her fellow Christians due to her advanced pregnancy,[411] and explains in a fascinating aside that the execution of a pregnant woman would have been unlawful (*quia non licet*

festival, and Christians were therefore moved to a military prison. See Rebillard (2017), 313 n. 83. For the argument that the reference to Geta's birthday proves that the text was written shortly after the events it describes, see Barnes (1968^b), 525.

406 *Passio Perpetuae et Felicitatis* 16.2. For the prevalence of magical thinking in the period, see den Boeft and Bremmer (2010), 60–2. The tribune's apparent fear that Christians might escape may suggest a parallel to Acts 12.3–19, in which Peter is said to have been liberated from prison by an angel.

407 The idea that refusal to participate in traditional religious practices was at least part of the issue may also be inferred from the narrator's claim that Christians were dressed up as priests of Saturn and priestesses of Ceres before being thrown to the beasts, see *Passio Perpetuae et Felicitatis* 18.4. For a more elaborate discussion of the readings found in various manuscripts, see Rebillard (2017), 323 n. 115.

408 See Barnes (1985), 70 for the relevance of the name *Vibia Perpetua*. Perpetua's husband is not mentioned, despite the fact that she is said to have been married in *Passio Perpetuae et Felicitatis* 2.

409 Barnes (1985), 148 and Rives (1996), 22.

410 *Passio Perpetuae et Felicitatis* 18.9, 20.2, and 21.7.

411 *Passio Perpetuae et Felicitatis* 15.2.

praegnantes poenae repraesentari).[412] While we are subsequently told that Felicitas miraculously gave birth just in time,[413] we have every reason to suspect that Hilarianus would indeed have postponed her execution if this had not been the case. Whether this event actually took place or not, it is nonetheless telling that the execution of a pregnant woman is presented as an act of excessive cruelty even for an apparently rather severe official like Hilarianus. It should also be noted that the number of accused appears to have been rather limited: the editor mentions the names of only six accused Christians without clear reference to any others, while Perpetua's account repeatedly refers to deacons who were able to enter and leave the prison in order to attend to her needs.[414] The other first-hand account, which is said to have been written by one Saturus, likewise makes mention of church officials 'on the outside',[415] and the narrator's account explains that Felicitas' daughter was raised by a *soror* as her own.[416] While this may refer to her biological relative, no possessive pronoun is present in the text, and it is thus equally possible that the child was instead taken in by another Christian woman. In fact, this may be more likely due to Felicitas' status as a slave: it is uncertain whether her relatives would have been available, or allowed, to care for the child. Although it remains unclear why these specific people were arrested, it seems certain that, on this occasion at least, Hilarianus' actions against the Christians were relatively limited in scope. When his name is once more connected to legal interactions with the Christians of his province, by contrast, the events in question do appear to have affected larger parts of the Christian community—although they were notably directed at property rather than people (Appendix 3.22). The conflict appears to have centred on Christian ownership of specific grounds they used for burials, and while this issue appears to have caused some disturbance, no mention of executions is made.[417] Even within Hilarianus' own time as magistrate, then, we find that the treatment of Christian communities could differ widely, depending on the circumstances.

[412] See Rebillard (2017), 321 n. 103. In his *Ad Sabinum*, Ulpian indeed mentions a similar regulation, which also postponed the torture of pregnant women until they had given birth. See *Digesta* 48.19.3.

[413] *Passio Perpetuae et Felicitatis* 15.5–7.

[414] *Passio Perpetuae et Felicitatis* 2, 3.7, 6.7. Visitors from outside the prison do not appear to have been uncommon—see for instance Acts 24.23 and Lucianus, *De morte Peregrini* 12–13.

[415] *Passio Perpetuae et Felicitatis* 13.1

[416] *Passio Perpetuae et Felicitatis* 15.7.

[417] Tertullian, *Ad Scapulam* 3.1. Tertullian does not tell us if Hilarianus himself was indeed directly involved, only that these events took place during his tenure as *praeses*. No further information about the event is given, and it remains unclear why the Christian burial grounds became the source of a dispute. It is possible that the local Christian communities held meetings there, which may have seemed sinister and potentially dangerous to their non-Christian neighbours. For the connection between Christian meeting places and burial sites, see MacMullen (2009), especially 51–67, where the churches of North Africa are discussed and the passage from *Ad Scapulam* is explicitly referenced. For the connection between Tertullian's Hilarianus and the magistrate in the *Passio*, see Rives (1996), 4.

4.11 The Road to a General Law?

In spite of this substantial diversity in the treatment of Christians by Roman officials, a number of alleged attempts to create a more uniform, coherent policy have also been dated to the same period. Accounts of such measures come from a number of different sources, and their reliability differs substantially. A telling example of this is a measure ascribed to Emperor Septimius Severus, which is mentioned in the *Historia Augusta* (Appendix 3.23).[418] The reference itself is brief, barely a sentence long, and declares that [*Severus*] *Iudaeos fieri sub gravi poena vetuit. Idem etiam de Christianis sanxit.* While some have accepted this measure as authentic,[419] it has since been soundly rejected by the overwhelming majority of scholars for a number of different reasons, of which the work's relatively late date, and therefore the significant change in political circumstances at the time of its writing, is only one.[420] It is also remarkable that Tertullian, who would have been alive at the time this supposed edict would have been issued, makes no mention of a measure of this scope, and even (although perhaps implausibly) suggests that Severus was inclined to defend certain Christians with whom he was familiar.[421] Thus, while it seems all but certain that a number of interactions between Christians and the Roman authorities took place during Severus' reign, it remains exceedingly unlikely that an edict by the emperor himself was responsible.

Accounts of a more positive imperial attitude towards Christianity present in the *Historia Augusta* must likewise be treated with strong suspicion. It seems unlikely, for instance, that Elagabalus ordered the *devotio* of the Christians to be transferred to Rome alongside the *religiones* of both Jews and Samaritans, so that they might be incorporated in the temple of his own personal cult (Appendix 3.24). On a practical level, it is difficult to imagine a tangible aspect of any of these religious movements that might be placed among the sacred objects of the other

[418] Scriptor Historiae Augustae, *Septimius Severus* 17.1. For a more elaborate discussion on the treatment of Christianity in this work, see Stertz (1977).

[419] Frend (1965), 319–23 and Keresztes (1979), 308. See Frend (1965), 341 n. 138 for the outright rejection of the idea that this measure may have been an invention.

[420] For the dating of the work towards the end of the fourth century CE, see Stertz (1977), 710, who at p. 698 notes that the edict is frequently rejected but makes no firm personal pronouncement on the matter. For rejections of the edict, see Barnes (1968[a]), 40–1 and (1968[b]), 526; Molthagen (1970), 39–43; Rives (1996), 19; Ste Croix (1974[a]), 224 n. 66; and others. See Honoré (1987), 164 for the idea that the author's attitude towards Christianity was strongly shaped by the political developments of his own time.

[421] See Barnes (1968[a]), 41 and Rives (1996), 19, the former of which holds that this measure would only have banned conversion to Christianity, whereas 'being Christian' would have become legal. The measure, then, would have been a relatively positive one. It seems unwise, however, to place this level of trust in the author of the *Historia Augusta*. While Eusebius, *Historia Ecclesiastica* 6.1.1, 6.2.2, 6.7, and 6.8.7 appears to provide some corroboration for the actions against Christians that may have resulted from the edict, it has been remarked that the examples he mentions seem to come from Alexandria exclusively. See Molthagen (1970), 40 and Rives (1996), 19. See Tertullian, *Ad Scapulam* 4.6 for Severus' alleged defence of certain upper-class Christians.

cults in which the emperor expressed an interest,[422] and no other source mentions the event. The frequency of references to Christianity in the biography of Alexander Severus,[423] as well as the emperor's known preference for syncretism,[424] by contrast, has by some been believed to lend credibility to the idea that he indeed adopted a lenient attitude towards members of the Christian community (Appendix 3.25). Alexander supposedly incorporated elements of both Christianity and Judaism in his own religious life alongside more traditionally Roman elements, and is said to have referenced the beliefs and practices of these groups.[425] On another occasion, we are told that he chose the side of a Christian community in a legal dispute about land.[426] However, the reason he allegedly gave for this is hardly indicative of an overly positive attitude towards Christianity, as he apparently said that it was better for the site to be used for the worship of some god, whichever one it was, rather than for the building of a cook-shop (*rescripsit melius esse, ut quemadmodumque illic deus colatur, quam popinariis dedatur*).[427] Finally, we are told that Alexander kept Jewish privileges intact, and likewise tolerated Christianity, although it may be implied that he did not necessarily accept conversion (*Christianos esse passus est*).[428] While it has been argued that these accounts are at least partially credible,[429] their origins in Alexander's highly dubious section of the *Historia Augusta* ultimately means that they cannot be taken seriously.[430] In addition, it should be noted that the phrasing of the passage is hardly indicative of a far-reaching measure, or indeed any concrete regulation at all. Rather, the account seems to imply that Alexander Severus simply took no action towards Christians, which even if we do take the *Historia* at face value

[422] Scriptor Historiae Augustae, *Antoninus Heliogabalus* 3.5. Barnes (1968ª), 41–2 rejects the existence of such a measure outright. Stertz (1977), 699 likewise expresses scepticism but does not completely dismiss the idea that these events may have taken place.

[423] Scriptor Historiae Augustae, *Alexander Severus* 22.4, 29.2, 43.6, 45.7, 49.6, 51.7–8.

[424] Stertz (1977), 702–3. For the view that the Severans came to know certain Christians personally, and therefore adopted a more lenient attitude, see Molthagen (1970), 51–2.

[425] In Scriptor Historiae Augustae, *Alexander Severus* 29.2, it is said that Alexander Severus kept statues of both Christ and Abraham in his *lararium*. In chapter 43.6, we are told that Alexander wanted to place Christ 'among the gods', but was prevented from doing so because of a prediction that this would result in the entire empire becoming Christian and abandoning all other gods, which he apparently found objectionable despite his supposed positive attitude towards Christianity. In chapter 45.7, we are told that Alexander cited the Jewish and Christian practices of openly announcing who had been named priest in order to support his own policy of publicly proclaiming the names of newly appointed governors. The tone of the passage implies that he did so in a slightly derogatory way, implying that if even Christians and Jews observed this practice, surely the Roman authorities should, too. Chapter 51.7–8, finally, tells us that Alexander sometimes cited the so-called golden rule ('do not unto others what you do not wish them to do unto you', see e.g. Matthew 7.12), which the author claims he had first heard from either a Jewish or a Christian teacher.

[426] Scriptor Historiae Augustae, *Alexander Severus* 49.6.

[427] See Stertz (1977), 705–6 for the view that this passage fits the author's attitude towards Christians, which was hardly positive but ultimately rather indifferent.

[428] Scriptor Historiae Augustae, *Alexander Severus* 22.4.

[429] Stertz (1977), 700–1.

[430] Barnes (1968ª), 42, who also dismisses the other mentions of Christianity in the account. For the use of distinctly fictitious elements in Alexander's biography, see Rohrbacher (2015), 13 and Syme (1968), 78, 168–72.

indicates indifference rather than an explicitly favourable policy and leaves open the possibility that Christians continued to face difficulty on a local level.[431]

A final passage that makes mention of a 'general law' concerning Christianity can be found in Eusebius' account of the reign of Maximinus Thrax (Appendix 3.27).[432] Here, the emperor is once again described as having an overtly negative attitude towards the Christian communities of his empire and is said to have taken strongly repressive measures in order to prevent their beliefs from spreading. Interestingly, Maximinus' measure is said to have targeted the leaders of the church in particular, which seems to make it a predecessor, or at least a parallel, to one of the edicts mentioned in Eusebius' description of Emperor Diocletian's so-called 'Great Persecution'.[433] If Eusebius is to be believed, Maximinus was particularly disturbed by the fact that these Christian leaders were responsible for teaching others the gospel (*αἴτιοι τῆς κατὰ τὸ εὐαγγέλιον διδασκαλίας*), and therefore, it is implied, for the continuing spread of Christianity. If such a measure did indeed exist, it therefore appears to have been intended not only to curb the growth of Christianity but also to dismantle existing Christian communities from the top down. The reliability of Eusebius' account of these events, however, has repeatedly been called into question.[434] While it is generally accepted that some Christians were targeted during the reign of Maximinus Thrax, the scant available evidence strongly point to the absence of empire-wide regulations, which suggests that we are once again dealing with localized waves of popular accusations at best.[435] It has likewise been remarked that a number of Christian leaders were indeed deported from Rome, although they were notably not executed, and their numbers appear to have been rather limited.[436] These arguments once again suggest a diverse range of Christian experiences, and make the promulgation of an empire-wide edict targeting the clergy unlikely.

[431] In the unlikely case that the phrasing in the *Historia Augusta* is indeed authentic, this might be seen as an example of tolerance in the literal sense of the word. See Garnsey (1984) for an exploration of the concept of toleration in the ancient world, which takes as its starting point the idea that toleration 'implies disapproval or disagreement, coupled with an unwillingness to take action'. For this definition, see p. 1.

[432] Eusebius, *Historia Ecclesiatica* 6.28. While Eusebius also mentions that Philippus Arabs had Christian sympathies (see book 6.34), he makes no mention of any legal consequences attached to such convictions—if they indeed existed. It is therefore unnecessary to further discuss the account in this context. It should be noted, however, that Eusebius does believe that Decius' edict was in part a response to his predecessor's more pro-Christian stance, as shown in book 6.39, thus implausibly repeating the motivations he ascribed to Maximinus Thrax in book 6.28.

[433] Eusebius, *Historia Ecclesiastica* 8.2.5 and 8.6.8–9, as well as Eusebius, *De Martyribus Palestinae*, prologue. Rives (1999), 142 n. 39 mentions that Maximinus' measure has also been seen as a precedent for the edict of Decius.

[434] e.g. Barnes (1968ᵃ), 43; Clarke (1966); Molthagen (1970), 52–8; Rives (1999), 142 n. 39. Sordi (1983), 92 holds that actions against individual Christians did take place but were political and personal, rather than religious, in nature, while also doubting their longevity.

[435] See Clarke (1966), 447.

[436] Clarke (1966), 451–2.

The credibility of these various accounts about wide-ranging measures on Christianity, then, is ultimately extremely limited. Interestingly, however, there are also more reliable indications that attempts were indeed being made to create more coherence in the legal treatment of Christians, and to clearly and systematically discuss the appropriate course of action for governors who became involved in trials against them. According to Lactantius, the Roman jurist Ulpian devoted part of the seventh book of his *De Officio Proconsulis* to a collection of imperial rescripts which dealt with the Christians, apparently in an attempt to determine how they should be punished (Appendix 3.26).[437] The exact contents of the measures cited by Ulpian, or indeed their original authors, are now lost—as is hardly surprising, since these parts of the jurist's work would certainly not have been incorporated in the *Digesta*.[438] Nevertheless, the fact that he chose to collect these regulations is illuminating in many ways. It is particularly notable that Lactantius mentions a collection of rescripts, rather than any other type of legal document. If he is indeed using technical legal terminology, this would then suggest that Ulpian was relying on pronouncements on individual cases for his analysis, and would therefore likely have been unaware of the existence of any definitive, centralized proclamation on the subject of Christianity.[439] Furthermore, the existence of such a collection of rescripts may well suggest that the legal basis for interactions between Christians and the Roman authorities was still to some extent uncertain in the early decades of the third century CE. Ulpian's work appears to have been intended as a guideline for provincial governors who were uncertain on how to handle specific situations they were faced with. It is therefore very well possible that the rescripts he collected were not common knowledge—as was likely the case for many of the precedents on other legal questions in his writings.[440] In fact, it is possible that the cited measures were originally diverse in nature, since Lactantius refers to punishments (*poenae*) in the plural, which has been seen as an indication that Christians could be punished in a number of

[437] Lactantius, *Divinae Institutiones* 5.11.19: *Domitius [Ulpianus] de officio pronconsulis libro septimo rescripta principum nefaria collegit, ut doceret quibus poenis affici oporteret eos qui se cultores dei confiterentur.* Much of Ulpian's treatise on the duties of the proconsul is now lost, but the known parts of its seventh book reference measures against divination, as well as sacrilege, unlawful associations, and *maiestas.* It is in itself interesting that Christianity was apparently included in the same part of Ulpian's analysis, and although it would be unwise to draw far-reaching conclusions from this observation, one might speculate that this sheds some light on the way in which Christians were viewed in this period.

[438] A similar remark is made by Nogrady (2006), 74–5, who also discusses a number of known rescripts that may have been included. This attempt must, however, remain largely speculative, since we can hardly assume to be aware of all rescripts on the subject, or indeed the argument Ulpian was attempting to construct, from the limited number of sources currently available to us.

[439] Beard, North, and Price (1998), 239; Nogrady (2006), 75; Rives (1996), 21; Ste Croix (1974[a]), 223.

[440] For the suggestion that *De Officio Pronconsulis* would have been consulted when 'normal practice' proved unworkable, see Beard, North, and Price (1998), 239. For the idea that these precedents were still non-binding, see Rives (1996), 21.

different ways, both before and after Ulpian's attempt at systematization.[441] Whether or not his suggestions were indeed being used, however, still seems to have depended on the individual judgements of the various provincial governors.

4.12 Conclusion

Over the course of this chapter, we have discussed the various legal interactions between Christians and the Roman authorities that took place between the first century and the first half of the third century CE. During this period, Christianity developed from a relatively small group of devotees primarily originating from Judea, and later Asia Minor, to a much more significant movement that was to varying degrees present throughout the empire. The interactions that occurred over the course of this development overwhelmingly took the form of trials, in which charges were brought forward against Christian individuals or against smaller and larger groups of people who were connected to the Christian community. On a select number of occasions, we also find references to measures that were intended to regulate such trials by imposing procedural limitations. These regulations could limit the active involvement of the Roman authorities, ban the use of anonymous accusations, or demand that any charges that were brought forward were investigated during proper legal proceedings before a Roman magistrate. Other types of measures, by contrast, are comparatively rare, although a number of important sources containing oblique references to financial measures against Christian communities suggest that they did indeed exist. It can therefore hardly be stressed enough that we simply do not have access to a complete overview of all legal interactions involving Christians that historically took place, and that we are instead dealing with a limited selection of sources. Similarly, it should be noted that a significant number, although certainly not all, of these sources were written, or at least cited and contextualized, by Christian authors, whose particular interest in narratives of heroic martyrdom is likely at least partially responsible for the comparative prevalence of trials, and particularly of executions, in the available material. Nevertheless, it remains possible to detect the mechanisms, attitudes, and procedures that governed interactions between Christians and the relevant authorities. Our corpus includes texts whose authorship is ascribed to Roman magistrates alongside the aforementioned accounts by Christian authors, and it is furthermore likely that even the latter would have had a vested interest in making their accounts of martyrdom more credible by presenting them in a legal setting that was both recognizable and realistic. In addition, the events known to us involved a wide variety of Christian communities and

[441] Nogrady (2006), 75.

took place in a number of different Roman provinces, which has allowed us to more precisely determine what effect temporal and regional differences may have had on the treatment of Christians.

Throughout this analysis, it has become abundantly clear that legal interactions between Christians and the Roman authorities were from the very beginning heavily embedded in the particular communities from which they emerged. In geographical terms, this means that the measures that are reliably known to us were generally limited to a single province at most, and on a significant number of occasions even applied to a single city. This pattern is especially visible in the early days of the Christian community: the various difficulties Paul and his followers encountered overwhelmingly involved the local authorities of the cities they visited, and the measures ascribed to Emperor Nero likewise show no sign of having been applicable beyond the borders of the city of Rome. However, this pattern continues to be relevant in later periods as well: Pliny's interactions with Christians were limited to his province of Bithynia-Pontus, the violence against Christians in Gaul—destructive as it may have been—was limited to Lyon, and possibly Vienne, and the various trials referenced by Tertullian likewise show no sign of having been the result of any measure that transcended the province of Africa in which they took place. Elsewhere, then, Christians may well have been able to live their lives without facing legal accusations. It therefore need not come as a surprise that the initiative for measures against Christians was also predominantly local, as has been rightly observed in previous scholarship, and that the inhabitants of the relevant provinces or cities were a centrally important factor in most of the available cases—not just by bringing forward charges and instigating legal proceedings as private accusers but also by creating a climate in which such charges were likely to be accepted by Roman officials. By contrast, the number of reliable instances in which the emperor became involved in proceedings against Christians is significantly more limited, and such interventions always appear to have been prompted by questions or appeals referencing events from specific regions. In this context, it is particularly telling that Ulpian's lost analysis of the legal treatment of Christians appears to have been based on a collection of imperial rescripts, rather than any other kind of measure: while this indicates that Christianity was almost certainly on different emperors' agendas, it also strongly suggests that they themselves did not take the initiative. The imperial measures that are known to us furthermore generally seem to have been concerned with ensuring adherence to proper legal and administrative procedures. With the exception of Marcus Aurelius' rescript to Lyon, which in any case is known only in a briefly paraphrased form, all available rescripts emphasize the importance of formal legal proceedings and upholding public order, while judgement on the individual case under consideration tends to be left to the local Roman officials who had initially requested the emperor's opinion. The involvement of the various Roman governors mentioned in our sources likewise appears to have been prompted by requests of the local population: as far as we can tell, governors did not generally operate proactively, but instead interacted with Christians primarily when a case against them was brought forward—although we are not always made privy to the way in which this occurred. The theory that interactions between Christians and the Roman authorities generally took place within the framework of the *cognitio* procedure, then, continues to hold up, which in turn suggests that trials against Christians were, in this regard at least, part of the established legal patterns in the provinces.

The precise way in which such trial proceedings took shape, however, has been shown to have been strongly subject to negotiation between all levels of government. Within the framework of the *cognitio* procedure, the governor had a wide range of options to respond to charges against Christians, and his decision-making process involved a number of different factors. It should first be noted that legal actions against Christians frequently do not appear to have involved the entire Christian community of a specific region, but were instead more often targeted at specific individuals, while other Christians were personally unaffected. Although this was certainly not universally the case, martyr narratives like those of Polycarp, Ptolemaeus, Perpetua, the unnamed Christians mentioned in Tertullian's *Ad Scapulam*, Justin Martyr, and possibly the Scillitan Christians do suggest that legal actions against Christians could be, and frequently were, less far-reaching than is often assumed, both in terms of their temporal scope and in the number of individuals involved. In addition, although it is not always possible to determine why specific Christian individuals drew the attention of their accusers, it may be tentatively suggested that, alongside potential personal motivations, visibility and perceived actions against the stability of the community may have been a contributing factor to such interactions, as seems to have been the case for, among others, Polycarp and Ptolemaeus.

Notably, we find little to no indication that those who accused Christians, whether as individuals or as a group, explicitly referenced any form of precedent in order to instigate measures against them. Instead, they generally appear to have focused on suggesting that Christians were in some way 'other' and therefore didn't 'belong', by pointing out things like perceived religious deviance, potential political disloyalty, and at times by voicing accusations of criminal or otherwise dangerous behaviour, like the use of magic, suspicious meetings, and, famously, cannibalism and incest. Such arguments occurred in various configurations, and furthermore appear to have gained force when the socio-political environment in which these accusations were being made was in some way subject to tensions. This is likely to have been the case for the anti-Christian measures issued under Nero, and we furthermore find references to the idea that Christians were targeted in the aftermath of natural disasters like earthquakes and failed harvests or other general crises. While Roman administrators may at times have rejected individual charges, as appears to have been the case in Pliny the Younger's famous

Christian letter, such arguments nevertheless frequently appear to have convinced them that Christians posed a threat to public order and the stability of the province, which it was their primary duty to maintain. Although Christian communities themselves are never reported to have instigated the disturbances, many governors appear to have seen their deviance and refusal to participate in general society, rather than the actions instigated by the general population, as the primary cause of unrest—or indeed the obstacle that had to be overcome to regain stability and control.

In this context, it should be noted that the influence of local magistrates operating in the relevant communities was a particularly powerful one. Cases like the execution of Polycarp and the events in Lyon serve to demonstrate that the local governing elite could lend significant credibility to charges against Christians in the eyes of Roman governors, who may have found it difficult to contradict eminent members of the local population, and would therefore likely have considered taking action against Christians an appropriate way to maintain the authority of their government and to avoid complaints about their administration—especially when the plaintiffs held public office. Roman governors therefore had to balance the arguments and wishes of the local population and its leaders with their own concerns about public order, and on occasion with the views of the emperor—a process that could have a variety of outcomes, ranging from larger-scale measures against the Christians of the region, to trials against certain individuals, and likely to *de facto* non-intervention. As was the case for the local population, explicit references to the use of legal precedent rarely appear in the available sources as part of governor's considerations. While the example of Pliny the Younger shows that Roman magistrates were even at this relatively early date to some extent aware of the fact that Christians could, and had been, brought to trial, and that they used this knowledge as a precedent in the most general sense of the word, there is little to suggest that they had concrete knowledge of the procedures that had been followed in these earlier cases. Instead, our sources repeatedly show that governors felt the need to consult the current emperor about the particular situation they were faced with, which suggests that they were unaware of any established procedure. Likewise, we find no indication that the emperors who received such questions referenced each other's rescripts in their responses. Instead, they overwhelmingly focused on maintaining proper procedure, and in addition seem to have emphasized different elements of these proceedings depending on the specific questions that were posed to them. It thus becomes clear that the legal treatment of Christians remained largely discretionary and subject to negotiation for a long time (as is also made clear by the fact that Ulpian felt the need to collect a number of different imperial rescripts in an attempt to create coherence at the beginning of the third century CE), and that all levels of the empire's government continued to be involved in these negotiations. Certainly, the measures attributed to Nero are never referenced in later proceedings, which strongly speaks against the idea that measures against Christians were in a legal sense an *institutum Neronianum*. Furthermore, while many trials to some extent show similarities to the procedure discussed by Pliny and Trajan, it is ultimately similarly unlikely that Trajan's response was widely seen as a landmark decision. Indeed, the measure is never referenced by Roman authors, and appears to have been equally unfamiliar to later Roman officials, who as mentioned felt the need to consult their emperors for themselves about the appropriate course of action within a relatively short period after the rescript had been issued. At the very most, then, Pliny's conduct may later have come to be seen as exemplary due to its unusually thorough description of the relevant proceedings.

The important role of negotiation in the known proceedings also sheds an interesting light on the well-known distinction between the *nomen ipsum* and *flagitia cohaerentia nomini*, which has been central to the debate surrounding the legal basis for trials against Christians since Pliny's day. While it is true that 'being Christian' more often than not appears to have been the official charge, as is demonstrated by the fact that Christians could avoid punishment by participating in the famous sacrifice test, accusations of criminal or otherwise unwanted behaviour played a significant part in arguing why that charge should be accepted as valid grounds for a trial by the governor. The two categories therefore cannot be entirely separated within a Roman legal context: the sheer prevalence of references to criminal behaviour, political disloyalty, and religious deviance in both Christian apologetic writings and in the available accounts of trials against Christians serves to confirm that such accusations were considered to be deeply relevant to the legal proceedings, even if some of them constituted social, rather than criminal offences. For this reason, it would be too simple to argue that Christians were convicted simply for 'being Christian': this may be true if we look exclusively at the ultimate verdict, but the rest of the proceedings as they appear in our sources cannot fully be explained by that charge alone.

It furthermore deserves to be emphasized that legal interactions between Christians and the Roman authorities could take markedly different shapes and have different results. As becomes clear from the attempt to seize Christian burial grounds mentioned by Tertullian—and is implied by Melito's references to Christians suffering financially rather than physically—not all such confrontations resulted in lives hanging in the balance. Even for Christians who were brought to trial, we find a number of indications that no specific punishment was ever put in place, either by law or by precedent. The possibility for a punishment more lenient than execution continued to exist for a long time, as becomes clear from the various governors mentioned in *Ad Scapulam*, as well as Hadrian's rescript to Minucius Fundanus, where the nature of the punishment is decidedly left open. On other occasions, we furthermore find brief references to the idea that Christians could also be banished, or temporarily imprisoned, which speaks against the idea that Christians always paid the ultimate price for their beliefs. It is also notable that the methods of capital punishment, when it was meted out, differed significantly. While some Christians do appear to have been sent *ad leones*, as the famous phrase goes, it should be noted that burning and beheading are also mentioned as potential methods of execution, and that the social status of the accused did not always matter. Although the governor of Lyon made a distinction between those who were Roman citizens and those who were not, the account of Perpetua's death suggests that this was not always the case, while the martyr narrative of the Scillitan Christians suggests that the accused were all beheaded despite their apparently low social status. We repeatedly find references to the local population attempting to influence the method of execution, and on a number of occasions this appears to have worked—which once again serves to demonstrate the importance of negotiation between various legal actors in cases involving Christians. The outcome of interactions between Christians and the Roman authorities, then, hardly appear to have been as uniform as is often assumed.

There were, however, a number of limits a Roman magistrate on any level had to contend with. The general legal framework, for instance regarding the treatment of Roman citizens, was likely established in the imperial *mandata* or the provincial edict, and various imperial rescripts serve to further emphasize the importance of proper procedure. In particular, they repeatedly underline that it was essential for accusations to be made within the context of a formal trial, which meant that the accuser could be held personally responsible for the charges he brought forward. Although references to punishments for false accusers are noticeably rare, and are seldom expanded upon in the sources available to us, *Ad Scapulam* and the rescript to Minucius Fundanus do seem to suggest that the possibility existed, and was likely occasionally enforced. The need for a proper procedure also appears to have included the possibility of denial or recantation. On a number of occasions, we hear that the accused were repeatedly given the chance to deny the allegations against them, and the governor who oversaw the trial of the Scillitan Christians even offered a significant period of time for reconsideration. When they deemed it necessary, governors could also bring in witnesses to further investigate the accusations against Christians, as was the case both in Pliny's investigation and during the events in Lyon. In this context, the use of the so-called sacrifice test is also particularly relevant. This method was indeed often used to determine if the accused truly rejected Christianity, and as such served as part of the magistrate's truth-finding tools and as an argument for the defence that could be used to demonstrate that the accused had indeed been re-integrated into general society, rather than as a punishment in itself. However, its employment does not appear to have been universal—or indeed uniform. Tertullian mentions that one of the governors he describes in his *Ad Scapulam* did not direct a recanting Christian to sacrifice, and while this reference emphasizes that the procedure was indeed common enough to be used as a familiar point of reference, it was apparently by no means inescapable. The inhabitants of Lyon only appear to have demanded sacrifice at the very end of the proceedings, and apparently only did so with regard to Christians who had retracted their previous recantation. Although it is difficult to find a discernible pattern, it is likewise notable that the object of sacrifice seems to differ from case to case, and from trial to trial: while Trajan encouraged Pliny to employ sacrifices 'to our gods', other governors appear to have preferred sacrifices 'for the well-being of the emperor', thus adding a more explicit dimension of political loyalty. Others again chose different tests to determine if the accused had truly given up Christianity. Polycarp, for example, was asked to renounce Christians as atheists, and to swear by the *genius* of the emperor, rather than to participate in sacrifice, and Pliny himself mentions the cursing of Christ as a potential option. For Christians, however, any of these options would have been unacceptable.

Just as the various known measures against Christians found their origins in local circumstances, so too do they appear to have been largely locally enforced. We repeatedly hear that local magistrates, and sometimes the general population, were involved in the enforcement of the verdict, although the governor's staff generally likewise appears to have been an active participant. The one significant exception to this course of action consisted of Roman citizens, about whose fate the imperial authorities generally appear to have been consulted—either by sending the accused to Rome or through enquiry by letter. The initiative for such consultations generally appears to have been taken by the responsible governor without interference by local authorities, and references to attempts by the accused to appeal the verdict are noticeably rare. While the book of Acts makes it clear that Paul had the opportunity to appeal to a higher authority, we find no mention of such an attempt in later trials against Christians. It seems likely that this is at least partially due to the fact that many of our sources are especially focused on the idea of martyrdom, and therefore tend to paint Christians as highly accepting of their fate. However, it is very likely that great diversity existed within Christian communities, and that some decided to recant rather than adhering to their beliefs to the end.

The works of many Christian apologists may likewise be seen in this context, and they serve to demonstrate that some Christians did indeed attempt to change the position of their communities by winning the support of the Roman authorities—whether emperor or governor. This is perhaps most obvious in the case of Melito of Sardis, who directly references current events in his appeal to Emperor Marcus Aurelius, but other apologists, too, appear to have made similar, or more far-reaching, attempts. Notably, a number of these apologists attempted to make rather extensive use of precedents, both in order to prove that only 'bad' emperors acted against the Christians, and by using the rescripts of better-loved emperors as an authoritative argument to encourage a more positive attitude.

Likewise, they frequently respond to the arguments of their accusers by rejecting the idea that Christians were involved in criminal activity, and furthermore regularly insist that Christians very much 'belonged' in the Roman world. This was sometimes done by emphasizing how Christians had aided the Roman authorities, and on other occasions by attempting to frame Christianity in Roman terms—for instance as an ancestral religion in the case of Justin's companions, or as a philosophical school in the case of Melito's apology. However, we have no record of any such appeal having had a concrete effect, and on the whole they do not appear to have been particularly successful. This may at least in part be due to the fact that the imperial rescripts that could conceivably be used as an authoritative precedent for a more lenient treatment were, as discussed, more focused on procedure than outcome, and were therefore not unambiguously positive. In addition, it seems unlikely that the emperors to whom such petitions were addressed were willing to interfere in what they generally appear to have seen as the business of the respective provincial governors.

Ultimately, then, the legal treatment of Christians in the Roman world was likely much more diverse than at first seems to have been the case. This pluriformity is visible not only in the variety of arguments that were used to instigate trials against Christians but also in the existence of other types of measures aimed at Christian communities, as well as the differences in procedure and in the outcomes of such procedures. The fact that the number of people involved was often relatively small, while periods of increased legal activity were overwhelmingly temporary and local in nature, furthermore speaks against the idea that any sort of policy with regard to Christianity was consistently enforced, or indeed that Christians were a particular point of concern for the Roman authorities. The position of Christians in the Roman world, it has become clear, was repeatedly up for renegotiation, and for this reason it is difficult to maintain that Christianity was an 'illegal' religion as such, as deeply threatening as the situation of various Christian communities in the empire may have been. Instead, their treatment appears to have depended strongly on local factors and the arguments brought forward by the different parties involved.

Marginalized Religion and the Law in the Roman Empire. K. P. S. Janssen, Oxford University Press.
 DOI: 10.1093/9780191946400.003.0005

Conclusion

5.1 Marginalized Religion in the Roman Empire

In a religious landscape as wide-ranging and diverse as that of the Roman Empire, it is hardly surprising that the characteristics and limits of acceptable religious behaviour became the subject of disagreement and debate. The process of determining what fit, in whole or in part, within the religious 'mainstream', and what was relegated to the margins, was not a straightforward one: it involved a wide variety of societal groups and individuals and was furthermore closely intertwined with other social, cultural, and political circumstances. As a result, the exact considerations and values that influenced Roman attitudes towards various individual religious groups often remain opaque. In some cases, however, the subject found its way into the legal sphere, and it is here that the societal factors that shaped the position of these religious movements within wider Roman society rise to the surface more clearly than perhaps anywhere else. This study therefore aimed to examine the ways in which marginalized religious groups were embedded in, and interacted with, the Roman legal system of the imperial period, and to provide a systematic analysis of the interactions between such groups and the Roman authorities by reconnecting them to the wider legal and administrative context in which they occurred. This endeavour, it has been argued, requires both an understanding of the legal and administrative framework of the Roman Empire in general, and a comparative approach that allows us to look beyond the treatment of specific individual groups, and to provide a broader perspective on the legal position of religious beliefs and practices that in one way or the other fell beyond the scope of Roman 'normality'. The juxtaposition of several well-attested religious communities allows us to discuss legal measures involving these groups not as isolated phenomena (or, particularly in the case of early Christianity, as anomalous or unique by default), but instead as a part of the Roman religious and legal landscape, which originated not simply from specific ideological objections against a particular group, but rather from an array of shared underlying considerations, mechanisms, and procedures. In order to get a firm grasp of these guiding principles, it has been suggested, it is furthermore necessary to take all stages of the legal process into account: by focusing not just on the contents of legal measures dealing with marginalized religious groups but also on their origins and implementation, we can more thoroughly position these regulations within their wider societal context.

Each of the chapters in this study, then, has in its own way served to further elucidate the administrative and judicial framework in which interactions between marginalized religious groups and the Roman authorities took place. Chapter 1 discussed the various procedures, institutions, mechanisms, practices, and legal actors that collectively shaped the way in which the Roman imperial authorities governed the territories under their jurisdiction. As we have seen, the governance of the empire depended not just on the emperor and the central Roman authorities but also on provincial governors and other, lower officials. These various layers of government were strongly interdependent and furthermore frequently appear to have operated on a reactive (rather than proactive) basis, relying strongly on the initiative and input of the general population—and particularly local elites. The recurring process of negotiation and renegotiation between these different actors was essential for maintaining and restoring stability in the provinces and for shaping the actions and attitudes of Roman administrators. This process likewise contributed to an important degree of institutionalized flexibility that allowed for significant legal diversity within the empire, which is reflected in the continued existence, in whole or in part, of the local customs, laws, and privileges of certain cities or communities, and especially in the fact that many of the measures taken by the Roman authorities were strongly tailored to specific temporal and local circumstances. The subsequent analyses of the Roman authorities' known interactions with diviners (Chapter 2), Jewish communities (Chapter 3), and early Christians (Chapter 4) in turn served to further illustrate how the treatment of religious groups could be influenced by the general principles discussed in the first chapter. While the legal position of these groups was far from identical, they together nevertheless shed a light on the various factors that contributed to the particular treatment of communities that were perceived to fall outside the boundaries of accepted Roman religious practices, and thereby on the spectrum of perceived religious 'otherness'.

5.2 Geographical and Temporal Scope

Like so many of the Roman authorities' administrative actions, interactions between marginalized religious groups and the Roman authorities were firmly embedded in the temporal and geographical circumstances under which they occurred. As a result, legal measures dealing with these groups were overwhelmingly local in nature, as well as of limited duration. In the case of diviners, we have seen that the majority of known legal interactions between those who were in some way involved in the practice and the Roman authorities occurred within Italy, or even the city of Rome specifically, and that the few measures that are said to have applied to the provinces were likewise limited in scope. The types of interactions that appear in the available sources similarly reflect the circumscribed nature of these attempts at regulation: overwhelmingly, they took the shape of either trials against individual diviners and those who consulted them, which may well have taken the form of a *cognitio* procedure, or of expulsion measures targeting private practitioners in a designated region. Both types of measures, it may be argued, were by their very nature aimed at specific cases, while the evidence for the existence of empire-wide bans on particular divinatory practices rests on very shaky historical ground—especially in the case of Augustus' alleged attempt to limit the contents and circumstances of divinatory enquiries (Appendix 1.5). Measures against diviners were repeated and re-issued with a frequency that was remarked upon even by Roman authors like Tacitus and Ulpian, and the known expulsions of diviners from Italy and the city of Rome in particular (Appendices 1.2, 1.3, 1.7, 1.8, 1.20, 1.28, 1.29) appear to have been intended as temporary measures to safeguard public order, which ceased to be upheld as soon as the immediate perceived need for them had passed—as was the case for similar attempts to expel members of the city's Jewish community (Appendices 2.4, 2.45, 2.52). In the same vein, trials that involved the divinatory practices of the accused have been shown to have overwhelmingly treated such accusations as supporting evidence for particular allegations of *maiestas* or other types of alleged disruptive behaviour that threatened the stability of the Roman state, rather than evolving into a formal charge in itself that found its basis in a long-standing law banning specific types of divination, as has often been assumed.

The existence of a durable 'general law' is even more doubtful in the case of early Christianity, and there is very little to suggest that the Roman authorities were pursuing a consistent policy of repression and persecution against the movement, or indeed that Christianity was an illegal religion as such. Up to the middle of the third century CE, the known cases all applied to specific cities, or provinces at most, and Christians who lived elsewhere in the empire may well have escaped legal interactions with the Roman authorities. Trials against Christians have been shown to have overwhelmingly taken place in the context of the *cognitio* procedure—as was common for a great many legal proceedings that took place in the provinces. Procedures involving Christians therefore generally occurred only when a charge was brought forward by members of the local population and subsequently accepted by the Roman governor, making them deeply rooted in specific regional circumstances. The limited scope of anti-Christian proceedings is likewise underscored by the fact that the number of Christians targeted by any particular interaction could vary significantly: while the events in Lyon in 177 CE (Appendix 3.17) involved large parts of the local Christian population, we have likewise seen that measures were frequently aimed at significantly smaller groups, or even at specific individuals (Appendices 3.11, 3.13, 3.15, 3.18, 3.20, and 3.21)—thus demonstrating that Christians, like those involved in divination, could be targeted not only for their perceived outsider-status as a group but also on more specific, even personal, grounds.

The surviving measures involving Judaism, while often being supportive rather than repressive in nature, were normally likewise originally taken with the Jewish communities of specific cities or provinces in mind, and the texts of the specific rulings that are available to us frequently explicitly mention the region to which the measure was meant to be applied. Although important evidence exists to suggest that such precedents could be passed on and applied to other parts of the empire, and that the Roman authorities on occasion acknowledged the transregional connections between various Jewish communities, both to their benefit and to their detriment, this does not appear to have occurred on a systematic basis for most of the period under discussion. Indeed, with the notable exception of the Jewish Tax (Appendix 2.56), the creation of large-scale measures rarely appears to have been the original intent. In addition, measures attempting to guarantee the rights and privileges of various Jewish communities in the empire do not appear to have been systematically enforced. The available sources repeatedly reference measures that had fallen into disuse, as well as subsequent requests for their revival. While these requests frequently appear to have been granted, the need for the repetition of such measures nevertheless suggests that their implementation was not closely monitored by the Roman authorities, and instead depended strongly on local circumstances. In general, then, it has become clear that measures dealing with particular religious groups were not, as a rule, systematic in nature, but were instead applied when, and where, they were deemed to be necessary.

5.3 Legal Actors and Negotiations

Given the fact that legal interactions with marginalized religious groups were so strongly embedded in their particular temporal and local circumstances, it need hardly come as a surprise that we find ample evidence for the involvement of a variety of different legal actors in both the creation and implementation of the relevant measures. With the exception of expulsions from the city of Rome, which generally appear to have been instigated by Roman magistrates, the initiative for the majority of these interactions lay not with the Roman authorities, whether central or provincial, but instead with the inhabitants of specific communities—and particularly their local elites. This has been most clearly demonstrated in the case of Jewish communities, who not only faced local attacks on their position with some frequency but also actively took part in negotiations for the protection of their ancestral customs and privileges themselves, as is repeatedly shown both in the documents transmitted by Flavius Josephus, as well as the sources dealing with the Alexandrian riots of 38 CE. The same pattern may be observed in legal actions against Christians, which as discussed were widely instigated by members of the general population. Furthermore, the inhabitants of a particular town or province could exert notable influence on the character of the resulting measures, especially with the support of the local elite. However, as we have seen, non-Christians were not the only ones to take this route: as has become clear from the example of apologists like Melito of Sardis and Tertullian, Christians themselves could likewise take an active role in the negotiation process and could attempt to improve the position of their communities. Both in the case of Christians and Jewish communities attempting to safeguard their ancestral customs, then, Roman authorities could be confronted with conflicting factions among the local population, each attempting to make a case for the course of action its members saw as most beneficial. The involvement of the regular inhabitants of the empire is less prominently present in the treatment of diviners, which may be at least partially due to the fact that most known interactions took place in Rome, and therefore fell more immediately within the central authorities' sphere of influence. Nevertheless, some hints of bottom-up initiative are visible even here, and trials that in some way involved the divinatory practices of the accused, like those against Christians, normally appear to have been instigated by private accusers, as was common for Roman legal proceedings.

Excepting those instances in which representatives of the central authorities were present in a particular region, cases that occurred in the provinces involving all of the religious groups under discussion were commonly initially taken up by local Roman officials—in many of the known cases the governor. The governor could then choose to pass on the requests or complaints made by the local population to a higher authority, in some cases the emperor, but initial investigations on a more local scale do not appear to have been uncommon. In a notable number of known instances, such investigations appear to have involved an opportunity for the competing sides to make their case and present their arguments, which suggests that governors made attempts to prevent disturbances or the escalation thereof on a local level and made use of local expertise to determine what the best course of action might be. The influence of the general population, then, did not end once the attention of Roman officials had been drawn to their request, but was instead often essential in shaping the attitude of the responsible magistrate, and even the way in which the resulting measures were implemented. As has been remarked, the reiteration of specific measures was likewise overwhelmingly the result of requests by the relevant communities, rather than of the continued interest of Roman officials, which meant that measures on marginalized religious groups were not just subject to negotiation, but to renegotiation as well.

This is not to say, however, that measures on particular religious groups were shaped exclusively by negotiations between one or more specific communities and local Roman officials. In certain cases, the latter could—and evidently did—consult the central authorities, either because a request to this effect was made by the relevant community, or because they were dealing with a matter that they did not know how to resolve themselves, or that might pose increased risk to the stability of the region. Important examples of this may be found in cases where diviners from the provinces were said to have made predictions about the imminent death of the emperor—which were seen as a threat to the stability of Roman rule and were therefore soon relegated to the capital—and especially in the disturbances surrounding the Jewish community of Alexandria (Appendices 2.46 and 2.48), in which two subsequent emperors became involved at the request of local delegations when the prefect proved unable to manage the situation effectively. In the case of Christians, too, emperors have been shown to have become involved only at the request of lower officials. Interactions between the Roman authorities and religious groups therefore appear to have conformed to the wider framework of Roman provincial administration, and frequently involved negotiations between different legal actors, in which balancing the various interests involved often proved to be crucial for the exact way in which the resulting measures took shape.

5.4 Arguments and Underlying Considerations

Throughout these negotiations regarding the contents and implementation of legal measures dealing with marginalized religious groups, a number of arguments and underlying considerations frequently reoccur, and as a result contributed significantly to shaping the Roman authorities' attitudes and actions. Each in their own way deals with the idea that certain groups fell outside the accepted societal boundaries of the Graeco-Roman world and therefore did not 'belong', which shaped the treatment of all three groups discussed in this study both directly and subtextually. The general sense of suspicion with which these groups were regarded has been illustrated by a notable number of examples, particularly in the case of the Jewish community of Alexandria, which was openly accused of not 'belonging' in its home city in both a social, political, and religious sense. The repeated appeals of other Jewish communities to the Roman authorities display similar struggles for inclusion with their non-Jewish neighbours, while the known expulsion measures against both Jews and diviners made the perceived outsider status of groups that were in one way or the other considered deviant, literal. References to Christians being accused of abandoning traditional religious practices, which are most prominently present in Pliny the Younger's account of the trials in his province, likewise show that the question of who 'belonged' played an important role in shaping the legal treatment of marginalized religious groups and could feature explicitly in their interactions with the Roman authorities.

On other occasions, however, the issue of 'belonging' was addressed in different ways. In this regard it is especially important to note that measures aimed at the repression of particular religious groups were frequently linked by perceived threats to public order or the stability of Roman rule to which the group(s) in question were believed to have contributed. Indeed, accusations of criminal, or otherwise disruptive, behaviour appear in accounts of legal interactions between the Roman authorities and members of religious groups with some frequency. Significant examples of this may be found in the conflicts between Jewish and non-Jewish inhabitants of Antioch during the Great Revolt (Appendices 2.54 and 2.55), where the Jewish community was accused of attempting to commit arson, but earlier attempts to prevent Jewish communities from sending money to the Temple in Jerusalem (Appendices 2.7, 2.37, and 2.38) and even Nerva's reference to *calumnia* related to the Jewish Tax (Appendix 2.61) suggest that the alleged disruption could take many forms, and could even be financial in nature. Most especially, accusations of deviant divinatory practices were presented in conjunction with—and in support of—more formal charges of attempting to cause harm to members of the imperial family with almost unmissable frequency, and the few known examples of legal proceedings dealing with the practice that involved members of lower social classes likewise suggest a perceived connection between divination and doing harm. In the case of Christians, the importance of this particular argument becomes most visible in the prevalence of accusations of criminal behaviour and political disloyalty, which appear with notable frequency in both Christian apologetic writings and the available accounts of trials against Christians. Such accusations were widely used from early on and served to convince Roman governors that charges of 'being Christian' should be accepted as legally valid, as well as administratively beneficial. As a result, the traditional distinction between the *nomen ipsum* and the *flagitia cohaerentia nomini* as the legal basis for trials against Christians cannot be strictly upheld: 'being Christian' became closely associated with accusations of criminal or otherwise disruptive behaviour, which, as in the case of private divinatory practitioners, served to make Christians a viable target for legal measures even when no evidence for concrete misbehaviour could be found.

The vulnerability of perceived religious outsiders furthermore appears to have been increased during periods of aggravated social tension, such as during or in the aftermath of a war, fire, or natural disaster, and expulsions of religious groups in particular were regularly ordered in times of socio-political instability. During such periods of disruption, religious groups that were thought to deviate from the established norm were furthermore more likely to be met with hostilities, which were, in turn, more likely to elicit a response from the Roman authorities. A number of conflicts between Jewish communities and the non-Jewish inhabitants of various cities appear to have been triggered or aggravated by disturbances of the established order, whether locally or on a larger scale, and Christians sources similarly report that their communities became particularly vulnerable to hostilities in the wake of a natural disaster. As we have seen, upholding public order and the stability of Roman rule was of central importance to the Roman authorities, and in this context, conflicts between different factions in a certain city or region would have been of particular concern. Roman intervention, whether by the emperor or by lower magistrates, was therefore frequently prompted by an outbreak of socio-political difficulties or the immediate threat thereof. This worry regarding factional conflicts appears to have contributed greatly to a variety of prominent measures, including Claudius' letter to Alexandria and the various notable attempts by the Roman authorities to safeguard proper procedure in trials against Christians, which could serve to limit the scope of the resulting measures. The attitudes of the Roman authorities towards marginalized religious groups, then, show a strong overriding concern for the stability of the empire—as did Roman administration in general.

The outcome of interventions by the Roman authorities, and the character of the resulting measures, could furthermore be influenced by the concrete legal and administrative resources the various parties had at their disposal. Firstly, the existence and availability of previous rulings that might serve as potential precedents could help religious communities, or those who sought to take action against them, to convince the Roman authorities of the appropriateness of the proposed course of action. This negotiation tool is particularly prevalent in cases related to the rights and customs of Jewish communities, who could not only reference their long-standing ancestral customs with familiar phraseology that would have resonated throughout the Mediterranean, but have also been shown to have referred to pre-existing measures and rights granted by previous governors or emperors with some frequency—even in parts of the empire other than the one to which such measures originally applied. While early Christian groups, by contrast, did not have access to such favourable precedents, we nevertheless find some evidence of Christian authors referring to earlier legal measures. They did so both in order to suggest that attempts to repress Christianity originated with so-called 'bad emperors', and to prove that Roman officials had on occasion been lenient—although the latter precedents were originally focused on procedure rather than outcome, and therefore did not constitute unambiguous evidence. Nevertheless, these types of arguments show that Christians were not fully positioned outside the Roman legal system, but instead attempted to participate in and interact with it in ways that suited the needs and interests of their communities.

The legal treatment of particular religious groups could furthermore be strongly affected by the extent to which they had access to established institutions, as well as leadership structures that were recognizable to the Roman authorities. The availability of a firmly rooted, authoritative diplomatic infrastructure helped to facilitate the incorporation of the group in question within the Roman administrative framework, and thus made it easier for that community's voice to be heard, while its absence could have noticeable detrimental effects. Both Jewish communities and those who attempted to repress their religious practices employed this mechanism with some regularity, while diviners, who are best described as a much more loosely affiliated amalgamation of practitioners, very likely lacked the tools to achieve similar results. In this case, however, the prevalence, popularity, and established character of divination both throughout the ancient world in general, and in the Roman Empire in particular, likely served to limit the scope of measures against those involved in it. While the practice could indeed be seen as disruptive, or even dangerous, its sheer popularity would likely have made sweeping bans difficult to uphold, and possibly even undesirable, for most of the principate, and individual diviners may furthermore well have derived protection from their connection to specific members of the Roman elite. In the case of early Christianity, we find that those who favoured anti-Christian measures could very well include members of the local governing elite, as well as local law enforcement. Christians themselves lacked access to such support, and Christian apologetic authors appear to have attempted to compensate for this by arguing that Christians, rather than being the potentially dangerous outsiders they were made out to be, could easily be incorporated within familiar Roman frameworks. This of course included elaborate denials of the various crimes of which Christians were accused, but also attempts to re-cast Christianity in terms that would be both acceptable and understandable to the Roman authorities, like an ancestral religion or indeed a philosophical school. While this approach does not appear to have been able to compensate for the lack of established institutions and recognizable leadership, it is nonetheless telling that Christian authors attempted to employ it, and tried to cast themselves not as 'outsiders' but as part of the wider Roman religious landscape.

While each of the aforementioned arguments and negotiation tools repeatedly appears in the available sources, it should be noted that they rarely occur in isolation. Instead, they were frequently combined and used to support one another, and might likewise work in different directions when utilized by opposing parties in the debate. The ultimate outcome of legal interactions between members of religious groups and the Roman authorities, then, continued to vary strongly on a case-to-case basis, which reflects the wider legal diversity of the Roman world.

5.5 Slow Emergence of Procedure

The flexibility and diversity of these legal interactions is likewise reflected in the fact that clear, established procedures for the treatment of particular religious groups in the Roman world emerged only gradually, over the course of a significant period of time. The aforementioned fragmentary temporal and geographic nature of the known interactions between the Roman authorities and all three of the groups discussed in this study indicates that none of the latter's legal treatment was founded in a single legal measure, and their diverse character serves to further illustrate this point. As we have seen, divinatory practices were regulated by both trials and expulsions, as well as attempts to limit access to certain relevant texts, and on occasion to specific types of consultations, while no fixed punishment for perceived divinatory transgressions can be detected. Attempts to determine how such practices should be penalized appear to have first emerged in the works of the third-century jurists, who notably still appear to have had differing opinions on the issue. Before that time, however, it remains unclear how such decisions were reached, and whether specific criteria were applied. The same holds true for early Christianity: there is important evidence to suggest that measures against Christians did not always end in execution but could also have a less lethal outcome (Appendices 3.20, 3.22, and possibly 3.10). It is furthermore telling that the scope of these interactions could likewise vary significantly, and that imperial authorities especially appear to have been more concerned with safeguarding proper procedure than with establishing concrete regulations on what the legal position of Christians should be, which could result in markedly different approaches. Similarly, measures involving the treatment of the empire's various Jewish communities were concerned with a wide variety of customs, depending on the individual circumstances of each particular case. Alongside such interactions, the outcomes of which are generally represented as favourable to the Jewish communities in question, we furthermore find reports of expulsions and a number of other measures, like the Jewish Tax (Appendix 2.56), that suggest that Roman involvement could impact the life of Jews in the Roman Empire in both positive and negative ways.

For all of these groups, then, the creation of coherence between such disparate measures was a slow process. The idea that the customs and privileges of Jewish communities were protected by a charter (or even a Jewish *Magna Carta*) of some sort may be soundly rejected, as has been proposed before, and the necessity to actively safeguard Jewish religious practices is very likely attested even in the late second century CE, when the topic of circumcision was repeatedly revisited (Appendices 2.64–2.66). The legal treatment of divination remained without a clear, unambiguous legal foundation for a similarly lengthy period of time. Even in the third century CE, Roman jurists were well aware that the specific grounds for taking action against diviners had long been in question, and their discussions of the issue suggest that the debate was still ongoing (Appendices 1.42 and 1.44). The importance of negotiation, and the apparent pluriformity of measures aimed at Christians, furthermore speak against the common idea that the Roman authorities soon adopted a relatively systematic approach to Christianity—an assumption that remains either implicitly or explicitly present in many studies on the subject, despite the fact that the so-called 'general law' theory is now commonly rejected. The letters between Pliny the Younger and Emperor Trajan (Appendices 3.8 and 3.9) in particular are often seen as a centrally important 'landmark' precedent, but this seems to be due more to their rather unique status as a remarkably complete source deriving more or less directly from Roman administrative practice, than to any concrete evidence for their continued use by later Roman officials. There is nothing to suggest that later magistrates were aware of the correspondence, or even Trajan's rescript on its own, and the emperor's ruling furthermore hardly appears to have been systematically followed. It is particularly telling that governors in Asia and Lyon (Appendices 3.10 and 3.17) seem to have found it necessary to once again consult their respective emperors about the correct treatment of Christians within a few decades of the exchange, which serves to aggravate existing doubts regarding the extent to which previous rulings would have been widely available to either Roman magistrates or the general population of the empire. Pliny himself does, however, refer to a general awareness of the fact that Christians had been tried and convicted in the past, and it is this type of precedent in the most general sense of the word that seems to have been most influential on the part of the Roman officials. The approximate knowledge of previous measures thus likely served to validate actions against Christians in the eyes of Roman governors, rather than prescribing their exact nature and character, while emperors were by all appearances more concerned with proper procedure and the stability of the provinces than with the particular outcome of individual trials. As was the case for measures involving diviners, then, coherent procedures for the legal treatment of Christians appear to have emerged only gradually, and were likely deduced by retroactively combining a variety of different measures—a similarity that is further underscored by the fact that the legal basis for measures against both groups (the knowledge or practice of divination vis-à-vis the *nomen ipsum* or *flagitia cohaerentia nomini* for Christians) was a point of explicit debate for Roman officials. The corpora of legal measures involving all three groups thus collectively serve to demonstrate, firstly, that the legal treatment of religious groups could become subject to the same attempts by Roman jurists to retroactively systematize a series of individual cases that may be observed in other areas of Roman law, but especially that measures were created on an *ad hoc* basis without such attempts at coherence for significant periods of time. These measures exhibited a degree of diversity in both origins, character, and application that suggests that the legal treatment of these groups was not so much the result of a concrete, systematic policy, but rather on specific ways in which they were embedded in the administrative and legal framework of the Roman world at various points in time.

5.6 Tests and Recantations

The fact that the character and implementation of measures dealing with religious groups were tailored to the particular contexts in which they occurred may also be observed in the existence of a number of additional procedures that helped the authorities to determine who was to be targeted by the measure in question and who was not. In a number of interesting cases, we hear about the use of certain tests, which were tailored to expose members of the relevant groups by demanding participation in religious practices or behaviours from which the group in question was required to abstain. While it is important to remember that these tests unavoidably involved significant legal pressures, and could even come with the threat of physical violence, they also served to facilitate an opportunity to avoid punishment by way of cooperation. The very existence of such tests, then, demonstrates that measures aimed at non-normative religious groups were not necessarily in the first instance intended as punishment for past behaviour. Instead, as we have seen, in certain cases those who were in danger of being included in groups that were being targeted by repressive measures could acquire an exemption by renouncing their connection to the group in question, even if they were known to have belonged to that group in the past. This once again emphasizes that measures dealing with religious groups were frequently in large part inspired by a desire to maintain or restore the status quo—which on occasion could be used to the advantage of the perceived religious 'outsiders' themselves in a very practical, although not systematic, way.

The most striking example of this may be found in the legal treatment of early Christianity, which has become closely associated with both the famous sacrifice test and the explicit discussion of recantation within trial proceedings. Although it is important to remember that no fixed procedures for this existed—the sacrifice test was not uniformly employed and could in fact take a variety of shapes—this association is far from unwarranted: such procedures appear in the available sources related to early Christianity with notable frequency from the Pliny–Trajan correspondence onwards, and are certainly linked to the treatment of early Christians significantly more often than they are to that of other contemporary religious groups. This does not mean, however, that they were unique to it. Diviners, like Christians, were explicitly or implicitly given the chance to escape punishment by giving up their religious practices with some frequency, despite the fact that both groups had become closely associated with disruptive, and potentially even criminal, behaviour. The most clear-cut evidence for this may be found in the expulsion of diviners from the city of Rome under Tiberius (Appendices 1.7 and 1.8), in which diviners could give up their profession in exchange for a pardon. In this particular instance, the option for a formal recantation is said to have been specifically requested by diviners themselves, but it is very likely that diviners could also escape being swept up in repressive measures in similar, though less official, ways at other points in time, as for instance during the aftermath of Q. Aemilius Saturninus' ban on divination in Egypt (Appendix 1.40). Diviners as a group were not particularly recognizable, and, since no single method of gaining access to hidden knowledge appears to have been targeted, it would have been relatively easy for those who wanted to avoid expulsion to become invisible by giving up their practice and disappearing into obscurity—which may serve to explain why expulsion of diviners proved to be widely ineffective.

Diviners, then, to an extent appear to have been able to shed their religious practices of their own volition, although it must be repeated that such recantations were prompted by the imminent threat of expulsion or other forms of repression. The same *a fortiori* holds true for Jewish communities in the Roman world, who were not offered the chance to abandon their religious practices at their own request. Instead, the known tests to determine who was Jewish and who was not were imposed on them, either by Roman or by local authorities. The most prominent example of this may be found in the tests used to determine who was liable to pay the so-called Jewish Tax during the reign of Domitian (Appendix 2.59), which focused on circumcision and therefore did not offer Jewish men the same opportunity to distance themselves from their religious practices that was afforded to diviners—and to those who sympathized with Judaism but had not been circumcised. On other occasions, however, the tests that were employed focused on the consumption of pork (Appendix 2.46) or on participation in traditional Greek sacrifices (Appendix 2.54). Both of these types of tests suggest that one's status as a religious 'outsider' was not permanently determined by past behaviour but could instead be revoked by participation in accepted religious practices. The (forced) abandonment of Jewish customs, then, may be seen as an attempt not only to determine who belonged to a group that was perceived to deviate from societal norms but also to force compliance with the religious and socio-political status quo.

5.7 Marginalized Religion and the Law: A Wider Framework

What, then, can we learn from studying the legal treatment of various marginalized religious groups in the Roman world, not in isolation but rather in conjunction with each other? As has become clear from the various analyses in this study, the known legal interactions between each of these respective groups and the Roman authorities share a number of important similarities, both with measures involving other religious groups and with Roman administrative practices in general. Up to the middle of the third century CE, legal measures that in some way involved marginalized religious groups were almost exclusively highly limited in scope, both in a temporal and a geographical sense, and were strongly shaped by the particular circumstances from which they emerged. Negotiation and a strong degree of institutionalized flexibility were therefore central to shaping the legal position of all of these groups, and the arguments and procedures that shaped this process were likewise strongly similar, and reflected concerns and consideration that were very much alike. This included a strong preoccupation with upholding public order and societal cohesion, which is very likely to have contributed to the repeated occurrence of semi-legal tests to establish whether specific individuals belonged to religious groups that were considered to be disruptive, as well as the space (or indeed pressure) for members of these groups to distance themselves from practices that were unfavourably regarded. More standardized, established procedures emerged only gradually, and their appearance in later sources is best understood as later attempts to retroactively create cohesion between what were originally broad collections of disparate measures. By adopting a comparative approach, then, it becomes clear that the legal treatment of religious groups cannot be regarded as an isolated, unique area of Roman governance, but was instead in many ways strongly integrated within other areas of Roman law and administration—nor can the treatment of any of these groups be rightfully considered to have been wholly distinct or unique.

All this is not to say, of course, that the treatment of diviners, Jewish communities, and early Christians was in all respects identical either—which, given the profound importance of negotiation and the particular circumstances of each individual interaction, could hardly have been the case. Certainly, the fact that Jewish communities had access to organizational structures and formal representatives that were recognizable to the Roman authorities generally allowed them to be more easily incorporated in the existing legal framework, as did the availability of positive precedents. Such tools of negotiation were not available for early Christians, while those who opposed them could on an important number of occasions count on the backing of the local elite. Diviners likewise lacked such structures, which may serve to explain why their legal interactions with the Roman authorities generally took a more repressive turn, but did benefit from the wider prevalence of divination throughout the Graeco-Roman world, and furthermore from the fact that their religious practices did not demand exclusivity and were more easily shed or disguised. This may serve to explain why trials dealing with the practice were more often focused on specific behaviours rather than more general accusations, and why execution, as far as we can tell from the available sources, was more prevalent in trials against Christians. What stands out most, however, is that the underlying legal and administrative mechanisms, structures, and principles that shaped legal interactions between the Roman authorities and the aforementioned religious groups did not differ in any significant way: the treatment of all three groups discussed in this study was primarily intended to safeguard established religious and socio-political structures, whether this meant repression of certain practices in the form of expulsion or trials, or incorporation of the group in question—either by acknowledging its position, or by pressuring its members to conform.

Marginalized Religion and the Law in the Roman Empire. K. P. S. Janssen, Oxford University Press.
 DOI: 10.1093/9780191946400.003.0006

Appendices

The following appendices contain an overview of the known legal interactions between the Roman authorities and the different religious groups that are discussed in this study. They are primarily intended to serve as an accessible point of reference to the reader, as well as a tool for further study and comparison. The interactions listed in each appendix have been ordered chronologically insofar as possible, although the exact order of events is sometimes obscure, particularly when multiple cases involving the same group are believed to date from the same year. However, since the especially densely occupied periods overwhelmingly encompass measures that are discussed by the same author(s), particularly in the case of interactions with Jewish communities, it has generally proved possible to list these cases in the order in which they are presented by the relevant sources where the available evidence lacks specificity. Interactions for which no specific date can be determined are listed at the end of the tenure of the Roman emperor or magistrate involved. In cases where important difficulties with regard to the reliability of the sources emerged, and where the occurrence of a particular interaction (or indeed its relevance to the chapter in question) is in substantial doubt, this has been indicated by placing round brackets, or parentheses, around the alleged date of the event in question. In order to simplify the use of the appendices, each case has furthermore been assigned a numerical code consisting of the number of the appendix in which it appears, and its chronological position within that list (e.g. 1.1, 2.1, 3.1, etc.). These codes are referenced in relevant locations throughout this study.

The cases listed in these appendices have been collected from a survey of the available sources, alongside previous scholarship. A number of studies have been particularly useful in this process. The overview in Appendix 1 (Divination) is based on the various inventories presented in Frederick Cramer,[1] although a different set of descriptive categories has been introduced to better suit the needs of the present study. Furthermore, certain expulsion measures that were originally included in Cramer's study are here omitted, due to the fact they did not apply to divination but instead to some other practice that was subjected to regulations implemented by the Roman authorities. Certain primary sources cited by Cramer have likewise been disregarded for similar reasons, while a number of references that were unavailable or overlooked at his time of writing have been added. In the case of Appendix 2 (Judaism), the measures cited by Flavius Josephus in books 14 and 16 of his *Antiquitates Iudaicae* have been helpfully catalogued by Miriam Pucci Ben Zeev, and her dating of the relevant events has generally been adhered to, unless otherwise indicated.[2] It should also be noted that a number of interactions that appear in this appendix also appear in Appendix 3 (Christianity), due to the fact that the Roman authorities did not initially make a clear distinction between Jewish and Christian groups. These cases are therefore discussed from different perspectives in both chapters, and thus appear in both appendices.

[1] Cramer (1954). [2] Pucci Ben Zeev (1998).

The various Christian martyr narratives referenced in Appendix 3 may be found in a number of editions, each of which makes its own selection of texts. The work of Herbert Musurillo continues to be frequently cited and contains all martyr narratives discussed in Chapter 4,[3] but more recent, and more thoroughly annotated, editions were published by, for example, Bastiaensen, Rebillard, and Seeliger and Wischmeyer.[4]

[3] Musurillo (1972).
[4] Bastiaensen (1987); Rebillard (2017); Seeliger and Wischmeyer (2015).

APPENDIX 1

Divination

No.	Date	Type	Sources	Officials/ Institutions	Applicability	Terminology	Circumstances and Contents
1.1	213 BCE	Confiscation of divinatory texts and restriction of ritual	Livy, *Ab Urbe Condita* 25.1.6–12.	Senate; *praetor urbanus* Marcus Aemilius (or Atilius)	Rome	*sacrificuli*; *vates*	Unrest in Rome due to war. Books on prophecy and ritual are to be handed in, and sacrifice according to foreign rituals is banned.
1.2	139 BCE	Expulsion	Valerius Maximus, *Facta et Dicta Memorabilia* 1.3 (*De Superstitionibus*).3.	*Praetor peregrinus* Cnaeus Cornelius Hispalus (or Hispanus)	Rome and Italy	*chaldaei*	Diviners are expelled from Rome and Italy, possibly due to complaints or disturbances caused by false predictions.
1.3	33 BCE	Expulsion	Cassius Dio, *Historiae Romanae* 49.43.5.	Aedile Marcus Agrippa	Rome	ἀστρολόγοι; γόητες	Diviners are expelled as part of a wider programme intended to restore public order and win popular favour.
1.4	12 BCE	Confiscation of divinatory texts	Suetonius, *De vita Caesarum: Augustus* 31.1; Tacitus, *Annales* 6.12.	*Pontifex Maximus* Augustus	Rome	*fatidicorum librorum* (Suet.)	Books on divination are collected and destroyed, with the exception of the Sibylline books (if they were deemed genuine). These 'approved' books are placed in the temple of Apollo.
1.5	(11 CE)	Regulation of divinatory enquiries	Cassius Dio, *Historiae Romanae* 56.25.5–6.	Augustus (by imperial edict?)	Unspecified	μάντεις	Ban on enquiries about the death of any individual, and on divination without witnesses. Possibly repeated in 1.10.

Continued

Continued

No.	Date	Type	Sources	Officials/ Institutions	Applicability	Terminology	Circumstances and Contents
1.6	16 CE	Trial involving consultation of diviners	Cassius Dio, *Historiae Romanae* 57.15.4; *Fasti Amiternini*, CIL 1_2, p. 244; Seneca, *Epistulae* 70.10; Suetonius, *De vita Caesarum: Tiberius* 25.1; Tacitus, *Annales* 2.27–32; Velleius Paterculus, *Historia Romana* 2.130.3.	Senate; Tiberius	Marcus Scribonius Libo Drusus; in Rome	*chaldaei*; *magi*; *somniorum interpretes* (Tac.)	Tacitus suggests that Libo was brought to trial on the basis of certain divinatory enquiries, although this was likely not the formal charge. The other sources reference charges of treason, but make no mention of divination.
1.7	16/17 CE[1]	Expulsion	Cassius Dio, *Historiae Romanae* 57.15.8–9; Suetonius, *De vita Caesarum: Tiberius* 36; Tacitus, *Annales* 2.32; Ulpian, *De Officio Proconsulis 7* in *Leg. Mos. et Rom. Coll.* 15.2.1.	Senate; Tiberius (by *senatus consultum*)	Rome and Italy	*ἀστρολόγοι*; *γόητες* (Cass. Dio); *mathematici* (Suet.); *mathematici*; *magi* (Tac.); *mathematici*; *chaldaei*; *arioli et ceteri* (Ulp.)	Diviners expelled from Rome and Italy. Tacitus links these events to the trial of Drusus in 1.6, as well as to the execution of two diviners in 1.9. Dio mentions execution for foreign diviners and expulsion from Rome for citizens. Suetonius simply mentions expulsion. Possibly repeated in 1.8.
1.8	16/17 CE	Expulsion	Cassius Dio, *Historiae Romanae* 57.15.8–9; Tacitus, *Annales* 2.32.	Senate; Tiberius (by *senatus consultum*)	Rome and Italy	*ἀστρολόγοι*; *γόητες* (Cass. Dio); *mathematici*; *magi* (Tac.)	Likely a repetition of 1.7, which may have proved ineffectual. Dio makes an explicit distinction between two measures; Tacitus' version is less clear.
1.9	16/17 CE[2]	Execution of diviners	Tacitus, *Annales* 2.32.	Unspecified	Lucius Pituanius and Publius Marcius; in Rome	*mathematici*; *magi*	Likely related to 1.7, although it remains unclear why these two diviners were punished separately.

[1] See Goodyear (1981), 284–5 and Ripat (2011), 119–20 for the issue of the date.
[2] While Tacitus dates this event to 16 CE, its possible connection to the Tiberian expulsion(s) suggests that it may have taken place in 17 CE instead.

No.	Date	Type	Sources	Officials/ Institutions	Applicability	Terminology	Circumstances and Contents
1.10	19 CE?[3]	Regulation of divinatory enquiries	Suetonius, *De vita Caesarum: Tiberius* 63	Tiberius	Likely Rome	*haruspices*; *oracula*	Possibly a reiteration of 1.5. The consultation of diviners without the presence of witnesses is banned and oracles near the city are closed. Consultations about an individual's death are not mentioned.
1.11	19 CE	Confiscation of divinatory texts	Cassius Dio, *Historiae Romanae* 57.18.4–5.	Tiberius	Likely Rome	–	Tiberius investigates divinatory texts circulating in the city in response to a dire prediction, and has unauthorized works destroyed. Likely repetition of 1.4, and connected to 1.14.
1.12	20 CE	Trial involving consultation of diviners	Suetonius, *De vita Caesarum: Tiberius* 49.1; Tacitus, *Annales* 3.22–3.	Senate; Tiberius	Aemilia Lepida; in Rome	*chaldaei* (Tac.)	Tacitus mentions a number of charges, including 'enquiries against the imperial family'. However, the focus is on poisoning, which is the only charge referenced by Suetonius.
1.13	(26 CE)	Trial	Cassius Dio, *Historiae Romanae* 59.19.1; Tacitus, *Annales* 4.52.	Unspecified; possibly Tiberius	Claudia Pulchra; in Rome	–	Dio mentions no charge, but Tacitus seems to focus on adultery, alongside poisoning and magic against the emperor. No mention of divination is made.
1.14	32 CE	Regulation of divinatory texts	Tacitus, *Annales* 6.12.	Tiberius	Likely Rome	–	Tiberius rebukes a tribune of plebs for entering a prediction ascribed to the Sibyl into the official collection without his knowledge or involvement. In doing so, he references Augustus' earlier measure 1.4. Likely connected to 1.11.

[3] Date suggested by Kippenberg (1997), 154.

Continued

Continued

No.	Date	Type	Sources	Officials/ Institutions	Applicability	Terminology	Circumstances and Contents
1.15	(32 CE)	Trial	Seneca Maior, *Suasoriae* 2.22; Tacitus, *Annales* 6.9.	Senate	Mamercus Aemilius Scaurus; in Rome	–	Both authors only mention *maiestas*.
–	(34 CE)	Trial	Cassius Dio, *Historiae Romanae* 58.24.3–5; Tacitus *Annales* 6.29.	Unspecified	Mamercus Aemilius Scaurus; in Rome	–	Both sources mention adultery with Claudia Livia Julia (Livilla) as the formal charge, although a tragedy composed by the accused seems to have been the original cause of disfavour. Tacitus mentions Scaurus' involvement in magical rites.
1.16	(40/1 CE)	Trial against a diviner	Cassius Dio, *Historiae Romanae* 59.29.4.	Caligula; likely also *praefectus Aegypti* Gaius Vitrasius Pollio	Apollonius; from Egypt	*προλέγειν*	Diviner from Egypt makes predictions about the violent death of Caligula (possibly during the unrests in Alexandria) and is brought to Rome to be tried there. The execution is never carried out. Note the similarities to 1.34.
1.17	47 CE	Trial involving divination	Tacitus, *Annales* 11.4.	Senate	The brothers Petra; in Rome	*praedicere*	Two brothers are brought to trial, according to Tacitus because they had facilitated an affair between the actor Mnester and Poppaea Sabina Maior, a rival of Empress Messalina. The charge against them, however, is that one of them had a politically charged dream about Emperor Claudius, which causes both brothers to be executed.

No.	Date	Type	Sources	Officials/ Institutions	Applicability	Terminology	Circumstances and Contents
1.18	49 CE	Trial involving consultation of diviners	Tacitus, *Annales* 12.22.	Senate; Claudius	Lollia Paulina; in Rome	*chaldaei*; *magi*; *Apollinis Clarii simulacrum*	Accusations of consulting diviners, as well as Apollo, on the subject of the imperial marriage.
1.19	52 CE	Trial involving consultation of diviners	Tacitus, *Annales* 12.52.	Unspecified	Furius Camillus Scribonianus and his mother Vibia; in Rome	*chaldaei*	Scribonianus allegedly consulted astrologers about the health of the emperor and is banished alongside his mother. His family was strongly connected to rebellion, even raising an army some ten years earlier.
1.20	52 CE	Expulsion	Cassius Dio, *Historiae Romanae* ep.61.33.1; Tacitus, *Annales* 12.52.	Senate; Claudius (by *senatus consultum*)	Rome and Italy	ἀστρολόγοι (Cass. Dio); *mathematici* (Tac.)	Diviners expelled from Italy. Tacitus claims the measure was both harsh and ineffective, and may suggest a connection to 1.19.
1.21	(53 CE)	Trial	Tacitus, *Annales* 12.59.	Senate	T. Statilius Taurus; in Rome	–	Accusation of extortion and (according to Tacitus) especially *magicas supersitiones*. No clear mention of divination.
1.22	(54 CE)	Trial	Suetonius, *De vita Caesarum: Nero* 7.1; Tacitus, *Annales* 12.65.	Unspecified	Domitia Lepida; in Rome	–	Lepida is accused of using magic against Agrippina, and imperfect control of her slaves in Italy. There is no clear mention of divination in either source.
1.23	Pre 66 CE	Banishment of diviner	Tacitus, *Annales* 16.14.	Unspecified	Pammenes; in Rome (?)	*chaldaei*	Mention of a diviner in exile, although no further details are provided. Connection to 1.24.

Continued

Continued

No.	Date	Type	Sources	Officials/ Institutions	Applicability	Terminology	Circumstances and Contents
1.24	66 CE	Accusations related to consultation of diviners	Tacitus, *Annales* 16.14.	Likely Nero	P. Anteius and Ostorius Scapula; in Rome (?)	–	Mention of consultations about the accused's own welfare and that of the emperor. No official trial takes place. Connection to 1.23.
1.25	66 CE	Trial involving consultation of diviners	Cassius Dio, *Historiae Romanae* ep.62.26.3; Tacitus, *Annales* 16.23 and 16.30–2.	Senate	Barea Soranus and his daughter Servilia; in Rome	*μάγευμα* (Cass. Dio); *magi* (Tac.)	Tacitus claims the father was accused of instigating rebellion in his province. His daughter allegedly consulted diviners about the welfare of her father. Both are executed in connection to a larger conspiracy. Dio states only that the father practised some form of magic via his daughter.
1.26	(68 CE)	Expulsion	Cod. Paris. suppl. gr. 607A.	Nero (by imperial edict)	Rome and Italy	*ἀστρολόγοι; γόητες*	Reference to an expulsion of diviners from Italy without further context. Likely a wrongly dated reference to 1.28.
1.27	(Pre-69 CE?)	Banishment of diviner	Juvenal, *Saturae* 6. 557–9; Plutarch, *Galba* 23.4; Suetonius, *De vita Caesarum: Otho* 4.1 and 6.1; Tacitus, *Historiae* 1.22.	Unspecified	Ptolemy Seleucus (?); in Rome (?)	*mathematici* (Juv.); *μάντεις; χαλδαῖοι* (Plut.); *mathematici* (Suet.); *mathematici* (Tac.)	All sources mention Seleucus' attempts to urge Otho to seize the throne, but his punishment generally goes unmentioned. Juvenal's reference seems to imply multiple banishments but is ultimately unclear.

No.	Date	Type	Sources	Officials/ Institutions	Applicability	Terminology	Circumstances and Contents
1.28	69 CE	Expulsion; possibly executions of diviners	Cassius Dio, *Historiae Romanae* ep.64.1.4; Suetonius, *De vita Caesarum: Vitellius* 14.4; Tacitus, *Historiae* 2.62; Zonaras 11.15.D.	Vitellius (by imperial edict)	Rome and Italy	*mathematici* (Tac.); *mathematici* (Suet.); ἀστρολόγοι (Cass. Dio); ἀστρονόμοι; γόητες (Zon.)	Tacitus mentions an expulsion from Italy without further context, while Suetonius also includes the execution of astrologers and authors of invective without a trial. Dio claims that the astrologers retaliated. Zonaras alone mentions two separate expulsions of astrologers and sorcerers respectively, but his late date makes this doubtful.
1.29	70 CE	Expulsion	Cassius Dio, *Historiae Romanae* ep.65.9.2.	Vespasian (by imperial edict)	Rome	ἀστρολόγοι	Expulsion of diviners from Rome, although Vespasian appears to have used divination himself.
1.30	89 CE?	Banishment and trial involving consultation of diviners	Cassius Dio, *Historiae Romanae* ep.67.12.2–4; Suetonius, *De Vita Caesarum: Domitianus* 10.3; cf. Suetonius, *De vita Caesarum: Vespasianus* 14.	Domitian	Mettius Pompusianus; in Rome	ἀστρολόγοι	Pompusianus is linked to divination in both sources, but this was likely combined with other accusations. Dio states that the accused was first banished, then executed.
1.31	(89/90 CE)	Expulsion	Jerome, *Chronicon* AD 89–90.	Domitian (by imperial edict)	Rome	*mathematici*	Expulsion of diviners and philosophers from Rome, without further context. Possibly repeated in 1.32.

Continued

Continued

No.	Date	Type	Sources	Officials/ Institutions	Applicability	Terminology	Circumstances and Contents
1.32	(93 CE)	Expulsion	Jerome, *Chronicon* AD 93–4; *Suda* on Domitian.	Domitian (by imperial edict)	Rome	*mathematici*	Possibly repetition of 1.31, although both references are questionable. Cassius Dio, Pliny the Younger, Philostratus, and Suetonius mention an expulsion of philosophers exclusively.
1.33	96 CE	Execution of a diviner	Cod. Paris. suppl. gr. 607A; Cassius Dio *Historiae Romanae* ep.67.16.3; Suetonius, *De vita Caesarum: Domitianus* 15.3.	Domitian	Ascletario; in Rome	*mathematici* (Suet.)	All sources mention that Domitian ordered the diviner to predict the manner of his own death, and then had him slain to prove predictions about his own approaching death false. However, none mentions a real trial. The name of the diviner is in doubt.
1.34	96 CE	Trial against a diviner	Cod. Paris. suppl. gr. 607A; Cassius Dio, *Historiae Romanae* ep.67.16.2; Suetonius, *De vita Caesarum: Domitianus* 16.1.	Domitian; likely also the local Roman governor	Larginus Proculus; from Germania	*προλέγω* (Cass. Dio); *haruspex* (Suet.)	Dio's account shows strong similarities to 1.16 in that the diviner was convicted but survived due to the death of the emperor. Suetonius mentions only that the soothsayer was convicted, but gives no further details.

No.	Date	Type	Sources	Officials/ Institutions	Applicability	Terminology	Circumstances and Contents
1.35	(137 CE?)[4]	Trial involving consultation of diviners	Cassius Dio, *Historiae Romanae* ep.69.17.1; Scriptor Historiae Augustae, *Hadrianus* 23.3.	Likely Hadrian	Pedanius Fuscus; in Rome	*praesagia; ostenta* (SHA)	Dio mentions only that Fuscus and his grandfather were executed because they disagreed with the emperor's choice of successor. The SHA suggests that Fuscus wanted imperial power, and therefore consulted diviners.
1.36	(Pre-*c.* 155 CE)	Regulation of divinatory texts	Justin Martyr, *1 Apology* 44.12	Unspecified	Unspecified	–	Justin suggests that people who read oracular texts were condemned to death.
1.37	138–61 CE	Unspecified; measure against diviners	Ulpian, *De Officio Proconsulis* 7 in *Leg. Mos. et Rom. Coll.* 15.2.4.	Antoninus Pius (by rescript to governor Pacatus)[5]	Gallia Lugdunensis	–	Ulpian claims to cite a rescript sent to the governor, but gives no indication of where his own analysis stops and where the transcript of the imperial order begins. As a result, the contents of the measure are unclear.
1.38	175 CE?	Banishment of diviner	*Digesta* 48.19.30; Tertullian, *De Idolatria* 9.2; Ulpian, *De Officio Proconsulis* 7 in *Leg. Mos. et Rom. Coll.* 15.2.5. Cf. Scriptor Historiae Augustae, *Marcus Aurelius* 13.6.	Marcus Aurelius (by rescript)	Unnamed diviner; from an unknown location	*vaticinati* (Ulp.)	Ulpian mentions the expulsion of a single diviner in connection to the rebellion of Avidius Cassius. The passage from the *Digesta* confirms that Marcus Aurelius ordered an expulsion of some kind. Tertullian provides only a vague reference.

[4] This date is given by Potter (1994), 161. Cramer (1954), 268 suggests 138 CE.
[5] The argument that we are dealing with a rescript, rather than a decree, is made in Nogrady (2006), 196n.950.

Continued

Continued

No.	Date	Type	Sources	Officials/ Institutions	Applicability	Terminology	Circumstances and Contents
1.39	(189 CE?)	Trial involving consultation of diviners	Scriptor Historiae Augustae, *Septimius Severus* 2.8–4.3.	Unnamed praetorian prefect under Commodus	Septimius Severus; in Rome	*astrologi*; *mathematici*; *vates*; *chaldaei*	Septimius Severus is allegedly tried, but acquitted, for receiving predictions about his imperial future.
1.40	199 CE	Regulation of divinatory practices	P. Yale Inv. 299.	*Praefectus Aegypti* Q. Aemilius Saturninus	Egypt	*μαντεία*; *χρησμοί*; *κωμασία*	Diviners in Egypt are threatened with capital punishment if they do not abandon their profession. Various types of divination are mentioned, including local Egyptian practices.
1.41	205 CE	Trial involving consultation of diviners	Cassius Dio, *Historiae Romanae* ep.77.8.1; Scriptor Historiae Augustae, *Septimius Severus* 15.5.	Senate; Septimius Severus	Popilius Pedo Apronianus; trial in Rome *in absentia*	*chaldaei*; *vates* (SHA)	Combined charge of divination and magic: the accused's nurse apparently dreamed that he would become emperor, and he himself applied magic to this end.
1.42	Early third century CE	Legal analysis	Ulpian, *De Officio Proconsulis* 7 in *Leg. Mos. et Rom. Coll.* 15.2.	Ulpian	–	*mathematici*; *chaldaei*; *arioli et ceteris*; *vaticinatores*	Ulpian states that diviners of all kinds are to be banished and relieved of their possessions if they are citizens, and killed if they are not. He references a legal debate about whether the knowledge or practice of divination is to be banned, and furthermore argues that divinatory consultations should be punished according to the nature of the enquiry, stating that enquiries about the death of the emperor are to be punished more severely than questions about oneself and one's relatives.

No.	Date	Type	Sources	Officials/ Institutions	Applicability	Terminology	Circumstances and Contents
1.43	Early third century CE	Punishment of diviners	Ulpian, *Ad Edictum* 77 in *Digesta* 47.10.15.13.	Unknown (possibly by imperial rescript)[6]	–	*astrologus vel qui aliquam illicitam divinationem pollicetur* (?)	The passage suggests a legal procedure for retaliating against a diviner who falsely accused someone of being a thief. Since the passage is likely redacted, the nature of this procedure is now impossible to determine.
1.44	Third century CE	Legal analysis	Pseudo-Paul, *Sententiae* 5.21.	Pseudo-Paul	–	*mathematici*; *harioli*; *haruspices*; *vaticinatores*; *divinatio*	Pseudo-Paul notes that diviners (*vaticinatores*) should be expelled due to concerns for public order, and adds that first-time offenders should be flogged and expelled from the city. Those who persist are thrown in prison or sent into exile. It is also noted that consultations about the welfare of the emperor (or, for slaves, that of their master) warrant capital punishment. The jurist recommends against possessing any knowledge about divination at all.

[6] For the theory that the passage was edited to reference the later imperial *constitutiones* rather than a rescript, see Sánchez-Moreno Ellart (2009), 207–8 and 221–2.

APPENDIX 2

Judaism

No.	Date	Type	Sources	Officials/ Institutions	Applicability	Terminology	Circumstances and Contents
2.1	161 BCE	Political treaty	1 Maccabees 8.17–32; Flavius Josephus, *Antiquitates Iudaicae* 12.10.6 (414–19).	Senate (by *senatus consultum*)	Judea/Judas Maccabeus	*Ἰουδαῖοι* (Macc.); *Ἰουδαῖοι* (Jos.)	Treaty of allegiance between Rome and the Maccabees against the Seleucid Empire. Mutual support is promised where possible. Connection to 2.2, 2.3, 2.5, and 2.6.
2.2	161 BCE[1]	Diplomatic missive	Flavius Josephus, *Antiquitates Iudaicae* 14.10.15 (233).	Consul (?) Gaius Fannius, son of Gaius; message to the magistrates of Cos	Cos	*Ἰουδαῖοι*	Gaius Fannius asks the magistrates of Cos to respect the decision of the senate in 2.1 and to grant the Jewish ambassadors safe passage. Note that Cos is not yet part of the empire nor of the Seleucid sphere of influence. Connection to 2.1, 2.3, 2.5, and 2.6.
2.3	144 BCE[2]	Political treaty	1 Maccabees 12.1–4; Flavius Josephus, *Antiquitates Iudaicae* 13.5.8 (163–5 and 169–70).	Senate	Judea/Jonathan Apphus	*Ἰουδαῖοι* (Macc.); *Ἰουδαῖοι* (Jos.)	League of friendship from 2.1 is renewed. The senate also gives the ambassadors letters to guarantee their safe conduct in- and outside of the Roman territories. Connection to 2.1, 2.2, 2.5, and 2.6.
2.4	139 BCE	Expulsion	Valerius Maximus, *Facta et Dicta Memorabilia* 1.3 (*De Superstitionibus*).3.	*Praetor peregrinus* Cnaeus Cornelius Hispalus (or Hispanus)	Rome	*Iudaei*	Expulsion of Jews from Rome due to the alleged spread of Jewish rites.

[1] Gera (1998), 310.

[2] Baltrusch (2002), 98.

No.	Date	Type	Sources	Officials/ Institutions	Applicability	Terminology	Circumstances and Contents
2.5	134–104 BCE	Political treaty	Flavius Josephus, *Antiquitates Iudaicae* 13.9.2 (259–66).	Senate	Judea/Hyrcanus I	*Ἰουδαῖοι*	League of friendship from 2.1 is renewed. The senate will later deliberate about the delegation's other questions (restoration of lands, etc.). Praetor Fannius, son of Marcus, ensures the delegation's safe passage home. Connection to 2.1, 2.2, 2.3, and 2.6.
2.6	134–104 BCE[3]	Political treaty	Flavius Josephus, *Antiquitates Iudaicae* 14.10.22 (247–55).	Magistrates of Pergamum (by *ψήφισμα*)	Pergamum	*Ἰουδαῖοι*	Pergamum decrees that it will follow Roman example and enter into a league of friendship with Judea. Connection to 2.1, 2.2, 2.3, and 2.5.
2.7	62 BCE	Restriction on Jewish customs	Cicero, *Pro Flacco* 67–9.	Governor Lucius Valerius Flaccus (by edict)	Asia	*Iudaei*	Ban on exporting gold from Asia, by which the Jewish Temple Tax is particularly affected. Earlier measures by the senate regarding the export of gold may have served as precedent but no specifics are given. Protests by Jewish community of Rome break out in response.
2.8	49 BCE	Protection of Jewish customs	Flavius Josephus, *Antiquitates Iudaicae* 14.10.13 (228–9).	Consul Lucius Lentulus	Ephesus	*Ἰουδαῖοι*	Jews who are Roman citizens are exempt from military duties because of their religious beliefs. Connection to 2.9, 2.10, 2.11, 2.13, and 2.14.

[3] Rajak (2002[b]), 308.

Continued

Continued

No.	Date	Type	Sources	Officials/ Institutions	Applicability	Terminology	Circumstances and Contents
2.9	49/48 BCE	Protection of Jewish customs	Flavius Josephus, *Antiquitates Iudaicae* 14.10.13 (230).	Legate and propraetor Titus Ampius Balbus; message to the magistrates, council and people of Ephesus	Ephesus	Ἰουδαῖοι	Balbus passes on Lentulus' orders from 2.8. He mentions that he himself has petitioned the consul and others to obtain the exemption from military service. No mention of Roman citizenship is made. Connection to 2.8, 2.10, 2.11, 2.13, and 2.14.
2.10	49/48 BCE	Protection of Jewish customs	Flavius Josephus, *Antiquitates Iudaicae* 14.10.14 (231–2).	Legate Marcus Piso; message by the magistrates of Delos (and Sardis)	Unspecified, but likely Delos (and Sardis)	Ἰουδαῖοι	On the basis of 2.8, the Roman legate has issued the order that Jews who are Roman citizens are exempt from military duty and should not be bothered about this issue. The Delian magistrates confirm this order, as do the people of Sardis. Connection to 2.8, 2.9, 2.11, 2.13, and 2.14.
2.11	49 BCE	Protection of Jewish customs	Flavius Josephus, *Antiquitates Iudaicae* 14.10.16 (234).	Consul Lucius Lentulus	Ephesus	Ἰουδαῖοι	A shorter version of the exemption from military service in 2.8. Connection to 2.8, 2.9, 2.10, 2.13, and 2.14.
2.12	49 BCE	Protection of Jewish customs	Flavius Josephus, *Antiquitates Iudaicae* 14.10.17 (235).	Proquaestor and propraetor Lucius Antonius; message to the magistrates, council and people of Sardis	Sardis	Ἰουδαῖοι	Message to officials in Sardis concerning a petition requesting that Jews should be allowed to hold their own assemblies according to their ancestral laws, and should have access to their own meeting place to judge internal legal issues. This request has been granted.

No.	Date	Type	Sources	Officials/ Institutions	Applicability	Terminology	Circumstances and Contents
2.13	49 BCE	Protection of Jewish customs	Flavius Josephus, *Antiquitates Iudaicae* 14.10.18 (236–7).	Lucius Lentulus; petition by Marcus Publius, son of Spurius; Marcus, son of Marcus; Lucius, son of Publius on behalf of Dositheos the Alexandrian	Unspecified, but likely Asia	*Ἰουδαῖοι*	Likely a description of the petition that led to Lentulus' decision in 2.8. One Dositheos (likely Jewish himself) appears to have intervened in the matter of military service on behalf of those Jews who were Roman citizens. Connection to 2.8, 2.9, 2.10, 2.11, and 2.14.
2.14	49 BCE	Protection of Jewish customs	Flavius Josephus, *Antiquitates Iudaicae* 14.10.19 (237–40).	Lucius Lentulus (by *δόγμα*)	Ephesus	*Ἰουδαῖοι*	Longest version of the exemption from military service presented in 2.8. Connection to 2.8, 2.9, 2.10, 2.11, and 2.13.
2.15	*c.* 47 BCE	Political treaty	Flavius Josephus, *Antiquitates Iudaicae* 14.10.1 (185).	Gaius Julius Caesar; petition by Hyrcanus II	Judea/Hyrcanus II	–	Request to confirm friendship and allegiance.
2.16	(*c.* 47 BCE?)	Confirmation of citizenship	Flavius Josephus, *Antiquitates Iudaicae* 14.10.1 (188); *Contra Apionem* 2.4 (37).	Gaius Julius Caesar or Augustus?	Alexandria	*Ἰουδαῖοι*	Claim that Caesar (or Augustus) confirmed the right to citizenship of all Alexandrian Jews and inscribed this on a bronze tablet.
2.17	47 BCE	Political treaty	Flavius Josephus, *Antiquitates Iudaicae* 14.10.2 (190–5).	Gaius Julius Caesar; message to the magistrates, council and people of Sidon	Sidon	*Ἰουδαῖοι*	Caesar orders Sidon to set up a bronze tablet proclaiming the status of Hyrcanus and Caesar's friendship and allegiance with him. Hyrcanus is granted the right to judge Jewish matters, although it is unclear if this applies to Judea alone or to the Diaspora as well. No stationing of troops or money is to be demanded. Connection to 2.18, 2.19, 2.20, 2.26, and 2.27.

Continued

Continued

No.	Date	Type	Sources	Officials/ Institutions	Applicability	Terminology	Circumstances and Contents
2.18	47 BCE?	Political treaty	Flavius Josephus, *Antiquitates Iudaicae* 14.10.3 (196–8).	Gaius Julius Caesar; possibly the senate?[4]	Sidon, Tyre, and Ascalon	Ἰουδαῖοι	Likely an abbreviated version of 2.17. Hyrcanus is described as protector of all Jews who are unjustly treated. Connection to 2.17, 2.19, 2.20, 2.26, and 2.27.
2.19	47 BCE?	Political treaty	Flavius Josephus, *Antiquitates Iudaicae* 14.10.4 (199).	Gaius Julius Caesar; possibly the senate?[5]	Judea/Hyrcanus II	–	Caesar confirms Hyrcanus and his descendants as high priests. Connection to 2.17, 2.18, 2.20, 2.26, and 2.27.
2.20	47 BCE?	Political treaty	Flavius Josephus, *Antiquitates Iudaicae* 14.10.6 (202–10).	Gaius Julius Caesar; possibly the senate?[6]	Judea/Hyrcanus II?	Ἰουδαῖοι	Some regulations regarding taxes, which do not have to be paid in the Sabbath year; no troops should be raised from the Jewish territories; Joppa is given to Hyrcanus, as well as a number of villages and possessions in Syria and Phoenicia; Jewish rights remain in effect, as do privileges previously granted by the Roman senate; some privileges are granted to Hyrcanus and family. Connection to 2.17, 2.18, 2.19, 2.26, and 2.27.
2.21	47/46 BCE	Protection of Jewish customs	Flavius Josephus, *Antiquitates Iudaicae* 14.10.8 (215); possibly also Suetonius, *De vita Caesarum: Iulius* 42.3.	Gaius Julius Caesar	Rome	Ἰουδαῖοι	Caesar bans all *collegia* in the city of Rome, except those of notable antiquity. The Josephus text suggests that Jews are exempt.

[4] See Pucci Ben Zeev (1998), 55.
[5] See Pucci Ben Zeev (1998), 68.
[6] See Pucci Ben Zeev (1998), 80.

No.	Date	Type	Sources	Officials/ Institutions	Applicability	Terminology	Circumstances and Contents
2.22	47/46 BCE	Protection of Jewish customs	Flavius Josephus, *Antiquitates Iudaicae* 14.10.20 (241–3).	Governor Gaius Rabirius, son of Gaius; letter from the magistrates of Laodicea	Laodicea	*Ἰουδαῖοι*	Envoys from Hyrcanus have brought a letter declaring that the governor allowed Jews to observe the Sabbath and perform their ancestral rites. Delegates from Tralles objected but were overruled, and the governor was asked to write to Laodicea as well. Laodicea promises to observe these rulings.
2.23	Post-June 47 BCE?	Protection of Jewish customs	Flavius Josephus, *Antiquitates Iudaicae* 14.10.23 (256–8).	People of Halicarnassus (by *ψήφισμα*)	Halicarnassus	*Ἰουδαῖοι*	Following Roman example, Halicarnassus decides to allow Jews to perform their devotions and observe their festivals and religious gatherings. They may also build places of prayer. Anyone who prevents them should be fined.
2.24	Post-October 47 BCE?	Protection of Jewish customs	Flavius Josephus, *Antiquitates Iudaicae* 14.10.24 (259–61).	Magistrates, council, and people of Sardis (by *ψήφισμα*)	Sardis	*Ἰουδαῖοι*	Jewish delegation has asked the council of Sardis for permission to maintain their customs, to hold meetings, and to judge their own legal cases, referencing decisions made by the city in the past and a proclamation by the Roman senate restoring their rights. They also request a location to offer sacrifices and prayers. Permission is granted, and market officials are ordered to provide suitable food.

Continued

Continued

No.	Date	Type	Sources	Officials/ Institutions	Applicability	Terminology	Circumstances and Contents
2.25	46–44 BCE?	Protection of Jewish customs	Flavius Josephus, *Antiquitates Iudaicae* 14.10.21 (244–6).	Governor Publius Servilius Galba; message to the magistrates, council, and people of Miletus	Miletus	*Ἰουδαῖοι*	Response to a petition. Jews have been prevented from observing the Sabbath, performing their ancestral rights, and managing their produce. The governor has heard the two parties and determines that Jews should be allowed to follow their own customs.
2.26	44 BCE	Political treaty	Flavius Josephus, *Antiquitates Iudaicae* 14.10.5 (200–1).	Gaius Julius Caesar; possibly the senate?[7]	Judea	*Ἰουδαῖοι*	Walls may be built around Jerusalem and Hyrcanus is in charge of the city. Some tax regulations are issued. Connection to 2.17, 2.18, 2.19, 2.20, and 2.27.
2.27	44 BCE	Political treaty	Flavius Josephus, *Antiquitates Iudaicae* 14.10.7 (211–12).	Gaius Julius Caesar; speech before the senate; possibly the senate (by *senatus consultum*)	Judea/Hyrcanus II	*Ἰουδαῖοι*	Caesar recommends that Hyrcanus and his people should be formally thanked for their help and loyalty. Connection to 2.17, 2.18, 2.19, 2.20, and 2.26.
2.28	44 BCE	Political treaty	Flavius Josephus, *Antiquitates Iudaicae* 14.10.10 (219–22).	Senate (by *senatus consultum*)	Judea/Hyrcanus II	*Ἰουδαῖοι*	Caesar's decrees regarding Judea are confirmed by the senate at the behest of Mark Antony and Dolabella, since they had not yet been entered in the records. This is likely a response to a delegation sent by Hyrcanus.
2.29	43 BCE	Protection of Jewish customs	Flavius Josephus, *Antiquitates Iudaicae* 14.10.11 (223–4).	Governor Dolabella of Asia; petition by Hyrcanus II	Asia	*Ἰουδαῖοι*	Petition to exempt Jews (likely specifically those living in Asia) from military service and to maintain their native customs. Connection to 2.30.

[7] See Pucci Ben Zeev (1998), 74.

No.	Date	Type	Sources	Officials/ Institutions	Applicability	Terminology	Circumstances and Contents
2.30	43 BCE	Protection of Jewish customs	Flavius Josephus, *Antiquitates Iudaicae* 14.10.12 (225–7).	Governor Dolabella of Asia; message to the magistrates, council and people of Ephesus	Asia	*Ἰουδαῖοι*	Response to the petition in 2.29. Dolabella exempts Jews from military service because of the Sabbath and dietary restrictions. He also grants them the right to meet for holy rites and to perform sacrifices. He bases this on proclamations of governors before him and asks local Ephesian officials to spread these instructions. No mention is made of consultations with central Roman authorities. Connection to 2.29.
2.31	42 BCE	Protection of Jewish customs	Flavius Josephus, *Antiquitates Iudaicae* 14.10.25 (262–4).	People of Ephesus (by *ψήφισμα*); Roman governor	Ephesus	*Ἰουδαῖοι*	The city's Jewish community asked the governor for permission to observe the Sabbath and their native customs. Since this permission has been granted, Ephesus repeats the command.
2.32	42/41 BCE	Protection of Jewish customs	Flavius Josephus, *Antiquitates Iudaicae* 14.10.8 (213–16). Cf. Philo of Alexandria, *Legatio ad Gaium* 311–12.	Octavian? Message to the magistrates, council and people of Paros (or Parium)[8]	Parium (or Paros); Delos and other surrounding islands	*Ἰουδαῖοι*	Response to a Jewish embassy, which claimed that Jews had been prevented from observing their rites and customs. The measure stipulates that they should be allowed to collect their money and hold common meals. Reference to Caesar's measures mentioned under 2.21.

[8] See Eckhardt (2018^{b}), 64–5; Pucci Ben Zeev (1998), 110.

Continued

Continued

No.	Date	Type	Sources	Officials/ Institutions	Applicability	Terminology	Circumstances and Contents
2.33	*c.* 41 BCE	Political treaty	Flavius Josephus, *Antiquitates Iudaicae* 14.12.3 (306–13).	Mark Antony; message to Hyrcanus II; delegation on behalf of Hyrcanus II	Judea/Hyrcanus II	Ἰουδαῖοι	Response to an embassy asking for renewal of the treaty of friendship between Judea and Rome. Jews who were sold as slaves by Gaius Cassius are to be released. Privileges granted by Antony and Dolabella are confirmed. Tyre should cease hostilities and give back conquered territories. Connection to 2.34, 2.35, and 2.36.
2.34	*c.* 41 BCE	Political treaty	Flavius Josephus, *Antiquitates Iudaicae* 14.12.4 (314–18).	Mark Antony; message to the magistrates, council and people of Tyre	Tyre	Ἰουδαῖοι	Envoys from Hyrcanus have complained that territories have been conquered by Tyre. Antony orders that these should be given back. Connection to 2.33, 2.35, and 2.36.
2.35	*c.* 41 BCE	Political treaty	Flavius Josephus, *Antiquitates Iudaicae* 14.12.5 (319–22).	Mark Antony; message to the magistrates, council and people of Tyre	Tyre	Ἰουδαῖοι	Order to give back territories and possessions, and release slaves. Connection to 2.33, 2.34, and 2.36.
2.36	*c.* 41 BCE	Political treaty	Flavius Josephus, *Antiquitates Iudaicae* 14.12.6 (323).	Mark Antony; message to the people of Sidon, Antioch, and Aradus	Sidon, Antioch, and Aradus	–	Order to give back territories and possessions, and release slaves. Connection to 2.33, 2.34, and 2.35.
2.37	14 BCE?	Protection of Jewish customs	Flavius Josephus, *Antiquitates Iudaicae* 16.6.4 (167–8). See also Flavius Josephus, *Antiquitates Iudaicae* 12.3.2 (125–8) and 16.2.3–5 (27–65).	Marcus Agrippa; message to the magistrates, council, and people of Ephesus	Ephesus	Ἰουδαῖοι	Jews of Asia should be granted the right to control the sacred money meant for the Temple in Jerusalem. Those who steal this money are to be treated as temple robbers. Agrippa has also written to the praetor to make sure that Jews do not have to appear in court during the Sabbath. Connection to 2.38, 2.39, 2.40, 2.41, and 2.42.

No.	Date	Type	Sources	Officials/ Institutions	Applicability	Terminology	Circumstances and Contents
2.38	14 BCE?	Protection of Jewish customs	Flavius Josephus, *Antiquitates Iudaicae* 16.6.5 (169–70).	Marcus Agrippa; message to the magistrates, council, and people of Cyrene	Cyrene	Ἰουδαῖοι	This Jewish community has complained that the money meant for the Temple was taken from them. Agrippa orders that it should be restored. Reference to a previous (though likely recent) letter from Augustus to the praetor of Libya regarding the Jews of Cyrene. Connection to 2.37, 2.39, 2.40, 2.41, and 2.42.
2.39	12 BCE	Protection of Jewish customs	Flavius Josephus, *Antiquitates Iudaicae* 16.6.2 (162–5); Philo of Alexandria, *Legatio ad Gaium* 291; 311–13.	Augustus	Asia	Ἰουδαῖοι (Jos.)	Augustus notes that Jews have been seen as allies since the time of Caesar. They should be allowed to maintain their ancestral customs and should be allowed to send money to Jerusalem. Jews also should not be compelled to appear in court during the Sabbath. Their sacred money and books are inviolable. Whoever breaks these rules, shall be seen as sacrilegious. Connection to 2.37, 2.38, 2.40, 2.41, and 2.42.
2.40	12 BCE?	Protection of Jewish customs	Flavius Josephus, *Antiquitates Iudaicae* 16.6.3 (166).	Augustus; letter to Governor Gaius Norbanus Flaccus	Asia	Ἰουδαῖοι	Flaccus is made aware that Jews should be allowed to send sacred money to Jerusalem without hindrance. Connection to 2.37, 2.38, 2.39, 2.41, and 2.42.
2.41	12 BCE?	Protection of Jewish customs	Flavius Josephus, *Antiquitates Iudaicae* 16.6.6 (171). Cf. Philo of Alexandria, *Legatio ad Gaium* 314–16.	Governor Gaius Norbanus Flaccus; message to the magistrates and council of Sardis (and Ephesus)	Sardis (and Ephesus)	Ἰουδαῖοι (Jos.); Ἰουδαῖοι (Phil.)	Flaccus passes Augustus' message stating that Jews should be allowed to send sacred money to Jerusalem without hindrance on to Sardis. Philo's citation addresses Ephesus. Connection to 2.37, 2.38, 2.39, 2.40, and 2.42.

Continued

Continued

No.	Date	Type	Sources	Officials/ Institutions	Applicability	Terminology	Circumstances and Contents
2.42	4 BCE?	Protection of Jewish customs	Flavius Josephus, *Antiquitates Iudaicae* 16.6.7 (172–3).	Governor Julius Antonius; message to the magistrates, council and people of Ephesus	Ephesus	Ἰουδαῖοι	Response to a delegation of the Jews of Asia, who had brought missives from Agrippa and Augustus giving them the right to maintain their own customs and to send sacred money to Jerusalem. The governor confirms this previous decision. Connection to 2.37, 2.38, 2.39, 2.40, and 2.41.
2.43	27 BCE–15 CE	Protection of Jewish customs	Philo of Alexandria, *Legatio ad Gaium* 158.	Augustus	Rome	Ἰουδαῖοι	Augustus determines that Jews of Rome can receive donations of money or corn on another day if the distribution of such grants takes place during the Sabbath.
2.44	27 BCE–15 CE	Grant of political privileges	Flavius Josephus, *Antiquitates Iudaicae* 19.5.2 (283); Philo of Alexandria, *In Flaccum* 74.	Augustus (by *mandata* to Marcus Magius Maximus?)	Alexandria	Ἰουδαῖοι (Jos.) Ἰουδαῖοι (Phil.)	According to Philo, a γερουσία is appointed after the death of the ethnarch, likely at the community's request. Josephus references the continued appointment of ethnarchs.
2.45	19 CE	Expulsion	Cassius Dio, *Historiae Romanae* 57.18.5a; Flavius Josephus, *Antiquitates Iudaicae* 18.3.5 (83–4); Philo of Alexandria, *Legatio ad Gaium* 160; Seneca, *Epistulae* 108.22; Suetonius, *De vita Caesarum: Tiberius* 36; Tacitus, *Annales* 2.85.	Senate; Tiberius (by *senatus consultum* or edict)	Rome	Ἰουδαῖοι (Cass. Dio); τὸ Ἰουδαϊκὸν (Jos.); Ἰουδαῖοι (Phil.); *Iudaei* (Suet.); *Iudaei* (Tac.)	Expulsion of Jews from Rome, possibly combined with conscription of young men of fighting age.

No.	Date	Type	Sources	Officials/ Institutions	Applicability	Terminology	Circumstances and Contents
2.46	38–40 CE[9]	Embassy	Flavius Josephus, *Antiquitates Iudaicae* 18.8.1 (257–60); Philo of Alexandria, *In Flaccum* and *Legatio ad Gaium*.	Caligula; delegations from Alexandria	Alexandria	Ἰουδαῖοι (Jos.) Ἰουδαῖοι (Phil.)	Delegations are sent to Rome by various factions to ask for assistance in the resolution of the conflict between Greek and Jewish Alexandrians.
2.47	39–40 CE[10]	Breach of Jewish customs	Flavius Josephus, *Antiquitates Iudaicae* 18.8.2–9 (261–309); Philo of Alexandria, *Legatio ad Gaium* 200–348.	Caligula	Jerusalem; likely noticeable effects elsewhere	–	Placing of a statue of Caligula in the Temple in Jerusalem in response to an incident in Jamnia. Local officials try to stop this from happening.
2.48	41 CE	Protection of Jewish customs; resolution of conflict	Flavius Josephus, *Antiquitates Iudaicae* 19.5.2 (279–85); P.Lond. 6.1912.	Claudius; message to Alexandrian delegations	Alexandria and Syria	Ἰουδαῖοι (Jos.) Ἰουδαῖοι (P.Lond.)	Claudius' resolution of the riots in Alexandria, in two noticeably different versions. In both cases, the measure is a response to a petition and states that Jews should be allowed to maintain their rights, although no new privileges are granted.
2.49	41 CE	Protection of Jewish customs	Flavius Josephus, *Antiquitates Iudaicae* 19.5.3 (286–91).	Claudius; petition by Agrippa and Herod	Throughout the empire	Ἰουδαῖοι	At the request of kings Agrippa and Herod, the privileges of the Alexandrian Jews become valid for Jews throughout the empire. Claudius references the various proclamations made by Augustus. Jews should be allowed to maintain their ancestral customs.

[9] Harker (2008), 14.

[10] Harker (2008), 14.

Continued

Continued

No.	Date	Type	Sources	Officials/ Institutions	Applicability	Terminology	Circumstances and Contents
2.50	41 CE?[11]	Restriction on Jewish customs	Cassius Dio, *Historiae Romanae* 60.6.6.	Claudius	Rome	*Ἰουδαῖοι*	Claudius forbids the Jewish community of Rome to hold meetings but does not expel it due to its size.
2.51	41/2 CE	Protection of Jewish customs	Flavius Josephus, *Antiquitates Iudaicae* 19.6.3 (300–11).	Governor Publius Petronius of Syria; message to the leaders of Dora	Dora	*Ἰουδαῖοι*	At the request of King Agrippa I, the governor writes to Dora in anger because they had set up a statue of the emperor in the synagogue. The governor references Claudius' edict granting Jews permission to maintain their ancestral customs (possibly 2.48 and/or 2.49), which had also been invoked by Agrippa when pleading his case.
2.52	49 CE[12]	Expulsion	Acts, 18.1–3; Suetonius, *De vita Caesarum: Claudius* 25.4.	Claudius	Rome	*Ἰουδαῖοι* (Acts); *Iudaei impulsore Chresto* (Suet.)	Expulsion of Jews from Rome, according to Suetonius because they caused disturbances 'at the instigation of Chrestus'. Christian involvement has been suggested, but deliberate targeting is unlikely. See Appendix 3.3.
2.53	*c.* 59–60 CE?	Limitation of citizenship	Flavius Josephus, *Antiquitates Iudaicae* 20.8.7 (173–8) and 20.8.9 (183–4); Flavius Josephus, *Bellum Iudaicum* 2.13.7 (266–70) and 2.14.4–5 (284–92).	Nero	Caesarea	*Ἰουδαῖοι*	At the request of Greek Caesareans, Nero takes away the citizenship of the Jewish inhabitants of the city. Religiously inspired riots follow.

[11] Barclay (1996), 305–6; Botermann (1996), 134–5; Cappelletti (2006), 87–8; Gruen (2002), 37; Smallwood (1976), 212–16.
[12] Barclay (1996), 305–6; Cappelletti (2006), 87–8; Gruen (2002), 38; Smallwood (1976), 212–16.

No.	Date	Type	Sources	Officials/ Institutions	Applicability	Terminology	Circumstances and Contents
2.54	67–9 CE	Protection of Jewish customs; breach of Jewish customs	Flavius Josephus, *Antiquitates Iudaicae* 12.3.1 (120); Flavius Josephus, *Bellum Iudaicum* 7.3.3 (46–53).	Governor Gaius Licinius Mucianus of Syria; local officials	Antioch	Ἰουδαῖοι	Jews are forced to sacrifice and banned from observing the Sabbath during a time of conflict, but maintain the right to buy their own oils, after a Greek petition to revoke it.
2.55	70 CE	Protection of Jewish customs	Flavius Josephus, *Antiquitates Iudaicae* 12.3.1 (121–4); Flavius Josephus, *Bellum Iudaicum* 7.5.2 (100–11).	Titus	Antioch (and Alexandria)	Ἰουδαῖοι	Response to a petition by the Greeks of Antioch. Titus refuses to expel Jews from the city and even confirms the rights they had previously had. A similar story is told about Alexandria.
2.56	71 CE[13]	Taxation	Appianus, *Syriaca* 50.251–3; Cassius Dio, *Historiae Romanae* ep.65.7.2; Flavius Josephus, *Bellum Iudaicum* 7.6.6 (218); Origen, *Epistula ad Africanum* 14.	Vespasian	Throughout the empire	Ἰουδαῖοι (App.); Ἰουδαῖοι (Cass. Dio); Ἰουδαῖοι (Jos.)	Introduction of the two denarii tax known as the Jewish Tax, which replaces the yearly tax meant for the Temple in Jerusalem.
2.57	73 CE	Destruction of sacred space	Flavius Josephus, *Bellum Iudaicum* 7.10.2–4 (420–36).	Vespasian	Leontopolis	Ἰουδαῖοι	Forced closure and demolition of the 'alternative' Jewish temple in Leontopolis. Notably, synagogues of nearby cities are not reported to have been closed.

[13] See Heemstra (2010), 10.

Continued

Continued

No.	Date	Type	Sources	Officials/ Institutions	Applicability	Terminology	Circumstances and Contents
2.58	73 CE	Accusation of conspiracy	Flavius Josephus, *Bellum Iudaicum* 7.11.1–4 (437–51); Flavius Josephus, *Vita* 76 (424–5).	Governor Catullus of Libya	Cyrene, Alexandria, and Rome	*Ἰουδαῖοι*	The governor of Libya accuses several prominent Jews of Alexandria and Rome of working with the *sicarii*. The accused are not convicted, but no real actions against the governor are undertaken either.
2.59	81–96 CE	Taxation	Suetonius, *De vita Caesarum: Domitianus* 12.1–2.	Domitian	Throughout the empire?	*Iudaei*	Stricter enforcement of the Jewish Tax. Connection to 2.60 is unlikely. Christian involvement has been suggested but remains uncertain. See Appendix 3.7.
2.60	(81–96 CE)	Trials involving Jewish sympathies	Cassius Dio, *Historiae Romanae* ep.67.14.1–2 and ep.68.1.2; Suetonius, *De vita Caesarum: Domitianus* 15.1.	Domitian	Rome	*Ἰουδαῖοι* (Cass. Dio)	Possible, but ultimately uncertain, accusations of Jewish sympathies against members of the Roman elite, including Flavius Clemens, in the context of political trials. Christian involvement has been suggested but remains unlikely. See Appendix 3.7.
2.61	96 CE	Taxation	Cassius Dio, *Historiae Romanae* ep.68.1.2; various coins.	Nerva	Throughout the empire?	*Ἰουδαῖοι*	End of Domitian's harsh enforcement of the Jewish Tax and the related malicious accusations.
2.62	131 CE?	Foundation of colony	Cassius Dio, *Historiae Romanae* ep.69.12.1; Eusebius, *Historia Ecclesiastica* 4.6.4.	Hadrian	Jerusalem	*Ἰουδαῖοι* (Eus.)	Jerusalem is re-founded as Aelia Capitolina. Sources disagree about whether this was a cause or consequence of the Bar Kokhba Revolt.

No.	Date	Type	Sources	Officials/ Institutions	Applicability	Terminology	Circumstances and Contents
2.63	(Post-136 CE?)	Expulsion	Eusebius, *Historia Ecclesiastica* 4.6.3–4; Justin Martyr, *1 Apology* 47.4–6; Justin Martyr, *Dialogue with Trypho* 16.	Hadrian	Jerusalem	*Ἰουδαῖοι* (Eus.)	Dubiously authentic banishment of Jews from Jerusalem.
2.64	*c.* 130–8 CE?	Restriction on Jewish customs	*Digesta* 48.8.4.2; Scriptor Historiae Augustae, *Hadrianus* 14.2.	Hadrian (by rescript)	Throughout the empire?	*Iudaei* (SHA)	Ban on castration, which possibly included circumcision. Connection to 2.65 and 2.66.
2.65	138–61 CE	Protection of Jewish customs	*Digesta* 48.8.11; possible connection to pseudo-Paul, *Sententiae* 5.22.4?	Antoninus Pius (by rescript)	Throughout the empire?	*Iudaei* (Dig.); *Iudaei* (Paul)	Jews are permitted to circumcise their own children, but no-one else. Possibly an amendment of 2.64. Connection to 2.64 and 2.66.
2.66	(193–211 CE)	Ban on conversion	Scriptor Historiae Augustae, *Septimius Severus* 17.1. Possible connection to pseudo-Paul, *Sententiae* 5.22.3?	Septimius Severus	Throughout the empire?	*Iudaei* (SHA); *Iudaei* (Paul)	Conversion to Judaism becomes illegal. The same measure is said to have applied to Christianity. See Appendix 3.23. Possible connection to 2.64 and 2.65.
2.67	198–211 CE	Protection of Jewish customs	*Digesta* 50.2.3.3.	Septimius Severus and Caracalla	Throughout the empire?	*Qui Iudaicam superstitionem sequuntur*	Jews are permitted to hold public office, but only those that do not force them to violate their ancestral customs.
2.68	213 CE	Trial on inheritance	*Codex Iustiniani* 1.9.1.	Caracalla (by rescript)	Cornelia Salvia; in Antioch	*Iudaei*	The emperor decides that a legacy left to the Jewish community of Antioch cannot be accepted.

APPENDIX 3

Christianity

No.	Date	Type	Sources	Officials/ Institutions	Applicability	Terminology	Circumstances and Contents
3.1	(30–7 CE?)	Ban on trials against Christians	Eusebius, *Historia Ecclesiastica* 2.2; Jerome, *Chronicon* AD 35; Tertullian, *Apologeticus pro Christianis* 5.2.	Tiberius (by edict?)	Throughout the empire?	*Χριστιανοί* (Eus.); Christiani (Jer.); Christiani (Tert.)	Tiberius attempts to ban the punishment of Christians but is met with opposition from the senate. It is highly unlikely that this event ever took place.
3.2	40–60 CE?	Trials and expulsions of a small number of Christians	Acts 4.1–22, 5.17–42, 6.11–8.1, 8.1–3, 12.1–4, 13.44–50, 14.1–6, 14.19–20, 16.16–40, 17.1–13, 18.12–17, 19.23–41, 21.27–28.31.	Various	Paul (and followers); in various locations	–	Paul is regularly faced with trials and expulsions on the basis of various accusations made by the local population (Jewish or Greek) of a number of cities, who seek to remove him for causing unrest. On some occasions the Roman authorities become involved.
3.3	(49 CE)	Expulsion	Acts, 18.1–3; Suetonius, *De vita Caesarum: Claudius* 25.4.	Claudius	Rome	*Ἰουδαῖοι* (Acts); *Iudaei impulsore Chresto* (Suet.)	Expulsion of Jews from Rome, according to Suetonius because they caused disturbances 'at the instigation of Chrestus'. However, it is unlikely that Christians were deliberately targeted. Cf. Appendix 2.52.

No.	Date	Type	Sources	Officials/ Institutions	Applicability	Terminology	Circumstances and Contents
3.4	(54–68 CE?)	Trial against a single Christian	1 Clement 5.4; Acts of Peter 33–41; Apocalypse of Peter 14.4–6; Apocryphon of James 5.9–20; Ascension of Isaiah 4.2–3; Eusebius, *Historia Ecclesiastica* 2.25.5–8 and 3.1.2–3; Ignatius of Antioch, *passim*; John 13.36–38 and 21.18–19; Lactantius, *De Mortibus Persecutorum* 2; Tertullian, *passim*.	Nero?	Peter; location uncertain	–	According to many Christian traditions, Peter was martyred, possibly in Rome during the reign of Nero. However, details about the circumstances that led to his conviction are lacking. The connection to 3.6 and the Great Fire is sometimes made but is tenuous at best.
3.5	(54–68 CE?)	Trial against a single Christian	1 Clement 5.5; Acts of Paul; Eusebius, *Historia Ecclesiastica* 2.25.5–8 and 3.1.2–3; Ignatius of Antioch, *Letter to the Ephesians* 12; Jerome, *De Viris Illustribus* 5; Lactantius, *De Mortibus Persecutorum* 2; Tertullian, *De Praescriptione Hereticorum* 36 and *Scorpiace* 15.	Nero?	Paul; location uncertain	–	According to many Christian traditions, Paul was martyred, possibly under Nero, likely by beheading. However, details about the legal proceedings are hard to come by. The connection to 3.6 and the Great Fire is sometimes made but is tenuous at best.
3.6	64 CE?	Measure against larger group of Christians	Suetonius, *De vita Caesarum: Nero* 16; Tacitus, *Annales* 15.44; Tertullian, *Ad Nationes* 1.7.8–9 and *Apologeticus pro Christianis* 5.3.	Nero	Rome	*Christiani* (Suet.); *Chrestiani* (Tac.); *Christiani* (Tert.)	Nero takes action against the Christians of Rome, which likely involves executions. The connection to the Great Fire is made only by Tacitus, and the nature of the Christians' crimes is the subject of debate. The connection of this measure to 3.4 and 3.5 is highly uncertain.

Continued

Continued

No.	Date	Type	Sources	Officials/ Institutions	Applicability	Terminology	Circumstances and Contents
3.7	(81–96 CE)	Measure against larger group of Christians?	Cassius Dio, *Historiae Romanae* ep.67.14.1–2 and ep.68.1.2; Eusebius, *Historia Ecclesiatica* 3.17–18; Suetonius, *De vita Caesarum: Domitianus* 12.1–2 and 15.1; Tertullian, *Apologeticus pro Christianis* 5.4.	Domitian	Throughout the empire?	*Ἰουδαῖοι* (Cass. Dio); *τῆς εἰς Χριστὸν μαρτυρίας ἕνεκεν* (Eus.); *Iudaei* (Suet.)	Possible, although ultimately uncertain, targeting of Christians in the context of Domitian's strict enforcement of the Jewish Tax, or of trials against members of the Roman elite, which were likely political in nature. Cf. Appendices 2.59 and 2.60.
3.8	*c.* 110–13 CE	Trials against larger group of Christians	Pliny the Younger, *Epistulae* 10.96.	Governor Pliny the Younger of Bithynia et Pontus; letter to emperor Trajan	Bithynia et Pontus	*Christiani*	Pliny asks Trajan's advice on how to deal with denunciations of Christians in his province, describing his course of action so far, which includes trials and executions. Answer follows in 3.9.
3.9	*c.* 110–13 CE	Regulation of legal proceedings against Christians	Pliny the Younger, *Epistulae* 10.97	Trajan; rescript to governor Pliny the Younger of Bithynia et Pontus	Bithynia et Pontus	*Christiani*	Trajan confirms Pliny's procedure described in 3.8 but adds that it is impossible to make general pronouncements on the subject. He also adds that anonymous accusations are not to be accepted, and that Christians are not to be sought out.
3.10	122/3 CE	Regulation of legal proceedings against Christians	Eusebius, *Historia Ecclesiastica* 4.8.6–4.9.3 and 4.26.10; Justin Martyr, *1 Apology* 68.3–70.4 (including Appendix).	Hadrian; rescript to Governors Serennius (?) Granianus and Minucius Fundanus of Asia	Asia	*Χριστιανοί* (Eus.); *Χριστιανοί* (Just.)	Hadrian has received a message from his governor regarding the correct procedures for dealing with Christians. Hadrian insists on proper proceedings, rejecting 'petitions and shouts', and states that Christians can be punished only if a formal case can be made that they have broken the law. He does not explain which laws are meant, stating that it is up to the governor to convict or acquit.

No.	Date	Type	Sources	Officials/ Institutions	Applicability	Terminology	Circumstances and Contents
3.11	*c.* 157 CE[1]	Trial against a single Christian	Eusebius, *Historia Ecclesiastica* 4.15; *Martyrium Polycarpi.*	Governor Statius Quadratus of Asia	Polycarp; in Smyrna	*Χριστιανοί*; *ἄθεοι* (Eus.); *Χριστιανοί*; *ἄθεοι* (MP)	Polycarp is tried and executed for being a Christian after the mob calls for him specifically, but other executions are also mentioned. Christians are repeatedly referred to as atheists.
3.12	(152–61 CE?)[2]	Regulation of legal proceedings against Christians	Eusebius, *Historia Ecclesiastica* 4.12–13 and 4.26.10; Justin Martyr, *1 Apology* (Appendix).	Antoninus Pius? (by rescript)	Asia? Possibly also Greek provinces	*Χριστιανοί* (Eus.)	Antoninus allegedly forbids the inhabitants of the province to take legal measures against the Christians, apparently during a time of unrest. An exception is made for Christians who plot against the Roman state. Those who do make accusations are to be punished. The authenticity of this passage is dubious.
3.13	*c.* 146–60 CE	Trials against small number of Christians	Eusebius, *Historia Ecclesiastica* 4.17; Justin Martyr, 2 *Apology* 2.	Urban prefect (Quintus Lollius?) Urbicus	Ptolemaeus, Lucius and an unnamed third Christian; in Rome	*Χριστιανοί* (Eus.); *Χριστιανοί* (Just.)	Ptolemaeus is arrested because he caused a Christian woman to divorce her non-Christian husband and is subsequently executed. Lucius and another unnamed Christian are executed for standing up for him. No consequences for the woman are mentioned.
3.14	161–80 CE	Measure against larger group of Christians	Eusebius, *Historia Ecclesiastica* 4.26.5–6.	Unknown; possibly local officials	Asia	–	Melito of Sardis, as cited by Eusebius, makes reference to 'new decrees' causing trouble for Christians in Asia and asks for the emperor's help. The exact contents and origins of these measures are unknown.
3.15	163–8 CE	Trial against small number of Christians	Eusebius, *Historia Ecclesiastica* 4.16; *Acta Iustini.*	Urban prefect (Quintus Junius?) Rusticus	Justin Martyr and companions; in Rome	*Χριστιανοί* (Eus.); *Χριστιανοί* (AI)	Trial of a select number of Christians. Tenuous connection to an order regarding compulsory sacrifice, which may have been an imperial edict. The prefect also enquires about meeting places, and methods of spreading Christianity.

Continued

[1] Barnes (2010), 49. For alternative suggestions, see Dehandschutter (1993), 497–501. For the doubtful authenticity and historicity of the text, see Moss (2010[a]).
[2] Authenticity doubted by Barnes (1968[a]), 38; Millar (1977), 560; Williams (2012), 199 n. 55. Attributed to the time of Marcus Aurelius by Coleman-Norton (1966), 8–13.

Continued

No.	Date	Type	Sources	Officials/ Institutions	Applicability	Terminology	Circumstances and Contents
3.16	(169–75 CE)	Regulation of legal proceedings against Christians	Eusebius, *Historia Ecclesiastica* 5.5.1–6; Justin Martyr, *1 Apology* (Appendix); Tertullian, *Apologeticus pro Christianis* 5.6–7 and *Ad Scapulam* 4.6.	Marcus Aurelius	Throughout the empire	*Χριστιανοί* (Eus.); *Χριστιανοί* (Just.); *Christiani* (Tert.)	Marcus Aurelius is said to have stopped trials against Christians by ordering that any accusers should be punished. This is highly dubious, especially given the many differing accounts.
3.17	177 CE	Trials against larger group of Christians	Eusebius, *Historia Ecclesiastica* 5.1.3–5.2.8.	Unknown governor of Gallia Lugdunensis; Marcus Aurelius; local officials	Larger group of Christians; in Lyon (and Vienne)	*Χριστιανοί* (Eus.);	Actions against Christians instigated by the local community before the arrival of the governor. A second trial under the governor takes place, who then consults the emperor about certain aspects of the procedure he means to follow. A number of Christians are executed.
3.18	July 180 CE	Trial against small number of Christians	*Passio Martyrum Scilitanorum.*	Governor Publius Vigellius Saturninus of Africa	Small group of named Christians in Africa	*Christiani*	A small group of Christians are tried and executed. The governor repeatedly offers imperial clemency and a chance to recant, but the Christians refuse.
3.19	(*c.* 180 CE)	Trial against a single Christian	Eusebius, *Historia Ecclesiastica* 5.21; *Acta Apollonii* (multiple versions).	Governor/urban prefect Perennis; senate (in certain versions)	Apollonius; either in Rome or in Asia	*Χριστιανοί* (AA)	Apollonius is accused of being a Christian and is questioned by the prefect and the senate after having been given some time to reconsider and a lengthy debate. The legal basis for his conviction differs significantly depending on the version of the story one adheres to.
3.20	*c.* 180–212 CE?[3]	Various trials against individual Christians	Tertullian, *Ad Scapulam* 4.3.	Various Roman governors of Africa	Africa	*Christiani*	Tertullian makes mention of Roman officials who, for various reasons, refused to hear cases against individual Christians or otherwise displayed leniency during these proceedings.

[3] Not all magistrates mentioned by Tertullian can be reliably dated. This date is therefore based on the range between the earliest known tenures and the date of *Ad Scapulam*. For the latter, see Barnes (1985), 55.

No.	Date	Type	Sources	Officials/ Institutions	Applicability	Terminology	Circumstances and Contents
3.21	*c.* 203/4 CE[4]	Trial against smaller number of Christians	*Passio Perpetuae et Felicitatis.*	Procurator Publius Aelius Hilarianus	Perpetua, Felicitas, and others; in Carthage	*Christiani*	A number of Christians are condemned to the arena. They are moved to different jails in succession. Few details about the trial are given, only that Perpetua and others are repeatedly encouraged to sacrifice.
3.22	*c.* 204 CE?[5]	Targeting of Christian burials	Tertullian, *Ad Scapulam* 3.1.	Governor Publius Aelius Hilarianus	Carthage?	–	Potential attempt to deprive Christians of their burial grounds. No other details are given.
3.23	(193–211 CE)	Ban on conversion	Scriptor Historiae Augustae, *Septimius Severus* 17.1.	Septimius Severus (by edict?)	Throughout the empire?	*Christiani*	Conversion to Christianity becomes illegal. The same law is said to have applied to Judaism, although the source is highly suspect. Cf. Appendix 2.66.
3.24	(218–22 CE)	Favourable measure	Scriptor Historiae Augustae, *Antoninus Heliogabalus* 3.5.	Elagabalus	Unspecified	*Christiana devotio*	According to a suspect account, the rites of Jews, Christians, and Samaritans were transferred to Rome in order to be included in Elagabalus' own cult.
3.25	(222–35 CE)	Favourable attitude	Scriptor Historiae Augustae, *Alexander Severus* 22.4, 29.2, 43.6, 45.7, 49.6, 51.7–8.	Alexander Severus	Unspecified	*Christiani*	This dubious account reports several instances in which Alexander seemed to show an interest in Christianity, a case in which he ruled in their favour regarding their claim to a piece of land in Rome, and an assertion that he 'left Christians alone' that is not otherwise explained.
3.26	Pre-early third century CE	Various unspecified measures	Lactantius, *Divinae Institutiones* 5.11.19.	Various unknown Roman officials (by rescript), as recorded by Ulpian	Likely various origins	*cultores dei*	According to Lactantius, the seventh book of *De Officio Proconsulis* contained rescripts against Christians by a number of emperors. No further details are given.
3.27	(235–8 CE)	Execution of clergy	Eusebius, *Historia Ecclesiastica* 6.28.	Maximinus Thrax (by edict)	Unspecified	–	According to Eusebius, Maximinus ordered the Christian clergy to be executed. No external evidence for this claim exists.

[4] For the date of the martyrdom, see Barnes (1985), 267 and (2010), 304–7, as well as Rebillard (2017), 296.
[5] Since Publius Aelius Hilarianus is referred to as procurator in the *Passio Perpetuae et Felicitatis* 6.3 but is called a governor (*praeses*) by Tertullian, it is possible that he is describing a slightly later event. This, however, is by no means certain.

References

In case multiple works by a particular author were published in the same year, a letter in superscript (*a, b, c*) *is added after the year of publication as a distinguishing factor in both footnotes and bibliography.*

Abusch, Ra'anan, 'Negotiating Difference. Genital Mutilation in Roman Slave Law and the History of the Bar Kokhba Revolt', in Peter Schäfer (ed.), *The Bar Kokhba War Reconsidered* (Tübingen, 2003), 71–91.

Alessandri, Salvatore, 'La Presunta Cacciata dei Giudei da Roma nel 139 a. Ch.', *Studi Classici e Orientali* 17 (1968), 187–98.

Allard, Paul, *Histoire des Persécutions d'après les Documents archéologiques*, vol. 1: *Histoire des Persécutions pendant les deux premiers Siècles* (4th edn, Paris, 1911).

Alonso, José Luis, 'Juristic Papyrology and Roman Law', in Paul J. du Plessis, Clifford Ando, and Kaius Tuori (eds), *The Oxford Handbook of Roman Law and Society* (Oxford, 2016), 56–69.

Alonso, José Luis, 'The Constitutio Antoniniana and Private Legal Practice in the Eastern Empire', in Kimberley Czajkowski, Benedikt Eckhardt, and Meret Strothmann (eds), *Law in the Roman Provinces* (Oxford, 2020), 44–64.

Alpers, Michael, *Das nachrepublikanische Finanzsystem. Fiscus und Fisci in der frühen Kaiserzeit* (Berlin, 1995).

Alston, Richard, 'Philo's *In Flaccum*. Ethnicity and Social Space in Roman Alexandria', *Greece and Rome* 44:2 (1997), 165–75.

Ameling, Walter (ed.), *Inscriptiones Judaicae Orientis*, vol. 2: *Kleinasien* (Tübingen, 2004).

Amelotti, Mario, 'Reichsrecht, Volksrecht, Provinzialrecht. Vecchi Problemi e Nuovi Documenti', *Studia et Documenta Historiae et Iuris* 65 (1999), 211–15. <https://sites.unipa.it//dipstdir/portale/romano/elenco%20pup%20testo%20pieno/AMELOTTI/reichsrecht.html> (accessed 9 Nov 2015).

Anderson, Gordon L., 'The Legal Basis for the Treatment of Christianity, 30–312 C.E.', PhD dissertation, University of Minnesota, 1986.

Ando, Clifford, *Imperial Ideology and Provincial Loyalty in the Roman Empire* (Berkeley, 2000).

Ando, Clifford, 'The Administration of the Provinces', in David Potter (ed.), *A Companion to the Roman Empire* (Oxford, 2006), 177–92.

Ando, Clifford, 'Jewish Privilege', review of Goodman (2007[a]), *Times Literary Supplement* 5427 (6 April 2007), 6–7.

Ando, Clifford, *The Matter of the Gods* (Berkeley, 2008).

Ando, Clifford, 'Imperial Identities', in Tim Whitmarsh (ed.), *Local Knowledge and Microidentities in the Imperial Greek World* (Cambridge, 2010), 17–45.

Ando, Clifford, *Law, Language, and Empire in the Roman Tradition* (Philadelphia, 2011).

Ando, Clifford, 'Exemplum, Analogy, and Precedent in Roman Law', in M. Lowrie and S. Lüdemann (eds), *Exemplarity and Singularity. Thinking through Particulars in Philosophy, Literature, and Law* (London, 2015[a]), 111–22.

Ando, Clifford, *Roman Social Imaginaries. Language and Thought in the Context of Empire* (Toronto, 2015[b]).

Ando, Clifford, 'Legal Pluralism in Practice', in Paul J. du Plessis, Clifford Ando, and Kaius Tuori (eds), *The Oxford Handbook of Roman Law and Society* (Oxford, 2016[a]), 283–93.

Ando, Clifford, 'The Rites of Others', in Alison Keith and Jonathan Edmondson (eds), *Roman Literary Cultures. Domestic Politics, Revolutionary Poetics, Civic Spectacle* (Toronto, 2016[b]), 254–77.

Ando, Clifford, 'Petition and Response, Order and Obey. Contemporary Models of Roman Government', *Journal of Epigraphic Studies* 7 (2024), 129–44.

Applebaum, Shim'on, *Jews and Greeks in Ancient Cyrene* (Leiden, 1979).
Ash, Rhiannon (ed.), *Tacitus. Annals, Book XV* (Cambridge, 2018).
Aubé, Benjamin, *Histoire des persécutions de l'église jusqu'à la fin des Antonins* (Paris, 1875).
Aubert, Jean-Jacques, 'The Setting and Staging of Christian Trials', in Fransesco De Angelis (ed.), *Spaces of Justice in the Roman World* (Leiden, 2010), 277–309.
Audin, Amable, 'L'Amphithéâtre des Trois Gaules à Lyon. Nouvelles campagnes de fouilles (1971–1972, 1976–1978)', *Gallia* 37 (1979), 85–100.
Avidov, Avi, *Not Reckoned Among the Nations* (Tübingen, 2009).
Bablitz, Leanne, 'Roman Courts and Private Arbitration', in Paul J. du Plessis, Clifford Ando, and Kaius Tuori (eds), *The Oxford Handbook of Roman Law and Society* (Oxford, 2016), 234–44.
Balsdon, John Percy Vyvian Dacre, and Andrew Lintott, 'maiestas', in *Oxford Classical Dictionary Online* (Oxford, 2016). <https://oxfordre.com/classics/view/10.1093/acrefore/9780199381135.001.0001/acrefore-9780199381135-e-3890>.
Baltrusch, Ernst, *Die Juden und das Römische Reich. Geschichte einer konfliktreichen Beziehung* (Darmstadt, 2002).
Bang, Peter Fibiger, 'The Roman Empire II. The Monarchy', in Peter Fibiger Bang and Walter Scheidel (eds), *The Oxford Handbook of the State in the Ancient Near East and Mediterranean* (Oxford, 2013), 412–72.
Barclay, John M. G., *Jews in the Mediterranean Diaspora. From Alexander to Trajan, 323 BCE–117 CE* (Edinburgh, 1996).
Barclay, John M. G., *Negotiating Diaspora. Jewish Strategies in the Roman Empire* (London, 2004).
Barclay, John M. G., *Flavius Josephus*, vol. 10: *Against Apion, Translation and Commentary* (Leiden, 2007).
Barclay, John M. G., 'Jews and Christians in the Eyes of Roman Authors c. 100 CE', in P. J. Tomson and J. Schwartz (eds), *Jews and Christians in the First and Second Centuries. How to Write Their History* (Leiden, 2014), 313–26.
Barnes, Timothy D., 'Legislation against the Christians', *Journal of Roman Studies* 58 (1968[a]), 32–50.
Barnes, Timothy D., 'Pre-Decian *Acta Martyrum*', *Journal of Theological Studies* 19 (1968[b]), 509–31.
Barnes, Timothy D., 'Eusebius and the Date of the Martyrdoms', in Jean Rougé and Robert Turcan (eds), *Les Martyrs de Lyon – 177* (Paris, 1978), 137–43.
Barnes, Timothy D., *Tertullian: A Historical and Literary Study* (rev. edn, Oxford, 1985).
Barnes, Timothy D., *Early Christian Hagiography and Roman History* (Tübingen, 2010).
Barton, Carlin A., and Daniel Boyarin, *Imagine No Religion. How Modern Abstractions Hide Ancient Realities* (New York, 2016).
Barton, Tamsyn S., *Ancient Astrology* (New York, 1994[a]).
Barton, Tamsyn S., *Power and Knowledge. Astrology, Physiognomics, and Medicine under the Roman Empire* (Ann Arbor, 1994[b]).
Barton, Tamsyn S., 'Augustus and Capricorn. Astrological Polyvalency and Imperial Rhetoric', *Journal of Roman Studies* 85 (1995), 33–51.
Bastet, Frédéric L., and Hendrik Brunsting, *Corpus Signorum Classicorum* (Zutphen, 1982).
Bastiaensen, Antoon A. R. (ed.), *Atti e passioni dei martiri* (Milan, 1987).
Bauckham, Richard J., 'The Martyrdom of Peter in Early Christian Literature', in Wolfgang Haase (ed.), *Aufstieg und Niedergang der Römischen Welt* II.26.1 (Berlin, 1992), 539–95.
Baudy, Dorothea, 'Prohibitions of Religion in Antiquity. Setting the Course of Europe's Religious History', in Clifford Ando and Jörg Rüpke (eds), *Religion and Law in Classical and Christian Rome* (Stuttgart, 2006), 100–14.
Bauman, Richard A., *Crime and Punishment in Ancient Rome* (London, 1996).
Baumann, Uwe, *Rom und die Juden. Die römisch-jüdischen Beziehungen von Pompeius bis zum Tode des Herodes, 63 v. Chr.–4 v. Chr.* (Frankfurt am Main, 1983).

Baviera, Johannes (ed.), *Fontes Iuris Romani Antejustiniani*, vol. 2: *Auctores* (Florence, 1940).

Beard, Mary, 'The Cult of the 'Great Mother' in Imperial Rome. The Roman and the Foreign', in J. Rasmus Brandt and Jon W. Iddeng (eds), *Greek and Roman Festivals. Content, Meaning, and Practice* (Oxford, 2012), 323–53.

Beard, Mary, John North, and Simon Price, *Religions of Rome*, vol. 1: *A History* (Cambridge, 1998).

Beerden, Kim, *Worlds full of Signs. Ancient Greek Divination in Context* (Leiden, 2013).

Beggio, Tommaso, 'Epigraphy', in Paul J. du Plessis, Clifford Ando, and Kaius Tuori (eds), *The Oxford Handbook of Roman Law and Society* (Oxford, 2016), 43–55.

Behrends, Okko, Rolf Knütel, Berthold Kupisch, and Hans Hermann Seiler (eds), *Corpus Iuris Civilis. Text und Übersetzung*, 5 vols (Heidelberg, 1995–2012).

Bendlin, Andreas, 'Religion, Violence, and the Diasporic Experience. The Jewish Diaspora in Flavian Rome and Puteoli', in Jitse H. F. Dijkstra and Christian R. Raschle (eds), *Religious Violence in the Ancient World. From Classical Athens to Late Antiquity* (Cambridge, 2020), 133–76.

Benko, Stephen, *Pagan Rome and the Early Christians* (Bloomington, 1984).

Berger, Adolf, *Encyclopaedic Dictionary of Roman Law* (Philadelphia, 1991).

Bernard, Seth G., 'Food Distribution and Immigration in Imperial Rome', in Luuk de Ligt and Laurens E. Tacoma (eds), *Migration and Mobility in the Early Roman Empire* (Leiden, 2016), 50–71.

Bickerman, E., 'The Name of Christians', *Harvard Theological Review* 42:2 (1949), 109–24.

Bilde, Per, 'Philo as a Polemist and a Political Apologist. An Investigation of his Two Historical Treatises *Against Flaccus* and *The Embassy to Gaius*', in G. Hinge, J. A. Krasilnikoff, and M. S. Jensen (eds), *Alexandria. A Cultural and Religious Melting Pot* (Aarhus, 2009), 97–114.

Billings, Drew W., *Acts of the Apostles and the Rhetoric of Roman Imperialism* (Cambridge, 2017).

Bisbee, Gary A., *Pre-Decian Acts of Martyrs and Commentarii* (Philadelphia, 1988).

Blant, Edmond le, 'Note sur les bases juridiques des poursuites dirigées contre les martyrs', *Comptes rendus des séances de l'Académie des Inscriptions et Belles-Lettres* 10 (1866), 358–73.

Bodel, John, 'The Publication of Pliny's Letters', in Ilaria Marchesi (ed.), *Pliny the Book-Maker. Betting on Posterity in the Epistles* (Oxford, 2015), 13–108.

Boeft, Jan den, and Jan N. Bremmer, 'Notiunculae martyrologicae III. Some Observations on the Martyria of Polycarp and Pionius', *Vigiliae Christianae* 39:2 (1985), 110–30.

Boeft, Jan den, and Jan N. Bremmer, 'Notiunculae martyrologicae IV', *Vigiliae Christianae* 45:2 (1991), 105–22.

Boeft, Jan den, and Jan N. Bremmer, 'Notiunculae martyrologicae V', *Vigiliae Christianae* 49:2 (1995), 146–64.

Boeft, Jan den, and Jan N. Bremmer, 'Notiunculae martyrologicae VI. Passio Perpetuae 2, 16 and 17', in J. Leemans (ed.), *Persecution and Martyrdom in Late Antique Christianity* (Leuven, 2010), 47–63.

Boman, J., 'Inpulsore Cherestro? Suetonius' *Divus Claudius* 25.4 in Sources and Manuscripts', *Liber Annuus* 61 (2011), 355–76.

Boni, Luis Alberto de, 'O Estatuto jurídico das perseguições dos Christãos no Império Romano', *Trans/Form/Ação* 37 (2014), 135–68.

Borleffs, Jan W. Ph., 'Institutum Neronianum', in Richard Klein (ed.), *Das frühe Christentum im römischen Staat* (Darmstadt, 1971), 217–35.

Botermann, Helga, *Das Judenedikt des Kaisers Claudius. Römischer Staat und Christiani im I. Jahrhundert* (Stuttgart, 1996).

Boudreaux, Petrus (ed.), *Catalogus Codicum Astrologorum Graecorum*, vol. 8: *Codicum Parisinorum partem quartam* (Brussels, 1921). <https://archive.org/stream/cataloguscodipart408bruxuoft>.

Bowden, Hugh, 'Before Superstition and After. Theophrastus and Plutarch on *Deisidaimonia*', in S. A. Smith and Alan Knight (eds), *The Religion of Fools. Superstition Past and Present* (Oxford, 2008), 56–71.

Bowersock, Glen W., *Hellenism in Late Antiquity* (Ann Arbor, 1990).

Bowman, Alan K., 'Provincial Administration and Taxation', in Alan K. Bowman, Edward Champlin, and Andrew Lintott (eds), *The Cambridge Ancient History*, vol. 10: *The Augustan Empire, 43 BC–AD 69* (Cambridge, 1996), 344–70.

Burden-Strevens, Christopher, 'Introduction', in Christopher Burden-Strevens and Mads Lindholmer (eds), *Cassius Dio's Forgotten History of Early Rome the Roman History. Books 1–21* (Leiden, 2019), 1–23.

Bradley, Keith R., 'Suetonius, *Nero* 16.2. "Afflicti suppliciis Christiani"', *Classical Review* 22 (1972), 9–10.

Braund, S. M. (ed.), *Juvenal and Persius*, Loeb Classical Library (Cambridge, MA, 2004).

Bremmer, Jan N., 'Atheism in Antiquity', in M. Martin (ed.), *The Cambridge Companion to Atheism* (Cambridge, 2006), 11–26.

Bremmer, Jan N., 'Early Christian Human Sacrifice between Fact and Fiction', in Agnes A. Nagy and Francesca Prescendi (eds), *Sacrifices humains. Dossiers, discours, comparaisons* (Turnhout, 2013), 165–76.

Bremmer, Jan N., 'Greek and Latin Narratives about the Ancient Martyrs. Oxford early Christian texts', review of Rebillard (2017), *Bryn Mawr Classical Review* 2019:02:37 (2019). <https://bmcr.brynmawr.edu/2019/2019.02.37/> (accessed 9 March 2022).

Bremmer, Jan N., 'The First Pogrom? Religious Violence in Alexandria in AD 38?', in B. Schliesser, J. Rüggemeier, T. J. Kraus, and J. Frey (eds), *Alexandria. Hub of the Hellenistic World* (Tübingen, 2021), 245–59.

Brinks, C. L., '"Great is Artemis of the Ephesians". Acts 19:23–41 in Light of Goddess Worship in Ephesus', *Catholic Biblical Quarterly* 71:4 (2009), 776–94.

Briscoe, John (ed.), *Valeri Maximi facta et dicta memorabilia. Libri I–VI*, Bibliotheca Teubneriana (Stuttgart, 1998).

Broughton, T. R. S., and Marcia L. Patterson, *The Magistrates of the Roman Republic*, vol. 1: *508 BC–100 BC* (New York, 1951).

Bruce, I. A. F., 'Nerva and the *Fiscus Iudaicus*', *Palestine Exploration Quarterly* 96 (1964), 34–45.

Bruun, Christer, 'Roman Government and Administration', in Christer Bruun and Jonathan Edmondson (eds), *The Oxford Handbook of Roman Epigraphy* (Oxford, 2015), 274–98.

Bryen, Ari Z., 'Martyrdom, Rhetoric, and the Politics of Procedure', *Classical Antiquity* 33:2 (2014^a), 243–80.

Bryen, Ari Z., 'The Law in Many Pieces', *Classical Philology* 109:4 (2014^b), 346–65.

Buck, P. Lorraine, 'Voluntary Martyrdom Revisited', *Journal of Theological Studies* 63:1 (2012), 125–35.

Buitenwerf, Rieuwerd, *Book III of the Sibylline Oracles and its Social Setting* (Leiden, 2003).

Bulhart, Vinzenz, and Phillipus Borleffs (eds), *Quinti Septimi Florentis Tertulliani opera pars quatra. Ad martyras, ad Scapulam, de fuga in persecutione, de monogamia, de virginibus velandis, de pallio, de paenitentia* (Vienna, 1957).

Burgess, Richard W., *Studies in Eusebian and Post-Eusebian Chronography* (Stuttgart, 1999).

Burton, G. P., 'Proconsuls, Assizes and the Administration of Justice under the Empire', *Journal of Roman Studies* 65 (1975), 92–106.

Burton, G. P., 'The Imperial State and its Impact on the Role and Status of Local Magistrates and Councillors in the Provinces of the Empire', in Lukas de Blois (ed.), *Administration, Prosopography and Appointment Policies in the Roman Empire* (Leiden, 2001), 202–14.

Burton, G. P., 'The Roman Imperial State (A.D. 14–235). Evidence and Reality', *Chiron* 32 (2002), 249–80.

Buschmann, Gerd, *Martyrium Polycarpi. Eine formenkritische Studie* (Berlin, 1994).

Butterweck, Christel, *'Martyriumssucht' in der Alten Kirche? Studien zur Darstellung und Deutung frühchristlicher Martyrien* (Tübingen, 1995).

Cairns, John W., and Paul J. du Plessis (eds), *Beyond Dogmatics. Law and Society in the Roman World* (Edinburgh, 2007).

Callewaert, C., 'Les premiers chrétiens furent-ils persécutés par édits généraux ou par mesures de police?', *Revue d'Histoire Ecclésiastique* 2 (1901), 771–97.

Callewaert, C., 'Les premiers chrétiens furent-ils persécutés par édits généraux ou par mesures de police?', *Revue d'Histoire Ecclésiastique* 3 (1902), 5–15, 324–8, and 601–14.
Callewaert, C., 'De la Méthode dans la Recherche de la Base juridique des premières Persécutions', *Revue d'Histoire Ecclésiastique* 12 (1911), 5–16 and 633–51.
Capogrossi Colognesi, Luigi, *Law and Power in the Making of the Roman Commonwealth*, trans. Laura Kopp (Cambridge, 2014).
Cappelletti, Silvia, *The Jewish Community of Rome. From the Second Century B.C. to the Third Century C.E.* (Leiden, 2006).
Carrier, R., 'The Prospect of a Christian Interpolation in Tacitus, Annals 15.44', *Vigiliae Christianae* 68:3 (2014), 264–83.
Cary, Earnest (ed.), *Dionysius of Halicarnassus. Roman Antiquities Books 1–2*, vol. 1, Loeb Classical Library (Cambridge, MA, 1937).
Cary, Earnest, and Herbert B. Foster (eds), *Cassius Dio. Roman History*, Loeb Classical Library, 9 vols (Cambridge, MA, 1914–27).
Castritius, Helmut, 'Judenvertreibungen im römischen Reich', *Aschkenas. Zeitschrift für Geschichte und Kultur der Juden* 16:2 (2006), 277–89.
Chilver, G. E. F., *A Historical Commentary on Tactius' Histories I and II* (Oxford, 1979).
Clarke, G. W., 'Some Victims of the Persecution of Maximinus Thrax', *Historia. Zeitschrift für Alte Geschichte* 15:4 (1966), 445–53.
Coarelli, Filippo, *I Santuari del Lazio in Età Repubblicana* (Rome, 1987).
Cohen, Shaye J. D., *The Beginnings of Jewishness. Boundaries, Varieties, Uncertainties* (Berkeley, 1999).
Coleman, Kathleen M., 'Bureaucratic Language in the Correspondence between Pliny and Trajan', *Transactions of the American Philological Association* 142:2 (2012), 189–238.
Coleman-Norton, Paul R. (ed.), *Roman State & Christian Church. A Collection of Legal Documents to A.D. 535*, 3 vols (London, 1966).
Colin, Jean, *L'Empire des Antonins et les Martyrs Gaulois de 177* (Bonn, 1964).
Collins, John J., 'Anti-Semitism in Antiquity? The Case of Alexandria', *Archiv für Religionsgeschichte* 7:1 (2005), 86–101.
Colson, F. H., *Philo. Every Good Man is Free; On the Contemplative Life; On the Eternity of the World; Against Flaccus; Apology for the Jews; On Providence*, Loeb Classical Library (Cambridge, MA, 1941).
Colson, F. H., *Philo. On the Embassy to Gaius; General Indexes*, Loeb Classical Library (Cambridge, MA, 1962).
Conrat, M., *Die Christenverfolgungen im römischen Reiche vom Standpunkte des Juristen* (Leipzig, 1897).
Conway, R. S., and S. K. Johnson (eds), *Titi Livi Ab Urbe Condita. Books XXVI–XXX*, Oxford Classical Texts (Oxford, 1963).
Conway, R. S., and C. F. Walters (eds), *Titi Livi Ab Urbe Condita. Books XXI–XXV*, Oxford Classical Texts (Oxford, 1963).
Cook, John Granger, *Roman Attitudes Toward the Christians* (Tübingen, 2010).
Corke-Webster, James, 'A Literary Historian. Eusebius of Caesarea and the Martyrs of Lyon and Palestine', *Studia Patristica* 66:14 (2013), 191–202.
Corke-Webster, James, 'The Early Reception of Pliny the Younger in Tertullian of Carthage and Eusebius of Caesarea', *Classical Quarterly* 67:1 (2017[a]), 247–62.
Corke-Webster, James, 'Trouble in Pontus. The Pliny-Trajan Correspondence on the Christians Reconsidered', *Transactions of the American Philological Association* 147:2 (2017[b]), 371–411.
Corke-Webster, James, 'By Whom Were Early Christians Persecuted?', *Past & Present* 261:1 (2023), 3–46.
Cortés-Copete, Juan Manual, 'Koinoi Nomoi. Hadrian and the Harmonization of Local Laws', in Olivier Hekster and Koenraad Verboven (eds), *The Impact of Justice on the Roman Empire* (Leiden, 2019), 105–21.
Cotterrell, Roger, *The Sociology of Law. An Introduction* (London, 1984).

Cotton, Hannah M., 'The Guardianship of Jesus Son of Babatha. Roman and Local Law in the Province of Arabia', *Journal of Roman Studies* 83 (1993), 94–108.
Cotton, Hannah M., 'A Cancelled Marriage Contract from the Judaean Desert', *Journal of Roman Studies* 84 (1994), 64–86.
Cotton, Hannah M., 'The Impact of the Documentary Papyri from the Judaean Desert on the Study of Jewish History from 70 to 135 CE', in Aharon Oppenheimer (ed.), *Jüdische Geschichte in hellenistisch-römischer Zeit* (Munich, 1999), 221–36.
Cotton Paltiel, Hannah M., and Avner Ecker, 'Reflections on the Foundation of Aelia Capitolina', in Giovanni Alberto Cecconi, Rita Lizzi Testa, and Arnaldo Marcone (eds), *Past as Present. Essays on Roman History in Honour of Guido Clemente* (Turnhout, 2019), 681–95.
Courtney, Edward, *A Commentary on the Satires of Juvenal* (Berkeley, 2013).
Crake, J. E. A., 'Early Christians and Roman Law', *Phoenix* 19:1 (1965), 61–70.
Cramer, Frederick H., *Astrology in Roman Law and Politics* (Philadelphia, 1954).
Crawford, M. H., *Roman Statutes*, vol. 1 (London, 1996).
Cresci Marrone, Giovannella, Alessandro Stroppa, and Francesca Rohr Vio, *Cassio Dione. Storia Romana, Libri 52–56* (Milan, 1998).
Crook, J. A., *Law and Life of Rome* (London, 1967).
Crook, J. A., 'Legal History and General History', *Bulletin of the Institute of Classical Studies* 41 (1996), 31–36.
Croteau, Shelly Jeanne, 'Marcus Aurelius and the Accidental Martyrs of Lyons. A.D. 177', PhD dissertation, University of Missouri-Columbia, 1992.
Cumont, Franz, *Astrology and Religion among the Greeks and Romans* (New York, 1912).
Czajkowski, Kimberley, *Localized Law. The Babatha and Salome Komaise Archives* (Oxford, 2017).
Czajkowski, Kimberley, 'Jewish Associations at Alexandria?', in Benedikt Eckhardt (ed.), *Private Associations and Jewish Communities in the Hellenistic and Roman Cities* (Leiden, 2019[a]), 76–96.
Czajkowski, Kimberley, 'The Limits of Legal Pluralism in the Roman Empire', *The Journal of Legal History* 40:2 (2019[b]), 110–29.
Czajkowski, Kimberley, '"Synagogues" in Ptolemaic and Early Roman Egypt', in Lutz Doering and Andrew R. Krause (eds), *Synagogues in the Hellenistic and Roman Periods. Archaeological Finds, New Methods, New Theories* (Göttingen, 2020), 295–312.
Czajkowski, Kimberley, and Benedikt Eckhardt, 'Law, Status and Agency in the Roman Provinces', *Past & Present* 241:1 (2018), 3–31.
Czajkowski, Kimberley, and Benedikt Eckhardt, 'Introduction', in Kimberley Czajkowski, Benedikt Eckhardt, and Meret Strothmann (eds), *Law in the Roman Provinces* (Oxford, 2020), 1–15.
Czajkowski, Kimberley, Benedikt Eckhardt, and Meret Strothmann (eds), *Law in the Roman Provinces* (Oxford, 2020).
Dando-Collins, Stephen, *The Great Fire of Rome. The Fall of the Emperor Nero and his City* (Cambridge, MA, 2010).
Davenport, Caillan, 'The Conduct of Vitellius in Cassius Dio's "Roman History"', *Historia. Zeitschrift für Alte Geschichte* 63:1 (2014), 96–116.
Davies, Jason P., *Rome's Religious History. Livy, Tacitus and Ammianus on Their Gods* (Cambridge, 2004).
De Angelis, Franscesco (ed.), *Spaces of Justice in the Roman World* (Leiden, 2010).
Dehandschutter, Boudewijn, 'The Martyrium Polycarpi. A Century of Research', in Wolfgang Haase (ed.), *Aufstieg und Niedergang der Römischen Welt* II.27.1 (Berlin, 1993), 485–522.
Dehandschutter, Boudewijn, 'A Community of Martyrs. Religious Identity and the Case of the Martyrs of Lyons and Vienne', in Johan Leemans (ed.), *More than a Memory. The Discourse of Martyrdom and the Construction of Christian Identity in the History of Christianity* (Louvain, 2005), 3–22.
Delehaye, Hippolyte, *Les Passions des Martyrs et les Genres Littéraires* (Brussels, 1966).

Delia, Diana, 'The Population of Roman Alexandria', *Transactions of the American Philological Association* 118 (1988), 275–92.
Delia, Diana, *Alexandrian Citizenship during the Roman Principate* (Atlanta, 1991).
Demougin, Ségolène, 'Proconsuls d'Asie sous Septime Sévère. Les gouverneurs de la province de 200 à 211', *Bulletin de la Société Nationale des Antiquaires de France* (1996), 323–33.
Desanti, Lucetta, *Sileat Omnibus perpetuo Divinandi Curiositas. Indovini e Sanzioni nel Diritto Romano* (Milan, 1990).
Díaz Fernández, Alejandro, 'When did a Provincia become a Province? On the institutional Development of a Roman republican Concept', in Alejandro Díaz Fernández (ed.), *Provinces and provincial Command in the republican Period. Genesis, Development and Government* (Seville, 2021), 41–69.
Dibelius, Martin, 'Rom und die Christen im ersten Jahrhundert', in Richard Klein (ed.), *Das frühe Christentum im römischen Staat* (Darmstadt, 1971), 47–105.
Dickie, Matthew W., *Magic and Magicians in the Greco-Roman World* (London, 2001).
Dickie, Matthew W., 'Magic in the Roman Historians', in Richard L. Gordon and Francisco Marco Simón (eds), *Magical Practice in the Latin West* (Leiden, 2010), 79–104.
Dijkstra, Jitse H. F., and Christian R. Raschle, 'General Introduction', in Jitse H. F. Dijkstra and Christian R. Raschle (eds), *Religious Violence in the Ancient World. From Classical Athens to Late Antiquity* (Cambridge, 2020), 1–14.
Dinkler, Michal Beth, 'Genre Analysis and Early Christian Martyrdom Narratives. A Proposal', in Joel Baden, Hindy Najman, and Eibert Tigchelaar (eds), *Sibyls, Scriptures, and Scrolls*, vol. 1 (Leiden, 2016), 324–36.
Dmitriev, Sviatoslav, *City Government in Hellenistic and Roman Asia Minor* (Oxford, 2005).
Dolganov, Anna, 'Reichsrecht and Volksrecht in Theory and Practice. Roman Law and Litigation Strategy in the Province of Egypt (P. Oxy. II 237, P. Oxy. IV 706, SB XII 10929)', *Tyche* 34 (2019), 27–60.
Domenicucci, Patrizio, *Astra Caesarum. Astronomia, astrologia e catasterismo da Cesare a Domiziano* (Florence, 1996).
Dondin-Payre, M., 'Notables et Élites dans les Trois Gaules', in L. de Ligt and E. A. Hemelrijk (eds), *Roman Rule and Civic Life. Local and Regional Perspectives* (Amsterdam, 2004), 357–71.
Dorey, Thomas Alan (ed.), *Titi Livi Ab Urbe Condita. Libri XXIII–XXV*, Bibliotheca Teubneriana (Leipzig, 1976).
Drinkwater, J. F., 'A Note on Local Careers in the Three Gauls under the Early Empire', *Britannia* 10 (1979), 89–100.
Drogula, Fred K., 'The Office of the Provincial Governor under the Roman Republic and Empire (to AD 235). Conception and Tradition', PhD dissertation, University of Virginia, 2005.
Drogula, Fred K., 'From the Beginning. The Origins of the Provincia and its unique Advantages in republican Rome', in Alejandro Díaz Fernández (ed.), *Provinces and provincial Command in the republican Period. Genesis, Development and Government* (Seville, 2021), 19–40.
Dunn, Geoffrey D., 'Rhetorical Structures in Tertullian's Ad Scapulam', *Vigiliae Christianae* 56:1 (2002), 47–55.
Dunn, James D., *Jews and Christians. The Parting of the Ways, A.D. 70 to 135* (Tübingen, 1992).
Dunn, James D., 'Who did they think Jesus was?', in *Jesus Remembered* (Grand Rapids, 2003), 615–704.
Dunn, James D., *The Acts of the Apostles* (rev. edn, Grand Rapids, 2016).
Du Plessis, Paul J. 'Introduction', in Paul J. du Plessis (ed.), *New Frontiers. Law and Society in the Roman World* (Edinburgh, 2013), 1–5.
Du Plessis, Paul J. 'Introduction', in Paul J. du Plessis (ed.), *Cicero's Law. Rethinking Roman Law of the Late Republic* (Edinburgh, 2016), 1–7.
Du Plessis, Paul J., Clifford Ando, and Kaius Tuori (eds), *The Oxford Handbook of Roman Law and Society* (Oxford, 2016).
Durkheim, Émile, 'La sociologia e il suo dominio scientifico', *Revista italiana di sociologia* 4 (1900), 127–48.

Eck, Werner, 'Jahres- und Provinzialfasten der senatorischen Statthalter von 69/70 bis 138/139', *Chiron* 13 (1983), 147–237.

Eck, Werner, 'Consules Ordinarii und Consules Suffecti als Eponyme Amststräger', *Epigrafia. Actes du colloque en mémoire de Attilio Degrassi* (Rome, 1991), 15–44.

Eck, Werner, 'Provincial Administration and Finance', in Alan K. Bowman, Peter Garnsey, and Dominic Rathbone (eds), *The Cambridge Ancient History*, vol. 11: *The High Empire,* AD *70–192* (Cambridge, 2000), 266–92.

Eck, Werner, *Rom und Judaea* (Tübingen, 2007).

Eck, Werner, 'Diplomacy as Part of the Administrative Process in the Roman Empire', in C. Eilers (ed.), *Diplomats and Diplomacy in the Roman World* (Leiden, 2009), 193–207.

Eck, Werner, 'Die römischen Repräsentanten in Judaea. Provokateure oder Vertreter der römischen Macht?', in Mladen Popović (ed.), *The Jewish Revolt against Rome* (Leiden, 2011), 45–68.

Eck, Werner, 'Der Bar Kokhba-Aufstand der Jahre 132–136 und seine Folgen für die Provinz Syria Palaestina', in Werner Eck (ed.), *Judäa – Syria Palästina* (Tübingen, 2014), 229–44.

Eck, Werner, 'The Emperor, the Law and Imperial Administration', in Paul J. du Plessis, Clifford Ando, and Kaius Tuori (eds), *The Oxford Handbook of Roman Law and Society* (Oxford, 2016), 98–110.

Eckhardt, Benedikt, 'Rom und die Juden. Ein Kategorienfehler?', in Görge K. Hasselhoff and Meret Strothmann (eds), *Religio Licita? Rom und die Juden* (Berlin, 2017), 13–53.

Eckhardt, Benedikt, 'Der Staat, das Recht und die Christen', in Benedikt Eckhardt and Clemens Leonhard (eds), *Juden, Christen und Vereine im römischen Reich* (Berlin, 2018[a]), 25–60.

Eckhardt, Benedikt, 'Synagogen, Vereine und ihr Platz in der antiken mediterranen Gesellschaft', in Benedikt Eckhardt and Clemens Leonhard (eds), *Juden, Christen und Vereine im römischen Reich* (Berlin, 2018[b]), 61–95.

Eckhardt, Benedikt, 'Who Thought that Early Christians Formed Associations?', *Mnemosyne* 71:2 (2018[c]), 298–314.

Eckhardt, Benedikt, 'Associations beyond the City. Jews, Actors and Empire in the Roman Period', in Benedikt Eckhardt (ed.), *Private Associations and Jewish Communities in the Hellenistic and Roman Cities* (Leiden, 2019), 115–56.

Eckhardt, Benedikt, 'Synagogues as Associations in the Roman Empire', in Lutz Doering and Andrew R. Krause (eds), *Synagogues in the Hellenistic and Roman Periods. Archaeological Finds, New Methods, New Theories* (Göttingen, 2020), 313–37.

Eckhardt, Benedikt, and Clemens Leonhard, 'Fazit und Ausblick', in Benedikt Eckhardt and Clemens Leonhard (eds), *Juden, Christen und Vereine im römischen Reich* (Berlin, 2018), 331–8.

Edmondson, Jonathan, 'The Roman Emperor and the Local Communities of the Roman Empire', in J. L. Ferrary and J. Scheid (eds), *Il princeps romano. Autocrate o magitrato? Fattori giuridici e fattori sociali del potere imperial da Augusto a Commodo* (Pavia, 2015), 701–29.

Edwards, Mark, 'The First Millennium', in S. Bullivant and M. Ruse (eds), *The Oxford Handbook of Atheism* (Oxford, 2013), 152–63.

Ehrman, Bart D., *Jesus. Apocalyptic Prophet of the New Millennium* (Oxford, 1999).

Ehrman, Bart D., *Forgery and Counterforgery. The Use of Literary Deceit in Early Christian Polemics* (Oxford, 2013).

Eilers, C., *Roman Patrons of Greek Cities* (Oxford, 2002).

Elliot, Thomas, 'Epigraphic Evidence for Boundary Disputes in the Roman Empire', PhD dissertation, University of North Carolina at Chapel Hill, 2004.

Erdkamp, Paul, *The Grain Market in the Roman Empire* (Cambridge, 2005).

Eshel, H. 'The Bar Kochba Revolt, 132–135', in S. T. Katz (ed.), *The Cambridge History of Judaism*, vol. 4 (Cambridge, 2006), 105–27.

Evans, Craig A., 'Prophet, Sage, Healer, Messiah, and Martyr. Types and Identities of Jesus', in Stangley E. Porter and Tom Holmén (eds), *Handbook for the Study of the Historical Jesus*, vol. 2 (Leiden 2011), 1217–43.

Fantham, Elaine (ed.), *Ovid. Fasti Book IV* (Cambridge, 1998).

Färber, Roland, *Römische Gerichtsorte. Räumliche Dynamiken von Jurisdiktion im Imperium Romanum* (Munich, 2014).
Feldman, Louis H., *Jew and Gentile in the Ancient World* (Princeton, 1993).
Feldman, L. H., R. Marcus, H. St. J. Thackeray, and A. Wikgren (eds), *Josephus. Jewish Antiquities*, Loeb Classical Library, 9 vols (Cambridge, MA, 1930–65).
Fenechiu, Carmen, 'Narrating Dreams in the Annals', in Ioan Piso, Viorica Rusu-Bolindet, Rada Varga, Silvia Mustaţă, Eugenia Beu-Dachin, and Ligia Ruscu (eds), *Scripta Classica* (Cluj-Napoca, 2011), 201–6.
Fisher, C. D., *Cornelii Taciti Annalium, ab excess divi Augusti Libri*, Oxford Classical Texts (Oxford, 1906).
Fisher, C. D., *Cornelii Taciti Historiarum Libri*, Oxford Classical Texts (Oxford, 1911).
Fishwick, Duncan, 'The Temple of the Three Gauls', *Journal of Roman Studies* 62 (1972), 46–52.
Fishwick, Duncan, 'The Severi and the Provincial Cult of the Three Gauls', *Historia. Zeitschrift für Alte Geschichte* 22 (1973), 627–49.
Fishwick, Duncan, 'The Federal Cult of the Three Gauls', in Jean Rougé and Robert Turcan (eds), *Les Martyrs de Lyon – 177* (Paris, 1978), 33–45.
Fögen, Marie Theres, *Die Enteignung der Wahrsager. Studien zum kaiserlichen Wissensmonopol in der Spätantike* (Frankfurt am Main, 1993).
Forsythe, Gary, *Livy and Early Rome. A Study in Historical Method and Judgement* (Stuttgart, 1999).
Frakes, Robert M., *Compiling the Collatio Legum Mosaicarum et Romanarum in Late Antiquity* (Oxford, 2011).
Frankfurter, David, 'Voices, Books, and Dreams. The Diversification of Divination Media in Late Antique Egypt', in Sarah Iles Johnston and Peter T. Struck (eds), *Mantikê. Studies in Ancient Divination* (Leiden, 2005), 233–54.
Frankfurter, David, 'Religious Practice and Piety', in Christina Riggs (ed.), *The Oxford Handbook of Roman Egypt* (Oxford, 2012), 319–36.
Frend, W. H. C., *Martyrdom and Persecution in the Early Church. A Study of a Conflict from the Maccabees to Donatus* (Oxford, 1965).
Frend, W. H. C., 'The Failure of the Persecutions in the Roman Empire', in M. I. Finley (ed.), *Studies in Ancient Society* (London, 1974), 263–87.
Frend, W. H. C., 'Martyrdom and Political Oppression', in Philip F. Esler (ed.), *The Early Christian World*, vol. 2 (London, 2000), 815–39.
Frend, W. H. C., 'Persecutions. Genesis and Legacy', in M. M. Mitchell and F. M. Young (eds), *The Cambridge History of Christianity*, vol. 1: *Origins to Constantine*, (Cambridge, 2006), 503–23.
Freudenberger, Rudolf, 'Die Acta Justini als historisches Dokument', in Karlmann Beyschlag, Gottfried Maron, and Eberhard Wölfel (eds), *Humanitas – Christianitas* (Witten, 1968), 24–31.
Freudenberger, Rudolf, 'Die Akten der scilitanischen Märtyrer als historisches Dokument', *Wiener Studien* 7 (1973), 196–215.
Freyburger, Marie-Laure, and Jean-Michel Roddaz, *Dion Cassius. Histoire Romaine, Livres 48 et 49*, Collection des Universités de France/Budé (Paris, 1994).
Freyne, Sean, 'The Revolt from a Regional Perspective', in Andrea M. Berlin and J. Andrew Overman (eds), *The First Jewish Revolt. Archaeology, History and Ideology* (London, 2002), 43–56.
Frier, Bruce W., *The Rise of the Roman Jurists. Studies in Cicero's Pro Caecina* (Princeton, 1985).
Fuchs, Harald, 'Tacitus über die Christen', *Vigiliae Christianae* 4 (1950), 65–93.
Fuhrmann, Christopher, *Policing the Roman Empire* (Oxford, 2012).
Fuhrmann, Christopher, 'Police Functions and Public Order', in Paul J. du Plessis, Clifford Ando, and Kaius Tuori (eds), *The Oxford Handbook of Roman Law and Society* (Oxford, 2016), 297–309.
Furneaux, Henry, *The Annals of Tacitus*, vol. 2: *Books 11–16* (Oxford, 1891).

Galsterer, Hartmut, 'Roman Law in the Provinces. Some Problems of Transmission', in M. H. Crawford (ed.), *L'Impero Romano e le strutture economiche e sociali delle province* (Como, 1986), 13–27.

Galsterer, Hartmut, 'The Administration of Justice', in Alan K. Bowman, Edward Champlin, and Andrew Lintott (eds), *The Cambridge Ancient History*, vol. 10: *The Augustan Empire, 43 BC–AD 69* (Cambridge, 1996), 397–413.

Galsterer, Hartmut, 'Local and Provincial Institutions and Government', in Alan K. Bowman, Peter Garnsey, and Dominic Rathbone (eds), *The Cambridge Ancient History*, vol. 11: *The High Empire, AD 70–192* (Cambridge, 2000), 344–60.

Gambash, Gil, Haim Gitler, and Hannah M. Cotton, 'Iudaea Recepta', *Israel Numismatic Research* 8 (2013), 89–104.

Gambash, Gil, *Rome and Provincial Resistance* (New York, 2015).

Gambetti, Sandra, *The Alexandrian Riots of 38 C.E. and the Persecution of the Jews. A Historical Reconstruction* (Leiden, 2009).

Garnsey, Peter, 'The Criminal Jurisdiction of Governors', *Journal of Roman Studies* 58 (1968), 51–9.

Garnsey, Peter, 'Legal Privilege in the Roman Empire', in M. I. Finley (ed.), *Studies in Ancient Society* (London, 1974), 141–65.

Garnsey, Peter, 'Religious Toleration in Classical Antiquity', in W. J. Sheils (ed.), *Persecution and Toleration* (Oxford, 1984), 1–27.

Garnsey, Peter, *Famine and food-supply in the Graeco-Roman world. Responses to Risk and Crisis* (Cambridge, 1988).

Garnsey, Peter, 'Roman Citizenship and Roman Law in the Late Empire', in Simon Swain and Mark Edwards (eds), *Approaching Late Antiquity* (Oxford, 2004), 133–55.

Garnsey, Peter, and Richard Saller, *The Roman Empire. Economy, Society and Culture* (London, 1987).

Gera, Dov, *Judaea and Mediterranean Politics, 219 to 161 B.C.E.* (Leiden, 1998).

Getty, Robert J., 'Nero's Indictment of the Christians in A.D. 64. Tacitus' *Annals* 15.44.2–4', in Luitpold Wallach (ed.), *The Classical Tradition. Literary and Historical Studies in Honor of Harry Caplan* (Ithaca, 1966), 285–92.

Geus, Klaus, 'Die "Weltkarte" und das Verbrechen des Mettius Pompusianus. Ein Vorschlag', in Emilio Suárez de la Torre, Isabel Canzobre Martínes, and Carmen Sánchez Mañas (eds), *Ablanathanalba. Magia, Cultura y Sociedad en el Mundo Antiguo* (Madrid, 2019), 175–83.

Giaro, Tomasz, 'Iulius IV.16: I. Paulus, Roman jurist, approx. AD 150–230', in *Brill's New Pauly Online* (2006). <http://dx.doi.org/10.1163/1574-9347_bnp_e600580>.

Gibson, Roy K., *Man of High Empire. The Life of Pliny the Younger* (New York, 2020).

Gibson, Roy K., and Ruth Morello, *Reading the Letters of Pliny the Younger. An Introduction* (Cambridge, 2012).

Gizewski, Christian, 'Comitia', in *Brill's New Pauly Online* (2006). <https://doi.org/10.1163/1574-9347_bnp_e303480>.

Glare, P. G. W., *Oxford Latin Dictionary* (8th edn, Oxford 1982).

Glay, M. le, 'Le Culte imperial à Lyon, au IIe Siècle Ap. J.C.', in Jean Rougé and Robert Turcan (eds), *Les Martyrs de Lyon – 177* (Paris, 1978), 19–31.

Glover, T. R., and Gerald H. Rendall (eds), *Tertullian. Apology and De Spectaculis; Minucius Felix. Octavius*, Loeb Classical Library (Cambridge, MA, 1931).

Goldsworthy, Adrian, *The Roman Army at War. 100 BC–AD 200* (Oxford, 1996).

Goodman, Martin, *The Ruling Class of Judea. The Origins of the Jewish Revolt against Rome, A.D. 66–70* (Cambridge, 1987).

Goodman, Martin, 'Diaspora Reactions to the Destruction of the Temple', in James D. G. Dunn (ed.), *Jews and Christians. The Parting of the Ways, A.D. 70 to 135* (Tübingen, 1992), 27–38.

Goodman, Martin, 'Trajan and the Origins of the Bar Kokhba War', in Peter Schäfer (ed.), *The Bar Kokhba War Reconsidered* (Tübingen, 2003), 23–9.

Goodman, Martin, 'The *Fiscus Iudaicus* and Gentile Attitudes to Judaism in Flavian Rome', in Jonathan Edmondson, Steve Mason, and James Rives (eds), *Flavius Josephus and Flavian Rome* (Oxford, 2005), 167–77.

Goodman, Martin, *Rome and Jerusalem. The Clash of Ancient Civilizations* (New York, 2007[a]).
Goodman, Martin, 'The Meaning of *Fisci Iudaici Calumnia Sublata* on the Coinage of Nerva', in J. Schwartz, S. J. D. Cohen, and L.H. Feldman (eds), *Studies in Josephus and the Varieties of Ancient Judaism* (Leiden, 2007[b]), 81–9.
Goodman, Martin, 'The Roman State and Jewish Diaspora Communities in the Antonine Age', in Yair Furstenberg (ed.), *Jewish and Christian Communal Identities in the Roman World* (Leiden, 2016), 75–83.
Goodyear, F. R. D. (ed.), *The Annals of Tacitus. Books 1–6*, vol. 2: *Annals 1.55–81 and Annals 2* (Cambridge, 1981).
Gordon, R., '*Superstitio*, Superstition and Religious Repression in the Late Roman Republic and Principate (100 BCE–300 CE)', in S. A. Smith and Alan Knight (eds), *The Religion of Fools. Superstition Past and Present* (Oxford, 2008), 72–94.
Gordon, R., 'The Roman Imperial Cult and the Question of Power', in J. A. North and S. R. F. Price (eds), *The Religious History of the Roman Empire* (Oxford, 2011), 37–70.
Goulder, Michael D., 'Did Peter ever go to Rome?', *Scottish Journal of Theology* 57:4 (2004), 377–96.
Gradel, Ittai, *Emperor Worship and Roman Religion* (Oxford, 2002).
Green, Steven J., *Disclosure and Discretion in Roman Astrology* (Oxford, 2014).
Grégoire, Henri, 'Procès-verbaux des Séances de la Société Théonoé. Séance du 8 Octobre 1956', *Nouvelle Clio. Revue Mensuelle de la Découverte Historique* 7–9 (1955–7), 298–304.
Griffin, Miriam, 'The Flavians', in Alan K. Bowman, Peter Garnsey, and Dominic Rathbone (eds), *The Cambridge Ancient History*, vol. 11: *The High Empire, AD 70–192* (Cambridge, 2008).
Groag, Edmund, 'Furius: 50', in *Paulys Realencyclopädie der classischen Altertumswissenschaft* VII.1 (Stuttgart, 1910), 351.
Gross, Simcha, 'Hopeful Rebels and Anxious Romans. Jewish Interconnectivity in the Great Revolt and Beyond', *Historia. Zeitschrift für Alte Geschichte* 72:4 (2023), 479–513.
Grothoff, Kyle, 'Astrology in Augustan Rome. A Cultural History', PhD dissertation, Indiana University 2016.
Gruen, Erich S., *Studies in Greek Culture and Roman Policy* (Leiden, 1990).
Gruen, Erich S., *Diaspora. Jews Amidst Greeks and Romans* (Cambridge, MA, 2002).
Gruen, Erich S., *Rethinking the Other in Antiquity* (Princeton, 2011).
Gruen, Erich S., 'Caligula, the Imperial Cult, and Philo's *Legatio*', *The Studia Philonica Annual* 24 (2012), 135–47.
Guettel Cole, Susan, 'Professionals, Volunteers, and Amateurs. Serving the Gods *kata ta patria*', in Beate Dignas and Kai Trampedach (eds), *Practitioners of the Divine* (Cambridge, MA, 2008), 55–72.
Günther, Sven, 'The *Fiscus Iudaicus*. A Hypothetical Scholarly Construct', in Görge K. Hasselhoff and Meret Strothmann (eds), *Religio Licita? Rom und die Juden* (Berlin, 2017), 175–90.
Guterman, Simeon L., *Religious Toleration and Persecution in Ancient Rome* (London, 1951).
Häger, Hans-Joachim, 'Das Briefcorpus des jüngeren Plinius. Neuere Tendenzen in Altertumswissenschaft und Didaktik', *Gymnasium. Zeitschrift für die Antike in der deutschen Bildung* 122:6 (2015), 559–96.
Haighton, Angela, 'Roman Methods of Authentication in the First Two Centuries AD', *Journal of the Society of Archivists* 31 (2010), 29–49.
Halbertsma, Ruurd B., *Beeldhouwkunst uit Hellas en Rome* (Amsterdam, 1995).
Halbertsma, Ruurd B., *Scholars, Travellers and Trade. The Pioneer Years of the National Museum of Antiquities in Leiden, 1818–1840* (London, 2003).
Hansen, C. M., 'The Number of the Myth. A Defence of the Ahistoricity of the Neronian Persecution', *Journal of Early Christian History*, 13:2 (2023[a]), 2–21. Accessed in early view version via <https://doi.org/10.1080/2222582X.2023.2208316>.
Hansen, C. M., 'The Problem of Annals 15.44. On the Plinian Origin of Tacitus's Information on Christians', *Journal of Early Christian History* 13:1 (2023[b]), 62–80.
Hare, Douglas R. A., *The Theme of Jewish Persecution of Christians in the Gospel According to St. Matthew* (Cambridge, 1967).

Harker, Andrew, *Loyalty and Dissidence in Roman Egypt* (Cambridge, 2008).
Harker, Andrew, 'The Jews in Roman Egypt. Trials and Rebellions', in Christina Riggs (ed.), *The Oxford Handbook of Roman Egypt* (Oxford, 2012), 277–87.
Harnack, Adolf, 'Das Edict des Antoninus Pius', in Oscar von Gebhardt and Adolf Harnack, *Texte und Untersuchungen zur Geschichte der altchristlichen Literatur*, vol. 13.4a (Leipzig, 1895).
Harries, Jill, 'Introduction. The Background to the Code', in Jill Harries and Ian Wood (eds), *The Theodosian Code. Studies in the Imperial Law of Late Antiquity* (London, 1993), 1–16.
Harries, Jill, *Law and Empire in Late Antiquity* (Cambridge, 1999).
Harries, Jill, *Cicero and the Jurists. From Citizens' Law to the Lawful State* (London, 2006).
Harries, Jill, *Law and Crime in the Roman World* (Cambridge, 2007).
Harries, Jill, 'Triple Vision. Ulpian of Tyre on the Duties of the Proconsul', in Jesper Majbom Madsen and Roger David Rees (eds), *Roman Rule in Greek and Latin Writing. Double Vision* (Leiden, 2014), 193–209.
Harrill, J. Albert, *Paul the Apostle. His Life and Legacy in Their Roman Context* (Cambridge, 2012).
Harvey, A. E., *A Companion to the New Testament* (Cambridge, 2004).
Hasselhoff, Görge K., and Meret Strothmann, 'Religio Licita. Rom und die Juden', in Görge K. Hasselhoff and Meret Strothmann (eds), *Religio Licita? Rom und die Juden* (Berlin, 2017), 1–12.
Hauken, Tor, *Petition and Response. An Epigraphic Study of Petitions to Roman Emperors, 181–249* (Athens, 1998).
Heemstra, Marius, *The Fiscus Judaicus and the Parting of the Ways* (Tübingen, 2010).
Heemstra, Marius, 'The *Fiscus Judaicus*. Its Social and Legal Impact and a Possible Relation with Josephus' Antiquities', in P. J. Tomson and J. Schwartz (eds), *Jews and Christians in the First and Second Centuries. How to Write Their History* (Leiden, 2014), 327–47.
Hekster, Olivier, *Rome and Its Empire. AD 193–284* (Edinburgh, 2008).
Hekster, Olivier, 'Imagining Power. Reality Gaps in the Roman Empire', *Babesch* 86 (2011), 111–25.
Hekster, Olivier, and John Rich, 'Octavian and the Thunderbolt. The Temple of Apollo Palatinus and Roman Traditions of Temple Building', *Classical Quarterly* 56:1 (2006), 149–68.
Hengel, Martin, *Judentum und Hellenismus. Studien zu ihrer Begegnung unter besonderer Berüksichtigung Palästinas bis zur Mitte des 2. Jh.s v. Chr.* (Tübingen, 1973).
Hengel, Martin and C. K. Barrett, *Conflicts and Challenges in Early Christianity* (Harrisburg, 1999).
Henten, J. W. van, and Friedrich Avemarie, *Martyrdom and Noble Death. Selected Texts from Graeco-Roman, Jewish, and Christian Antiquity* (London, 2002).
Herz, Peter, 'Emperors. Caring for the Empire and Their Successors', in Jörg Rüpke, *A Companion to Roman Religion* (Malden, 2007), 304–16.
Heubner, Henricus (ed.), *P. Cornelii Taciti libri qui supersunt*, vol. 1: *Ab Excessu Divi Augusti*, Bibliotheca Teubneriana (Stuttgart, 1983).
Honigman, Sylvie, 'The Shifting Definition of Greek Identity in Alexandria through the Transition from Ptolemaic to Roman Rule', in B. Schliesser, J. Rüggemeier, T. J. Kraus, and J. Frey (eds), *Alexandria. Hub of the Hellenistic World* (Tübingen, 2021), 125–43.
Honoré, Tony, 'Scriptor Historiae Augustae', *Journal of Roman Studies* 77 (1987), 156–76.
Honoré, Tony, *Ulpian. Pioneer of Human Rights* (Oxford, 2002).
Honoré, Tony, *Justinian's Digest. Character and Compilation* (Oxford, 2010).
Hooker, Morna D., 'Artemis of Ephesus', *Journal of Theological Studies* 64:1 (2013), 37–46.
Horbury, William, *Jewish War under Trajan and Hadrian* (Cambridge, 2014).
Horst, Pieter W. van der, 'The first Pogrom. Alexandria 38 CE', *European Review* 10:4 (2002), 469–84.
Horst, Pieter W. van der, *Philo's Flaccus. The First Pogrom, Introduction, Translation, and Commentary* (Leiden, 2003).

Huebner, Sabine R., *Papyri and the Social World of the New Testament* (Cambridge, 2019).
Humfress, Caroline, *Orthodoxy and the Courts in Late Antiquity* (Oxford, 2007).
Humfress, Caroline, 'Law and Custom under Rome', in A. Rio (ed.), *Law, Custom and Justice in Late Antiquity and the Early Middle Ages* (London, 2011), 23–49.
Humfress, Caroline, 'Law's Empire. Roman Universalism and Legal Practice', in Paul J. du Plessis (ed.), *New Frontiers. Law and Society in the Roman World* (Edinburgh, 2013), 73–101.
Hurlet, Frédéric, 'Justice, Res Publica and Empire. Subsidiarity and Hierarchy in the Roman Empire', in Olivier Hekster and Koenraad Verboven (eds), *The Impact of Justice on the Roman Empire* (Leiden, 2019), 122–37.
Hyamson, Moses (ed.), *Mosaicarum et Romanarum Legum Collatio* (London, 1913).
Ibbetson, David, 'High Classical Law', in Alan Bowman, Averil Cameron, and Peter Garnsey (eds), *The Cambridge Ancient History*, vol. 12: *The Crisis of Empire, AD 193–337* (Cambridge, 2005), 184–99.
Ibbetson, David, 'Sources of Law from the Republic to the Dominate', in David Johnston (ed.), *The Cambridge Companion to Roman Law* (Cambridge, 2015), 25–44.
Ihm, Maximilianus (ed.), *C. Suetoni Tranquilli opera*, vol. 1: *De Vita Caesarum Libri VIII*, Bibliotheca Teubneriana (Leipzig, 1908).
Isaac, Benjamin, 'Roman Religious Policy and the Bar Kokhba War', in Peter Schäfer (ed.), *The Bar Kokhba War Reconsidered* (Tübingen, 2003), 37–54.
Israelowich, Ido, 'The Rain Miracle of Marcus Aurelius. (Re-)Construction of Consensus', *Greece and Rome* 55:1 (2008), 83–102.
Jackson, John (ed.), *Tacitus, The Annals*, vol. 5: *Books XIII–XVI*, Loeb Classical Library (Cambridge, MA, 1937).
Janssen, K. P. S., '"All Turned on Us Like Beasts". Legal Negotiation and the Persecution of Lyon and Vienne', in Markus Tiwald and Jürgen K. Zangenberg (eds), *Early Christian Encounters with Town and Countryside. Essays on the Urban and Rural Worlds of Early Christianity* (Göttingen, 2021[a]), 299–319.
Janssen, Renske, 'Christenen in Bithynia-Pontus. De Plinius-Trajanus correspondentie als context voor de christenbrieven', *Lampas. Tijdschrift voor Classici* 54:3 (2021[b]), 330–50.
Johne, Klaus-Peter, 'Historia Augusta', in *Brill's New Pauly Online* (18 Sept 2017). <https://doi.org/10.1163/1574-9347_bnp_e515750>.
Johnston, David, *Roman Law in Context* (Cambridge, 1999).
Johnston, Sarah Iles (ed.), *Religions of the Ancient World* (Cambridge, MA, 2004).
Jolowicz, H. F., *Historical Introduction to the Study of Roman Law* (2nd edn, Cambridge, 1954).
Jolowicz, H. F., and Nicholas, B., *Historical Introduction to the Study of Roman Law* (3rd edn, Cambridge, 1972).
Jones, Brian W., *The Emperor Domitian* (London, 1992).
Jones, Christopher P., 'Juristes romains dans l'Orient greque', *Comptes rendus de l'Academie des Inscriptions et Belles-Lettres* 151 (2007), 1331–59.
Jones, Christopher P., 'The Historicity of the Neronian Persecution. A Response to Brent Shaw', *New Testament Studies* 63 (2017), 146–52.
Jones, Frederick, 'Naming in Pliny's Letters', *Symbolae Osloenses* 66 (1991), 147–70.
Juster, Jean, *Les Juifs dans l'Empire romain. Leur condition juridique, économique et sociale*, 2 vols (Paris, 1914).
Kaiser, Wolfgang, 'Justinian and the Corpus Iuris Civilis', in David Johnston (ed.), *The Cambridge Companion to Roman Law* (Cambridge, 2015), 119–48.
Kasher, Aryeh, *The Jews in Hellenistic and Roman Egypt. The Struggle for Equal Rights* (Tübingen, 1985).
Kaster, R. A. (ed.), *C. Suetoni Tranquilli. De Vita Caesarum Libros VIII et De Grammaticis et Rhetoribus Librum*, Oxford Classical Texts (Oxford, 2016[a]).
Kaster, R. A., *Studies on the Text of Suetonius' 'De Vita Caesarum'* (Oxford, 2016[b]).
Kelly, Benjamin, 'Riot Control and Imperial Ideology in the Roman Empire', *Phoenix* 61:1 (2007), 150–76.

Kelly, Benjamin, *Petitions, Litigation, and Social Control in Roman Egypt* (Oxford, 2011).

Kelly, Benjamin, 'Policing and Security', in Paul Erdkamp (ed.), *The Cambridge Companion to Ancient Rome* (Cambridge, 2013), 410–24.

Kelly, Benjamin, 'Repression, Resistance and Rebellion', in Paul J. du Plessis, Clifford Ando, and Kaius Tuori (eds), *The Oxford Handbook of Roman Law and Society* (Oxford, 2016), 374–85.

Kelly, Gordon P., *A History of Exile in the Roman Republic* (Cambridge, 2006).

Keresztes, Paul, 'Hadrian's Rescript to Minucius Fundanus', *Latomus* 26 (1967[a]), 54–66.

Keresztes, Paul, 'The Emperor Hadrian's Rescript to Minucius Fundanus', *Phoenix* 21:2 (1967[b]), 120–9.

Keresztes, Paul, 'The Massacre at Lugdunum in 177 A.D.', *Historia. Zeitschrift für Alte Geschichte* 16 (1967[c]), 75–86.

Keresztes, Paul, 'Marcus Aurelius a Persecutor?', *Harvard Theological Review* 61:3 (1968), 321–41.

Keresztes, Paul, 'The Emperor Antoninus Pius and the Christians', *Journal of Ecclesiastical History* 22:1 (1971), 1–18.

Keresztes, Paul, 'The Jews, the Christians, and Emperor Domitian', *Vigiliae Christianae* 27:1 (1973), 1–28.

Keresztes, Paul, 'The Imperial Roman Government and the Christian Church', in H. Temporini and W. Haase (eds), *Aufstieg und Niedergang der Römischen Welt* II.23.1 (Berlin, 1979), 247–315 and 375–86.

Kierdorf, Wilhelm, 'Quellen und Quellenkritik', in Walter Eder (ed.), *Staat und Staatlichkeit in der frühen römischen Republik* (Stuttgart, 1990), 200–7.

Kierdorf, Wilhelm (ed.), *Sueton. Leben des Claudius und Nero* (Paderborn, 1992).

Kippenberg, Hans G., 'Magic in Roman Civil Discourse. Why Rituals could be Illegal', in Peter Schäfer and Hans G. Kippenberg (eds), *Envisioning Magic* (Leiden, 1997), 137–63.

Klingshirn, William E., 'Christian Divination in Late Roman Gaul. The *Sortes Sangallenses*', in Sarah Iles Johnston and Peter T. Struck (eds), *Mantikê. Studies in Ancient Divination* (Leiden, 2005), 99–128.

Knapp, Robert, 'Legally Marginalised Groups. The Empire', in Paul J. du Plessis, Clifford Ando, and Kaius Tuori (eds), *The Oxford Handbook of Roman Law and Society* (Oxford, 2016), 362–73.

Kneppe, Alfred, 'Die Gefährdung der securitas. Angst vor Angehörigen sozialer Randgruppen der römischen Kaiserzeit am Beispiel von Philosophen, Astrologen, Magiern, Schauspielern und Räubern', in Ingomar Weiler and Hans Graßl (eds), *Soziale Randgruppen und Aussenseiter im Altertum* (Graz, 1988), 165–76.

Knopf, D. Rudolf (ed.), *Ausgewählte Märtyrerakten* (Tübingen, 1913).

Koestermann, Erich, 'Ein folgenschwerer Irrtum des Tacitus (Ann. 15,44,2 ff.)?', *Historia. Zeitschrift für Alte Geschichte* 16 (1967), 456–69.

Koestermann, Erich (ed.), *Cornelius Tacitus. Annalen, Buch 14–16* (Heidelberg, 1968).

Kokkinia, C., 'Ruling, Inducing, Arguing. How to Govern (and Survive) a Greek Province', in Luuk de Ligt, E. A. Hemelrijk, and H. W. Singor (eds), *Roman Rule and Civic Life. Local and Regional Perspectives* (Amsterdam, 2004), 39–58.

Kovács, Péter, *Marcus Aurelius' Rain Miracle and the Marcomannic Wars* (Leiden, 2009).

Kraemer, David, 'Jews in Palestine', in Paul Erdkamp and Claire Holleran (eds), *The Routledge Handbook of Diet and Nutrition in the Roman World* (London, 2018), 208–17.

Laes, Christian, and Johan Strubbe, *Youth in the Roman Empire* (Cambridge, 2014).

Lampe, Peter, *Die stadtrömischen Christen in den ersten beiden Jahrhunderten* (Tübingen, 1989).

Lampe, Peter, *From Paul to Valentinus. Christians at Rome in the First Two Centuries*, trans. Michael Steinhauser (Minneapolis, 2003).

Lane, E. N., 'Sabazius and the Jews in Valerius Maximus. A Re-examination', *Journal of Roman Studies* 69 (1979), 35–8.

Lane Fox, Robin, *Pagans and Christians* (London, 1986).

Lapin, Hayim, *Rabbis as Romans. The Rabbinic Movement in Palestine, 100–400 C.E.* (Oxford, 2012).

Last, H., 'Christenverfolgung II (juridisch)', in Theodor Klauser, Ernst Dassmann, Franz Joseph Dölger, et al. (eds), *Reallexikon für Antike und Christentum*, vol. 2 (Stuttgart, 1954), 1208–28.
Lavan, Myles, 'Pliny Epistles 10 and Imperial Correspondence. The Empire of Letters', in Alice König and Christopher Whitton (eds), *Roman Literature under Nerva, Trajan and Hadrian. Literary Interactions AD 96–138* (Cambridge, 2018), 280–301.
Lendon, J. E., *Empire of Honour. The Art of Government in the Roman World* (Oxford, 1997).
Leppin, Harmut, 'Old Religions Transformed. Religions and Religious Policy from Decius to Constantine', in Jörg Rüpke (ed.), *A Companion to Roman Religion* (Malden, 2007), 96–107.
Lesaffer, Rendall, *Inleiding tot de Europese Rechtsgeschiedenis* (Leuven, 2004).
Lewis, Carlton Thomas, and Charles Short, *A Latin Dictionary* (rev. edn, Oxford, 1975).
Liddell, Henry George, Robert Scott, and Henry Stuart Jones, *A Greek–English Lexicon* (9th edn, Oxford, 1968).
Liebs, Detlef, *Die Jurispurdenz im spätantiken Italien. 260–640 n. Chr.* (Berlin, 1987).
Liebs, Detlef, *Römische Jurisprudenz in Africa* (Berlin, 2005).
Liebs, Detlef, *Hofjuristen der römischen Kaiser bis Justinian* (Munich, 2010).
Liebs, Detlef, *Summoned to the Roman Courts* (Berkeley, 2012).
Linder, Amnon, 'The Legal Status of the Jews in the Roman Empire', in Steven T. Katz (ed.), *The Cambridge History of Judaism*, vol. 4 (Cambridge, 2006), 128–73.
Linder, Amnon, 'The Legal Status of Jews in the Byzantine Empire', in Robert Bonfil, Oded Irshai, Guy G. Stroumsa, and Rina Talgam (eds), *Jews in Byzantium. Dialectics of Minority and Majority Cultures* (Leiden, 2011), 149–217.
Lintott, Andrew, *Violence in Republican Rome* (Oxford, 1968).
Lintott, Andrew, *Imperium Romanum. Politics and Administration* (London, 1993).
Lintott, Andrew, *The Constitution of the Roman Republic* (Oxford, 1999).
Lintott, Andrew, 'Crime and Punishment', in David Johnston (ed.), *The Cambridge Companion to Roman Law* (Cambridge, 2015), 301–31.
Löhr, Winrich A., 'Der Brief der Gemeinden von Lyon und Vienne', in Damaskinos Pandreou, Wolfang A. Bienert, and Knut Schäferdiek (eds), *Oecumenica et Patristica* (Stuttgart, 1989), 135–49.
Lund, A. A., 'Zur Verbrennung der sogenanten Chrestiani (Tac. Ann. 15.44)', *Zeitschrift für Religions- und Geistesgeschichte* 60:3 (2008), 253–61.
Mace, Hannah, 'Astrology and Religion in Late Antiquity', in Josef Lössl and Nicholas J. Baker-Brian (eds), *A Companion to Religion in Late Antiquity* (Newark, 2018), 433–51.
McLaren, James S., 'Jews and the Imperial Cult. From Augustus to Domitian', *Journal for the Study of the New Testament* 27:3 (2005), 257–78.
McLaren, James S., 'Going to War against Rome. The Motivation of the Jewish Rebels', in Mladen Popović (ed.), *The Jewish Revolt against Rome* (Leiden, 2011), 129–53.
MacMullen, Ramsay, *Enemies of the Roman Order. Treason, Unrest and Alienation in the Empire* (Cambridge, MA, 1966).
MacMullen, Ramsay, *The Second Church. Popular Christianity A.D. 200–400* (Atlanta, 2009).
Marcovich, Miroslav (ed.), *Hippolytus. Refutatio Omnium Haeresium* (Berlin, 1986).
Marcovich, Miroslav (ed.), Athenagoras. *Legatio pro Christianis* (Berlin, 1990).
Marcovich, Miroslav (ed.), *Iustini Martyris Apologiae pro Christianis* (Berlin, 1994).
Marshall, Anthony J., 'Flaccus and the Jews of Asia (Cicero "Pro Flacco" 28.67–69)', *Phoenix* 29:2 (1975), 139–54.
Martin, Dale B., *Inventing Superstition. From the Hippocratics to the Christians* (Cambridge, MA, 2006).
Mason, Steve, *Flavius Josephus. Translation and Commentary* (Leiden, 1999–2022).
Mason, Steve, 'Jews, Judeans, Judaizing, Judaism. Problems of Categorization in Ancient History', *Journal for the Study of Judaism* 38:4 (2007), 457–512.
Mason, Steve, 'What is History? Using Josephus for the Judaean-Roman War', in Mladen Popović (ed.), *The Jewish Revolt against Rome* (Leiden, 2011), 155–240.

Mason, Steve, 'Why Did Judaeans Go to War with Rome in 66–67CE? Realist-Regional Perspectives', in P. J. Tomson and J. Schwartz (eds), *Jews and Christians in the First and Second Centuries. How to Write Their History* (Leiden 2014), 126–206.

Mason, Steve, *A History of the Jewish War.* AD *66–74* (Cambridge, 2016).

Matthews, John, 'The Making of the Text', in Jill Harries and Ian Wood (eds), *The Theodosian Code. Studies in the Imperial Law of Late Antiquity* (London, 1993), 19–44.

Mazzoli, Giancarlo, 'E Il Principe Risponde. Tra Penegirico e Libro X dell'Epistolario Pliniano', in Luigi Castagna and Eckhard Lefèvre (eds), *Plinius der Jüngere und seine Zeit* (Munich, 2003), 257–66.

Merola, Giovanna D., 'Perspectives', in Kimberley Czajkowski, Benedikt Eckhardt, and Meret Strothmann (eds), *Law in the Roman Provinces* (Oxford, 2020), 486–94.

Merrill, Elmer Truesdell, *Essays in Early Christian History* (London, 1924).

Meshorer, Ya'akov, *The Coinage of Aelia Capitolina* (Jerusalem, 1989).

Metzger, Ernest, 'Roman Judges, Case Law, and the Principles of Procedure', *Law and History Review* 22:2 (2004) 243–75.

Metzger, Ernest, 'Litigation', in David Johnston (ed.), *The Cambridge Companion to Roman Law* (Cambridge, 2015), 272–98.

Meyer, Elizabeth A., *Legitimacy and Law in the Roman World. Tabulae in Roman Belief and Practice* (Cambridge, 2004).

Meyer, Elizabeth A., 'Evidence and Argument. The Truth of Prestige and its Performance', in Paul J. du Plessis, Clifford Ando, and Kaius Tuori (eds), *The Oxford Handbook of Roman Law and Society* (Oxford, 2016), 270–82.

Miethling, Mirjam, and Eddie Hartmann, 'Die Soziologie und ihr Wissenschaftsbereich (1900)', *Berliner Journal für Soziologie* 19:2 (2009), 164–80.

Migdał, Justyna Ewa, 'Magic as an Element of Political Debate in the Historiography and Imperial Biography of the 1st–5th Centuries AD', PhD dissertation, University of Kraków 2020.

Millar, Fergus, *A Study of Cassius Dio* (Oxford, 1964).

Millar, Fergus, 'The Emperor, the Senate and the Province', *Journal of Roman Studies* 56 (1966), 156–66.

Millar, Fergus, *The Emperor in the Roman World. 31* BC–AD *337* (London, 1977).

Millar, Fergus, 'Trajan. Government by Correspondence', in Fergus Millar, Hannah M. Cotton, and Guy M. Rogers (eds), *Rome, the Greek World, and the East*, vol. 2: *Government, Society and Culture in the Roman Empire* (Chapel Hill, 2004), 23–46.

Millar, Fergus, 'Rome in Greek Culture. Cassius Dio and Ulpian', in Lucio Troiani and Giuseppe Zecchini (eds), *La Cultura Storica nei primi due Secoli dell'Impero Romano* (Rome, 2005), 17–40.

Miller, David M., 'The Meaning of *Ioudaios* and its Relationship to Other Group Labels in Ancient "Judaism"', *Currents in Biblical Research* 9:1 (2010), 98–126.

Miller, David M., 'Ethnicity Comes of Age. An Overview of Twentieth-Century Terms for *Ioudaios*', *Currents in Biblical Research* 10:2 (2012), 293–311.

Miller, David M., 'Ethnicity, Religion and the Meaning of *Ioudaios* in Ancient "Judaism"', *Currents in Biblical Research* 12:2 (2014), 216–65.

Minns, D. P., 'The Rescript of Hadrian', in S. Parvis and P. Foster (eds), *Justin Martyr and His Worlds* (Minneapolis, 2007), 38–49.

Minns, Denis, and Paul Parvis (eds), *Justin, Philosopher and Martyr. Apologies* (Oxford, 2009).

Mitteis, Ludwig, *Reichsrecht und Volksrecht in den östlichen Provinzen des römischen Kaiserreichs* (Leipzig, 1891).

Moehring, Horst R., 'The *Acta pro Judaeis* in the *Antiquities* of Flavius Josephus. A Study in Hellenistic and Modern Apologetic Historiography', in Jacob Neusner (ed.), *Christianity, Judaism and Other Greco-Roman Cults*, vol. 3 (Leiden, 1975), 124–58.

Moeller, Walter O., 'The Trinci/Trinqui and the Martyrs of Lyons', *Historia. Zeitschrift für Alte Geschichte* 21 (1972), 127.

Molthagen, Joachim, *Der römische Staat und die Christen im zweiten und dritten Jahrhundert* (Göttingen, 1970).

Molthagen, Joachim, 'Die ersten Konflikte der Christen in der griechisch-römischen Welt', *Historia. Zeitschrift für Alte Geschichte* 40:1 (1991), 42–76.
Mommsen, Theodor, *Römisches Staatsrecht*, 3 vols (Leipzig, 1871–88).
Mommsen, Theodor, 'Der Religionsfrevel nach römischem Recht', *Historische Zeitschrift* 28 (1890), 389–429. <https://archive.org/details/derreligionsfre00mommgoog/page/n19> (accessed 9 Jan 2019).
Mommsen, Theodor, *Römisches Strafrecht* (Leipzig, 1899).
Mommsen, Theodor, Paul Krueger, Rudolf Schoell, and Wilhelm Kroll (eds), *Corpus Iuris Civilis*, 3 vols (Berlin, 1895; repr. Cambridge, 2014).
Monat, P. (ed.), *Firmicus Maternus. Mathesis*, vol. 1: *Livres 1–2*, Collection des Universités de France/Budé (Paris, 1992).
Morgan, Gwyn, 'Omens in Tacitus' Histories I–III', in Robin Lorsch Wildfang and Jacob Isager (eds), *Divination and Portents in the Roman World* (Gylling, 2000), 25–42.
Morgan, Gwyn, *69 A.D. The Year of the Four Emperors* (Oxford, 2006).
Morrell, Kit, 'Petitioning for Change in the Republican Empire', in Roman M. Frolov and Christopher Burden-Strevens (eds), *Leadership and Initiative in Late Republican and Early Imperial Rome* (Leiden, 2022), 433–53.
Moss, Candida R., 'On the Dating of Polycarp. Rethinking the Place of the Martyrdom of Polycarp in the History of Christianity', *Early Christianity* 1:4 (2010[a]), 539–74.
Moss, Candida R., *The Other Christs. Imitating Jesus in Ancient Christian Ideologies of Martyrdom* (Oxford, 2010[b]).
Moss, Candida R., *Ancient Christian Martyrdom. Diverse Practices, Theologies, and Traditions* (New Haven, 2012[a]).
Moss, Candida R., 'The Discourse of Voluntary Martyrdom. Ancient and Modern', *Church History* 81:3 (2012[b]), 531–51.
Moss, Candida R., *The Myth of Persecution. How Early Christians Invented a Story of Martyrdom* (New York, 2013).
Mrozewicz, Leszek, *Roman Empire during the Reign of the Flavians* (Warsaw, 2010).
Murison, Charles (ed.), *Suetonius. Galba, Otho, Vitellius* (London, 1992).
Musurillo, Herbert (ed.), *Acts of the Pagan Martyrs* (Oxford, 1954).
Musurillo, Herbert (ed.), *Acts of the Christian Martyrs* (Oxford, 1972).
Mynors, R. A. B. (ed.), *C. Plini Caecili Secundi Epistularum libri decem*, Oxford Classical Texts (Oxford, 1963).
Nadeau, Yvan, *A Commentary on the Sixth Satire of Juvenal* (Brussels, 2011).
Nelson, Hein Leopold Wilhelmus, *Überlieferung, Aufbau und Stil von Gai Institutiones* (Leiden, 1981).
Neugebauer, O., and H. B. van Hoesen (eds), *Greek Horoscopes* (Philadelphia, 1959).
Niese, B., 'Bemerkungen über die Urkunden bei Josephus Archaeol. B. xiii. xiv. xvi', *Hermes* 11 (1876), 466–88.
Nippel, Wilfried, *Public Order in Ancient Rome* (Cambridge, 1995).
Nixey, Catherine, *The Darkening Age. The Christian Destruction of the Classical World* (London, 2017).
Noethlichs, Karl Leo, *Das Judentum und der römische Staat. Minderheitenpolitik im antiken Rom* (Darmstadt, 1996).
Nogrady, Alexander, *Römisches Strafrecht nach Ulpian. Buch 7 bis 9 De officio proconsulis* (Berlin, 2006).
Nongbri, Brent, 'Dislodging "Embedded" Religion. A Brief Note on a Scholarly Trope', *Numen* 55:4 (2008), 440–60.
Nongbri, Brent, *Before Religion. A History of a Modern Concept* (New Haven, 2013).
Noreña, Carlos F., 'The Social Economy of Pliny's Correspondence with Trajan', *American Journal of Philology* 128:2 (2007), 239–77.
Nörr, Dieter, 'Zur Reskriptenpraxis in der hohen Prinzipatszeit', *Zeitschrift der Savigny-Stiftung für Rechtsgeschichte. Romanistische Abteilung* 98 (1981), 1–46.

Norris, Richard A., Jr, 'The Apologists', in Frances Young, Lewis Ayres, and Andrew Louth (eds), *The Cambridge History of Early Christian Literature* (Cambridge, 2004), 36–44.

Oakman, Douglas E., 'Culture, Society and Embedded Religion in Antiquity', *Biblical Theology Bulletin. Journal of Bible and Culture* 35:1 (2005), 4–12.

Odahl, Charles M., 'Government IV: Christianity. A: Patristic and Orthodox Churches', in E. Ziolkowski, B. Walfish, J. Schröter, T. Römer, B. Matz, J. LeMon, and C. Furey (eds), *Encyclopedia of the Bible and Its Reception*, vol. 10 (Berlin, 2015), 737–9.

Oehler, Franz, John E. B. Mayor, and Alexander Souter (eds), *Q. Septimi Florentis Tertulliani Apologeticus* (Cambridge, 1917).

Öhler, Markus, 'Pliny and the Expansion of Christianity in Cities and Rural Areas of Pontus et Bithynia', in Markus Tiwald and Jürgen K. Zangenberg (eds), *Early Christian Encounters with Town and Countryside. Essays on the Urban and Rural Worlds of Early Christianity* (Göttingen, 2021), 269–97.

Oliver, J. H. and R. E. A. Palmer, 'Minutes of an Act of the Roman Senate', *Hesperia* 24 (1955), 320–49.

Oppenheimer, Aharon, 'The Ban on Circumcision as a Cause of the Revolt. A Reconsideration', in Peter Schäfer (ed.), *The Bar Kokhba War Reconsidered* (Tübingen, 2003), 55–69.

Orlin, Eric M., *Temples, Religion and Politics in the Roman Republic* (Leiden, 1997).

Orlin, Eric M., *Foreign Cults in Rome. Creating a Roman Empire* (New York, 2010).

Oudshoorn, Jacobine G., *The Relationship between Roman and Local Law in the Babatha and Salome Komaise Archives* (Leiden, 2007).

Overman, J. Andrew, 'The First Revolt and Flavian Politics', in Andrea M. Berlin and J. Andrew Overman (eds), *The First Jewish Revolt. Archaeology, History and Ideology* (London, 2002), 213–20.

Pandey, Nandini B., 'Caesar's Comet, the Julian Star, and the Invention of Augustus', *Transactions of the American Philological Association* 143:2 (2013), 405–49.

Parássoglou, G. M., 'Circular from a Prefect. *Sileat omnibus perpetuo divinandi curiositas*', in Ann Ellis Hanson (ed.), *Collectanea Papyrologica. Texts Published in Honor of H.C. Youtie*, vol. 1 (Bonn, 1976), 261–74.

Parke, H. W., *The Oracles of Apollo in Asia Minor* (London, 1985).

Parke, H. W., *Sibyls and Sibylline Prophecy in Classical Antiquity* (London, 1988).

Parvis, Paul, 'Justin, Philosopher and Martyr. The Posthumous Creation of the Second Apology', in S. Parvis and P. Foster (eds), *Justin Martyr and His Worlds* (Minneapolis, 2007), 22–37.

Parvis, Sara, 'The Martyrdom of Polycarp', *The Expository Times* 118:3 (2006), 105–12.

Peachin, Michael, 'Jurist and the Law in the Early Roman Empire', in Lukas de Blois (ed.), *Administration, Prosopography and Appointment Policies in the Roman Empire* (Leiden, 2001), 109–20.

Pearce, Sarah, 'Jerusalem as "Mother-City" in the Writings of Philo of Alexandria', in John M. G. Barclay, *Negotiating Diaspora. Jewish Strategies in the Roman Empire* (London, 2004), 19–36.

Perry, Jonathan S., '*Collegia* and their Impact on the Constitutional Structure of the Roman State', in Paul J. du Plessis, C. Ando, and K. Tuori (eds), *The Oxford Handbook of Roman Law and Society* (Oxford, 2016), 137–48.

Petersen, Anders Klostergaard, 'Alexandrian Judaism. Rethinking a Problematic Cultural Category', in G. Hinge, J. A. Krasilnikoff, and M. S. Jensen (eds), *Alexandria. A Cultural and Religious Melting Pot* (Aarhus, 2009), 115–43.

Petersen, Anders Klostergaard, 'Imagine No Religion. How Modern Abstractions Hide Ancient Realities', review of Barton and Boyarin (2016), *Bryn Mawr Classical Review* 2017:06:14 (2017). < https://bmcr.brynmawr.edu/2017/2017.06.14/> (accessed 7 Feb 2022).

Petersen, Jens, *Recht bei Tacitus* (Berlin, 2019).

Pölönen, J., 'The Case for a Sociology of Roman Law', in M. Freeman (ed.), *Law and Sociology* (Oxford 2006), 398–408.

Pölönen, J., 'Framing "Law and Society" in the Roman World', in Paul J. du Plessis, C. Ando, and K. Tuori (eds), *The Oxford Handbook of Roman Law and Society* (Oxford, 2016), 8–17.

Potter, David, *Prophets and Emperors. Human and Divine Authority from Augustus to Theodosius* (Cambridge, MA, 1994).

Power, T., 'Suetonius' Tacitus', *Journal of Roman Studies* 104 (2014), 205–25.

Price, S. R. F., *Rituals and Power. The Roman Imperial Cult in Asia Minor* (Cambridge, 1984).

Pucci Ben Zeev, Miriam, 'Caesar and Jewish Law', *Revue Biblique* 102 (1995) 28–37.

Pucci Ben Zeev, Miriam, *Jewish Rights in the Roman World. The Greek and Roman Documents Quoted by Flavius Josephus* (Tübingen, 1998).

Pucci Ben Zeev, Miriam, *Diaspora Judaism in Turmoil, 116/117 CE. Ancient Sources and Modern Insights* (Leuven, 2005).

Rabello, Alfredo Mordechai, 'The Legal Condition of the Jews in the Roman Empire', in Hildegard Temporini (ed.), *Aufstieg und Niedergang der Römischen Welt* II.13 (Berlin, 1980), 662–762.

Rajak, Tessa, 'Jewish Rights in the Greek Cities under Roman Rule. A New Approach', in William Scott Green (ed.), *Approaches to Ancient Judaism*, vol. 5: *Studies in Judaism and its Greco-Roman Context* (Atlanta, 1985), 19–36.

Rajak, Tessa, 'Jews, Pagans and Christians in Late Antique Sardis. Models of Interaction', in *The Jewish Dialogue with Greece and Rome* (Leiden, 2002[a]), 447–62.

Rajak, Tessa, 'Was there a Roman Charter for the Jews?', in *The Jewish Dialogue with Greece and Rome* (Leiden, 2002[b]), 301–33.

Rajak, Tessa, 'Document and Rhetoric in Josephus. Revisiting the "Charter" for the Jews', in Shaye J. D. Cohen and Joshua D. Schwartz (eds), *Studies in the Varieties of Ancient Judaism* (Leiden, 2007), 177–89.

Rajak, Tessa, 'The Mediterranean Jewish Diaspora in the Second Century', in James Carleton Paget and Judith Lieu (eds), *Christianity in the Second Century. Themes and Developments* (Cambridge, 2017), 39–56.

Raschle, Christian R., 'The Expulsion of Isis Worshippers and Astrologers from Rome in the Late Republic and Early Empire', in Jitse H. F. Dijkstra and Christian R. Raschle (eds), *Religious Violence in the Ancient World. From Classical Athens to Late Antiquity* (Cambridge, 2020), 87–105.

Rasmussen, Susanne William, *Public Portents in Republican Rome* (Rome, 2003).

Rathbone, Dominic, 'Egypt, Augustus and Roman Taxation', *Cahiers du Centre Gustav Glotz* 4 (1993), 81–112.

Rea, John, 'A New Version of P. Yale Inv. 299', *Zeitschrift für Papyrologie und Epigraphik* 27 (1977), 151–6.

Rebillard, Éric, *Greek and Latin Narratives about the ancient Martyrs* (Oxford, 2017).

Rebillard, Éric, 'Response: Rebillard on Bremmer on Rebillard, Greek and Latin Narratives about the Ancient Martyrs', response to Bremmer (2019), *Bryn Mawr Classical Review* 2019:03:12 (2019). <https://bmcr.brynmawr.edu/2019/2019.03.12/> (accessed 9 March 2022).

Rebillard, Éric, *The Early Martyr Narratives. Neither Authentic Accounts nor Forgeries* (Philadelphia, 2020).

Reichert, Angelika, 'Durchdachte Konfusion. Plinius, Trajan und das Christentum', *Zeitschrift für die Neutestamentliche Wissenschaft und die Kunde der älteren Kirche* 93:3–4 (2002), 227–50.

Richardson, John, 'The Administration of the Empire', in J. A. Crook, Andrew Lintott, and Elizabeth Rawson (eds), *The Cambridge Ancient History*, vol. 9: *The Last Age of the Roman Republic, 146–43 BCE* (Cambridge, 1994), 564–98.

Richardson, John, 'Roman Law in the Provinces', in David Johnston (ed.), *The Cambridge Companion to Roman Law* (Cambridge, 2015), 45–58.

Richardson, John, 'Provincial Administration', in Paul J. du Plessis, Clifford Ando, and Kaius Tuori (eds), *The Oxford Handbook of Roman Law and Society* (Oxford, 2016), 111–23.

Riggsby, Andrew, 'Public and Private Criminal Law', in Paul J. du Plessis, Clifford Ando, and Kaius Tuori (eds), *The Oxford Handbook of Roman Law and Society* (Oxford, 2016), 310–21.

Ripat, Pauline, 'Expelling Misconceptions. Astrologers At Rome', *Classical Philology* 106:2 (2011), 115–54.

Ritner, Robert K., 'Egyptian Magical Practice under the Roman Empire. The Demotic Spells and their Religious Context', in W. Haase and H. Temporini (eds), *Aufstieg under Niedergang der römischen Welt* II.18.5 (Berlin, 1995), 3333–79.

Ritter, Bradley, *Judeans in the Greek Cities of the Roman Empire. Rights, Citizenship, and Civil Discord* (Leiden, 2015).

Rives, James B., 'Piety of a Prosecutor', *Journal of Early Christian Studies* 4:1 (1996), 1–25.

Rives, James B., 'The Decree of Decius and the Religion of Empire', *Journal of Roman Studies* 89 (1999), 135–54.

Rives, James B., 'Flavian Religious Policy and the Destruction of the Jerusalem Temple', in Jonathan Edmondson, Steve Mason, and James Rives (eds), *Flavius Josephus and Flavian Rome* (Oxford, 2005), 145–66.

Rives, James B., 'Magic, Religion, and Law. The Case of the *Lex Cornelia de Sicariis et Veneficiis*', in Clifford Ando and Jörg Rüpke (eds), *Religion and Law in Classical and Christian Rome* (Stuttgart, 2006), 47–67.

Rives, James B., *Religion in the Roman Empire* (Malden, 2007).

Rives, James B., 'Diplomacy and Identity among Jews and Christians', in Claude Eilers (ed.), *Diplomats and Diplomacy in the Roman World* (Leiden, 2009), 99–126.

Rives, James B., '*Magus* and its Cognates in Classical Latin', in Richard L. Gordon and Francisco Marco Simón (eds), *Magical Practice in the Latin West* (Leiden, 2010), 53–77.

Rives, James B., 'Magic in Roman Law. The Reconstruction of a Crime', in J. A. North and S. R. F. Price (eds), *The Religious History of the Roman Empire* (Oxford, 2011[a]), 71–108.

Rives, James B., 'The Persecution of Christians and Ideas of Community in the Roman Empire', in G. Cecconi (ed.), *Politiche religiose nel mondo antico e tardoantico. Poteri e indirizzi, forme del controllo, idée e prassi di tolleranza* (Bari, 2011[b]), 199–216. <https://www.academia.edu/5382548/The_Persecution_of_Christians_and_Ideas_of_Community_in_the_Roman_Empire> (accessed 12 Dec 2018).

Rives, James B., 'Animal Sacrifice and Political Identity in Rome and Judaea', in P. J. Tomson and J. Schwartz (eds), *Jews and Christians in the First and Second Centuries. How to Write Their History* (Leiden, 2014), 105–25.

Rizakis, Athanasios, 'Urban Elites in the Roman East. Enhancing Regional Position and Social Superiority', in Jörg Rüpke (ed.), *A Companion to Roman Religion* (Malden, 2007), 317–30.

Rizzi, Marco, 'Hadrian and the Christians', in Marco Rizzi (ed.), *Hadrian and the Christians* (Berlin, 2010), 7–20.

Robinson, David M., 'A New Latin Economic Edict from Pisidian Antioch', *Transactions and Proceedings of the American Philological Association* 55 (1924), 5–20.

Robinson, J. Armitage, *The Passion of S. Perpetua* (Cambridge, 1891).

Robinson, Olivia F., *The Criminal Law of Ancient Rome* (Baltimore, 1995).

Robinson, Olivia F., *The Sources of Roman Law. Problems and Methods for Ancient Historians*, online edition (London, 1997).

Robinson, Olivia F., 'The Role of Delators', in J.W. Cairns and Paul J. du Plessis (eds), *Beyond Dogmatics. Law and Society in the Roman World* (Edinburgh, 2007), 206–20.

Rocca, Samuele, *In the Shadow of the Caesars. Jewish Life in Roman Italy* (Leiden, 2022).

Roddaz, Jean-Michel, *Marcus Agrippa* (Rome, 1984).

Rogers, R. S., 'The Date of the Banishment of the Astrologers', *Classical Philology* 26:2 (1931), 203–4.

Rogers, R. S., *Criminal Trials and Criminal Legislation under Tiberius* (Middletown, 1935).

Rohrbacher, David, *The Play of Allusion in the Historia Augusta* (Madison, 2015).

Rolfe, J. C. (ed.), *Suetonius. Lives of the Caesars; Lives of Illustrious Men*, vol. 2, Loeb Classical Library (rev. edn, Cambridge, MA, 1997).

Roselaar, Saskia T., 'Local Administration', in Paul J. du Plessis, Clifford Ando, and Kaius Tuori (eds), *The Oxford Handbook of Roman Law and Society* (Oxford, 2016), 124–36.

Roueché, Charlotte, 'The Functions of the Governor in Late Antiquity. Some Observations', *AnTard* 6 (1998), 31–6.

Rougé, Jean, 'Aspects économiques du Lyon antique', in Jean Rougé and Robert Turcan (eds), *Les Martyrs de Lyon – 177* (Paris, 1978), 47–63.

Rowe, Greg, 'Laws, Lawmaking and Legal Documents', in Christer Bruun and Jonathan Edmondson (eds), *The Oxford Handbook of Roman Epigraphy* (Oxford, 2015), 299–318.

Ruelle, Carolus Aemilius (ed.), *Catalogus Codicum Astrologorum Graecorum*, vol. 8: *Codicum Parisinorum partem secundam* (Brussels, 1911). <http://www.hellenisticastrology.com/ccag/CCAG08Part2.pdf> (accessed 18 Sept 2017).

Rüfner, Thomas, 'Imperial Cognitio Process', in Paul J. du Plessis, Clifford Ando, and Kaius Tuori (eds), *The Oxford Handbook of Roman Law and Society* (Oxford, 2016), 257–69.

Ruggiero, F. (ed.), 'Atti dei martiri Scilitani. Introduzione, testo, traduzione, testimonianze e commento', *Atti della Accademia Nazionale dei Lincei* 9:1:2 (1991), 36–140.

Rüpke, Jörg, *Die Religion der Römer* (Munich, 2001).

Rüpke, Jörg, 'Roman Religion' in Harriet I. Flower (ed.), *The Cambridge Companion to the Roman Republic* (Cambridge, 2004) 179–96.

Rüpke, Jörg, *From Jupiter to Christ. On the History of Religion in the Roman Imperial Period*, trans. David M. B. Richardson (Oxford, 2014).

Rüpke, Jörg, *Pantheon. Geschichte der antiken Religionen* (Munich, 2016[a]).

Rüpke, Jörg, *Religious Deviance in the Roman World. Superstition or Individuality*, trans. David M. B. Richardson (Cambridge, 2016[b]).

Rutgers, Leonard Victor, 'Roman Policy toward the Jews. Expulsions from the City of Rome during the First Century C.E.', in Karl P. Donfried and Peter Richardson (eds), *Judaism and Christianity in First-Century Rome* (Grand Rapids, 1998), 93–116.

Samberger, Ch., W. Seyfarth, and E. Hohl, *Scriptores Historiae Augustae*, 2 vols, Bibliotheca Teubneriana (Stuttgart, 1997).

Sánchez-Moreno Ellart, C., 'Ulpian and the Stars. The *actio iniuriarum* against the astrologer; some reflections about d.47.10.15.13 (Ulp.lib.77 ad edictum)', *Iuris Antiqui Historia* 1 (2009), 195–222.

Sandwell, I., 'Outlawing "Magic" or Outlawing "Religion"? Libanius and the Theodosian Code as Evidence for Legislation against "Pagan" Practices', in W. V. Harris (ed.), *The Spread of Christianity in the first Four Centuries. Essays in Explanation* (Leiden, 2005), 87–123.

Santalucia, Bernardo, *Studi di Diritto penale Romano* (Rome, 1994).

Santangelo, Federico, 'Law and Divination in the Late Roman Republic', in Olga Tellegen-Couperus (ed.), *Law and Religion in the Roman Republic* (Leiden, 2012), 31–54.

Santangelo, Federico, *Divination, Prediction and the End of the Roman Republic* (Cambridge, 2013).

Schäfer, Peter, *The History of the Jews in Antiquity. The Jews of Palestine from Alexander the Great to the Arab Conquest* (London, 1995).

Schäfer, Peter, *Judeophobia. Attitudes towards the Jews in the Ancient World* (Cambridge, MA, 1997).

Scheda, Gunther, 'Nero und der Brand Roms', *Historia. Zeitschrift für Alte Geschichte* 16 (1967), 111–15.

Schiavone, A., *The Invention of Law in the West*, trans. J. Carden and A. Shugaar (Cambridge, MA, 2012).

Schiemann, Gottfried, 'Institutiones', in *Brill's New Pauly Online* (2006). <https://doi.org/10.1163/1574-9347_bnp_e525090>.

Schiller, A. Arthur, 'Custom in Classical Roman Law', *Virginia Law Review* 24:3 (1938), 268–82.

Schmitt, T., 'Des Kaisers Inszenierung. Mythologie und neronische Christenverfolgung', *Zeitschrift für Antikes Christentum* 16 (2012), 487–515.

Schröder, Bernd, *Die 'väterlichen Gesetze'* (Tübingen, 1996).

Schubert, Christoph (ed.), *Minucius Felix. Octavius* (Freiburg, 2014).

Schulz, Fritz, *Classical Roman Law* (Oxford, 1951).

Schulz, Verena, *Deconstructing Imperial Representation. Tacitus, Cassius Dio, and Suetonius on Nero and Domitian* (Leiden, 2019).

Schuol, Monika, *Augustus und die Juden. Rechtsstellung und Interessenpolitik der kleinasiatischen Diaspora* (Frankfurt am Main, 2007).

Schwartz, Daniel R., *Agrippa I. The last king of Judaea* (Tübingen, 1990).

Schwartz, Daniel R., 'Philo and Josephus on the Violence in Alexandria in 38 C.E.', *The Studia Philonica Annual* 24 (2012), 149–66.

Schwartz, Matthew B., 'Greek and Jew. Philo and the Alexandrian Riots of 38–41 CE', *Judaism* 49:2 (2000), 206–16.

Schwartz, Seth, *The Ancient Jews from Alexander to Muhammad* (Cambridge, 2014).

Scurlock, Joann, '167 BCE. Hellenism or Reform', *Journal for the Study of Judaism* 31 (2000), 125–61.

Sedley, David, 'From the Pre-Socratics to the Hellenistic Age', in S. Bullivant and M. Ruse (eds), *The Oxford Handbook of Atheism* (Oxford, 2013), 139–51.

Seeliger, Hans Reinhard and Wolfgang Wischmeyer, *Märtyrerliteratur* (Berlin, 2015).

Seeman, Chris, and Adam Kolman Marshak, 'Jewish History from Alexander to Hadrian', in John J. Collins and Daniel C. Harlow (eds), *Early Judaism. A Comprehensive Overview* (Cambridge 2012), 30–69.

Seland, Torrey, 'Philo and the Clubs and Associations of Alexandria', in John S. Kloppenborg and S. G. Wilson (eds), *Voluntary Associations in the Graeco-Roman world* (London, 1996), 110–27.

Seland, Torrey, 'The Alexandrian Riots of 38 C.E. and the Persecution of the Jews. A Historical Reconstruction. Supplements to the Journal for the Study of Judaism 135', Review of Gambetti (2009), *Bryn Mawr Classical Review* 2010:12:63 (2010). <https://bmcr.brynmawr.edu/2010/2010.12.63/> (accessed 9 March 2022).

Shannon-Henderson, Kelly E., *Religion and Memory in Tacitus' Annals* (Oxford, 2019).

Shaw, Brent D., 'The Passion of Perpetua', *Past & Present* 139:1 (1993), 3–45.

Shaw, Brent D., 'Judicial Nightmares and Christian Memory', *Journal of Early Christian Studies* 11 (2003), 533–63.

Shaw, Brent D., 'The Myth of the Neronian Persecution', *Journal of Roman Studies* 105 (2015), 73–100.

Shaw, Brent, D., 'Response to Christopher Jones: The Historicity of the Neronian Persecution', *New Testament Studies* 64 (2018), 231–42.

Sherk, R. K., *Roman Documents from the Greek East* (Baltimore, 1969).

Sherwin-White, A. N., 'The Early Persecutions and Roman Law Again', *Journal of Theological Studies* 3:2 (1952), 199–213.

Sherwin-White, A. N., *Roman Society and Roman Law in the New Testament* (Oxford, 1963).

Sherwin-White, A. N., *The Letters of Pliny. A Historical and Social Commentary* (Oxford, 1966).

Sherwin-White, A. N., 'Why Were the Early Christians Persecuted? An Amendment', in M. I. Finley (ed.), *Studies in Ancient Society* (London, 1974), 250–5.

Sherwin-White, A. N., *Roman Foreign Policy in the East. 168 B.C. to A.D. 1* (London, 1984).

Shotter, D. C. A., 'The Trial of M. Scribonius Libo Drusus', *Historia. Zeitschrift für Alte Geschichte* 21:1 (1972), 88–98.

Shotter, D. C. A., *Tacitus. Annals IV* (Warminster, 1989).

Shotter, D. C. A. (ed.), *Suetonius. The Lives of Galba, Otho and Vitellius* (Warminster, 1993).

Simon, Marcel, 'Jupiter-Yahvé', *Numen* 23:1 (1976), 40–66.

Simons, Benedikt, *Cassius Dio und die Römische Republik. Untersuchungen zum Bild des römischen Gemeinwesens in den Büchern 3–35 der Rōmaïka* (Berlin, 2009).

Sirks, A. J. B., 'The Sources of the Code', in Jill Harries and Ian Wood (eds), *The Theodosian Code. Studies in the Imperial Law of Late Antiquity* (London, 1993), 45–67.

Sirks, A. J. B., 'Making a Request to the Emperor: Rescripts in the Roman Empire', in Lukas de Blois (ed.), *Administration, Prosopography and Appointment Policies in the Roman Empire* (Leiden, 2001), 121–35.

Sirks, A. J. B., 'Public Law', in David Johnston (ed.), *The Cambridge Companion to Roman Law* (Cambridge, 2015), 332–52.

Slootjes, Danielle, 'The Governor as Benefactor in Late Antiquity', in Luuk de Ligt, E. A. Hemelrijk, and H. W. Singor (eds), *Roman Rule and civic Life. Local and regional Perspectives* (Amsterdam, 2004), 59–75.

Slootjes, Danielle, *The Governor and his Subjects in the Later Roman Empire* (Leiden, 2006).

Smallwood, E. Mary, *The Jews under Roman Rule. From Pompey to Diocletian* (Leiden, 1976).

Smits, Nicolaas, *Mosaicarum et Romanarum Legum Collatio* (Haarlem, 1934).

Smuts, F., 'Waarvan is die Christene voor Plinius aangekla?', *Acta Classica* 8 (1965), 71–85.

Sogno, Cristiana, 'Astrology, Morality, the Emperor, and the Law in Firmicus Maternus' "Mathesis"', *Illinois Classical Studies* 30 (2005), 167–76.

Sordi, Marta, *The Christians and the Roman Empire*, trans. Annabel Bedini (London, 1983).

Sordi, Marta, 'Plinio, Traiano e i Christiani', in Luigi Castagna and Eckhard Lefèvre (eds), *Plinius der Jüngere und seine Zeit* (Munich, 2003), 267–78.

Southern, Pat, *The Roman Army. A Social and Institutional History* (Oxford, 2007).

Spinelli, Tommasso, and Gian Luca Gregori, '(Un)-damning Subplots. The Principate of Domitian between Literary Sources and Fresh Material Evidence', *Illinois Classical Studies* 44:2 (2019), 242–67.

Spruit, J. E., et al. (eds), *Corpus Iuris Civilis. Tekst en vertaling*, 12 vols (Zutphen, 1993–2011).

Spruit, J. E. and K. E. M. Bongenaar, *Gaius en Paulus. Verzameling van prae-Justiniaanse juridische geschriften met vertaling in het Nederlands*, vol. 2: *Het Erfdeel van de klassieke Romeinse Juristen* (Zutphen, 1984).

Stadter, Philip A., 'Pliny and the Ideology of Empire. The Correspondence with Trajan', *Prometheus: Rivista di studi classici* 32 (2006), 61–76.

Ste Croix, G. E. M. de, 'Why Were the Early Christians Persecuted?', in M. I. Finley (ed.), *Studies in Ancient Society* (London, 1974[a]), 210–49.

Ste Croix, G. E. M. de, 'Why Were the Early Christians Persecuted? A Rejoinder', in M. I. Finley (ed.), *Studies in Ancient Society* (London, 1974[b]), 256–62.

Stern, Menahem (ed.), *Greek and Latin Authors on Jews and Judaism*, vol. 1: *From Herodotus to Plutarch* (Jerusalem, 1974).

Stern, Menahem (ed.), *Greek and Latin Authors on Jews and Judaism*, vol. 2: *From Tacitus to Simplicius* (Jerusalem, 1980).

Stern, Menahem (ed.), *Greek and Latin Authors on Jews and Judaism*, vol. 3: *Appendixes and Indices* (Jerusalem, 1984).

Stertz, S. A., 'Christianity in the Historia Augusta', *Latomus* 36 (1977), 694–715.

Streeter, Joseph, 'Introduction. De Ste. Croix on Persecution', in G. E. M. de Ste Croix, Michael Whitby, and Joseph Streeter (eds), *Christianity, Persecution, Martyrdom, and Orthodoxy* (Oxford, 2006), 3–34.

Swan, Peter Michael, *The Augustan Succession. A Historical Commentary on Cassius Dio's Roman History Books 55–56, 9 B.C.–A.D. 14* (Oxford, 2004).

Syme, Ronald, *Tacitus*, vol. 2 (Oxford, 1958).

Syme, Ronald, *Ammianus and the Historia Augusta* (Oxford, 1968).

Syme, Ronald, 'The Early Tiberian Consuls', *Historia. Zeitschrift für Alte Geschichte* 30:2 (1981), 189–202.

Tacoma, Laurens E., *Moving Romans. Migration to Rome in the Principate* (Oxford, 2016).

Taylor, Tristan S., 'Social Status, Legal Status and Legal Privilege', in Paul J. du Plessis, Clifford Ando, and Kaius Tuori (eds), *The Oxford Handbook of Roman Law and Society* (Oxford, 2016), 349–61.

Tcherikover, Victor, *Hellenistic Civilization and the Jews* (Philadelphia, 1959).

Tcherikover, Victor A., and Alexander Fuks, *Corpus Papyrorum Judaicarum*, vol. 1 (Cambridge, MA, 1957).

Tcherikover, Victor A., and Alexander Fuks, *Corpus Papyrorum Judaicarum*, vol. 2 (Cambridge, MA, 1960).

Tellegen-Couperus, O., and J. W. Tellegen, 'Artes Urbanae. Roman Law and Rhetoric', in Paul J. du Plessis (ed.), *New Frontiers. Law and Society in the Roman World* (Edinburgh, 2013), 31–50.

Thackeray, H. St. J. (ed.), *Josephus. The Life; Against Apion*, Loeb Classical Library (Cambridge, MA, 1926).

Thackeray, H. St. J. (ed.), *Josephus. The Jewish War*, Loeb Classical Library, 3 vols (Cambridge, MA, 1927–8).

Thomasson, Bengt E., *Die Statthalter der römischen Provinzen Nordafrikas von Augustus bis Diocletianus*, vol. 1 (Lund, 1960[a]).

Thomasson, Bengt E., *Die Statthalter der römischen Provinzen Nordafrikas von Augustus bis Diocletianus*, vol. 2 (Lund, 1960[b]).

Thompson, James Westfall, 'The Alleged Persecution of the Christians at Lyons in 177', *American Journal of Theology* 16 (1912), 359–84.

Thompson, James Westfall, 'The Alleged Persecution of the Christians at Lyons in 177. A Reply to Certain Criticisms', *American Journal of Theology* 17 (1913), 249–85.

Trebilco, Paul R., *Jewish Communities in Asia Minor* (Cambridge, 1991).

Tsafrir, Yoram, 'Numismatics and the Foundation of Aelia Capitolina. A Critical Review', in Peter Schäfer (ed.), *The Bar Kokhba War Reconsidered* (Tübingen, 2003), 31–6.

Tuori, Kaius, 'The *ius respondendi* and the Freedom of Roman Jurisprudence', *Revue Internationale des Droits de l'Antiquité* 51 (2004), 295–337.

Tuori, Kaius, 'Legal Pluralism and the Roman Empires', in J. W. Cairns and Paul J. du Plessis (eds), *Beyond Dogmatics. Law and Society in the Roman World* (Edinburgh, 2007), 39–52.

Tuori, Kaius, *The Emperor of Law. The Emergence of Roman Imperial Adjudication* (Oxford, 2016).

Urso, Gianpaolo, 'The Origin of the Consulship in Cassius Dio's Roman History', in Hans Beck, Antonio Duplá, Martin Jehne, and Francisco Pina Polo (eds), *Consuls and Res Publica. Holding High Office in the Roman Republic* (Cambridge, 2011), 41–60.

Versnel, H. S., 'Some Reflections on the Relationship Magic–Religion', *Numen* 38:2 (1991), 177–97.

Vittinghoff, F., 'Christianus sum. Das "Verbrechen" von Außenseitern der römischen Gesellschaft', *Historia. Zeitschrift für Alte Geschichte* 33 (1984), 331–57.

Vogt, J., 'Christenverfolgung I (historisch)', in Theodor Klauser, Ernst Dassmann, Franz Joseph Dölger, et al. (eds), *Reallexikon für Antike und Christentum*, vol. 2 (Stuttgart, 1954), 1159–208.

Vonken, Paul (ed.), *Asser 10–I. Algemeen deel Internationaal Privaatrecht* (Deventer, 2013).

Voorst, Robert E. van, *Jesus Outside the New Testament* (Grand Rapids, 2000).

Walsh, Joseph, and Gunther Gottlieb, 'Zur Christenfrage im zweiten Jahrhundert', in Gunther Gottlieb and Pedro Barceló (eds), *Christen und Heiden in Staat und Gesellschaft des zweiten bis vierten Jahrhunderts. Gedanken und Thesen zu einem schwierigen Verhältnis* (Munich, 1992), 3–86.

Walsh, Patrick G. (ed.), *Titi Livi Ab Urbe Condita. Libri XXVIII–XXX*, Bibliotheca Teubneriana (Leipzig, 1986).

Wardle, D. (ed.), *Valerius Maximus. Memorable Deeds and Sayings, book 1* (Oxford, 1998).

Wardle, D. (ed.), *Cicero on Divination. De Divinatione, book 1* (Oxford, 2006).

Warmington, B. H. (ed.), *Suetonius. Nero* (2nd edn, London, 1999).

Wartelle, André (ed.), *Saint Justin. Apologies* (Paris, 1987).

Waszink, J. H. and J. C. M. van Winden, *Tertullianus. De Idololatria, Critical Text, Translation and Commentary* (Leiden, 1987).

Watson, Alan, *The State, Law and Religion. Pagan Rome* (Athens, GA, 1992).

Watson, Alan, *The Spirit of Roman Law* (Athens, GA, 1995).

Watson, Alan, 'Law and Society', in J. W. Cairns and Paul J. du Plessis (eds), *Beyond Dogmatics. Law and Society in the Roman World* (Edinburgh, 2007), 9–35.

Weber, Winfried, 'Die Suche nach dem Petrusgrab. Zu den archäologischen Untersuchungen im Bereich der Confessio von St. Peter', in Stefan Heid (ed.), *Petrus und Paulus in Rom. Eine interdisziplinäre Debatte* (Freiburg, 2011), 67–113.

Weikert, Christopher, 'Nach der Tempelzerstörung. Die *gens Flavia* und die Juden', in Görge K. Hasselhoff and Meret Strothmann (eds), *Religio Licita? Rom und die Juden* (Berlin, 2017), 159–74.

Weksler-Bdolah, Shlomit, *Aelia Capitolina. Jerusalem in the Roman Period in the Light of Archaeological Research* (Leiden, 2020).
Wellesley, Kenneth, *The Year of the Four Emperors* (London, 2000).
Wendt, Heidi, '*Ea Superstitione.* Christian Martyrdom and the Religion of Freelance Experts', *Journal of Roman Studies* 105 (2015[a]), 183–202.
Wendt, Heidi, '*Iudaica Romana.* A Rereading of Evidence for Judean Expulsions from Rome', *Journal of Ancient Judaism* 6:1 (2015[b]), 97–126.
Wendt, Heidi, *At the Temple Gates. The Religion of Freelance Experts in the Roman Empire* (Oxford, 2016).
Whittaker, Molly, *Jews & Christians. Graeco-Roman Views* (Cambridge, 1984).
Wilcken, Ulrich, 'Zu den Edikten', *Zeitschrift der Savigny-Stiftung für Rechtsgeschichte: Romanistische Abteilung* 42 (1921), 124–58.
Wildfang, Robin Lorsch, 'The Propaganda of Omens. Six Dreams Involving Augustus', in Robin Lorsch Wildfang and Jacob Isager (eds), *Divination and Portents in the Roman World* (Gylling, 2000), 43–56.
Wilken, Robert L., *The Christians as the Romans Saw Them* (New Haven, 1984).
Wilker, Julia, 'God is with Italy Now. Pro-Roman Jews and the Jewish Revolt', in Benedikt Eckhardt (ed.), *Jewish Identity and Politics between the Maccabees and Bar Kokhba* (Leiden, 2012), 157–87.
Willems, Constantin, 'Kognitionsprozess', in Ulrike Babusiaux, Christian Baldus, Wolfgang Ernst, Franz-Stefan Meissel, Johannes Plaschek, and Thomas Rüfner (eds), *Handbuch des Römischen Privatrechts*, vol. 1 (Tübingen, 2023), 492–510.
Williams, M. H., 'The Expulsion of the Jews from Rome in A.D. 19', *Latomus* 48:4 (1989), 765–84.
Williams, M. H., 'Domitian, the Jews and the "Judaizers". A Simple Matter of Cupiditas and Maiestas?', *Historia. Zeitschrift für Alte Geschichte* 39:2 (1990), 196–211.
Williams, Travis B., *Persecution in 1 Peter. Differentiating and Contextualizing Early Christian Suffering* (Leiden, 2012).
Williamson, Callie, *The Laws of the Roman People. Public Law in the Expansion and Decline of the Roman Republic* (Ann Arbor, 2005).
Williamson, Callie, 'Crimes against the State', in Paul J. du Plessis, Clifford Ando, and Kaius Tuori (eds), *The Oxford Handbook of Roman Law and Society* (Oxford, 2016), 333–44.
Wiseman, T. P., 'A Debate on the Temple of Apollo Palatinus. Roma Quadrata, Archaic Huts, the House of Augustus, and the Orientation of Palatine Apollo', *Journal of Roman Archaeology* 25 (2012), 371–87.
Wlosok, Antonie, 'Die Rechtsgrundlagen der Christenverfolgungen der ersten zwei Jahrhunderte', in Richard Klein (ed.), *Das frühe Christentum im römischen Staat* (Darmstadt, 1971), 275–301.
Wolf, Joseph Georg, 'Documents in Roman Practice', in David Johnston (ed.), *The Cambridge Companion to Roman Law* (Cambridge, 2015), 61–84.
Wolff, Hans Julius, *Das Problem der Konkurrenz von Rechtsordnungen in der Antike* (Heidelberg, 1979).
Woolf, Greg, 'Pliny's Province', in: T. Bekker-Nielsen (ed.), *Rome and the Black Sea Region. Domination, Romanisation, Resistance* (Aarhus 2006), 93–108.
Yaron, Reuven, 'Reichsrecht, Volksrecht and Talmud', *Revue Internationale des Droits de l'Antiquité* 11 (1964), 281–98.
Zangenberg, Jürgen K., 'Fragile Vielfalt. Beobachtungen zur Sozialgeschichte Alexandrias in hellenistisch-römischer Zeit', in Tobias Georges, Felix Albrecht, and Reinhard Feldmeier (eds), *Alexandria* (Tübingen, 2013), 91–107.
Zangenberg, Jürgen K., 'Peace from the Ashes. Commemorating the Wars in the East, the Centre, and the West of the Roman Empire during the "Long Year of the Four Emperors" (68–70 CE)', in Joel Baden, Hindy Najman, and Eibert Tigchelaar (eds), *Sibyls, Scriptures, and Scrolls*, vol. 2 (Leiden, 2016), 1418–52.
Zanker, Paul, *The Power of Images in the Age of Augustus*, trans. Alan Shapiro (Ann Arbor, 1988).
Zeiller, J., 'Nouvelles observations sur l'origine juridique des persécutions contre les Chrétiens aux deux premiers siècles', *Revue d'Histoire Ecclésiastique* 46 (1951), 521–33.

Zeiller, J., 'Institutum Neronianum. Loi fantôme ou Réalité?', *Revue d'Histoire Ecclésiastique* 50 (1955), 393–9.
Ziethen, Gabriele, *Gesandte vor Kaiser und Senat. Studien zum römischen Gesandtschaftswesen zwischen 30 v. Chr. und 117 n. Chr.* (St Katharinen, 1994).
Zollschan, Linda T., 'A Bronze Tablet from the Church of San Basilio in Rome', *Classica et Mediaevalia* 63 (2012), 217–45.
Zollschan, Linda T., 'The Conclusion of the First Jewish Revolt. Interpreting IVDAEA RECEPTA', *Israel Numismatic Research* 14 (2019), 97–116.
Zulueta, Francis de (ed.), *The Institutes of Gaius*, 2 vols (Oxford, 1946–53).
Zwierlein, Otto, *Petrus in Rom. Die literarischen Zeugnissen, mit einer kritischen Edition der Martyrien des Petrus und Paulus auf neuer handschriftlicher Grundlage* (Berlin, 2009).
Zwierlein, Otto, *Petrus und Paulus in Jerusalem und Rom. Vom neuen Testament zu den apokryphen Apostelakten* (Berlin, 2013).

Index

Note: Notes are indicated by "n." following the page numbers.

Since the index has been created to work across multiple formats, indexed terms for which a page range is given (e.g., 52–53, 66–70, etc.) may occasionally appear only on some, but not all of the pages within the range.